Paulo Afonso B. Duarte · Rui Albuquerque ·
António Manuel Lopes Tavares
Editors

Portugal and the Lusophone World

Law, Geopolitics and Institutional Cooperation

palgrave
macmillan

Editors
Paulo Afonso B. Duarte
Universidade Lusófona
Porto, Portugal

Rui Albuquerque
Universidade Lusófona
Porto, Portugal

António Manuel Lopes Tavares
Universidade Lusófona
Porto, Portugal

ISBN 978-981-99-0454-9 ISBN 978-981-99-0455-6 (eBook)
https://doi.org/10.1007/978-981-99-0455-6

This Palgrave Macmillan imprint is published by the registered company Springer Nature Singapore Pte Ltd.
The registered company address is: 152 Beach Road, #21-01/04 Gateway East, Singapore 189721, Singapore

Portugal and the Lusophone World

To all the victims of the war

Foreword by Professor Francisco José B. S. Leandro

International relations in the Lusophere is a neglected area of study in terms of its volume of publications in the English language, but it has been growing in political and economic importance: The Lusophone space shares a common language, traces of a common history, and coastal geographies as it encompasses places accessed by Portugal's historical seafaring expeditions. This space, currently composed of nine sovereign states—Angola, Brazil, Cabo Verde, Equatorial-Guinea, Guinea-Bissau, Mozambique, Portugal, Timor-Leste, and São Tomé and Príncipe—across four continents, therefore holds remarkable potential in both regional and global dimensions. The Lusophere covers 7.2% and 5.48% of the world's land and maritime space, respectively, providing access to 2.9 billion consumers through regional economic communities; the Portuguese language is the most spoken language in the southern hemisphere; and, formally—in addition to the above nine states—the Community of Portuguese-speaking Countries has 35 "associate observer" states, and 106 "consultative observer" international entities.

The growing public and academic interest in post-colonial studies and international studies of the Lusophere has been a long time in the making: First, since 1975, there had been a series of Portuguese-speaking sovereign states forming, before the subsequent creation of the Community of Portuguese-speaking Countries in 1995. Then, in 2003, the Forum for Economic and Trade Cooperation between China and Portuguese-speaking Countries (Forum Macao) was established by the People's Republic of China, to facilitate scholars, students, institutions, as well as the general public to uncover and discover new areas of interest. Such areas now include (1) the identity, existence, and development of Portuguese-speaking countries from a post-colonial perspective; (2) the economic, political, geopolitical, legal, and social relations between the Portuguese-speaking countries; (3) the economic and social-political spaces of influence of the Portuguese-speaking countries; (4) particular groups of states sharing common characteristics the Portuguese-speaking Small Developing Island States; and (5) the Portuguese-speaking countries' bilateral and multilateral relations with major regional and global actors such as the European Union, the US, and the People's Republic of China. These areas are gaining importance in the context of international studies.

This especially timely manuscript, *Portugal and the Lusophone World: Law, Geopolitics and Institutional Cooperation*, is honoured to be published by the internationally renowned Palgrave Macmillan, and is in English. It covers four thematic areas: (1) Legal issues within the Lusophone world; (2) Portugal and the Lusophone world; (3) The Atlantic and the Lusophone world; and (4) Influence and Institutional cooperation in the Lusophone world. In particular, this volume contributes substantially to fields of studies concerning law, the role of the Portuguese Republic, influence from certain Lusophone institutions, and the importance of the middle and south Atlantic.

Economic, diplomatic, and language cooperation, blue economy, maritime security, spatial development initiatives, the Belt and Road Initiative, Forum Macao, energy, and soft power are among the topics discussed and debated in this publication, which, though revolving mainly around Africa, Brazil, and the South Atlantic, has not neglected the Pacific, where Timor-Leste's candidacy for ASEAN membership will prove to be significant for the region and beyond. All of these discussions remind us of the once heated debates regarding development, cooperation, and dependency, which have since triggered different narratives and diverse perspectives. More importantly, such research will contribute to deepening our understanding of the existing Lusophone order, offering a better grasp of not only the Lusosphere's reality but also the plethora of opportunities and pathways that it brings to the global community for states to develop mutual benefits. As such, this book is most academically relevant and valuable to current studies and discourse on international relations. It is therefore our sincere hope that the book will be recommended to the widest possible readership, thereby allowing it to induce and catalyse more academic interest on research associated with the Portuguese-speaking states.

Francisco José B. S. Leandro
Associate Professor with
Habilitation and Associate Dean
of the Institute for
Portuguese-speaking Countries
City University of Macau
Macao, China

Foreword by Professor Li Xing

This book takes a hybrid and holistic approach to a wide scope of perspectives that encompass history, law, and geopolitics of Portugal and the Community of Portuguese Language Countries, known as the Lusophonia. I believe that this book represents one of the pioneering efforts in its intellectual devotion to the "globalization" of the Lusophone World. One particular issue that I want to emphasize in writing this foreword is the increasing connections between China and the Lusophone community.

In October 2003, perhaps unnoticed by the rest of the world, Macao—a Special Administrative Region of the People's Republic of China (SAR)—hosted the first ministerial meeting of the Forum for Trade and Economic Cooperation between China and Portuguese-speaking Countries (Angola, Brazil, Cape Verde, China, Guinea-Bissau, Mozambique, Portugal, East Timor, and São Tomé and Príncipe joined the Forum at a later point). Since Portuguese is one of its official languages, Macao is seen by the Chinese government as a link to facilitate and consolidate the commercial and economic relations between China and the Portuguese-Speaking countries. It was also named "Forum Macao". Identified as a multilateral and intergovernmental mechanism for cooperation, the formation of the Forum was promoted by the Central Government of China, with the coordination of other Portuguese-speaking countries. The main objective of Forum Macao is to contribute to the development and strengthening of commercial and economic relations between China and its other members.

Ten years after Forum Macao, Chinese President Xi Jinping first announced China's grand "going out" idea of the "Belt and Road Initiative" (BRI) in 2013, followed by the launch of a series of development projects across Asia, Europe, Africa, and Latin America. The BRI is an infrastructure project attempting to link Eurasia. It has two routes: one is the land route, called Economic Belt of the New Silk Road (consisting of six economic corridors), and the other is the sea route, called the twenty first Century Maritime Silk Road. Globally, so far about 138 countries have signed a Memorandum of Understanding with China on the BRI. It is widely perceived, at least by the developing world, that the BRI is China's international cooperation strategy to enhance global connectivity, communication, and cooperation, so as to foster a more balanced and equitable world system.

However, the BRI has been seen by the West as China's most ambitious geopolitical initiative of the age. Such a grand geopolitical strategy is aimed at (1) exporting the Chinese development model; (2) spreading the Chinese mode of capital accumulation; (3) extending Beijing's geopolitical sphere of influence; (4) fostering new norms of international economic cooperation; and (5) promoting a new world order with Chinese characteristics. As the Chinese government and academia keep promoting the BRI in ever higher profile, the EU and the US are starting to deliberate their own blueprints for global infrastructure investment programmes, such as the EU's "Global Gateway" and the US' "Build Back Better World". Especially in the current era of growing strategic competition between China and the US, their rivalry is driven by shifting power dynamics and competing visions of the future of the international order. For the US, the BRI is no doubt a leading indicator of the scale of China's global ambitions, and it will reshape the world economy and crown China as the new centre of capitalism and globalization.

The capitalist world history shows that world orders, disorders, or reorders have always resulted from the disturbing dynamics unleashed by the rise of new powers and the resistance of established powers. Today China is seen both by the US and the EU as a "systemic rival". It implies that the impact of China's challenge to the existing world order does not only represent some functional redistribution of comparative advantage (hard power) within the existing world order. Rather, it symbolizes more serious structural changes—*a paradigm shift*—in which the institutions and regimes as well as the norms and values grounded on the existing world order need to be redefined.

The capitalist world economy is conceptualized as a dynamic one in which nation's change of positions within its structural morphology is possible, but difficult, by taking advantage of global capital mobility and relocation of production. This explains that the change of positions in the global division of labour and the change of patterns of competition and competitiveness is the *dynamic nature* of the capitalist world economy. "Room for maneuver" refers to the external conditions for "upward mobility" in the world capitalist economy that is conducive to internal development. Historically, it was in such pivotal moments that opportunities for upward mobility within the system were generated and regenerated, such as the US historical role in the industrialization of East Asia as well as China's current role in the Global South. "Promotion by invitation" refers to the upward mobility path brought about by the rise of a new emerging economy of global scale, whose economic outward expansion is favourable to global capital mobility and production relocation, such as China's BRI project.

What is the implication to the Lusophone countries which are covered in this book? "Seizing the opportunities" indicates nation's internal capability to take advantage of a new situation or condition taking place in the international political economy and to adjust its internal development mobility accordingly. It is important for Lusophone countries to understand China's grand strategic objective of shaping the world reordering through occupying a leading position in the emerging world order and providing alternative "public goods". I believe that it is in the political and economic interest of Lusophone countries to find strategic convergence with China's global strategy so as to improve their "upward mobility" by enlarging their "room for maneuver" in a new era of global transformation.

Portugal is one of the 57 founding member countries of the Asian Infrastructure Investment Bank (AIIB) and one of the first European states to sign a Memorandum of Understanding on jointly advancing the construction of the Belt and Road and the first EU country to establish a "blue partnership" with China. Since the BRI was initiated, China–Portugal investment cooperation has scored sound economic and bilateral benefits, with substantial progress in third-party market cooperation. As the *China Daily* (December 21, 2021) concludes, "China-Portugal relations will sail toward a more splendid future, not only better benefiting the two peoples, but also contributing more to the building of a community with a shared future for humanity".

Li Xing
Professor
Department of Politics
and Society
Aalborg University
Aalborg, Denmark

Final Words

Organizing this book was a huge task, despite being a very enriching one. In the process, we found obstacles although we believed that our sacrifice and resilience would be worth it. Therefore, we thank all those who believed as well that together we would come up with this book, particularly when there is no comprehensive, updated, and holistic work on the subject. We acknowledge that a lot more could be said regarding the role of Asia within the Lusophone World, despite the core of Lusophony as well as the bulk of geoeconomics and geopolitics are currently (and will likely remain so in the following decades) concentrated in both South American and African shores of the Atlantic Ocean. Brazil alone is an outstanding market of approximately 200 million people, while Angola, Mozambique, and other Portuguese-Speaking African countries are rich in raw materials which become increasingly important in a planet of scarce resources and where demand is bound to raise dramatically. This is mainly due to an insatiable China, which looks for new markets, as well as human and economic (in which energy security is included) instruments to feed the largest population in the world and to pursue the development of the country. In the process, security of sea lanes of communication in the vast Atlantic becomes a relevant issue when it comes to ensure an uninterrupted access to sources. All these issues help understand the relevance of the Lusophone Atlantic, which is not however limited to maritime or land logistics. In fact, institutional cooperation is crucial, as we have seen, to strengthen the ties of the Lusophone countries. Associated to it comes soft power or, in other words, a quest for influence in world politics, in which the Portuguese language—already one of the most spoken languages in the world—is well positioned to become even more relevant in the following years. All these factors may help bring momentum to the Lusophony and to the Lusophone world which is something yet to accomplish in all its splendour, as the *Fifth Empire* in its spiritual dimension, has always inspired to believe.

In light with the aforementioned, we dare to say that this book does not offer a single conclusion, nor imposes any view. Instead, it aims to contribute to improve knowledge on the Lusophone World, its actors, dynamics, difficulties, opportunities, and challenges. All in all, we aim to inspire others to continue to delve into this promising path of research, by further complementing it according to the lines of thought that this book inaugurated, or building new ones. The goal is not to compete but rather to cooperate in order to join efforts, authors, and inputs to help disseminate both Lusophony and Lusophone World to regions and peoples all over the world, while improving knowledge on the Lusophone countries themselves about the current developments on Law, Geopolitics, and Institutional Cooperation arousing from its inside.

A final word to show our solidarity with all those who have been forced to leave their land, or who have lost their relatives in the war. Our hearts are with the children, mothers, disabled, and victims of the Russo-Ukrainian conflict.

The Editors,
Paulo Afonso B. Duarte
Rui Albuquerque
António Manuel Lopes Tavares

Introduction

This book aims to fulfil a serious need for a consistent and comprehensive publication which combines an analysis of Law, Geopolitics, and Institutional cooperation within the Lusophone world. In this sense, this monograph uses a terminology related to the fields of international politics, namely the aforementioned ones. Given the lack of existence in English of previous literature on such topics, the reader's profile for such a book is heterogeneous and thus far from being limited to citizens of Portuguese-speaking countries. Indeed, the audience is global. In fact, on the one hand, the reader expects to hear for the first time something relatively new, while on the other hand there is the other reader who is already acquainted with some aspects addressed by the book, although he expects to deepen his knowledge on them.

Geopolitically, the Lusophone world encompasses a set of countries and peoples whose mother tongue, currently or officially, is Portuguese. Directly linked to this, *Lusophony* can also be interpreted as a feeling, a soul, and a desire to live together, sharing a common past. Lusophony and the Lusophone World must be understood in the light of globalization and interdisciplinarity in which they aim to consolidate a community of identity, in addition to the linguistic factor. Each Lusophone country has its own identity, which explains that the Lusophone World is formed by a multicultural reality. However, the fact that Portugal is the country whose history made the existence of the Lusophone World possible cannot be ignored in this book. In fact, it was not only the place where the Portuguese language was born, but also the departing point of the caravels that provided the meeting of cultures and civilizations, which in turn produced the cultural and affective traits that connect the Lusophone World. This book's originality lies in its hybrid and holistic approach, offering the readers complementary, intertwined, and multilevel perspective on Law, Geopolitics, and Institutional Cooperation regarding the Lusophone World. Based on the contribution of respected scholars in the field from all over the world, as well as on their diverse education and professional experiences, this book helps the readers to comprehend, recognize, identify, discuss, form their own opinion, and consequently contribute to the ongoing debate about the Lusophone World in this new century. More precisely it aims to deepen knowledge on the legal, social, historical, geopolitical, and geoeconomic development processes of the Lusophone World.

The book is divided into three parts. In a first part, the book will address the legal and political issues within the Lusophone Space. Thus, in the first chapter, José Oliveira Rocha investigates the feasibility of the Portuguese legal system in the former African colonies. As the author argues, the importation of institutions, as well as legal systems in the postindependence period, suffered from dysfunctions that must be analysed in order to discuss the viability of the Portuguese legal system in the former African colonies. Then, in a second chapter, Fabio D'Avila and Rodrigo de Oliveira debate the onto-anthropological foundation of criminal law in Brazil, namely its fundamentals, presence, and innovation. In so doing, and drawing on the lack of studies on the subject, the authors aim at responding to the following research question: What is the main contribution of the onto-anthropological foundation to contemporary criminal law in Brazil? In the third chapter, Nuno Castro Marques analyses the various economic laws in the Portuguese-speaking countries, taking competition laws as central points of work and comparison. Also, this chapter covers the existing legal framework and law enforcement practice of authorities and courts, in addition to introducing a debate on how existing rules and procedures in Portugal have influenced other Portuguese-speaking countries. In turn, Paulo Cardinal drives us to an important part of the Lusophone world which is not located in the Atlantic, unlike the other cases presented so far, but which nonetheless deserves attention due to its unique and challenging status anchored in the "One Country, Two Systems" principle: Macau. Even though Macau's Law was basically imported from Portugal, recent developments explain that continuity and linkage to Portuguese Law has been the subject of challenges and criticism albeit mostly in a political rather than technical way. Thus, Cardinal's question seems to be at the same time interesting and topical: What will be the road ahead? In order to complement the legal issues previously addressed, we could not end this first part of the book without looking at the place and role of Portugal within the international relations of the Lusophone World. Thus, in Chapter 6 António Manuel Lopes Tavares and José Manuel Duarte de Jesus aim to identify the pillars of Portuguese Foreign Policy from what they call the first period of globalization until the current world order. As main conclusion, the authors argue that Portugal's key geography based on both land and sea has been an omnipresent feature in shaping the country's Foreign Policy. This helps to pave the way for the next chapter to focus on reframing Portuguese Foreign Policy (PFP) after 1974. In viewing the Lusophone discourse as instrument of a global coloniality of power, Marcos Farias Ferreira addresses the question of how, with the formal end of colonial rule in 1974, PFP has been working as an ordering tool of global coloniality vis-à-vis former African colonies and Timor, a role that has been enabled by neoliberalism as the structuring principle of today's globalizing world. Finally, in the following chapter, Carmen Amado Mendes and Xuheng Wang analyse how China's interactions with the Portuguese-speaking world may affect Portugal's opportunities in formulating its foreign policy both towards China and the Portuguese-speaking countries.

The second part of the book, called *The Atlantic and the Lusophone World*, looks beyond Portugal to the vastness of the Lusophone World that is concentrated in and along the coast of the Atlantic Ocean as a space of transformation at the level of geoeconomics and geopolitics, able to bring important opportunities and challenges to Portuguese-Speaking Countries in this new century. In the first chapter of the third part, Jorge Tavares da Silva, Paulo Afonso B. Duarte, and Rui P. Pereira highlight the Portuguese maritime priorities in the Atlantic, with special focus on the challenges and opportunities generated by the growing Chinese presence in that Ocean. Finally, the conclusion sums up the main findings and points towards avenues of future research on these topics. The next chapters focus on the role of South Atlantic and Africa within/for the Lusophone World. By adding China to the equation, José Bessa Maia brings an added-value to the research, namely by exploring the multifaceted repercussions of China's engagement in the

Lusophone countries located in the South Atlantic. Considering that most of the Portuguese-speaking countries are located in the South Atlantic and that China is now also one of the largest trading partners and investors in South America and sub-Saharan Africa, the author argues that the China factor is leading to a reconfiguration of forces in the region. Based on this assumption, characterized by a hegemonic competition between the US and China, the following chapter, by Daniel Cardoso, analyses how these dynamics affect Brazil's and Portugal's stakes in this geopolitical area. The author provides pertinent and topical insights on the opportunities and challenges in maritime cooperation between the two countries in various areas, encompassing infrastructure, science, and technology, in addition to defence. Still in the realm of maritime cooperation, in the next chapter Sabrina Medeiros and Danielle Pinto examine Lusophone cooperation frameworks and the expansion of the Atlantic Maritime Security. The authors argue that the Portuguese-Speaking countries' maritime frameworks can boost Atlantic cooperation and ensure the cooperation nexus's continuing synergy within European security patterns and boundaries. In the following chapter, Francisco José B. S. Leandro and Yichao Li delve deeper into Chinese growing influence—namely through the Belt and Road Initiative (BRI)—in the African Portuguese-Speaking Countries (APSCs). The authors examine China's investment plans in Africa in a geoeconomic analysis with regional perspectives, associating Lusophony, geoeconomics, regional economic communities with the context of national development plans to answer the question: To what extent does the BRI contribute to designing the development of the APSCs regional economic space? This topic is particularly relevant in the context of the development of the Portuguese language in Africa, in which Portugal and more recently Brazil have been playing an important role. This being said, what is often neglected by literature on the Lusophone World is that Brazil's interests, despite historically more recent than the Portuguese ones, have become more and more important and diversified in the South Atlantic. That is why in their chapter, Flávio Thales, Giorgio Romano, and Mojana Vargas investigate the determinants of Brazil's approach to the African continent as a strategic option during two specific moments: the 1970s, particularly in the Ernesto Geisel government (1974–1979), and during the presidency of Luiz Inácio Lula da Silva (2003–2010). These are divided into three perspectives: geopolitical considerations, economic interests, and racial identity. In the next chapter, Cátia Miriam Costa provides the reader with a proposal for a modern state and society in the Lusophone context, by focusing on the Angolan case. The author concludes that the nativist movement in the country endeavoured to shape Angolan identity, the idea of the modern state, and introduced a connection to a broader Lusophone geopolitical space.

The next chapters address the Lusophone World from the perspective of defence. Thus, João Paulo Madeira analyses Cabo Verde's geopolitical position in the Mid-Atlantic, in the attempt to answer the following research question: what should Cabo Verde's role be in combating terrorism and transnational organized crime, including maritime piracy, human trafficking, smuggling of illegal migrants, drug trafficking and money laundering that threaten the security of Atlantic littoral states? The author concludes that the country enjoys a geostrategic position and that it constitutes one of its most relevant assets, despite scarce resources. This position raises special interest from both NATO and US partners in terms of the possibility of signing agreements and consolidating partnerships with a view to ensuring an adequate level of security at its external borders. Particular attention is given as well by Emilio Zeca to Mozambique Geopolitics in the Lusophone World, who analyses the challenges and perspectives for Mozambique geopolitics in the Lusophone world basing on historical, defence, and security aspects, on one hand, and the international strategic insertion, opportunities, and challenges for Mozambican state in this geopolitical space, on another hand. Continuing with Mozambique, Célia Taborda explores a very topical issue related to the terrorist conflict in Cabo Delgado. As she notes, since independence, Mozambique has signed several cooperation agreements in the areas of defence and security with Portugal. Therefore, this chapter analyses the ongoing Luso-Mozambican cooperation in this conflict in Cabo Delgado and the involvement of Portuguese diplomacy in the response to this conflict. Continuing with Mozambique, Francisco Proença and Sónia Ribeiro focus on an interesting albeit less studied approach in the framework of the Lusophone Geopolitics, which is related to the blue economy and maritime security in Mozambique. Departing from the concept of Blue Geopolitics, the authors focus on both blue economy and security to reflect on Mozambique's contemporary geopolitical challenges and development opportunities. As they argue, control of the Mozambique Canal and the Development Corridors, as well as the energy offshore resources potential, represent new opportunities for the nation's economy, but also challenges to security.

The third part of the book addresses the *Influence and Institutional Cooperation in the Lusophone World*. Firstly, José Paulo Esperança analyses the challenges for the Portuguese language to establish its role as a language of knowledge, despite its predicted rise of the number of speakers as a mother tongue. He concludes that without appropriate incentives and the build-up of a common market for knowledge through the geographically dispersed Lusophone community, the role of Portuguese as a language of science will lag behind its overall presence as a language currently shared by about 260 million native speakers. Secondly, João Mourato Pinto and Laura C. Ferreira-Pereira explore the Portuguese Science Diplomacy and the European Union's External Science activities with Lusophone Africa. Their study demonstrates that Portuguese science diplomacy is a centrepiece of a developing relationship between EU and Lusophone Africa based on a co-building approach. This is only possible because Portugal besides having direct access to EU funding, has showed the capacity to influence the content of normative conditionalities underlying European science programmes and initiatives implemented in Portuguese-speaking African countries. In so doing, Portugal has been ultimately contributing to improve the EU's standing as a "model power" in the Lusophone world. In the next chapter, Fernanda Ilhéu carries out an interesting comparison between the (British) Commonwealth of Nations and the CPLP—Community of Portuguese-Speaking Countries. She investigates the circumstances in which they were created, ranging from the origins of the British and Portuguese Empires through to their decolonization processes, and examines how they impacted the creation of these organizations and their objectives, as well as their problems and their organization structures. She then proceeds to analyse their future prospects, in accordance with the Diasporas Networks Theory. In a separate chapter, José Palmeira continues the analysis on the CPLP which struggles with the geostrategic dilemmas of its member states. The question is to what extent the CPLP consolidates itself as a multi-continental organization capable of maximizing the power of its member states and influencing the international system. José Palmeira arrives at the conclusion that it is possible to state the exercise of a CPLP Soft Power on a global scale, under the effect of a Portugal-Brazil-Angola strategic triangle. Still in the realm of CPLP, the following chapter, by Pedro Seabra and Rafael Mesquita, explore whether the creation of the CPLP has fostered closer ties between this set of countries in key multilateral platforms by quantitively analysing voting patterns at the United Nations

General Assembly in the last two decades. Their results demystify broader claims of privileged relations, yet still point to considerable room for manoeuvre in institutionally dense formats such as the UN.

Moving to another field of cooperation, in the next chapter, Carla Fernandes and António Paulo Duarte focus on a different (despite interesting) field related to the Lusophone World—the Geopolitics of Energy—particularly when the current global warming scenario requires an accelerated transition to a sustainable model based on renewable energy sources. The authors examine Portuguese-speaking countries in terms of energy "access and security" using the WEF Energy Transition Index, assessing not only how their energy system is performing, but also their potential to change the energy paradigm. Fernandes and Duarte conclude that, despite their potential of their energy sources, the Portuguese-speaking countries, with the exception of Portugal and Brazil, are gradually moving towards the transition process. The book could not end without a reference to the role of Asia in the Lusophone World, as evidence of its vastness. That is why Pedro Paulo dos Santos concentrates his attention on the so-called Forum Macao. More specifically, through reviewing the importance that Portuguese-speaking countries present to China and analysing Forum Macao's documentation, his research unveils the forum's purpose and the roles that it plays both in the Lusophone World and in China's foreign policy. Finally, still keeping the eye on Asia, Francisco José B. S. Leandro, José Leandro, and Carlos Branco discuss the geopolitics of Timor-Leste in the context of the Belt & Road Initiative vis-à-vis ASEAN and CPLP. They address the role of Timor-Leste within the Maritime Silk Road strategy in the context of the relations between China and the Community of Portuguese Language Countries (CPLP).

The authors would like to thank Palgrave for its receptiveness towards their proposal. We honestly hope that our contribution aims to expand the debate on the potential and vastness of the Lusophone World, as reflected in our concern to invite authors from different parts of the Lusophone Word, such as Portugal, Latin America, Africa, and Asia.

The Editors,
Paulo Afonso B. Duarte
Rui Albuquerque
António Manuel Lopes Tavares

Contents

Editors and Contributors

About the Editors

Paulo Afonso B. Duarte received his Ph.D. in Political Science from Catholic University of Louvain (Belgium). He is Assistant Professor at Universidade Lusófona do Porto and Invited Assistant Professor of Political Science and International Relations at the University of Minho where he teaches various courses at both graduate and postgraduate levels, and conducts research in the domains of International Relations and China studies. Paulo Afonso B. Duarte is the co-editor of *The Belt and Road Initiative: An Old Archetype of a New Development Model* (Palgrave, 2020, with Francisco José B. S. Leandro), and co-editor of the Palgrave Handbook *of Globalization with Chinese Characteristics: The Case of the Belt and Road Initiative* (upcoming), with F. Leandro and E. Galan. He has acted as invited revisor for Geopolitics (Taylor & Francis), Sage journals, and Peter Lang, among others, under his field of expertise, which is China's Belt and Road Initiative (BRI). He conducted extensive on-the-ground research in several Central Asian countries with scholarship granted by Calouste Gulbenkian Foundation, besides having been granted with scholarship from both the People's Republic of China and the Republic of China to carry out research both in Beijing and Taipei. He is the author of the first book on China's BRI in all Lusophone space (*A Faixa e Rota Chinesa: a convergência entre terra e mar*, 2017, launched in Macau and Rio de Janeiro) as well as of a book (*Metamorfoses* *no Poder: Rumo à Hegemonia do Dragão?*) with foreword and presentation by current President of Portugal, Marcelo Rebelo de Sousa (2014). He is often invited to cooperate with national and International media on BRI-related issues, and he is a weekly political analyst at Mozambique's TV programme *Observatório Internacional*. His most recent publications include Duarte, P. (2021). "The Soft Power of China and the European Union in the context of the Belt and Road Initiative and Global Strategy". *Journal of Contemporary European Studies*, with Ferreira-Pereira; and Duarte, P. (2021). "China and the Belt and Road Initiative in Europe: The case of Portugal" In Ntousas and Minas (eds.). *The European Union and China's Belt and Road Impact, Engagement and Competition*. Routledge (co-authored with Ferreira-Pereira, L.). Duarte, P. (2023). A 'Soft' Balancing Ménage à Trois? China, Iran and Russia Strategic Triangle vis-à-vis US Hegemony. *Journal of Asian Security and International Affairs* (with Papageorgiu, M. & Mamad, E.).

Rui Albuquerque has a degree in Law and a Master's and Ph.D. in Political Science and International Relations. Specialist in the History of Law and Political Thought, as well as in Constitutional and Political Law of the European Union, he is an integrated member of CEAD—Francisco Suárez Center for Advanced Studies in Law and Deputy Director of the Faculty of Law and Political Science of the University Center of Porto of the Lusofona University. Regularly publishes books and scientific articles, as well as intervenes in the public space with opinion articles, conferences, and lectures.

António Manuel Lopes Tavares received his Ph.D. in Political Science, International Relations and Citizenship from Universidade Lusófona do Porto. He is the Director of the course in Political Science and Electoral Studies and responsible for the following courses: Lusophone Studies, European Studies and International Relations, postgraduate studies in International Relations, Political Diplomacy and Economics as well as Social Service. He is both a Specialist Professor in Social Work and Orientation and an Assistant Professor at Universidade Lusófona do Porto where he teaches several curricular units at both graduate and postgraduate levels. Since 2013, António Manuel Lopes Tavares has been a Visiting Professor for several reputable Universities in Portugal where he teaches curricular units that fall under three pillars: Health Care Management, Human Resources and Governance, and Health Policies. He has a special interest in investigation research in the subjects of Political Science and International Relations with emphasis on the functioning of the political system. From his published work, he is the author of *Na balança do tempo da política*, (Âncora, Lisbon, 2019); *Coabitação Política em Portugal na Vigência da Constituição de 1976*, (Almedina, 2016); *The Misericórdias mission before the community and the State, in the minutes of the IX National Congress of the Misericórdias*, (UMP, Braga, 2010); *Sustainability of the Misericórdias in the current state of affairs, in the minutes of the II Congress of the Misericordias of the North*, (UMP, Braga, 2006). *He was also the Co-Author of Colectânea de legislação florestal*, (Forrestis and AEDRL, Association for Regional and Local Law and Studies, November 2018); *Segurança e Defesa Nacional - um conceito estratégico*, (Almedina, 2013); *Nato: Desafios no atual quadro internacional*, (Personal Edition, Porto, 2012). António Manuel Lopes Tavares also coordinated a cycle of debates: *Which Social State? The responses of the Solidarity Sector - Misericórdia do Porto and União das Misericórdias Portuguesas* (Porto, 2013). In 2021 he was a keynote speaker at the XXI Health Forum, in Lisbon; Chronicles of a pandemic foretold, with the topic *A new Social model or a new Governance model*? He holds positions as an Associate Director of the Journal 1820 Political Science and a Member of the Scientific Council of Revista do CEPESE.

Contributors

Carlos Martins Branco is a Major-General (retired) with the Portuguese army. He is an integrated researcher with the Portuguese Institute of International Relations (IPRI) and associated researcher with the National Defense Institute (IDN). He has authored two books and more than 70 scientific papers and essays on conflict resolution, security, and defence matters published in books, periodicals, and daily news, and has co-edited four books. He lectures at various higher education and defence institutions on security and defence, and international relations (United Nations Peacekeeping, NATO, CSDP, and Conflict Resolution), and was scientific co-director of postgraduate studies on Media and Crisis Management, in Instituto Superior de Ciências Sociais, do Trabalho e da Empresa (ISCTE). He was deputy director of the Portuguese War College and is a member of various think tanks and civic organizations.

Paulo Cardinal is invited teacher at the Faculty of Law of Macau University, Visiting Lecturer, Faculty of Law, Hong Kong University, Visiting Academic, University of Saint Joseph, Macau. He has been teaching, namely, Constitutional Law, International Law, and Comparative Law courses, both at undergraduate and Master's programmes. He has published intensively on Macau Law.

Daniel Cardoso is Assistant Professor of International Relations at Autonomous University of Lisbon and Vice-Director of Observare-Observatory of Foreign Relations. He received his Ph.D. in Political Science and International Relations from the Free University of Berlin (Germany). He was a post-doctoral researcher at IPRI-NOVA (Portugal), guest researcher at Fudan University, Shanghai (China), and Guest Assistant Professor at the NOVA University of Lisbon and at the University of Coimbra (Portugal). Daniel Cardoso was a researcher in the project on the role of Macau in China's relations with the Portuguese-speaking countries, funded by the Portuguese national funding agency for Science, Research and Technology and hosted by the University of Coimbra. He researches on governance and foreign policy, with a special focus on Brazil, Portugal, and China. He has authored the book *Capitalising on Constraint: Bailout Politics in Eurozone Countries* (Manchester University Press, 2021). His research has been published in several scientific journals such as *Third World Quarterly*, *South European Society and Politics*, *Contexto Internacional*, and *East Asia Journal*.

Cátia Miriam Costa is a researcher at the Centre for International Studies and an invited Assistant Professor at Iscte-Instituto Universitário de Lisboa. She is also the co-ordinator of two European Union EARSMUS+ Projects and the Chair of Global Ibero-America (European Institute of International Relations: Salamanca/Stockholm). She has participated in several international projects supported by national and international institutions (FCT—Portugal, CYTED, COST) and published in national and international scientific journals and books (https://ciencia.iscte-iul.pt/authors/catia-costa/cv). She was the advisor to the Secretary of State of Internationalization in the 22nd Government of the Portuguese Republic. She specialized in discourse analyses, international communication, and China's foreign policy. She holds a Ph.D. in Literature, a Master's in African Studies, and a degree in International Relations. Her Ph.D. thesis centred on the proto-nationalist movements in Angola and how literary and journalist discourse became determinant to claiming political autonomy and independence.

Jorge Tavares da Silva is a visiting Assistant Professor at the University of Aveiro and at the University of Coimbra. He is a researcher at the Unit on Governance, Competitiveness and Public Policies (GOVCOPP). Holds a Ph.D. in International Relations from the Faculty of Economics at the University of Coimbra (Portugal), in the specific field of International Politics and Conflict Resolution. He is a founding member of the Observatory of China (Portugal) and the Center for Studies and Research on Security and Defence of Trás-os-Montes and Alto Douro (CEIDSTAD). He is also a member of the European Association for Chinese Studies (EACS), the Association of Chinese Political Studies (ACPS), and scientific member of Tempo Exterior (Spain). He is author of multiple articles and chapters of books in international journals on political, economic, and social issues facing contemporary China. He is author of the book *BRICS and the New International Order* [Portuguese] (Caleidoscópio, 2015) and co-author of the book *Em Bicos de Pés e de Olhos em Bico—Experiences and Living Together between Chinese and Portuguese* [Portuguese] (Mare Liberum, 2012) and *Role and Impact of Tourism in Peacebuilding and Conflict Transformation* (IGI global, 2020).

Fabio Roberto D'Avila received his Ph.D. in Criminal Law from the University of Coimbra in 2004. From 2006 to 2007 he developed postdoctoral research at University of Frankfurt a. M. with the support of the Alexander von Humboldt Foundation (AvH). Fabio Roberto D'Avila is Full Professor of Criminal Law at the Pontifícia Universidade Católica do Rio Grande do Sul (PUCRS) where he teaches various courses at both graduate and postgraduate levels and conducts research in the domains of Criminal Sciences. He is also President of the Instituto Eduardo Correia (IEDC), Brazilian Representative in the European Group for Legal Initiatives against Organized Crime (Europäischer Arbeitskreis zu rechtlichen Initiativen gegen die Organisierte Kriminalität—EAK) and criminal attorney in Brazil.

Rodrigo Moraes de Oliveira received his Ph.D. in Criminal Law from the Pontifícia Universidade Católica do Rio Grande do Sul (PUCRS) in 2015. He is Professor of Criminal Law of the Pontifícia Universidade Católica do Rio Grande do Sul (PUCRS) where he teaches various courses at both graduate and postgraduate levels and conducts research in the domains of Criminal Sciences. Rodrigo Moraes de Oliveira is also President of the Instituto Transdisciplinar de Estudos Criminais (ITEC), Coordinator of Post-Graduation Course in Controllership, Compliance and Audit at the Pontifícia Universidade Católica do Rio Grande do Sul (PUCRS) and criminal attorney in Brazil.

Pedro Paulo dos Santos is a Ph.D. candidate at the Institute for Research on Portuguese-speaking Countries, City University of Macau, China. He is currently a lecturer and researcher at City University of Macau, teaching English and Portuguese languages, where he has been lecturing for 9 years. He has had articles presented in international conferences in Singapore, Hong Kong, or Macao. His most recent publication was as co-editor in Leandro, F., Santos, P. P., Li, Y. book entitled China and the Portuguese-Speaking Small Island States: From sporadic bilateral exchanges to a comprehensive multilateral platform. His main research areas are People's Republic of China, Portuguese-speaking countries, great bay areas, and Chinese forums.

António Paulo Duarte received his Ph.D. degree from the Institute of Contemporary History (IHC), NOVA *School of Social* Sciences and *Humanities* (NOVA FCSH), and a Master's in Strategy from the Institute of Social and Political Sciences of the University of Lisbon (ICS-UL). He has a Degree in History from the University of Lisbon. He is currently Assistant Professor at the Portuguese Military Academy (AM) and Visiting Professor at NOVA FCSH. Previously he was an integrated researcher at the National Defense Institute from 2022, where he was co-ordinator of the Energy Security group research and a teacher in various courses at both graduate and postgraduate levels at Nova University. His main research focuses on military history and strategy, and energy security. He's the author of multiple articles and chapters of books, with his most recent published article entitled "Energy Security Strategies: A Conceptual Interpretation", in Teresa Rodrigues e Carla Fernandes (Ed.) *The Future of Energy: Prospective Scenarios on EU-Russia Relations*, Nova Science Publishers: New York, 2019, pp. 3–32; and "A Humanidade Demiúrgica sobre o Signo do Aniquilamento: Uma Reflexão Holística sobre o Conceito de Estratégia de Segurança Energética" (Demiurgic Humanity on the Sign of Annihilation: A Holistic Reflection on the Concept of Energy Security Strategy), *Nação e Defesa*, nº 153, 5ª Série, agosto de 2019, pp. 9–48. He also has publications on the history of war, strategic theory, and Portugal's geopolitics. One of the last articles is “Exercício Comparativo: Os Pequenos Beligerantes na Primeira Guerra Mundial” [Comparative Exercise: The Little Belligerents (small powers) in World War I], in Ana Paula Pires, António Paulo Duarte e Bruno Cardoso Reis, *A Inserção Internacional das Pequenas Potências: Primeira Guerra Mundial* (The International Insertion of the Small Powers: World War I), Instituto da Defesa Nacional, Lisboa, 2019, pp. 39–132.

José Paulo Esperança is the Vice-President of the Foundation for Science and Technology (FCT). He is Full Professor of Finance and former Dean of the ISCTE Business School as well as former Pro-Rector for International Relations and Entrepreneurship at ISCTE-IUL. He cofounded AUDAX-ISCTE, an associated centre focused on entrepreneurship and family business and BGI, a new ventures accelerator. He got a Ph.D. in economics from the European University Institute, Florence on The Investment Decision by Service Multinationals. His research interests include innovation and small business financing, corporate governance and the impact of language commonality on international business. Outside of Portugal he has taught and consulted in China, Angola, Mozambique, Cabo Verde, Brazil, and the US. He is the co-author of several books on the value of the Portuguese language and research papers in Applied Financial Economics, Corporate Governance, Emerging Markets Review, International Journal of Organizational Analysis, Journal of Business Research, Journal of Small Business and Enterprise Development, Management International Review, Management Research, and Research in International Business and Finance.

Marcos Farias Ferreira has Ph.D. in Social Sciences and International Relations from the Technical University of Lisbon, and MScEcon in International Politics from Aberystwyth University. He is senior lecturer at the School of Social and Political Sciences, University of Lisbon, where he teaches different courses both at undergraduate and postgraduate levels, viz. International Relations Methodology, International Politics, Portuguese Foreign Policy, Russia and Post-Soviet Politics. Marcos F. Ferreira was the leading researcher of the Portuguese Foundation for Science and Technology (FCT) financed project “Observatory of Human Security” (2010-2015). In the last twenty years he conducts regular political analysis on international affairs for different media outlets, viz. RTP, SIC, Radio France International and France24 en español. Marcos F. Ferreira is co-editor of Emancipating the World. Critical Theory and International Relationd (Almedina, 2021) and author of Christians and Pepper. The Via Media in the Theory of International Relations of Adriano Moreira (Almedina, 2007). He has been invited to peer review for, among others, Asian Review of Women's Studies, Social Anthropology/Anthropologie Sociale, Italian Journal of International Affairs, Portuguese Review of Asian Studies, University of Coimbra Press. Current research interests revolve around the methodological agenda of visual global politics. Marcos F. Ferreira is the author of feature and short documentary films, viz. La Toma (89', Portugal/Nicaragua, 2011), Revolusión (122', Portugal/Nicaragua, 2014), Esperance (9', Portugal/Rwanda, 2015). Latest academic publications include Ferreira, M. and Dawar, A. (2021). "Impact of Emergency Cash Assistance on Gender Relations in the Tribal Areas of Pakistan" in Asian Journal of Women's Studies, Vol. 27 No. 3; Ferreira, M. and Dawar, A. (2021). "New Winners and Losers in North Waziristan. Understanding Tensions Between Top-Down Projects and Local Knowledge in the Post-Conflict Setting (2015-2019)" in Cogent Social Sciences, Vol. 7 No. 1; Ferreira, M. and Dawar, A. (2021). "'State-Security First' and the Militarization of Development. Local Perceptions on Post- Conflict Reconstruction Policies in Pakistan's Tribal Areas (2015-2019)" in Forum for Development Studies, Vol. 48 No. 2.

Carla Fernandes received her Ph.D. in International Relations from NOVA *School of Social* Sciences and *Humanities* (NOVA FCSH), with the thesis "China Today - Energy Needs and International Relations. Relations with Portuguese-speaking Countries". She also received a Master's Degree in Chinese Studies from Aveiro University and various courses in Chinese Language, Culture, and History from the University of Macau and the University of Kunming, China. She is an Invited Assistant Professor of the Faculty of Social Sciences and Humanities of the NOVA University since 2006, where she teaches various courses at both graduate and postgraduate levels. She has also participated in lectures and courses at the Instituto Universitário Militar (IUM) and courses at the Instituto Defesa Nacional (IDN) and several universities. She is an integrated researcher at Instituto Português de Relações Internacionais (IPRI-NOVA) where she conducts research in the domains of China studies and energy security. She coordinated the Fundação para a Ciência e Tecnologia (FCT) funded research project "The Geopolitics of Gas and the Future of the Euro-Russian relations", which analysed the geopolitics of gas in the Euro-Russian relationship, based on the elaboration of future scenarios for the Euro-Russian energy relationship, from 2016 to 2018. She has several publications and has organized and delivered lectures and communications on her areas of research: energy security, energy geopolitics, and the People's Republic of China. She is often invited to cooperate with national and international media on energy security. Her most recent publications include Fernandes, Carla (2021). "China's Energy Security and Portugal in the BRI". In Sofia Gaspar (ed.). *The Presence of China and the Chinese Diaspora in Portugal and Portuguese-speaking Territories*. Leiden: Brill, pp. 127–150; Fernandes, Carla (2020). "A Cooperação Energética China-África: das energias fósseis às energias limpas". Relações Internacionais. Lisboa: IPRI, pp. 27–41; Fernandes, Carla (2019). China energy security and Portuguese-speaking countries. Fernanda Ihéu, Francisco José B. S. Leandro e Paulo Duarte, Suma Oriental-Lisboa, pp. 121–135. Carla Fernandes & Teresa Rodrigues (ed.). *The Future of Energy: Prospective Scenarios on EU-Russia Relations*. Nova Science Publishers: New York.

Laura C. Ferreira-Pereira received her Ph.D. in International Relations from the University of Kent at Canterbury (UK). She is Full Professor of Political Science and International Relations of the University of Minho where she teaches various courses at both graduate and postgraduate levels, and conducts research in the domains of International Relations and European Union Studies. Laura Ferreira-Pereira is the editor of *Portugal in the European Union: Assessing Twenty-Five Years of Integration Experience* (Routledge, 2014) and co-editor of *The European Union's Strategic Partnerships: Global Diplomacy in a Contested Worl*d (Palgrave Macmillan, 2021). She has acted as the leading guest editor of Special Issues published in *European Security* (2012) and *Cambridge Review of International Affairs* (2016). She is also contributor to other leading journals such as *Journal of Common Market Studies*, *Cooperation and Conflict*, *Journal of Contemporary European Studies*, *International Politics and Journal of European Integration*, among others; and has published in several edited volumes. Her current research explores the EU's strategic partnership diplomacy and relations with the Lusophone world; Europeanization within and beyond Europe; comparative regional integration (with an emphasis on security and defence); Brexit and small states; China in global affairs and Luso–Chinese relations. Laura Ferreira-Pereira is a member of the editorial boards of the journals *Contemporary*

Politics and *Global Society*. She is a founding member of the European International Studies Association (EISA).

Flávio Thales Ribeiro Francisco Ph.D. Professor in undergraduate studies on International Relations and graduate studies on World Political Economy (EPM) at the Federal University of ABC (UFABC). His research fields are in Racial Relations, Race and International Relations, Black Diaspora, and Brazil–Africa Relations. Author of *O Novo Negro na Diáspora* (2020) and *Laços Atlânticos: imigração africana em São Paulo*, (2008).

Francisco Proença Garcia is currently Associate Professor with Habilitation and Dean for Faculty at the Institute of Political Studies of the Portuguese Catholic University; Visiting Academic at University of Saint Joseph (Macau), Instituto Universitário Militar (Lisbon) and Mozambique Catholic University (Beira). Among other duties, he served as national representative in the Science and Technology Organization/North Atlantic Treaty Organization (2014–16), Head of the Department of Postgraduate Studies of the Military Academy (2014), Advisor of the Chief of the Army Staff (2011–14); Military Advisor to the Portuguese Delegation to the North Atlantic Treaty Organization and the European Defense Agency (2008–11), President of the Scientific Council of the Higher Institute of Business Communication (2013); Vice-President of the Army Research Center (2002 and 2014), Planning Officer of the PKF/UNTAET Central Sector Command Headquarters in Timor-Leste (2001). Francisco Proença Garcia is Academic of the International Academy of Portuguese Culture and Director of the Lisbon Geographical Society. It has 16 books and several dozens of published scientific articles in the areas of International Relations, Security Studies, and African Studies. His most recent books are titled: Authoritarian Power and the challenges to liberal democracy (2022), Aletheia, Lisbon.

Fernanda Ilhéu received her Ph.D. in Business Administration and Marketing from the University of Seville (Spain). She also graduated in Economics from ISEG/Lisbon's School of Economics and Management of Lisbon University; post-graduated in Marketing and Export Management at the Cambridge Institute of Massachusetts and got a Master's degree in Strategic Management at Lisbon's Higher Institute of Business and Labor Sciences (ISCTE). Presently she lectures post-graduated programmes at ISEG Executive Education, and at ISEG she is also a researcher at CEsA—Centre of African Studies and Development. She is a Board Member of Jorge Álvares Foundation and the President of the Board of Directors of the New Silk Road Friends Association a Portuguese Portugal's Think Tank on BRI. She lived in Macau 18 years executing roles of great responsibility in both the private and public sectors and lectured in Macau University. She is author and co-author of several books and scientific articles on China's economy and business, on BRI, and on China and Portuguese-Speaking Countries relations.

José Manuel Duarte de Jesus was born in Portugal, December 1935. Graduated in History and Philosophy in the University of Lisbon in 1960; post-graduated in Philosophy (Mathematical *Logic: "R. Carnap: Language, Meaning and Truth"*) in 1978; Ph.D. in International Relations at the Universidade Nova, Lisbon, in 2009. He joined the diplomatic service in 1961. As diplomat he was posted in Rabat, Bonn, Lille (France), Frankfurt, Prague, Brussels (EEC) and was appointed Ambassador to Kinshasa, Brazzaville, Bujumbura, Kigali, Bangui, Beijing, Ulan Bator, Pyong Yang, and Ottawa. He left the Diplomatic Career for political reasons between 1965 and 1974 and during this period he was active in the financial sector in Germany and Belgian; he was President of the "Fund of Commodities", and General manager of the "General Commodities Corporation". As a retired Ambassador, he was Chairman of the Declassification Committee (Public Disclosure of Classified Documents) in the Ministry of Foreign Affairs in Lisboan, and now he is research fellow at the Asian Institute (ISCSP) of the Lisboa University and at the IPRI, Portuguese Institute of International Relations, University Nova in Lisboan. He was an invited Professor at the University of Aveiro, University Nova in Lisboa and IUM, Military University Institute. All my published books are listed in ORCID.

Francisco José B. S. Leandro received a Ph.D. in political science and international relations from the Catholic University of Portugal in 2010. From 2016 to 2017 he took part in a post-doctoral research programme on State monopolies in China—One belt one road studies. In 2014, 2017, and 2020, he was awarded the Institute of European Studies in Macau (IEEM)'s Academic Research Grant, which is a major component of the Asia-Europe Comparative Studies Research Project. From 2014 to 2018, he was the Programme Coordinator at the Institute of Social and Legal Studies, Faculty of Humanities at the University of Saint Joseph in Macau, China. He is currently Associate Professor with Habilitation and Associate Dean of the Institute for Research on Portuguese-Speaking Countries at the City University of Macau (China). His most recent books are titled: *Steps of Greatness: The Geopolitics of OBOR* (2018), University of Macau; *The Challenges, Development and Promise of Timor-Leste* (2019), City University of Macau; *The Belt and Road Initiative: An Old Archetype of a New Development Model* (2020), Palgrave Macmillan; and *Geopolitics of Iran* (2021), Palgrave Macmillan; *Disentangled Visions on Higher Education: Preparing the Next Generation* (2022), Peter Lang Publishers. Francisco José B. S. Leandro is member of OBSERVARE (Observatory of Foreign Relations), which was founded in 1996 as a centre for studies in International Relations at the Autonomous University of Lisbon, Portugal.

José Eduardo Garcia Leandro is a Lieutenant-general (retired) with the Portuguese Army. He was Chief of Staff to the Governor of Timor (1968/70) and between 1974 and 1979 he was Governor of Macau. Garcia Leandro was a professor at the Portuguese Army War College (1991/93) as well as its Deputy Director and Director (1996/2000), National Defense Institute Director (2001–2004), and Guest Professor at ISCSP (1999–2005) and at Universidade Autónoma de Lisboa (1992/93). Between 2003/2009 he was a visiting professor at Instituto de Estudos Políticos da Universidade Católica Portuguesa; since 2009 he has been a member of the Consultative Council at Instituto Superior de Ciências de Informação e Administração de Aveiro (ISCIA). He currently holds the position of President of the Board of Trustees at Fundação Jorge Álvares, is a member of the Board of Trustees at Fundação Casa de Macau, and is a Correspondent Member of the International Academy of Portuguese Culture. In 1999 he coordinated the book *Portugal and the 50 years of Atlantic Alliance* published by the Ministry of Defense of Portugal, and in 2011 he authored the book *Macau During the Portuguese Revolution—1974/1979*, published by Gradiva Editions.

Yichao Li received her Ph.D. degree from the Institute for Research on Portuguese-speaking Countries, City University of Macau. She also received a Master's degree in comparative civil law (in Chinese) from the University of Macau, and a Bachelor's of Law from Nanjing University of Information Science & Technology, China. In 2020, she was awarded the Institute of European Studies in Macau (IEEM) Academic Research Grant, which is a major component of the Asia-Europe Comparative

Studies Research Project. Her current research interests are the Belt and Road Initiative and Portuguese-speaking countries. Her latest publications include Li, Y., & Vicente, M. (2020), "Chinese partnerships and the Belt and Road Initiative: a synergetic affiliation", in Leandro, F. & Duarte, P. (eds.), *The Belt and Road Initiative: An Old Archetype of a New Development Model* (Palgrave Macmillan); and Li, Y. (2021), "Chinese Partnerships with Portuguese-Speaking Small Island Developing States: Past, Present and Future Perspectives", in Leandro, F., Paulo, P. & Li, Y. (eds.), *China and the Portuguese-Speaking Small Island States: From Sporadic Bilateral Exchanges to a Comprehensive Multilateral Platform* (City University of Macau). She is an associate researcher of OBSERVARE (Observatory of Foreign Relations), which was founded in 1996 as a centre for studies in International Relations at the Autonomous University of Lisbon, Portugal.

João Paulo Madeira (Portugal) is Assistant Professor and Coordinator of the International Relations and Diplomacy Program at the University of Cabo Verde (Uni-CV). He is associate researcher at the Centre for Public Administration and Public Policies (CAPP-ISCSP-UL). He holds a Ph.D. in Social Sciences from the University of Lisbon (ISCSP-UL), and has completed a post-doctoral mobility programme at FCT NOVA University with the support of the Calouste Gulbenkian Foundation in partnership with the Network of Environmental Studies of the Portuguese-Speaking Countries (REALP).

José Nelson Bessa Maia is an economist with an M.A. in Economics and who holds his Ph.D. in International Relations from the University of Brasilia (UnB). He is a retired auditor for finance and controlling of the Brazilian Ministry of Economy. He was director of foreign affairs office of the Brazilian State of Ceará (1995–2006). Was the Brazilian official representative at the G20 Framework Working Group (2012–2015). He was a senior advisor, from January 2016 until January 2019 at the International Secretariat for International Affairs (SEAIN) of the Ministry of Planning, Budget and Management of Brazil. He was co-ordinator for international financial markets at the Secretariat for International Economic Affairs in the Ministry of Economy of Brazil (2019–2021). Mr. Maia was Brazil's official co-ordinator for preparation of the Brazilian chapter in the BRICS Report, a Policy-oriented study of Brazil, Russia, India, China, and South Africa with special focus on synergies and complementarities, published by the Oxford University Press (2012). Has 11 books published in Brazil in co-authorship or as sole author in areas such as International Relations, Regional History, Genealogy, and Public Governance and many articles published in Brazil and abroad. His current research explores International Relations Theory; International Economic and Financial Governance; Paradiplomacy and China in global affairs, Latin America, and Lusophone–Chinese relations. José Nelson Maia is now an international consultant with expertise in International Economy and Geopolitics.

Nuno Castro Marques holds a degree in Law from the Faculty of Law of Porto of the Portuguese Catholic University; a postgraduate degree in European Studies from the Institute of European Studies at the Catholic University of Louvain; an LL.M. in EU Law from the Faculty of Law of the University of Coimbra and a Ph.D. in Law from the Porto School of the Faculty of Law of the Portuguese Catholic University. He is a Professor at the Faculty of Law and Political Science at the ULP, at the Faculty of Economics at the University of Porto and at the Porto School at the Faculty of Law at the Portuguese Catholic University. He is deputy director of the ULP Law Review, editor for the health area of the Journal of Competition & Regulation, and an investigation co-ordinator at the Francisco Suárez Center for Advanced Studies in Law (CEAD-Francisco Suárez). He is also a lawyer working mainly in the areas of economic, corporate and contract law, European law, and with a special focus on competition law and regulation, and has been previously a legal officer at the European Commission, a senior legal officer at the Portuguese Competition Authority and a director at the Health Regulatory Authority.

Sabrina Evangelista Medeiros received her Ph.D. in Political Science from IUPERJ (IESP), during which she was a fellow at WZ Berlin, from DAAD. She was an Associate Professor at the Brazilian Naval War College (licensed since 2020) and one of the founders of the Maritime Studies Program (Master's and Ph.D.) and the Laboratory of Simulations and Scenarios. She was also a professor at Rio de Janeiro Federal University (UFRJ), and the Inter-American Defense College, as part of the Organization of American States. She is currently Professor at Lusófona University and associate researcher at the InterAgency Institute and the Portuguese National Defence Institute. She leads the GIRI-hub lab at Lusófona University and her main publications are in defence and security economics, cooperation, and gamification & decision-making process.

Carmen Amado Mendes is President of the Macau Scientific and Cultural Centre. Tenured Associate Professor of International Relations, accredited at the School of Economics of the University of Coimbra, where she established the course "China and the Portuguese-speaking Countries in World Trade". Principal Investigator at the University of Coimbra on a project on the role of Macau in China's relations with the Portuguese-speaking countries, funded by the Portuguese national funding agency for Science, Research and Technology. Former head of the International Relations department at the same university. Holds a Ph.D. degree from the School of Oriental and African Studies, University of London, a Master's degree from the Institute of Higher European Studies, University of Strasbourg, and a Bachelor's degree from the Institute of Social and Political Sciences, University of Lisbon. Author of *China and the Macau Negotiations, 1986–1999* (HKUP) and *China's New Silk Road: An Emerging World Order* (Routledge), among other publications, see: www.uc.pt/feuc/carmen.

Rafael Mesquita obtained his Master's and Ph.D. in Political Science at the Federal University of Pernambuco (UFPE), Recife, Brazil, having also spent part of his Ph.D. at the German Institute of Global and Area Studies (GIGA) and the Latin American Centre in Oxford. He was an Associate Research Fellow at the GIGA (2018) and is currently a researcher at the "Núcleo de Estudos de Política Comparada e Relações Internacionais" (NEPI, UFPE). He is Assistant Professor of International Relations at UFPE focusing on the topics of international organizations, rising powers, and quantitative methods. He has published on *International Studies Quarterly*, *Third World Quarterly*, *Revista Brasileira de Política Internacional*, and *Bulletin of Latin American Research*, among other journals.

José Palmeira holds a Ph.D. in Political Science and International Relations from the University of Minho (Portugal), where he is Assistant Professor in the Department of Political Science and member of the Centre for Research in Political Science, being co-editor of *Perspectivas—Journal of Political Science*. The main research interests lie in the areas of geopolitics, strategy, and Portuguese foreign policy. He is the author of several scientific publications and conferences in his areas of expertise and a regular commentator on national and international politics in the Portuguese media.

Rui P. Pereira born in 1970, holds an M.A. in European Studies from the Portuguese Catholic University (2006–2008) and Postgraduate Degrees in Modern China (ISCSP/UTL, 2003) and International Economic Relations (ISEG/UTL, 2001–2002). He has a degree in International Relations from Lusíada University of Lisbon (1989–1994). He completed FORGEP—Training in Public Management for Intermediate Managers in the Public Service (National Institute of Administration, 2009) and the National Defense Auditors Course (National Defense Institute, 2008–2009). He is currently the Head of the International Relations Division at the Directorate-General for Economic Activities—Ministry of Economy. He is the Focal Point of the Forum for Economic and Trade Cooperation between China and the Portuguese-Speaking Countries (Macau Forum). He is a Founding Member of the Observatory of China—Association for Multidisciplinary Investigation of Chinese Studies in Portugal, and a Member of the Association of Friends of the New Silk Road. He has several articles and chapters of books published on themes related to China, including bilateral relations with Portugal, the European Union, and African countries.

João Mourato Pinto graduated in International Relations from the University of Coimbra (Portugal) and holds a Master's degree in International Relations—European Studies from both this university and Sciences Po Bordeaux (France). Currently, João Mourato Pinto is based at the University of Minho where he is a member of the Research Center in Political Science, a professor of diplomacy, and a Ph.D. candidate studying the global actorness of the European Union, especially towards Brazil and South America. He was a member of a research project on the EU's Strategic Partnerships funded by the Portuguese Foundation of Science and Technology (FCT) and has worked at the European Research Council (European Commission). Additionally, he is a former President of the Erasmus Student Network (2017–2019), where he has worked to increase access to and the quality of higher education student exchanges worldwide. His main research interests are EU external action, Brazilian foreign policy, South American regionalism, and diplomacy.

Daniele Jacon Ayres Pinto is a Professor at the Department of Economics and International Relations of the Federal University of Santa Catarina/UFSC. She has a Post-Doc Research in Military Science at Brazilian Army Command and General Staff School—ECEME, and she received her Ph.D. in Political Science from UNICAMP, as she received her Master's Degree in International Relations—Peace and Security—from the University of Coimbra. She has a Bachelor's in International Relations from the University of Coimbra and has a Specialist degree in Human Rights and Democracy from the Faculty of Law of the University of Coimbra/FDUC. She leads the Research Group in Strategic Studies and Contemporary International Politics—GEPPIC—and is an associate researcher at the InterAgency Institute. Currently, she is a vice-president of the Brazilian Association of Defence Studies—ABED. Danielle has experience in the areas of International Power and Policy Studies, Peace and Security Studies with emphasis on Mediation of International Conflicts, State Power Building, Smart Power, Cyber defence and cybersecurity, Power and International insertion of Brazil.

Sónia Ribeiro holds a Ph.D. (2010) and Master's (2000) in European Studies in the Institute of European Studies of the Portuguese Catholic University and a degree in International Relations (1997) of Lusíada University of Porto. She is a visiting Professor at the Institute of Political Studies of 9*+- the Portuguese Catholic University and Coordinator of the Research Line in Maritime Affairs, since 2011. She has coordinated various advanced programmes within the UCP Institute of European Studies, and since 2014 has coordinated the Advanced Program in Sea Studies and coordinates, since 2015, the Post-graduation in Sea Sciences & Business Administration. Sónia is Consultant and Executive Project Manager at SaeR—Society of Strategic Assessment and Risk since September 2000, specializing in the areas of Geopolitics and Prospective, Strategic Planning, Strategic Evaluation, and Regional Development.

José A. Oliveira Rocha holds a law degree from the University of Coimbra, and received a Ph.D. in Political Science from the University of South Carolina (USA). He is Full Professor of Political Science and Public Policy at the Lusófona University of Porto, and member of the Research Center in Political Science, University of Minho, Braga, Portugal. Outside of Portugal, he was professor of Law in Macau University and professor of Public Administration in Brazil, and cooperates actively with researchers in Mozambique. His research interests include public administration and public policies. He is author of several books in Political Science (Ciência Política no Séc. XXI, 2022), Public Policy (Gestão do Processo Político e Políticas Públicas, 2010), and Public Management (Gestão Pública, Modelos e Práticas, 2010, e Gestão de Recursos Humanos e Direito da

Função Pública, 2021) and a long series of research papers published on high quality academic journals.

Maria do Rosário Anjos Ph.D. in Public Law (2011), is Associate Professor at the Faculty of Law and Political Science of the Lusófona University of Porto (ULP) and Director of the 2nd Cycle of Studies in Law of the ULP. She is Vice Dean of Lusófona of Porto since November 2021. She Graduated in Law from the Portuguese Catholic University (1989) and Postgraduate in European Studies from the Portuguese Catholic University. She holds a Master's degree in Public Administration from the School of Economics and Management of the University of Minho (1998) and a Ph.D. in Special Public Law from the Faculty of Law of the University of A Coruña, Spain. She is a representative of the Faculty of Law and Political Science for International Relations; Lawyer and member of BAR association (since 1989); Arbitrator in Administrative and Tax matters at Administrative Arbitration Center (CAAD), in Lisbon. She is also arbitrator judge at the Dispute Resolution Center of the Bar Association, operating in the Regional Center of The OADV of Lisbon and in National Arbitration Center (CAN), operating with AICCOPN - National Association of the Civil Construction and Public Works Industry. She is member of the Portuguese Tax Association, the International Tax Association, and the Portuguese Association of Public Markets (APMEP), among others; Trainer of the Training Center of the Bar Association, in the Porto Internship Center, in Administrative and Tax Procedural Practices; Member of the Advisory Board of Administrative and Tax Courts (North) by indication of the Bar Association. She is a member of the Portuguese Tax Association and the International Tax Association. In November 2021 she became Vice-Rector of the Lusophone University of Porto. Maria do Rosário Anjos is author and co-author of several publications, in book, scientific article and others available in: Maria do Rosário Anjos (9C1A-8286-1349) | CIÊNCIAVITAE (cienciavitae.pt).

Giorgio Romano Schutte Ph.D. Associate Professor in undergraduate studies on International Relations and Economics and graduate studies on International Relations (PRI) and World Political Economy (EPM) at the Federal University ABC (UFABC). His research fields are in International Political Economy, Geopolitics of Energy, and China and Brazil Foreign Policy. He has work experience in trade unions and local and federal government. He is author of A dinâmica dos investimentosprodutivos chineses no Brasil (2020) and The challenge to US hegemony and the "Gilpin Dilemma", RBPI, 2021. He is a research fellow of the National Council of Technological and Scientific Development (CNPq) since 2018.

Pedro Seabra is a researcher at the Centre for International Studies of the University Institute of Lisbon (CEI-Iscte) and a Guest Assistant Professor at Iscte-IUL. He currently serves as an Adviser to the Minister of National Defence of Portugal. He holds a Ph.D. in Political Science, with a specialization in International Relations, from the Institute of Social Sciences, University of Lisbon (ICS-ULisboa). He was previously a researcher at the National Defence Institute, as well as a Visiting Professor at the Institute of International Relations of the University of Brasília (IREL-UnB). He is a former Nuclear Security Fellow of the School of International Relations-Getúlio Vargas Foundation (FGV), SUSI Fellow of the US State Department, and Leibniz-DAAD Research Fellow of the German Institute of Global and Area Studies (GIGA). His areas of expertise focus on multilateralism, South Atlantic regional dynamics, and defence cooperation in Africa and he has published in such outlets as *Cambridge Review of International Affairs*, *African Security*, *South African Journal of International Affairs*, *Journal of Interventation and Statebuilding*, *International Studies Quarterly* and *International Politics*. In 2021 he co-edited the volume, *Brazil-Africa Relations in the 21st Century: From Surge to Downturn and Beyond*, published by Springer.

Célia Taborda Silva holds a Ph.D. in Contemporary History from University of Porto, Faculty of Letters, and a Master's Degree in Modern and Contemporary History from University of Porto, Faculty of Letters. She is Associate Professor at Lusófona University of Porto (ULP) and Vice-President of Portuguese Association of Vine and Wine (APHVIN/GEHVID). Previously she was Assistant Professor at Catholic University of Porto. Currently she is a researcher at CICANT—The Centre for Research in Applied Communication, Culture, and New Technologies and researcher associate at CEAUP—Center of Africana Studies of the University of Porto. Author of books, book chapters, and several articles in national and international scientific journals, her research interests focus on History, social movements, society, and politics. Simultaneously, she participated in diverse international and national conferences and integrated diverse scientific committees and events organization. Her most recent publications include Silva, C.T. (2021). Democracy and Popular Protest in Europe: The Iberian Case (2011). *European Journal* *of Social Sciences*, *4*(2), 97–109; Silva, C.T. (2020). Social movements in Europe, from the past to the present. *European Journal of Social Science Education and Research September*, 5(3), 17–26.

Mojana Vargas Correia Silva Ph.D. Assistant Professor in undergraduate studies on International Relations at the Federal University Paraiba (UFPB). Her research fields are in African Politics, Africa in Brazilian Foreign Policy, Race and Internacional Relations. Author of "O ensino e a pesquisa em relações internacionais no Brasil – sentidos e desafios da decolonialidade", Oasis 2020.

Xuheng Wang is Ph.D. Candidate in International Relations—International Politics and Conflict Resolution, at the Faculty of Economics of the University of Coimbra (FEUC) and the Centre for Social Studies (CES) of the University of Coimbra. Currently researching the role of Macao in the relations between China and the Portuguese-speaking Countries (PSCs) from the perspective of Chinese paradiplomacy. Holds a Master's degree in Marketing and attended the Advanced Course "China and the Portuguese-speaking Countries in World Trade" at FEUC. Holds a Bachelor's degree in Business Administration in Marketing from the School of Business of the Macao Polytechnic Institute.

Emilio J. Zeca received his Ph.D. in International Strategic Studies from the Universidade Federal do Rio Grande do Sul—Brazil in 2018. Currently, he is researcher at Department of Peace and Security at Center for Strategic and International Studies—CEEI/UJC and teacher of Security Studies at Joaquim Chissano University—Mozambique. His most recent books are: *Civil-Military Relations in CPLP: The Role in Promoting Peace, Security and Stability* (2022); "Intelligence Services in Mozambique: Institutions, Dynamics and Operations" (2021); "Elements for Understanding and Analyzing Mozambique's Foreign Policy and Diplomacy" (2020); and "Mozambique: Energy Resources and Foreign Policy" (2016). He is Editor of Mozambican Journal of International Studies (*Revista Moçambicana de Estudos Internacionais*—RMEI).

List of Figures

Transition to a New Geopolitics of Energy: The Lusophone World

The Role of Forum Macao in the People's Republic of China Foreign Policy

The Geopolitics of Timor-Leste: Belt & Road Initiative (B&RI), ASEAN and CPLP

List of Tables

The Geopolitics of the Portuguese Language: Knowledge and Influence

Transition to a New Geopolitics of Energy: The Lusophone World

The Role of Forum Macao in the People's Republic of China Foreign Policy

Legal Issues and Politics Within the Lusophone World

The Feasibility of the Portuguese Legal System in the Former African Colonies

José A. Oliveira Rocha

Introduction

To discuss the viability of the Portuguese legal system in the former Portuguese colonies in Africa (PALOPs) implies an analysis of the theory of circulation and diffusion of legal models. This approach, also known as legal transplantation, contains the idea of the movement and flow of legal paradigms and legal ideas across national borders.

The literature does not abound on this matter. If we put aside the works on the reception of Roman law, the first author to raise the problem was Frederick Walton (1927), who advances the thesis of the non-interference of culture in the transfer of legal norms between societies. According to the same author, there are "legal constructions" that are not intrinsically linked to a particular society. This approach was further developed by Watson (1983), who underlined that this kind of "loan" does not mean the recipient's full understanding. It is an automatic process.

In the opposite sense, Kahn-Freund (1974) states that the social environment where the norms are transferred is decisive. On the other hand,

J. A. O. Rocha (✉)
University of Minho, Braga, Portugal

P. A. B. Duarte et al. (eds.), *Portugal and the Lusophone World*,
https://doi.org/10.1007/978-981-99-0455-6_1

one must take into account the nature of the company that produced the same standards. This approach is due to Montesquieu, who stated in the *Esprit des Lois*:

> … The political and civil laws of each nation… must be so clean to the people for whom they are made, that it is a great coincidence that those from one nation may suit another.

According to this theory, Watson (1983) refers to legal transplantation only when the process involves the simultaneous transfer of social models, of which the legal system is a component. In his opinion, there is no strict correlation between law and social, political and economic circumstances. Law would be autonomous and operates in its own sphere, differently from other social institutions.

As a way to harmonize the two views, Sacco (1991) insists that it is necessary to distinguish the different legal formats, since there are legal forms capable of being transferred from one system to another. But, in fact, few legal systems can produce exportable formats.

In the same vein, Graziadei (2015) identifies three important factors of legal change: the imposition by force, the exporter's prestige and the idea of connection to economic performance. And, in fact, legal transplants were almost always the result of the use of force. This was the case with Roman law and, more recently, with the extension of German law to Austria and the imposition of Soviet law on the popular republics of continental Europe.

Another relevant contribution is due to Gunther Teubner (1998) who criticizes the previous theories, as they start from the misconception that the material being transferred will reach its destination, playing the same role and acting under the same conditions as before.

In fact, the transplanted element will arrive at the new system, not as a natural element of it, but as a "legal irritant"; will have to be the subject of a deconstruction process, without which the assimilation of imported legal forms will not occur.

Assuming a different methodology, Riggs (1964) argued that imported political, administrative or legal models, when in contact with traditional structures, undergo a process of refraction, giving rise to societies that are distinguished from traditional ones, but that also do not identify with the exporters (See Fig. 1).

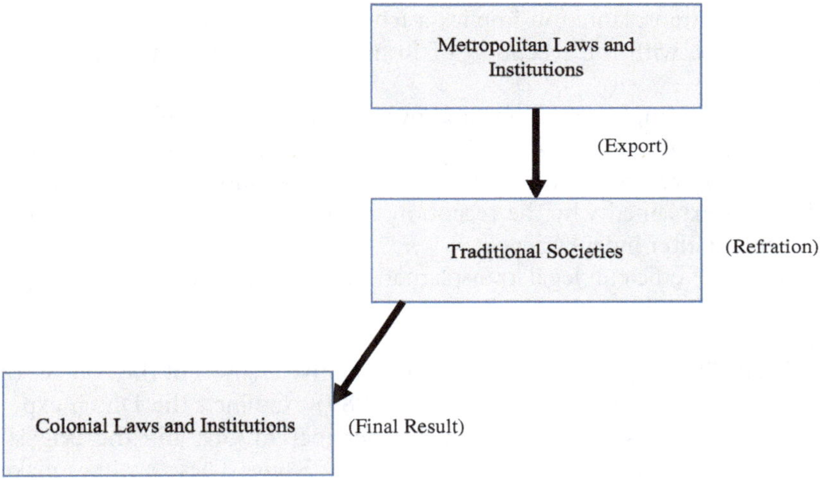

Fig. 1 Legal circulation between the metropolis and the colonies (*Source* Adapted from Riggs [1964])

Administrative and procedural practices and routines do not follow the legislator's intentions, nor do they simply represent traditional thinking. This explains why Portuguese law, although derived from Roman law and belonging to the civil law family, is not to be confused with other continental European rights.

Heady (1986) also argues that, despite the adoption of legal and institutional models in the colonizing country, prismatic societies maintain traditional values. Thus, for example, the merit system is, as a rule, subverted, giving preference to family members and members of the same tribe; on the other hand, correction is part of the political and legal system. There is always a discrepancy between form and reality.

The concept of transplantation goes beyond just exporting, insofar as it implies a certain degree of transformation of the society, must be associated with a change in the social structure (Rocha 1991). However, the success of this transfer is linked, simultaneously, to the export of a certain ideology. That happened, for example, with the adoption of the democratic model in China with Sun Yat-Sen's bourgeois revolution, or in Japan during the opening to the West.

Second, transplantation implies a lengthy process of acculturation, as was the case with the reception of Roman law. And yet, it is subject to distortions.

Third, the implementation of a given legal system is only feasible if it enjoys political legitimacy, that is, if the recipient society accepts the new model as more economically appropriate and because it enjoys prestige. Thus it is explained why the reception of the colonizer's juridical system accelerated after independence.

Fourthly, efficient legal transplantation is not possible without legal operators, familiar and trained in the imported model. Jurists can acclimatize foreign legal models to social institutions.

Finally, it is important to make a comparative analysis of the contact of different legal models. Alberto Costa (1989) examined the Dutch experience in Sri Lanka, the Portuguese experience in Goa and the English experience in Malaysia, Singapore and Hong Kong. These analyses make it possible to draw several conclusions. First, there is a connection between law and language; the second conclusion is that knowledge of an imported legal system necessarily implies the existence of legal practitioners. For example, the disappearance of the Portuguese law in Goa can be attributed, to a large extent, to the progressive occupation of judicial functions by jurists trained under the "Common law".

To answer the initial question about the viability of the Portuguese legal system in the former African colonies, it is important to analyze the colonization process. In fact, the implementation of the Portuguese legal model should be considered as part of a broader process of political, economic and cultural colonization.

Portuguese Colonization: Duality of Law

The colonization system that most influenced the Portuguese system was carried out by France, which foresaw the existence of a dual legal system: the laws of the metropolis applied only to French colonists, while the "indigenous" ones, remained subject to customary rights. In the event of conflict, the principle of applying French law, in the name of the "colonial public order", was in force.

Although the contacts between Portugal and Africa date back to the fifteenth century, effective colonization started by the end of the nineteenth century, under pressure from the Berlin Conference (1884–1885), which demanded effective occupation and not just the invocation of the so-called "historical rights". It was just in the last decades of the nineteenth century and in the first two decades of the twentieth that the Portuguese armed forces in the African colonies of Portugal conducted a vast set of military operations, of very unequal scale, known as Pacification and Occupation Campaigns. As regards concretely to Mozambique, both to the south and to the north, they were administered directly; in the center and in the north, the territory was leased to private firms, some of which not only exploited the territory economically, but also ensured administrative authority. The role of these private companies followed the so-called "*prazos*" (concessions made by the local chiefs), which allowed the administration and enforcement of justice, created in the seventeenth century, but which lasted until the twentieth century (Rocha e Zavale 2020).

Following the effective occupation, the Portuguese State opted for the differentiation between Europeans and Africans. The former was subject to European law and institutions; and the latter to customary rights and traditional authorities, legitimized by colonial power. Some Africans, a small minority, who knew how to read and write fluent Portuguese and hold jobs in the colonialist economy started to be "assimilated", but still maintaining a lower position than Europeans (Newit 1997).

The Indigenous Labor Code of 1928 and the Indigenous Statute of 1929, following the 1899 Labor Law and other diplomas, articulated the relationship between colonialists and the colonized. The latter were forced by the Colonial Administration to perform various types of work. Recruitment was done by "*cipaios*" (local soldiers, belonged to the colonial administration), who worked in rural areas. Traditional authorities served as intermediaries between colonial power and indigenous peoples. The indigenous political system subordinated the natives of the colonies to the local authorities who administered justice in collaboration with the colonial authorities.

Traditional authorities were particularly important in matters such as access to land, family issues, debts, bodily harm, property, health and petty theft. Thus, one can say that civil issues and minor crime were the responsibility of traditional authorities, which followed tribal traditions (Santos 2006).

The use of traditional customs and structures of tribal power constituted an integral part of colonial power. According to Acemoglou and Robinson (2010), the colonizing countries exported extractive institutions to the colonized countries in Africa, designed to exploit the colonial wealth. These institutions are part of the legal system used by the colonialists. As for the local legal norms, they are adjusted and made dependent on the objectives of the colonizers. Thus, according to the same authors, a dual legal system and a dual economy were created. This dual model had its peak in apartheid in South Africa.

To quote Mamdavi (2001), in the indirect colonization model there is not a single customary law. Each ethnic group has its own law. The tribes in Africa corresponded, in a broad sense, to the nations in Europe. And in some cases, such as in northern Mozambique and Guinea-Bissau, this mosaic of tribes has become more complex as some of these tribes are Islamized. Each African colony can be seen as an ethnic federation, with many native authorities.

In this legal mosaic, traditional authorities are particularly relevant. Many of these authorities are ancestral, but others have been legitimized by colonial powers. Traditional authority, known as "*régulo*", does not function as a first instance in conflict resolution. In terms of conflict resolution, judicial cases were presented, first, to the so-called "*cabos da terra*", who worked as subordinates to the "*régulo*". Only if these authorities could not solve the problem, the cases would be presented to the traditional authority, the "*régulo*". Concerning procedural law, it was used to follow simple rules: it is immediate, simple, public and relatively transparent (Meneses et al. 2003).

If we examine the content of customary African rights, two observations can be made at the outset: first, the idea of tradition as a set of practices, norms and values that go back to immemorial antiquity. Examples are the concept of non-privatization of land; another example is the emphasis on corporal punishment. Second, although Europeans arrived in Africa, they conceived of tradition as immutable, there was no fixed body of traditional norms, but several conflicting traditions supported by various authorities (Araújo 2008).

Two observations can be drawn. Firstly, we are dealing with an indirect type of government that presupposes the existence of two legal orders: one European and several native ones. Portuguese colonization adopts the doctrine of assimilation that allowed the transition of indigenous people to full citizenship, with obedience to certain requirements. On the contrary, direct government is associated with the English colonies and presupposes the existence of a single legal order.

The end of the indigenous regime in 1961, a solution imposed by anti-colonial pressure, did not bring about substantial changes in terms of legal dualism. The Decree-Law 43893 contains only one article in which the Statute of the Indigenous is revoked. However, the preamble attempts to justify this policy change. The Portuguese tradition of respect for the private law of the populations incorporated in the Portuguese State is highlighted. The Indigenous Statute would be a manifestation of this policy. However, international criticism has insisted on a change of policy. Indeed, this is the reason for the change, despite insisting that this change corresponds to a movement to subject the entire population to the same political status.

In other words, the so-called indigenous people started to be considered citizens without going through the assimilation process, even though the fact that they continue to be governed by customary rights. The Portuguese authoritarian, autocratic and corporatist state regime that prevailed in Portugal between 1933 and 1974 ("Estado Novo") adhered to Gilberto Freyre's luso-tropicalism thesis, which defended the construction of a multiracial Portuguese nation. At the same time, it extolled the mildness of Portuguese colonialism, when compared to other colonialisms. But dualism continued. It was just a new guise to avoid international campaigns against colonial policy.

Post-independence Period

According to Mamdavi (2001), African countries, following its independence, can be divided into two categories: conservative states and radical states. The former states defend the idea of customary law, with an authentic African tradition; in practice, however, they reproduced the legal dualism of the colonial period. Traditional chiefs remained the same as in colonial times. In turn, the radical states, as a rule of a single party, proceeded to dismantle the customary authorities. Portuguese-speaking African countries (PALOPs) followed this guide.

As for Mozambique, which we are examining in a special way, the post-colonial government established a rupture with the colonial heritage, having sought the construction of a socialist state and a "New Man". As stated by Samora Machel, the mythical figure who led the Mozambican War of Independence, the objective was the creation of a nation from Rovuma to Maputo, going through the destruction of the "colonial State".

While the colonizer's language and law were seen as instruments for the creation of a centralized nation and state, the traditional Authorities were ostracized because they had collaborated with the colonizer. On the other hand, traditional rights were banned because through this recognition the country was fragmented. In place of the traditional authorities, dynamization groups were created, linked to the central state and Frelimo transmission belts.

In terms of judicial organization, popular courts were created at different levels (Araújo 2008). The Supreme People's Court was at the top of the hierarchy; then the provincial popular courts; district people's courts; and, finally, the neighborhood or local people's courts.

In all echelons, non-professional judges participated, elected by popular assemblies to exercise judicial functions. At the base of the pyramid, the judicial function was performed exclusively by elected judges who tried small crimes according to common sense and justice, whenever the parties could not be reconciled.

The objective was to build a legal system that rejected the dualism between a state right for elites and other rights for the population; and it supposed the recreation of a single right for the entire Mozambican society, from Rovuma to Maputo. The phrase of Samora Machel: "for the nation to be born, the tribe must die" clearly expresses this political objective. However, this did not imply that traditional authorities had disappeared from the judicial map. Some of them adjusted to the new reality; others passed to Renamo, the second largest Mozambican political party.

Period of Liberal Democracy and Market Economy

Even in the 1980s, Frelimo was forced to acknowledge the failure of economic policies. In addition, the war with Renamo has aggravated the problems. Hence, at the end of the eighties, Mozambique, like other African countries, was forced to turn to international organizations for help, namely the World Bank and the International Monetary Fund. These institutions made their aid dependent on changing the economic model, from socialist to liberal, or from a centralized economy to a market economy.

From a political point of view, the one-party state has evolved into a model of liberal, multi-party democracy with free elections (See Table 1).

Table 1 PALOPS political development trajectory

Political system	*Juridical system*	*International politics*
1. Colonial state since mid-twentieth century until 1975	Legal dualism (*Indirect Rule*)	War of independence that begins in the 60s, and continues until 1975
2. Independence: Socialist State • Single Party regime • Centralized Economy	State unification; a single legal order. Denial of traditional rights	Cold War period. Liberation Movements supported by the USSR in the construction of the post-independence state
3. Economic and political liberalization since 1990	Recovery of traditional authorities and local rights	Political pluralism is imposed by donor institutions

Source Author

In Mozambique, the 1990 Constitution enshrined the principle of the separation of powers. The independence of the courts was translated into a new Organic Law of the Courts of 1992. According to this law, the elected judges start to intervene only in the first instance judgments and in matters of fact (art. 10). Community Courts were created by the same diploma. They judge on the basis of customs and practices about small civil conflicts and minor crimes. These courts are also expected to seek, in the first place, to reconcile the parties.

With regard to traditional authorities, having found that the attempt to abolish them constitutes a problem, progress has been made toward their recognition, as these continued to exist. Recognition was made by Law 3/94 and Law 2/97. In addition to performing administrative functions, they also perform judicial functions.

Subsequently, the Decree 15/2000 seeks to qualify the traditional authorities, including the traditional chiefs, recognized by colonialism, and the secretaries of the neighborhood or village of the time of the socialist period.

Recently, there have been advances in the recognition of Mozambican legal and judicial plurality. The latest constitutional revision emphasizes that “the State recognizes the various normative and conflict resolution systems that coexist in Mozambican society, insofar as they do not contradict the fundamental values and principles of the Constitution” (article 4).

The proposal of the Administration of Justice system introduced an articulation between the community courts and the judicial courts (See Fig. 2).

As noted before, the transplantation of a certain legal system implies the existence of legal operators, familiar and trained in the imported model. These operators exist in all former African colonies.

In Mozambique, the Faculty of Law was created even before independence with a program similar to that of Portuguese law schools. The faculty was, however, closed between 1983 and 1987. The law schools served as a vehicle for the permanence of Portuguese law of the Roman-Germanic family.

In addition to law schools, Judicial Studies Centers were created in all former colonies, with the responsibility of training future judges, prosecutors and other legal operators (Trindade and Pedroso 2003).

B. Sousa Santos (2006) carried out, together with his team, a detailed investigation in Mozambique about the legal system. They verified that

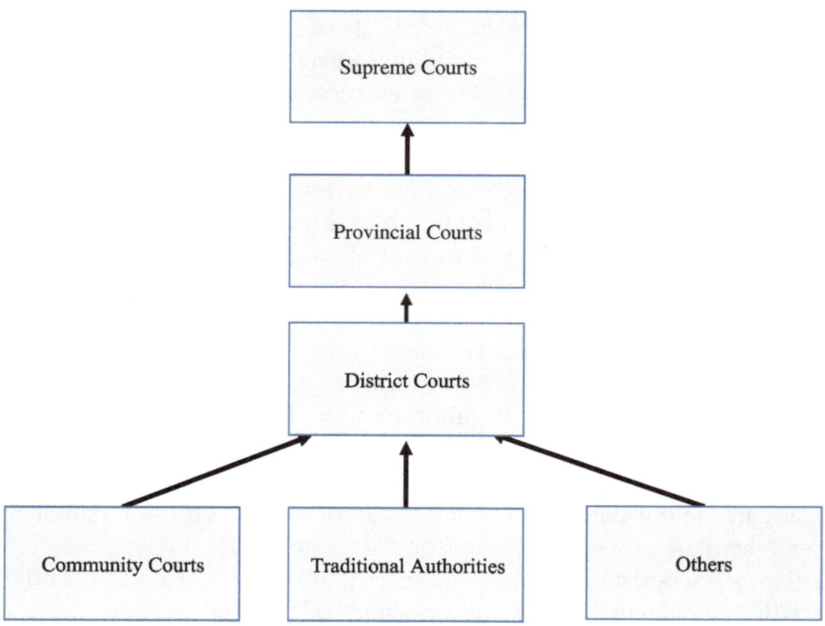

Fig. 2 Judicial pluralism in Mozambique (*Source* Author)

the official system is only part of the country's legal system. Supranational laws, introduced by donor institutions, as well as NGOs, are now part of the Mozambican legal system. Community courts and other forms of conflict resolution are also included. Furthermore, in the case of Mozambique, this country is influenced by common law both in the field of contracts and in the legislative process. It is also important to underline the revival of Muslim culture and law in the north and regions of central Mozambique. The same is true in Guinea-Bissau, where part of the population is Islamized.

It follows that many authors (vd. Sousa Santos 2006) consider Mozambique to be a heterogeneous state, without unity in the legal system, since there are different legal orders, although there is cross-fertilization among them.

Other researchers reject the concept of legal pluralism, arguing that there are no rights (European, customary, indigenous, Islamic) and stressing the existence of a single legal order—colonial law (Roberts and Mann 1991).

Reference to Other Ex-colonies Beyond Mozambique

The analysis made so far approached the case of Mozambique, but it is also valid for the other former Portuguese colonies in Africa.

Thus, in what concerns Angola, the 2010 Constitution states in article 7: "The validity and legal force of the custom that is not contrary to the Constitution, nor does not violate the dignity of the human person, is recognized". The Constitution also defines the traditional Authorities in article 224° as "entities that personify and exercise power within the respective traditional political-community organization".

Custom, as a source of law, ranges from its rejection in the post-independence period, through ignorance to its constitutional recognition and the acceptance of legal pluralism (Silva 2015).

In Guinea-Bissau, the weight of traditional authorities is even more important than in Angola, or Mozambique, for two reasons. Firstly, because the weight of European law is less and also because the tribes are better structured and participate directly in the political process. In addition, in Islamized areas, which represent more than a third of the population, the sphere of influence of the rulers has been replaced by that of the religious authorities (Carvalho 2000).

In Cape Verde, the official courts are an instance of appeal, given the importance of informal conflict resolution mechanisms. We are moving, albeit without official recognition, toward legal pluralism. Moreover, popular courts were replaced by community courts in the early 90s (Varela 2004).

Finally, the colonization of S. Tomé and Príncipe has different contours from the other former Portuguese colonies in Africa. The population of S. Tomé is the result of slavery, forced labor and labor import contracts, destined to work in the coffee and cocoa plantations. These workers from the African coast, and above all from Angola, were subjected to an uprooting process that destroyed traditional values and norms (Nascimento 2020).

Despite this, there are four Creole languages, according to the origin of its inhabitants and resulting from the crossing with the language of the colonizers. Among the ethnic groups, the "*Angolars*" are relevant. In this context, traditional rights also exist, although with less relevance.

Conclusion

Whatever the thesis adopted—legal pluralism, or colonial law—it is unclear that Portuguese law endures, as such, in the PALOPs. It is certain that there are favorable factors, such as language, creation of Law Schools, Centers of Judicial Studies, as well as the influence of Portuguese doctrine and jurisprudence.

But traditional rights are of relevant importance, tending to inform the legal culture of the future. In part of Mozambique, as well as in Guinea-Bissau, Islamic law has a very important influence.

Secondly, and although the laws of the colonial metropolis continue to be imported, they are only formally applied, since they suffer a refraction during the importation process (Riggs 1964).

With time, it will be more proper to speak of Mozambican law, Angolan law, etc., although integrated into the family of "civil law" and close to Portuguese law, from which they received and continue to receive influence.

Of course, the investigation is purely institutional. It would be important to analyze the registration of sentences, in which the meaning of European law takes on new contours in contact with customary rights and how they adjust to the so-called "State law". B. Sousa Santos (2006) uses the concept of legal hybridization in order to show the porosity of the borders between the different legal orders.

References

Acemoglou, D. and J. Robinson. 2010. "Why is Africa Poor?" *Economic History and Developing Regions*. Vol. 25 (1): 21–50.

Araújo, Sara. 2008. "Pluralismo Jurídico em África: Ficção ou Realidade". *Revista Crítica de Ciências Sociais*. Nº 83: 1–14.

Carvalho, Clara. 2000. "A Revitalização do Poder Tradicional e os Regulados Manjaco da Guiné-Bissau". *Etnográfica*. Vol. 1V (1): 37–59.

Costa, Alberto. 1989. "Contributo para a definição de uma Política de direito para Macau, à luz de Outras Experiências de Raiz Europeia na Região". *Relatório do Governo de Macau*.

Graziadei, Michele. 2015. "Comparative Law as a study of Transplants and Receptions". *The Oxford Handbook of Comparative Law*. Oxford University Press.

Heady, Ferrel. 1986. *Public Administration: A Comparative Perspective*. 3rd edition. New York: Marcel Dekker, Inc.

Kahn-Freund, Otto. 1974. "On Uses and Misuses of Comparative Law". *Modern Law Review*. Vol. 37.

Mamdavi, M. 2001. "Beyond Settler and Native as Political Identities: Overcoming the Political Legacy of Colonialism". *Comparative Studies in Society and History*. Vol. 43: 651–664.

Meneses, Maria Paula, J. Fumo, G. Mobilana and C. Gomes. 2003. "As Autoridades Tradicionais no Contexto do Pluralismo Jurídico". In B. Sousa Santos e J. Trindade, eds. *Conflito e Transformação Social: uma Paisagem das Justiças em Moçambique*. Porto: Afrontamento.

Nascimento, A. 2020. "Escravatura, Trabalho Forçado e Contratos de Trabalho em S. Tomé e Príncipe nos séculos XIX–XX. Sujeição e Ética Laboral. *Africana Studies*. 1–36.

Newit, M. 1997. *História de Moçambique*. Lisboa: Europa-América.

Riggs, Fred W. 1964. *Administration in Developing Countries: The Theory of Prismatic Society*. Boston: Houghton Mifflin Company.

Roberts, Richard and Kristin Mann. 1991. *Law in Colonial Africa*. Portsmouth, N. H. Heineman Education Books.

Rocha, J. A. Oliveira. 1991. "A Viabilidade do Sistema Jurídico de Macau". *Administração*. Vol. IV. Nº 13/14: 541–557.

Rocha, J. A. Oliveira Rocha e G. Jonas Zavale. 2020. *Introdução à Administração Pública de Moçambique*. S. Paulo: Novas Edições Académicas.

Sacco, Formants. 1991. "A Dynamic Approach to Comparative Law". *Journal of Comparative Law*. Vol. 9, Nº 3: 343–401.

Santos, B. Sousa. 2006. "The Heterogeneous State and Legal Pluralism in Mozambique". *Law and Society Review*. Vol, N° 1: 39–75.

Silva, C. Buritz. 2015. "O Costume Como Fonte de Direito na Ordem Jurídica Plural Angolana". *Revista de Direito de Língua Portuguesa*. N° 5: 7–64.

Teubner, Gunther. 1998. "Legal Irritants: Good Faith, in British Law or Unifying Law Ends After New Divergences". *Modern Law Review*. Vol. 61: 11–32.

Trindade, J. Carlos e João Pedroso.2003. "The judicial System: Structure, Education and Legal Training". In B. Sousa Santos e João Trindade (org.). *Conflito e Transformação Social: Uma Paisagem das Justiças em Moçambique*. Porto: Afrontamento.

Varela. O. Bartolomeu. 2004. "A Extinção dos Tribunais Populares e Cabo Verde Perante o Processo de Globalização Hegemónica do Direito: Reinvenção contra-hegemónica e Mito, ou Realidade?" *VIll Congresso Luso-Afro-Brasileiro de Ciências Sociais*. Coimbra, 16–18 de September, 2004.

Walton, Frederick. 1927. "The Historical School of Jurisprudence and Transplantation of Law." *Journal of Comparative Legis and International Law*. Vol. 9, N° 1.

Watson, A. Alan. 1983. "Legal Changes: Sources of Law and Legal Culture". *University of Pennsylvania Law Review*, pp. 131 e sgts.

The Onto-Anthropological Foundation of Criminal Law in Brazil

Fabio Roberto D'Avila and *Rodrigo Moraes de Oliveira*

Introduction: Portuguese Influence on the First Laws of Brazil

The history of Brazilian criminal codification dates back to the beginning of the nineteenth century when Brazil, which had recently become independent from Portugal, was still under the aegis of the Laws of the Kingdom or, more precisely, with regard to criminal law, under the aegis of Book V of the Legal Code of King Philip I of Portugal (in Portuguese *Ordenações Filipinas*). In the beginning of that century, after having been in force for more than two hundred years, the harshness of the old Book V was no longer in line with the new political and social condition of Brazil and, even less, with the arising liberal ideals and principles (Bruno 1967, p. 174; Silva 1943, p. 5). The content of Book V was extremely outdated when, in 1822, Brazil became independent from Portugal by

F. R. D'Avila (✉) · R. M. de Oliveira
Pontifícia Universidade Católica do Rio Grande do Sul (PUCRS), Porto Alegre, Brazil
e-mail: fabio.davila@pucrs.br

R. M. de Oliveira
e-mail: rodrigo.oliveira@pucrs.br

P. A. B. Duarte et al. (eds.), *Portugal and the Lusophone World*,
https://doi.org/10.1007/978-981-99-0455-6_2

an act of Emperor Pedro I and also began to seek autonomy in legislative terms as a means of establishing the national identity.

In this sense, the Constitution of 1824 was the landmark of Imperial Brazil. It had a prominent liberal accent and was in harmony with the political and legal aspirations of the time. The Constitution of the Empire provided a broad list of individual rights and guarantees under article 179. And, under item 2 of article 179 it provisioned 'no law will be established without it having public utility', showing this Political Charter had a clear influence of Jeremy Bentham's philosophy which is well-founded on the notion of utility (Garcia 1952, p. 120). And, under the other items, the political commitment of the country with principles and values that would shape the first Brazilian Penal Code could be perceived. In other words, the new Constitution had provided all that would be necessary to welcome a modern criminal law. Which, in fact, came to be.

The first project for a Brazilian Penal Code was presented to the Chamber of Deputies on 4 May 1827 by Bernardo Pereira de Vasconcelos (Pierangeli 2004, p. 66). A few days later, on 15th May, the also Deputy José Clemente Pereira submitted a preliminary draft project for the Penal Code, only to submit his own Penal Code project to the Chamber on the following day (Bruno 1967, p. 178). Although the latter was accepted for consideration by the bicameral Commission created to review the proposals, it was not as significant as Pereira de Vasconcelos' project, which was indeed decisive for the legislating efforts that resulted in the enactment of the Penal Code of 1830 (Pierangeli 2004, p. 66).

Pereira de Vasconcelos was, as was Clement Pereira, a graduate from the Faculty of Law at the University of Coimbra (Gauer 2001, p. 305)—the institution which at the time echoed the teachings of the renowned Professor Pascoal de Mello Freire. Professor Mello Freire had solid Enlightenment thought and was particularly influenced by the work of Cesare Beccaria. At the time, the Professor was the person most largely responsible for the dissemination of liberal ideals and for the humanization of criminal law in light of the principles of The Enlightenment in Portugal (Pierangeli 2004, pp. 68–69). He had been entrusted by Maria I of Portugal with the task of preparing a project to replace the Legal Code of King Philip I in Portugal. Although the proposed project had admitted many concessions in order to make liberal ideals compatible with the then political and historical context of Portugal it was too advanced for the times and ended up not succeeding (Pierangeli 2004, p. 69).

On the other hand, in Brazil things were different. As aforementioned, the Constitution of 1824 had opened the doors to a liberal Penal Code that would consecrate the principles and aspirations of penal Enlightenment, which, in fact, resulted in being positively reflected in the legislative process itself. Pereira de Vasconcelos' project of unquestionable liberal accent was well-received. The most controversial issue established regarded the death penalty, which was maintained due to a small majority vote cast by parliamentarians, and which had been required by the conservatives on the grounds that order among the slaves needed to be maintained (Garcia 1952, p. 123), and for that reason it was abolished for political crimes—which, considering the times, was already a major advance—and was maintained for other crimes, under the condition of it being submitted to the Moderating Power (Jiménez de Asúa 1950, p. 1046).

On 16 December 1830, the first Brazilian Penal Code, the Penal Code of the Empire, was sanctioned. Locally celebrated as a liberal code of high quality and rather advanced for the times literature (Bruno 1967, p. 178; Garcia 1952, pp. 123–124; Noronha 1959, p. 79), the Code of the Empire achieved great repercussion in the international scenario and would come to influence the Spanish Code of 1848 (Jiménez de Asúa 1950, p. 1046) and, consequently, several other Latin American Penal Codes that sought inspiration in the criminal legislation of Spain (Garcia 1952, p. 123; Pierangeli 2004, p. 73). At the same time, the first Penal Code of Brazil revealed that the ties that united the two nations were even stronger. Aside from the political arena, the legal matters of Brazil and Portugal had much in common and would still have much more in common ahead.

This chapter falls exactly at this point. It seeks to review the main lines of the onto-anthropological foundation of criminal law developed in Portugal by José de Faria Costa by taking into account its significant repercussion in Brazil. It aims to answer the following guiding question: What is the main contribution of the onto-anthropological foundation to contemporary criminal law?

The Onto-Anthropological Foundation of José De Faria Costa

Crime and punishment—as it is well known—are the core categories of criminal law (Faria Costa 2017, p. 12). It is from them that the normative expression and dogmatic structure of criminal law stems from. It is from them that criminal law gains existence within the universe of law.

The essentiality of these two ideas, however, goes far beyond the leading role it plays within the formal dimension of criminal law. The way crime and punishment are conceived by the criminal system is directly linked to the way the system itself is thought out and structured, as well as to the solutions it (the system) offers. In other words, the output of the penal system—both what it seeks and what it delivers in terms of conflict resolution—depends on how the ideas of crime and punishment are received and articulated by the penal system. And from that, nothing escapes—nothing, ranging from the measure of the penalty to the definition of a new crime, including, for example, fundamental elements such as the criteria for objective imputation, the limits of the attempt or the dogmatic contours of the mens rea. These are all, without exception, manifestations at a practical level of a state of matters that precede them, of a deeper level arrangement, in which the conceptions of crime and punishment encounter the foundation and function of criminal law.

At a remarkable conference held in 2000, Faria Costa shed light on what one might call a key idea. According to him, the rationale behind criminal law order can take two paths, 'It is either extracted from the consequences of the norm, that is, in this sense, from the punishment or, conversely, critical attention is supported by the object of the norm, that is, by *Unrecht*' (Faria Costa 2002, p. 9). Each path is responsible for a precise way of understanding and structuring criminal law. The former seeks legitimacy in a consequential/functionalist matrix, the latter, in an ontological matrix (Faria Costa 2002, p. 9).

The last decades have been a stage for the widespread rise in consequential matrix thought. Although it has been shaped by different lines, criminal functionalism has been markedly present when positions are taken on the main issues of recent history, such as terrorism. Whether regarding the doctrine-theory scope or whether regarding the multiple levels of execution of criminal practices, functionalist thinking has dominated decision-making and the elaboration of strategies in both the national and international scenarios. Criminal law was thought and shaped by punishment. Punishment—*rectius*, the sanctioning logic and everything useful and good that is believed to be able to be obtained from it—has not only dominated criminal policy but has also made criminal law an instrument of its implementation.

There is no intention, for obvious reasons, to take stock of the leading role of functional thinking here. Gone are the days when the goodness of a given way of thinking implied the failure or the necessary illegitimacy of other ways of thinking. It is necessary to recognize, however, that every path proposes (and leads to) a destination. More than that. It is committed to a certain course. Something which is actually revealed in the governing question itself. 'What is the law for?' With this question, as rightly noted by Castanheira Neves there is an attitude of legal functionalism before the law. An attitude that clearly puts 'an asymmetry in which the constitutive autonomy of input is sacrificed for the optimization of output' (Castanheira Neves 1998, p. 26), which speaks for itself. The onto-anthropological foundation is established within another horizon. In an authorial work, Faria Costa reveals a new view on criminal law, giving back to crime or, more precisely, to *Unrecht* (wrongdoing) its lost protagonism: *Unrecht*, and not punishment, is positioned at the center of criminal thought.

This repositioning, on the one hand, is a starting point for countless practical consequences, both in terms of crime and punishment. On the other hand, it is also the point of arrival. This is because in Faria Costa's formulation, *Unrecht* embodies something that precedes it and gives it shape. It is the penal-dogmatic expression of the 'perversion or rupture' of the onto-anthropological matrix relationship of care-of-danger (Faria Costa 2002, p. 13). A fundament that refers us to philosophy and, with it, to the question about the meaning of the Being and its relationship with care and that finds, although it finds multiple sources inside and outside philosophy, in Heideggerian Sorge one of its core categories.

In an interesting excerpt from Being and Time, Heidegger makes use of an old Fable from Hyginus, fable # 220, to shed some light on his understanding of 'care' (Sorge).

> Once when 'Care' was crossing a river, she saw some clay; she thoughtfully picked up a piece and began to shape it. While she was meditating on what she had made, Jupiter came by. 'Care' asked him to give it spirit, and this he gladly granted. But when she wanted her name to be bestowed upon it, he forbade this, and demanded that it be given his name instead. While

> 'Care' and Jupiter were disputing, Earth arose and desired that her own name be conferred on the creature, since she had furnished it with part of her body. They asked Saturn to be their arbiter, and he made the following decision, which seemed a just one: 'Since you, Jupiter, have given its spirit, you shall receive that spirit at its death; and since you, Earth, have given its body, you shall receive its body. But since 'Care' first shaped this creature, she shall possess it as long as it lives. And because there is now a dispute among you as to its name, let it be called '*homo*', for it is made out of *humus* (earth). (Heidegger 1962, p. 242)

One can tell from this important allegory that it was Care who was the first to shape man and thus it became the source of the Being of man. It is by the hands of Care that man comes to be the Being and, as such and through justice, in an immutable connection to its first source, Care will possess man for as long as he lives. Or, as said by Heidegger, 'the entity is not released from this source but is held fast, dominated by it through and through as long as this entity "is in the world." "Being-in-the-world" has the stamp of "care", which accords with its Being' (Heidegger 1962, p. 243). It is therefore not in the matter that constitutes the Being, herein represented by *humus,* but in the Being of the Being-there, as a contribution of Care. A decision which is, by no chance, delivered by Saturn. It is Saturn, or Time, who is called to be the arbiter of the dispute and it is he who imposes to the Being, for as long as it lives, the connection to Care, its source. It is, in this well-characterized call to history that, therefore, the Being of the Being-there will be hopelessly connected to the Being-towards-death.

Stein highlights that differently from the allegory of the Cave and the allegory of the Dove, the allegory of Care does not seek to establish a theory of knowledge from ontology as Plato does, and, far less, to draw the limits of an ontology from the theory of knowledge as Kant intends, but it only seeks to introduce, by overcoming the other two allegories, a 'description of man placed before the fact that he is a Being-in-the-world, as a Thrown-being and as a Being-towards-death, before a finite task, in which he has ever since the beginning been engaged in as care' (Stein 2005, p. 100).

Putting it straightforward: man is care. This bold assertion, when observed from the onto-anthropological perspective of Faria Costa, takes on such a wealth of developments that it could not possibly be developed in its entirety here. It is important, however, for us to consider herein its matrix lines, starting with the way care is understood.

In Faria Costa's work, care is not only an existential category, but also, and fundamentally, a relational category. It is an essential element of existence that is only revealed in its fullness in the person of the other, in the relationship that stems from the other and becomes possible (Faria Costa 1992, p. 250, footnote 87). Within this horizon, to be yourself is to look after oneself. But it also means to be the Being-with and, therefore, in this opening of the Being to the other, to look after oneself also means to look after the other, as a fundamental expression of the Being-in-the-world that, at being, projects itself, in its fragility, on the other, and looks after oneself in the care-for-the-other.

The act of Being-in-the-world—which is always an action of Being-with—throws Being-there into a web of reciprocal relationships of care that structure and give consistency to the community Being. Individual care, the care of self towards self, as said by Faria Costa, only finds any 'meaning if it opens up to the care for others, because it is also only in this way, only within this reciprocity, that safety, the lack of care and the lack of danger are found', in a community which, without question, is built amidst dangers (Faria Costa 1992, p. 319).

Indeed, danger and care are dimensions of the same reality. It is in danger and for danger that care finds its reason for being and, therefore, care is always care-of-danger (Faria Costa 1992, p. 327). And it is in this indivisible unit that the care-of-danger takes itself on as an ontological matrix of the Being-there-different in the context of a community. This ontological matrix, with its legal-normative resonance, allows us to find the very ontological foundation of criminal law. 'The Being-there-different and the legal community behind it become (are the) ontological structures of care-of-danger' (Faria Costa 1992, p. 327).

This ontological relationship that throws the I out of itself towards the encounter of the other, in which and through which the Being-in-the-world unveils itself and gets to know itself, confers existence, as aforementioned, to a web of reciprocal care which structures the community Being. And it is precisely within the harmful oscillation of the web of care and, therefore, in the harmful oscillation of the onto-anthropological matrix relationship of care-of-danger that criminal law, via its characteristic signs, will seek the elements that inform its fundamental nucleus, *Unrecht*. In this perspective, *Unrecht* is first of all the criminal law expression for the harmful oscillation of the tension that arises from the onto-anthropological relationship of care-of-danger. Obviously, it is not just any oscillation, but that which in the eyes of the historically situated community is regarded as unbearable.

Criminal law, as a point of convergence of the principles of safety and culpability (Faria Costa 1992, pp. 248–249), is the fragmentary expression of the order of values that the objectification of care brings about, and its unbearable violation is reported by *Unrecht* (Faria Costa 1992, p. 251). Harm (understood as injury or danger) to legal goods arises in that context as the legal form of the perception of the intolerable impact of the matrix relationship of care-of-danger. An opening which, in sight of the criminal law categories of legal good and harm, can only come to be in an evidently indirect way.

For all this, in an onto-anthropological understanding of criminal law, *Unrecht*, more than ever, takes on the central role in the dogmatic structure of crime. *Unrecht* is the radiating center of opposition to not only the normative teleology, but also to the very function of criminal law, revealed in the fundamental forms of harm to legal goods (D'Avila 2005, pp. 90–179). An evident throwback to the result (*rectius*, legal result), that is, to an understanding of *Unrecht* built based on the harmful result. It is not, however, an *Unrecht* that ends in the exasperation of the harmful result but an *Unrecht* that also and necessarily opens up to the meaning of criminal conduct in itself, but which does so on the basis of the permanent presence of the harmful result.

Regarding punishment, the unfolding of the onto-anthropological foundation is no less important.

Punishment is conceived as the legal response to the rupture of the matrix relationship of care-of-danger caused by crime. Punishment takes on the role of an element to restore the broken balance, thus converting itself into a good. In this horizon, punishment is a good (Faria Costa 2005, pp. 223–224). A good that returns to the past, to the crime as a breach of the original care (Faria Costa 2005, pp. 223–224). It is therefore a neo-retributive conception of punishment. A conception that finds its fundamental pillars in the ideas of responsibility and equality. As explained below.

Without freedom and autonomy there is no responsibility. If, under concrete circumstances, it is not possible to choose and decide, there is no responsibility. In these cases, a person does not only not 'respond to his own critical and self-reflective consciousness' (Faria Costa 2005, p. 226), but also does not respond 'to the critical consciousness that the community itself represents' (Faria Costa 2005, p. 226). The person is 'foreign to the normative discourse that has its epicenter in the solid – and legally sustained – idea of responsibility' (Faria Costa 2005, p. 226).

Under this framework of analysis, the 'punishment applied or to be applied' must look to the past, observe the criminal fact and its context, because, only then, will the punishment be an expression of the responsibility of the agent. It is 'in the past place of the rupture of the primal relationship of care-of-danger that cause is, that the core of everything is' (Faria Costa 2005, p. 227). This is why the onto-anthropological foundation opposes to the validity of preventionist discourses in the foundation of criminal punishment. It is 'illogical or incomprehensible'—says Faria Costa—'to apply punishment and say that it is being applied with the intent that others do not commit crimes or with the aim of replacing the counter-factic validity of the norm' (Faria Costa 2005, p. 227). Such a way of looking at punishment admits not only the punishing of innocent persons but also punishing beyond the responsibility of the condemned (Faria Costa 2005, p. 227). Which very well concludes that 'the idea of retribution is the one that best addresses the fundamental aspect which the principle of responsibility represents' (Faria Costa 2005, p. 227).

Equality, in turn, corresponds to a double and just individual expectation: the expectation of each individual to be treated by others on equal footing and of each individual in relation to the community, as a legally and politically organized power, in the sense that it also treats each of its members equally (Faria Costa 2005, p. 228). These two planes (vertical and horizontal) are bound in such a way that for the 'identity effect that equality enhances in the horizontal relationship with the "other", there must also be a corresponding identity consequence of equal treatment in the course of a lifetime' (Faria Costa 2005, p. 228).

Equality implies trust, an aggregating element of the legal and political community. Everyone must trust that their acts will be treated equally (Faria Costa 2005, p. 228). So much so that the 'breakdown of a relationship of trust in equal treatment of what is equal and in the unequal treatment of what is unequal is a step towards the abyss of social disintegration' (Faria Costa 2005, p. 228).

It is, therefore, to this extent, that equality connects to the theme of the foundation of punishment. If the social body is founded on a community of meaning, one cannot admit that penalties varying in degree and quality be applied to facts that are materially equal, under the penalty of violating this sense (on retreating from equality and betraying the trust of all). The assignment and distribution of punishment (and, therefore, the idea of distributive justice therein) implies compliance with the principle of equality (Faria Costa 2005, p. 229).

Therefore, the relationship of the individual with the punishment will not be (*rectius:* cannot be) that of a mere object, receptacle, functional appendix of its exercise, the chosen one upon who to produce an effect of prevention. He is 'the responsible citizen who has the right to undergo fair punishment because all the punishments that equally correspond to criminally relevant behavior' (Faria Costa 2005, p. 229), that which today is also placed as a refraction of the culture of fundamental rights itself, and 'the result of a profound and correct idea of what is a truly Democratic Rule of Law' (Faria Costa 2005, p. 230).

The Onto-Anthropological Foundation in Brazil: Presence and Innovation

Our times, as we put it, are times strongly marked by functional thinking, by that which Heidegger once called the thinking that calculates (*das rechnende Denken*) (Heidegger 2000, p. 13). That does not mean, however, that there is no fertile ground for other ways of understanding the world and, along with it, criminal law itself. The onto-anthropological foundation is undoubtedly one way.

In the last two decades, the onto-anthropological foundation has sparked the interest of Brazilian researchers and jurists. Especially in the south of Brazil, there is already a significant number of books, articles and scientific research developed based on this precise foundation. Writings that, have no place within the boundaries of this essay, can otherwise be dimensioned owing to their diverse themes. They comprehend themes ranging from fundamental questions to practical applications, projecting both on general institutions such as culpability and self-responsibility, as well as on important fields of criminal law (such as economic criminal law) and criminal procedure (Moura 2015, pp. 23–24, footnote 25; 2021, pp. 110–111, footnote 4).

The importance of these set of writings speaks for itself. It is eloquent in the sense it asserts the seminal character of Faria Costa's works in Brazil. However, defining the main contribution of his work is no easy task.

Given its philosophical nature, the contribution of Faria Costa's thought does not end in a single aspect or in a single premise but is surprising at multiple levels. Something which, indeed, supports everything so far discussed herein. This finding, however, does not prevent us from deeming it possible to lead the multiple levels of his normative expression to a common denominator, to a precise way of seeing and understanding a Being and the world. The onto-anthropological foundation is, first of all, a claim to a way of looking at, to a way of conceiving the world and the Being-person-in-the-world from the point of the relationship with the other. A horizon in which the Being only is because it also is-in-the-other. And that, in this genesis relationship, conceives a world in which we are not in-ourselves, but we are for-and-to-others.

This way of understanding the human condition in the world is, of course, not limited to criminal law. In criminal law, as previously seen, there is already a number of practical developments regarding the understanding of crime and punishment, as well as studies that seek to further them. The horizon, however, is broader. And it finds, in other fields of science, elements of support. As for instance in the neurosciences, which deserve special attention.

In the field of cognitive neuroscience, recent research has attested to the existence of an effective neural network that connects one person to another. These findings have become available due to technological advances that have made it possible to monitor brain activity on an fMRI Scanner—functional magnetic resonance scanner. In this regard, it is worth mentioning three research studies, even if only briefly.

In a historical study published in 2004 in the journal Science, a group of researchers lead by social neuroscientist Tania Singer proposed something innovative. Instead of studying only one single brain as had been the standard in neuroscience investigations, a couple was placed within the scanner environment with the objective of investigating 'neuronal processes underlying empathic emotions, that is emotions I feel for another person', but which in reality 'are not mine' (Cognitive Neuroscience Society 2013, accessed: 27 December 2021). Therefore, a phenomenon of a marked social nature. And surprising results were obtained.

The first investigations involved 16 couples who were invited to participate in experiments in which a woman's brain activity was monitored by magnetic resonance imaging while painful stimuli were applied to her and her partner through electrodes attached to the back of the hand (Singer et al. 2004, p. 1158). The man was positioned next to the scanner in such a way that the woman could see through a mirror system her and her partner's right hand and thus follow the moments when the painful stimuli were applied (Singer et al. 2004, p. 1158). This made it possible to compare pain-related brain activity in her (self) context (i.e., the direct pain she felt) and in his (other) context (the pain he felt) (Singer et al. 2004, p. 1158).

Before the trial, some believed they would find an 'empty brain'. Findings, however, were the opposite. Neural responses demonstrated that 'empathy activates parts of the pain-related neural network associated with emotions', devoid, however, of a sensory experience. In other words, the woman felt the pain of her partner (Cognitive Neuroscience Society 2013, accessed: 27 December 2021). Although she was not feeling the electric stimulus when she learned her partner was in pain, she also felt pain.

To this extraordinary finding about empathy from a neurological perspective, new experiments followed, now with the aim of better understanding how empathic responses of the brain are modulated. And, once again, impressive results were obtained. In studies published in 2006 (Singer et al. 2006, pp. 466–469) and 2010 (Hein et al. 2010, pp. 149–160), evidence was presented to support that neuronal responses related to empathy are influenced both by the perception of justice and by the fact that the affected person belongs to or does not belong to the same group.

The consequences of such discoveries are countless. What matters to us, however, within the limits of this essay, is a particular aspect. The fact that such findings both redimension the concepts of empathy and compassion in the field of the sciences and, at the same time, attest to the exhaustion of certain explanatory models and, with them, of a certain *Menschenbild*. Relating to economics, it is no longer possible to speak of a *homo economicus*; in the same way that, in law, there is no longer room for strictly instrumental reasoning. And not only that, social structures established from the exploration of the other, based on the reification/objectification of the other, the rejection, the belittling and the annihilation of the other become, in this new horizon, self-destructive mechanisms. Mechanisms that can no longer find a place and that cannot even guide the search for solutions to the major problems of our time.

The onto-anthropological foundation, due to all the explained, more than theorizing about a better and fairer arrangement for criminal issues, seems to anticipate the claim for a new *Menschenbild*, which is currently supported and strengthened by other areas of knowledge. A *Menschenbild* no longer centered on individual interests, no longer limited by the other but *built from the point of the other that is also I*, to reveal new visions on our human condition in society. A new and definitive step towards a better understanding of our existence and towards the meaning that this existence demands.

That is, therefore, what we feel is the main contribution of the onto-anthropological foundation of Faria Costa. When we say we feel, we mean to say that while his work is seminal today it is also a formulation that is work in progress being built by other hands and, therefore, is also subject to the misunderstandings and imperfections of those who are toiling on it. The approaches made here based on neuroscience are a sufficient example of this. They relate to ongoing investigations being carried out in the south of Brazil. Investigations that single-handedly and further support the strength and innovative potential of the onto-anthropological foundation of Faria Costa.

Conclusion

In the last two decades, the onto-anthropological foundation has sparked the interest of Brazilian researchers and jurists, especially in the south of Brazil. The already significant number of writings that deal directly or indirectly with this precise foundation account for its importance and innovative character in addition to bringing together, once again, the legal matters of Brazil and Portugal.

Given the nature of the onto-anthropological foundation, its contribution is surprising at multiple levels. This, however, does not prevent us from deeming it possible to lead the multiple levels of its normative expression to a common denominator, to a precise way of seeing and understanding the person and the world. The onto-anthropological foundation is, first of all, a claim to a way of looking at, to a way of conceiving the world and the Being-person-in-the-world from the point of the relationship with the other.

This manner of understanding the human condition in the world is not limited to criminal law and is not alone. It is in harmony with propositions stemming from other areas of knowledge such as current studies in cognitive neuroscience concerning the concepts of empathy and compassion.

Considered in its deepest essence, the onto-anthropological foundation, is more than a theory on the foundation of criminal law, it is revealed as an effective proposition for a new *Menschenbild*. A *Menschenbild* no longer centered on individual interests, no longer limited by the other, *built from the point of the other that is also I*, to reveal new visions on our human condition in society.

References

Bruno, A. (1967) *Direito penal.* Tomo 1. 3rd ed. Rio de Janeiro, Forense.

Castanheira Neves, A. (1998) Entre o "legislador", a "sociedade" e o "juiz" ou entre "sistema", "função" e "problema". Os modelos actualmente alternativos da realização jurisdicional do direito. *Boletim da Faculdade de Direito* [Coimbra]. 74, 1–44.

Cognitive Neuroscience Society. *Feeling Others' Pain: Transforming Empathy into Compassion.* (2013) [Online]. Available at: https://www.cogneurosociety.org/empathy_pain/ (Accessed: 27 Dec 2021).

Costa e Silva, A. J. da. (1943) *Código Penal.* Vol. I. São Paulo, Editora Nacional.

D'Avila, F. R. (2005) *Ofensividade e crimes omissivos próprios.* Contributo à compreensão do crime como ofensa ao bem jurídico. Stvdia Ivridica 85. Coimbra, Coimbra Editora.

Faria Costa, J. de. (1992) *O perigo em direito penal.* Contributo para a sua fundamentação e compreensão dogmáticas. Coimbra, Coimbra Editora.

Faria Costa, J. de. (2002) Ilícito-típico, resultado e hermenêutica. Ou o retorno à limpidez do essencial. *Revista Portuguesa de Ciência Criminal.* 12, 7–23.

Faria Costa, J. de. (2005) *Linhas de direito penal e de filosofia.* Alguns cruzamentos reflexivos. Coimbra, Coimbra Editora.

Faria Costa, J. de. (2017) *Direito penal.* Lisboa, Imprensa Nacional.

Garcia, B. (1952) *Instituições de direito penal.* Vol. I. Tomo I. São Paulo, Max Limonad.

Gauer, R. C. (2001) *A construção do Estado-Nação no Brasil.* A contribuição dos egressos de Coimbra. Curitiba, Juruá.

Heidegger, M. (1962) *Being and time*, translated by John Macquarrie & Edward Robinson. Cambridge, Blackwell.

Heidegger, M. (2000) *Gelassenheit.* 12th ed. Stuttgart, Günther Neske.

Hein, G., Silani, G., Preuschoff, K., Batson, C. D., Singer, T. (2010) Neural Responses to Ingroup and Outgroup Members' Suffering Predict Individual Differences in Costly Helping. *Neuron.* 68(1), 149–160.

Jiménez de Asúa, L. (1950) *Tratado de Derecho Penal.* Tomo I. Buenos Aires, Losada.

Moura, B. de O. (2015) *Ilicitude penal e justificação*. Reflexões a partir do ontologismo de Faria Costa. Coimbra, Coimbra Editora.

Moura, B. de O. (2021) Sobre as bases para uma concepção onto-antropológica do direito. In: Faria Costa, J. de, Moura, B. de O. ed. *Filosofia do direito*. Livro Segundo. Lisboa, Âncora Editora.

Noronha, E. M. (1959) *Direito penal*. Vol. I. São Paulo, Saraiva.

Pierangeli, J. H. (2004) *Códigos penais do Brasil*. Evolução histórica. 2nd ed. São Paulo, RT.

Singer, T., Seymour, B., O'Doherty, J. P., Kaube, H., Dolan, R. J., Frith, C. D. (2004) Empathy for Pain Involves the Affective but not Sensory Components of Pain. *Science*. 303, 1157–1162.

Singer, T., Seymour, B., O'Doherty, J. P., Stephan, K. E., Dolan, R. J., Frith, C. (2006) Empathic neural responses are modulated by the perceived fairness of others. *Nature*. 439(26), 466–469.

Stein, E. (2005) *Seis estudos sobre "Ser e Tempo"*. 3rd ed. Petrópolis, Vozes.

The Base Erosion and Profit Shifting: A View of Portugal and Brazil

Maria do Rosário Anjos

Introduction

International taxation as we have understood that term to describe the reconciliation of countries intersecting tax claims, is quite simple and very difficult at the same time.

In a free and globalized market context, the problems of international taxation acquire greater relevance and are essential to ensure effective free competition. Special relations between countries with strong historical affinities, such as the Lusophone countries, can also be a problem if they are not aligned with international good practice rules. Nevertheless, there are ever only three key questions: (1) Where was the taxpayer when he earned income?; (2) Where did the taxpayer conduct activities to generate the income he earned; (3) Where did the activities to generate income take place?

The first two questions became more interesting due to the internationalization of business models and activities. These questions—rooted

Present Address:
M. do Rosário Anjos (✉)
Universidade Lusófona Do Porto, Porto, Portugal
e-mail: p2476@ulusofona.pt

P. A. B. Duarte et al. (eds.), *Portugal and the Lusophone World*,
https://doi.org/10.1007/978-981-99-0455-6_3

in the 1920 policy of the League of Nations—have recently become of utmost relevance.

The Organization for Economic Cooperation and Development (OECD) has been developing multilateral initiatives in order to respond to some of the challenges posed by increasing attention to substance, coherence, and transparency requirements for taxation. The goal is to promote an effective international collaboration to end tax avoidance. This instrument of international tax regulation, called "Base Erosion and Profit Shifting – BEPS" has been instrumental in alleviating the extremely negative effects of the phenomenon of base erosion.

Globalization has profoundly changed the rules of play in the international economy. A new world order, new challenges, and new difficulties have arisen as well as new strategies to avoid the consequences of global free competition. Fiscal policy is a crucial tool in a new global competition model, in special for regions with a high level of economic integration, as the European Union (EU). In this context tax harmonization is extremely important to prevent distortions of competition in the European market. But the difficulties are evident and there are several misunderstandings between member states about this issue. The fight against tax base erosion is not easy even in the EU. Creating and developing the EU fiscal system is not only an economic, but also an important political process. Generally, the fiscal system rests on the institutions and instruments necessary for the implementation of fiscal policy on a certain area. Creating an institutional fiscal infrastructure at a supranational level of the EU is rather complex and limited due to globalization fiscal trends, but also given the political complexity of the integration of traditionally independent EU member countries (Haan and Sturm 1994). The problem is that in economies with high level of integration, the budgetary and fiscal discipline is crucial for the success of the process (Anjos 2021).

We can say that the EU has done everything to achieve its goals in the economic realm, but did all this without a real tax harmonization in the euro zone. This was and is one of the biggest mistakes in the European construction process, because the lack of an appropriate European fiscal policy and tax harmonization had as result the worsening of budgetary indiscipline, the increase in public debts of some member states, and the use of the tax system as an instrument of unfair competition between member countries. In this context, BEPS Action 4 is crucial to discipline the fiscal competition between countries in a globalization era. This process is stronger than EU measures to fiscal policy and tax harmonization.

We can say that this contemporary idea of tax multilateralism remains a goal for the future. Indeed, the fundamental issue of tax base erosion remains unresolved and has been a factor in unfair tax competition between countries that are partners in international transactions and activities. Indeed, after so many years of international efforts to address these issues, it seems that when we find a solution to them, new problems soon arise. And the truth is that countries have been unable to react as quickly as possible to new problems and challenges in international taxation. Reality always runs faster than the law. On the other hand, we have to understand that international law is soft law, which means that it is always very difficult to act against any country that breaks the law. That's why the OECD has been a great force in the fight against tax evasion, as an international organization with great power to influence its member countries.

As of 4 November 2021, 137 countries and jurisdictions joined a new two-pillar plan to reform international taxation rules and ensure that multinational enterprises pay a fair share of tax wherever they operate. Some of the Lusophone countries are among the 141 members of OECD/G20 inclusive within the framework of BEPS. Brazil has been assuming a peculiar position, because it is not among these countries (Malek and Brenttzen 2021).

This study aims to analyze how the implementation of the Base Erosion and Profit Shifting (BEPS Action 4) has been done in Lusophone countries, with special focus on Portugal and Brazil. This is one of BEPS's actions, under the supervision of the OECD, which addresses the problem of limiting interest deductions.

The fundamental question of research is to understand how governments can become more agile, efficient, and effective in responding to this important international action to combat tax erosion and unfair tax competition. It is very important to understand how Portugal influences and determines the other positions of the Lusophone countries and vice versa. Portugal's current position as an EU member state is an important motivating factor for other Portuguese-speaking countries to intensify their economic relations with Portugal and bridge the EU market. Therefore, it is quite important to understand whether the special relationship between Portugal and Brazil can be an easy way to break the rules.

BEPS: Concept, Mission, and Overview

First, it is important to be aware of the relevance of BEPS concept and mission. BEPS Action 4 was a very important measure to guarantee transparency and rule of law in tax systems, interest deductibility, and a loyal free competition both in the EU and in the global order (OECD 2015).

According to OECD, the domestic tax base erosion and profit shifting (BEPS) stemming from multinational corporations' exploiting gaps and mismatches between different countries' tax systems, affect all countries. Developing countries higher reliance on corporate income tax means they suffer from BEPS disproportionately. Within the Lusophone space, there are special relations between countries that share history, language, culture, and economic interests (IFA 2019).

Businesses operate internationally, so governments must act together to tackle BEPS and restore trust in domestic and international tax systems. According to the OECD (2021) report, BEPS practices cost countries $100–240 billion in lost revenue annually, equivalent to 4–10% of global corporate income tax revenues (IFA 2019, p. 11).

The Action 4 recommendations aim to limit base erosion, through the use of interest expense in order to achieve excessive interest deductions or to finance the production of exempt or deferred income (Stanley and Shah 2015). The work by the Inclusive Framework member jurisdictions on Action 4 resulted in the 2015 OECD report *Limiting Base Erosion Involving Interest Deductions and Other Financial Payments* (OECD 2021), according to which:

> Action 4 "focuses on best practices in the design of rules to prevent base erosion and profit shifting using interest and other financial payments economically equivalent to interest. Its stated goal is described in the following Action: Develop recommendations regarding best practices in the design of rules to prevent base erosion through the use of interest expense, for example through the use of related-party and third-party debt to achieve excessive interest deductions or to finance the production of exempt or deferred income, and other financial payments that are economically equivalent to interest payments".

The work will evaluate the effectiveness of different types of limitations. In connection with and in support of the foregoing work, transfer pricing guidance will also be developed regarding the pricing of related-party financial transactions, including financial and performance guarantees, derivatives (including internal derivatives used in intra-bank dealings), and captive and other insurance arrangements.

In working together in the OECD/G20 Inclusive Framework on BEPS, 141 countries and jurisdictions did assume the commitment to implementing 15 actions to tackle tax avoidance, improve the coherence of international tax rules, ensure a more transparent tax environment. BEPS Action 4 is one of them and aims to limit base erosion involving interest deductions and other financial payments.

The OECD/G20 Base Erosion and Profit Shifting Project is based on two pillars of intervention to address the tax challenges arising from the digitization of the economy. The first is the introduction of a more aggressive legal regime against base erosion. And the 2nd pillar is the introduction of legal rules to combat profit shifting. This legal regime based on these two pillars of intervention is called the OECD/G20 Inclusive Framework on Base Erosion and Profit Shifting (IF).

A detailed implementation plan is provided by OECD that since the beginning of this Action is monitoring its implementation. Revenue will be sourced to the end market jurisdictions where goods or services are used or consumed. To facilitate the application of this principle, detailed source rules for specific categories of transactions will be developed.

Moreover, segmentation will only occur in exceptional circumstances where, based on the segments disclosed in the financial accounts, a segment meets the rules of the scope. The marketing and distribution of profits is a safe harbor. Where the residual profits of an MNE are already taxed in a market jurisdiction, a trading and profit distribution safe harbor will limit the residual profits attributed to the market jurisdiction by a fixed amount. Further work will be undertaken on the safe harbor design, including to consider the global scope.

Elimination of double taxation of profit allocated to market jurisdictions will be relieved using either the exemption or credit method. The entity (or entities) that will bear the tax liability will be drawn from those that earn residual profit. Tax certainty will benefit from dispute prevention and resolution mechanisms, which will avoid double taxation in a mandatory and binding manner.

Disputes will be solved in a mandatory and binding manner, without delaying the substantive dispute prevention and resolution mechanism. An elective binding dispute resolution mechanism will be available only for issues related to tax amount. The eligibility of a jurisdiction for this elective mechanism will be reviewed regularly; jurisdictions found ineligible by a review will remain ineligible in all subsequent years (Anjos 2019).

The application of the arm's length principle to in-country baseline marketing and distribution activities will be simplified and streamlined, with a particular focus on the needs of low-capacity countries.

The tax compliance will be streamlined (including filing obligations) and allows to manage the process through a single entity. The Multilateral Convention (MLC) will require all parties to remove all "Digital Services Taxes" and other relevant similar measures with respect to all companies, and to commit not to introduce such measures in the future. No newly enacted Digital Services Taxes or other relevant similar measures will be imposed until 31 December 2023.

A detailed implementation plan is set out in the design "Pillar Two". Countries are free to apply the income tax to corporations headquartered in their country even if they do not meet the threshold. Government entities, international organizations, non-profit organizations, pension funds, or investment funds that are Ultimate Parent Entities (UPE) of a Multinational Enterprise (MNE) Group or any holding vehicles used by such entities, organizations, or funds are not subject to the "GloBE rules". The "GloBE rules" also provide for an exclusion for international shipping income using the definition of such income under the OECD Model Tax Convention.

To ensure that the administration of the "GloBE rules" is as targeted as possible, and to avoid compliance and administrative costs that are disproportionate to the policy objectives, the implementation framework will include safe harbors and/or other mechanisms.

The taxing right will be limited to the difference between the minimum rate and the tax rate on the payment. The minimum rate for the STTR will be 9%. Implementation Pillar Two should is expected to come into force in 2023, with the UTPR coming into force in 2024. This is a summary of the results of BEPS actions in recent years. This is an overview about the results of BEPS actions in the last years.

The Action 4 recommendations aim to limit base erosion using interest expense to achieve excessive interest deductions or to finance the production of exempt or deferred income. The work by the Inclusive Framework member jurisdictions on Action 4 resulted in the 2015 OECD report *Limiting Base Erosion Involving Interest Deductions and Other Financial Payments*.

Brief History of BEPS Action 4

In July 2013, the OECD published an Action Plan on Base Erosion and Profit Shifting (BEPS), which set out 15 BEPS actions. Then, on 5 October 2015 the OECD and the G20 published final reports along with an explanatory statement outlining consensus recommendations that had been reached as part of the BEPS project. Links to the final reports can be found below under the relevant actions.

Since October 2015, the OECD and G20 have continued to undertake further work on many of BEPS's actions through the BEPS "Inclusive Framework". The Inclusive Framework brings together a much larger group of countries than those involved in agreeing the recommendations published in 2015, enabling additional countries to take part in the ongoing BEPS work on an equal footing with OECD and G20 members, provided they commit to the BEPS minimum standards.

Action 4 aims to limit base erosion involving interest deductions and other financial payments. A final report on Action 4, which was published as part of the OECD's 5 October 2015 package of final reports, includes recommendations for domestic rules to restrict interest deductions by reference to a proportion of the profits of an entity or group. The report recommends a fixed ratio rule that would allow an entity to deduct interest and other financial payments up to a fixed percentage of its earnings before interest, tax, depreciation, and amortization (EBITDA) and a group ratio rule that would allow groups with higher levels of external debt to deduct net interest (Anjos 2021).

An updated report on Action 4 was released by the OECD on 22 December 2016. The report includes further guidance on the design and operation of the group ratio rule and suggests approaches to deal with the risks posed by the banking and insurance sectors.

As with Actions 2 and 3, discussed above, the EU has subsequently introduced requirements that are similar to the recommendations in the Action 4 report. ATAD 1 required EU member states that did not already have rules as effective as those set out in the Directive to introduce a fixed-rate interest rule, like what was already recommended from 2019. The rule limits the deduction of (net) interest expense to 30% of an entity's EBITDA.

On 11 February 2020, the OECD released final guidance on the transfer pricing aspects of financial transactions. The guidance forms follow-up work in relation to Action. One of the main goals of the OECD analysis report was to determine which countries adopted BEPS Action 4 in substance (OECD 2021).

Multinational groups may achieve favorable tax results by adjusting the amount of debt in a group entity. BEPS risks in this area may arise in three basic scenarios:

1. Groups placing higher levels of third-party debt in high tax countries;
2. Groups using intragroup loans to generate interest deductions in excess of the group's actual third-party interest expense;
3. Groups using third-party or intragroup financing to fund the generation of tax-exempt income.

This is an important question because the use of third-party and related-party interest is perhaps one of the simplest of the profit-shifting techniques available in international tax planning (Lang 2014). The fluidity and fungibility of money make it a relatively simple exercise to adjust the mix of debt and equity in a controlled entity. In particular, the deductibility of interest expense can give rise to double non-taxation in both inbound and outbound investment scenarios. The interest payments are deducted against the taxable profits of the operating companies, while the interest income is taxed at comparatively low tax rates or no rates at all at the level of the recipient. This is even though in some situations the multinational group may have little or no external debt.

Tying a solution, the 2015 Action 4 report on Limiting Base Erosion Involving Interest Deductions and Other Financial Payments focused on the use of all types of debt giving rise to excessive interest expense or used to finance the production of exempt or deferred income. This report established rules linking an entity's net interest deductions to its level of economic activity within the jurisdiction, which is measured according to taxable earnings before interest, depreciation, and amortization (EBITDA). This approach includes three elements: a fixed ratio rule based on a benchmark net interest/EBITDA ratio; a group ratio rule which may allow an entity to deduct more interest expense depending on the relative net interest/EBITDA ratio of the worldwide group; and targeted rules to address specific risks.

As of mid-2019, several OECD and Inclusive Framework members had adopted interest limitations rules or were in the process of aligning their domestic legislation with the recommendations of Action 4. From the commencement of 2019, all EU Member States have been applying an interest cap that restricts a taxpayer's deductible borrowing costs to generally 30 percent of the taxpayer's earnings before interest, tax, depreciation, and amortization (EBITDA). Various other countries have also taken steps to limit interest deductibility (e.g., Argentina, India, Malaysia, Norway, South Korea) or are in the process of aligning their domestic legislation with the recommendations of Action 4 (e.g., Japan, Peru, Viet Nam).

The latest edition of Corporate Tax Statistics published in July 2020 collected, for the first time, information on interest limitation rules, which can assist in understanding progress related to the implementation of BEPS Action 4. The data highlights that interest limitation rules can limit base erosion via the use of interest expense to achieve excessive interest deductions or to finance the production of exempt or deferred income. It also shows that information on the presence and design of interest limitation rules is available for 134 Inclusive Framework jurisdictions, of which 67 had interest limitation rules in place in 2019.

This is a work in progress and until December 2022 a final report will be published to disseminate the most up-to-date information on the subject. Portugal has reasonably respected all OECD impositions. However, some questions have arisen in relation to its privileged relations with Portuguese-speaking countries that have undertaken to stay out of this commitment, such as Brazil.

Implementing BEPS in Portugal and Influence on Lusophony Countries

The Community of Portuguese-speaking Countries (CPLP) was born as a pact of friendship and solidarity **between equals.** This is our main force.

Unlike other communities also based on language, but based on old political ties and an in-depth dissemination of the common language, the CPLP does not act as a centralist model in which the ancient metropolis radiates to its periphery both its economic prosperity and its cultural value. On the contrary, the CPLP assumes the purpose of strengthening and expanding from the sum of the potentialities and the vast wealth that are found in the diversity of the eight member states that constitute it, with full respect for the sovereignty of each one.

Constituted by several states, but with Brazil and Portugal assuming strategic positions, the decisions taken by the CPLP member states affect all others and can have an impact on the relations of these states with the rest of the world. Thus, the international position that each of the CPLP member states takes on the BEPS commitments is relevant due to the consequences in the international community and may favor unfair tax competition.

The CPLP defends and welcomes the dissimilarity it contains, and it is for it to take an active role in the defense of diversity. This structuring principle is also valid in the context of economic decisions taken before the international community. But Lusophony is the construction of a space, the "Lusophone Space" because it speaks the Portuguese language, and that is a cultural, economic, political, and strategic space that can and must have its own personality and word in the contemporary world. Moreover, it is the geostrategic dimension that is essential and, therefore, Lusophony is essentially a matter of economic and political geostrategy, which gives meaning to everything else (Bellan 2012).

In this context, we can say that the OECD should be aware of the negative effects that may result from the special relations between two Lusophone countries, such as Portugal and Brazil, knowing that the first fully assumed the commitment imposed by ACTION 4 of the BEPS, and the second chose not to do so. Moreover, the economic relations of foreign investment between these two Lusophone countries are very significant. This results in two important questions:

1. Is it possible for Brazil to benefit from the advantages of the action, overcoming the disadvantages?
2. What is Portugal's role in facing this problem?

To answer these questions, we need to observe and understand the reasons why Brazil stays out of the BEPS Action 4 commitment.

The Special Case of Brazil

Among other actions needed to combat tax base erosion and profit transfer, the BEPS Action Plan identifies "Action 4 – Limit base erosion via interest deductions and other financial payments". This is clear, at least, since 2015 (OECD 2021).

Action 4 addresses the tax deductibility of certain charges arising from financial transactions, such as the payment of interest and other compensation, e.g., financial and enforcement guarantees, and other insurance systems, in particular between related entities, in which case the deductibility of such payments may give rise to or contribute to double-tri-taxation of income (Torres 2012).

In fact, in the case of financing from an entity resident in a low-tax jurisdiction to a related entity resident in a high taxation jurisdiction, the payment of interest may lead to excessive deductions within the sphere of the paying entity, without the corresponding inclusion of income in the sphere of the entity receiving the payment, i.e., the beneficiary. On the other hand, and from the point of view of outbound investments, an entity may resort to indebtedness to finance the generation of an exempt income or defer its taxation (Elali 2010).

Thus, Action 4 seeks to make recommendations on the development of international anti-abuse standards aimed to prevent the erosion of the tax base, by deducting interest and other economically equivalent financial compensation, which are misused to obtain excessive deductions or to finance the production of an income exempt or postponed taxation. In this context, most jurisdictions already have such anti-abuse rules, including Brazil, which in its domestic legislation already contains important anti-abuse rules and, we can say that many of them are like those defined by the OECD. This reality mitigates the perverse effects of Brazil's position vis-à-vis BEPS Action 4.

According to the IFA (2019), the most important thing is to pay attention to the changes in the legislation currently in force in several states. In fact, some jurisdictions have unilaterally strengthened the domestic rules of limitation to the deductibility of financial charges, a fact which corroborates the relevance of BEPS in practical terms. It should be noted that three different approaches to combating the excessive deduction of interest charges have been highlighted in the international political debate.

The first approach is to take anti-abuse rules aimed at limiting the deduction of interest from a group perspective by limiting deductions made by the group in its entirety to the amount of interest actually paid to third parties.

The second approach concerns the possibility of limiting the interest deductibility of each entity, based on a fixed relationship between revenue, assets, or capital. Finally, the third approach provides for the possibility of drawing up specific rules aimed to challenge specific abusive situations. This approach is still in the process of further development/implementation (Rinninsland and Lobo 2015).

This matter is so important for international trade and foreign investment that some multinational economic agents to anticipate the impact of this Action 4, identify financial transactions potentially subject to the application of this anti-abuse regulation, with the aim of assessing the need to re-equate its corporate structure and the financing model itself. And from this point of view, it is indifferent to the investor whether the contracting country is bound by BEPS Action 4, because what really matters is whether the state of its head office is bound.

Obviously, for foreign investment made by Brazilian companies abroad, the non-adoption of BEPS Action 4 constitutes an advantage, since the control of the Brazilian State over the erosion of the tax base is much smaller. But this is a question of internal governance and only the Brazilian institutions can change this status quo. At the end of the day, the problem is to guarantee "sustainability, typically expressed as a concern for future generations, pointing in the direction of assuring that taxpayers, in each time period, contribute to public expenditures, from which they derive benefits in accordance with their share in those benefits" (Oliveira 2020).

In other words, at the proper time Brazil will find a way to keep moral and fair taxation aligned with OECD countries, and increase its internal economic and social development. It is a matter of time.

Trying to systematize the situation in the case of Brazil, we can conclude:

1. Formally, Brazil is not implementing any BEPS recommendation, but the reality shows some domestic legislation similar or inspired by it.
2. Brazil does not follow the OECD Guidelines for transfer pricing.
3. As far as we know, there will not be a substantial change due to BEPS in Brazil.

Findings

It is fundamental to reduce the gaps between some countries' tax law to fight against base erosion and profit shifting (BEPS).

Multinational companies that exploit gaps and mismatches between the tax systems of different countries affect all countries and that is why BEPS Action 4 is so important to combat these unfair behaviors.

All countries all over the world use their jurisdictions to compete among themselves, fighting for more foreign investment and capital. Tax policy is part of that competition. The question is to find the way to impose a fair tax competition. BEPS Action 4 is a part of the solution but must be completed with some other actions to get good results.

Existence of special relations between Lusophone states, like Portugal and Brazil, can provide some unfair use of tax system, if both are not aligned with OECD rules to combat the erosion of the tax base. In this case, Portugal, as a member of the OECD fully committed to the implementation of BEPS Action 4, must ensure transparency and fairness in international transactions and investments with Lusophone countries. As far as Portugal is an EU member state, it is mandatory to assure a free and loyal international competition between member states. It means that it is necessary to impose, even to CPLP member states, the international rule of law. Although we try to achieve harmonization, there will always be competitiveness. Most likely, in ten years, even the rules of BEPS Action 4 will change. In fact, in the last decade, as we have seen, the rules have been revised and changed a few times.

With this framework, we conclude that Portugal has adopted all measures in accordance with the BEPS Action 4 agenda. Brazil, for its part, has been a strong and committed partner in the implementation of several BEPS actions, but regarding Action 4, the country has not yet implemented any measure. Nevertheless, regardless Action 4, Brazil has thin capitalization rules that apply to intercompany foreign loans. The rules are based on debt-equity ratios, with more stringent rules applying to intercompany loans with a party resident in a tax haven jurisdiction.

It is important to note that India joined the global tax deal under the G20-OECD Inclusive Framework on Base Erosion and Profit Shifting (BEPS). It seeks to reform international tax rules and ensure that multinational companies pay their fair share wherever they operate. This means that there is a tendency to extend the number of countries to adhere to the BEPS commitments.

A frequent question is to know what the BEPS minimum standards are. Answering this question the BEPS Associates committed to the four minimum standards, namely countering harmful tax practices (Action 5), countering tax treaty abuse (Action 6), transfer pricing documentation and country-by-country reporting (Action 13), and improving dispute resolution mechanisms (Action 14).

Another conclusion is that investment funds should be used not for tax evasion, but for good and genuine commercial reasons. Lusophone solidarity should be used for the good of the Lusophony, instead of driving big capital on tax evasion and hiding schemes of corruption or other criminal purposes.

Therefore, funds should be scrutinized under lighter conditions where tax issues are concerned but must always be scrutinized. BEPS Action 4, with all reforms operated since 2015, is an important instrument to get some credibility and equity to international affairs, as foreign investments and international transactions. So, all members of OECD that adopted the commitment to implementation must be, as well, the guarantee that all parts in the game respect the rule of law in the international field.

Loyalty, transparency, and commitment between parts are essential to ensure a fair and democratic game. In international commerce this is fundamental. Tax system must be respected and be a road to progress and sustainable development. It can be a key to a better governance.

Acknowledgements The author acknowledges that this study was conducted with the support of CEAD—Centro de Estudos Avançados em Direito, Faculty of Law and Political Science at Lusófona University of Porto – Por, Porto, Portugal.

References

Anjos, M. R. (2019). Free Competition and Fiscal Policy in European Union. In D. Dukic, T. Studzieniecki & J. Grzinic (Eds.), *Economic and Social Development 49th International Scientific Conference on Economic and Social Development*. Varazdin: Varazdin Development and Entrepreneurship Agency.

Anjos, M. R. (2021). Globalization, fiscal policy and free competition: The impact in EU. SHS Web of Conferences 92, 0 (2021) Globalization and its Socio-Economic Consequences 2020. https://doi.org/10.1051/shsconf/20219208001.

Bellan, D. V. (2012). *Estudos Avançados de Direito Tributário*. Rio de Janeiro: Elsevier, Brasil.

Elali, A. (2010). *Incentivos fiscais internacionais*. São Paulo: Quartier Latin, Brasil.

Haan, J., Sturm, J. (1994). The Political and Institutional Constraints of Fiscal Policy in the European Union. *Public Choice Review*, 80(1–2), 157–172.

IFA – International Fiscal Association. (2019). Report. London Proceedings Congress, FSC. Netherlands.

Lang, M. (2014). *BEPS Action: Introducing an Antiabuse Rule in Tax Treaties*. Tax Notes International, London. UK.

Malek, B., Brenttzen, S. (2021). *Congress Report IFA 2019*. FSC Certified paper. Netherlands.

OECD. (2015). International Collaboration to End Tax Avoidance. Available: https://www.oecd.org/tax/beps/.

OECD. (2021). Limiting Base Erosion Involving Interest Deductions and Other Financial Payments, Action 4 - 2015 Final Report. Available: Limiting Base Erosion Involving Interest Deductions and Other Financial Payments, Action 4 - 2015 Final Report | OECD/G20 Base Erosion and Profit Shifting Project | OECD iLibrary (oecd-ilibrary.org).

Oliveira, M. O. (2020). Sustainable Tax Systems. ESD Porto International Conference. Book of Proceedings. Varazdin ed. Croatia,

Rinninsland, R. G., Lobo, K. (2015). *US-Based Pushback on BEPS*. Intertax, New York. USA.

Stanley, C. R., Shah, S. (2015). *B.E.P.S. Action 4: Limit Base Erosion via Interest Payments and other Financial Payments*. Insights Volume 2 Number 1. IFA Report 2015.

Torres, R. (2012). *Planejamento Tributário:* elisão abusiva e evasão fiscal. Rio de Janeiro: Elsevier. Brasil.

Economic Law: A Focus on Lusophone Competition Laws

Nuno Castro Marques

Introduction

Legal frameworks for competition defence usually prohibit abuse of dominance practices and agreements between undertakings that restrict or distort competition.

That is the result of a worldwide inspiration concerning competition defence, with the recognized genesis of antitrust law going back to the United States of America (US) and to its still-in-force Sherman Act of 1890. Section I of Sherman Act prohibits "[…] every contract, combination in the form of trust or otherwise, or conspiracy in restraint of trade or commerce among the several states; or with foreign nations […]", and Section II prohibits all conducts of "[…] monopolise, or attempt to monopolise, or combine or conspire with any other person or persons, to monopolise any part of the trade or commerce among several states, or with foreign nations […]" (Amato 1997).

N. C. Marques (✉)
Centro de Estudos Avançados em Direito Francisco Suárez, Lisboa, Portugal
e-mail: nmarques@spm-advogados.com

Cejea, Porto, Portugal

P. A. B. Duarte et al. (eds.), *Portugal and the Lusophone World*,
https://doi.org/10.1007/978-981-99-0455-6_4

As to the European reality, the work developed, essentially between 1930 and 1950, by the German Ordoliberalism of the Freiburg School, considering competition defence as a (the) way to avoid monopolies and excessive corporate power capable of harming the welfare of society, decisively conformed firstly the German law but, most importantly, the European integration (Hildebrand 2002; Gal 2004; Pera 2008). First launched with the Treaty of Paris of 1951, establishing the European Coal and Steel Community (ECSC), and substantially developed with the Treaty of Rome of 1957 and establishment of the European Economic Community, competition defence acquired a fundamental importance in European soil. Nowadays Article 101 of the Treaty on the Functioning of the European Union (TFEU) prohibits "all agreements between undertakings, decisions by associations of undertakings and concerted practices which may affect trade between Member States and which have as their object or effect the prevention, restriction or distortion of competition within the internal market" and Article 102 states that "Any abuse by one or more undertakings of a dominant position within the internal market or in a substantial part of it shall be prohibited as incompatible with the internal market in so far as it may affect trade between Member States".

The principle of competition is central to any economic model and as Mcnulty (1968) points out, it is structural to all economic reasoning even when not clearly specifying it. It is therefore open to the interpenetration of international sources and solutions from different legal systems. Notwithstanding the fact that different national social, political and economic environments demand accurate legal transplants so to correctly adapt imported solutions to the legal tradition, culture, structuring principles and systemic congruence of the receiving legal system, continued experience demonstrates that competition is particularly suited to this common inspiration.

The widespread acceptance for the need to implement competition legal regimes is also an international trend concerning the recognition of the harm for societies deriving from anti-competitive practices. So, the special gravity of cartel practices is internationally recognized—see the Recommendation of the Council concerning Effective Action against Hard Core Cartels. Paris: OCDE (1998), where it is stated that "[…] hard core cartels are the most egregious violations of competition law […]" (p. 2), or Defining Hard Core Cartel Conduct. ICN (2005), considering an "[…] worldwide consensus […] on the recognition that hard core cartels harm consumers and damage economies" (p. 5)—, being considered highly detrimental to society but also to international trade—Gal (2010, p. 58) considers cartels as the "primary evil of global trade", Harding (2011, p. 247) as "cancers on the open market economy" and "supreme evil of antitrust", and Jones & Williams (2014, p. 100) as the "most egregious violation of competition law"—, and even a global trend towards its criminalization can be identified. At the heart of the globalization of competition defence regimes in national legal systems is thus an effort—mainly promoted by the US but supported by the EU—to promote awareness of the international community for the importance of prohibiting and sanctioning anti-competitive practices—(Kovacic 2006; Joshua et al. 2008).

With such a worldwide background, it is crucial to understand how Lusophone countries stand in terms of competition defence. Even though competition laws are frequently studied, the present chapter brings the innovation of comparing Portuguese and Brazilian competition laws on specific subjects relating to the promotion of effectiveness of competition defence, such as the settlement procedure and the leniency regime, allowing to assess their developments on the present moment against the most evolved systems.

The analysis is based on a comparative legal research method, with the direct study of the existing competition laws in Lusophone countries, and the chapter is organized as follows. Section two presents the actual existing competition laws in Lusophone countries and the recognized influence of Portuguese competition law relating to some of them. In the third section, the evolution of the Portuguese competition regime since its beginning to the present is presented. The fourth section is dedicated to the comparison of the Portuguese and Brazilian competition laws, and section five closes the chapter with the conclusions.

Portuguese Competition Law: Influence on Other Lusophone States

Portugal and some Lusophone countries are in line with the international tendency for competition defence, although at different stages concerning implementation and maturity of their competition legal regimes.

Portugal was the first Lusophone country to implement a competition defence system, in 1983 through Decree-Law n.º 422/83, of 3.12, in the course of its preparation for EU membership, and since then it has followed the evolution that the EU itself has been introducing towards the constant improvement in the effectiveness of the application of competition defence regimes.

In Brazil, the competition defence regime was introduced in 1990 (Law n° 8137, of 12.27.1990), and it is also recognized it has been strongly influenced by external or international tendencies relating to the introduction of modern instruments (so-called "tool kit") for an effective competition defence—for an analysis of the evolution of Brazilian competition law, see Carvalho (2013). Some of its mechanisms such as the leniency regime compare adequately "to the recommendations of the literature concerning the already well-established themes" (Pinha 2018, p. 156), and a broader analysis of the set of sanctions available in the Brazilian legal system reveals that the "path followed by the Brazilian antitrust authority does not detach from a global trend, marked by a considerable increase of the pecuniary sanctions imposed, mainly, on legal entities"—Cruvinel (2020, p. 145).

With regard to Mozambique, it was through Law n.° 10/2013 that the legal regime for competition was established and establishing the Authority Competition Regulator (ARC), which is responsible for its application. The Mozambican competition law is directly inspired by the legislation in force in Portugal—(Henriques 2013).

Lastly, the Angolan Competition Defence System is structured in the Law n.° 5/18, of 10 May ("Law of Competition"), and in the Presidential Decree n.° 240/18, of 12 October ("Competition Law Regulation"), and notwithstanding the explicit recognition that the Angolan economy is a developing economy posing the need for a special need for specific adaptation, it is also recognized that "it was built on the European model" and partially following the Portuguese Competition Law (Fonseca 2019).

Having that background evidencing that the Portuguese competition law is generally recognized as an inspiration for the Lusophone countries, with the note that in relation to the Brazilian reality there is also some influence of the US system as a result of being a legal system that opted for the criminalization of anti-competitive practices.

Constitutional and Legal Framework of Competition Defence in Portugal

Protection of competition represents in Portugal a duty to guarantee "the efficient functioning of markets so as to ensure balanced competition between undertakings, to repress monopolistic forms of organization, abuses of dominant position and other harmful practices of general interest" (Article 81, f) of Constitution). Competition defence is a social and economic fundamental principle, related with economic and individual freedom of initiative—see Marques (2002).

Whilst the constitutional support goes back to 1976, the first Portuguese competition law (PCL) was only approved in 1983 (PCL 1983) and motivated by the accession process to the EEC, in 1985–1986. A first change in the PCL occurred in 1993 (PCL 1993) but a strong motivation to enhance competition defence, alongside the 2003 "modernization" process of the EU competition law, indeed came into force with the creation of Portuguese Competition Authority (PCA), replacing formers Directorate-General for Competition and Competition Council, through the Decree-Law n.° 10/2003, and the PCL 2003 was passed. The later was revoked and replaced by the actual PCL (2012).

As in EU competition law, PCL 2012 prohibits agreements between undertakings, concerted practices and decisions by associations of undertakings which by object or effect prevent, distort or restrict competition in whole or in part of the domestic market (Article 9), thus adapting to the national market Article 101 TFEU, and the prohibition of abuse of a dominant position in the domestic market or in a substantial part of it is previewed (Article 11) in similar terms of Article 102 TFEU. PCL also establishes the prohibition of abuse of economic dependence. PCL 2012 adds a prohibition for one undertaking or more undertakings to abuse the economic dependence under which any of its supplier or customer may find itself as a result of the fact that any equivalent alternative is not available, to the extent that such a practice affects the way the market or competition operate (Article 12), and the Portuguese competition defence legal order also provides for a merger control system and a State Aid monitoring system.

Portugal was one of those European countries opting to introduce a misdemeanour law ("Regime Geral das Contra-Ordenações e Coimas", aproved by Decree-Law 433/82, with the last amendment introduced by Law 109/2001, of 24.12), inspired by the German "Ordnungswidrigkeit" law—on the Portuguese misdemeanour institute, see e.g. (Faria Costa 1998; Figueiredo Dias 1998; Lumbrales 2006; Albuquerque 2011; Vilela 2013a, 2013b, 2014; Brandão 2016). PCL 1983 classified competition law infringements as misdemeanours (hereafter called as administrative offences). In PCL 2012, Article 67 states that infringements to PCL and to EU competition law where its enforcement is carried out by the PCA shall be deemed as administrative offences and Article 68 (1), (a) and (b) establish that infringements of Articles 9 and 11 (and 12) and also Articles 101 and 102 TFEU, when enforced by the PCA according to Article 3 (1) of Regulation 1/2003, are also sanctioned with a (similar) fine.

Liability for competition law infringements is applicable over natural and legal persons, as well as undertakings and associations (even if with no legal status). Legal persons are deemed responsible for the administrative offences when committed in their name and in their collective interests by their responsible or by anyone acting under their authority—Article 73 (1), (2). Fines cannot exceed 10% of the undertaking's turnover for each of the undertakings concerned or, in the case of associations of undertakings, the aggregate turnover of the associated undertakings (Article 69 (2)). As to the fine applicable to natural persons, it cannot exceed 10% of their annual income in the last full year when the prohibited practice occurred (Article 69 (4)).

Criteria for the concrete setting of fine are the seriousness of the infringement in terms of its effect on competition in the domestic market; the nature and size of the market affected; the duration of the infringement; the degree of involvement in the infringement by the party concerned; the advantages obtained by the infringer with the competition infringement, when such advantages can be identified and calculated; the behaviour of the infringer in eliminating the prohibited practices and repairing the damage caused to competition; the economic situation of the infringer; previous competition infringements committed; and the assistance given to the PCA throughout the proceedings (Article 69 (1)). Based on this set of criteria, the PCA adopted its "Guidelines on the methodology to be used in the application of fines".

Alongside the fine(s), PCA can also apply accessory sanctions—when the seriousness of the infringement so justifies—, such as the publication of an extract of the sanctioning decision in the Official Journal and in a newspaper with a large circulation in the relevant geographical market at the expense of the party concerned or even a ban up to a maximum of two years on the right to take part in procedures for public contracts or procedures involving the award of licences or authorizations where the infringement that has led to the application of a fine has occurred during or because of such type of procedures (Article 71 (1), (a), (b), (2)). This latter accessory sanction was firstly introduced upon approval of the new Public Contracts Code of 2008, where an amendment was introduced into PCL 2003, adding an accessory sanction making it possible to impose a prohibition to participate up to two years in public tenders, public concessions or other public contracts to undertakings considered to have infringed competition law in the preparation and/or execution of a public tender (typically in situations of bid rigging).

When and if justifiable, also a periodic penalty sanction, up to a maximum of 5% of the average daily turnover, can be imposed per day of late payment in case of non-compliance with a PCA decision that has imposed a sanction or the adoption of specific measures (Article 72).

Time barrier (statute of limitation) for the adoption of a sanctioning decision is five years for the most important competition infringements, such as Articles 9 or 11 of PCL and 101 or 102 of the TFEU, with time limit for proceedings being (i) interrupted by the notification of a statement of objections and (ii) suspended for the period when a PCA decision is subject of judicial review or in those cases where the PCA has initiated administrative offence proceedings for infringement of Articles 101 and 102 of the TFEU but subsequently acquires the information that another NCA has initiated proceedings concerning the same facts and articles of the TFEU and notifies the party concerned pursuant to Article 13 (1) of Regulation 1/2003 (Article 74 (1), (3), (4), (5)).

The decisions handed down by the PCA are subject to appeal and judicial review by the Competition, Regulation and Supervision Court, and normally have no suspensive effects (Article 84). The appeal against final decisions of PCA shall be lodged within 30 working days (Article 87 (1)) and the Competition, Regulation and Supervision Court has full jurisdiction to review PCA decisions imposing a fine or a periodic penalty payment, and can reduce or increase the amount of the fine or of the periodic penalty payment (Article 88 (1)).

Judgements of the Competition, Regulation and Supervision Court are subject to appeal to the Court of Appeal that shall be the court of final instance (Article 89 (1)).

How Portuguese and Brazilian Regimes Compare

Portuguese competition legal framework has greatly evolved over the past years. Mostly due to the EU influence, Portugal has been adopting modern instruments idealized in recent years to promote effectiveness of competition defence, such as the settlement procedure and the leniency regime. Brazil is also the other example of a Lusophone country that is on the upfront line of modernity of its competition defence regime, but presents a fundamental difference deriving from the fact that is a criminal-based system. It is therefore interesting to compare the two models, highlighting their capability to inspire other Lusophone countries depending on the option made between a misdemeanour law or a criminal law-based system.

Actual PCL previews either a settlement procedure during the investigation phase (Article 22), either the possibility for the case closing under the acceptance of conditions by the undertaking (Article 23). Starting with the latter, Portuguese Competition Authority may accept commitments proposed by the undertaking under investigation that is likely to eliminate the effects on competition arising from the practices in question, closing the case by imposing conditions aimed at ensuring compliance with the proposed commitments. The Portuguese Competition Authority decision closing the case makes the commitments mandatory and the case can only be reopened within a maximum period of two years if there has been a substantial change in the factual situation on which the decision was based, if the conditions are not met, or if the archiving decision was based on false, inaccurate or incomplete information (Article 23(7)), but in any case, the verification of compliance with the conditions prevents the reopening of the process (Article 23(9)).

Basically, it is an "import" to Portugal of the same possibility previewed in European competition law and established in art. 9 of Regulation 1/2003. And since such a decision is a decision that closes an investigation and does not conclude that an infringement exists, subject to the application of the commitments, there is a transparency rule imposed prior to its adoption, allowing for any injured parties to comment on the relevant aspects of it (Article 23(4)).

As for the settlement procedure, it also constitutes an "import" of the solution introduced in European competition law, this time by means of an amendment to Article 10A to Commission Regulation (EC) No. 773/2004 when amended by Commission Regulation (EC) No. 622/2008. The difference—which is important—consists in the fact that such Art. 10A of the Commission Regulation (EC) No. 773/2004 establishes that the settlement procedure applies only for cartels, whilst the PCL establishes the procedure for all anti-competitive offences established in section II of chapter II of the PCL, which means that in European competition law the settlement procedure was introduced as a "support" to the leniency regime, applicable only to cartels, whereas in the PCL is capable of "supporting" the negotiated resolution of almost all competition cases.

The settlement procedure may originate at the initiative of the Competition Authority or at the request of the undertaking investigated (Article 22 (1), (2)), and are based on carrying out "conversations" that will eventually end up in the presentation of a transaction proposal by the undertaking.

If accepted the transaction proposal is converted into a final condemnatory decision with the payment of the fine applied, the facts not being able to be re-assessed, nor the facts confessed may be judicially challenged (Article 22 (12), (13)).

The settlement procedure, in a first assessment, would be an approximation to the plea-bargaining model in force in the US, that would have been transplanted by the Commission to European competition law and, subsequently, to the PCL. However, this is only partially true and regarding the concept of negotiation of acknowledgement of guilt and reduction of the sanction, and not so regarding the model itself. In fact, the original plea-bargaining system is based on a tripartite model between the accuser or public prosecutor (prosecutor), the defendant and the court, in which the first two can develop conversations aimed at acknowledging the defendant's guilt (plead guilty) before the court, accompanied by a reduction of the concrete sanction to be proposed by the prosecutor to the court. And it is always a recommendation or proposal, as it is always up to the court to decide to accept the proposed plea agreement, that is, it is always up to the court to decide on the sanction to apply (via acceptance or rejection of the proposed agreement)—see (Ferro 2005, pp. 451–459; Wils 2006, pp. 345–366; 2008, pp. 335–351; Georgiev 2007, pp. 995–1013; Cellere & Mezzapesa 2009, pp. 604–609; Dekeyser & Roques 2010, pp. 819–842; Schinkel 2011, pp. 461–481).

However, what is established in the Portuguese legal system is different, as it refers to the administrative phase of a sanctioning process, in which the conversations occur between the administrative entity having the powers of investigation, prosecution and decision, and that through of the transaction procedure, the "accuser and decision maker" is allowed to negotiate with the defendant and if a transaction in completed the conviction is non-appealable to the Courts. In our opinion, it is a solution that should be improved in terms of robustness, transparency and should preview the right to appeal.

As to the Brazilian legal system, the Competition Defense Law (Law 12.529/11) also provides in Article 85 the figure of what he calls "Cease Commitment" and which refers to the possibility of "Conselho Administrativo de Defesa Económica" (CADE) being able to accept commitment(s) to cease the practice under investigation or its harmful effects, whenever, in a judgement of convenience and opportunity duly reasoned, it is considered that it meets the interests protected by law. The openness to opportunity is expressed here, and the commitment is reinforced by the fact that it should identify the obligations that the undertaking shall respect as well the amount of the fine in the event of total or partial non-compliance with the obligations contained in the commitment.

The commitment to terminate the practice is public and the agreement must be published on the CADE website, constitutes an extrajudicial enforceable title, and the administrative proceedings will be suspended during implementation of the commitment and until it is fulfilled. If, on the other hand, there is a breach of the conditions established in the commitment, CADE will apply not only the sanctions provided for therein, but it will proceed with the administrative proceeding and other administrative and judicial measures for its execution.

Regarding what will correspond to the settlement procedure itself, considering that the system is a hybrid one, adding criminal to administrative sanctions, it is determined that a Specialized Federal Attorney's Office works within CADE, being responsible to promote court settlements in proceedings relating to infractions against the economic order, with the authorization of the Court (Article 15, VI, of Law 12.529/11). Brazilian law provides several mechanisms that fall under the concept of "negotiated justice" (also established in Law 9.099/95 for criminal settlements and conditional suspension of the process, and in Law 12.850/2013 regarding non-criminal prosecution agreement recently introduced by Law 13.964/2019 in the so-called "Anti-Crime Package").

The criminal settlement incorporates the idea of consensus, establishing the principle that the process will be guided by the criteria of orality, simplicity, informality, procedural economy and speed, seeking, whenever possible, conciliation or transaction (Article 2 of Law 9.099/95), previewing such settlement possibility for criminal offences of lesser offensive potential, that is, criminal offences for which the law imposes a maximum penalty of not more than two years, cumulative or not with a fine. However, given the sanctioning framework provided namely for cartels, the plea-bargaining ("delação premiada") rewarding collaboration established in Law 12.850/13, amended by Law No. 13.964/19, is defined in Art. 3-A as the procedural legal business and means of obtaining evidence, which presupposes public utility and interest. In the rewarded collaboration agreement, the collaborator must relate all the illicit facts for which he or she contributed, and indicate the evidence and supporting evidence. (§ 3 and 4 of Article 3-B). Following this phase, the judge may, at the request of the parties, grant a judicial pardon or reduce by two-thirds the penalty of deprivation of liberty, provided that some of the following results from this collaboration: the identification of other co-authors and participants in the criminal organization and the criminal offences committed by them; revealing the hierarchical structure and division of tasks of the criminal organization; the prevention of criminal offences arising from the activities of the criminal organization; and/or the total or partial recovery of the proceeds or profit from the criminal offences committed by the criminal organization.

A last and brief reference to the novel non-criminal prosecution agreement, contained in Article 28-A introduced in the Code of Criminal Procedure by Law 13.964/19, which now provides that if the person investigated confesses the practice of criminal offence without violence or serious threat and with a minimum sentence of less than four (4) years, the Public Prosecutor's Office may propose a non-criminal prosecution agreement if deemed sufficient for disapproval and prevention of the crime, and provided that the investigated complies with the conditions established by the Public Prosecutor's Office in the agreement, namely regarding the repair of the damage, except in the case of impossibility to do so.

Conclusion

Within Lusophone countries, Portuguese and Brazilian legal systems shall be considered to be well developed in terms of competition defence.

Indeed, the actual legal framework for competition defence in Portugal is at a level already justifying the discussion about its real nature, with some authors considering that it establishes quasi-criminal sanctions. The nature of quasi-criminal sanctions is often used by several authors to qualify EU sanctions for violation of Articles 101 and 102 of the TFEU.

As for the defence of cartel criminal sanctions in EU Competition law, albeit considering that penalties for violation of European competition law are (still) purely administrative ones, see e.g., Whelan (2007, p. 24). In Portugal, Moura e Silva (2011) makes reference to the "quasi-criminal nature of competition infringements in Portugal" and Gageiro (2009, p. 55) argues that several sanctions imposed by international authorities are possible to be considered as "criminal sanctions by nature" (criminal in nature). But what is underlined is that several authors refer to sanctions set out in European competition law—and therefore without even considering sanctions over individuals such as in PCL—as criminal (or at least quasi-criminal) sanctions, with Möschel (2011, p. 371) emphatically arguing that "fines of an exorbitant scope [applied in the European competition law] have effects identical, or at least similar, to criminal sanctions. Any other perception would be a life lie".

Notwithstanding the discussion over the real nature of sanctions, the straightforward and undisputed conclusion is that at every amendment in PCL, increased powers for the competition defence enforcement and competition infringements sanctioning were introduced, which also opens the debate about if this movement has been accompanied by the necessary adjustments in terms of the rights of defence—see Castro Marques (2019, pp. 356–375). As for Brazil, the criminal nature for competition defence is already established, as thus both countries had implemented robust legal regimes that are needed for an effective (general and special) prevention of economic offences.

The Portuguese legal regime is however the most preferred to be the inspiring system to other Lusophone countries, either due to its EU context and origin, either precisely due to the fact that it is not (still) a criminal-based system. In the initial phases of implementation of competition defence regimes (and) on developing economies countries, it seems advisable not to opt straightforward for a criminal-based model and to start with an administrative-based one, to create a competition culture within society, to proceed with a strong advocacy policy and afterwards eventually evolve to the criminalization of the competition defence regime.

Acknowledgements The author acknowledge that this study was conducted with the support of CEAD—Centro de Estudos Avançados em Direito, Lusófona University of Porto, Faculty of Law and Political Science, Porto, Portugal.

Orcid ID—http://orcid.org/0000-0001-8250-6002 Ciência ID—4C1A-CD19-A402.

References

Albuquerque, P. P. d. (2011). Comentário do Regime Geral das Contra-Ordenações à luz da Constituição da República e da Convenção Europeia dos Direitos do Homem. Lisboa: Universidade Católica Editora.

Amato, G. (1997). Antitrust and the Bounds of Power—The Dilemma of Liberal Democracy in the History of the Market. Oxford: Hart Publishing.

Brandão, N. (2016). Crimes e contra-ordenações: da cisão à convergência material - ensaio para uma recompreensão da relação entre o direito penal e o direito contra-ordenacional. Coimbra: Coimbra Editora.

Carvalho, E. L. F. (2013). A política antitruste no Brasil e o combate a cartéis à luz do novo Cade. Revista de Defesa da Concorrência, 1(2), 74–91.

Castro Marques, N. (2019). Contributo para a Autonomia do Direito Nacional da Concorrência - em particular na criminalização dos cartéis. Porto: Universidade Católica Editora.

Cellere, S. M. d., & Mezzapesa, G. (2009). The Commission's settlement package: EU- US comparison. European Competition Law Review, 30(12), 604–609.

Cruvinel, R. (2020). Definindo sanções ótimas a práticas anticompetitivas e corruptas: a punição a indivíduos por meio de mecanismos alternativos. Revista de Defesa da Concorrência, 8(2), 144–163.

Dekeyser, K., & Roques, C. (2010). The European Commission's settlement procedure in cartel cases. Antitrust Bulletin, 55(4), 819–842.

Faria Costa, J. d. (1998). O direito penal económico e as causas implícitas de exclusão da ilicitude. In Direito Penal Económico e Europeu: Textos Doutrinários (Vol. Volume I, pp. 413–429). Coimbra: Coimbra Editora.

Ferro, M. S. (2005). Committing to Commitment Decisions—Unanswered Questions on Article 9 Decisions. European Competition Law Review, 26(8), 451–459.

Figueiredo Dias, J. d. (1998). O Movimento de Descriminalização e o Ilícito de Mera Ordenação Social. Direito Penal Económico e Europeu: Textos Doutrinários, Vol. I - Problemas Gerais, pp. 19–33.

Fonseca, S. L. R. (2019). A Lei da Concorrência Angolana e o Desafio do Mercado Informal. Universidade Católica Portuguesa.

Gageiro, A. (2009). Modelos de direito estrangeiro na perspectiva do enforcement (E.U.A./R.U./Europa Continental). In M. F. D. Palma, Augusto Silva; Mendes, Paulo Sousa, (coord.) (Ed.), Direito Sancionatório das Autoridades Reguladoras (pp. 41–74). Coimbra: Coimbra Editora.

Gal, M. S. (2004). Monopoly Pricing as an Antitrust Offense in the U.S. and the EC: Two Systems of Belief About Monopoly. The Antitrust Bulletin, Spring-Summer, 343–384.
Gal, M. S. (2010). Free Movement of Judgments: Increasing Deterrence of International Cartels Through Jurisdictional Reliance. Virginia Journal of International Law, 51(1), 57–94.
Georgiev, G. S. (2007). Contagious Efficiency: the Growing Reliance on U.S.-Style Antitrust Settlements in EU Law. Utah Law Review, 971–1037.
Harding, C. (2011). Cartel Deterrence: The Search for Evidence and Argument. Antitrust Bulletin, 56(2), 345–376.
Henriques, F. d. A. (2013). A Nova Lei da Concorrência de Moçambique. Guia para empresas & negócios em Moçambique.
Hildebrand, D. (2002). The European School in EC Competition Law. World Competition, 25(1), 3–23.
ICN, I. C. N.-. (2005). Defining Hard Core Cartel Conduct—Effective Institutions—Effective Penalties. Luxembourg.
Jones, A., & Williams, R. (2014). The UK Response to the Global Effort Against Cartels: Is Criminalization Really the Solution? Journal of Antitrust Enforcement, 2(1), 100–125.
Joshua, J. M., Camesasca, P. D., & Jung, Y. (2008). Extradition and Mutual Legal Assistance Treaties: Cartel Enforcement's Global Reach. Antitrust Law Journal, 75(2), 353–397.
Kovacic, W. E. (2006). An Integrated Competition Policy to Deter and Defeat Cartels. Antitrust Bulletin, 51(4), 813.
Lumbrales, N. B. M. (2006). Sobre o Conceito Material de Contra-Ordenação. Lisboa: Universidade Católica Editora.
Marques, M. M. L. (2002). Um Curso de Direito da Concorrência. Coimbra: Coimbra Editora.
Mcnulty, P. J. (1968). Economic Theory and the Meaning of Competition. Quarterly Journal of Economics, 82(4), 639–656.
Möschel, W. (2011). Fines in European Competition Law. European Competition Law Review, 32(7), 369–375.
Moura e Silva, M. (2011). Anti-cartel Enforcement in Portugal: A Short Chronicle of an Uphill Struggle. European Competition Law Review, 32(1), 37–41.
OCDE. (1998). Recommendation of the Council Concerning Effective Action Against Hard Core Cartels. Paris: OCDE.
Pera, A. (2008). Changing Views of Competition, Economic Analysis and EC Antitrust Law. European Competition Journal, 4(1), 127–168.
Pinha, L. C. (2018). Qual a contribuição da Teoria dos Jogos para os programas de leniência? Uma análise aplicada ao contexto brasileiro. Revista de Defesa da Concorrência, 6(1), 156–172.

Schinkel, M. P. (2011). Bargaining in the Shadow of the European Settlement Procedure for Cartels. Antitrust Bulletin, 56(2), 461.

Vilela, A. (2013a). Crime e contraordenação: por morrerem algumas andorinhas pode acabar a primavera. Revista da Faculdade de Direito da Universidade Lusófona do Porto, 2(2), 194–206.

Vilela, A. (2013b). O Direito de Mera Ordenação Social: Entre a Ideia de "Recorrência" e a de "Erosão" do Direito Penal Clássico. Coimbra: Coimbra Editora.

Vilela, A. (2014). A Segunda parte do regime geral do ilícito de mera ordenação social: um direito processual muitas vezes ignorado. Revista da Faculdade de Direito da Universidade Lusófona do Porto, 4, 2–10.

Whelan, P. (2007). A Principled Argument for Personal Criminal Sanctions as Punishment under EC Cartel Law. The Competition Law Review, 4(1), 7–40.

Wils, W. P. J. (2006). Settlements of EU Antitrust Investigations: Commitment Decisions Under Article 9 of Regulation No. 1/2003. World Competition, 29(3), 345–366.

Wils, W. P. J. (2008). The Use of Settlements in Public Antitrust Enforcement: Objectives and Principles. World Competition, 31(3), 335–351.

The Role and Influence of Portuguese Law in the Macau SAR of People's Republic of China: Issues and Perspectives

Paulo Cardinal

Introduction

The Macau Special Administrative Region of the People's Republic of China, was established on 20 December 1999 and enjoys a unique and challenging status. Guaranteed for a period of at least 50 years, anchored in the "One Country, Two Systems" formula, firstly guaranteed by the Joint Declaration, an international treaty deposited by both contracting parties at the United Nations, stating that after the establishment of the SAR, the laws, decree laws, administrative regulations and other provisions previously in force in Macau shall be maintained. The legal system receives a continuity guarantee, not as an untouchable set of various pieces of legislation, but as a whole, its spirit, its principles. It was mostly imported from Portugal or strongly influenced by it and it showcases a guarantee of Law as Law proper and a legal system with Rule of Law. All of these, nevertheless, operates vis-à-vis a multicultural socio-cultural background that is, mainly, dominated by a Chinese population

P. Cardinal (✉)
Faculty of Law, University of Macau, Macau, China

Faculty of Law, University of Hong Kong, Hong Kong, China

P. A. B. Duarte et al. (eds.), *Portugal and the Lusophone World*,
https://doi.org/10.1007/978-981-99-0455-6_5

with a presence of Confucianism within its legal culture (Godinho 2011) or, in other words, this blending of cultures and peoples characterizes Macau and includes and defines "*the organization and the functioning of Macau's legal and judicial systems*" (Halis 2019). Lately, in a context of increasing pressure on the SAR's autonomy, this continuity and linkage to Portuguese Law has been subjected to challenges.

Besides, one must note that in terms of constitutional law and political regimes, what is promised is a political system that does not endeavour autocracy, and it purports some degree of separation of powers. The Basic Law is purported to have a normative effect and to be present in the Macau legal system, but not solely as, or reduced to, a sort of generic guideline devoid of proper legal effects and thus, among other consequences, not enforceable by the courts.

What will the road ahead be? Will this linkage—along with its connatural characters and guarantees—survive up until, at least, 2049 or, inversely, will this connection be severed and, potentially, will the Macau legal system move more and more, in a previously untoward way, to the realms of Chinese legal system contemporary characterization? A Chinese legal system that purports an amalgam of formal Roman-German characteristics, a presence of traditional law elements rooted mainly on Confucianism, a revisitation and revivalism of the *nefarious* Legalist school—"*In the twentieth century not a few scholars dubbed Legalists 'totalitarians' (…). Some of the aspects of the Legalist program—a powerful state that overwhelms society, rigid control over the populace and the administrative apparatus, harsh laws, and the like—seem to lend support to this equation.*" (Pines 2014)—, socialist law elements and, therefore, for instance, the place and role of law being subdued, the *Rule of Law* ceding to the *Rule by Law*, the inexistence, formally and substantially, of judicial independence, and so on.

And, in the same stance, will the Macau Basic Law, resorting now to the famous ontological classification of constitutions advanced by Karl Loewenstein, departing from a normative *constitution—lato sensu* or functional sense (Cardinal 2010; Alexandrino 2013)—be metamorphosed, by the end of the road, into a nominal or a semantic one?

Brief Historical Contextualization[1]

Macau, a tiny territory laying in the south of China, inhabited largely by Chinese ethnic people, is a Special Administrative Region of the People's Republic of China (PRC), since 20 December 1999, thus ending several centuries of Portuguese official dominance not mattering now for the purposes of this paper under what juridical title. For instance international treaties, neither its scope and variances, as, for example exemption of Portuguese Law application to Chinese Imperial subjects thus establishing a system of mixed jurisdiction (up until the end of eighteenth century, with both Portuguese and Chinese authorities exercising jurisdiction. The Portuguese had jurisdiction over the Portuguese community and certain aspects of the overall territory's administration, but no real sovereignty), and theoretical justification or models, such as *condominium*, *leased territory*, *internationalized territory*, *colony*, *territory under (transitory) Portuguese Administration*. For the last half millennium, Macau has thus existed in a strange state of individuality and disconnection *vis-à-vis* greater China and, for several centuries, up until the last days of 1999, it has been effectively separated from China, and connected to a small and far way State, Portugal, albeit as an autonomous entity.

Some have referred to the history of Macau as a history of anomaly (Wills/Van Dyke 2000) and absurdity (Cabrita 2002). This anomalous history provides some clues as to why a miniscule piece of land has achieved such extensive autonomy within one of the giants of the world and, naturally, moving to our topic, it also provides explanations to the presence and significance of Portuguese Law in a faraway *Ausland* inhabited mostly by a non-Portuguese population.

In the official, yet disputed, Portuguese version, a naval victory over the pirate fleets that had been disturbing trade on the southern coast of China was the reason why the Chinese emperor authorized the establishment of the Portuguese presence in Macau in 1557. For more than two centuries the Portuguese established in Macau administered their interests in an autonomous fashion. In Asia, the attentions of Portuguese imperial

[1] In this chapter we are following closely our accounts put forward in "Continuity and Autonomy—Leading Principles Shaping the Fundamental Rights Constitutional System in the Macau Special Administrative Region", 2008.

power were concentrated on India and Macau was too small, too far away, and too difficult to communicate with to care about.

The Chinese authorities continued to collect certain land and customs taxes, and the Portuguese continued to pay rent to China until 1849, when they abolished the Chinese customs. In 1887 the Chinese government recognized the Portuguese right of "perpetual occupation" of Macau in an international agreement and agreed that Macau was the same as any other Portuguese possession, with the proviso that Portugal would never surrender Macau to a third party without China's permission. Despite the existence of this treaty, the political status of Macau henceforth remained a subject of dispute.

Following the Portuguese Revolution of 25 April 1974, that reinstated a democratic regime, Portugal and China established diplomatic relations in 1979 and both countries expressed interest in finding a mutually agreeable solution to Macau's status—noting that the Joint Declaration states: "*The Government of the People's Republic of China and the Government of the Republic of Portugal have reviewed with satisfaction the development of the friendly relations between the two Governments and peoples since the establishment of diplomatic relations between the two countries and agreed that a proper negotiated settlement by the two Governments of the question of Macau, which is left over from the past, is conducive to the economic growth and social stability of Macau*"; negotiations began in 1985, a year after the signing of the Sino-U. K. Joint Declaration, and in 1987 the Joint Declaration of the Portuguese Republic and the People's Republic of China on the Question of Macau, a formal international treaty, with binding effects, deposited by both contracting parties at the United Nations (United Nations—Treaty Series • Nations Unies—Recueil des Traités, Vol. 1498 1–25805, pp. 228 and ff.), was signed agreeing that Macau would return to China and thus it became a Chinese territory under Portuguese administration up until it returned to China. This new state of affairs was duly reflected in the Portuguese Constitution, namely by stating that Macau was under temporary Portuguese Administration and thus, not a part of Portuguese territory.

The SAR, the Joint Declaration, and the Basic Law Pointing the Continuity Principle

On 20 December 1999, Macau went from being a territory under Portuguese administration to the resumption of sovereignty by the People's Republic of China as a Special Administrative Region (SAR), in accordance with the Joint Declaration. This eloquently specifies that the SAR will enjoy a high degree of autonomy and will incorporate the basic policies stated in the Joint Declaration into a Basic Law thus effectively materializing the famous formula "One Country, Two Systems" in Macau.

It is important to take notice of some of those twelve basic policies (in twelve autonomous *subparagraphs* of point 2 of the Joint Declaration and later on further elaborated by the PRC in Annex I of the Joint Declaration and it is of juridical relevance to state that the Annex is still a part of this international treaty) established in the international treaty (and consequently later inscribed in the Basic Law the Joint Declaration offspring, one may say) that impact more strongly our topic:

- The Macau SAR will be vested with executive, legislative, and independent judicial power, including that of final adjudication.
- The current social and economic systems in Macau will remain unchanged, as shall the existing way of life. The laws in force will remain basically unchanged. The Macau SAR will, in accordance with the law, ensure all the rights and freedoms of the inhabitants and other individuals in Macau.
- The maintenance of public order in the Macau SAR will be the responsibility of the Government of the Macau SAR.
- And lastly, but definitely not the least, the basic policies and the related clarifications set forth in annex I to the Joint Declaration will be stipulated, in a Basic Law of the Macau SAR and will remain unchanged for 50 years.

As Deng Xiaoping eloquently stated "*We have solemnly promised that our policy towards Hong Kong will remain unchanged for 50 years after 1997. Why 50 years? There is a reason for that. Not only do we need to reassure the people of Hong Kong, but we also have to take into consideration the close relation between the prosperity and stability of Hong Kong and the strategy for the development of China. (...) As a matter of fact, 50 years is only a vivid way of putting it. Even after 50 years our policy will not change either. That is, for the first 50 years it cannot be changed, and for the second there will be no need to change it. So this is not just idle talk*" (Xiaoping 1994).

The Annex I elaborations, in paragraph III, further state that "*After the establishment of the Macau Special Administrative Region, the laws, decree laws, administrative regulations and other provisions previously in force in Macau shall be maintained, save for any that contravene the Basic Law and subject to any amendment by the Macau Special Administrative Region legislature (…) The laws of the Macau Special Administrative Region shall comprise the Basic Law, the laws previously in force in Macau and laws enacted by the Macau Special Administrative Region legislature as above.*"

Consequently, the Basic Law establishes: "*The laws, decrees, administrative regulations and other normative acts previously in force in Macau shall be maintained, except for any that contravenes this Law, or subject to any amendment by the legislature or other relevant organs of the Macau Special Administrative Region in accordance with legal procedures*", article 8. See also, "*The laws in force in the Macau Special Administrative Region shall be this Law, the laws previously in force in Macau as provided for in Article 8 of this Law, and the laws enacted by the legislature of the Region*", article 18, and, "*Upon the establishment of the Macau Special Administrative Region, the laws previously in force in Macau shall be adopted as laws of the Region except for those which the Standing Committee of the National People's Congress declares to be in contravention of this Law*", article 145. All these, albeit denting in some measure the initial principle, reaffirm the principle of continuity of the legal system of Macau.

These normative precepts, of international and constitutional nature, embody what is called the principle of continuity in the field of the legal system.

In truth, a paramount principle in general, the maintenance of the way of life principle, itself also a legal concept (Tong 2012), as well as in the fields of the legal system and others such as on fundamental rights is the principle of continuity. As mentioned elsewhere, this apex principle of continuity *allows the preservation of the Portuguese legal heritage and influence, which remains strong in Macau's legislation, judiciary and legal profession* (Halis 2019). As seen from the above cited legal narratives, one is dealing with the continuity of the social system, of the economic system and also of the normative acts basically unchanged. Or, as one author put it, it was envisaged a "*high degree of continuity*" (Crawford 2005).

This principle is also referred to, sometimes, as the principle of the inalterability of the essential. However, it does not affirm itself as absolute, meaning that the principle of continuity does not have to be read as meaning pure or absolute intangibility. It does not claim to be synonymous with intangibility in as much as the contracting parties had intended to prevent an undesirable sclerosis of the legal system. In truth, this characteristic of elasticity, though limited one must say, of the principle of continuity, presents itself as an added guarantee to the effective survival of the legal system since it allows it, without abdicating its essential characteristics, to adapt to the natural and unexpected evolution of the social system where it is inserted. If it is the *veritas* that the legal system will have to be maintained, although not in absolute terms, it is equally true that it could only be modified with respect to the limits established in the Joint Declaration. One has to point out that the limit to the fullness of the principle of continuity cannot be reduced to only the thesis of the maintenance of the laws, saved in that to oppose the Basic Law or that it will be subject to posterior alterations; otherwise, that will simply mean carrying out the emptiness of that apex principle and consequently be rendered useless. One indeed has to admit the possibility of the introduction of those alterations; however, it is not permissible for these alterations to consubstantiate basic changes. With this, we mean that the general principles that characterize and shape the Macau legal system cannot be disregarded, and neither can the diverse legal regimes be disregarded as well—for example, of the fundamental rights in general—they cannot have their *ratio* deviated or overwhelmed. In other words, the essential content of a given juridical regimen will have to be respected and kept.

It was already stated with good reasoning that a*s* for the concept of "*laws in force*" we understand it in a broad meaning, encompassing not only the formal aspect—written laws—but also the spirit of the legal system, its internal logic, its own dogmatic concepts, and all the rest that provides life and sense to the legal order previously existent at the date of transfer of the exercise of sovereignty (Alves 2001).

Thus, the principle of continuity—of the present social and economic systems, and in order to secure this, the laws currently in force will remain basically unchanged—constitutes a master guarantee of the transition process as we envisage it.

On the other hand, but intimately connected to it, one must point out that, contrary to what, to a certain extent, is common, the legal order of the sovereign applies, or so tends to, unlimitedly and unrestricted to the subnational entities, at least in the subject matters reserved to the centre. However, with the SAR's example, we do not find such schemes except for some limited PRC constitutional norms, the Basic Law (and in here with constraints applicable to the sovereign power due to the need to obey the Joint Declaration's twelve basic policies) and a few sovereignty legislations that must be identified and, in a sense, incorporated by the Basic Law itself and via a special procedure of application. PRC's national laws will not apply, apart from those listed in Annex III to the Basic Law. In this sense, there is an extremely limited and low-grade intervention in the Macau legal system, thus the expression of Macau legal system "*immunity from Chinese Law*" (Olivetti 2009).

In some areas, such as the fundamental rights, one can express a principle of *self-containment and of absolute exclusivity* resting upon Macau legislation, besides the Basic Law and international treaties, as well as a *principle of local philosophy in the interpretation and integrative methods*, in order to comply with the autonomic fundamental rights system, there is to be no importation of rules, methods of interpretation, methods, and theories of fundamental rights that are observed in the PRC; on the contrary, the matrix must be the western idea of fundamental rights fully embodied in the Macau legal order before 1999. This is particularly important as these embody an extremely different general approach to the subject matter when compared to that of the SAR.

The system envisaged by both the international treaty and the subsequent Basic Law clearly promises and points to a system endowed and directed by the Rule of Law, thus purporting what we can call a *Rechtregion*—in a regionalized synonymy with *Rechtstaat*. The courts are independent, every normative act must be in conformity with the Basic Law, a system of fundamental rights is in place and the principle of safeguarding is expressly established, the Government must abide by the law, a specific separation of powers frame is established, there is no retroactivity of criminal law, especially in typifying crimes, the presumption of innocence is guaranteed, human dignity, equality, and non-discrimination are all expressly established, and so on.

The Macau Legal System Panoramic Characterization and Its Place in the Legal Families Discourse

We have seen that the legal system receives, under the umbrella of the "One Country, Two Systems" formula, a guarantee of continuity which should mean the inalterability of the essential, the maintenance of its characteristics, that is, *v.g.* its principles, values and axioms, methods, legal institutes.

The Macau legal system after the Joint Declaration was signed, was in many areas identical to the Portuguese one, for instance its Civil Code and its Commercial Code were the Portuguese ones, whereas in some other areas, were identical to previously enshrined in Portugal and Portuguese legislation—no longer in force at the time in Portugal—such as the criminal procedure code. There was also in place a system of appeals—namely in private law, criminal law, and administrative law matters, as well as in constitutional review issues—to Portuguese courts. This, naturally, meant a potential identity verified also in *jurisprudence*.

However, gradually, Macau gained more and more autonomy in order to prepare for the future and subsequently the links to Portuguese courts were mostly severed.

On the other hand, and in spite of the Joint Declaration not fulminating with the non-continuity of the legislation approved by Portuguese law-makers, such as the Republic Assembly, it was stated that by virtue of sovereignty issues the legislation approved in Portugal would no longer be fit to continue in force in Macau after the establishment of the SAR. Henceforth, a complex and demanding process of so-called localization ensued. Then in the final years of Portuguese administration, a huge *redecoration* effort of the legal system took place. The five big codes—Civil, Commercial, Criminal, Civil Procedure, Criminal Procedure—were created and approved locally, as well as a number of other *minor* codes such as the Administrative Procedural Code, the Administrative Procedure Code, and several registration codes.

The major, huge influence, in truth in the spirit of what was established in the Joint Declaration, of these new codes was Portuguese Law at the time in force in Portugal. As stated by Jorge Godinho, "*In terms of detailed content, the legal system of Macau, as it exists today, is generally based on the Portuguese legal system. Although differences between both legal systems have always existed, and are now increasing rapidly, the very strong similarity is undeniable. This is clear from the fact that most codes, while not being exactly equal, are based on those in force in Portugal, of which they represent updated and modernized versions*" (Godinho 2007). As elsewhere stated, the Portuguese legal and judicial systems, with their perspectives, principles, and structures served as models for those of Macau and Macau's legislation and judiciary are based on a Portuguese matrix (Halis 2019).

Regarding other new legislation approved already in the realm of the Macau SAR one could also see the continuous influence of Portuguese Law. For example, the data protection law (Law 8/2005), in which the formal proposal claims that Portuguese Law was one of the most immediate and direct sources of inspiration.

In the field of the *case law*, regarding the Macau supreme court, that is the Court of Final Appeal, in a study covering a period between 2002 and 2011, one finds that "*there was a steady reference to Portuguese legal doctrine, and in many of these, reference was made also to Portuguese jurisprudence*" (Mancuso 2013; see, also Halis 2019).

It is also noteworthy to mention the possibility and opening to foreign judges in Macau, that is judges from Portugal, as stated in the Joint Declaration (Annex I, IV) and in the Basic Law (article 87). At present, there are still a few judges from Portugal sitting at Macau first instance court and at Macau Court of Second instance but no longer at the Court of Final Appeal. This door opening to foreign judges clearly connects with the "One Country, Two systems" policy and several of its corollaries such as the existence and guarantee of a differentiated legal system *vis-à-vis* the Mainland one, the multivalent principle of continuity of the way of life, of the legal system, of the fundamental rights, and the principle of independence of the judiciary. The recourse to foreign judges can be seen as ancillary to better fulfilling these principles.

All of the above should not come as a surprise as it fully embodies the juridical promises of the Joint Declaration regarding the maintenance of the way of life, of the social system, of the legal system, and its (almost entirely) inoculation of immunization from Chinese Law. Thus, even after 1999, or better said, particularly after 1999, these links to Portuguese Law, albeit naturally different in nature and obviously devoid of any power from Portuguese legislators, are presupposed to be maintained and are one of the core elements of the "Second system" segment of the formula "One Country, Two systems".

In another perspective, these legal solutions and methods, doctrinarian works, and jurisprudence *communion* between Macau and Portuguese Law, call for what we can address as a sort of *specific and reinforced role or function of comparative law* for, and in, the Macau legal system, namely, anchored in the above-said continuity principle mandate, especially in its substantial understanding, besides a usual comparative law function, in the sense that comparative law is essential to determine the meaning and scope of the norms and institutes of national law. Whenever these reflect principles also enshrined in the Law of another country or countries or that have been received from them: Comparative Law is, to this extent, an interpretive element of the law (Vicente 2019).

Placing the Macau legal system in the geo-legal atlas should thus, *prima facie*, not be particularly difficult given its intimate connection with the Portuguese one which is clearly a member of the Roman-German or Civil legal family. As said, "*The legal system of Macau is part of the group or 'family' of civil law or Roman-German legal systems*" (Godinho 2007; see also, Correia 2013).

We have elsewhere proposed the same affiliation (Cardinal 2010), stating that the Macau legal system is deeply rooted in the Portuguese legal system. Portugal is, as known, firmly situated in the civil law legal family and hence shares its most outstanding characteristics, such as written law, and by far the most important source of law, written constitutional texts, broad codification, relatively low importance of judicial decisions, if compared to common law legal systems. This circumstance naturally places Macau in the civil law legal family—at least from a strict formal stance—thus with closer ties with the Mainland legal system than Hong Kong's legal system, at least from a formal point of view. However, as to be seen further ahead, maybe this placing is not that clear, after all.

It seems true to say that the level of "purity" in being a member of the Roman-German legal family is slightly less now than before due to some intersections with the Chinese legal system. However, the number of formal intersections is relatively low and are notably under a *numerus clausus* system; that is, those intersections are constitutionally limited due to a system of expressly built bridges and thus expressly identifies the access of Chinese law into the Macau legal system and the strict rules of legitimization of its application, such as ambit, procedures, occurrence of given exceptional circumstances, participation of subnational bodies, etc. One should point out that the idea of an "enclaved" and *immune* different legal system thriving within and along a "sovereign major" legal system pertaining to a diverse legal family, and maintaining its own identity *vis-à-vis* the centre legal system, is not something totally new and unique.

Nevertheless, a few words of some contention to the above remarks should now be brought forward.

Firstly, being true that the classical René David *legal families* proposal (David and Brierley 1978)—basically a distinction between civil law and common law—remains to this day the most used, traditional, and well-known in comparative law and elsewhere, "*Still, David's family pictures continue to rule comparative lawyers from the terminal phase of their lives, if not from their graves. Its continued influence is demonstrated by the difficulties in overcoming the common law-civil law taxonomic divide as the main comparative classification tool*" (Castellucci 2012). It is also undeniable that René David's classification of legal families, among other reasons, should be revised because the *juridical atlas* is different nowadays and there is an abundance of dissent in comparative law when one comes to the taxonomy of legal systems. New approaches, namely less Eurocentric, and new proposals are being made, namely resorting to other variables or elements of analysis.

That is the case, to be brief, for example, of Ugo Mattei, moving away from a Eurocentric perspective and pointing to three distinct patterns: professional rule of law, political rule of law, and traditional rule of law and Macau would sit on the first pattern (Mattei 1997), regarding H. Patrick Glenn classifications, Macau would be positioned in "*the centrality of the person*" one (Glenn 2010), Esin Örücü, in which, basically, all systems are mixed and there are no pure legal families (Örücü 2004), Mathias M. Siems (2016), invoking several innovative elements and variables imported from other sciences, and bringing the idea of clusters, and Macau would sit in the first one. The rise of the hybrid or mixed legal systems theories, for the purposes of this paper we consider synonyms, should also be taken into consideration here.

Secondly, in face of all dissent, of all obstacles, of all shortcomings of the taxonomy effort, the fact is some authors put forward the question—*Classification of Legal Families Today: Is it time for a memorial hymn?* (Husa 2004).

Thirdly, the classic classifications of legal families, due to a phenomenon one can call as the *capture* of comparative law by *privatists*, in spite of the fact that comparative law was born in the realms of public law. In Aristotle, especially in his *Politics*, notably in its Book II, we already find true comparison between constitutions accompanied by conclusions on similarities and differences, opinions, explanations. Much later, again, it is in the fields of public law that one witnesses firm comparative law approaches, for instance, Jean Bodin, XVI century, with his *Juris universi distributivo*, *Methodus ad facilem historiarum cognitionem* and, *De republica libri sex*, 1576, usually known in English as the *Six Books of the Commonwealth*, Montesquieu, *The Spirit of Laws* 1748, and with the imagined *Persian Letters* 1721, P. Anselm Feuerbach, in the beginnings of 1800, dealing with compared criminal law, an unescapable name in comparative law history some even stating that he was the first to conceive the science of comparative law (Hug, 1932). Nevertheless, the usual taxonomies are based almost exclusively in the fields of private law, and, one must stress, are not serviceable when one moves to, for example, comparative constitutional law.

A very simple example will show that the traditional main divide within general comparative law—common law versus civil law. is unserviceable to comparative constitutional law. For instance, in a general comparative law approach, if one compares the legal systems of, say, Australia and Spain, one would easily determine that these two belong to two very different legal families, hence there will be much more differences than similarities. However, if one puts the glasses of comparative constitutional law, the conclusion will be the opposite: both belong to the family of democratic and rule of law systems, and not in the autocratic circle, that is, both are constitutional democracies being thus placed on different sides of the normal comparative law, however standing on the same side of the political regimes division.

As emphasized by Uwe Kischel, "*Comparative law is possible and is pursued in all legal fields. The suggestion that comparative law plays a smaller role outside private law (and in particular in public law), is a rumour which is as false as it is persistent. However, it tends to circulate only among purely private-law oriented jurists*" (Kischel 2019).

This said, even if *brevitatis causa*, one probably needs to somehow empirically (at the moment) rethink the place of Macau in the legal taxonomies.

If one looks at the big field of private law—mostly civil and commercial branches of law—plus the sources of law system—emphasis on legislation, reduced relevance of case law, and wide codification—one could with some ease conclude that Macau belongs still with the Roman-German legal family, or the professional rule of law pattern, or the European legal culture cluster. However, with the presence of some hints of some hybridity due to the application of some Mainland legislation and the penetration of some Mainland doctrine. Regarding Hong Kong, and due to the exercise of several official interpretations and later legal developments, one is faced with clear legal infiltrations that moved Hong Kong's legal system towards a clear case of hybrid system. Ignazio Castellucci, tells us about Macau and its lower resistance to legal infiltration from Mainland China and that the absence of the stare decisis principle made it much easier for the Macanese courts to smoothly implement policies and legal doctrines consistent with the new political environment after the handover to China (Castellucci 2012). Or, for instance, especially in the public law fields, wondering if Macau is becoming a hybrid system or moving towards the Rule of Political Law pattern (Godinho 2011).

When one moves to the fields of public law, namely constitutional law and especially in the sensitive field of fundamental rights, both in jurisprudence, *e.g.* particularly, the decisions of the Court of Final Appeal case 94/2019, it deals with freedom of demonstration, specifically the permit regarding public gatherings intended to demonstrate solidarity with protesters in Hong Kong, and case 58/2020, where, again, one is dealing with freedom of demonstration, the court upheld the government's refusal to prohibit said demonstration. Both cases had a rare dissent vote and signified a departure from previously *guarantistic* or *pro libertate* approaches to this fundamental right. See also the August 2021 decision of the same court confirming the exclusion of several candidates to the Legislative Assembly elections, including several that used to run for previous elections and some that were elected, using unheard and strange argumentation and concluding, basically retroactively, that the would-be candidates were unfaithful to Macau and against the CCP, hence disqualifying them.

And in legislation related to criminal law and criminal procedure law, bearing more and more a mark of securitization, one can detect, with a special relevance recently, a path of moving towards the characteristics of the Chinese legal system, thus rendering Macau clearly as a *legal system in a voyage*, in transition from what was and is supposed to be to something else.

The Macau Basic Law, contrary to what is the reality of the PRC Constitution, it has been indeed a law with normative effect and is enforceable namely by the courts. This contrasts, as known, with the PRC constitution which is basically unenforceable by the courts, "*It is conventional wisdom that China's Constitution is unenforceable and plays little role in China's legal system, other than as a symbolic document*" (Lin/Ginsburg 2015).

A *propos*, we bring in here the famous tripartite classification of constitutions—normative, nominative, and semantic—by Karl Loewenstein (2018). Even if the Macau Basic Law is not a *stricto sensu* Constitution, one can consider it a *lato sensu* one or *functional* one (Alexandrino 2013).

On the other hand, being true that the Basic Law is a domestic law from the PRC—not a Portuguese one—the fact remains that it is enacted pursuant and in obedience to the bilaterally created (China and Portugal) Joint Declaration and thus, it embodies, namely in the consecration and densification of the twelve basic policies, also a spirit of Portuguese Law, hence, it still makes sense to bring this analysis to this paper.

This is an ontological classification since it mainly analyses and concentrates on the *de factum*, real effectiveness of the constitutional text, and the way in which it is assimilated by society. In our view, this classification seems to be regaining importance, having its relevance reinforced in face of new trends such as constitutions without constitutionalism, negating the core roles of constitutions and Rule of Law but, at the same time, keeping up appearances, and so on. As known, for the normative constitution, Loewenstein uses the analogy of a suit that perfectly fits its user, for the nominal constitution, he compares them to a badly tailored suit, for instance the size is too big or too small for the user and, semantic constitution, that Lowenstein also calls it "pseudo-constitution" where politics override the Law and he compares them with a mere carnival dress or a disguise.

Naturally one can recall here the dilemma of constitutions without constitutionalism. Macau Basic Law was supposed to be, as far as one can understand the transition process and the Joint Declaration, a normative constitution. What one should ask now is, if the suit still fits?

In short, bringing together the whole of Macau legal system, we would say that, in varying degrees, the Macau legal system is probably better qualified now as a legal system with a strong Roman-German basis, or Rule of Professional Law basis, or placed in the legal tradition of the centrality of the person (and so on, as seen). However it contains, more and more, relevant elements characteristic of other legal systems and, hence, it presents itself now more adequately as a hybrid system, or on a path to it.

For instance, focusing on constitutional law aspects Eric C. Ip tells us about a hybrid constitutionalism regarding the SAR's (Ip 2019).

As stated by Jorge Godinho, the "*general and commonly held assumption is that Macau is a part of the Roman-German family of legal systems. This assumption is questioned and discussed from a broad perspective. First, it is necessary to also take developments in the field of public law into account, which comparative lawyers not always do, remaining focused on private law. Second, is also necessary to abandon the Eurocentric approach implied in the division between civil law and common law and use a more comprehensive taxonomy. Third, it is also necessary to take into account the broader role of law in society*", and further saying, that, in general, Macau is still a Roman-German legal system as a result of the Portuguese legacy, based in the rule of law. However, "*Macau law has now elements of socialist legal systems and of course legal-cultural traits common to East Asia*", concluding that Macau Law is in a transition from West to East and will always be a hybrid, showing a peculiar mix of influences, Roman-German, Confucian, Socialist, which may actually vary in each area of the law (Godinho 2011).

Perspectives of the Future Role of Portuguese Law and a Lusophone Legal Family? Some Tentative Conclusions

Shortly after the Joint Declaration, on various hypothetical scenarios regarding the Macau legal system, including the loss of its legal system identity, Oliveira Rocha, pointed to three possibilities or scenarios: absorption by the Chinese Law, desegregation, and replacement by the common law, particularly in areas in the orbit of business law, and the survival of the Macau legal system as it is (Rocha 1991).

To preserve in the Macau legal system the Portuguese matrix signifies, immediately, a logical corollary of the maintenance of the way of life in general, and of the laws previously in force in particular, principles stated in the Joint Declaration. The maintenance of this matrix is, in itself, a constitutive component of the particular identity of Macau—second system—within the framework of the "One Country, Two Systems" apex formula.

On the other hand, in complement, the use of Portuguese as a technical-juridical language is one of the characteristics of Macau, revealing the origins of the system previously in force and maintaining the unity of the judiciary language and thus assuring, both from the doctrine stance and the jurisprudence stance, the intrinsic relationship with the original system (Lin 2007) also stressing the role of the Portuguese language (Cordeiro 2010).

At this point, it might be worthwhile to mention a possible subfamily within the civil law legal family—a *Jus-Lusophony* subfamily (Cardinal 2010), or some other *common-identity* search approaches focusing on this Lusophone *sphere*. For example, a *legal community* albeit not presenting a specific or typic conception of the Law, (Vicente 2013), an *autonomous Lusophone system proper within the large Roman-German family* (Cordeiro 2010), *a more connected juridical Lusophone family within the Roman-German family* (Santos 2003), a *common normative soul* (Castro 2003). Or, somehow on the other *spectrum*, in the neighbourhood of Vicente's above-mentioned position, acknowledging an influence of Portuguese Law on other Lusophone systems as well as several similarities. Yet several legal systems in Africa, for example Mozambique, have a strong presence of customary and informal law, for instance regarding land rights, thus making it not possible to speak about a family or subfamily (Jerónimo 2015).

Moving towards the constitutional law meso-comparison, one finds, for example, the possible unveiling of a constitutional law Lusophone legal family, albeit with some doubts (Gouveia 2006) *a Lusophone Ius publicum particularly engaged in the Human Rights protection* (Castro 2003), a *constitutional jus commune* endowed with a *common scientific language* (Amaral 2002).

We purport, not without some doubts, a subfamily that is bounded by language, institutionalized in an international organization—the CPLP—but also by a strong common asset in history and law. It is an *acquis* that originated from Portugal and was then imposed at the first stage and later assumed by the Portuguese-speaking countries and jurisdictions. If the answer is in the affirmative, Macau can also claim to be a full member. Naturally, the concrete density of commonness varies from, for example, Brazil to (probably the less common) Cape Verde, which is surely one of the legal systems sharing a larger commonality with the "reference point". Probably, the intensity level of this commonality will also vary from one branch of law to another. Moreover, within a branch of law, it may be possible to find nuances. For instance, in the field of fundamental rights text, pretext, and possibly also in the context, there is a popular sharing among several Lusophony jurisdictions due, namely, to the irradiating force of the Portuguese constitutional system of fundamental rights.

This aspect is of great importance in several notes. For example, there is a common academic doctrine even though the specific written law has some variances. For a place such as Macau, which has a small legal community, this aspect is of high relevance. With probably less importance, but still relevant, one can also have access to certain judicial decisions of the common law of Lusophony on several domains of the Law.

In short, Macau is not an isolated or insular legal system surrounded and overwhelmed by "strange" and dissimilar legal systems that, hence, bear the risk of losing its own legal system identity. After all, the legal identity of Macau—and its multiple differentiation *vis-à-vis* the Mainland one—can and should be seen as a key question which protects society (Berlie 2016) and this intrinsic comparative law connection to Lusophone Law, Portugal, and others, should be effectively maintained, and devoid of any political approach such as neo-colonialism and other pretexts to simply bury the past and the international commitments and promises, and can be one, or the, key factor to avoid a result that some describe as an *Isolated Island of Law* and a *Machine without a Ghost* (Tong/Wu 2013).

In truth, as a renowned expert in Macau Law said, the comparative reference is evidently not restricted to Portugal and may occur in relation to the growing doctrinal and jurisprudential production in Portuguese from other legal systems, especially in Lusophone Africa (Godinho 2011).

Getting back to the supra mentioned recent judicial and legal evolution towards a different and divergent path and conception of Law and principles should thus not be expanded and, on the contrary, be reversed. In doing so, both the Joint Declaration and the Basic Law would be more clearly observed and respected as well as the continuity of the legal system and its matrix better upheld.

As said elsewhere, in the face of harmonization trends with China, a keen awareness of the above-seen comparative characteristics of the Macau system *versus* the Mainland one will always be extremely useful when questioning what should or should not be approved or what should work in a similar way on both sides of the border (Godinho 2011).

The maintenance of the Macau legal system characteristics and principles showcases a guarantee of Law conceived as Law proper and with long established and anticipative guarantees, and a legal system endowed with Rule of Law. This maintenance can promote trust, call investments, and shows the will and the capacity to fulfil international obligations.

As argued many years ago (Cardinal 1998), the preservation of the Portuguese matrix is, above all, a logical corollary guarantee to maintain Macau's way of life, given by the Joint Declaration. It is a component of Macau's identity that is intended to be maintained and is an important historical legacy. As a result of this attachment to the Portuguese legal matrix, one will achieve the maintenance of Macau's legal system within the Roman-Germanic family, or *equivalent* taxonomies, such as the Rule of Professional Law pattern, and, in consequence, with even more emphasis on the Lusophone subfamily, or community or similar.

At the end of the day, the above is, after all, the essence of the promised One Country, Two Systems political-juridical formula, along with the maintenance of the Macau "Way of life".

Acknowledgements The author expresses his thanks to Jonathan Owens, M.Sc., Professor at the Macau Anglican College, for this paper's English proof-reading.

References

Alexandrino, José Melo (2013), *O sistema de direitos fundamentais na Lei Básica da Região Administrativa Especial de Macau*, Centro de formação jurídica e judiciária.

Alves, Leonel (2001), 'A Região Administrativa Especial de Macau e os trabalhos da Comissão Preparatória', *BFDM,* 12.

Amaral, Maria Lúcia (2002), 'Será necessária uma harmonização das Constituições para dar efectividade ao exercício dos direitos de participação política?', in *Estatuto Jurídico da Lusofonia*, AAVV, Coimbra Editora.

Aristotle (1999), *Politics*.

Berlie, Jean (2016), 'Macau's Legal Identity', *Asian Education and Development Studies*, Vol. 5 No. 3, 2016.

Bodin, Jean (1576 [2012]), *Les Six Livres de la République*.

Cabrita, Eduardo (2002), 'International and Constitutional Limitations on the Autonomy of the Macau Special Administrative Regio', *Macau Law Journal*, special issue.

Cardinal, Paulo (1998), '*Determinantes e Linhas de Força das Reformas Legislativas em Macau*', Administração, vol. X, n.º 40.

Cardinal, Paulo (2008), 'Continuity and Autonomy—Leading Principles Shaping the Fundamental Rights Constitutional System in the Macau Special Administrative Region', *La ciencia del derecho procesal constitucional. Estudios en homenaje a Héctor Fix-Zamudio en sus cincuenta años como investigador del derecho*, T. IV, Derechos fundamentales y tutela constitucional, Ferrer Mac-Gregor, E./Zaldívar Lelo de Larrea, A., (coord.), UNAM, IMDPC, Marcial Pons.

Cardinal, Paulo (2010), 'Fundamental Rights in Macau: From Territory Under Portuguese Administration to Special Administrative Region of the PRC', in *Studies on Macau Civil, Commercial, Constitutional and Criminal Law*, Jorge Godinho (editor), Lexisnexis.

Castellucci, Ignazio (2012), 'Legal Hybridity in Hong Kong and Macau', *McGill Law Journal*, 665.

Castro, Paulo Canelas De (2003), 'A Comunidade dos Países de Língua Portuguesa: para um discurso jurídico sobre a sua identidade e um seu programa de acção', in *Colóquio de Direito Internacional. Comunidade dos Países de Língua Portuguesa*, AAVV, Coimbra, Almedina.

Cordeiro, António Menezes (2010), 'O Sistema Lusófono de Direito', *Revista da Ordem dos Advogados*, Ano 70, 2010, available at https://portal.oa.pt/publicacoes/revista-da-ordem-dos-advogados-roa/ano-2010/ano-70-vol-iiv-2010/actualidade/antonio-menezes-cordeiro-o-sistema-lusofono-de-direito/.

Correia, Paula (2013), 'The Macanese Legal System: A Comparative Law Perspective', in *New Frontiers of Comparative Law*, Lexisnexis.

Crawford, James (2005), *Rights in One Country: Hong Kong and China*, Hochelaga Lectures, Faculty of Law, HKU.

David, René/Brierley, John E.C (1978), *Major Legal Systems in The World Today.*

Glenn, H. Patrick (2010), *Legal Traditions of the World: Sustainable Diversity in Law*, Oxford UP.

Godinho, Jorge (2007), *Macau Business Law and Legal System*, LexisNexis, Hong Kong.

Godinho, Jorge (2011), Uma Soberania, Dois Sistemas Sociais, Três Tradições Jurídicas: O Sistema Jurídico De Macau E a Família Romano-Germânica. Available at SSRN: https://ssrn.com/abstract=2532944.

Gouveia, Jorge Bacelar (2006), *As Constituições dos Estados de Língua Portuguesa*, 2.ª ed., Coimbra, Almedina

Halis, Denis De Castro (2019), *Between Two Systems of Law: Administrative Law Litigation in Macau's Court of Final Appeal*, Universidade Estácio de Sá.

Hug, Walther (1932, April), 'The History of Comparative Law', *Harvard Law Review*, Vol. 45, No. 6, April 1932.

Husa, Jaakko (2004), 'Classification of Legal Families Today - Is It Time for a Memorial Hymn?', R.I.D.C.

Ip, Eric C (2019), *Hybrid Constitutionalism—The Politics of Constitutional Review in the Chinese Special Administrative Regions*, Cambridge UP.

Jerónimo, Patrícia (2015), *Lições de Direito Comparado.*

Kischel, Uwe (2019), *Comparative Law*, Oxford UP.

Lin, Yan/Ginsburg, Tom (2015), 'Constitutional Interpretation in Lawmaking: China's Invisible Constitutional Enforcement Mechanism', *The American Journal of Comparative Law*, Vol. 63, No. 2, Spring.

Lin, Zhu (2007), 'A situação da língua chinesa nas sentenças judiciais de Macau – duma perspectiva dos direitos fundamentais', *Administração*, 75.

Loewenstein, Karl (2018), *Teoría de la Constitución*, 1965, Editorial Ariel, 2018 Macqueen, Norman (1985), 'Macao: End of a Special Case', *The World Today*, Vol. 41.

Mancuso, Salvatore (2013), 'The Use of Comparative Law by the Judiciary in Macau', in *New Frontiers of Comparative Law*, Lexisnexis.

Mattei, Ugo (1997), 'Three Patterns of Law: Taxonomy and Change in the World's Legal Systems', *American Journal of Comparative Law.*

Montesquieu, C. L. S (1721), *Persian Letters*, Penguin Classics (1973).

Montesquieu, C. L. S (1748), *The Spirit of Laws*, Lonang Institute (2003).

Olivetti, Marco (2009), 'The Special Administrative Regions of the PRC in Comparison with Autonomous Regions Models', in *One Country, Two Systems, Three Legal Orders—Perspectives of Evolution*, J. Oliveira/P. Cardinal (eds.).

Örücü, Esin (2004), 'Family Trees for Legal Systems: Towards a Contemporary Approach', in *Epistemology and Methodology of Comparative Law*, Mark van Hoecke (ed.).

Pines, Yuri (2014), 'Legalism in Chinese Philosophy', First published Wed Dec 10, 2014; Substantive Revision Fri Nov 16, 2018, Stanford Encyclopedia of Philosophy.

Rocha, Oliveira (1991), 'A viabilidade do sistema jurídico de Macau', *Administração*, 13.

Santos, António Marques Dos (2003), '*As Relações Entre Portugal, A Europa e o Mundo Lusófono e as Suas Repercussões No Plano Jurídico*', Lusíada, Direito.

Siems, Mathias M (2016), 'Varieties of Legal Systems: Towards a New Global Taxonomy', *Journal of Institutional Economics*, Vol. 12, No. 3, September 2016.

Tong, Io Cheng (2012), 'The Basic Law and the Chinese of Macau', in *The Chinese of Macau a Decade after the Handover*, Berlie, J. A. (Ed.), Proverse, Hong Kong.

Tong, Io Cheng/Wu, Yanni (2013), 'Legal Transplant and the On-Going Formation of Macau Legal Culture', in *New Frontiers of Comparative Law*, Lexisnexis.

Vicente, Dário Moura (2013), 'The Common Law of Portuguese-Speaking Countries and Territories', in *New Frontiers of Comparative Law*, Lexisnexis.
Vicente, Dário Moura (2019), *Direito Comparado*, Vol. I, Almedina.
Wills, John/Van Dyke, Paul (2000), 'Strange Shores: 442 Years of Anomaly in Macau, and Counting…', *Harvard Asia Pacific Review*, Summer 2000.
Xiaoping, Deng (1994), *Selected Works of Deng Xiaoping*, Vol. III, p. 262, Beijing.

The Pillars of Portuguese Foreign Policy: From the First Globalisation to the Twenty-First Century

António Manuel Lopes Tavares and José Manuel Duarte de Jesus

Introduction

We do not think it is possible to examine the main lines of foreign policy of any country, in this case, Portugal, without contextualising this policy in a perspective of the world paradigm in which it is inserted.

On the other hand, addressing this problem without also contextualising it from a historical perspective would be too basic. In terms of international relations, it will always be naive and dangerous to analyse the present, forgetting the more or less distant past and, in the case of Portugal, without going back a few centuries. The vicissitudes of the Portuguese case, a country that has had stable borders for hundreds of years and with a very specific geographical position, in regard to

A. M. L. Tavares (✉)
Universidade Lusófona—Centro Universitário do Porto, Porto, Portugal
e-mail: antonio.tavares@ulusofona.pt

J. M. D. de Jesus
Institute of Oriental Studies, ISCSP-University of Lisbon, Lisbon, Portugal
e-mail: Duarte.jesus@sapo.pt

P. A. B. Duarte et al. (eds.), *Portugal and the Lusophone World*,
https://doi.org/10.1007/978-981-99-0455-6_6

the European continent and the Atlantic Ocean, are factors that gave it a geostrategic continuity, which necessarily adapted to the World Orders or paradigms that followed one another through the centuries. This geostrategic continuity is embodied in the current major axes of Portuguese foreign policy.

In this brief chapter we seek to analyse the nature, the secular identity, as well as the pillars on which the Portuguese foreign policy is based. Every foreign policy of a country, or a group of countries, is part of what we call a World Order. Any World Order can be divided into several phases. Likewise, any World Order has periods of transition from one paradigm to another, and periods in which it asserts itself at the peak of a stable paradigm. To a World Order corresponds a certain dominant political ideology, but it is composed at its base by a culture and an ethic.

The continuity and permanence, in various forms, of our foreign policy is based on the fact that our country has contributed to the formation of a World Order, which has conditioned and formatted our own foreign policy. As a general rule, a World Order has geographical conditions at its origin that shape its geostrategy. In the case of Portugal, the basic conditioning factors that influence its geostrategy are composed of its huge border to the Atlantic. This fact, together with political factors, the marriage of João I, and the Alliance with England, constituted the first step towards the consolidation of the first pillar of our foreign policy, the Atlantic pillar. In this chapter, we seek to analyse how this window came to provide a second pillar of our policy, namely globalisation and multiculturalism.

The size of our country did not encourage us to exercise a policy of hard power, i.e. an Empire. We quickly opted to build a commercial emporium in Africa, Asia, and the Americas. We forged a soft power structure based on increasingly multicultural networks, with obvious exceptions, but until today we have sought to circumvent bipolar models of World Orders.

Our European dimension has always been far from the great confrontations that have marked central European politics for centuries. Our European dimension was based on relations with the Vatican—the "United Nations" of other times—which allowed us to legitimise our intercontinental policy. Recently, in a very different World Order, our European option no longer conflicted with our other strategic options. Thus, the three great dimensions of our foreign policy have been consolidated in a new paradigm—the Atlantic, which is embodied in NATO, in the

European Union and the multicontinental structure, embodied in the Community of Portuguese-speaking countries (CPLP). Within the framework of this last figure of our foreign policy, we cannot forget our *Shadow Empire*, everything that we left behind in the African continent and in Asia and that cannot be defined within the framework of Politics/Power or the major economy. It is a network that is revealed in the language, in family habits, in religious beliefs, and in daily life. This informal network can and must be an instrument of our foreign policy in many and varied dimensions, particularly in the cultural and commercial dimensions.

This being said, this chapter aims to identify the pillars of Portuguese Foreign Policy from what we call the first globalisation until the current World Order. To achieve this goal, we will begin by defining the concept World Order and Diplomacy in the Global World. Then, we will describe the main pillars of diplomacy, as the key instrument to carry out any Foreign Policy. Additionally, we will analyse the Portuguese Foreign Policy and the role of Portugal in the world from the moment of empire building (1415) to the restitution of Macao to China (1999). In revisiting the first globalisation to the current World Order, we list the different networks Portugal is part of: the institutional networks as well as the informal networks, as its *Shadow Empire*. Finally, we will attempt to define the guiding principles that could model a potential Portuguese Foreign Policy in our Global World Order. As main conclusion, we argue that Portugal's key geography based on both land and sea has been an omnipresent feature in shaping the country's Foreign Policy.

World Order and Diplomacy: A Background

The concept of World Order is generally used today by historians and political analysts based on the principles defined in the Westphalia Treaty, in the seventeenth century. It has been used as an analytic instrument in International Relations. It became a common reference since it was used by Henry Kissinger in his famous book entitled "World Order", published in 2014.

Before introducing some details concerning the actual World Order, let us make some considerations about the scope of this concept, which includes several components. The main component is the political, economic, and geostrategic one. Parallel to this, we can find several others of a more regional or even national character. These complex forms constitute what we could name as "cultures" in the paleoanthropological sense. Among them, we find the so-called *common sense*, with different values, according to geographical areas and cultures. The common sense is the way common people see the world we live in. This *common sense*, where some values vary according to the mainstream ideologies of the period and area are of great importance to the sustainability of a certain World Order. As an example, we can refer to the prevailing values of the western *common sense* during our Keynesian capitalist society after World War II that prevailed until the seventies, and the evolution of these values after a neoliberal capitalist society and a consequent deregulated market replaced that first period. This same principle applies, as an example, to the *common sense* of the Chinese society during this same post-World War II period, where different cultural, political, and economic values prevailed.

Let us come to the main component of the so-called post-Westphalia World Order in our western world. It established, so to speak, the rules of the game of International Relations, ethic norms that should give the possibility to the main actors of the period—the sovereign states—to keep balanced relations between them and peace. Later, Great Britain introduced the concept of Balance of Power some countries of which like the United States of America never used, as its foreign policy is dominated by the wish to crusade for their internal values around the world (Kissinger 1988).

The old-World Order was legitimised by the Vatican, which lasted for centuries in Europe and a new legitimacy in International Relations was thus created. This new legitimacy was based on two theoretical principles the *Nation State* and the *Balance of Powers*. This paradigm remained until a new World Order tries the new concept of *Multilateralism* to solve international conflicts that the first one was unable to overcome. We should never forget that if we look backwards, we find several other World Orders—Regional Orders—such as the Roman Empire in parts of Europe, the Middle East, and Africa or the Persian Empire, and further East we find the Chinese Empire with its tributary states. In each one of these World Orders, we find different political and economic systems with specific rules and paradigms through which they tried to solve problems concerning the different nations that build those main actors.

Nowadays, with the disappearance of the bipolar system, tensions and a great number of conflicts that hid behind the two major players—the United States and the Soviet Union—spread all over, taking different forms.

Multilateralism has tried, with little success, to minimise such a "World Disorder", and a new factor, the globalisation and the digital network, produced a new factor, which we call *simultaneity.* An event x in a specific part of the world has a simultaneous effect on the whole world.

In this emerging framework, a new great power arises, China and Asia, in general. Fortunately, the new Chinese leadership seems to bet on multilateralism. The new pandemic makes the present world situation even more complicated and unpredictable. Further to these circumstances, there are permanent sources of tension such as Taiwan, the Middle East, and even conflicting ones such as Ukraine. In short, we are living in a Global World Order in transition with many unknowns.

Now let us try to define diplomacy in the framework of the World Order/disorder as we have just described. Diplomacy is the instrument used by the Foreign Policy of a state or a group of states to negotiate conflicts of interest to obtain a win/win situation with the final objective of preserving peace. Nevertheless, diplomacy can also be misused by states to justify international criminal actions. This is the negation of the purpose and nature of diplomacy.

There are several enemies of peace and negotiation in our present World Order. Money and Power are two of them. As Karl Popper (1973, p. 128) says in his "The Open Society and Its Enemies", money (capital) "becomes dangerous if it can buy power, either directly, or by enslaving the economic weak who must sell themselves in order to live". We can identify several of the crises we have today in different regions of the globe, where we can apply this reasoning to explain them. But, as Karl Popper (1973, p. 270) points out in the same book, "the history of power politics is nothing but the history of international crime and mass murder". Let us give an example of such a situation that happened not long ago: the Iraq war (2013–2017). Two countries forged a fake reason to justify a war that killed approximately 450,000 people, among them some 200,000 civilians who died from violence. The main fake reason to justify the war was the existence of weapons of mass destruction, which were obviously never found, and end a regime that committed outrageous human rights abuses. This is an example of misuse of diplomacy in the preparation of a criminal war that killed many more people than the Sadat regime itself and left a chaotic situation in the country that lasts until today. It was the example in which the aggressor was one of the great world actors, the United States. In the current case of Ukraine, the aggressor was another of the great world actors, the Russian Federation (Ferrow 2018; Chomsky and Waterstone 2021).

But having these circumstances in mind, diplomacy continues to be the only instrument that exists since there are human communities, and the only alternative to the use of force. With the evolution of human society, the complexity of relations among nations, the globalisation and the progress of technology, diplomacy is nowadays the object of scientific studies in the framework of International Relations. As such, the practice of diplomacy is based on three pillars:

1. *Public Diplomacy* to build a positive image of the state or the entity using diplomacy.
2. *Information* that requires a permanent dialogue with Intelligence services.
3. *Negotiation* whether bilateral or multilateral is the most important of the three pillars.

A complete and well-founded information is necessary for any decision-making process. The negotiation is the most important part of diplomatic practices because it is through negotiation that we can arrive at a win/win settlement of any conflict. It is difficult to have a fair and good negotiation without good information. Portugal and other countries that lived long periods under a dictatorship had difficulties to create a professional and reliable new Information Service. Portugal has the image of a good international negotiator, as shown by the negotiations between Portugal and China concerning the *handover* of Macao. Both parts knew how to handle the difficult problem of interculturality and conduct the negotiations keeping in mind the interests of both parts considering the short- and long-term future of the friendly relation of the two countries. Moreover, both countries were conscious that there were no Best Alternative(s) to a Negotiated Agreement (BATNA) (Mendes 2013).

Portugal in the First Globalisation

After having described the main pillars of Global Order and Diplomacy in the previous section, we will now highlight the main historical contours of Portuguese diplomacy and Foreign Policy in the period of the first globalisation.

In politics constancy means, not always doing the same thing, but always wanting the same thing. Mazarin[1]

How to found, expand, consolidate, and maintain a state with relevance and influence in international politics has been for Portugal one of the most difficult and arduous tasks, throughout its history. When, in 1415, the Portuguese forces conquered Ceuta, one of the most surprising strategic options of this small European country began.

Independent since 1143, Portugal is one of the most ancient nations in Europe and its borders have long been consolidated. On account of the Treaty of Tagilde, signed on 10 July 1372, King Ferdinand I of Portugal signed with delegates from John of Gant, Duke of Lancaster, the first agreement that set the foundations of the legal basis for the future treaty of LusoBritish alliance in 1373, which would later take shape on 12 May 1386 in the Treaty of Windsor, the oldest alliance between two states.

Once this alliance had been forged, thus averting the Castilian danger, and due to the policy, which allowed the development of the *Pinhal de Leiria*, initiated by King Denis I, Portugal established the conditions for the creation of a war navy with scientific pretensions for the discovery of the seas.

The strategic creation of a "nautical school", known as the *School of Sagres*, promoted by Prince Henry the Navigator, provided the tools for the affirmation of a new geopolitical and geostrategic reality in a world emerging from the Middle Ages.

The first sharing of sovereignty of the seas came with the signing of the Treaty of Tordesillas, on 7 June 1494, which allowed Portugal and Castile to divide the lands "discovered and undiscovered" by both Crowns outside Europe. The territories east of the meridian, defined as 370 leagues west of the island of Santo Antão (Cape Verde), belonged to Portugal while those to the west belonged to Castile.

We are in a time of transition, in international relations, between the hegemony of the Papacy and the affirmation of the secular power of monarchs. The policy of expansion that followed had always had a great impact on the affirmation of Portugal's sovereignty before the world and other nations. Between 1498 and 1500, with the discovery of the sea route to India and the "finding" of Brazil, the domination of trade routes

[1] Jules Mazarin known as Cardinal Mazarino (1602–1661) was Prime Minister of France.

and the transfer to Europe of unique merchandise was consolidated, along with the labour force that enabled property owners to accumulate wealth due to the slavery regime.

From Portuguese India the British Empire will be born owing to Catherine of Braganza's dowry, which included the city of Bombay, in consequence of her marriage to Charles II of England. The maritime dimension present in the History of Portugal allows us to assert an external projection of power that, influenced by the mutations of the times, also enables the development of the strategic vectors of the Portuguese external policy.

The colonisation of more than five centuries, from Goa to Brazil, through Africa to Malaysia, Timor or Macao, was not exempt from errors or accidents throughout the whole process until the end of the Empire by the twentieth century. On that account, it was possible to create innovative trade routes, as an alternative to the Silk Routes promoted by Marco Polo, which China now intends to implement again (in a project called Belt and Road Initiative), in order to bring boats with gold for the churches and palaces of the European continent, besides contributing to the reunion of peoples and to the multiplication of the gathering of races.

Afonso de Albuquerque consolidated this expansionist vocation by combining it with a strategic option when he conquered Hormuz, therefore controlling access to the Persian Gulf, as well as Malacca, whose straits controlled the connection between the Pacific and Indian Oceans via the South China Sea.

Its geostrategic lesson is still observed today by the United States Navy. As Basil Liddel Hart (1895–1970) states (cit. in Reis 2019, p. 17), "while the horizons of strategy are limited by war, grand strategy looks beyond war to peace" contributing to "the security and prosperity" of a state.

This seems to be a contradiction as Portugal, since 1961, had been engaged in a three-front war in Africa, saw Goa, Damão, and Diu invaded by the Indian Union, and was, in diplomatic terms, "proudly alone", in the words of the dictator Salazar (1889–1970). It is clearly known that the impact of that war in Africa destroyed generations of young people, decimated the peace of families and postponed or annihilated many life projects. The context of the Cold War inhibited and allowed this development. With the end of World War II and thanks to its geographical position, Portugal joined the founding group of NATO—North Atlantic Treaty Organisation, despite not being a democracy and not having any military power of interest. The vulnerability of the West in integrating Portugal into NATO ended up creating the conditions for a modernisation of its Armed Forces and for the entrance of new ideas that accompanied the arrival of modern military equipment.

It is clear that this ambiguous position eventually led to a division between "Africanists" and "Europeanists", which Franco Nogueira (1987), as Minister of Foreign Affairs, headed in order to eradicate the fear that without the Empire, Portugal would collapse. His vision of Portuguese Foreign Policy enabled him to say that

> an era with flashes of grandeur, a style of government where there was a sense of measure and elegance of form, a conception of life based on certainties, a vision of Portugal drawn from history, mistakes and shadows without doubt, but it was a whole policy where firmness and courage played a major role. A turning point, in short, let's have new times, new truths. (Nogueira 1987, p. 316)

This division was accelerated by Marcelo Caetano who, in 1972, sought a proximity agreement with the former EEC. In fact, Salazar had already proposed, by Minister Correia de Oliveira, the opening of a consultation period with the EEC after the entry of Portugal into EFTA.[2]

With the military coup of 25 April 1974, the Empire inevitably ended and, consequently, a cycle that had begun in 1415 finished. After the fall of the Berlin Wall (1989) and the end of the Cold War, the African colonies were to remain in the Soviet sphere; Timor was invaded by Indonesia and Macao was to await instructions from Beijing.

By 1822, Brazil had already split from the Kingdom of Portugal and the Algarves, following the liberating movement of Simon Bolivar in Latin America. We can clearly perceive how Portugal needed to find another national design, in this case Europe, to continue its geostrategic role.

Pillars of the Current Portuguese Foreign Policy

Continuing the analysis initiated in the previous section, we will now focus on the most recent features and contours of Portuguese Foreign Policy. The Portuguese presence in the world since the fifteenth century has ended up developing an idea of genetic code that affirms the strategic

[2] Letter dated 18 May 1962 addressed to the former President of the European Economic Community, Maurice Couve de Murville, former French Foreign Minister.

vectors of its foreign policy. Portugal was no longer just a European country, through its Commercial Emporium and the networks thus created, it has become a small European country with a global dimension, covering the Americas, Africa, and Asia. These historical circumstances explain the main axes of our current Foreign Policy, which we can state as follows:

1. The Atlantic dimension and the Atlantic islands, making Portugal a member of NATO.
2. The African Asian and Brazil connection. This aspect makes us an active member of the CPLP (Community of Portuguese-Speaking Countries) and explains our good ancient relations with China.
3. More recently, the European option of 1986 that made Portugal an active member-state of the European Union.

Some of these aspects interact with each other. The European Option: For centuries we had a global strategy where Europe was not the main dimension. Salazar assumed a position of neutrality during World War II and took refuge in the idea of a colonial empire. The European option comes after the 1974 revolution. The Atlantic dimension has its roots in the old English alliance. In the present framework a new geostrategic dimension emerges and beyond NATO, this Atlantic dimension is also a *window* for our special relations with Brazil, Africa, and Asia. This is an important third aspect of Portuguese Foreign Policy.

The transatlantic dimension of our foreign policy adds value to our position within the framework of the European Union. Within the multiple aspects that characterise the European Union's relationship with the countries of Asia, the Caribbean and the Pacific—the ACP—Portugal is one of the members of the European Union that plays a role that must be recognised in our foreign policy.

In a difficult framework that characterises Europe's relations with China, Portugal, the oldest European country to have several dimensions of relationship with China, can and does play an important role. Macao plays an equally important role in this good relationship with China in general and the surrounding region of Macao. The so-called Macao Forum is yet another triangular relationship network: China–Portugal—CPLP. If Portugal, from the fifteenth and sixteenth centuries, started a process of globalisation from the West, China, a few centuries before, started a process of globalisation from the East with the so-called First Silk Road. This is how Portugal accompanies the so-called Belt and Road Initiative in different ways.

Also related to Portuguese foreign policy, we would like to mention an element in addition to the CPLP, which we would call our *Shadow Empire*, in Africa and in Asia. The concept of *Shadow Empire* was first used by the historian Georges Winius (1991a, b) in 1991 and is intimately linked to his other concept of Expansion, meaning the way how the Europeans penetrated non-European territories creating a not simply national view of cultures. As he says in one of his famous interviews, with Leonard Blussé, the problem is to avoid seeing all national histories unconnected to anyone else´s history, because since the Expansion we are all connected, and Portugal has today a large unofficial *Shadow Empire*.

As António Manuel Hespanha (2019, p. 26) puts it very well,

> the Atlantic is not just an area of expansion of European culture, a space of travel linking metropolitans and settlers, but an autonomous theater for the new birth of forms of life and representations, cultural events, in which contributions from both sides coalesce...In this scenario, the protagonism goes to the mestizos.

This shadow empire forms a cultural network spread across the most diverse territories in Africa, India, Ceylon, Southeast Asia, China, and Japan, among others. This unofficial Empire was built based on shared social cultures and values under the ambiguity of several political situations. So, in parallel to the formal empire, a shadow empire was created that, in several regions, lasts until our days. This aspect is or should be an important dimension of our foreign cultural and economic policy.

Portugal remains faithful to a multidimensional tradition of its foreign policy, Atlantic, European, Afrasian, where the Lusophony plays an important role with its different networks. We have left in Africa and Asia a cultural and social informal heritage close to daily and intimate life of different populations and therefore lasting for generations; values concerning family relations, religious practices, kitchen recipes, popular proverbs, music, language (crioulos); so, this is not a "political or economic" network, but a human transnational and multicultural network, essential for establishing a constructive dialogue.

In many of these places, we are not known as "Portuguese", but as *Nasrani* in Persia, *Kriston, Kristang* in Malaysia, *Mzungo* in Zambia,

Falangxi in China, *Tongomanos* in Guinea and Angola, *and Protuket* in Siam, among others. Professor David Knoke, from the University of Minnesota, has, in many of his books and essays, explored the economic and political importance of what he called "strategic power networks". This concept is now frequently used in economics and also in certain aspects of soft power policy.

According to David Knoke (2012), these networks are fundamentally shaped: In people; In groups, in the broad sense of this concept; In political, economic, academic, and social organisations; And in populations, language, and culture in the broad sense of this concept.

Separated in time, the presence in NATO dates back to 1949, the entry in Europe to 1985 and the CPLP to 1994. There is a line of coherence in the development of these policies and a wide consensus in Portuguese society that the two major parties, PS and PSD, know how to interpret in a consensual way. The Portuguese communities scattered throughout the world show a tolerant form of participative integration in local life.

According to the current Minister of Foreign Affairs, Augusto Santos Silva (2020, p. 149),

> Portugal is, along with Spain, the main link between Europe and Latin America; and it is, with France or Belgium, a platform for interaction with the whole African continent. It does not act alone. In fact, the Community of Portuguese Speaking Countries, comprising 280 million people spread over nine countries, all of them maritime, located in four continents, America, Africa, Europe and Asia, is a cooperative environment of enormous potential (...) for a global action focused on the oceans.

Thus, Portugal presents itself as a small power that knows how to use the "soft power" that Joseph S. Nye, Jr. refers to as the ability to seduce through its culture, in its political values and the expression of its foreign policy. In accordance with Nye the "soft power is a dance that requires partners" (Nye 2012, p. 106).

The fact that two Portuguese politicians, José Manuel Durão Barroso and António Guterres, have held important positions in supra-national or international organisations, such as President of the European Commission or Secretary General of the United Nations, reinforces this idea that Portugal is a country that makes it possible to create bridges of variable geometry between peoples.

The participation in peace or humanitarian aid missions as part of the UN Blue Helmets has helped to highlight the applicability of the Portuguese Armed Forces. The Portuguese migratory dynamics, between the fifteenth and twenty-first centuries, as Vitorino Magalhães Godinho said, are a "structural constant" of our collective life and explain this aggregative capacity of the language that is also projected in the Portuguese communities. The Portuguese diaspora represents, if we also add the non-Portuguese nationals, almost five million people distributed around the planet.

From the combination of these efforts was born a strategic concept to consolidate a nation, where its military, scientific-technological, and maritime power evolved over time and often put at risk its sovereignty and national independence, although it also provided a role of facilitator of international relations.

According to Hans Morgenthau (cit. in Gaspar 2021, p. 49),

> realism assumes that the character of a foreign policy can only be ascertained by examining political acts and the foreseeable consequences of those acts. (...) we are in the position of a Statesman who has to confront himself with a given foreign policy problem in certain circumstances and ask what are the rational alternatives from which he can choose to deal with the problem...

This realism has dominated our understanding of Portuguese foreign policy and its international positioning. Portugal is a member of both the NATO military alliance and the European Union, two pillars of the democratic transatlantic community. It has set up the CPLP as a Portuguese-speaking community and, thanks to it, supports and strengthens the communities in the diaspora. It develops the community of IberoAmerican countries, continues an active presence with forces deployed in UN military missions. Portuguese is spoken by 225 million people, equivalent to 3.6% of the world population.

The central parties of the democratic political system, the PS and PSD, maintain and support a consensual and coherent line in defence of these strategic vectors of Portuguese foreign policy.

Over the centuries, with its strengths and weaknesses, opportunities and threats, Portugal has followed a path combining strength, security, and power according to each situation, which has left an indelible mark on the heritage of Humanity.

Adriano Moreira (2009, p. 385), however, alerts us to a

> severe crisis in the entering of the third millennium, once expired the secular national strategic concept, which also seems to awaken an understanding that the conjuncture is radically new comparing to the secular experience that the demands of the state threaten to place it in the category of a meagre state, whether in the definition in progress of the internal hierarchies of Europe, or in the hierarchy of Europe in the world power as far as the strategic, scientific, technical and economic balances are concerned.

Will this be the new geopolitical challenge for Portugal in the balance of its geostrategic choice in the twenty-first century? Only time will tell. In this time of pandemic caused by COVID-19, the new challenges to Portuguese foreign policy are immense.

In the words of Fernandes (2008, p. 308) one of the answers to these challenges will be

> in the global conjuncture we are living in, the role and the importance of Portugal in the system of international relations depends a lot on its political capacity to articulate the interaction of the three strategic triangles in which it is inserted. And this capacity should be used to bring its economic dimension closer to its political dimension, in order to prevent Portugal from continuing to live among the rich by playing the poor.

Conclusion

Given the maritime option or the deepening of relations with Europe, in the fifteenth century Portugal chose to develop new maritime knowledge and become the first medieval European power to develop a policy of expansion towards North Africa.

Portugal's geostrategic positioning, its historical heritage, which determined its pluricontinental policy, without ever ceasing to be a European country, shaped a multi-secular identity. These facts contributed to a more global view of its position in the world and, consequently, in the definition of its foreign policy and diplomacy. The presence of Portugal in the world through its foreign policy has been consolidated in the twenty-first century by means of its policy of alliances based on a strategic tripod involving NATO, the European Union, and the CPLP (Community of Portuguese-Speaking Countries). Portugal thus presents itself deeply against Salazar's foreign policy, during the final phase of the New State, when it claimed to be "proudly alone".

Beyond this institutional policy, Portugal also bases its diplomacy on some privileged relations—historical legacies—with countries such as China and India, particularly through Macao and Goa.

In addition to this configuration of our foreign policy, we must add the informal network that Portugal has in Africa, Latin America, the Indo-Pacific and which constitutes our shadow empire. This network has no direct political or economic weight, but nevertheless presents itself as a "strategic-power-network", which can and should constitute an important element in our diplomatic dialogue in a vast region of the world. As part of a policy of alliances, Portugal has drawn on its capacity for institutional dialogue with other nations to develop its ability to build consensus, of which the election of António Guterres as UN Secretary General seems to be the most relevant example. Whether with China, in the Pacific, or with the United States, in the Atlantic, Portugal has shown that it is attentive to the new winds of globalisation that will be blowing on the liberal international order after the Ukraine–Russia war.

References

Chomsky, N. e Waterstone M. (2021). *As Consequências do Capitalismo*. Editorial Presença.

Farrow, R. (2018). *War on Peace: The End of Diplomacy and the Decline of American Influence*. William Collins.

Fernandes, A. J. (2008). *As relações internacionais e Portugal – da Europa do Mundo ao Mundo da Europa*. Lisboa, Prefácio.

Gaspar, C. (2021). *Teoria das Relações Internacionais: textos clássicos*. Lisboa: Livros Horizonte.

Hespanha, A. (2019). *Filhos da Terra*. Tinta da China.

Kissinger, A. (1988). UK: Diplomacy. Simon & Schuster.

Knoke, D. (2012). *Changing Organizations – Business Networks in the New Political Economy*. New York: Routledge.

Mendes. C. (2013). *Portugal, China and Macau Negotiations* 1986–1999. Hong Kong: RASHKSS.

Moreira, A. (2009). *A circunstância do Estado Exíguo*, Lisboa: Diário de Bordo.

Nogueira, F. (1987). *Um político confessa-se. Diário 1960–1968*. Porto: Civilização.

Nye, J. (2012). *O futuro do poder*. Lisboa: Temas e Debates.

Popper, K. (1973). *The Open Society and its Enemies*, vol. II. Routledge.

Reis, B. (2019). *Pode Portugal ter uma estratégia?* Lisboa: Fundação Francisco Manuel dos Santos.

Santos Silva, A. (2020). *Evoluir.* Lisboa: Tinta da China.

Winius, G. (1991a). Interview. "On Discovering the Expansion of Europe", https://www.Cambridge.org/core

Winius, G. (1991b). "Portugal Shadow Empire in the Bay of Bengala", *Revista de Cultura*, 13 & 14. Instituto Cultural de Macau.

Reframing Portuguese Foreign Policy After 1974: The Lusophone Discourse as Instrument of a Global Coloniality of Power

Marcos Farias Ferreira

Introduction

The evolving relationship between Portugal and the Lusophone world is one of the most salient topics in the literature about Portuguese foreign policy (PFP). More than salient, this topic can be said to enjoy a high degree of consensuality on its significance for the national interest (MacQueen, 1985; Cravinho, 2005; Pinto, 2005; Cravo, 2012; Moreira, 2014; Reis and Oliveira, 2018; Pavia, 2019c; Raimundo, 2019; Dias, 2019). However, most of this literature continues to adopt positivist/rationalist approaches and methods for foreign policy analysis and has proved unable to problematize the subreptitious entanglement

M. Farias Ferreira (✉)
Instituto Superior de Ciências Sociais e Políticas, Universidade de Lisboa, Lisbon, Portugal
e-mail: marcosfariasferreira@gmail.com

P. A. B. Duarte et al. (eds.), *Portugal and the Lusophone World*,
https://doi.org/10.1007/978-981-99-0455-6_7

between discourse and power and, more critically, the intersubjective processes through which colonial dynamics, identities and hierarchies have been incorporated, sedimented and reproduced, until today, through the practices of PFP. Seeking to tackle this issue, this chapter provides a reappraisal of PFP after 1974 through the lenses of postcolonial and decolonial perspectives. It provides a critical analysis of PFP that considers both academic discourse and official discourse as constitutive elements of foreign policy practice. Consequently, the chapter addresses the question of how, with the formal end of colonial rule in 1974, PFP has been working as an ordering tool of global coloniality vis-à-vis former African colonies and Timor, a role that has been enabled and consolidated by neoliberalism as the structuring principle of today's world. Then, the overarching goal here is to foster reflexive modes of thinking about PFP in ways that recognize the political role of public discourses in the reproduction of simplistic political agendas, and help questioning the practices and relations they serve.

The chapter is structured in three parts. Part I contextualizes the debate about discourse, identity and PFP in the context of regime change and structural constraints produced by the international system. It contrasts conventional modes of inquiry in International Relations, often associated with positivist/rationalist methods and epistemologies, with more critical-cum-reflexive approaches that seek to understand the conditions that make foreign policy possible. Part II builds upon this analysis to offer an assessment of the literature on PFP as part of foreign policy practice. Adopting the method of narrative literature review, it surveys key works about the role of the Lusophone world in the reframing of PFP after 1974. It shows that while the traditional research line has been increasingly interested in utilizing social constructivist insights that foreground the role of foreign policy in identity-building, and question the role of discourses and ideas in constituting the global order, it is still unable to question how foreign policy practices, including official discourses and academic research, have functioned to preserve the workings of coloniality. Engaging with this issue, I argue, requires a more systematic engagement with interpretive research strategies that are particularly tailored to explore foreign policy as a meaning-making practice, but also with decolonial modes of knowledge production that can serve the goal of overriding global injustices, unbalances and systemic distortions.

Part III extends this assessment by focusing on the 'values debate' about the ethical character of PFP after 1974, and then identifies the normative framing of the current Lusophone discourse. Through a critical discourse analysis, it shows how official statements and strategic documents have operated to forge multilateral relationships based on formal equality among sovereigns, wherein Portugal can consolidate its image and influence in the international system while helping to teach and socialize its Lusophone partners into the rules and ideas of the (civilized) global liberal order. Going against the grain of conventional PFP literature, this part underlines the discursive continuum, rather than rupture, linking pre- and post-1974 discourses that are often manifested in statements concerning former colonies but also, and more visibly, in the strategic articulation with the two other main discursive spaces, viz. 'Europe' and the 'Transatlantic community'. As shown clearly by the depth of vision and concepts in official documents and texts by political elites (Ferreira, 1976; Gama, 1985; Barroso, 2000; Silva, 2020), the African/Lusophone strategy is always subordinated to the other two vectors, i.e., it is instrumental vis-à-vis the international image Portugal wants to project as normative power within the hegemonic liberal order. Even if PFP is based on a stable matrix composed of three vectors, its core is defined by a crucial interest in attaching the country's identity, decision-making apparatus and political culture to the institutional mechanisms and cultural frames of a hegemonic liberal West. The chapter concludes by reflecting on the complicity of academic research with the perpetuation of colonizing mechanisms, and posits the need for critical thought and deeper public debate in the quest for decolonizing PFP, and in the multiple arenas of theory, agenda, discourse and practice.

Part I

An 'Almost Aristocratic Condition': The Discursive Framing of Identity Through PFP

Addressing the Council of National Defence (CDN) in 1988, in the context of the sweeping transformations the country was going through after the EU accession (1985), the then Portuguese Minister of Foreign Affairs (MNE) Deus Pinheiro (1988, p. 15) made it clear that changes in foreign policy after dictatorship were more a matter of expediency, efficiency and resources than the re-orientation of national goals and worldview.

Overviewing PFP in historical terms, he underlined that.

> [o]ur history and culture have made the Portuguese people a crucial reference in world history. Let us assume this almost aristocratic condition! Let us stop walking headlong low, apologizing for having been a colonial power [...].

As the example shows, foreign policy is instrumental not only for the projection of the national interest onto the international system but also, and more crucially, for the re-production of a meaningful and efficient discourse about the national community, its national interests and, more broadly still, its place, role or mission in the concert of nations (Burchill, 2005; Guzzini, 2012). As stressed by Morin and Paquin (2018, p. 267), "[f]oreign policy is far more effective at reproducing identity on a continual basis than any other public policy". Therefore, foreign policy cannot be understood merely as being about a specific agenda of conflict and cooperation to be implemented, by a sovereign, through the mobilization of material resources in a circumscribed period of time; rather, it is about the construction of collective identity but also of the subjective feelings of political elites vis-à-vis national specificities and their nation's international insertion (Mendes, 2018). That is why the study of foreign policy must also cover the structures of meaning that political elites inhabit and that become normalized and institutionalized through practice and some degree of will and choice (Smith, 2001).

More deeply into the structure of political ontology, foreign policy is about the sense of community itself, historical-philosophical discourses about collective survival and the capacity to thrive, as well as geopolitical ideas about a global order, i.e., how the world works/ought to work. The post-positivist literature has illustrated fruitfully the ways in which geopolitical frameworks are constitutive of national and group identities (Dalby, 1991; Sidaway and Power, 2005), how these frameworks and discourses are produced, reproduced and consumed as an active process (Anderson, 1991; Ó Tuathail and Agnew, 1992), how group identities become entrenched through the mass consumption of foreign policy (Campbell, 1992). However, conventional perspectives have more often treated foreign policy as a taken-for-granted analytical concept (Leira, 2019), a specialist field understandable only if articulated by political elites and their rationality (Garskarth, 2006), and proved unwilling/incapable of problematizing identity and its relationship with power/knowledge production and exploring deeper epistemological layers going beyond the causality of foreign policy design and implementation. Moreover, and as underlined by Roxanne Doty (1993, p. 297), which is largely illustrative of the Portuguese case, "the study of foreign policy has been largely unaffected by the critical insights offered by post- positivism". By problematizing causality, this chapter aims at uncovering the conditions of possibility for PFP beyond a rationalist approach.

The close ties connecting mainland Portugal to different communities along the Atlantic Ocean and beyond, through colonialism and colonial rule, have forged powerful domestic consensus about identity and politics that outlived the end of dictatorship in 1974. As a result, the independence of African colonies in 1975 contributed to produce what João Gomes Cravinho (2005, p. 90) identifies as a 'national psychology'. In spite of that, foreign policy analyses henceforth have been unwilling/incapable of problematizing conventional positivist/rationalist approaches which limit their focus to explaining why particular decisions were made that caused specific courses of action and legitimizing the persistence of a certain structure of interests (Mendes, 2018; Pureza, 2019). Taking into consideration regime change in Portugal during the twentieth century as explanatory variable (Telo, 2000; Ferreira, 2006; Rato 2008; Cravo, 2012), extant analyses have been unable to go beyond explaining why "a certain policy decision was predictable given a particular set of circumstances" (Doty, 1993, p. 298). Therefore, this chapter is aimed at opening up thinking space about PFP through theoretical and methodological perspectives that reject the reproduction of conventional research strategies based on simplistic epistemologies and the legitimation of entrenched discourses that they serve. Rather, and drawing on Doty, I argue that it is crucial to investigate *how* foreign policy subjectivities and meanings have been socially constructed and so deeply entrenched that even if colonial rule was superseded, a broader coloniality of power is clearly identifiable as constitutive of current diplomatic practices and relations with former colonies, as well as racialized relations within the community itself.

Therefore, this chapter is about exploring postcolonial PFP, i.e., foreign policy after the colonial rule, and how a certain form of coloniality of power has become entrenched and renewed through emerging articulations of *Portugueseness* and the concomitant psychic-material relationship with former colonies. In addition, it is also about the national interest and Portugal's role within the current liberal global order, stabilized and consolidated since the 1970s. But it is also about illuminating the structural embeddedness of deeply ingrained ideas and a set of practices, more often presented and justified in the grammar of the sovereign's individual agency, interest and values (Cravo and Freire, 2014). Doing so allows us to lay bare a discursive continuum running through colonial and postcolonial foreign policies which is constitutive of both hegemonic identities in Portugal and the relationship to former colonies, and colonized identities more broadly, in what has come to be known as the Lusophone world. The Lusophone world does not exist in a vacuum; it must be given a certain meaning, consistently, that fits the interests and worldview of PFP. This stresses the need to investigate the foreign policy and postcolonial identity shift after 1974–1976 from the vantage point of those structural constraints posed by deeper ideas and practices pertaining to the domain of coloniality understood as the intrinsic logic of Modernity-cum-Western civilization. Concomitantly, it questions the ways in which they help to reproduce existing inequalities. Drawing on Bhabha (1986) and Mignolo (2021), coloniality can be said to operate like the unconscious in Freud; one cannot see it but it works its way through a multiplicity of tools, viz. diplomatic, military, cultural, commercial, linguistic, humanitarian. I argue then that PFP after 1974 has been instrumental in re-inventing coloniality within a particular neoliberal globalizing frame.

Postcolonial Portugal taken broadly is especially illustrative for investigating foreign policy as discourse about identity and politics, not from the vantage point of methodological individualism, or the strictly material structure of a conventional/realist balance of power, but from that of a coloniality of power and knowledge as the symbolic/material global structure and order. Consequently, this chapter problematizes a set of interrelated discursive practices, including both formal and informal, political-cum-diplomatic and academic, that lay bare the imbrication between knowledge and postcolonial power, the symbolic and the material, and function to order, articulate and enact specific conceptions of Portuguese identity that foreclose alternative, more inclusive, views of Portugueseness and the role of Portugal within the global order. Therefore, postcolonial and decolonial literature has a central role for the kind of critical foreign policy analysis I want to develop here, and the interpretivist modes of inquiry that assist it methodologically. The basic assumption is that *colonialism* (equated here with *colonial rule* for the sake of the argument) and *coloniality* (the broader material, ideological, unconscious logic of Western civilization enveloping the whole world) can be distinguished but have been equally imbricated in the construction of modern states and societies, both in the centre and in the margins/peripheries of the Westphalian international system (Quijano, 1988). Another assumption is that the postcolonial break with colonial rule, occurring in Portugal in 1974–1975, triggered a shift in identity and politics, and a reconstruction of foreign policy, consistent with and not at all opposed to the building blocks of a structured sense of self and community and the deeper, hegemonic and unconscious international/global structures. Therefore, I sustain that the discursive shift/break in Portuguese foreign policy after 1974–1976 operates via the articulation of three discursive spaces, viz. 'Europe', 'The Lusophone world' and 'The Transatlantic community', but only at the surface of politics. In other words, this so-called post-authoritarian shift in PFP discourse and practice epitomizes a performative shift at best, not ethical, and is constituted by rather entrenched ideas/practices operating at a deeper, structural level of politics.

Similar to the Lusophone world, the current discourse of PFP and the interests that underpin it cannot be taken as an ontological given, which makes it more difficult to approach as a clear break with past discourses. It is part and product of a broader context, within which Portugueseness, as a social identity, has been dialectically reconfigured in ways that reflect the interaction between the pragmatic interests of the Portuguese nation-state and the constraints imposed by an evolving global order. Academic work took an important role in this process by helping systematizing this narrative, and making the policy shifts it entails appear as something rational, natural and necessary.

Before going deeper into literature and the discursive practices of foreign policy, it is necessary to investigate further the entrenched character of foreign policy and the geopolitical discourse about *Portugueseness* as social identity. Concomitantly, this study examines Portugal's role within the international system, not from the traditionally accepted foundationalist and materialist vantage point of the permanent national interest but from that of the constraints of deeper ontological structures operating in ideological, material and knowledge dimensions. By layering over the literature review and the analysis of the discourse permeating current foreign policy strategic texts and official documents, the argument illustrates how the above-mentioned discursive shift has represented, more than a transformation or revolution, the mere strategic catching up with and adaptation to the structural rules of the liberal international system, after decades of conservatism, resistance to change and outright tension with the principles of the consolidating liberal order. The very idea of a Lusophone world as superseding centuries of colonialism ought to be read as such, i.e., the catching up with the idea that language, culture, public diplomacy and multilateralism can be used as relevant resources in order for a nation to carve out its way into contemporary global politics. According to this, the liberal order has not only pushed for a different relationship within coloniality between Portugal and former colonies; it has structurally allowed and facilitated the reframing of coloniality ties. When Portugal came to be fully integrated into the Western liberal world, it ceased to be the master of colonies and colonized peoples to become their mentor, teacher and socializer (Chandler, 2010; Cravo and Freire, 2014; Cravo, Lopes and Roque, 2018; Mendes, 2018).

Therefore, and drawing on Bhabha, Mignolo and Quijano's quasi-Freudian and structuralist conception of the coloniality of power and knowledge, I argue that the uneasiness of the conventional literature to problematize the relationship between discourse and power in postcolonial PFP is a gap that ought to be explored and bridged from within the academia but also in more public debates. That literature is mainly individualist, methodologically speaking, i.e., approaching change from the vantage point of agency and political voluntarism, and ontologically materialist. Even when exogenous structures are considered in a determining way (Moreira, 2005), they are taken as causal, impending on the diminishing material capabilities of the Portuguese state. Instead, I explore a constructivist approach that takes seriously the constraints of ideas, practices and structural power over agency and political will but sees alternative pathways as feasible and necessary from an openly normative point of view. Extant literature takes state power and policies as given and does not problematize the production and reproduction of structural power (Barnett and Duvall, 2005) in the form of ideas about power itself, criss-cross inequalities, discriminations and systemic distortions for which particular foreign policies are a tool. At that normative level, the ultimate goal here is to problematize coloniality itself as a set of global diplomatic practices and therefore establish the theoretical conditions of possibility for the academia to ask *how* PFP could become decolonial in postcolonial times.

Part II

'Portugal is not a Small Nation': The Literature on PFP as Practice

From a post-positivist approach, academic writing does not exist outside the world. To write *about* the world is also to write *the* world. What we write about and, more crucially, how we write it is also a practice of bringing a certain world into being (Smith, 2004). This also holds for academic inquiry on PFP. Although the discourse of PFP has already been framed in terms of the nation's insertion in international systems throughout the historical process (Macedo, 1987; Telo, 2000; Teixeira, 2010), the structuralist and constructivist consequences of this framing have been neglected, or at least developed solely in the context of a realist-cum-materialist approach. It is the case of Martínez (1985) in his massive *História Diplomática de Portugal*. In the introduction, the author underlines this gap in the study of foreign policy as a most important shortcoming, in the sense of what he identifies as the trend to study political developments in Portugal as unconnected to the international context. However, and as a conventional realist, Martínez (1985, p. 13) understands this context solely in the strict material sense of the clash among great powers, their military capabilities and dynastic/national interests, i.e., the European and later global balance of power, so that "national independence seems to derive merely from the opposition of external interests". Writing at a moment of national crossroads (ten years after the end of war in Africa and the independence of colonies, and on the eve of the signing of the Accession Treaty to the European Communities), Martínez sets out to uncover (or rather reconstitute) what he calls the 'Portuguese truth'. The context is that of the fear of an impoverished community, even one emptied out of its essence, as it were, probably incapable of sustaining the legitimate aspirations of its members, who would be sentenced henceforth to roam the world for individual salvation, detached from all kinds of national connections. In this book, which remains the most thoroughgoing study of Portuguese diplomacy, Portuguese national essence and the capacity to survive in a dangerous, anarchic world are placed at the centre of politics, such that "the evolution of Portuguese community is not easily intelligible apart from the study of international frameworks" (Martínez, 1985, p. 11). In this context, extra European territories and colonies are perceived as the most valuable resource and guarantee in the recurrent game of national survival, independence and collective purpose (a meaning-making game in a more constructive perspective).

More recently, Teixeira (2010) draws explicitly on the assumption that PFP and diplomacy must be contextualized historically according to the nation's insertion in international frameworks, showing a more refined approach to the interplay between agency and structure and the role of ideas therein. However, his analysis does not seek to problematize mechanisms of identity reconfiguration, opting for a conventional explanation of foreign policy in strictly causal terms. Following Macedo (1987), the author underlines the continental pressure (the European balance of great powers) over Portuguese politics and the maritime alternative as geopolitical opposites and frames over time, causing the strategic options in the long term that he identifies as the structures or models of Portugal's international insertion. The three models identified are the *medieval*, the *classic* and the *democratic*. The classic model, from the fifteenth century until 1974, is characterized by un-variables, viz. the material and ideational contention between continental and maritime strategic options; the retreat and disengagement from European politics; and the Atlantic strategic vector. In Teixeira's own phrasing, this leads to the affirmation (or structuring) of an Atlantic and colonial Portugal, but the internal processes of identity shifting due to the development of colonial expansion and rule are not questioned nor clarified. Likewise, the shift to the democratic model of foreign policy is assumed to have occurred, as in a simple cause-effect chain, pushed by the political will encapsulated in the 1974 programme of the revolutionary Armed Forces (MFA), viz. decolonization, democratization, development. Therefore, colonial rule is represented as an unproblematic device or mechanism used to exert power over non-European others, rather than a new and complex context of meaning that, during centuries, operated deep into the structure of collective identities, both in Portugal and in Africa, reconstituting in turn the idea of politics and the sense of collective purpose. By stressing the democratic nature of the shift occurring after 1974, the author in fact forecloses the space for discussing and developing new articulations of coloniality through PFP.

Martínez (1985) explores this individual and collective mental process at the very beginning of his book, from his own personal experience, but giving it no place in the analysis other than that of a fleeting biographic, nostalgic footnote. The case is made about the well-known map of

Portugal and its colonies superimposed on the map of Europe (accompanied by the caption *Portugal is not a small Nation!*), a composition authored by Henrique Galvão for the First Portuguese Colonial Exhibition, held in Porto in 1934 (Sidaway and Power, 2005, p. 537), crucial in the meaning-making machine of the Portuguese *Estado Novo political regime*. In the former's words, "[a]s for me, I believed in my childhood, by staring at a map that hanged frequently in public places, and in which our overseas possessions overlapped with Europe, that Portugal was not a small Nation" (Martínez, 1985, p. 7). Reflecting on the political role of cartography under *Estado Novo*, Sidaway and Power (2005, p. 536) underline that the caption "reinforces the cartographic expression and disclaims Portuguese anxieties about the place of the country in the geopolitical order of things". Drawing on the same map, Reis and Oliveira (2018, pp. 632–633) has underlined that this mythical side of empire in its late colonial stage was both the product of *Realpolitik* and the awareness "of the importance of the cultural or ideational dimension of imperialism" and that even "major crises often involve the refashioning of identity rather than a complete break [...]". This is a critical point, for the shift *performed* in PFP in 1974–1976 did pick up on the importance of the cultural and ideational dimensions of power in international relations, of which the creation of a Lusophone community would be a central project later on. But, as the example shows, the transition to democracy does not necessitate a complete break in foreign policy (Gorjão, 2005).

Clarifying the priorities and geographical axes of the democratic model of PFP after colonial rule, Teixeira converges with other authors (Moreira, 2000; Pereira, 2006; Freire and Brito, 2010; Sá, 2016; Costa Pereira, 2018; Seabra, 2019; Pavia, 2019a) in underscoring three main vectors, and often the balance among them: 'Europe', the 'Atlantic/NATO' and 'Africa', especially the postcolonial relations with Portuguese- speaking countries. Portugal is presented, historically, as an Atlantic and colonial country seeking, at times, continental (meaning European) compensation and shifting, since the 1974 break, to being a European country seeking to take profit (within European politics) of its Atlantic position and historic relations with postcolonial countries (Ferreira, 1976; Teixeira, 2010; Cravo, Lopes and Roque, 2018; Seabra, 2019; Raimundo, 2019). However, this break only finds its unequivocal way, according to Teixeira, with the end of the pre-Constitutional period (1974–1976). These two/three years were marked by indefinition and parallel diplomacy outside the Ministry (Rezola, 2016), resulting in deep contestation around Portugal's insertion in international frameworks, a balance that until 1976 swayed to the side of those favouring a non-aligned foreign policy vis-à-vis the geopolitical blocks and powers of the day. Teixeira (2010, p. 54) presents it *ex post facto,* as condemned to be superseded in short time (from 1976 on) by a "rigorous and univocal definition" of Portugal's external position as a Western country, both European and Atlantic. During the time span of provisional governments (1974–1976)

> Portuguese foreign policy was moving in a Third-Worldist direction, towards the development of privileged relations with the nations emerging from Portuguese decolonization. It was the last avatar, socialising in that occasion, of the thesis of Portugal's 'African vocation'.

Curiously enough, the author considers the left leaning, Third-Worldist MFA foreign policy as the last expression of an African vocation supposedly running through Portuguese history since the end of the Middle Ages but then interrupted abruptly, as it were, in 1976, by the clarification of Portuguese domestic politics in favour of liberal democracy and the global market.

In a similar way, Reis and Oliveira (2018, p. 635) underscore the influence of Third- Worldism in PFP between 1974 and 1976, with a strong dimension of cultural identification, "formalized in several cooperation agreements with the newly independent African countries which provided for the dispatch of Portuguese aid workers (*cooperantes*), as well as various mechanisms of technical assistance and cultural exchange". Rezola (2016, p. 31) considers this strategy as part of "a struggle for a more just international order [...]", while sticking to previous commitments within NATO. According to Pinheiro (1988, p. 15), "[n]ever in the past has there been a place in Portugal for Third-Worldism, and most probably never will be, because the doors of the First World start opening up". The same thesis is defended by José Medeiros Ferreira (1976, p. 19), MNE in 1976, for whom the Third-Worldist option was the product of a "resentful country", fading while the European strategy started materializing. This in fact performs a discursive re-articulation of PFP within the liberal order in a clear functionalist way. Therefore, and from the 1980s on, the official approach consolidates that sees the Portuguese nation-state aiming at being readmitted into a liberal globalizing system, whose multiple constitutive parts work together to promote solidarity and stability and to implement the principles of liberal peace, reshaping the links with former colonies in the spirit of formal equality among nations (Gama, 1985).

Therefore, the literature on PFP has converged to assess Portugal's new regime and model of insertion in international frameworks, consolidating after 1976, as emerging with a clean slate in terms of colonial record, in sharp contrast to previous regimes and their foreign policies, marked by colonial rule and interests. This has been part clearly of a narrative of legitimation that uses democracy as a shade to avoid problematizing how coloniality works globally (and accelerates in times of neoliberal globalization), what the full insertion of Portugal in the liberal order has meant in that respect, and how the new foreign policy options have been articulated and made coherent inside that web of meaning or discourse. This liberal reading of the PFP shift after 1976 is half utopian and half instrumental, as far as the relationship with former colonies is concerned. As an example of how the conventional literature has framed this subject, and after underlining that Portugal's national interest within the European framework resides in taking advantage of the Atlantic position and postcolonial relations, Teixeira (2010, p. 54) remarks the purely consensual and evenly balanced nature of relations with former colonies: "[i]f on top of the European option and the Atlantic vector we add up the relationship of friendship and cooperation with the new Portuguese-speaking African Nations (PALOP), and the renewed relationship with Brazil, we find the crucial strategic lines of the democratic foreign policy". This kind of discourse has been accommodated into official documents recently, viz. the *Strategic Concept of National Defence* (Government of Portugal, 2013), in revision in 2023, and the *Strategy of Portuguese Cooperation 2030* (Government of Portugal, 2022).

By underscoring this kind of shift, both academic elites and political/diplomatic officials has ended up converging to consolidate the new discourse enveloping relations with former colonies—*Lusofonia*, the 'Lusophone world'—as driven by a foreign policy of values, in sheer contrast to the interests of colonial rule. Therefore, the final institutionalization of the Community of Portuguese Speaking Nations (CPLP) in 1996, after more than ten years of diplomatic consultations, came to structure the democratic discourse of PFP and articulate it with the discourse of liberal humanitarian internationalism (Paris, 1997; Dunne and McDonald, 2013) based on a global responsibility to manage and govern challenges arising from global imbalances and unequal development, as well as from political and natural disasters (Gama, 2001). In this context, it is meaningful to bring back to the debate Sidaway and Power (2005, p. 527) and their critical study of twentieth-century Portuguese geopolitical writings, which in their words "enables wider reflections on empires, 'race', and the geopolitical". Particularly important in terms of the argument I put forward here, the authors underline that membership of the EU, in the 1980s, and the formalization of CPLP in the 1990s, rested on a fundamental re-inscription of Portuguese identity narratives and the re-working of functional ties among independent countries in a Lusophone world. Therefore, I argue, this reframing would be conceived of as the ideational foundation for claiming the role of Portugal as bridge between continents (approached not only as cultural building blocks but also as the different constitutive and functional parts of the liberal global order), as well as the central role of CPLP in structuring cooperation among regional economic blocks.

Part III

The Social Framing of a Lusophone Discourse

Apart from postcolonial and decolonial theory, this chapter draws on the added value of critical discourse theory, and interpretivism as social ontology, in order to open up theoretical space for a post-positivist analysis of PFP and its discourse on the Lusophone world. Critical discourse theory helps scrutinize the articulations of language and action in foreign policy agendas, such that the emphasis is placed "on the *semantic*, *pragmatic*, and *rhetorical aspects* in the construction of social structures and identities [...]" (Torfing, 2005, p. 23). Taking discursive practices seriously leads us to understand that power is dispersed but not less "productive of subjects and their worlds" (Doty, 1993, p. 302), and is deeply imbricated in presenting meanings, identities and interests as fixed and stable. Therefore, discursive spaces both frame, order and determine—they structure—the limits and possibilities of social identities and the policies they make possible. This analysis takes advantage also of interpretivism's ability to "cast fresh light on the ideational basis of political activity" (Bevir et al., 2015, p. 6) and the acknowledgement that ideational/normative structures are no less real for being in the minds of political agents and their discourses. These are both contingent and contested, as they operate intersubjectively and therefore are prone to change. The clarification of these assumptions is crucial before identifying a Lusophone discourse and its co-constitutive relation with PFP.

The literature about PFP is framed since the 1990s by what I put forward as a *functionalist-idealist* discourse. On the one hand, postcolonial Portugal is rediscovered as a country with the potential to *articulate* different interests and political spaces within the post-1989 liberal order (Moreira, 2000); on the other, a *global vocation* is stressed in direct articulation with the maritime tradition and renewed responsibility to uphold multilateralism globally and development in Africa and the former colonies (Vasconcelos, 1991; Maltez, 2002; Moreira, 2009; Pinto, 2013; Pavia, 2019b), one "shaped by immutable eternal influences" (Gaskarth, 2006, p. 332). This has been approached as geopolitical destiny and upheld by all Portuguese governments, both centre-right and centre-left, after 1976 (Pureza, 2019). In turn, political and academic elites have accommodated it easily into the framing of a 'foreign policy of values' suggesting that the promotion abroad of human rights, democracy and the rule of law have become the *raison d'être* of foreign policy itself (Teixeira, 2010; Rezola, 2016; Silva, 2018; Mendes, 2018; Dias, 2019). Concomitantly, the central role of Portuguese language is stressed in this context and articulated as a vehicle for the promotion of liberal values in the world at large (Moreira, 2014; Silva, 2020). Following this line, the former Director-General of Foreign Policy at the Ministry of Foreign Affairs Pedro da Costa Pereira (2018, p. 282) wrote recently that

> the promotion of multilateralism, allied with a foreign policy based on values and dialogue, and the insertion in multiple political spaces at the global level, has led the country to be perceived by many other countries as an entity available and willing to voice their concerns, without a selfish national agenda, focused instead on the promotion of the common good and the respect for international rules.

Therefore, it is possible to affirm that 'values through language' becomes the ideational/normative structure of a Lusophone discourse, that both shapes and is shaped by the daily practices of the PFP, and is therefore accompanied by a set of material resources.

However undeveloped and uncritical, the talk of a shift towards a foreign policy of values after 1974 marks the acute consciousness of the importance of culture and identity for a state's efficient image within a globalizing political system. According to Juliet Kaarbo (2003, p. 159), contemporary political options of major powers reveal a struggle over identity and its influence on foreign policy, so that "questions 'Who are we?' and 'How are we perceived by others?' seem to be prominent factors influencing the external behaviour of these states and their internal policymaking processes". Recognizing that foreign policy starts with the clarification of national interests, Teixeira (2010) is equivocal however about how to frame the relationship between interests and values, suggesting that the latter should not be ignored but instead balanced with the former in order to meet the challenge of chasing economic gain *and* at the same time standing up for the promotion of human rights and the rule of law. Accordingly, one of the biggest successes in PFP is deemed to be the 'diplomacy of values' deployed at the end of the 1990s, vis-à-vis the independence of East Timor (Gorjão, 2001; Gama, 2002; Cravo and Freire, 2014). Writing ten years after the events, Teixeira makes this a founding myth for the democratic model of PFP by making 'values' the frame for relations with developing countries. Therefore, the African or Lusophone vector in post-1974 PFP is noted generally in the literature as deriving not from naked *Realpolitik*, geostrategic or geoeconomic interests, but instead "from considerations of humane, linguistic, cultural, historical nature and 'affection'" (Pavia, 2019b, p. 184). As soon as October 1976, at the 31st UN General Assembly, MNE José Medeiros Ferreira (1981, p. 149) referred to "a solidarist and economic geopolitical space" linking democratic Europe to African Nations, for whose articulation Portugal could be of great assistance. In a way, this argument draws on the Luso-tropicalist myth of Portugal as a good colonizer (Bastos, 2019), from whose assumption "followed the claims about empire not being an actual empire but a unique multiracial Nation across continents [...]", and projects into the future the new role of the Portuguese Nation as a benevolent partner vis-à-vis former colonies and the African continent as a whole (Barroso, 2000; Vitorino, 2000; Seabra, 2019). In the words of Jaime Gama (2001, p. 251), MNE at the time of CPLP's institutionalization, this political process "contributes to consolidate the common values of all those who find in the Portuguese language a fundamental trait of their specific identity". From a more critical perspective, feeding this myth of a benevolent colonizer has served the purpose of softening potential tensions within the Portuguese-speaking world—but within Portuguese domestic politics as well—and reproducing, uncritically, a certain form of coloniality of power and knowledge.

I sustain therefore that the Lusophone discourse has been framed uncritically, based on the reconstruction of the international role of Portugal as benevolent partner for multilateralism and liberal peace, and claiming to operate ***not*** through ***Realpolitik*** or naked national interests, like other former colonizers, but instead through the cultural and public diplomacy of values and a common language. Drawing on Diez (2013), and contrarily to the common view accepted by political elites, this discourse frames PFP and is used as a particular tool of Western liberal hegemonic interests and values. In the Gramscian sense, it is not hegemony in itself, meaning it does not own hegemony; it can acquire hegemonic status but does not make Portugal a hegemon in the individualist/neorealist sense of state agency. A foreign policy of values framing the Lusophone discourse uncovers then "a relation in which those subject to hegemony consent to the same conceptions of society, broad problem definitions and principled solutions" (Diez, 2013, p. 200). This is the same argument used in the critical reading by Pureza (2019, p. 9) vis-à-vis MNE Santos Silva's arguments: "Sure, what is at stake in foreign policy statements as the kind Augusto Santos Silva synthesises in commitments to the European construction and Transatlantic ties is the expression of the hegemony of a type of society. And that is a disputed hegemony". Speaking about the ethical dimension of foreign policy is always controversial, as the critique of Blair's in the Britain of the early 2000s shows (Williams, 2002; Chandler, 2003; Wheeler and Dunne, 2004; Abrahamsen, 2005; Gaskarth, 2006). What stands out from this debate, and is even more appalling in the Portuguese case, is the lack of depth and debate itself about the statements conveying a 'foreign policy of values', especially in the discourse of, and relationship with, the Lusophone world. As underscored by Gaskarth (2006, p. 326), "[f]ew questioned who should be authorized to make policy decisions, where this authority derives from, who should be consulted, and even how they might be held accountable afterwards". The literature on PFP has accepted mostly uncritically the official Lusophone discourse and neglected these questions vis-à-vis specific facts and political practices, like the kind involved in development cooperation and the use of security forces in peacekeeping/peacebuilding missions. From a critical perspective, a more holistic idea of ethics is needed which takes practice seriously and questions the structures of meaning that political and academic elites inhabit and are not used to investigate.

Up until now, the Lusophone discourse has been framed systematically along three material-symbolic dimensions, corresponding roughly to what MNE Santos Silva (2018) identified recently as the 'differentiating resources' of PFP, viz. the role of the armed/security forces in the promotion of international peace and stability, development cooperation and the international role of the Portuguese language. From a decolonial perspective, this discourse illustrates how "the rhetoric of modernity regarding salvation, peace, progress, democracy, human rights, development, rough and dangerous states, etc., hides or diverts attention from global designs advanced by the logic of coloniality" (Mignolo, 2021, p. 183). One such very vocal example is the recent investigation of the alleged smuggling of drugs, gold and diamonds by the Portuguese UN peacekeepers in the Central African Republic, and the concomitant official anxieties about its impact on the discourse of Portugal as co-producer of international security and development, and the necessity to reaffirm publicly the reasons beyond Portugal's participation in international peace missions (Duarte, 2021). In an estimated illegal trade of €500 million, *Operação Miríade* took up to investigate the collusion of local actors with Portuguese military forces and transnational actors operating in the global market, allegedly laundering money through the purchase of bitcoins, and raising high-level concerns about the international image of the Portuguese armed forces as a foreign policy tool (Lusa, 2021). This has proved to be an especially embarrassing episode for Portuguese diplomacy, showing the importance of scrutinizing all PFP actors in terms of the impact of their practices and relations on the field, and not just of official documents or stated goals.

Each of these three dimensions is both material and symbolic, in that they are the product of a social framing of specific interests, identities and capabilities. Ideas have a special function in this type of political construction because "they empower actors through discourse, and because they shape the identities which determine individual and state interests" (Temperley, 2013, p. 1). However, and as Robert Cox (1996) has underlined, historical structures are always specific configurations of forces consisting of material capabilities, ideas and institutions. The Lusophone discourse is clearly about the liberal articulation of multilateralism, solidarism and humanitarianism as symbolic-material spaces, in which Portugal-cum-Western modern nation-state operates in order to produce and distribute status, power and security within a liberal global order, aligning with the hegemonic powers of the day (Amaral,

2002; Cravo, 2012) and the accepted models of interventionism (Gama, 1997; Pinto, 2012; Cravo et al., 2018). Theoretically, it is a resource that can be used by all Portuguese-speaking states in different degrees, but it is within the practice and institutional framework of PFP that the potential of this discourse has been developed more fully. Inside it, it becomes the hegemonic product of articulating particular ideas of international legitimacy with the mobilization of the material capabilities (military cooperation, development aid, cultural consistency, humanitarian assistance) necessary to act on their behalf (Chandler, 2010). The full range of discursive practices identified above are conveyed and structured through the web of meaning (re)produced through an official Portuguese language. None of these dimensions has been more unreflexively and uncritically received within PFP literature than language, overlooking completely the contributions of postcolonial studies on the construction of the colonial discourse through the Imaginary (Bhabha, 1986), the role of language and metalanguage for the control of cultural variety and difference (Makoni and Pennycook, 2006; Souza and Guilherme, 2019), or the interconnections among language, ideology and the politics of neoliberal globalism (Joseph, 2006; Flores, 2013; Kubota, 2014).

The exception must be made for Martins et al. (2020) who have analysed recently the role of language in the context of Portuguese cooperation as a political construct invested with symbolic power, according to Bourdieu's perspective, and have contributed to denaturalize it as a neutral tool and instead stressed its constitutive effects vis-à-vis the Lusophone discourse, PFP and CPLP. Drawing on Boaventura Sousa Santos (2009), they underscore critically how Portuguese language operates as a tool of epistemic dominance, refashioning in fact the hierarchical mechanisms of cultural coloniality under the guise of multilateral consensus and multiple-state interest. The conventional approach notwithstanding focuses on the Portuguese language as strategic asset for PFP, and a mark and justification for Portugal's global vocation, but does not see it as an instrument of naked Portuguese interest; it represents language with a messianic tone, as common legacy and asset for Portuguese-speaking Nations and peoples in a globalizing world (Maltez, 2002; Carneiro, 2006; Pinto, 2011; Moreira, 2014), a tool for peace, development and democracy (Government of Portugal, 2006; Palma, 2006; Moreira, 2007).

Echoing the conventional approach, MNE Santos Silva (2020, p. 30) has identified the kernel of the Lusophone discourse as a shared legacy of language and values structuring cooperation among Portuguese-speaking Nations in vital areas of interest, viz. security, nation-building, economic growth, but extending cooperation and influence beyond the language area to countries "in the Maghreb and Southern, Eastern and West Africa". The Lusophone discourse appears clearly as a new grammar for the long-standing African 'vocation', a discourse in which Portugal assumes a pivotal role for coordinating Europe- Africa relations and mobilizes new and old forms of diplomacy to communicate its position vis-à-vis different publics. As an example, the Maghreb is conceived of strategically as "the nearer abroad" (Brito, 2005, p. 159) with the production of regional security taken as the opportunity to play a relevant role, both bilaterally and multilaterally, in the global order (Government of Portugal, 2013). Therefore, a decolonial study about the discursive practices inherent to the concept of a Lusophone world must analyse critically both the role of Portuguese security and defence cooperation (and development cooperation, broadly speaking) in the articulation of national interests with international (in)security practices and the fulfilment of international responsibilities, on the one hand, and the literature thereof, on the other (Teixeira, 2010; Cravo, 2012; Cravo and Freire, 2014; Carreiras, 2015; Bernardino, 2019; Dias et al., 2021).

More recently, Cravo et al. (2018, p. 188) have opened up the way for a more critical decolonial appraisal, albeit in a limited way, by studying peace promotion and development instruments in East Timor and Guinea-Bissau, in the context of PFP strategic cooperation programmes. In their study, cooperation outcomes are assessed as instrumental for Portugal's international reputation, and the promotion of the Portuguese language appears as a central interest and vehicle for balancing other powers' influence in different geostrategic areas. The authors deem the liberal approach to peace promotion and development a mechanism that can "reproduce the conditions for conflict" in the name of the West's values, geostrategic interests and hegemony. Crucially, they conclude that the instruments of Portuguese cooperation are not reflexive enough and demonstrate a 'neo-colonial' face, CPLP included. They reflect the priority of promoting Portuguese influence (language, law, security forces), often at the expense of the needs of vulnerable cooperation partners. The contradictions and fragilities of Portuguese cooperation strategies regarding the Lusophone world are stressed, in a critical way, by other authors too (Pureza et al., 2007; Nascimento, 2015; Seabra, 2019), who point at the need to go deeper in uncovering and investigating the enduring structures that order relations between Portugal and its former colonies in a globalizing world.

Conclusion

Drawing on a decolonial perspective and critical discourse analysis, this chapter has set out to address the question of how, after the formal end of colonial rule in 1974, PFP has been working as tool of global coloniality vis-à-vis its former colonies, a role consolidated within neoliberalism as the structuring principle of a globalizing world. Therefore, it addresses foreign policy analysis from a constructivist perspective that takes seriously the complex entanglement between discourse and power and, more critically, the intersubjective processes through which colonial dynamics, identities and hierarchies have been incorporated, sedimented and reproduced through the practices of PFP until today. Methodologically, this chapter has proceeded by considering both academic discourse and official discourse as constitutive elements of foreign policy practice in need of critical appraisal in order to uncover and investigate the enduring structures that order relations between Portugal and its former colonies. Finally, it has identified the framing of a Lusophone discourse as the particular set of ideas, practices and pragmatic tools of Western liberal hegemonic interests and values, in the Gramscian sense, meaning that the Lusophone discourse is not hegemony in itself but it can and do acquire hegemonic status within the dominant frame of power distribution and global legitimacy for the production of peace, security and development. The overarching goal of the argument is to foster reflexive modes of thinking about PFP in ways that (i) recognize the political role of conventional public discourses in the reproduction of simplistic political agenda; and (ii) question the practices and relations they serve. Therefore, the chapter advances the need to encourage critical thought and innovative academic methodologies that can influence public debate in the quest for an emancipatory and decolonizing PFP, in the multiple arenas of theory, agenda, discourse and practice.

References

Abrahamsen, R. (2005) 'Blair's Africa: The Politics of Securitization and Fear', *Alternatives: Global, Local, Political* 30 (1), pp. 55–80.

Amaral, D. F. (2002) 'Sobre a Política Externa Portuguesa', *Janus: Anuário de Relações Internacionais 2002*, viewed 5 December 2021, https://www.janusonline.pt/arquivo/2002/2002_3_2_4.html

Anderson, B. (1991) *Imagined Communities: Reflections on the Origin and Spread of Nationalism*. London: Verso.

Barnett, M. and Duvall, R. (2005) 'Power in International Politics', *International Organization* 59 (01), pp. 39–75.

Barroso, J. M. D. (2000) 'O Interesse Nacional e a Globalização', in Teixeira, N. S., Rodrigues, J. C. and Nunes, I. F. (eds.) *O Interesse Nacional e a Globalização*. Lisbon: Instituto de Defesa Nacional, pp. 129–141.

Bastos, C. (2019) 'Luso-tropicalism Debunked: Race, Racism, and Racialism in Three Portuguese-Speaking Societies', in Anderson, W., Roque, R. and Santos, R. (eds.) *Luso- tropicalism and Its Discontents. The Making and Unmaking of Racial Exceptionalism*. New York and Oxford: Berghahn.

Bernardino, L. (2019) 'As forças armadas como instrumento de política externa: contributos para a cooperação militar portuguesa em África', in Raimundo, A. (ed.) *Política Externa Portuguesa e África: Tendências e Temas Contemporâneos*. Lisbon: Centro de Estudos Internacionais-IUL, pp. 101–120.

Bevir, M., Daddow, O. and Schnapper, P. (2015) 'Interpreting British European Policy', *Journal of Common Market Studies* 2015 (53), pp. 1–17.

Bhabha,H. K. (1986) 'The Other Question: Difference, Discrimination and the Discourse of Colonialism', in Barker, F. et al. (eds.) *Literature, Politics and Theory*. London: Methuen, pp. 148–172.

Brito, N. F. (2005) 'Política Externa Portuguesa. O Futuro do Passado', *Relações Internacionais* 2005 (5), pp. 147–161.

Burchill, S. (2005) *The National Interest in International Relations Theory*. NY: Palgrave Macmillan.

Campbell, D. (1992) *Writing Security*. Manchester: Manchester University Press.

Carneiro, A. T. (2006) 'Uma Visão Geopolítica do Espaço de Língua Portuguesa', *Nação e Defesa* 2006 (114), pp. 99–139.

Carreiras, H. (2015) 'A dimensão sociológica das intervenções militares externas: As forças armadas portuguesas em missões internacionais', in Freire, R. (ed.) *Consolidação da paz e a sua sustentabilidade: As missões da ONU em Timor-Leste a contribuição de Portugal*. Coimbra: Imprensa da Universidade de Coimbra, pp. 123–156.

Chandler, D. (2003) Rhetoric without Responsibility: 'The Attraction of 'Ethical' Foreign Policy', *British Journal of Politics and International Relations* 5 (3), pp. 295–316.

Chandler, D. (2010) 'The Uncritical Critique of 'Liberal Peace'', *Review of International Studies* 2010 (36), pp. 137–155.

Costa Pereira, P. (2018) 'Portuguese Foreign Policy: Constraints and Responses', in Belli, B. and Nasser, F. (eds.) *The Road Ahead: The 21st-Century World Order in the Eyes of Policy Planners*. Brasília: Fundação Alexandre de Gusmão, pp. 269–285.

Cox, R. W. (1996) 'Social Forces, States, and World Orders: Beyond International Relations Theory', in Cox, R. W. and Sinclair, T. J. (eds.) *Approaches to World Order*. Cambridge: Cambridge University Press, pp. 85–124.

Cravinho, J. G. (2005) 'Les Relations Post-Coloniales Portugaises', *Pôle Sud* 2005/1 (22), pp. 89–100.

Cravo, T. (2012) 'Consolidating Partnerships: History and Geopolitics in Portugal's Twenty-First Century Foreign Policy', in Royo, S. (ed.) *Portugal in the Twenty-First Century, Politics, Society, and Economics*. NY: Lexingtin Books, pp. 215–244.

Cravo, T. and Freire, R. (2014) 'Portugal and East Timor: Managing Distance and proximity in Post-Colonial Relations', *European Review of International Studies* 1 (3), pp. 39–59.

Cravo, T., Lopes, P. and Roque, S. (2018) 'Portugal e a promoção da paz: uma análise crítica de percursos pós-coloniais', *e-cadernos CES* 2018 (29), pp. 169–196.

Dalby, S. (1991) Critical Geopolitics: 'Discourse, Difference, and Dissent', *Environment and Planning D: Society and Space* 9 (3), pp. 261–283.

Dias,A. M. (2019) 'A evolução da sociedade internacional africana e as suas implicações para a política externa portuguesa', in Raimundo, A. (ed.) *Política Externa Portuguesa e África: Tendências e Temas Contemporâneos*. Lisbon: Centro de Estudos Internacionais-IUL, pp. 49–71.

Dias, V. A., Freire, M. R. and Barradas, J. R. (2021) 'A Participação de Portugal em Missões Internacionais como Eixo Estratégico de Política Externa',*Nação e Defesa* 2021 (159), pp. 119–150.

Diez, T. (2013) 'Normative Power as Hegemony', *Cooperation and Conflict* 48 (2), pp. 194–210.

Doty, R. L. (1993) 'Foreign Policy as Social Construction: A Post-Positivist Analysis of U.S. Counterinsurgency Policy in the Philippines', *International Studies Quarterly* 1993 (37), pp. 297–320.

Duarte, J. C. (2021) 'Marcelo Rebelo de Sousa diz que reputação das Forças Armadas continua 'intacta'', *Observador* 16 November, viewed 25 November 2021, https://observador.pt/2021/11/16/marcelo-rebelo-de-sousa-diz-que-a-reputacao-das-forcas-armadas-continua-intacta/

Dunne, T. and McDonald, M. (2013) 'The Politics of Liberal Internationalism', *International Politics* 50 (1), pp. 1–17.

Ferreira, J. M. (1976) 'Relações Externas e Defesa Nacional',*Nação e Defesa* 1976 (1), pp. 16–23.
Ferreira, J. M. (1981) *Do Código Genético do Estado Democrático*. Lisboa: Contexto.
Ferreira, J. M. (2006) *Cinco Regimes na Política Internacional*. Barcarena: Fundamento.
Flores, N. (2013) 'The Unexamined Relationship between Neoliberalism and Plurilingualism: A Cautionary Tale', *TESOL Quarterly* 47 (3), pp. 500–520.
Freire, M. R. and Brito, R. R. (2010) 'Ensaio Bibliográfico. Estudos Sobre a Política Externa Portuguesa Após 2000', *Relações Internacionais* 2010 (28), pp. 157–179.
Gama, J. (1985) *Política Externa Portuguesa (1983–1985)*. Lisbon: Ministério dos Negócios Estrangeiros.
Gama, J. (1997) 'A Política Externa', *Nação e Defesa* 1997 (83), pp. 45–57.
Gama, J. (2001) *A Política Externa Portuguesa (1995–1999)*. Lisbon: Instituto Diplomático MNE.
Gama, J. (2002) *Política Externa Portuguesa (1999–2002)*. Lisbon: Instituto Diplomático MNE.
Gaskarth, J. (2006) 'Discourses and Ethics: The Social Construction of British Foreign Policy', *Foreign Policy Analysis* 2006 (2), pp. 325–341.
Gorjão, P. (2001) 'The End of a Cycle: Australian and Portuguese Foreign Policies and the Fate of East Timor', *Contemporary Southeast Asia* 23 (1), pp. 101–121.
Gorjão, P. (2005) 'Mudança de regime e política externa: Portugal, a Indonésia e o destino de Timor Leste', *Análise Social* XL (174), pp. 7–35.
Government of Portugal. (2006) *Uma Visão Estratégica para a Cooperação Portuguesa*. Lisbon: Ministério dos Negócios Estrangeiros.
Government of Portugal. (2013) *Strategic Concept of National Defence*. Lisbon: Conselho de Ministros.
Government of Portugal. (2022) *Strategy of Portuguese Cooperation 2030*. Lisbon: Conselho de Ministros.
Guzzini, S. (2012) 'The Argument: Geopolitics for Fixing the Coordinates of Foreign Policy Identity', in Guzzini, S. (ed.) *The Return of Geopolitics in Europe? Social Mechanisms and Foreign Policy Identity Crises* . Cambridge: Cambridge University Press, pp, 1–6.
Joseph, J. (2006) *Language and Politics*. Edinburgh: Edinburgh University Press.
Kaarbo, J. (2003) 'Foreign Policy Analysis in the Twenty-First Century: Back to Comparison, Forward to Identity and Ideas', *International Studies Review* 2003 (5), pp. 156–163.
Kubota, R. (2014) 'The Multi/Plural Turn, Postcolonial Theory, and Neoliberal Multiculturalism', *Applied Linguistics* 37 (4), pp. 474–494.

Leira, H. (2019) 'The Emergence of Foreign Policy', *International Studies Quarterly* 2019 (63), pp. 187–198.

Lusa. (2021) 'Operação Miríade. PSD e PCP alertam que caso tem impacto na imagem das Forças Armadas', *Expresso* 9 November, viewed 15 November 2021, https://expresso.pt/politica/2021-11-09-Operacao-Miriade.-PSD-e-PCP-alertam-que-caso-tem-impacto-na-imagem-das-Forcas-Armadas-b6ad0afd

Macedo, J. B. (1987) *História diplomática portuguesa: constantes e linhas de força*. Lisbon: Instituto de Defesa Nacional.

MacQueen, N. (1985) 'Portugal and Africa: The Politics of Re-Engagement' *The Journal of Modern African Studies* 23 (1), pp. 31–51.

Makoni, S. and Pennycook, A. (eds.) (2006) *Desinventing and Reconstituting Languages*. Clevedon: Multilingual Matters.

Maltez, J. A. (2002) *Curso de Relações Internacionais*. São João do Estoril: Principia.

Martínez, P. S. (1985) *História Diplomática de Portugal*. Lisbon: Verbo.

Martins, B., Silva, R. and Coelho, L. S. (2020) 'O poder simbólico e a cooperação portuguesa: Uma análise sobre o papel da língua', *Cadernos de Estudos Africanos* 2020 (39), pp. 17–30.

Mendes, P. E. (2018) 'Identidade, ideias e normas na construção dos interesses em política externa: o caso português', *Análise Social*, vol. LIII (2.º) 2018 (227), pp. 458- 487.

Mignolo, W. (2021) *The Politics of Decolonial Investigations*. Durham and London: Duke University Press.

Moreira, A. (2000) 'Situação internacional portuguesa', *Análise Social* XXXV (154–155), pp. 315–326.

Moreira, A. (2005) 'O papel da política externa portuguesa no mundo contemporâneo', in Requixa, M. M. (ed.) *Visões de Política Externa Portuguesa*. Lisbon: Sociedade de Geografia and Instituto Diplomático MNE, pp. 13–20.

Moreira, A. (2007) 'A Diplomacia Portuguesa', *Negócios Estrangeiros* 2007 (10), pp. 19–25.

Moreira, A. (2009) 'Portugal e a Geopolítica da Interculturalidade', *Povos e Culturas* 2009 (13), pp. 53–91.

Moreira, A. (2014) 'A Língua Transporta Valores', *Nação e Defesa* 2014 (138), pp. 244–253.

Morin, J.-F. and Paquin, J. (2018) *Foreign Policy Analysis. A Toolbox*. Cham: Palgrave Macmillan.

Nascimento, D. (2015) 'Para além das cinzas: Uma avaliação crítica da cooperação portuguesa para o desenvolvimento em Timor Leste', in Freire, R. (ed.) *Consolidação da paz e a sua sustentabilidade: As missões da ONU em Timor-Leste a contribuição de Portugal*. Coimbra: Imprensa da Universidade de Coimbra, pp. 99–122.

Ó Tuathail, G. and Agnew, J. (1992) 'Geopolitics and Discourse: Practical Geopolitical Reasoning and US Foreign Policy', *Political Geography* 11, pp. 190–204.

Palma, E. C. (2006) *Cultura, Desenvolvimento e Política Externa: Ajuda Pública ao Desenvolvimento nos Países Africanos Lusófonos*. Lisbon: Instituto Diplomático MNE.

Paris, R. (1997) 'Peacebuilding and the Limits of Liberal Internationalism', *International Security* 22(2), pp. 54–89.

Pavia, J. F. (2019a) 'Introdução', in Pavia, J. F. (ed.) *A Política Externa Portuguesa Contemporânea*. Lisbon: Universidade Lusíada, pp. 5–9.

Pavia, J. F. (2019b) 'O vector lusófono da política externa portuguesa', in Pavia, J. F. (ed.) *A Política Externa Portuguesa Contemporânea*. Lisboa: Universidade Lusíada, pp. 181–208.

Pavia, J. F. (2019c) 'A persistência duma dimensão africana na política externa portuguesa: o verdadeiro consenso nacional', in Raimundo, A. (ed.) *Política Externa Portuguesa e África: Tendências e Temas Contemporâneos*. Lisbon: Centro de Estudos Internacionais-IUL, pp. 29–48.

Pereira, M. F. (2006) 'Política externa portuguesa e Política Externa e de Segurança Comum da União Europeia', *Negócios Estrangeiros* 2006 (9), pp. 134–145.

Pinheiro, J. D. (1988) 'Grandes Eixos da Política Externa no Portugal de Hoje', *Nação e Defesa* 1988 (45), pp. 11–36.

Pinto, J. F. (2005) *Do Império Colonial à Comunidade dos Países de Língua Portuguesa: Continuidades e Descontinuidades*. Coimbra: Almedina and Instituto Diplomático MNE.

Pinto, J. F. (2011) 'Da CPLP à Comunidade Lusófona: o futuro da Lusofonia', *Revista Angolana de Sociologia* 2011 (7), pp. 107–118.

Pinto, J. N. (2013) *Portugal: Ascensão e Queda. Ideias e Políticas de uma Nação Singular*. Coimbra: Almedina.

Pinto, M. C. (2012) 'Portugal: A participação em missões de paz como factor de credibilização externa', *Janus* 3 (1), pp. 66–78.

Pureza et al. (2007) 'As novas operações de paz das Nações Unidas. Os casos de Angola, Timor Leste e Moçambique', *Oficina do CES* 290, viewed 4 December 2021, https://estudogeral.uc.pt/handle/10316/11084

Pureza, J. M. (2019) 'Quem é o interesse nacional?', *Le Monde Diplomatique*, Portuguese Edition 2019 (2), pp. 8–9.

Quijano, A. (1988) *Modernidad, Identidad y Utopía en América Latina*. Lima: Ediciones Sociedad y Política.

Raimundo, A. (2019) 'Política Externa Portuguesa e África: A necessidade de um olhar renovado', in Raimundo, A. (ed.) *Política Externa Portuguesa e África: Tendências e Temas Contemporâneos*. Lisbon: Centro de Estudos Internacionais-IUL, pp. 13–28.

Rato, V. (2008) 'A Revolução de Abril na Política Externa', in Almeida, J. and Ramos, R. (eds.) *Revoluções, Política Externa e Política de Defesa em Portugal: Séc. XIX-XX*. Lisbon: Edições Cosmos and IDN, pp. 195–222.

Reis, B. C. and Oliveira, P. A. (2018) 'The Power and Limits of Cultural Myths in Portugal's Search for a Post-Imperial Role', *The International History Review* 40 (3), pp. 631–653.

Rezola, M. I. (2016) 'Elementos para uma Política Externa do Portugal Democrático. O Legado de Medeiros Ferreira', *Relações Internacionais* 2016 (49), pp. 27–45.

Sá, T. M. (2016) *Política Externa Portuguesa*. Lisbon: Fundação Francisco Manuel dos Santos.

Santos, B. S. (2019) *O Fim do Império Cognitivo: A Afirmação das Epistemologias do Sul*. Coimbra: Almedina.

Seabra, P. (2019) 'Um produto de tempos passados? Portugal e África no domínio político-diplomático', in Raimundo, A. (ed.) *Política Externa Portuguesa e África: Tendências e Temas Contemporâneos*. Lisbon: Centro de Estudos Internacionais-IUL, pp. 73–99.

Sidaway, J. and Power, M. (2005) "'The Tears of Portugal': Empire, Identity, 'Race', and Destiny in Portuguese Geopolitical Narratives', *Environment and Planning D: Society and Space* 23 (4), pp. 527–554.

Silva, A. S. (2018) *Argumentos Necessários. Contributos Para a Política Europeia e Externa de Portugal*. Lisbon: Tinta da China and Instituto Diplomático MNE.

Silva, A. S. (2020) *Evoluir. Novos Contributos Para a Política Europeia e Externa de Portugal*. Lisbon: Tinta da China and Instituto Diplomático MNE.

Smith, S. (2004) 'Singing Our World into Existence: International Relations Theory and September 11', *International Studies Quarterly* 48 (3), pp. 499–515.

Smith, S. (2001) 'Foreign Policy Is What States Make of It: Social Construction and International Relations Theory', in Kubálková, V. (ed.) *Foreign Policy in a Constructed World*. Armonk, NY and London: Sharpe, pp. 38–55.

Souza, L. M. T. M. and Guilherme, M. (2019) *Glocal Languages and Critical Intercultural Awareness*. New York: Routledge.

Temperley, A. (2013) 'Ideas and Materials in IR', *e-IR* 3 July, viewed 25 November, Ideas and Materials in IR (https://www.e-ir.info/2013/07/03/ideas-and-materials-in-ir/)

Teixeira, N. S. (2010) 'Breve Ensaio Sobre a Política Externa Portuguesa', *Relações Internacionais* 2010 (28), pp. 51–60.

Telo, A. J. (2000) 'As relações externas da transição para a democracia', *Janus: Anuário de Relações Internacionais 1999/2000*, viewed 2 December 2021, https://www.janusonline.pt/arquivo/1999_2000/1999_2000_1_40.html

Torfing, J. (2005) 'Discourse Theory: Achievements, Arguments, and Challenges', in Howarth, D. and Torfing, J. (eds.) *Discourse Theory in European Politics*. Houndmills, UK and New York: Palgrave Macmillan, pp. 1–32.

Vasconcelos, A. (1991) 'Conclusion', in Maxwell, K. (ed.) Portuguese Defense and Foreign Policy Since Democratization. Camões Center Special Report No. 3, New York: Camões Center, pp. 80–92.

Vitorino, A. (2000) 'Política e Estratégia Nacionais Perante um Mundo em Globalização', in Teixeira, N. S., Rodrigues, J. C. and Nunes, I. F., *O Interesse Nacional e a Globalização*. Lisbon: Instituto de Defesa Nacional, pp. 142–157.

Wheeler, N. J. and Dunne, T. (2004) *Moral Britannia? Evaluating the Ethical Dimension in Labour's Foreign Policy*. London: Foreign Policy Centre.

Williams, P. (2002) 'The Rise and Fall of the "Ethical Dimension"', *Cambridge Review of International Affairs* 2002 (15), pp. 53–63.

Portugal and China Geopolitics: Avenues to Cooperation

Carmen Amado Mendes and *Xuheng Wang*

Acronym List

ANACOM	Autoridade Nacional de Comunicações
AUKUS	The trilateral security pact between Australia, the United Kingdom and the United States
BRI	"Belt and Road" Initiative
CPLP	Community of Portuguese Language Countries
CPTPP	Comprehensive and Progressive Agreement for Trans-Pacific Partnership
CCP	Chinese Communist Party
GDP	Gross domestic product
IMF	International Monetary Fund
INE	Instituto Nacional de Estatística

C. A. Mendes (✉)
Macau Scientific and Cultural Centre, Lisbon, Portugal
e-mail: carmen.mendes@fe.uc.pt

X. Wang
University of Coimbra, Coimbra, Portugal
e-mail: carol_wxh@foxmail.com

P. A. B. Duarte et al. (eds.), *Portugal and the Lusophone World*,
https://doi.org/10.1007/978-981-99-0455-6_8

NATO	North Atlantic Treaty Organization
OBOR	One Belt One Road
OECD	Organization for Economic Co-operation and Development

Introduction

When the US military evacuated from Afghanistan in 2021, international politics entered a new and complex stage of development. At the same time, concerns in the post-pandemic era as to how best to revive weakened economies emerged as a critical issue, and the future promises tremendous changes in the globalized world (Apolo and Jesus 2020). This chapter focuses on Portugal and the unique affiliation of nations spreading over three continents to which this EU-member state belongs, and their possible roles in China's geopolitical strategy. Portugal occupies an important geostrategic position. While the country's continental territory may be limited, it nevertheless possesses vast maritime and air territories (Correia 2002). Considered from a narrow perspective, Portugal is situated on the Atlantic seacoast of Europe, but when viewed in a global context it occupies a mid-point between Europe and the Americas, and between Europe and Africa, and is a hub for many important routes. These potential geographical advantages can play a significant role for Portugal in rebuilding its economy in the post-pandemic era. However, Portugal faces the predicament of being in need of considerable foreign investment.

Portugal's geographical situation cannot be considered without also reflecting upon Portugal's unique and abiding close relations with the Community of Portuguese Language Countries (CPLP), also known as the Portuguese-speaking world, or Lusophone world, that was founded in 1996. The nine members of the CPLP are, in alphabetical order, Angola, Brazil, Cap Verde, East Timor, Equatorial Guinea, Guinea-Bissau, Mozambique, Portugal, and São Tomé & Príncipe. In 2006 Macau was invited to request Associate Observer status, but a request has not yet been formalized by the Chinese government. There are furthermore twenty-seven countries that have been accorded Associate Observer status since 2006, including four African nations (Ivory Coast, Mauritius, Namibia, and Senegal), two Asian nations (India and Japan), and as of 2021 the United States of America. Interest in obtaining Associate Observer status at the CPLP is strong, and the organization may thus be understood to be viewed as having real global significance.

Issues faced by Portugal and the CPLP are similar to those faced by countries participating in the BRI. Investment, structural development, resource management, and global inter-connectivity are the paramount concerns. The significant scope of China's investment in the "Belt and Road" Initiative (BRI), has been the cause of extensive debate, and many voices have been raised advancing pros and cons, not least from China itself. As the geopolitical field may undergo a transformation, originating from this non-Western initiative, scholars in the field of geopolitics have called for more attention to be paid to non-Western geopolitical theories (Dodds 2001). With the ongoing implementation of the BRI, intensive discussions about China's geopolitical ambitions have been stimulated (W. Liu 2021), and the majority of Western authors view the BRI as China's geopolitical project, or at least a process leading towards a change in the global geopolitical landscape (Blanchard and Flint 2017; Flint and Zhu 2019; Heiduk and Sakaki 2019).

China has endeavoured to develop strong strategic links with Portugal and the Lusophone world. The importance of China's strategy towards the Lusophone world as an association, rather than through the one-to-one relations that China prefers, deserves attention. It is important to identify the economic issues that are increasingly important in the foreign policy strategies and so-called "economic diplomacy" of all the involved countries (Sá 2016, p. 65). How Portugal specifically defines its own sustainable identity affects its foreign policy. As with the rest of the world, Portugal's economic recovery is inseparable from its successful control of the COVID-19 pandemic, and the development of digitization and information technology can become a key development direction in the future. In 2021 there were Chinese commentators who held that cooperation between Portugal and China should be strengthened (*People's Daily* 2021–05–26, 2021–12–21), and that the Portuguese government should actively participate in multilateral financial institutions, but other voices warned that care had to be taken to avoid a fiscal crisis caused by excessive borrowing. At the same time, there was a high degree of consensus that Portugal should maintain and strengthen multilateral cooperation with the Lusophone world to combat the economic influence of the pandemic.

Economies After the Pandemic

The impact of the pandemic on Portugal and China may be different in scale, but essentially has wrought great changes in both countries, despite the fact that the Chinese economy was significantly more robust that the Portuguese. The pandemic has demonstrated the dramatic impact that urgent public health crises have on the globalized economy. Governments around the world have prepared emergency plans and aid plans to maintain their economic development (Fernandes 2020). China has deployed, and continues to deploy, a range of large-scale and severe blockades to control the health crisis. The Chinese government still finds itself forced to adopt strict restrictive measures in various regions, often at very short notice. One example will suffice. In September 2021 there were major lockdowns in Xiamen, Quanzhou, and Putian City in Fujian province, and simultaneously in Harbin in Heilongjiang province. All businesses were closed, travel severely restricted, and large-scale biochemical sterilization measures were taken (South China Morning Post, 28–09–2021). The steps taken by the Chinese authorities represent one approach, but many other countries have not followed the path taken by China, in attempting repeatedly to suppress the disease totally. In contrast to China's stringent restrictions, some smaller countries have successively, and successfully, announced a lifting of restrictions. Geir Bukholm of the Norwegian Institute of Public Health stated in 2021 that Norway had entered the next stage of the pandemic, and that "the new Corona can be treated as an ordinary seasonal respiratory disease, just like influenza and RS virus" (Fausko and Holmes 2021; Göteborgs-Posten 2021). Whether this optimism will be found to have been premature remains a matter of debate, and observation. This shows that in the post-pandemic era, countries may be expected to adhere to one of two strategies towards COVID-19 and its mutant forms. The first is to work towards the eradication of the virus, like China, Australia and New Zealand. The second is to treat the virus as if it were a form of virulent flu, and through the use of widespread vaccination, try to achieve a form of coexistence with the virus.

China's rigorous and restrictive quarantine measures have led to a reduction in consumer spending and major interruptions in production. Many small businesses and tourism companies have declared bankruptcy. According to data published by the *Economist* on March 16, 2020, five million people lost their employment in China in January and February that year, and this number is likely to exceed nine million (Economist Intelligence Unit 2020). Where scholars for several years have compared the slow-developing west with the economically vibrant east, and believed that the pandemic would also play a role in accelerating the shift of the global balance of power from west to east, recent news from China regarding power shortages, production slow-downs and stoppages, and lay-offs, coupled with the potential fall-out of the property development debt-repayment crisis, may render the optimism slightly premature. Indeed, the new question is whether we may expect the impact of the pandemic to have a sufficiently negative effect on Chinese production to slow global recovery.

There remain concerns that negative economic impact of the pandemic on the economies of the United States and the EU may be long-lasting. The unconventional fiscal and monetary measures adopted by many countries to support their businesses and households are considered to "be hard to reverse" (Economist Intelligence Unit 2020). In 2020 the view was that China and other fast-growing economies in Asia could experience a faster recovery, based on their fundamental advantages in strong investment, innovation, and productivity growth (Economist Intelligence Unit 2020), and that the pandemic would accelerate the shift of the economic centre of gravity and tilt the balance of power towards China and Asia (Bahi 2021). However, the above-mentioned recent crises, combined with a global shortage of computer chips have hit the Chinese production industries hard. China has acted tactically by seeking membership in the Comprehensive and Progressive Agreement for Trans-Pacific Partnership (CPTPP), imprudently declined by the Trump regime, but has been noticeably aggravated by the Australian, UK and US military pact (AUKUS) that once again brought to the fore China's fear of encirclement by superior naval forces. With global maritime transportation the key feature of the BRI, or the Maritime Silk Road as it is often referred to, and Eurasian rail transport an almost forgotten relic of the earlier OBOR, maritime issues are central to China's global strategic planning.

The pandemic has damaged many pillar industries in Portugal, and there is evidence that consumer discretionary spending has suffered an expected collapse. However, the consequences of the pandemic were not evenly distributed across the Portuguese economy. Problems were particularly serious in the tourism and service-oriented industries. While this was not unique to Portugal, from airlines to cruise lines, from casinos to hotels, the global tourism industry in general faced a catastrophic reduction in its activities of more than 90% (Fernandes 2020). The dependence of the Portuguese economy is well-known, and in 2019 tourism revenue accounted for almost 9% of the GDP. The global decline in tourism caused by the pandemic has obviously had a greater impact on Portugal than on countries more focused on production industries, and pessimistic predictions have been made that most of the lost output for the service-oriented economy will never recover (Fernandes 2020). According to survey data, the number of non-resident tourists to Portugal was expected to reach only 6.5 million in 2020, a decrease of 73.7% from 2019 (an increase of 7.9% in 2019) (INE 2020). According to the *Instituto Nacional de Estatística (INE)*, in 2021 the decline continued, with overnight stays of non-resident tourists decreasing 50.8% in the first half of the year, measured in year-on-year terms (*The Portugal News* 30.07.2021c).

What is clear is that the impact on Portugal's GDP and employment will be viewed as having been somewhere between a natural disaster and an economic recession. After a disaster, as long as sufficient funds are available, reconstruction will often bring economic growth, but when an economy goes into decline, recovery will take much longer. Considering the impact of isolation and the decline in trade and tourism, Portugal will still face severe challenges. The unemployment rate has risen, and in order to alleviate the crisis, budget deficits and public debt have also risen (Goulart 2020).

Portugal in the Post-Pandemic Global Environment

To fully comprehend the situation, it is necessary to consider Portugal's recent history, and specifically the role of the Azores in relation to current developments. From 1974 to 1999, after the disintegration of Portugal's multi-continental country, it was reduced to a nation possessing two island groups (the Azores and Madeira) lying off its coast in the Atlantic Ocean. This lead Portugal to completely reorient its national security policy (or geopolitical design), from being maritime-oriented to land-centric, and to focusing on telecommunications, and concentrating on its political position within the European Union (Morgado 2021). However, Portugal's maritime territory remains a singular advantage in a new and reformatted political structure. Portuguese foreign policy today is not only the result of its historical experience, but also the result of the tradition formed through it, and the power distribution that has been formed successively during its strategic participation in the international system. Portugal is a member of a number of important organizations, such as the European Union, NATO, the United Nations, and the CPLP (Adhitama 2019). These international organizations have not only shaped Portugal's current strategy, but also shaped Portugal's geopolitical views and perspectives. At present, it is difficult for the state to act as a single actor because it has become impossible for it to separate itself from these organizations.

The Azores and Technology

From the perspective of the United States, Portugal stands at the gateway to Europe. The Portuguese islands in the Atlantic Ocean are regarded as the European throat in maritime terms, and for air navigation. Consequently, the Azores located mid-way between the United States and Europe is the site of a major NATO air base (Morgado 2021). One key military facility of concern for the United States in the Air Force Base Lajes Field on Terceira Island in the Azores. From the First World War onwards to the contemporary ongoing war on terrorism, the aircraft and warships stationed by the US military in the Azores have played an indispensable role (Kochis 2020). The Azores constitutes a valuable communications hub and fuel depot (Amaral 2014), increasing the adaptability of US military planners, and enabling the United States to monitor maritime routes in the mid-Atlantic. Strategic considerations have consequently become a serious obstacle to any massive Chinese investment. While Lajes Field remains an important part of the extended frontier deployment of the United States, as far as Portugal is concerned the significance of the Azores seems to have become somewhat more oriented towards research and investment. In 2016, the Prime Minister of Portugal opened the door for China to increase its footprint in the Azores in the name of scientific research. He said: "Currently, the military use of US bases is not under consideration, and the EU research institute, the American research institute and the Chinese research institute are reusing the infrastructure for scientific research purposes" (Shi and Engle 2016).

Over the past ten years, Chinese officials have visited the Azores repeatedly. In June 2012, when Wen Jiabao, the then Premier of the State Council of China, returned to China from Chile, he made a short stop on Terceira Island. The visit included a delegation of more than one hundred

Chinese officials (Chang 2012). In July 2014, the General Secretary of the CCP Xi Jinping also made a short stop on Terceira Island on his return from Chile (Ames 2016), and in September 2016, Chinese Premier Li Keqiang made a two-day "technical stay" on Terceira Island after visiting Cuba. Before Premier Li's visit, twenty Chinese officials stayed in the Azores for a week, laying the foundation for this visit (Kates 2017). These repeated visits by the highest echelons of the Chinese leadership signify clearly that the Azores is of more than mere ephemeral interest to China—refuelling mid-Atlantic has not been a necessity for trans-Atlantic flights for many decades.

Whether it comes with a change in Portugal's attitude, or simply as a space that the United States is willing to abandon, any possibility to gain even an apparently insignificant and insubstantial presence on the Azores will be seen as a valuable opportunity by the Chinese leadership for a possible geostrategic advantage. As Michael Rubin (2015) pointed out regarding the advantage to be gained by a presence in the Azores, "Chinese aircraft can patrol the northern and central Atlantic, thereby cutting off air and sea traffic between the United States and Europe. Beijing can also deny access to the nearby Mediterranean. China can target the continental United States. Lajes is less than 2300 miles (or 3700 kilometres) from New York, which is shorter than the distance between Pearl Harbor and Los Angeles".

China's interest in the Azores does not only lie in its uniquely important geographical location, but also in its accompanying technical resources. In November 2018, Khalip (2018), the current Portuguese Minister for Science, Technology and Higher Education announced cooperation with China to develop micro-satellites. The Azores constitute the core of Portugal's space programme. The Portuguese Aerospace Agency, established in March 2019, has its headquarters on the island of Santa Maria in the Azores. Heitor also commented that the Azores has a particularly appropriate geographical and strategic location, and that the installation and operation of space infrastructure for launching satellites from the Azores can be a topic to be considered (Weitering 2019).

For Portugal, the important geographic and military position of the Azores brings considerable geopolitical advantages to it, and secures it a place in the process of maintaining relations both with the United States and China. For China, the Azores represents considerable opportunities, but also challenges. The infrastructure of scientific research and the accompanying technological value could have a great impact on the development of China's aerospace technology. But the similar emphasis that the United States attaches to this group of islands can also bring potential factors that seriously aggravate tensions between China and the United States. As Sino-US relations involve all aspects of politics and economy, the trade conflicts have exacerbated the tension between the two countries. It is not yet clear how China's interest in the Azores and possible future actions could, or will, trigger a reaction from the United States. But there is no doubt that the importance the United States attaches to the Azores will be one of the threats facing China, and that the interest of the United States in retaining and developing its relations with Portugal is indisputable.

However, it is important to note that technical cooperation has often occupied an important position in relations between Portugal and China, and technical cooperation between Portugal and China extends beyond the space programme in the Azores. As early as 1993, Portugal and China signed an intergovernmental science and technology cooperation agreement. Over the following years, scientific and technological cooperation between the two countries never came to a standstill. On October 31, 2018, a Sino-Portuguese Science and Technology Innovation Cooperation Seminar was held in Shanghai, at which Professor Paulo Ferrão, at that time Chairman of the Portuguese Science and Technology Foundation, expressed his vision of possible cooperation with China in the fields of renewable energy, biology, agriculture, ocean, and new materials (Shanghai Government 2018).

In 2016, Portuguese Prime Minister Antonio Costa said in an interview that Huawei had invested in technology and infrastructure in Portugal and established a technological innovation centre. In 2019, Huawei announced that it planned to open a 4G and 5G network technical support centre in Lisbon, which would be Huawei's first network technical support centre in Europe (Jornal de Negócios 2019). Both the Portuguese telecommunications operator NOS and Altice began cooperating with Huawei to jointly develop 5G network technology. On October 23, 2019, NOS announced that it had cooperated with Huawei to build the country's first 5G network in Matosinhos, located in northern Portugal (Jornal de Negócios 2019). NOS officially put into use the 5G network, providing a research base for 5G technology applications for local governments, enterprises, and research institutions, thereby establishing NOS at the forefront in 5G technology applications, and in a leading position in innovations such as smart cities. This seemed, at the time, to demonstrate a strong trend in the development of cooperation between China and Portugal in the use of Huawei technology.

However, this potential long-term development was suddenly interrupted. On May 15, 2020, the US Department of Commerce issued an announcement that it planned to restrict Huawei's ability to use US technology and software to design and manufacture semiconductors outside the United States (An 2020). Since 2018, media reports concerning potential national security threats from Chinese telecom suppliers have spread globally. The United States decided to mount a global effort to block Huawei's 5G network plans. The prohibition of US companies from supplying hardware and software to Huawei has severely weakened Huawei (Lysne et al. 2019), and as of July 2021 it is no longer one of the top smartphone producers.

The potential threats that Huawei claimed to pose were related to national security, since the company could harm individual countries through conducting espionage, and that the company entertained strategic interests. The core of these two lines of thinking is based on the same assumption—private enterprises are and will increasingly become tools used by the state to exercise power (Farrell & Newman 2019). In the digital age, as companies control and manage big data streams that are vital to society, the control of these companies can in turn become an important resource of power. Huawei's dominance in the 5G network and in the entire global communications infrastructure presented an important strategic advantage. Banning any supplier from providing equipment to Huawei, as the United States did, poses a clear political risk to other countries, and is particularly harmful to smaller countries with a high degree of dependence on foreign technology. This is a sensitive political decision, that transcends simple trade interests, and may well have consequences. Any country that chooses to prohibit Huawei from entering its 5G network risks alienating China (Lysne et al. 2019).

For Portugal, the situation is even more complicated. On July 30, 2020, the three operators NOS, Vodafone and Altice that dominate Portuguese mobile communications announced that although the Portuguese government had not issued any ban, they would cease using Huawei technology in the construction of the 5G core network. The services of these three operators cover almost all mobile communication users in Portugal (Wen and Zhao 2020). A NOS spokesperson stated that the company will select the "best partner" for each network component, but that it will "not use Huawei equipment" in the core network. A spokesperson for the Portuguese branch of Vodafone said that the parent company of Vodafone has announced that it will not use Huawei equipment in the core network, and "therefore, the Portuguese branch of Vodafone will not be an exception". The spokesperson said that Vodafone Portugal will cooperate with Ericsson for 5G network construction (Marcela 2020a).

Altice Portugal CEO Alexandre Fonseca made a similar statement as early as March of the same year, saying that the company would not include Huawei in the core network construction. Altice said at this time that the company's position will not change. After learning of the statements of the three operators, the Portuguese Minister of Planning and Infrastructure Nuno Santos responded quickly, stating that the matter has nothing to do with the Portuguese government's choice, or any mandatory requirements. In this matter, the Portuguese government has always been in line with EU directives (Reuters 2020). According to a news release on September 20, 2021, the Portuguese National Communications Authority has approved 5G technology trials in the 1800 MHz frequency band (ANACOM 2020). This should show that the three operators in Portugal are actually ready to commence 5G, but it has been claimed that they are not (Kang 2021). With the United States successfully restricting Huawei's hardware facilities, if Huawei cannot develop its own research and development, or obtain technical support to solve the problem elsewhere, the company's market share and competitiveness will continue to decline, and its future is placed at risk.

From a Portuguese perspective, reducing or ceasing cooperation with Huawei may help it to maintain its good relations with the United States, but the ban on Huawei could also have an impact on the Portuguese economy. The Portuguese financial media source *Dinheiro Vivo* quoted a report from the University of Oxford that 5G networks and related services have promoted Portuguese economic growth and brought with them 127,000 jobs. If Huawei's 5G network is excluded, depending on the cost situation, at most more than one million users may not be able to use the 5G network before 2023. In addition to 5G deployment delays caused by excluding Huawei, economic losses may also occur for Portugal, potentially amounting to between 100 million and over one billion euros in GDP growth by 2035, and an additional 30–95 million euros per year for the next ten years, in infrastructure costs (Marcela 2020b). Whether Portugal will be able to sustain such losses to its post-pandemic economy will certainly result in further discussions on the improvement of the Portuguese economy after the pandemic.

Tourism

The pandemic has had a significant effect on China's economic growth. The first quarter for 2021 contracted by 6.8% year-on-year. This is the worst performance of the Chinese economy since the establishment of the national accounting system in 1992 (K. Liu 2021). The most severely affected were the accommodation and catering industries, which contracted by 35.3%, followed by wholesale and retail industries. There are widespread reports that the impact on the hospitality industry has been devastating. According to the latest data for the Dragon Boat Festival from June 25 to 27, 2020, China's national tourism revenue has fallen by 68.8% year-on-year (People.com.cn 2020). China's ability to prevent and control the pandemic is seen as the biggest driving force for economic recovery, but the continuance of outbreaks in different parts of the country remain a significant worry. Claims were made by the National Bureau of Statistics of China in late March 2021, that the spread of the pandemic in China was basically halted, have proven to be premature. On a positive note, the Chinese GDP grew by 3.2% in the second quarter, turning from negative to positive. However, as noted above, a fresh outbreak in September 2021 showed that the struggle to control the disease has not achieved been entirely successful.

The economic situation in Portugal also improved in the first half of 2021. According to Eurostat, Portugal's gross domestic product (GDP) in the second quarter of 2021 increased by 4.9% compared with the previous quarter, making it the EU country with the second highest growth rate. In addition, the GDP of the Eurozone in the second quarter of 2021 increased by 14.3% compared with the same period in 2020, while that of the 27 EU countries was 13.8% (OECD 2021). The relaxation of border restrictions led the Portuguese government to express some optimism about the tourism industry. Rita Marques, Secretary of State for Tourism, stated that the "best estimate" of the national tourism industry by the end of 2021 pointed to a "20–30% increase" compared to 2020 (The Portugal News 2021b). For example, Portugal's popular tourist city, Madeira, showed good recovery in the summer of 2021 with 90% of hotels operating and "high occupancy rates" (The Portugal News 2021a). Since visitors to Portugal remain mainly EU citizens, the recovery of Portugal's tourism industry depends on EU pandemic control and corresponding policies. Chinese tourism to Portugal has hitherto been relatively negligible, and even once policies of "vaccine mutual recognition" and "international travel health certificate" have been implemented, Chinese tourists to Portugal can be predicted still to only visit Lisbon (INE 2020).

Investment in Energy

Chinese direct investment abroad has become, since WTO entry in 2001, a normal activity when it participates in the global economy (Fernandes 2021), and Chinese investment has become noticeably important for Portugal. As of 2018, China's investment in Portugal has exceeded 9 billion euros, making it the fifth largest country for Chinese investment destinations in Europe (Dinheiro 2019). The energy, power, finance, insurance and real estate sectors are China's main investment areas in Portugal. By way of comparison, as of 2019, Portugal's direct investment in China was only US$220 million. While this imbalance may appear predictable, given China's rapid economic growth, it is nevertheless remarkable and a budding source of concern. The result has been that in a relatively short period of time, a number of large Portuguese companies operating in strategic and sensitive industries have become partially or fully owned by Chinese companies. The situation is perhaps most noticeable in Chinese shareholding in Portuguese energy companies, where major investments are owned, for example, by two fully state-owned Chinese companies, namely China Three Gorges (Europe), S.A., and Orise, S.a.r.l., in which in each case a total of 28.25% of voting rights are directly attributable to the PRC (Fernandes 2021).

The background to this state of affairs lies in the austerity policy and extensive privatization plan that were implemented in 2011 to alleviate financial and economic crises in Portugal. The country received financial assistance and strict supervision from the International Monetary Fund, the European Commission and the European Central Bank. Chinese investors viewed this development as an opportunity to take advantage of the vulnerability of the Portuguese economy, as has also happened in other parts of Southern and Eastern Europe (J. P. T. Fernandes 2021).

Academic opinion holds that the national strategic sector, i.e. the sector where the Portuguese government plays a role, and the non-strategic sector operating in accordance with the market economy have not yet reached an agreement on energy (Fernandes 2021). There is also confusion between investment by foreign private enterprises and investment by government enterprises. This leads to a very important question as to whether the transfer of energy services and power networks related to national security to companies controlled by the Chinese government will result in serious security risks for Portugal.

From a geopolitical point of view, the autonomy of the energy sector and energy-related facilities can almost undoubtedly be considered as strategic and critical in a national security crisis (IMF 2019). Therefore, the general consensus is that the Portuguese government's views on the energy sector do not seem to be consistent. Should the state control and play a role in these sectors, or let these sectors operate in accordance with the logic of the market and the private economy? Another very important point is that China Three Gorges is not the same as a private company with foreign direct investment in the general sense. China Three Gorges is owned by the Chinese government. Is it really irrelevant to Portugal whether a large company that is important in terms of public service and energy security is directly owned by a country that is neither a member of the European Union, nor a political or military ally? Is the energy sector a potential problem for Portugal? It can be considered as a potential threat, but this threat largely depends on the relationship between China and Portugal.

Here we have to mention the United States. Portugal's risky balance between China and the United States is not less difficult than walking a tightrope stretched between two cliffs. On the one hand, the Azores is a key military base in the Atlantic Ocean. On the other hand, the energy sector that the country relies on to maintain normal operations is owned to a great extent by other nations.

Economic and commercial relations between Portugal and China cannot be separated from the current international environment. It is unrealistic to think that a small country has the ability and means to control international tensions. Even if a pessimistic view of reality is set aside, and the complex confrontation between the United States and China regarded as a "Thucydides trap" (Allison 2017), preventive measures will be necessary both at present and in the future. It is worth thinking about the strategic dilemmas that the EU and Portugal may face in the near future (Teixeira 2019). The new world order may not be easy for Europe to negotiate, and the EU is likely to become one of the victims of the competition that will arise. The United States and China will eventually force the EU to make a choice. This is the choice that Europeans will be unwilling to make, and delays may be predicted. Because both of the nations involved have substantial financial interests, any choice will mean losing something, but it is worth noting that the choice will ultimately transcend economics, and become a political issue.

The Lusophone World

Aside from the problems between the United States and China, we cannot omit consideration of the rest of the world, and in this chapter specifically the CPLP. As an important member of the CPLP, Portugal has strengthened its cooperation with the Lusophone world to jointly respond to the new world crisis. At present, China's influence in Lusophone Africa is significant. At the multilateral level, the Forum on China–Africa Cooperation, or FOCAC, which encompasses almost the entire African continent, did not pay special attention to Lusophone Africa, as suggested by the sixth ministerial meeting held in Johannesburg in 2015. However, the Forum for Economic and Trade Cooperation between China and the Portuguese-speaking Countries (also known as the "Macau Forum") took place in Beijing where its permanent secretariat is located in a Special Administrative Region of China. The Forum includeded all the Portuguese-speaking countries (Mendes 2017). China's main investment in Lusophone Africa has focused on the construction of infrastructure, such as commercial facilities, roads, airports, sewage treatment plants, etc. It also includes the establishment of deep-water ports to promote oil exports and maritime trade (Rotberg 2013). In this way, China's investments in Lusophone Africa are entirely the same as the sort of investments that occur in the BRI. The relationship between China and the two largest Portuguese-speaking African countries, Angola and Mozambique, focuses on China's energy security needs, and principally consists of natural resource extraction, without substantial industrial development in either country. In Mozambique, if we consider the value of loans, infrastructure projects and assistance provided through FOCAC, China is by far the most important Asian partner for the country. In addition to its principal interests in natural gas and coal, China is also interested in fisheries, agriculture, and timber, while building public infrastructure and exporting manufactured goods. With its development work in Luanda, Beijing has established its strongest relationship with an African nation. The framework is a credit line negotiated with post-war Angola, which desperately needs reconstruction, and is very similar to countless BRI projects. Investment by Chinese state-owned enterprises is claimed to be beneficial to infrastructure, transportation, and the oil and diamond sectors, while funds from credit lines are used for technical and social cooperation, including the construction of schools and medical facilities, public utility services such as water supply and sanitation, and human resource development training scheme (Kiala and Ngwenya 2011). However, as Maria Patricia Bejarano has noted, the "Angola Mode", whereby repayments for infrastructure projects or loans are repaid with natural resources, appears to have become a real burden for Angola, with Angola "trying to end this scheme as two-fifths of its external debt exists in the form of oil-backed loans owed to China", (Bejarano, 2020). Angola has certainly obtained much-needed infrastructure construction, but trade deals have brought with them corruption and have had "negligible impacts on poverty reduction" (Oya & Schaefer, 2019).

Conclusion

A degree of cooperation between Portugal and China would appear to be indispensable in the current state of affairs. But as mentioned previously with regard to energy investment, this involves not only commercial issues, but also political and national security issues. As the main shareholders of Portuguese energy companies, it is necessary to consider whether Chinese companies may pose any threat to Portuguese energy supplies, due to the current changing international situation. This is not to suggest that Portugal should restrict cooperation with China in this area, but rather contemplate means to avoid over-reliance on foreign investment. The same consideration holds true for BRI-related investments and loans. Over-dependence on one major financial source can result in complications. The Portuguese government needs to prevent excessive borrowing that may cause government financial deficits, which will affect the economic recovery after the pandemic has been brought under control. The state of technical cooperation between Portugal and China is still in the sway. However, restrictions on Huawei's 5G facilities have seen an impact on the relationship between China and Portugal. China's continued strong interest in gaining a footprint in the Azores, may alarm the United States and lead it to reinforce its wariness regarding China's activities in various fields in Portugal. The Portuguese government needs to be vigilant to avoid becoming drawn, against its will, into a dispute that might affect Portugal's own positive development. As an important member of the CPLP, Portugal might be prudent if it were able to encourage the members of the CPLP to enhance their mutual cooperation, and maintain a positive level of economic development through closer cooperation. In the same way, the problems faced by other Lusophone countries during and after the pandemic, or arising from financial risks faced by cooperation projects with China should be treated as being worthy of the Portuguese government's close attention.

Bibliography

Adhitama, M. R. (2019). Geopolitics of Portugal in Atlantic Sea. *IPTEK Journal of Proceedings Series*, *0*(6), 48. https://doi.org/10.12962/j23546026.y2019i6.6337

Allison, G. (2017). *Destined for war: Can America and China escape Thucydides's trap?* Boston, MA: Houghton Mifflin Harcourt.

Amaral, R. F. (2014). *U.S.–Portuguese relations and Lajes air field base.*

Ames, P. (2016). China's Atlantic stopover worries Washington. Retrieved from https://www.politico.eu/article/chinas-atlantic-stopover-terceira-worries-washington-li-keqiang-united-states/

An, M. (2020). The United States completely contained Huawei, the latest Huawei's response. Retrieved from https://news.stcn.com/sd/202005/t20200516_1808752.html

ANACOM. (2020). Auction of 5G and other relevant bands. Retrieved from https://anacom.pt/render.jsp?categoryId=416723

Apolo, I., & Jesus, L. (2020). The Strategic importance of Portugal for the European Union: The Portuguese Geopolitics towards the Atlantic South The Strategic importance of Portugal for the European Union : The Portuguese Geopolitics towards the Atlantic South.

Bahi, R. (2021). The geopolitics of COVID-19: US-China rivalry and the imminent Kindleberger trap. *Review of Economics and Political Science*, *6*(1), 76–94. https://doi.org/10.1108/reps-10-2020-0153

Bejarano, M. P. (2020). On the contentious subject of Chinese investment in Africa. Retrieved from https://thesecuritydistillery.org/all-articles/on-the-contentious-subject-of-chinese-investment-in-africa

Blanchard, J. M. F., & Flint, C. (2017). The geopolitics of China's maritime silk road initiative. *Geopolitics*, *22*(2), 223–245. https://doi.org/10.1080/14650045.2017.1291503

Chang, G. G. (2012). Red flag over the Atlantic. Retrieved from https://www.nationalreview.com/2012/11/red-flag-over-atlantic-gordon-g-chang/

Correia, P. P. (2002). Análise geoestratégica de Portugal. *Nação e Defesa.*

de Sá, T. M. (2016). *Política externa portuguesa.* Fundação Francisco Manuel dos Santos.

Dinheiro, V. (2019). Investimento chinês em Portugal superou os 9 mil milhões em 2018. Retrieved from https://www.dinheirovivo.pt/economia/investimento-chines-em-portugal-superou-os-9-mil-milhoes-em-2018-12805714.html

Dodds, K. (2001). Political geography III: Critical geopolitics after ten years. *Progress in Human Geography*, *25*(3), 469–484. https://doi.org/10.1191/030913201680191790

Economist Intelligence Unit. (2020). Geopolitics after Covid-19 : Is the pandemic a turning point ? 1–10.

Farrell, H., & Newman, A. L. (2019). Weaponized interdependence: How global economic networks shape state coercion. *International Security*, *44*(1), 42–79.

Fausko, L., & Holmes, M. C. S. (2021). FHI: We can now compare the coronavirus with the flu (FHI: Vi kan nå sammenligne coronaviruset med influensa). Retrieved from https://www.vg.no/nyheter/innenriks/i/ALEMnM/fhi-vi-kan-naa-sammenligne-coronaviruset-med-influensa

Fernandes, J. P. T. (2021a). Chinese economic diplomacy regarding Portugal: Promoting business or concealing geopolitical ambitions?. *International Politics*, *58*(1), 18–36.

Fernandes, J. P. T. (2021b). Siren song: Chinese economic diplomacy regarding Portugal (the case of the energy sector). *Journal of Public Affairs*, *21*(2). https://doi.org/10.1002/pa.2203

Fernandes, N. (2020). Economic effects of coronavirus outbreak (COVID-19) on the world economy Nuno Fernandes Full Professor of Finance IESE Business School Spain. *SSRN Electronic Journal, ISSN 1556–5068, Elsevier BV,* 0–29.

Flint, C., & Zhu, C. (2019). The geopolitics of connectivity, cooperation, and hegemonic competition: The Belt and Road Initiative. *Geoforum*, *99*(October 2018), 95–101. https://doi.org/10.1016/j.geoforum.2018.12.008

Göteborgs-Posten. (2021). Partying and dancing are encouraged when Norway reopens (Fest och dans uppmuntras när Norge öppnar igen).

Goulart, P. (2020). COVID and the challenges to the Portuguese economy Portugal risks a heavy toll on its economy but has shown resilience in the past (April).

Heiduk, F., & Sakaki, A. (2019). Introduction to the special issue—China's belt and road initiative: The view from East Asia. *East Asia*, *36*(2), 93–113. https://doi.org/10.1007/s12140-019-09312-y

IMF. (2019). IMF lending case study: Portugal. Retrieved from https://www.imf.org/en/Home

INE. (2020). *Tourism statistics (Estatísticas do Turismo).*

Jornal de Negócios. (2019). Matosinhos é a "primeira cidade" 5G em Portugal. Retrieved from https://www.jn.pt/economia/matosinhos-e-a-primeira-cidade-5g-em-portugal-11435892.html

Kang, Z. (2021). Portugal's self-testing of 5G means that Huawei completely missed the opportunity. Retrieved from https://new.qq.com/omn/20210921/20210921A00ZNV00.html

Kates, G. (2017). Defense dept. decision gives China chance for foothold between U.S. and Europe. Retrieved from https://www.cbsnews.com/news/azores-withdrawal-gives-china-foothold-between-us-europe/

Khalip, A. (2018). Portugal to build satellite launch pad, lab with China. Retrieved from https://www.reuters.com/article/us-portugal-websummit-space-idUSKCN1NB25K.

Kiala, C., & Ngwenya, N. (2011). *Angola's strategic co-operation with the BRIC countries. South African Foreign Policy and African Drivers Programme, South African Institute of International Affairs.*

Kochis, D. (2020). Lajes field: Why this airbase is important to US Strategic interests. *Heritage Foundation Backgrounder*, (3566), 2020–12.

Liu, K. (2021a). COVID-19 and the Chinese economy: Impacts, policy responses and implications. *International Review of Applied Economics*, *35*(2), 308–330. https://doi.org/10.1080/02692171.2021.1876641

Liu, W. (2021b). Confucian geopolitics or Chinese geopolitics? *Dialogues in Human Geography*, *11*(2), 265–269. https://doi.org/10.1177/20438206211017774

Lysne, O., Elmokashfi, A., Schia, N. N., Gjesvik, L., & Friis, K. (2019). Critical communication infrastructures and Huawei. In *TPRC47: The 47th Research Conference on Communication, Information and Internet Policy 2019.*

Marcela, A. (2020a). Altice. "Não temos Huawei no core" da rede 5G. Retrieved from https://www.dinheirovivo.pt/empresas/altice-nao-temos-huawei-no-core-da-rede-5g-12687286.html

Marcela, A. (2020b). Huawei. Exclusão da rede 5G pode ter impacto de 500 milhões no PIB nacional. Retrieved from https://www.dinheirovivo.pt/empresas/huawei-exclusao-da-rede-5g-pode-ter-impacto-de-500-milhoes-no-pib-nacional-12892919.html

Mendes, C. A. (2017). Asia in Lusophone Africa. In *Routledge handbook of Africa- Asia relations* (pp. 321–334).

Morgado, N. (2021). Portugal as an old sea power: Exploring the EU membership as geopolitical design, *8*(2), 59–73. https://doi.org/10.2307/JTMS.8.2.59

OECD. (2021). Economic forecast summary (May 2021). Retrieved from https://www.oecd.org/economy/portugal-economic-snapshot/

Oya, C., & Schaefer, F. (2019). *Chinese firms and employment dynamics in Africa: A comparative analysis*. IDCEA Research Synthesis Report, SOAS, University of London [online] Available from https://eprints.soas.ac.uk/34241/1/file141857.pdf.

People.com.cn. (2020). 端午假期旅游收入同比恢复 31.2% 节日效应明显 "Dragon boat holiday travel income recovered 31.2%" (in Chinese).

People's Daily (2021–05–26). China-Portugal ties set to help fuel East-West Cooperation (in English).

People's Daily (2021–12–21). China and Portugal are sailing toward a bluer future (in English).

Reuters. (2020). Telecomunicações portuguesas não terão Huawei nas redes core 5G. Não há "imposições" do Governo.

Rotberg, R. I. (2013). China and São Tomé. Retrieved from https://www.chinausfocus.com/foreign-policy/china-and-sao-tome

Rubin, & Michael. (2015). China may be trying to take over a critical U.S. Air Base in the Atlantic. Retrieved from https://www.businessinsider.com/china-may-be-trying-to-take-over-a-critical-us-air-base-in-the-atlantic-2015-11

Shanghai Government. (2018). The future can be expected! Sino-Portuguese scientific and technological innovation cooperation seminar held in Shanghai. Retrieved from http://stcsm.sh.gov.cn/xwzx/zt/2018pjcxlt/zxbd/20181101/0016-151726.html

Shi, T., & Engle, S. (2016). Portugal open to China investment in Azores as U.S. Sway Wanes. Retrieved from https://www.bloombergquint.com/politics/portugal-open-to-china-investment-in-azores-as-u-s-sway-wanes

Teixeira, N. S. (2019). O future da Europa. Retrieved from https://www.publico.pt/2019/05/08/mundo/opiniao/futuro-europa-1871751

The Portugal News. (2021a). Madeira tourism sector "recovering well." Retrieved from https://www.theportugalnews.com/news/2021-09-25/madeira-tourism-sector-recovering-well/62603

The Portugal News. (2021b). Tourism to grow by up to 30% in 2021. Retrieved from https://www.theportugalnews.com/news/2021-04-01/tourism-to-grow-by-up-to-30-in-2021/59060

The Portugal News. (2021c). Overnight stays of non-residents fell dramatically. Retrieved from https://www.theportugalnews.com/news/2021-07-30/overnight-stays-of-non-residents-fell-dramatically/61457.

Weitering, H. (2019). Portugal just launched a national space agency! Retrieved from https://www.space.com/portugal-launches-space-agency.html

Wen, X., & Zhao, D. (2020). Portuguese media say that rejecting Huawei's participation in 5G construction will harm the Portuguese economy. Retrieved from http://world.people.com.cn/n1/2020/0729/c1002-31801855.html

The Atlantic and the Lusophone World

China, Portugal and the Atlantic: The Shifting Geopolitics

Jorge Tavares da Silva, Paulo Afonso B. Duarte, and Rui P. Pereira

Introduction

While considerable attention has been paid to China's maritime ambitions in the conventional sea lanes of communication as well as through a potential, albeit seasonal Arctic route (Butt et al. 2020; Erickson and Wuthnow 2016), the Atlantic has been the object of scarce investigation, which is a gap that we are aware of and wish to respond to. An exception in this regard is the work of Goldstein (2017) who investigates whether China is crafting an Atlantic maritime strategy. In turn,

J. T. da Silva
University of Beira Interior, Covilhã, Portugal

P. A. B. Duarte (✉)
Lusophone University, Porto, Portugal
e-mail: duartebrardo@gmail.com; pauloduarte@eeg.uminho.pt; p5786@ulusofona.pt

R. P. Pereira
Ministério da Economia de Portugal, Lisbon, Portugal

P. A. B. Duarte
Minho University, Braga, Portugal

P. A. B. Duarte et al. (eds.), *Portugal and the Lusophone World*,
https://doi.org/10.1007/978-981-99-0455-6_9

Martinson (2019) explores China's stance as an Atlantic Naval Power, which has been further complemented by Ferreira-Pereira and Duarte's (2022) research on the relevance of the South Atlantic in China's Global Policy. This being said, when it comes to assessing Chinese interests in a specific part of the vast Atlantic, which is the Portuguese Sea, existing literature is scarce, with exceptions of the works of Duarte and Leandro (2020) or Silva and Pereira (2020). Although Portugal is a nation recognized for its relationship with the sea, after being part of the European construction process, the Atlantic option has lost some vigour. However, the political power intends to place the sea as a national goal, drawing up several official documents in order to define a strategy for the sector (Governo de Portugal 2021). This is due to the importance of the sea in the magnitude and prosperity of nations, as was defined by US strategist Alfred Mahan (1890). This author considered maritime power as a result of some strengths and factors, instruments and geographic circumstances that work together to achieve the domain of sea. For him it was essential to consider some elements: geographic position, physical configuration and territory extension; effective population to national psychology.

Drawing on the importance of the Sea both to Portugal and China, this chapter seeks to understand the shifting geopolitics in the Atlantic Ocean stemming from China's increasing interest in the Portuguese Sea. Thus, following this main goal, other secondary objectives arise, as best expressed by the following questions: What opportunities can the Portuguese Sea provide to Chinese interests? What geopolitical factors justify the Chinese presence in these waters? We shall see that the Chinese factor could bring geopolitical challenges to Portuguese Foreign Policy, as Lisbon is an important and traditional ally of both the United States (US) and NATO. The time frame that best serves this analysis is the one that follows the creation of the Belt and Road Initiative (BRI) in 2013, which includes, as we shall see, both the land and maritime corridors. Interestingly, Portugal has the perfect ingredients that China's BRI is looking for, due to its huge maritime platform as well as its geostrategic position between Europe, Africa and the Americas, together with its land connection to the rest of Europe.

We will use a qualitative analysis, based on hermeneutics, i.e. on understanding, composed both of primary sources, such as Portuguese and Chinese official sources and news agencies as well as of secondary sources drawing upon the most respected authors that have been producing knowledge on the topics that we address here, despite the fact that we believe that current literature does not yet properly address Chinese maritime initiatives in the Portuguese Sea and its inherent geopolitical contours and challenges. To achieve the above stated goals, this chapter has been structured as follows. In the first section, we will draw some considerations on the Atlantic essence of Portugal. In the second section, we will provide the reader with some background regarding the 21st Century Maritime Silk Road. The following section will address the so-called "Blue Partnership" between Portugal and China, while the last section analyses the contours and geopolitical implications of China's presence in the Portuguese Sea. The conclusion summarizes the main findings.

Portugal and the Atlantic: The Essence of a Nation

Portugal as a nation began essentially as an agricultural place, even though its lands are always bathed by the Atlantic Ocean. It was with the Aviz Dynasty (1385–1580) that this special relationship became closer and the country discovered its maritime vocation. The sea gained national interest in Portugal and from Lisbon led to the "globalization of inter-dependencies" (Moreira 2018, p. 55). Over time, Portugal gained a maritime mentality, and in the thirteenth century, it had already an intense commercial activity with northern Europe, England, Flanders and Normandy (Silva 2020). Although two ancestral traditions marked the essence of Western civilization—the Greco-Roman tradition and the Judeo-Christian tradition—we find a strong link with the maritime core (Espada 2014). The Atlantic constitutes a source of resources, a channel to transport people and goods, although potentially causing competition, threats to security and conflicts. The connection to the sea prevents Portugal's tendency from becoming a tiny state within the framework of the European Union (Moreira 2018).

The Atlantic offers to Portugal a huge central role in the relationship between Europe and the United States, but also interconnecting with other continents. It is important to remember that world trade is predominantly carried out by maritime transport, giving importance to countries with coasts and ports. In addition, the sea appears as an alternative to road transport that environmental public policies are trying to reduce. New European projects such as "motorways of the sea" are putting Portugal in an intermodal maritime-based logistic chain, in an attempt to develop a shipping arrangement in which goods are delivered directly from sender to receiver ("door-to-door service"), increasing efficiency of national ports (European Commission 2022).

In 2017, the Portuguese Ministry of the Sea outlined a strategy for increasing national port competitiveness, to be implemented within a decade (Diário da República 2017). Its main goals consisted of adapting infrastructure and equipment to increase the size of ships, demand and optimize connections to the hinterland; improving the operational conditions of the port units and creating platforms for technological acceleration and new skills in ports (ibidem).

In the report "Economic Recovery Plan" prepared by António Costa Silva (2020) for the Portuguese Government, regarding the post-pandemic context (Covid-19), the need to strengthen the national rail network in its connection to Spain, and the country's port capacity, with special emphasis on increasing the "radius of reach" to the port of Sines (Costa Silva 2020) appear:

> Exploring the maritime dimension of the country requires the reinforcement of investment in its port structures, in logistics platforms, in the expansion of quays and storage capacity, in cargo handling equipment, consolidating the country's role as a commercial and logistics platform, reinforcing its inclusion in global trade, energy, transport, technology and knowledge networks. This must be done in conjunction with the sea cluster, treating the sea as a crucial asset of the country's territory, sovereignty, economy and development.

The Portuguese port of Sines, according to the same report, should be equipped with an ore port terminal for the export of strategic mineral resources, essentially taking lithium into account. In addition, there is a need to:

> [C]onsolidation of a multipurpose national port hub that meets the demands of demand in the segments of commercial shipping, tourism, long and short-distance transport, considering ports for the integration of the logistics chains they serve, and completing them with the necessary investments. (Costa Silva 2020)

The idea of creating an industrial deployment area, concentrated around the deep-water ocean port in Sines dates back to the early 1970s, when Portugal was under the rule of Marcelo Caetano. At the time, almost half of the population was still engaged in agriculture, in a country that Silva Costa (1967) called in a small book as "macrocephalous", in a huge imbalance between Lisbon and the rest of the territory. Nowadays, port modernization in terms of digitalization, including investment in the 5G mobile communications network, is essential, with a view to gaining efficiency in processes, reducing costs and increasing competitiveness. The port of Sines currently has a weight of 1.5% in the national economy, represents 2% of employment and more than 56% of containerized cargo handled in commercial ports on the mainland. In this type of cargo, the growth of the last 15 years was reflected in the passage from 20,000 TEU, in 2004, to more than 1.75 million TEU, in 2018. It corresponds to an increase in the order of 8652.2% at an average annual rate of 37.6% (Expresso 2019). These maritime facilities were the ones that grew the most in terms of cargo handled in Europe, being also leaders in the same indicator in Portugal. Competition between ports is one of the factors that mark the dynamics of economic globalization and maritime transport, forcing Portugal to be strongly assertive in this area.

The port has no restrictions on the reception of any type of ship or cargo, a relevant factor in the context of the great international competitiveness in this area:

> [The port of Sines] has a "privileged geographical location, at the crossroads of the main commercial routes, which allow it to assert itself as the great hub of the Euro-Atlantic façade, offering regular connections to the main international consumption centers and providing companies located in its Hinterland with greater competitiveness in foreign markets". (Cacho 2020)

It is the main port on the Ibero-Atlantic front, whose geophysical characteristics have contributed to its consolidation as a national strategic asset, being, on the one hand, the main energy supply port in the country (oil and derivatives, coal and natural gas) and, on the one hand, it is already positioned as an important general/containerized cargo port with high growth potential to be an Iberian, European and world reference. It is a development hub for the region and for the country, capable of receiving oil, ore and bulk carriers. It has gained strategic relevance in view of the Atlantic valorization by the new infrastructures in Latin America. The port intends to be an Atlantic port of Europe, a fundamental link in the international logistics chains, enriched with the reinforcement of the container handling capacity of Terminal XXI (it has a storage area of 39.1 ha which makes it possible to provide a total capacity of 2100.000 TEU per year) (Cacho 2020; Porto de Sines 2022).

It is also important to mention the importance of the Azores archipelago in the Portuguese geopolitical context, reinforcing its central role in the Euro-Atlantic axis. The "Portuguese sea" has enormous energy, commercial, logistical, financial and, essentially, political potential (Lima 2016). The Chinese interest in the Azores archipelago is a proven fact, but not declared, due to the competitive environment that this country has with the United States (Rodrigues and Silva 2020). The Azores has gained relevance since Washington announced the reduction of its troops at Lajes Base (Alexender 2015). The United States has been neglecting Atlantic relations and has reinforced its presence in the Pacific. The Trump administration ended the Transatlantic Trade and Investment Partnership (TTIP) free trade project, which paradoxically promised to bring about an intensification of Euro-Atlantic trade. The possibility of underground storage of US fracking gas was open, which could serve as an alternative to European supplies of Russian gas. The war in Ukraine at the beginning of 2022, promised to reinforce this entire previous project. The apparent reduction of the United States in the Atlantic would be an opportunity for China. The archipelago with its nine islands has a privileged geographical position, which makes it immediately attractive as a manager of maritime power. The possibility of attracting Chinese companies is being discussed at the deep-water port in Vitória, on Terceira Island. Here, too, the interests shared with the United States end up hampering the progress of effective investment proposals (Silva 2020).

The national and international interest in the Atlantic has one matter that has become unavoidable to examine: the extension of the continental shelf under UN legislation. In the contemporary international-legal context, it corresponds to an opportunity that states have—in a peaceful way—to extend the area of sovereignty and jurisdiction over living and non-living resources of the bed and marine subsoil (Coelho 2017). A geological, economic, geostrategic and political wealth is available to Lisbon, to which countries, among others, such as China and the United States do not fail to pay particular attention. The Portuguese maritime space is rich in mineral resources and rare marine species, which can be used in medicine and pharmacology, which are currently included in the legal regime of the high seas. There is also a strong probability of the existence of hydrocarbons, natural gas, methane, ores in a state of high purity and hydrothermal vents (Madureira 2017). Portugal has a continental coastline of 942 square kilometres, which, together with the islands, constitutes an Exclusive Economic Zone (EEZ) with 1.72 million square kilometres (Público 2018a). This is the third largest EEZ in the European Union. In the case of enlargement of the Continental Shelf, it will increase from 18 to 40 times the land territory, which transforms 97% of Portugal into a maritime area. The maritime space resulting from the merger of the EEZ and the extension of the Continental Shelf (CP), to be approved by the UN, will be equivalent to the territory of India (Público, 2018a). It means that Portugal gains sovereign rights to prospect and exploit its natural resources beyond 200 nautical miles. In fact, the continental shelf comprises only the soil and subsoil (and not the water column), throughout the natural extension of its terrestrial territory. Portugal is obliged to show convincing technical and scientific arguments for the evaluators at the service of the UN to grant the extension proposal (EMEPC 2020; Madureira 2017).

The 21st Century Maritime Silk Road: The Rationale

To better understand Chinese maritime cooperation with Portugal, as well as Beijing's aspirations in the North Atlantic, this section will provide the reader with the background of China's 21st Maritime Silk Road, a component of China's Belt and Road Initiative.

With the exception of the maritime incursions of Admiral Zheng He, during the Ming Dynasty, China has traditionally emphasized land power and security issues over sea. In other words, China has predominantly been a continental power, with considerable buffer zones (e.g. the Xinjiang) providing security to its most eastern provinces. Nonetheless, Chinese elites' perception of the threats has significantly changed, with the 12th and 13th Five Year Plans reflecting a qualitative shift from land to sea in regard to the need to protect Chinese interests. Thus, in practice, Chinese strategic mindset has broadened to increasingly acknowledge the importance of the seas as part of a holistic and hybrid strategy in which sea and land are interdependent. Not surprisingly, China's Belt and Road Initiative, the flagship of nowadays' Chinese domestic and Foreign Policy, is in its essence a hybrid initiative. In fact, following Xi Jinping's visit to Kazakhstan in September 2013, from where he officially announced the Silk Road Economic Belt (Xinhua 2015), one month later, in October 2013, the Chinese President publicly presented the 21st Century Maritime Silk Road, during his visit to Jakarta (Ibidem). Therefore, the fact that the BRI is simultaneously land- and sea-oriented confirms the increasing importance of the sea to Chinese elites and strategic circles. After all, there is no way to deny that most of Chinese trade, and *lato sensu*, of the world's trade, is conducted by sea.

What is more, China has been particularly concerned with the so-called Malacca dilemma. The latter refers to the omnipresent fear within China's Foreign Policy that one day a rival power or coalition of powers may prevent Chinese ships from using the straits of Malacca (Duarte 2018). The latter is one of the world's most important chokepoints, as well as the main maritime passage between the Indian Ocean and the Pacific Ocean, through which most of the world trade circulates. Although the so-feared maritime blockade never materialized, this concern is nonetheless one of the drivers for China's *going out policy* in recent years, namely characterized by an unimpeded access to sources in order to mitigate the aforementioned Malacca dilemma (Duarte 2017). Despite China being already a great oil exporter until 1993, its unprecedented and rising consumption leads China to look abroad to meet its domestic needs. Nevertheless, China was a latecomer to the international oil market, when the most relevant oil fields had already been taken by the United States and some EU countries (Ibidem). That explains in part China's turn to the so-called rogue states. Regarding these, for instance, former Sudan or Libya provided China with a (quasi)monopoly in terms of access to and exploitation of oil, which offered Beijing great opportunities in terms of energy security, but also serious economic losses as those caused by the death of Gadaffi.

Coming back to the sea, Chinese naval doctrine is, to a large extent, inspired by US naval thinking, specifically, on Alfred Mahan's thesis. According to Mahan (1890), trade implies both a merchant navy and a navy capable of protecting it, as well as support points for resupply across the ocean. Such rationale thus provides the drivers for the so-called String of Pearls, which is an artificial coastline in the Indian Ocean, formed by support points (ports) along the main maritime arteries, which extend approximately from Myanmar to the Strait of Hormuz (Butt et al. 2020). Such an infrastructure network serves Chinese naval purposes, as it allows the Chinese navy to refuel, in addition to carrying out surveillance and protection missions of the sea lanes of communication, for longer periods and at larger distances from China. Despite Chinese naval assertiveness in the Indian Ocean being far less considerable when compared to the island-build-up that Beijing is undertaking in the East China Sea, it is nonetheless a motive for great concern to New Delhi. In practice, India tries to counterweight Chinese incursions in the Indian Ocean by joining Japan, Australia and the United States in naval drills in the Pacific Ocean, as well as in trying to dissuade the coastal states from the Indian Ocean, to be receptive to Beijing's combination of soft power and economic incentives (Duarte 2017).

Far away, in the remote Atlantic, despite this having been a region of scarce interest for the People's Liberation Army Navy (PLAN) which has the Pacific and to a lesser extent the Indian Ocean as main priorities, there seems to be a tendency for evolution. In fact, the vast Chinese diaspora which is often the object of violence and robbery in both African and Latin American shores of the Atlantic, as well as the increasing importance of ensuring oil and food security for China, have been turning Beijing's attention to the South Atlantic. Should there be a need of urgent evacuation of Chinese citizens living in the Western shores of Africa or in the Atlantic shores of Latin America, the fastest response from the PLAN, whose nearest base is in Djibouti, would take approximately two weeks to reach the South Atlantic (Ferreira-Pereira and Duarte 2022). But there is at least one more factor that has been rendering the Atlantic more appealing to Chinese naval calculus, at the same time that it shows a departure from the Chinese traditional bystander approach to the region to an emerging South Atlantic naval power. This factor comes from the awareness in Beijing (Martinson 2019; Ferreira-Pereira and Duarte 2022) that the South Atlantic can provide China with a complementary "exterior strategy" to help the PLAN alleviate US pressure in Chinese coastal waters. Such strategy consists of using the South Atlantic to "diffuse the attention of extra-regional powers away from China's maritime periphery", by mobilizing a "permanent fleet of 2–3 aircraft carrier strike groups" to the region, in an attempt to "deter and pin down US forces" (Martinson 2019, p. 28).

Although the Indian Ocean, the Pacific and the Atlantic are the conventional maritime arteries of international trade, the literature (see Zeng et al. 2020; Bennett et al. 2020) has been paying increasing attention (given the melting of polar ice caused by climate change) to alternative routes for the transit of goods between East and West. Thus if, in the past, the Arctic was mainly perceived with a mixture of curiosity and fascination, today it has become an increasingly closer and inseparable reality from China's long-term projection capacity. It is not a question of if, but when. In fact, it is imprudent to advance dates for the polar crossing to stop being only seasonal and allow a daily passage of goods in transit from the East to the West, and vice-versa. For now, what can be argued with certainty and credibility is that there is no consensus among experts about the effectiveness of using a polar route, which has nonetheless generated a rising use of the expression Polar Silk Road both by academics and Chinese official documents (Woon 2020; China's Arctic Policy 2018).

After having shed light on the contours of China's maritime aspirations within the framework of its 21st Century Maritime Silk Road, the following section focuses on the specific case of Portugal, namely on the so-called Blue Partnership between China and Lisbon.

The "Blue Partnership" Between Portugal and China

Portugal is an oceanic country, with a coastline of about 2500 km^2 and one of the biggest exclusive economic zones of the world, extending through 1.7 million km^2, including a vast diversity of ecosystems and resources. The Portuguese maritime triangle (continental part, Madeira and the Azores islands) constitutes 48% of total maritime waters under jurisdiction of the European Union (EU) Member-States in adjacent spaces to the European continent (Sea National Strategy 2021–2030).

Considering its privileged geographic and resources conditions as well as its long-standing maritime tradition, the sea economy has been increasing in importance. Currently, the annual turnover of maritime industry totals around 6 thousand million euros, representing about 3% of the country's Gross Domestic Product (GDP) and 4% of total exports (Ferreira 2021).

Apart from the economic dimension, the excellence of marine scientific research in Portugal has been attracting interest from other countries, including the People's Republic of China (PRC). For instance, in May 2016, a group of researchers from the PRC met with researchers from the University of the Azores, in Horta, Faial, to discuss scientific partnerships related to sea resources, namely the exploration of seabed minerals in the vast sea ground of the Azores (Portuguese-American Journal 2016).

One month later, in June 2016, the Minister of the Sea from the People's Republic of China, Wang Hong, visited the Azores Islands and afterwards took part in the 1st United Nations Ocean's Meeting Conference, which was held in Lisbon. On the fringes of the event, a Memorandum of Understanding (MoU) was signed between the Chinese Oceanic State Administration and the Portuguese Ministry of the Sea, establishing cooperation in the fields of blue economy, marine environmental protection, research and monitoring of the marine fund in international waters, marine technological sciences, training and education in sciences of the sea and management of marine biological resources (Silva and Pereira 2020).

As regards its implementation, it should be done through the organization of governmental delegations from both countries, exchange of scientists, professors and students, sharing of experimental data, research results, scientific information as well as the provision of equipment and services with a view to increasing ocean and space research and monitoring in the Atlantic. Other actions consist of jointly holding seminars and conferences, and also submitting joint proposals for projects and programmes from the European Union.

One year later, in October 2017, the Portuguese Minister of the Sea, Ana Paula Vitorino, headed a business mission to China, which culminated with the signature of an Action Plan in the field of the Blue Economy (also known as "Blue Partnership"), following the MoU signed in 2016. On this occasion, some sectors for potential business cooperation and investment were highlighted, namely ports, blue biotechnology, aquaculture and shipbuilding, and platform construction for oceanic renewables energies (Silva and Pereira 2020).

It is important to note that Portugal was the first European Union Member-State to sign a "Blue Partnership" with the People's Republic of China, as declared by the Chinese Vice-Minister of Foreign Affairs, Wang Chao, during a Press Conference on the preparation of the State Visit to Portugal from the Chinese President, Xi Jinping (Lusa, cit. by Público 2018b).

Additionally, during the visit of Xi Jinping to Portugal (4 and 5 December 2018), a Memorandum of Understanding on the Implementation Plan of STARLAB was signed, which foresees the establishment, in Portugal, of a Research Laboratory for Advanced Technology in the fields of Sea and Space, comprising areas such as 4D vision, development of satellite platforms or technologies for oceans monitorisation and surveillance (Silva and Pereira 2020).

This joint project is coordinated by the Portuguese Science and Technology Foundation and the Academy for Innovation in Microsatellites from the Chinese Science Academy (IAMCAS). According to Zhang Yonghe, director of IAMCAS, the laboratory is studying the climate change, the currents in deep ocean and the health of marine ecosystems, and its objective is to create technology that allows not only monitoring and protection of the oceans, but also the promotion of the sea economy sustainable development (Público 2021a).

Although STARLAB laboratory has been serving as a platform for cooperation between Portuguese and Chinese universities and research institutions, it should also be noted that some activities appear to be lagging behind, namely the Portuguese "Infante" microsatellite for maritime and land surface observation, to be completed until October 2021, which was not confirmed (so far, there is no estimate on the new date for its conclusion).

Despite the shortcomings, perspectives for bilateral cooperation look promising overall. In a recent International Conference on Portugal-China Cooperation held in Lisbon (14 and 15 December 2021), the Chinese Ambassador in Portugal, Zhao Bentang, highlighted the ongoing cooperation in the areas of sea protection and promotion, biodiversity preservation and maritime pollution combat as well as the exchanges between universities and research institutions from both countries for the development of the "blue economy" (Observador 2021).

At the same Conference, the Portuguese Minister of the Sea, Ricardo Serrão Santos, confirmed that the channels for scientific and technological cooperation between Portugal and China are already well established, but there is still much room for improvement. Among current opportunities for cooperation and Chinese investment, two stand out: the Sea National Strategy 2021–2030 (made public on 4 June 2021) and the Recovery and Resilience Plan (RRP), which has a Sea Component (no. 10) that foresees the creation of a Blue Hub encompassing the creation of a vast infrastructure network and technological poles in Alentejo and the Algarve, Peniche, Lisboa, Aveiro and Porto. Consequently, bilateral cooperation with China can be established in new and emerging areas and, at the same time, reinforced in others of mutual interest, namely blue biotechnology, oceanic renewable energies, aquaculture and fisheries (Conference recording available on YouTube 2021).

Thus, maritime cooperation is considered as an important element of bilateral cooperation between Portugal and China, and there are many complementarities to explore. Portugal has advantages in marine sciences research and China has the financial capacity to support scientific research projects. By joining efforts, both countries will have more opportunities to cooperate on maritime protection, marine resources development, maritime scientific research, maritime economy, construction and technological upgrade of ports infrastructure and facilities (Yu Hui *op cit* Ferreira 2021). As regards ports cooperation, the Chinese interest in the Port of Sines (the main Portuguese oceanic port) is well known. The Port of Sines weighs 1.5% of the Portuguese economy, 2% of total employment and represents more than 56% of total container handling capacity in the Portuguese ports. It is currently an energy asset for Portugal, the main international maritime platform for the movement of oil, refined products, LPG, Liquefied Natural Gas, petrochemical products and coal. The Port of Sines, including its Industrial and Logistics Zone at the rear, with more than 2000 ha, is already an international logistics platform with capacity to welcome the major players in the maritime, port, and industrial and logistics sectors (Silva and Pereira 2020).

As to Portugal, it has been expressed, on several occasions, the interest in the extension of the Belt and Road Initiative maritime route to the Atlantic, in order to include the Port of Sines. However, although China, as well as other relevant players (namely the United States), has repeatedly expressed its interest in the Port of Sines potentialities, the fact is that, until now, such interest has not materialized. For instance, in the context of the international public procurement for the construction and concession of the new Sines container terminal (Vasco da Gama), which was opened between October 2019 and April 2021, no proposals were presented (Público, 2021b).

China in the Portuguese Sea: Contours and Geopolitical Implications

Portugal has been considered a case study in all EU when it comes to assess the manifestations and receptiveness vis-à-vis China's presence in the framework of its BRI in EU's space. Ferreira-Pereira and Duarte (2021, p. 228) put forth two main reasons for this unique relation:

> Similarly to other EU member states, the first reason is linked to Beijing's preference for bilateralism in dealing with Lisbon in order to advance its BRI-related priorities and interests. The second reason, however, rests on

> the collaborative approach exhibited by Portuguese national authorities vis-à-vis Chinese bilateral initiatives since the beginning of the sovereign debt crisis. Eventually, such a bilateral approach enabled Beijing's authorities to explore possibilities and initiatives outside the framework of the existing EU-China Strategic Partnership and other cooperative multilateral arrangements like the Galileo Programme. The issuing of public debt in yuan and the monitoring of space as well as the Atlantic Ocean are cases in point.

One should recall here that it was the international bailout period (2011–2014) in which the Portuguese economy was facing hard times that triggered China's investments. While the centre-right government led by Passos Coelho had launched the controversial Gold Visa scheme through which several Chinese obtained Portuguese nationality, the centre-left Socialist government, in turn, had shown an increasingly receptive stance towards the BRI (Ferreira-Pereira and Duarte 2021). On the occasion of Chinese President Xi Jinping's visit to Portugal in December 2018, the two countries signed a memorandum of understanding to promote logistics, air, land and maritime cooperation under the BRI. In total, 17 bilateral agreements were signed covering various sectors (Jornal Económico 2018). Some of the topics covered by the agreements were particularly sensitive. This was the case of the joint project between China and Portugal—called STARLAB[1]—for microsatellite production as well as Ocean monitoring, in the face of scrutiny from European partners (Duarte 2020; Duarte and Leandro 2020).

It should be noted that Portugal has the third largest Exclusive Economic Zone (EEZ) in the EU, and may even double its maritime territory if the United Nations considers the proposal to enlarge the seabed, presented by Lisbon in 2009, to be legitimate. In the event of approval, a larger maritime area presupposes that there will also be a greater allocation of naval and air resources to monitor a large part of the Atlantic (bearing in mind that the size of the current EEZ is already

[1] If implemented, STARLAB would enable cooperation between Portugal and China on microsatellite launches and ocean monitoring. It should be borne in mind in this connection that one of the reasons given by the EU for suspending cooperation with China in developing the Galileo Programme (the EU's satellite navigation system) is precisely the fear of alleged espionage and strategic parity (shared, incidentally, by the US NASA, which also refuses to cooperate with China on space matters) that such cooperation is likely to offer Beijing. Portugal could therefore be the first EU country to set a precedent in such a sensitive matter, which, together with the other aspects mentioned, makes it to be seen as a case study in the EU Belt and Road.

significant for a country that has only two submarines). A larger maritime area also means a greater probability of finding and extracting riches from the bottom of the ocean, something that interests China in the context of its Belt and Road. Will Portugal be able to maintain the difficult balance between its interests and national sovereignty, its strategic commitments to the EU and NATO, and at the same time collaborate with China in monitoring the North Atlantic (NATO's privileged space)? This rhetorical questioning cannot be dissociated from point 10 of the bilateral agreements (which provides for the Memorandum between MEO and Huawei regarding the development of 5G technology), as a result of the tensions currently being felt both in the United States and in the EU and other countries. In short, Oceans, Space and 5G technology are precisely the forbidden fruit as the EU and the United States (metaphorically) conceive it, or also, the forbidden borders in Duarte and Leandro's (2020) vision.

All in all, China's presence in Portugal and Lisbon receptive stance towards the BRI can be seen as "a somewhat innovative factor in the country's contemporary foreign policy", which "has been characterized by long-standing advocacy of the US strategic interests inside and outside NATO, and also a politico-diplomatic alignment to preferences and concerns of leading European players such as Germany and France" (Ferreira-Pereira and Duarte 2021, p. 229). Lisbon has been actively criticized by former US Ambassador to Portugal, Mr George Glass, who has warned several times that "this Xi is not the China with whom the Portuguese have been trading for 500 years" (*apud* Diário de Notícias 2019, para.1, Author's translation).

One issue of promising importance when discussing the challenges and opportunities generated by the growing Chinese presence in the Atlantic Ocean is the Azores, more specifically the potential that the Lajes Field is likely to offer in the framework of the 21st Century Maritime Silk Road. Despite being for decades home to US 65th Air Base Wing, recent years have shown an unprecedented series of alleged "technical landings". Interestingly, Chinese President Xi Jinping himself had already landed in Lajes on 24 July 2014, where, among others, the then Deputy Prime Minister Paulo Portas was waiting for him. This episode is far from being a unique case, as the alleged technical stopovers, an expression with which Beijing officially justifies the visits of Chinese politicians to Terceira Island, have been following US gradual disinterest in the Lajes field, accompanied by a decrease of US military (Duarte 2020).

Chinese alleged technical stopovers at Lajes have aroused the concern of Devin Nunes, Republican Chairman of the House Intelligence Committee, as shown in his letter to then Secretary of Defence, Ashton Carter, on 20 September 2016:

> The Chinese delegation is in negotiations to expand China's investments and presence in the islands, including in the port of Terceira. [...] It has also expressed interest in using the airstrip at the Lajes Base. [...] The Chinese plans in the Azores aim to create a logistics and intelligence centre, which could eventually be expanded for other military purposes. (In *CBS News* 2017)

In practice, Terceira island is likely to help China kill two birds with one stone in the North Atlantic, insofar as, in addition to Lajes, Beijing is showing interest in the construction of a deep-water port at Praia da Vitória, which is the island's main port (Duarte 2020). On the other hand, the context seems to be favourable for the restructuring of the port of Praia da Vitória so that it can accommodate the largest cargo ships in the world, judging by the favourable conclusions of a technical opinion requested by the Chamber of Commerce of Angra de Heroísmo, released in 2018 (ibidem). Another factor that attests to the added value that the expansion and modernization of the port of Praia da Vitória may represent for Portugal is intrinsically linked to the relevance that Liquefied Natural Gas (LNG) has been acquiring nowadays, and even more in the ongoing search for alternatives for Russian gas to Europe. That is where geoeconomics and geopolitics meet with possible advantages for Portugal stemming from the use of Praia da Vitória for transhipment. After all, Nord Stream 2 will not be filled with Russian gas and the The United States has become an extraordinary gas exporter worldwide. In this sense, Russia's "special operation in Ukraine" could have set an unprecedented logistical opportunity for Portugal in the Atlantic. Only time will let us know.

Conclusion

This chapter has sought to analyse the challenges and opportunities generated by China's growing presence in the Atlantic, by focusing on the potential that Portugal may offer within Chinese maritime interests, as well as on how both Beijing and Lisbon may benefit from their Blue

Partnership. We have thus highlighted that Portugal was the first European Union Member-State to sign a "Blue Partnership" with the People's Republic of China. This can be explained through various reasons, namely the Portuguese privileged geographic and resources conditions and its long-standing maritime tradition, as well as the excellence of its marine scientific research.

Under the "Blue Partnership", bilateral cooperation with China can be developed in new and emerging areas, such as blue biotechnology, oceanic renewable energies, aquaculture and fisheries, taking advantage of opportunities resulting from the National Sea Strategy 2021–2030 and the Sea Component of the Portuguese Recovery and Resilience Plan. Additionally, maritime cooperation between both countries should also encompass ports, where there is still much room for improvement. This could involve, on the Portuguese side, the Ports of Sines, Douro-Leixões, Aveiro and Lisboa, to name just a few.

Scarce EU countries can provide China with a strategic foothold in-between land and Sea, such as Portugal. Certainly, Greece—with its Piraeus port—is also an exception that pleases the Chinese merchant navy which crosses the Suez Canal en-route to the Mediterranean. Nonetheless, Portugal's geostrategic location between the Americas, Africa and Europe has all assets to help China expand its Twenty-first-Maritime Silk Road to the North Atlantic. But in the process, the Portuguese Sea, one of the largest exclusive economic zones in the world (which may even double its maritime platform), may be forbidden waters for Beijing. In fact, despite the significant receptiveness that Lisbon has been showing towards China's BRI since the traumatic experience generated by post-2008 economic hardship, geography is insurmountable. That is, there is no way for Lisbon to deny that Portuguese waters are also NATO's waters and sphere of influence. This complicates Portuguese Foreign Policy, which so far has been smart and effective in dealing with US warnings and pressure to keep China outside the North Atlantic realm. It remains to be seen, however, for how long more Lisbon can continue to maximize its interests vis-à-vis China without testing Washington to the limit.

References

Alexander, D. 2015. "U.S. to cut European military bases as budgets shrink". https://www.reuters.com/article/us-usa-defense-europe-idUKKBN0KH18O20150108. Accessed May 8, 2022.

Bennett, M., et al. 2020. "The opening of the Transpolar Sea Route: Logistical, geopolitical, environmental, and socioeconomic impacts". *Marine Policy*. https://doi.org/10.1016/j.marpol.2020.104178

Butt, K., Kharl, S., and Bhatti, K. 2020. "String of pearls: Politics of ports in Indian Ocean". *South Asian Studies* (1026-678X), 35(1): 73–86.

Cacho, J. L. 2020. "As potencialidades do Porto de Sines". ADFERSIT—Associação Portuguesa para o Desenvolvimento dos Sistemas Integrados de Transportes. https://adfersit.pt/noticia/439/as-potencialidades-do-porto-de-sines. Accessed June 1, 2022.

CBS News. 2017. "Defense Dept. decision gives China chance for foothold between U.S. and Europe". Accessed May 3, 2022. https://www.cbsnews.com/news/azores-withdrawal-gives-china-foothold-between-us-europe/

China's Arctic Policy. 2018. The State Council Information Office of the People's Republic of China January 2018. Accessed May 4, 2022. http://english.www.gov.cn/archive/white_paper/2018/01/26/content_281476026660336.htm.

Coelho, P. 2017. "O Artigo 76.º da Convenção das Nações Unidas sobre o Direito do Mar—A Problemática da Aplicação Técnica de Conceitos Jurídicos pela (in)Controversa Comissão de Limites da Plataforma Continental". Tese de Doutoramento. Porto: Faculdade de Direito da Universidade do Porto.

Costa, S. 1967. *Portugal, País Macrocéfalo*. Mem Martins: Publicações Europa-América.

Costa Silva, A. 2020. "Visão Estratégica para o Plano de Recuperação Económica de Portugal 2020–2030". *Governo de Portugal*. https://www.portugal.gov.pt/download-ficheiros/ficheiro.aspx?v=%3d%3dBQAAAB%2bLCAAAAAAABAAzNDAytAQAziD%2fFAUAAAA%3d. Accessed June 1, 2022.

Diário de Notícias. 2019. https://www.dn.pt/mundo/este-xi-nao-e-a-china-com-quem-os-portugueses-tem-comerciado-durante-500-anos-10878774.html. Accessed May 3, 2022.

Diário da República. 2017. "Resolução do Conselho de Ministros" nº 175/2017, série I de 2017-11-24. https://dre.pt/dre/detalhe/resolucao-conselho-ministros/175-2017-114248655. Accessed February 11, 2022.

Duarte, P. 2017. *Pax Sinica*. Lisbon: Chiado Editora.

Duarte, P. 2018. "Whose Silk Road? The Chinese, US, European Union and Russian strategic projects for regional integration in Central Asia". In *The New Silk Road in the Context of East Asian Relations and Wider International Implications,* edited by Carmen Mendes, 38–49. Routledge.

Duarte, P. 2020. *De Lisboa a Pequim: Portugal na Faixa e Rota Chinesa*. Lisboa: Instituto Internacional de Macau.

Duarte, P., and Leandro, F. 2020. "The Ultimate European Border: The Belt and Road Initiative Discovers Portugal". In Duarte, P. and Leandro, F. (eds). *The Belt and Road Initiative—International Perspectives on an Old Archetype of a New Development Model*, 363–388. Singapore: Palgrave Macmillan.

EMEPC—Estrutura de Missão para a Extensão da Plataforma Continental. 2020. https://www.emepc.pt/. Accessed May 9, 2022.

Erickson, A., and Wuthnow, J. 2016. Barriers, springboards and benchmarks: China conceptualizes the pacific 'Island Chains'. *The China Quarterly*, 225: 1–22. https://doi.org/10.1017/S0305741016000011

Espada, J. 2014. *Portugal, a Europa e o Atlântico.* Lisbon: Alêtheia.

European Commission. 2022. "Motorways of the Sea". https://transport.ec.europa.eu/transport-modes/maritime/motorways-sea_en. Accessed February 11, 2022.

Expresso. 2019. "Sines. Terminal Vasco da Gama promete criar 1.350 postos de trabalho". https://expresso.pt/economia/2019-10-16-Sines.-Terminal-Vasco-da-Gama-promete-criar-1.350-postos-de-trabalho. Accessed May 9, 2022.

Ferreira, R. 2021. "China de olhos postos na transição digital, economia do mar e saúde em Portugal". O Jornal Económico. https://jornaleconomico.pt/noticias/china-de-olhos-postos-na-transicao-digital-economia-do-mar-e-saude-em-portugal-755602. Accessed January 11, 2022.

Ferreira-Pereira, L. C., and Duarte, P. 2021. "China and the Belt and Road Initiative in Europe: The case of Portugal". In Ntousas and Minas (eds). *The European Union and China's Belt and Road*, 218–234. Routledge.

Ferreira-Pereira, L. C., and Duarte, P. 2022. "The South Atlantic in China's Global Policy: Why It Matters?" In Duarte, P., Leandro, F. and Galán, E. (eds). *The Palgrave Handbook of Globalization with Chinese Characteristics*. Singapore: Palgrave Macmillan.

Goldstein, L. 2017. "Is China Crafting an Atlantic Maritime Strategy?" The National Interest. http://nationalinterest.org/feature/beijing-sea-china-crafting-atlantic-maritime-strategy-19622. Accessed May 18, 2022.

Governo de Portugal. 2021. "Resolução do Conselho de Ministros n.º 68/2021 sobre a Estratégia Nacional para o Mar". https://www.portugal.gov.pt/download-ficheiros/ficheiro.aspx?v=%3d%3dBQAAAB%2bLCAAAAAAABAAzNLQwsQQAODaj3AUAAAA%3d. Accessed May 18, 2022.

Guedes, A. 2012. "Geopolitical Shifts in the Wider Atlantic: Past, Present, and Future". In Richardson, J. et al. 2012. *The Fractured Ocean: Current Challenges to Maritime Policy in the Wider Atlantic*, 11–57. Wider Atlantic Series.

Jornal Económico. 2018. https://jornaleconomico.sapo.pt/noticias/do-comercio-a-educacao-conheca-os-17-acordos-de-cooperacao-assinados-entre-portugal-e-china-385631. Accessed May 2, 2022.

Lima, B. 2016. *Portugal e o Atlântico.* Lisboa: Fundação Francisco Manuel dos Santos.

Madureira, P. 2017. *A Plataforma Continental Portuguesa-Os Recursos Minerais Marinhos*. Lisboa: Academia das Ciências de Lisboa.

Mahan, A. 1890. *Influence of Sea Power Upon History, 1660–1783.* Boston: Little, Brown and Company.

Martinson, R. 2019. "China as an Atlantic Naval Power". *The RUSI Journal*, 164(7): 18–31. https://doi.org/10.1080/03071847.2019.1700684

Moreira, A. 2018. "*O Mar em Perspetiva*". *Cadernos Navais*, Centro de Estudos Estratégicos da Marinha, nº 50, outubro. Lisbon: Edições Culturais da Marinha.

Observador. 2021. "China quer mais parcerias e cooperação com Portugal". https://observador.pt/2021/12/14/china-quer-mais-parcerias-e-cooperacao-com-portugal/. Accessed January 12, 2022.

Porto de Sines. 2022. https://www.apsinesalgarve.pt/porto-de-sines. Accessed June 1, 2022.

Portuguese-American Journal. 2016. "President Vasco Cordeiro welcomes Chinese Minister of the Sea". https://portuguese-american-journal.com/china-president-vasco-cordeiro-welcomes-chinese-minister-of-the-sea-azores/. Accessed January 12, 2022.

Público. 2018a. "Extensão da plataforma continental vai estar fechada até 2021". https://jornaleconomico.sapo.pt/noticias/extensao-da-plataforma-continental-vai-estar-fechada-ate-2021-345332. Accessed June 1, 2022.

Público. 2018b. "Xi em Portugal: Pequim destaca cooperação com Lisboa em países terceiros". https://www.publico.pt/2018b/11/23/economia/noticia/xi-portugal-pequim-destaca-cooperacao-lisboa-paises-terceiros-1852203. Accessed January 11, 2022.

Público. 2021a. "Laboratório sino-português junta-se à iniciativa chinesa Uma Faixa, Uma Rota". https://www.publico.pt/2021a/12/10/ciencia/noticia/laboratorio-sinoportugues-juntase-iniciativa-chinesa-faixa-rota-1988072. Accessed June 1, 2022.

Público. 2021b. "Concurso para novo terminal do Porto de Sines encerra sem propostas". https://www.publico.pt/2021b/04/07/economia/noticia/concurso-novo-terminal-porto-sines-encerra-propostas-1957584. Accessed January 13, 2022.

Recuperar Portugal. 2021. "Resilience and recovery plan". C10 (Mar), https://recuperarportugal.gov.pt/c10-mar/?lang=en. Accessed January 15, 2022.

Rodrigues, C., and Silva, J. T. da. 2020, "Portugal, China and the US: A universalist's stance to get along with both powers". In Esteban, M. et al. (eds),

Europe in the face of US-China Rivalry, A report by the European Think-tank Network on China (ETNC), 131–135.

Sea National Strategy 2021–2030. Council of Ministers Resolution no. 68/2021, published at Diário da República, Series I, no. 108, 4 June 2021. https://dre.pt/dre/detalhe/resolucao-conselho-ministros/68-2021-164590045?_ts=1654214400034. Accessed January 10, 2022.

Serrão Santos, R. 2021. Speech at the 3rd International Conference on Portugal-China Cooperation. Lisbon, 14 and 15 December. https://www.youtube.com/watch?v=_kPYokghAeg. Accessed January 15, 2022.

Silva, A. C. 2020. "Visão Estratégica para o Plano de Recuperação Económica de Portugal 2020–2030". Report to Portuguese Government. https://www.portugal.gov.pt/download-ficheiros/ficheiro.aspx?v=%3d%3dBQAAAB%2bLCAAAAAAABAAzNDAytAQAziD%2fFAUAAAA%3d. Accessed February 11, 2022.

Silva, J. T. da. 2020. *Portugal-China—As Relações Luso-Chinesa, do Mundo Quinhentista ao Contexto Contemporâneo*. Macau: Instituto Internacional de Macau.

Silva, J. T. da, and Pereira, R. 2020. "China and the Portuguese Atlantic: The BRI´s last puzzle piece". Leandro, F., and Duarte, P. (eds.), *The Belt and Road Initiative—International perspectives on an old archetype of a new development model*, 389–409. Palgrave.

The 12th Five-Year Plan. 2011. "The 12th Five-Year Plan for economic and social development of the People's Republic of China". In *Central committee of the Communist Party of China*. Beijing. http://www.csrc.gov.cn/pub/csrc_en/newsfacts/release/201210/W020121010631355001488.pdf. Accessed May 4, 2022.

The 13th Five-Year Plan. 2016. "The 13th five-year plan for economic and social development of the People's Republic of China 2016–2020". *Compilation and Translation Bureau, Central Committee of the Communist Party of China*. Beijing. https://en.ndrc.gov.cn/policies/202105/P020210527785800103339.pdf. Accessed May 4, 2022.

Woon, C. 2020. "Framing the Polar Silk Road: Critical geopolitics, Chinese scholars and the (Re)positionings of China's Arctic interests". *Political Geography*, 78. https://doi.org/10.1016/j.polgeo.2019.102141.

Xinhua. 2015. "Chronology of China's Belt and Road Initiative". 28 March. http://www.xinhuanet.com/english/2015-03/28/c_134105435.htm. Accessed May 4, 2022.

Zeng, Q., et al. 2020. "The competitiveness of Arctic shipping over Suez Canal and China-Europe railway". *Transport Policy*, 86: 34–43. https://doi.org/10.1016/j.tranpol.2019.11.005;

Lusophone Connections and China's Growing Presence in the South Atlantic

José Nelson Bessa Maia

Introduction

For a long time, since the opening of the Suez canal in 1867, the South Atlantic has been losing relevance and becoming just a passageway for trade between Latin American countries and Europe, with little interaction between its margins in South America and West Africa.[1] The loss of strategic importance of the South Atlantic became even more visible with the opening of the Panama Canal in 1914, creating a so called "power void" in the South Atlantic (Penha 2011). However, this has changed in the beginning of twenty-first century as it has become an area of increasing exploration and extraction of strategic resources, as well as a projection space over Antarctica.

In fact, the South Atlantic is gradually becoming a geoeconomic space where strategic interests are associated with the intensification of trade flows, the discovery of important gas and oil reserves along the continental shelves; and the identification of mineral deposits, including in the area of international waters Abdenur and de Souza Neto (2013), Paulo

J. N. B. Maia (✉)
Brazil's Ministry of Economy, Brasília, Brazil
e-mail: nbessamaia@gmail.com

P. A. B. Duarte et al. (eds.), *Portugal and the Lusophone World*,
https://doi.org/10.1007/978-981-99-0455-6_10

Duarte (2016) and Mário Santos (2021). Whereas before, only the US and the UK were present over the region, today, China has reached South America and West Africa and is beginning to expand its presence on both sides of the South Atlantic. For Ralph Espach the Asian giant is now also one of the largest trading partners and investors in South America and sub-Saharan Africa, which is leading to a reconfiguration of foreign powers' presence in the region (Espach 2021). The arrival of the Chinese in the South Atlantic is already arousing an overreaction from the US concerned with losing its status and influence in the region.[2]

As a theoretical perspective this paper makes use of the liberal view of China's engagement in Africa based on how domestic variables influence state's foreign policy preference (Moravcsik 1997). According to Oscar Otele, this view is rooted in China's domestic modernization program started in the late 1970s (Otele 2020). The outcome of these economic reforms saw China increase its role in the global economy in 1980s and 1990s, so much that by the turn of twenty-first century the growth of Chinese market led to higher prices of primary commodities as well as strong demand for agricultural products driving China's interest in Africa.[3]

Still based on Oscar Otele, unlike the realist perspective that sees the Chinese as solely driven by the quest to access natural resources, the liberal perspective views Chinese actors as driven by the same motives as other Western actors. In fact, proponents of this view argue that Chinese companies are not yet able enough to compete on the same footing as Western companies, and therefore given that African continent offers low-cost markets, this allows them to gradually develop their capacity to also become global economic players (Corkin 2008; Haglund 2009).[4]

Amid the surging geopolitical context of dispute between the US and China in the South Atlantic, the Portuguese-speaking countries in the region find themselves in the crossroads to define to whom their allegiance is best served and advantageous. In addition to the South Atlantic Peace and Cooperation Zone (ZPCAS), an organization and a military alliance of 23 African and South American countries, created in 1986 through resolution of the U.N. general assembly on Brazil's initiative, the Portuguese-speaking countries in the region have their own organization: the Community of the Portuguese- speaking countries (CPLP). But despite some positive achievements, after 25 years of economic cooperation failure of CPLP, the members of the organization seem to be with their backs to each other.[5]

The surging presence of China in the South Atlantic rim and its remarkable capacity and scale of financial resources mobilization already bring a completely new dynamic that needs to be well understood so as to allow Portuguese-speaking countries, in particular the big ones, such as Brazil and Angola, to draw up relationship strategies with China that might maximize gains in their development processes without jeopardizing, however, their national security and sovereignty.

The article is divided into six sections. The first section introduces the topic of Lusophone connections and China's surging presence in the South Atlantic. The second one shows how the changes in the world geoeconomy have led China to occupy a position of global power and have strategic interests all over the oceans, which has led it to engage in several areas of the world far beyond the Asian waters, specially in the South Atlantic. The third section attempts to indicate how the Chinese engagement in the South Atlantic has been materialized in the last two decades. The fourth section discusses how the Lusophone connections in South Atlantic now operate.

The fifth section of this paper deals with the perception of risks of China's engagement in the South Atlantic by the different actors, especially in the Portuguese- speaking countries in the region. The final section concludes with comments about the need for China to either reconsider or rebuild its strategy in the South Atlantic in order to increase trade and investment ties not only with China but also to help promote more trade among the several Lusophone countries themselves in both sides of the Ocean and thus thereby creating conditions to take development and prosperity to all the stakeholders involved.

The Changes in Global Geoeconomy and Surging Engagement of China in the South Atlantic

It is widely known that China has become the powerhouse of the world because of its sustained high growth performance in the last 30 years. As China is now the second largest economy at market prices and the first one in purchasing power parity terms (IMF 2020), and the biggest exporter country in the world (Unctad 2021), it is natural and legitimate its intention to assume an increasing role in the world economic affairs (endnote 5).

The times of low profile of China in the geoeconomic diplomacy are gone. It became clear when the Chinese President Xi Jinping announced what is now known as the "Belt and Road Initiative" (BRI), launched in 2013, with the stated purpose of promoting the economic prosperity of the countries along the Belt and the Road path and regional economic cooperation, thereby strengthening exchanges and mutual learning between different civilizations, and enhancing the basis for world peace and development.

In fact, according to Elisabeth Economy (2022, p. 57), the BRI:

> not only offers a physical manifestation of Chinese centrality through three overland and three maritime corridors that will connect China to Asia, Europe, the Middle East, and Africa but also evokes historical memories of the Silk Road and of Chinese centrality during imperial times. In its original conception, the BRI was a vehicle for Chinese-led hard infrastructure development along the six corridors. Today, BRI offshoots include so-called digital, health, and polar Silk Roads, and all countries are welcome to participate.[6]

The current engagement of China in Africa is part of the new geopolitical activism of the country all over the world. Pursuant José Sales, in 2002, China began the gradual transition to its so called naval strategy of "far-seas operations", with the aim of expanding its capacity to project power in a maritime area beyond 1000 nautical miles from its mainland territory (Sales 2017). Some factors were responsible for this change in strategy: (i) the fact that China has resolved most of its land border disputes with the signing of treaties (except with India), while most Chinese disputes over maritime territories have not been resolved; (ii) the possibility of deterring the eventual US intervention in Taiwan island; (iii) China's greater integration into the world economy and global supply chains, which implies not only opportunities but also vulnerabilities when crises come up; and (iv) the high and sustained growth of the Chinese economy that contributed to the formation of a solid industrial and infrastructure basis, which has enabled the development of a navy based on a "far seas operations" strategy (Nan Li 2021).[7]

As highlighted by José Sales China's new naval power strategy has not been restricted to its Asian adjacent maritime space and, since 2008, its vessels have been operating on the east coastline of the African continent, especially on the coast of Somalia, participating in naval operations against piracy, protecting their shipping destined to the transportation of raw materials, manufactured goods and oil (Sales 2017). China even opened a military base in Djibouti in 2017. To make such a strategy in Africa possible Chinese authorities put in place a diplomatic arrangement for African countries: the Forum on China-Africa Cooperation (FOCAC), a successful instrument of Chinese soft power, founded in October 2000 at the first ministerial conference in Beijing. It aims to strengthen Sino-African economic cooperation and trade relationships to establish a new international order that will better reflect the needs and interests of China and Africa.[8]

In addition to FOCAC, China has also put in place since 2003 its own mechanism for expanding its relations with Portuguese-speaking countries, especially the African ones (PALOP): the so called Forum of Macao whose headquarters are in Macao, a former Portuguese colony transferred to China in 1999. The Forum of Macao represents a new form of trans-regional cooperation, with the establishment of regular contacts between the participants and the use of the Chinese economic power of attraction to gain space on the international stage. China has been gaining influence with the PALOP, gaining trust through the proximity established by the Forum, the changes that have been taking place in its image before the world (soft power) and the most advantageous and low-cost partnership, with which Brazil could hardly compete (Veloso 2015).[9]

The perception of surging engagement of China in the South Atlantic has been clearly noted by the academic community throughout the region, including in Africa but especially in South America. According to Abdenur and de Souza Neto (2013, p. 171) from Brazil:

> Overall, we note that not only has China's presence increased dramatically in the South Atlantic over the past ten years – as reflected in the rapid expansion of trade, the proliferation of businesses and investments, as well as the growth of the Chinese diaspora communities in the countries of Africa and the coasts of Latin America – but this presence has also undergone important qualitative changes. [translation from Spanish is ours]

Carlos Moneta and Sergio Cesarín (Moneta and Cesarín 2016, p. 11), from Argentina, argue that:

> For the economies of the region, China has become an ordering variable that defines an order of external regional priorities tending to achieve goals of growth and expansion of exports. Over the years, China is increasingly perceived as an engine of regional growth, a highly demanding market for

> raw materials and a partner inclined to promote "peripheral industrialization" processes through investments and credits. [translation from Spanish is ours]

Finally, Paulo Duarte (2016, p. 99), from Portugal, asserts that:

> We start from the conviction that currently the Atlantic rim is a space for the future, where the regions of the South are currently protagonists of a geopolitical reconfiguration, after which they have conquered a greater autonomy face to Europe and the United States. In the next decade, China can and should launch its anchor in a geostrategic scenario where the powers of the North Atlantic are losing ground. [translation from Portuguese is ours][10]

In sum, those views indicate that China is firmly engaged in occupying space in the South Atlantic by means of a network of relationships and arrangements with West African and South American countries and using the levers of its huge demand for commodities and capacity to deploy investment in infrastructure and providing official credits for the countries in the region.

Indications of China's Engagement in the South Atlantic Since 2000

The South Atlantic as a concept or region does not appear in Chinese foreign policy definitions. China has strategies for cooperation with regional organizations like the European Union as well as official White Papers on regions like Latin America and Africa. Both Africa and Latin America are important for China in its "South-South" diplomacy with developing countries. But so far, no official statements or documents seem to adopt the concept of the "South Atlantic". Though it does not use such a concept in official foreign policy, China maintains na increasing and strong cooperation ties with the countries that make up the region.[11]

What matters most is the fact that the engagement of China in the Atlantic South in the last 20 years has been clearly increasing and carries a strong economic feature that takes mostly the form of trade, investment, and finance in both sides of the Ocean, in West African and Mercosur member countries. It includes many countries beyond the Lusophony such as English and French-speaking African polities as well as Spanish-speaking countries of South America such as Argentina and Uruguay (Meza 2016).[12]

With regard to the Portuguese-speaking countries in the region (including Portugal that is located in the North Atlantic and Mozambique in the Indian Ocean), data show that trade with China has increased exponentially since the year 2000, especially with Angola and Brazil where the Chinese share in both export and import has augmented a lot making China the main market destination and the origin supplier for both countries. The small countries in the bloc (Cape Verde, Guinea-Bissau, and Sao Tome and Principe) have not followed suit because of their limited export capacity and small domestic markets. Portugal in turn has quintupled its export share to China in the period but it is still a mere 1% of all Portuguese exports and 3.7% of all its imports.

The Chinese engagement in foreign direct investment (FDI) in the Portuguese- speaking countries in the South Atlantic has been impressive in the last two decades. The FDI accumulated inflows reached USD 25 billion in Angola and USD 73.7 billion in Brazil accounting for 81% of all direct investment inflows in the bloc. Mozambique and Portugal received about USD 10 billion each one. Even the other smaller economies received considerable amounts of Chinese FDI if compared to their Gross Domestic Products.

As external financing is concerned, Chinese state-owned banks have lent USD 74.9 billions in the last 20 years to the Portuguese-speaking countries in the South Atlantic, particularly for Angola and Brazil which received more than 90% of the loans. Most of such huge resources have been channeled to finance infrastructure and investment in the petroleum companies of both countries.

It is worth mentioning that China's engagement in the West African coast, including the Portuguese-speaking countries, has focus on: (i) trade, based on the import of primary commodities, required for its economic growth and energy security, and the exportation of higher valued added manufactured products; and (ii) an expanding market for its companies, especially those in the civil construction sector, meeting the huge local demand for infrastructure works. According to Mário Santos (2021), not coincidentally, and as part of the Chinese strategy that privileges the sea as a vector of projection, there is a trend of undertaking numerous investments in port infrastructure works in several African countries in the South Atlantic rim.

Mário Santos further argues that China, which already exhibited strong presence in Africa as a whole, whether through trade, multiple investments, or cooperation in terms of defense, has been expanding its area of influence in the South Atlantic through the construction of numerous connective infrastructure projects in neighboring countries—mainly ports facilities and transport corridors—as examples: the construction by Chinese companies of the Caio Port terminal in Cabinda province in Angola and the expansion and management for 20 years of the Lobito port terminal in Benguela province also in Angola (Santos 2021) (endnote 12). China is committed as well to build a deep water port in São Tomé and Príncipe aimed at transforming the country into a platform for providing logistic services to Central and West African countries by serving as a transhipment site for containers and goods from various parts of the world to those countries.[13]

Lusophone Connections in South Atlantic: A New Role for the Community of the Portuguese-Speaking Countries

In multilateral terms, the connections among the Portuguese-speaking countries in the South Atlantic are exerted by above mentioned Community of Portuguese-Speaking Countries (CPLP), an international organization formed by the Portuguese-speaking countries, set up in 1996, whose objective is the "deepening of mutual friendship and cooperation between its members". The CPLP is financed both through the Executive Secretariat's operating budget, funded by mandatory contributions from member states, and through the Special Fund, fed by voluntary contributions and intended to fund cooperation programs, projects, and specific actions. Its headquarters are in Lisbon, Portugal.[14]

According to Figueiredo e Volante, the CPLP is a privileged forum for deepening relations between member states that benefit from common historical, ethnic, and linguistic ties (Figueiredo and Volante 2019). The organization focuses its actions on three general objectives: political-diplomatic concertation; cooperation in many areas, and the promotion and diffusion of the Portuguese language. Within the political conciliation framework, the coordination of positions in multilateral forums is emphasized, as well as the political cooperation during member state elections.

Regarding technical cooperation, it is noteworthy that the Portuguese-speaking African countries (PALOPs), together with East-Timor, are currently the main recipients of Brazilian South-South cooperation, which has prioritized capacity-building in areas such as education, food security, agriculture, health, and institutional strengthening, among others.[15]

Since 1996 heads of state in CPLP have come together every two years to assess progress and propose new projects for the Community. Although these meetings have taken place regularly, the institutionalization of the group occurred late, and its bylaws were formalized only in 2007, more than ten years after its creation. It was in this document that the operationalization of the different areas was established and the objectives were defined more clearly, outlining in general terms the role to be played by the Community, such as political-diplomatic concertation, cooperation in all domains, and the promotion of diffusion of the Portuguese language (CPLP 2015).[16]

Despite the progress in many areas of cooperation in CPLP, some members, especially African ones, have pushed for more focus on economic and business areas so as to improve the promotion of trade, investment, and financing mechanism inside the bloc.[17] The economic crises of Portugal in 2011–2012 and Brazil in 2014–2016 limited the resources and interests of both countries to speed up the economic agenda in CPLP in such a away that at the 2012 meeting in Luanda, Angola, the ministers presented just the guidelines but no specific actions. In 2016, the group of ministers met again, but no concrete measures resulted from the meeting. Thus, the absence of political leadership and economic dynamism mainly accounts for the modest achievements of this organization so far (Alves 2008). In fact, there was a slowdown in the development of CPLP's trade agenda that is reflected in the poor outcomes of the group's trade interchange, which has been increasing throughout the years, but is still limited when analyzed globally.[18]

As a matter of fact, the figures of intra-CPLP trade data from the last decade (2008–2019) show, with the exception of the smaller economies (Cape Verde and São Tome and Principe), that transactions between the member countries are very modest, not indicating a trend toward trade densification. It reveals otherwise the lack of promotion mechanisms and navigation lines between South America and West Africa countries necessary to increase the exports and imports and overcome the low dynamism of the demand for products from each country within CPLP with their partners (Maia 2020).[19]

In the context of weak trade and investment flows among CPLP countries, China's engagement in the South Atlantic arouses the interest of several countries in the region due to the possibility of increasing significantly their exports, receiving investments in infrastructure and other sectors, and obtaining higher levels of technical and financial cooperation.[20] In this sense, organizations such as the CPLP could avail of its secretariat structure to rationally assess the positive and negative aspects of this rapprochement with China and discuss with its members strategies to enhance the net gains for national development arising from this promising relationship with the emerging Asian great power and, at the same time, preserve the sovereignty and room for maneuver of each country, thus avoiding excessive economic dependence (Table 1).

Table 1 CPLP share in trade in some of its member countries, from 2008 up to 2019

	2008	*2012*	*2015*	*2019*
		Exports		
Angola	4.2	3.1	3.8	3.7
Brazil	1.9	1.2	0.8	0.8
Cape Verde	41.4	30.8	25.5	17.5
Guinea-Bissau	0.9	2.9	0.3	0.0
Mozambique	1.4	1.3	1.1	2.0
Portugal	7.8	9.6	6.9	3.0
Sao Tom and Principe	73.6	8.7	7.6	15.1
		Imports		
Angola	26.0	23.0	18.3	16.8
Brazil	1.9	0.6	0.8	0.6
Cape Verde	55.6	44.1	47.4	47.9
Guinea-Bissau	28.3	30.7	29.4	0.0
Mozambique	3.6	9.6	6.4	4.0
Portugal	3.2	6.6	3.8	2.8
Sao Tom and Principe	85.1	75.1	89.1	70.6

Source ITC/Comtrade; produced by the author

The Perception of Risks of Chinese Engagement in South Atlantic by Different Actors in the Portuguese-Speaking Countries

As it becomes more active internationally, China, such as any other major economy, begins to face increased risks to its nationals and assets abroad. In the South Atlantic, it faces threats that highlight risk exposure in financially and politically weak nation-states. The fact is that China's "going-out policy", adopted in 2002 to encourage its companies to internationalize operations, has led to significantly greater exposure of its nationals, companies, and finances to the headwinds of foreign unstable countries.

As China is now promoting its "Belt and Road" initiative (BRI), connecting Asia to foreign markets in Europe and Africa, even larger Chinese direct investment and development aid on the continent tend to increase and impose risks to Chinese nationals operating abroad (Parello-Plesner, 2016).

However, the other way round, the governments in the region also perceive risks stemming from the surging engagement of Chinese companies and banks operating in the diferente countries. The risks are of another nature and are often in the headlines of mass media and academic analysis. The risks perceived by Africans and South Americans have to do with concerns about the loss of sovereignty; the threat to national security, the scale of sale of national assets to Chinese investors as well as with debt overhang of credits provided with almost no conditionality.[21]

China's relationship with the Portuguese-Speaking African countries (PALOPs) follows China's own track-record of success in Africa as a whole and is explained by three main reasons: (i) China is not a new partner, since very early on it supported the independence of African countries from Portuguese colonialism; (ii) China does not try to impose its world vision or political model as a condition to support the development of African countries, unlike some Western nations; last but not least, (iii) China's investment responds to the structural needs of the countries that ask for this support, investing, in particular, in infrastructure required for the development of these countries (Lorido 2022).[22]

In the Brazilian defense epistemic community, for instance, José Sales (2017) argues that the increasing presence of China in the West African coast brings risks to Brazil because of conflict of interests in a region considered to be strategic to the Brazilian defense policy. For José Sales, the strong capacity of China to invest and finance projects in the West Coast African countries (not only in the Portuguese-speaking countries in the region) would tend to reduce the Brazilian influence and trade flows in the countries at stake. Specifically, José Sales (2017, p. 67) asserts that:

> China has flooded Africa with manufactured products of all kinds, cheap and of low quality, competing with Brazilian exports to that continent, which are predominantly from small value-added products. In this way, China has been one of the responsible for the decrease in the consumer market for Brazilian manufactured products, at the same time as it exerts strong pressure with its great demand for raw materials and agricultural products, compelling the country to enter the agribusiness sector, and contributing to the deindustrialization of Brazil and the reprimarization of its exports. [translation from the Portuguese is ours]

José Sales (2017) further mentions that the competition of China in African countries in mining and civil construction sectors is detrimental to Brazilian companies operating in the region where a situation of competition naturally arises, and disputes are likely to increase. Ultimately, Sales (2017) refers to risks for Brazil in terms of defense once the Chinese would be also suppporting the "militarization" of the Atlantic South by selling weapons to "autoritarian regimes in the region", leading to a climate of instability. Such a perception of instability could in its turn persuade other external powers (like the US, UK, and France) to increase their military presence in the surrounding West Africa coast, what is contrary to Brazilian interests and the general guidelines of the ZPCAS.

In the same rationale, Mário Santos (2021) argues that:

> The Brazilian strategy in the South Atlantic space is based on deterrence and cooperation, aiming to prevent conflicts or threats caused by the action of extra-regional powers in the region, which places Chinese geopolitical expansion as a major challenge for Brazilian aspirations in the South Atlantic. In this case, it can be inferred that a scenario of instability in the South Atlantic would be largely harmful to Brazil, not only from an economic point of view, but also in terms of Brazilian security. That said, the existence of extra-regional actors in the South Atlantic with interests not necessarily converging with Brazilians gives rise to growing concerns for Brazil, being an impact factor in the region, an aspect in which the Chinese presence in the South Atlantic space has to do with. [translation from the Portuguese is ours]

Paulo Duarte (2016, p. 119), in his turn, presents a positive appreciation that China's engagement in the Atlantic South could become a risk reducer by acting like a factor of check and balance in the region:

> The South Atlantic could be a good test of a modern China that wants to reactivate the historical ties that once linked the Middle Kingdom to the world. At a time when Africa and Latin America are facing concrete security problems, such as drug and human trafficking, money laundering, organized crime, rogue states and narco-states, among others, China can and must be an active partner in combating these scourges. Another concrete example is the resurgence of tensions between the the United Kngdom and Argentina, following the recent discovery of important energy reserves north of the Falklands. [translation from the Portuguese is ours]

As Angola is concerned, a Portuguese-speaking African country, Lucy Corkin (2013) argues that a wide range of diferente countries have demonstrated very different capabilities and experiences of engagement with China, and that Angola has been among the most successful in this. By examining China's involvement in Angola, she assessed how different African states exploit this relationship to their advantage. In the same line, Vera Daves, Angola's incumbent finance minister, considers that relations with China have been "very positive" for more than 20 years and that her country will continue to invest in this cooperation and friendship between the two countries, with emphasis on bilateral trade, financial and economic relations (newspaper *Visão*, 6 August 2021).[23]

Final Remarks and Policy Advice

China assumed an outstanding role at the beginning of the twenty-first century, becoming an important member of the international system, with power of influence over several countries, including those located in South America and West Africa. The growing political, economic, and diplomatic interaction between China in the South Atlantic region generated a new factor for reordering the international relations, since the rapprochement with China allowed African and South American countries to discharge from the traditional Western powers and thus trying to build a more mutually beneficial relationship with the great Asian emerging power.

China's political and economic penetration in Africa in the last 20 years have aroused much controversy in the current literature, with scholars, journalists, and policymakers seeking to assess the benefits and risks stem-mimg from this engagement. Whatever the case, China is developing a very successful economic diplomacy through cooperation, investment, trade, and finance in the African continent and by doing so is reinforcing its capacity in promoting South-South dialogue and reaffirming its "soft power" in terms of international relations (Alves 2008).[24]

Regarding China's surging economic and diplomatic presence in the South Atlantic there has been also a diversity of reactions, ranging from excitement to panic and uncertainty, and not just from Africans but from other actors of the international community, especially in Europe and the US. However, despite the caveats, for many Africans China is regarded as a welcomed competitor, positioned to provide Africa with leverage toward traditional donors and address the structural imbalances of the international economic system within which many African states complain about.

In fact, the presence of China in the South Atlantic region may become a single opportunity for all the stakeholders to overcome the problems of low economic integration and underdevelopment of many countries in both sides of the South Atlantic. The scale of resources and the power of the Chinese economy may make a difference in a region where most countries are poor (low per capita income) and have limited interaction (trade) among themselves. In this way, China might exert a positive influence on mobilizing production factors and finance required to generate stronger economic growth and development in the region.

However, for performing such a beneficial role in the South Atlantic China needs to either reconsider or rebuild its ongoing strategy in West Africa and in South America in order to redirect trade and investment ties of both subcontinents not only with China but also to help promote more trade among the several Portuguese-speaking countries themselves in both sides of the Ocean and thus thereby creating conditions to take development and prosperity to all the stakeholders involved.

China has been already doing a good work by investing in port infrastructure and logistics in both sides of the South Atlantic. But there is a missing link: the lack of navigation lines and export credits to encourage trade between both sides of the South Atlantic Ocean. Such as sustained by Maia (2020), given that China has already extended its "maritime Silk Road" component of BRI to Africa and South America, the Chinese could assume a driving role in the maritime connection between West Africa and South America in a unified perspective of South Atlantic.[25]

The engagement of China in this initiative would be not only important in economic and geopolitical terms because China would perform a starring role in the South Atlantic but also contribute to expand trade and speed up economic development in the countries of Mercosur and those of West Africa coast (not just the Portuguese-speaking countries in the area). Further, building a bridge linking East and West of South Atlantic is the bottom line required to develop a strong economic relationship between those two continental blocks that always look to each other through the seas but that have so little contact with each other. Undoubtedly this is a fascinating and thought-provoking topic for further research and policy-making debate.

Notes

1. According to ECLAC, the Panama Canal was built primarily with strategic military objectives in mind, making it easier to defend the coasts of the US by optimizing the use of its naval fleet and creating a strategic hemispheric defense center covering North and South America, as well as the Caribbean and the Pacific.
2. Both Abdenour and de Souza Neto (2013) and Mário Santos (2021) emphasize that the South Atlantic is becoming a maritime axis of great relevance, given that it has a large amount of energy resources, is an important maritime communication route and power projection space. Thus, China, which was already characterized by its strong presence in Africa, has been expanding its area of influence in the South Atlantic. However, this Chinese geopolitical expansion tends to clash with Brazilian interests in the region, given that Brazil has the South Atlantic as part of its strategic surroundings. In addition to them, as highlighted by Espach (2021), over the past 20 years, China's trade and investment with South America has surged, and it is now the region's top trade partner. China's Maritime Silk Road envisions a global network of Chinese-managed ports and sea routes flowing with Chinese cargo. Rich with resources, the South Atlantic offers various opportunities for China to exploit its strategic weight. Off the South American and West African coastlines lay vast undersea oil and gas fields, and the region's waters are rich in biodiversity.
3. On the discussion of different theories of International Relations for approaching Chinese engagement in Africa see Moravcsik (1997) and Otele (2020).

4. On the application of the Liberal theory of International Relations to the analysis of the China–Africa engagement Cf: (i) Corkin (2008) and Haglund (2009).
5. For details see: (i) The National Interest, 15 October, 2020, available at https://nationalinterest.org/feature/china-now-world%E2%80%99s-largest-economy-we-shouldn%E2%80%99t-be-shocked-170719; (ii) World Economic Outlook (2020), IMF, available at https://www.imf.org/en/Publications/WEO/Issues/2020/09/30/world-economic-outlook-october-2020; and (iii) Unctad, 27 April 2021, available at: https://unctad.org/news/china-rise-trade-titan.
6. All the countries belonging to CPLP are not countries with common borders. They belong to diverse economic and geopolitical spaces. Therefore, CPLP differently from the Francophonie or the Commonwealth is not a "natural" group of countries sharing common problems, other than those that are established in the bloc's objectives. The question here is not to have grandiose expectations. Therefore, it will be completely natural that development of each country will follow diverse paces and confront diverse scenarios. This is just a cooperation space, not a kind of economic organization or political integration project. For more see Klomegah (2021).
7. The BRI has in fact positioned China at the center of the international system, with its physical, financial, cultural, technological, and political influence flowing to the rest of the world. It is redrawing the fine details of the world's map, with new railroads and bridges, fiber-optic cables and 5G networks, and ports. By one assessment, the BRI now touches more than 60 countries and has exceeded $200 billion in Chinese investment.
8. Nan Li (2021) firstly shows that China's naval strategy has undergone two major changes: from "near- coast defense" prior to the mid-1980s to "near-seas active defense" after the mid-1980s, and then to the advancement of a "far-seas operations" strategy. Related to the evolution of naval strategy is the change in naval capabilities: from limited capabilities for coastal defense to more expansive capabilities to operate more effectively in China's near seas by the late 2000s.
9. According to Veloso (2015), the Forum of Macau would be harmful to the Brazilian interests, since it strengthens the presence of China in the African countries where Brazil has more influence (the PALOPs). This would be one of the reasons for the Brazilian diplomacy to resist to actively participate in the Forum. For the Brazilian Ministry of Foreign Relations supporting the Forum of Macao would be the same as supporting the inroad that China has been conquering in these countries of great strategic interest for Brazil.
10. The FOCAC is part of a growing trend of South-South cooperation that provides an alternative to traditional development assistance mechanisms.

The Forum meets every three years and has held meetings in Beijing in 2000; Addis Ababa, Ethiopia in 2003; Beijing in 2006; Sharm El-Sheik, Egypt in 2009; Beijing in 2012; and Johannesburg, South Africa in 2015. The 7th and the 8th Ministerial Conferences of FOCAC were at summit level and held, respectively, in Beijing in 2018 and 2021.

11. Cf. For more details see: Abdenur and de Souza Neto (2013), Monet and Cesarín (2016), and Paulo Duarte (2016).
12. See Parello-Plesner (2016); For more see: Raúl Bernal Meza (2016).
13. The Cabinda port project in Angola, undertaken by the Chinese Energy China Gezhouba Group, is expected to be completed in June 2022.
14. According to Expansão (2022), the China International Trust Investment Corporation (CITIC) and Shandong Port Group (SPG) consortium was the winner of the public tender for the management and operation of the Multipurpose Container and General Cargo Terminal, at the Commercial Port of Lobito, for a period of 20 years, surpassing the Philippine group ICTSI.
15. The CPLP was formally created by Angola, Brazil, Cape Verde, Guinea-Bissau, Mozambique, Portugal, and São Tomé and Príncipe. In 2002, after gaining independence, East-Timor was welcomed as a member country during the IV Conference of Heads of State and Government held in Brasília, Brazil. In July 2014, during the summit held in Dili, East-Timor, Equatorial Guinea, through consensus, was accepted as a full member of the CPLP.
16. In this context, due to economic dynamism and concertation processes, such as Mercosur and CPLP, the South Atlantic acquired great economic and strategic prominence, mainly due to its control of large amounts of living and non-living resources. Inserted in CPLP's geographical area there are the Campos Basin and the Pre-salt layer in Brazil, Cabinda in Angola, and the Gulf of Guinea, where Sao Tome e Principe is located.
17. The weak economic integration among CPLP countries and the low emphasis on this issue by the major countries of the bloc explain the stagnation perception made by analysts, such as See Ariane Figueira and Bernardo Silva-Rêgo (2018).
18. In 2015, the incumbent Cape Verde's Prime Minister, Mr. José Maria Neves, called on governments within the CPLP to "work together" with the private sector to enable financing for small- and medium-sized enterprises in those nations. "Regarding CPLP, we can create investment funds to support business initiatives within the CPLP, and we can create platforms to promote trade among countries", said the Cape Verdean Prime Minister. Mr. Neves added that the CPLP community "*only makes sense if it can ease the circulation of people and goods to increase trade, investment opportunities, jobs and growth*" in all the countries within the group. Cf. Cape Verde PM urges Lusophone countries to link with private sector.

19. Some analysts minimize the low profile of trade performance of the CPLP members given that the economic bias did not prove to be the main reason for the constitution of the bloc, despite keeping future promising perspectives in several sectors, where Brazil has sought to accompany, through the internationalization of its companies, in addition to bilateral, multilateral, and cooperation trade agreements.
20. According to Kamoche et al. (2021), the Africa–China engagement has important implications for Africa's economic fortunes. As Chinese businesses become significant players on the continent, there has been an important debate to identify appropriate analysis for an emergent and controversial phenomenon, and to shed light on how the Chinese presence is impacting the African investment and business landscape, including organizational and human resource practices.
21. The perception of risks by the African governments stemming from the engagement of Chinese companies and banks in the region has been highlighted by many analysts such as O Diabo (2015), Lechini (2013), Barría (2021), Sales (2017); and Alves (2008).
22. Cf. For a discussion on China's track-record of success in Africa, especially with the Portuguese-Speaking African countries (PALOPs) see Corkin (2013).
23. On how different African states exploit the relationship with China to their advantage see Lorido (2022).
24. Alves (2008) gives an insightful approach by which China has been so successful in African countries.
25. The lack of navigation lines and export credits to encourage trade between both sides of the South Atlantic is really a crucial issue that China should consider to consolidate its influence in the South America and West Africa. For more dicussion on this point see Altair Maia (2020).

References

Abdenur, Adriana; de Souza Neto, Danilo (2013). "La creciente influencia de China en el Atlántico Sur". *Revista CIDOB d'Afers Internacionals*, 102–103, 169–197.

Alves, Ana Cristina (2008). *Chinese Economic Diplomacy in Africa: The Lusophone Strategy*. In: *China Returns to Africa: A Rising Power and a Continent Embrace*. Oxford University Press.

Barría, Cecilia (2021). "A estratégica rede de portos que a China controla no mundo e avança até no Brasil". *BBC News Mundo*, https://www.bbc.com/portuguese/internacional-58982435. Accessed 10 Nov 2021.

Corkin, Lucy (2008). "Competition or Collaboration? Chinese & South African Transnational Companies in Africa". *Review of African Political Economy*, 35 (115), 128–134.

——— (2013). *Uncovering African Agency: Angola's Management of China's Credit Lines*. Farnham: Ashgate.

CPLP (2015). Permanent Secretariat Forum for Economic and Trade Co-operation. https://www.forumchinaplp.org.mo/cape-verde-pm-urges-lusophone-countries-to-link-with-private-sector/. Accessed 12 Nov 2021.

Economy, Elisabeth (2022). "Xi Jinping's New World Order", *Foreign Affairs*, 101 (1), https://www.foreignaffairs.com/articles/china/2021-12-09/xi-jinpings-new-world-order. Accessed 30 Jan 2022.

Espach, Ralph (2021). "A New Great Game Finds the South Atlantic". *Texas National Security Review*, https://warontherocks.com/2021/03/a-new-great-game-finds-the-south-atlantic/. Accessed 13 Jan 2022.

Expansão (2022). *Chineses ficam com a gestão do Porto do Lobito na fase final do concurso*, https://expansao.co.ao/angola/interior/chineses-ficam-com-a-gestao-do-porto-do-lobito-na-fase-final-do-concurso-106352.html. Accessed 18 Jan 2022.

Figueira, Ariane; Silva-Rêgo, Bernardo (2028). "The Economic Face of International Co-operative Arrangements: The Cases of IBSA and CPLP". *Contexto Internacional* 40 (1), 139–160.

Figueiredo, Eurico; Volante, Alexandre (2019). "The Community of Portuguese-Speaking Countries (CPLP) and the Strategy of Intelligence Power Projection of Brazil: An Analysis of the Brazilian Foreign Policy." *Revista da Escola de Guerra Naval*, 25 (1), 129–166.

Fórum de Cooperação China-África. https://bricspolicycenter.org/forum-de-cooperacao-china-africa-focac/. Accessed 18 Nov 2021.

Haglund, D. (2009). "In It for the Long Term? Governance and Learning Among Chinese Investors in Zambia's Copper Sector". *The China Quarterly*, 199, 610–626.

International Monetary Fund, World Economic Outlook (October 2020). "A Long and Difficult Ascent". *IMF*, https://www.imf.org/en/Publications/WEO/Issues/2020/09/30/world-economic-outlook-october-2020. Accessed 14 Nov 2021.

Kamoche, Ken; Gunessee, Saileshsingh; Kufuor, Nana K. (2021). "The Africa–China Engagement: Contemporary Developments and Directions for Future Research". *Africa Journal of Management*, 7 (4), 447–464.

Klomegah, Kester (2021). Community of Portuguese Language Countries (CPLP): Forging Cultural Unity in Economic Diversity, https://www.pressenza.com/2021/07/community-of-portuguese-language-countries-cplp-forging-cultural-unity-in-economic-diversity/. Accessed 12 Jan 2022.

Lechini, Gladys (2013). A China na África: discurso sedutor, intenções duvidosas. Rosario: *Revista Nueva Sociedad*, https://static.nuso.org/media/articles/downloads/3970_1.pdf. Accessed 15 Nov 2.

Li, Nan (2021). "The Evolution of China's Naval Strategy and Capabilities: From 'Near Coast' and 'Near Seas' to 'Far Seas'". *Asian Security*, 5 (2), 144–169, https://www.tandfonline.com/doi/abs/10.1080/14799850902886567?journalCode=fasi20. Accessed 17 Dec 2021.

Lorido, Rui (2022). Visão: *O desenvolvimento da China fortalece os países de língua portuguesa*. http://portuguese.cri.cn/news/world/408/20220107/726940.html. Accessed 29 Jan 2022.

Maia, Altair (2020). *ZPCAS a new deal for South Atlantic*. Columbia.

Meza, Raúl Bernal (2016). *Las Relaciones entre China y America Latina y la retórica "ganadores- ganadores"* in: Moneta, Carlos; Cesarín, Sergio [et al.]. *La Tentación Pragmática China - Argentina/América Latina: lo actual, lo próximo y lo distante*. Sáenz Peña: Eduntref.

Moneta, Carlos; Cesarín, Sergio et al (2016). *La Tentación Pragmática China - Argentina/América Latina: lo actual, lo próximo y lo distante*. Sáenz Peña: Eduntref.

Moravcsik, A. (1997). "Taking Preferences Seriously: A Liberal Theory of International Politics". *International Organization*, 51 (4), 513–553.

O Diabo (2015). "A ascenção do Império Colonial Chinês em Angola". O Diabo, https://jornaldiabo.com/internacional/china-angola-colonizacao/. Accessed 10 Dec 2021.

Oscar M. Otele. "Introduction. China-Africa Relations: Interdisciplinary Question and Theoretical Perspectives". *The African Review*, 47 (2020), 267–284.

Parello-Plesner, Jonas (2016). *China's Risk Map In the South Atlantic*. The German Marshall Fund of the United States – GMF, http://www.gmfus.org/listings/research/type/publication. Accessed 12 Nov 2021.

Paulo Duarte (2016). "As Incursões da China na América Latina e Atlântico Sul". *Marília: Brazilian Journal of International Relations (BJIR)*, 5 (1), 98–120.

Penha, Eli Alves (2011). *Relações Brasil-Africa e geopolítica do Atlântico Sul*. Salvador: Edufba.

Sales, José Carlos Cavalcanti (2017). A Expansão Chinesa na África e os Conflitos de Interesses com o Brasil na Costa Oeste Africana. Escola de Guerra Naval, https://www.marinha.mil.br/egn/sites/www.marinha.mil.br.egn/files/CPEM30%20TESE%20CMG%20SALES.pdf. Accessed 12 Oct 2021.

Santos, Mário (2021). "Brasil e China no Atlântico Sul: a expansão geopolítica chinesa e suas implicações para o Brasil". VIII Encontro Brasileiro de Estudos Estratégicos e Relações Internacionais, https://www.youtube.com/watch?v=a8X_jiPn5gs. Accessed 12 Nov 2021.

Unctad (April 2021). https://unctad.org/news/china-rise-trade-titan. Accessed 16 Nov 2021.

Veloso, Isabel (2015). "O Fórum Macau e a CPLP nas Estratégias de Cooperação Sul-Sul da China e do Brasil na África". São Paulo: *Perspectivas*, 45, 41–62.

"So Much Sea": Opportunities and Challenges in Portugal-Brazil Maritime Cooperation

Daniel Cardoso

Introduction

Portugal and Brazil have a long history of state-to-state relations. Culture has been traditionally the main driver of the relationship, but, in recent decades, there has been an effort to develop new areas of cooperation, ranging from science, technology, and education, to the economy, among others. This effort was based on a dense set of institutions, agreements, and exchanges already in place.

Even though the Atlantic Ocean is the geographic space connecting the two, maritime cooperation has not been a priority in the bilateral relationship. There is no specific agreement, document, or institution on this issue. There are a few initiatives that bring together the two countries on issues related to the sea, but they are far from constituting a consistent and coordinated bilateral approach to maritime affairs. Besides being the space that Brazil and Portugal share, the Atlantic Ocean is an area of

D. Cardoso (✉)
OBSERVARE-UAL / IPRI-NOVA, Lisbon, Portugal
e-mail: dcardoso@autonoma.pt

P. A. B. Duarte et al. (eds.), *Portugal and the Lusophone World*,
https://doi.org/10.1007/978-981-99-0455-6_11

crucial geopolitical and geoeconomic importance. Therefore, the room for cooperation between the two countries in the ocean is vast.

Against this background, the chapter will analyse the challenges and opportunities associated with maritime cooperation between Portugal and Brazil. There are several studies on the bilateral relationship, which makes it possible to have a general picture of this topic (Cervo and Calvet de Magalhães 2000; Fonseca 2010; Carvalho 2011; Ataíde 2016). The chapter contributes to this literature and expands it by specifically focusing on Portugal- Brazil maritime cooperation. It argues that this area has the potential to stimulate the relationship with possible positive spill-over effects to other areas, namely science and technology, economy, and security.

It is a qualitative study based on primary and secondary sources. All the treaties between Portugal and Brazil in recent years have been analysed as well as the official documents issued by the two countries in this area. Data was also collected from the website and publications of the institutions operating in this realm. Besides these primary sources, newspaper articles and other secondary sources were considered and analysed.

The chapter is organised as follows. The first section presents a brief historic overview of bilateral relations, focusing on recent developments. In the second section, the geopolitical and geoeconomic relevance of the Atlantic Ocean is examined. This analysis will provide the context for the evaluation of the maritime dimension of the bilateral relations, which will be done in the third section. The fourth section features an analysis of the risks and opportunities that increasing competition between China and the US poses to these two countries regarding maritime affairs. The chapter closes with a few concluding remarks.

History of Relations Between Portugal and Brazil

Portugal and Brazil have developed cordial and peaceful relations for the past two centuries. In the nineteenth century and for most of the twentieth century, these relations were mostly of cultural nature (Pato 2020). Bringing them together were historic, cultural, and language affinities. In economic and political terms, the two countries were distant (Cervo and Calvet de Magalhães 2000). Portugal was focused on its African colonies whereas Brazil was working to stabilise its borders and gain international relevance.

Against this background, the bilateral relations were marked by a difficulty to translate the rhetoric of fraternity and friendship between the two countries into concrete political and economic initiatives. Indeed, only recently did the two countries manage to significantly deepen their ties in these areas (Fonseca 2010). The end of the dictatorships in both countries in the 1970s and the 1980s as well as the liberalisation and internationalisation of their economies motivated by regional integration and international trade treaties favoured a rapprochement (Carvalho 2011). In addition to these conditions, it was crucial the stability that the new currency (Real) brought to the Brazilian economy. In this context, bilateral trade and economic investment increased, mostly towards the end of the 1990s. The role of Portugal was key in this context, especially during António Guterres's first mandate as prime minister. Guterres made Brazil a foreign policy priority for Portugal. Seizing this opportunity, several Portuguese companies such as EDP, PT, CIMPOR, Brisa, SONAE, and Águas de Portugal started or increased their investments in Brazil (Ataíde 2016). Furthermore, Portugal's rapid modernisation after accession to the European Economic Community (ECC) attracted workers from Brazil paving the way for an inversion of migration flows between the two countries. Whereas the traditional migration flow was from Portugal to Brazil, since the 1990s more and more Brazilians have chosen Portugal as their migration destination. According to the Portuguese National Statistics Institute (INE), the Brazilian community in Portugal double its size in the 1990s, totalling 22,000 people in 2001 (Pordata, n/d).

The increase in the flow of people, goods, and capital was accompanied by significant institutional developments. In 1991, the two countries signed the Framework Cooperation Agreement and held their first high-level bilateral summit in Brasília. Portugal became, at that point, the only European country with which Brazil had annual institutional exchanges (Ataíde 2016). Also in 1991, the first Iberian-American Summit takes place, showing that both Portugal and Spain were interested in complementing their European linkages with close ties with Latin American partners (Carvalho 2011). This multilateral trend in Portugal–Brazil relations was deepened in 1996 with the establishment of the Community of Portuguese Speaking Countries (CPLP). In 2000, Brazil and Portugal increased their institutional links by signing the Treaty of Friendship, Cooperation, and Consultation, which replaced several previous bilateral treaties, including a similar one from 1953 (Pato 2020). One of the main points of this treaty was the establishment of the Permanent Portuguese-Brazilian Committee to monitor the treaty and create a stable cooperation environment between the two countries. The work has been carried out in sub-committees including those on consulate issues, economy, culture, and education. In 2007, Brazil established a strategic partnership with the European Union (EU), an initiative launched during the Portuguese presidency of the Council of the EU.

Today, Portugal and Brazil have a relationship based on a broad institutional setting, which includes various bilateral agreements, a permanent committee, and regular summits (since 1991, there have been 12 summits). Migration continues to be an important driver of the relationship. The Brazilian community in Portugal amounts almost to 190,000 people. In economic terms, the results are mixed. Bilateral trade rarely reaches the 2 billion dollar mark. As of 2020, Brazil is only the 9th largest seller of goods and services to Portugal, and it is not among the 10 largest buyers of Portuguese products (Eurostat 2021). In terms of investment, the impetus of the mid-1990s did not last until today. Around 600 Portuguese companies are operating in Brazil, but the level of investment is low (França *apud* Ferreira 2021).

Given these features, scholars agree that Brazil is undoubtedly Portugal's main partner in Latin America and vice-versa (Cervo and Calvet de Magalhães 2000; Fonseca 2010; Carvalho 2011). However, the inconsistency in economic relations and the narrow political linkages also indicate that the bilateral partnership is not as strong as the one that the United Kingdom (UK) has with some of its former colonies like the United States (US) and Australia. This means that there is room for improvement in the bilateral relationship. One of these areas is maritime cooperation. The chapter turns to this dimension in the next sections.

The Geopolitical and Geoeconomic Relevance of the Atlantic

Oceans and seas, defined as the global ocean, cover 70% of the globe's surface and connect every continent and almost every country in the world. Indeed, only 41 states (defined as landlocked states) do not have access to the sea (Campos and Rodrigues 2020, p. 5). Oceans are also an essential element of life-support for our planet. As stated by the United Nations (2018), "they generate most of the oxygen we breathe, absorb a large share of carbon dioxide emissions, provide food and nutrients, regulate climate, and are important economically for countries that rely on tourism, fishing and other marine resources for income, and serve as the backbone of international trade". Around 80% of global trade by volume and over 70% of global trade by value are carried by sea and are handled by ports worldwide (UNCTAD 2018). This means that the world economy and globalisation depend on open, safe seas and oceans for free trade, transport, and economic development. Besides, oceans are crucial for global communication, since it is through the 750,000 miles of undersea cables that almost 95% of mobile and internet data is shared (Satariano 2019; Cerulus 2021). While new wireless and satellite technologies exist today, cables remain the fastest, most efficient, and least expensive way to send information across the ocean (Satariano 2019). All these dimensions are present in the most important international legal document regulating the oceans, the United Nations Convention on the Law of the Sea, from 1982 (Campos and Rodrigues 2020).

The conditions provided by the oceans are important for the environment, the economy, but also international politics (Cierco and Silva 2015). These conditions are the foundations of what is defined as sea or maritime power. Silva (2017, p. 238) defines sea power "as the ability of a state to exploit or influence the range of sea-related activities in the political, economic, social, environmental, and military domains. Naval power is the military component of sea power". Alfred Mahan, an American admiral, has produced some of the most important academic and policy work in this regard. In his book "The Influence of Sea Power upon History", Mahan explained that the best and most efficient way to project power internationally is through the sea (Mahan 2010). First, mastery of the sea means control of 7/10 of the surface of the globe. Second, the oceans constitute a continuous space that provides access to all continents and islands which is important for commerce, but also military aspects (Mahan 2010). To this point, Pezarat Correia (2002, p. 154) adds that, although through the air is also possible to reach every continent, by sea it is possible to transport a larger quantity of forces (human and material), and sea power can be converted into airpower (aircraft carriers) and the opposite does not happen.

In addition to some specificities, all the political, economic, and environmental characteristics mentioned above can also be found in the Atlantic, the second largest ocean in the world. It covers an area of 86 million and 560 thousand km^2 in size, about 24% of the earth's surface, spreading across 65 countries. Portugal and Brazil are important states in this context. The latter has 8000 km of coastline and 3,500,000 km^2 of maritime rescue area along the South Atlantic. The islands of Trindade and Martins Vaz, the eastern end of Brazil are located 1167 km from the Brazilian coast and 2400 miles from the African coast. The former has one of the most extensive exclusive economic zones (EEZ) in Europe, in part due to the territorial extent Azores and Madeira allow. The EEZ is an area of Portuguese sovereignty that includes the resources of the entire column of water and sea bed within the limit of 200 nautical miles beyond the coastline.

The Atlantic is a major route for trade between the northern and southern hemispheres, and Portugal and Brazil are no exception to this: in 2020, 95% of all the trade in goods between the two countries was done by sea (GEE 2021). For this reason, deep water ports are of crucial importance, especially Sines (in Portugal) and Santos (in Brazil). Cape Verde, which stands halfway between the two countries, is a promising important entrepôt. These three countries form a strategic triangle in the Atlantic with potential benefits to all of them. The commercial connections between the two sides of the Atlantic have also a dark side, in which organised crime engages in the illegal trafficking of people, weapons, and narcotics. This indicates the importance of maritime security in the Atlantic to respond to these transnational threats and others, such as piracy (Pires et al. 2020, p. 2; Seabra and Costa 2021, p. 11). Indeed, the major concern of the international community in terms of maritime piracy is in the Atlantic, specifically the Gulf of Guinea, (Guedes 2020, p. 112). According to the International Chamber of Commerce's International Maritime Bureau (IMB), out of the 135 crewmembers kidnapped from vessels around the world in 2020, 95% of them were kidnapped in the Gulf of Guinea (IMB 2021).

Besides being a fundamental trade route, the Atlantic Ocean is also a key in terms of energy resources both renewables (wind offshore, ocean waves, solar) and non-renewable. The Atlantic space holds 67% of technically recoverable shale gas reserves, 77% of installed solar power capacity, 64% of installed wind power capacity, and 59% of geothermal energy capacity (Kraemer and Stefes 2016). Additionally, in terms of offshore oil extraction, the most important area is the so-called Golden Triangle between the Gulf of Mexico, Brazil, and West Africa, including Angola (Zhang et al. 2019).

In the Atlantic Ocean, there are a high number of undersea cables connecting the three continents: America, Africa, and Europe. In the case of Brazil, the virtual digital connection with the other continents, including Europe, was always made with submarine cables going to the US as a crossing point. Recently, Brazil joined efforts with the EU to build a high- performance submarine cable between the cities of Fortaleza, in Brazil, and Sines, in Portugal (Ellalink, n/d). The project's main goals were for Brazil to have an alternative way to share virtual information with other great international players and to boost the development of cloud centres and data services around the cables' landing spots in Sines and Fortaleza (Cerulus 2021). The submarine cable was launched last June 1, 2021, and now represents the most critical way to connect Brazil to the world (Ayres 2021).

The Atlantic Ocean also displays some of the best places in the world, like the Azores Islands, to carry out oceanic and climatic research. This research is of crucial importance because, as put by Seabra (2021, p. 7), "a deep understanding of the oceans' behaviour is essential to prevent their destabilisation and to promote the fight against ocean pollution, acidification, loss of oxygen, and deterioration and destruction of the ecosystems and biodiversity".

Lastly, even though its centrality in world politics has been waning in recent years due to the growing importance of Asia and the Pacific (Reis 2015), the Atlantic remains geopolitically relevant. First and foremost, the Atlantic is a central transit point. It connects the EU and the US, the two most important markets in the world, and allies in the North Atlantic Treaty Organization (NATO). Furthermore, in the Southern part of the Atlantic, one can find three of the most relevant world hinges: the Cape of Good Hope, connecting the Atlantic and Indian Oceans; the Panama Canal; and the Strait of Magellan, which connects the Atlantic and Pacific oceans.

Maritime Cooperation Between Portugal and Brazil: The Missing Link

The previous section demonstrated the relevance of the oceans, in general, and of the Atlantic, in particular. In this section, cooperation between Portugal and Brazil in maritime issues, specifically regarding the Atlantic will be examined.

To assess the significance of maritime cooperation in Portugal–Brazil relations, we have analysed all the main legal bilateral documents signed between the two countries in the last decades. The first conclusion is that there is no specific agreement, memorandum of understanding (MoU), or any sort of formal bilateral document specifically on maritime issues. The only document which touches upon a related matter is the 2010 MoU on deepwater hydrocarbon exploration and production in the Atlantic (Lusa/Visão 2010). The MoU was signed following the discovery in 2007 of a vast offshore subsalt oil field by the Brazilian company, Petrobrás, together with foreign companies, including Petrogal, a subsidiary of the Portuguese oil company, GALP. The discovery, yielded as the largest oil discovery in 30 years, showed how advanced and sophisticated Petrobrás and Petrogal's technology for ultra-deepwater exploration was at that point, making them world leaders in this area (Offshore 2008). The MoU sought to deepen collaboration between the two states and their companies in terms of research and development to continue to develop this technology and ease the complexity and difficulty of ultra-deepwater oil exploration and extraction (Lusa/Visão 2010).

In the most important legal documents guiding the bilateral relationship, the 1991 Framework Cooperation Agreement and the 2000 Treaty of Friendship, Cooperation, and Consultation, there are just a few references to maritime issues. In the 1991 agreement, there is one article on the fishery in which the two countries state their commitment to collaborate economically, politically, and scientifically in this area. In the 2000 friendship treaty, there is no section or article about maritime matters, even though there are other areas specifically mentioned (justice, armed forces, environment, economy, and health, among others). In the treaty, there is no reference to the terms "ocean", "Atlantic" and "sea". Besides, as mentioned before, it was in the realm of the friendship treaty that the permanent bilateral committee was established. Associated with this committee, various sub-committees were created to carry out work on specific policy areas ranging from tourism and visas to science, technology, economy, and education. No sub-committee on maritime issues was created so far.

The analysis above shows that maritime cooperation has not been a priority in Portugal–Brazil relations. Nevertheless, there have been a few initiatives that offer promising avenues for more frequent and formal cooperation between the two countries in this regard. The first one is the Atlantic International Research Center (AIR Center), an intergovernmental-driven framework and institution, established in 2018. Among its founding members are Portugal, Brazil, Angola, Cape Verde, the US, and South Africa, among others. The AIR Centre's mission is to unleash the potential of the Atlantic to the benefit of society. In that sense, the centre is driven and at the same time supports emerging technological innovations and advances in data science to carry out research on the deep sea, space, climate, ocean, and energy in the Atlantic. The research centre was the outcome of a long process of scientific diplomacy, driven by the Portuguese Government, called Atlantic Interactions. Bringing together the various participants was the view that the Atlantic had great potential but was still understudied in terms of its natural resources, ecosystem dynamics, and interdependences with human activities. Therefore, a better understanding of the Atlantic, for the sustainable management of this common resource, required the alignment of research strategies through international cooperation. Azores, the Portuguese Archipelago, was chosen to be the centre's headquarters due to its privileged location in the Atlantic. Besides the headquarters in the Azores, the Air Centre also has offices in Lisbon and Brazil (Air Centre, n/d).

The second one is the Atlantic Center. Hosted by Portugal, this multinational agency seeks to produce knowledge about the Atlantic in the domain of maritime security, foster political dialogue, and promote defence capacity-building among Atlantic countries (Atlantic centre, n/d). Despite having distinct geopolitics and strategic context, countries from the North and South Atlantic have room for cooperation around common issues such as the protection of the maritime globalised system, the maritime scientific research, and the development of the Blue Economy (Silva 2020). These common issues are exacerbated by the various security priorities associated with the Atlantic today, such as protection from piracy and organised crime, prevention of Illegal, Unreported and Unregulated (IUU) fisheries, and protection of communication cables, among others. The centre expects to achieve its mission through the participation of several national military and civilian experts, from the Atlantic basin countries and partners, which include, so far, Brazil, Angola, Germany, Spain, Cape Verde, Morocco, UK, Cameroon, US, Uruguay, among others. The centre was officially launched in 2021 and its headquarters will be in the Azores, Portugal (Atlantic centre, n/d).

The third one is the work done within the Community of Portuguese Speaking Countries (CPLP). In this context, it is worth highlighting the "CPLP Strategy for the Oceans", prepared in 2009, and the "Meeting of Ministers of Maritime Affairs", which began in 2010 on a biennial basis (but which in the meantime failed as early as the 2014 meeting), the "Permanent Technical Secretariat for Maritime Affairs" and the project to create a "Maritime Strategic Information Observatory" (CPLP, n/d). However, these plans have not produced substantial results and, according to Graça (2018), that might be related to the slow decision-making and implementation process of the organisation.

The initiatives mentioned above are relevant per se, but they are not examples of a consistent, regular, and integrated maritime cooperation between Portugal and Brazil. That sort of cooperation does not exist between the two countries. In the remaining part of this section, we will analyse the possible reasons behind this.

Generally, progress in Portugal–Brazil relations occurs in the context of particular historic occasions and initiatives led by the will of specific leaders. That means that the bilateral relationship is marked by a lack of consistency and regularity (Fonseca 2010), which is also noticeable in the maritime domain. The initiatives mentioned above are promising avenues for bilateral cooperation, but there are not articulated, even though they all are related to the Atlantic. The lack of a more integrated and coordinated approach to maritime bilateral cooperation means that the synergies between these various initiatives are under-explored. This scenario could be overcome by adding institutional weight to the maritime domain, for example, with the creation of a sub-committee on maritime affairs in the permanent bilateral committee, which would follow the developments both in the Air Centre, and the Atlantic Centre, and the CPLP.

In the last decades, the foreign policy priorities of Brazil and Portugal have revolved mostly around their immediate neighbourhoods. Since 1991, Brazil has put regional integration through Mercosul and other institutions at the top of its international goals (Saraiva 2020). The same for Portugal regarding European integration since 1986 (Pitta e Cunha 2011). This meant that the continental dimension has been more preeminent in these countries' foreign policies than the maritime dimension. However, the latter was not completely disregarded by either of them. NATO is crucial for Portugal while links with Africa have been important for Brazil. CPLP is a relevant project for both countries.

Recently, Brazil and Portugal have put more emphasis on the maritime dimension of their foreign and defence policies, seeking to complement the priority given to the continental dimension (Pitta e Cunha 2011; Fonseca 2011). In the case of Brazil, the 2020 National Defence Strategy considers the Atlantic to be an area of strategic importance. The document highlights the relevance of animal and natural resources in this area, especially the reserves of oil and gas (Brazil 2020). The 2008

National Defence Strategy and the 2012 White Paper had both already elevated the South Atlantic to the same degree of importance previously accorded to the River Plate and the Amazon. To highlight its relevance, Brazilian authorities defined the Ocean Atlantic as “Blue Amazon”, a slogan designed to generate popular support for Brazil’s maritime power build-up (Silva 2013).

In the case of Portugal, the 2013 Strategic Concept of National Defence refers to the Atlantic as a vast geographical area of relevant strategic interest, highlighting the role of trade and the natural resources (Portugal, 2013). This re-orientation to the sea by Portuguese authorities has been more visible since the beginning of the twenty-first century, with the creation of specific national agencies and plans on maritime affairs (Silva 2020). Based on studies and surveys, both Brazil and Portugal have also asked the UN, under the auspices of the UN Convention on the Law of the Sea, to expand the outer limits of their continental shelves beyond 200 nautical miles. This extension would make it possible for the two countries to have further access to mineral resources and living organisms that exist on the seabed and in the subsoil (EMPC, n/d; Marinha, n/d). At the time of writing (February 2022), the UN has partially approved the Brazilian request and has not released the decision concerning the Portuguese request (EMPC, n/d; Marinha, n/d).

Various authors assert that this focus on the maritime dimension should be strengthened further. The argument is that Portugal is a peripherical state in the European Union, but it gains geopolitical relevance as a link between the Atlantic and Europe (Carvalho 2004; Pitta e Cunha 2004; Simões 2013; Cierco and Silva 2015; Graça 2018). However, when it comes to the relationship with Brazil, the possibility of Portugal serving as a link between Brasilia and Europe might be limited. First, as put by Valença Pinto, in times of globalisation and digitalisation, geography is important, but not a fatality. A country can be geographically peripherical, but central when it comes to the internet, intelligence, and knowledge (Valença Pinto 2015). Second, despite the historic links between the two countries, Brazil does not necessarily need Portugal to establish relations with the EU. For this reason, pursuing this strategy can be ineffective and, besides that, Portugal runs the risk of becoming a mere instrument, a channel, or a platform in the cooperation between Brazil and the EU. To be clear, Portuguese authorities must play a role in this setting, but it is necessary to be aware of the limitations and risks and have clarity regarding the national interests and strategies.

One of the reasons for the limited focus on maritime affairs in the relationship between Portugal and Brazil is the fact that they have different policy-making contexts and some divergent priorities and interests. In the case of Portugal, for example, its maritime strategy must take into consideration the EU stakes in this area, which include an Integrated Maritime Policy (European Union, 2007), a Maritime Strategy for the Atlantic Ocean Area (2011), and Maritime Security Strategy (European Union, 2014), among other initiatives. Portuguese authorities are, therefore, presented with the challenge of navigating this policy setting that can pose opportunities (since they can elevate the country's position in the Atlantic), but also risks (such as the decrease in the country's autonomy in this area).

In the case of Brazil, as pointed out by Reis (2015), it is important, above all, to understand the Southern and Northern parts as having specific and distinctive dynamics and demands. Regarding security, for example, there is no military alliance in South Atlantic, similar to the one in the north (NATO). The South Atlantic follows other types of institutional arrangements: one of the most relevant is Zona de Paz e Cooperação do Atlântico Sul (ZOPACAS), launched in 1986, by Brazil and which gathers African and South American countries (Seabra 2019). Relatively inactive in recent years, this informal mechanism remains a potential space for cooperation in this region.

For Brazil, therefore, given the different characteristics of the two parts of the Atlantic, it is necessary to consider the specific type of answers and solutions for each of them. In this context, an exclusive unified view of the Atlantic is, therefore, seen as counter- productive. Furthermore, the idea of unity in the Atlantic brings back memories of European and North American hegemonies in the area, which are to be avoided (Reis 2015). Given its economic and political weight, Brazil aims to function as a gatekeeper in the South Atlantic, which means that its interests and concerns must be taken into consideration by external actors. While this position does not close the door for a more holistic and integrated collaboration between Portugal and Brazil in maritime affairs, it does provide relevant clues on the expectations of the latter regarding this type of collaboration.

Lastly, the size of the Atlantic demands the mobilisation of vast military and economic resources both from Portugal and Brazil. The two countries have small fleets, depleting naval industries, and second-rank ports. They are both relevant actors in terms of science and technology related to the sea, but the room for development is ample. While this limitation of resources calls for cooperation, it also constrains the scope of joint initiatives. If collaboration in maritime affairs is to be deepened, optimal use of resources will be necessary.

This section analysed the cooperation between Brazil and Portugal in maritime affairs. It showed that, while the room for articulated, holistic, and coordinated cooperation between the two countries in this area exists, there are various hurdles in the way. In the next section, we will zoom out to examine how growing US-China competition in international affairs impacts the Atlantic Ocean and Portugal-Brazil cooperation in this realm.

The Atlantic in the Context of US-China Competition

Even though its importance has been waning in recent years due to the economic re- emergence of Asia-Pacific countries, especially China, the Atlantic remains geopolitically and geoeconomically relevant, as demonstrated in the previous sections (Reis 2015). Both the US and China have stakes in the region and, as the competition between the two of them increases, this will likely have an impact on the various aspects related to the Atlantic, including the cooperation between Brazil and Portugal. The competition is openly assumed by the US. In the recent report on Indo-Pacific published by the White House, the competition with China has been pointed out as one of the biggest challenges for the country (The White House 2022).

China is far from the Atlantic. However, due to its growing integration into the world economy, this region has become increasingly relevant to the Asian country. In terms of trade, China is a key partner for various Atlantic countries, including Portuguese-speaking countries. China is Brazil's most important trade partner since 2009 (Cardoso 2016) and is one of Portugal's top 10 exporters (Nunes 2021). Most of this trade is done by sea, therefore the importance of the Atlantic. In this sense, guaranteeing the freedom of the seas and the safe circulation of products is key to China's economy (Abdenur et al. 2014; Leandro and Duarte 2020a).

In recent years, China has also become a key investor in the two countries economies. Most of this investment goes to the energy sector. In the case of Brazil, China's investment in electricity and, especially oil, is of utmost relevance. Chinese state companies are very strongly present in the pre-salt basins along the coast of Brazil, the main source of oil for the South American country (Cardoso 2015). In the case of Portugal, Chinese companies have purchased stakes, among other sectors, in two energy-related companies, EDP and REN (Siying 2018).

These investments are likely to increase in the next years due to the Belt and Road Initiative (BRI). Launched in 2013 by China's president, Xi Jinping, the BRI, is a plan to further the links of China with the world through investments in infrastructure, mainly transportation corridors, such as rail, roads, seaports, airports, special economic zones, and dry ports, and is, therefore, composed of two main elements: the Silk Road Economic Belt, consisting of the land route; and the 21st Century Maritime Silk Road, the sea lanes (Leandro and Duarte 2020b).

Given the distance to China, the maritime dimension is the most relevant one for the relations between the Asian country and Portuguese-speaking countries, including Portugal and Brazil. Beijing has not shared many details on the maritime silk road, however, according to the Vision for Maritime Cooperation Under the Belt and Road Initiative, there will three blue economic corridors, being the most relevant for Portuguese-speaking countries the one connecting China-Pakistan, Bangladesh-China-India-Myanmar through the South China Sea and the Indian Ocean, and then continuing to the Mediterranean Sea and into the Atlantic and Africa (Songa and Fabinyia 2022).

Despite this potential, no specific infrastructure project in the realm of the BRI was carried out in Brazil and Portugal, even though the latter has officially joined the initiative in 2017 (Brazil has not signed an MoU with China in this regard). Nevertheless, given the position of Brazil and Portugal in the Atlantic and the intense economic relations with China, it is likely that the BRI will become more important for these countries in the next years. In the case of Brazil, there has been already Chinese investment in infrastructure, some of it directly related to maritime affairs. As mentioned before, Chinese companies are key players in the extraction of oil from the pre-salt basins along the Brazilian coast. In addition, Chinese companies have acquired stakes in the second most important Brazilian port in volume, Paranaguá, and there are conversations to acquire the port of São Luís (Canal Rural 2020; Portos e Navios 2019). This investment is important given the need for modernisation of Brazilian ports, however, it is worth bearing in mind that the history of Chinese investment in Brazil is marked by ups and downs. Many of the infrastructure projects ended up not being implemented. In 2010, for example, there was the possibility of China investing in a new port between Rio de Janeiro and São Paulo, which would become the main gateway for commerce between the two countries. The port was only partially developed and without Chinese funding (Cardoso 2015). By the same token, in 2015, Brazil and China announced the goal of building, with Chinese investment, a railroad from São Paulo to Peru, connecting the two sides of South America (Senado Notícias 2017). That project has not come to fruition either.

In the case of Portugal, there is no specific investment in infrastructure yet, but there have been conversations regarding Chinese investment in the port of Sines, close to Lisbon. The port is interesting for China because it can offer alternative access to the centre of Europe, not far from the Strait of Gibraltar, especially for commercial vessels crossing the Panama Canal. The port is Europe's nearest one to the Panama Canal and has the potential to become a link between maritime shipping and railroads on the European continent (Leandro and Duarte 2020a; Silva and Pereira 2020). Furthermore, differently from Brazil, Portugal has taken concrete steps with China in terms of maritime cooperation. The two countries have, since 2016, an MoU on Maritime Cooperation and have signed papers establishing a "blue partnership" in 2017 during the Blue Economy Partnership Forum held in China's southeast Fujian. Azores might also become an important link between the two countries, especially if the US withdraws its military base in Lajes (Leandro and Duarte 2020a; Silva and Pereira 2020).

All these movements have drawn the attention of the most important actor in the region, the US. Traditionally, the US sees the Atlantic as one of its areas of influence and considers that the stability of the region is crucial for its interests. Given the importance of the region, American authorities look with concern for China's increasing presence there. During the Trump administration, for example, there was pressure for Portugal not to develop projects with China, particularly in technological areas and in strategic assets involving the BRI (Silva and Pereira 2020). In the case of Brazil, American authorities have shown concern regarding the increasing presence of China in oil extraction along the Brazilian coast, competing with American companies' interests in the region (Cardoso 2017). Perhaps due to this increasing Chinese presence in the Atlantic, the US re-activated its 4th fleet in 2008 which was inactive since the 1950s (Sanchez 2016).

Given the increasing competition between China and the US, countries in the region must calculate how to promote their interests in this context. Pressure from both superpowers is likely to increase in the next years, especially as Portugal and Brazil seek to enlarge their continental shelves and cooperate further in oil extraction and communications via submarine cables. This context can be a window of opportunity for Portugal and Brazil to deepen bilateral cooperation since it would be a chance to strengthen their autonomy vis-a-vis the two superpowers.

Conclusion

The Atlantic Ocean is a key political and economic geographic space that connects more than 50 countries, including Portugal and Brazil. It is the source of natural resources, the space for channels of communication, and the exchange of goods. It offers promising conditions for research and technology development.

Even though Portugal and Brazil are connected by this Ocean, the cooperation between the two in maritime affairs is limited. There is no MoU, no agreement, or no specific institution in this field. This situation is more surprising given the long history of bilateral relations, the various institutional channels between the two, and the relevance of the sea in their public policies.

As demonstrated in the chapter, the lack of a coordinated and holistic bilateral approach to maritime affairs results from the general inconsistency in the bilateral relationship, lack of resources, divergent interests, priorities, and policy contexts. Brazil and Portugal have been carrying out relevant initiatives related to the sea (Air Centre, Atlantic Centre, public–private partnership in oil extraction, CPLP, and submarine cables) which testifies to the relevance of this space. However, the absence of an articulated approach to this field means that these various initiatives' potential synergies and spill-over effects are under-explored.

In recent years, the Atlantic Ocean has steadily become one of the hotspots of competition between China and the US. This new political scenario in the region necessarily presents a risk to the Atlantic countries, including Portugal and Brazil, since their national initiatives might clash with the interests of the two superpowers. However, this situation can also be a window of opportunity for Portugal and Brazil to develop more consistent collaboration in maritime affairs as they seek to consolidate agency and protect their national interests amid superpower competition.

References

Abdenur, Adriana Erthal, Folly, Maiara Moura, Kayo, Jordão Sergio A.S. and Maia, Pedro. (2014). "The BRICS and the South Atlantic: Emerging arena for South–South cooperation", *South African Journal of International Affairs*, 21(3), 303–319.

Agência Senado. (2017). "Ferrovia bioceânica é viável, dizem chineses em audiência pública", Notícias Senado, https://www12.senado.leg.br/noticias/materias/2017/04/18/ferrovia-bioceanica-e-viavel-dizem-chineses-em-audiencia-publica. Accessed on 4 Mar 2022.

Air Centre. (n/d). Air Centre, https://www.aircentre.org. Accessed on 4 Mar 2022.

Ataíde, Ânia. (2016). *Portugal-Brasil: uma análise das relações políticas e económicas (1991–2013)*, Dissertação de Mestrado, Faculdade de Ciências Sociais e Humanas da Universidade Nova de Lisboa.

Atlantic Centre. (n/d). Atlantic Centre, https://www.defesa.gov.pt/pt/pdefesa/ac/about. Accessed on 4 March 2022.

Ayres, Danielle Jacon Pinto. (2021). "The Europe and Brazil Submarine Cable Initiative: challenges and opportunities", *Policy Brief—Inter-Agency Institute.*

Brazil. (2020). *Estratégia Nacional de Defesa*. Brasília.

Campos, Adelino Santos de and Rodrigues, Teresa (2020). "Oceano global: quo vadis?",*Relações Internacionais*, 66, 5–10.

Canal Rural. (2020). "Entenda a participação da China no porto de Paranaguá",*Canal Rural*, https://www.canalrural.com.br/noticias/participacao-china-porto-paranagua/. Accessed on 4 Mar 2022.

Cardoso, Daniel. (2015). *Coping with a Rising Power: Understanding the making of Brazil's foreign policy towards China through network governance* [Ph.D. thesis, Free University of Berlin].

Cardoso, Daniel. (2016). "Network Governance and the Making of Brazil's Foreign Policy Towards China in the 21st Century", *Contexto Internacional*, 38(1), 277–312.

Cardoso, Daniel. (2017). "Between Dependence and Autonomy: Understanding Power Dynamics in Brazil-China Relations", *Global Dialogue*, 15(2), 11–14.

Carvalho, João Pedro a Silveira. (2004). "A política externa do XV governo constitucional", *In* Francisco Knopfli (org.), *As políticas exteriores de Brasil e Portugal: visões comparadas*. Lisboa: Instituto Superior de Ciências Sociais e Políticas.

Carvalho, Thiago. (2011). "Portugal e as relações Brasil-União Europeia (1986–2007)". *Relações Internacionais*, 29, 91–100.

Cerulus, Laurent (2021). "Portugal looks to rule the waves again (thanks to undersea data)". *Politico*. https://www.politico.eu/article/portugal-plugs-in-submarine-internet-cable/. Accessed on 4 Mar 2022.

Cervo, Amado Luiz; Calvet de Magalhães, José. (2000). *Depois das Caravelas. As relações entre Portugal e Brasil, 1808–2000*. EdUnb.

Cierco, Teresa and Silva, Jorge Tavares da. (2015). "Vetores geopolíticos do «mar português» face à visão integrada de um mar europeu". *Relações Internacionais,* nr. 46, 143–156.

Ellalink. (n/d). "The EllaLink Story So Far". https://ella.link/project-timeline/. Accessed on 4 Mar 2022.

EMPC. (n/d). "Estrutura de Missão para a Extensão da Plataforma Continental". https://www.emepc.pt. Accessed on 4 Mar 2022.

European Union. (2007). *Integrated Maritime Policy*. Brussels.

European Union. (2014). *Maritime Security Strategy*. Brussels.

Eurostat. (2021). "TopEU trading partners visualised". Eurostat. https://ec.europa.eu/eurostat/web/products-eurostat-news/-/wdn-20210405-%201?redirect=%2Feurostat%2F. Accessed on 4 Mar 2022.

Ferreira, Leonídio Paulo. (2021). "Temos 600 empresas de capital português atuando no Brasil e acreditamos que há espaço para mais". *Diário de Notícias*. https://www.dn.pt/internacional/temos-600-empresas-de-capital-portugues-atuando-no-%20brasil-e-acreditamos-que-ha-espaco-para-mais--13903136.html. Accessed on 4 Mar 2022.

Fonseca, Carmen. (2010). "Intenções versus desempenho: o Brasil na política externa portuguesa (1976-2007)". *Revista Brasileira de Política Internacional*, 53(2), 49–69.

Fonseca, Carmen. (2011). "O Brasil na Europa", *Relações Internacionais*, 17, 39–42.

GEE. (2021). "Comércio Internacional Portugal-Brasil". *GEE*. https://www.gee.gov.pt/pt/lista-publicacoes/estatisticas-de-comercio-bilateral/Brasil/1512-%20comercio-internacional-de-portugal-com-brasil/file. Accessed on 4 Mar 2022.

Graça. (2018). "Portugal e o Oceano Atlântico: os desafios estratégicos". *Lusíada. Economia & Empresa*, n.o 25, 73–85.

Guedes, Henrique Portela. (2020). "Maritime piracy in the Gulf of Guinea". *JANUS.NET, e- journal of International Relations,* 11(1), 112–119.

IBM. (2021). "Gulf of Guinea Records Highest Ever Number of Crew Kidnapped in 2020, According to IMB's Annual Piracy Report". *IBM*. https://www.icc-ccs.org/index.php/1301-gulf-of-guinea-records-highest-ever-number-of-crew-kidnapped-in-2020-according-to-imb-%20s-annual-piracy-report. Accessed on 4 Mar 2022.

Initiative: An Old Archetype of a New Development Model. Palgrave Macmillan, 389–410.

Kraemer, Andreas, and Stefes, Christoph. (2016). "The Changing Energy Landscape in the Atlantic Space". *In* Jordi Bacaria and Laia Tarragona (Eds.),

Atlantic Future—Shaping a New Hemisphere for the 21st century: Africa, Europe and the Americas, 88–102. CIDOB.

Leandro, Francisco and Duarte, Paulo. (2020a). "Intro". *In* Francisco Leandro and Paulo Duarte (eds.), *The Belt and Road Initiative: An Old Archetype of a New Development Model*. Singapore: Palgrave Macmillan, 11–24.

Leandro, Francisco and Duarte, Paulo. (2020b). "The Ultimate European Border: The Belt and Road Initiative Discovers Portugal".*In* Francisco Leandro and Paulo Duarte (eds.), *The Belt and Road Initiative: An Old Archetype of a New Development Model*. Singapore: Palgrave Macmillan, 363–388.

Lusa/Visão. (2010). "Portugal-Brasil: Países vão desenvolver programa para produção de hidrocarbonetos em águas profundas". *Visão*. https://visao.sapo.pt/lusa/2010-05-19-%20portugal-brasil-paises-vao-desenvolver-programa-para-producao-de-hidrocarbonetos-em-%20aguas-profundasf559924/. Accessed on 4 Mar 2022.

Mahan, Alfred. (2010). *The Influence of Sea Power upon History, 1660–1783*. Cambridge: Cambridge University Press.

Marinha. (n/d). "Marinha Brasileira". https://www.marinha.mil.br/secirm/leplac. Accessed on 4 Mar 2022.

Nunes, Flávio. (2021). "Saiba quais os dez países que mais "pesaram" nas importações e exportações nacionais". *ECO*. https://eco.sapo.pt/2021/04/05/saiba-quais-os-dez-paises-que-%20mais-pesaram-nas-importacoes-e-exportacoes-nacionais/. Accessed on 4 Mar 2022.

Offshore. (2008). "Pre-Salt Discoveries Continue in Brazil". *Offshore*. https://www.offshore-mag.com/geosciences/article/16761678/presalt-discoveries-continue-in-brazil. Accessed on 4 Mar 2022.

Pato, Rosa Ana. (2020). "A cultura dos dois lados do Atlântico: Um olhar sobre as relações ulturais luso-brasileiras entre 1945 e 1953". *Relações Internacionais*, 66, 127–140.

Pezarat Correia, Pedro de. (2002). *Manual de Geopolítica e Geoestratégia—Vol. I—Conceitos, Teorias e Doutrinas*. Quarteto.

Pires, Nuno Lemos, Reis, Bruno Cardoso, and Simão, Licínia (2020). "A Vision for the Atlantic Centre: Building up Resilience and Cooperative Security for a More Secure Ocean for All", *Atlantic Center Policy Brief*, 5.

Pitta e Cunha, Tiago de. (2004). "A importância estratégica do mar para Portugal". *Nação e Defesa*, n.º 108, 41–52.

Pitta e Cunha, Tiago de. (2011). *Portugal e o Mar—À Redescoberta da Geografia*. Fundação Francisco Manuel dos Santos.

Pordata. (n/d). População estrangeira com estatuto legal de residente: total e por algumas nacionalidades, Pordata. https://www.pordata.pt/Portugal/População+estrangeira+com+estatuto+legal+de+residente+total+e+por+algumas+nacionalidades-24-184449. Accessed on 4 Mar 2022.

Portos e Navios (2019). "China anunciará investimento bilionário em Porto de São Luís através da CCCC, dizem fontes". *Portos e Navios*. https://www.portosenavios.com.br/noticias/portos-e-logistica/china-anunciara-%20investimento-bilionario-em-porto-de-sao-luis-atraves-da-cccc-dizem-fontes. Accessed on 4 Mar 2022.

Portugal (2013). *Conceito Estratégico de Defesa Nacional*. Lisboa.

Reis, Bruno Cardoso. (2015). *A Centralidade do Atlântico: Portugal e o Futuro da Ordem Internacional*, IDN Cadernos, 10.

Sanchez, Alejandro. (2016). "The Uses of the US Navy's Fourth Fleet". SIMSEC. https://cimsec.org/opinion-uses-u-s-navys-fourth-flee/ Accessed on 4 Mar 2022.

Saraiva, Miriam Gomes. (2020). "The democratic regime and the changes in Brazilian foreign policy towards South America". *Brazilian Political Science Review* [online], 14(3).

Satariano, Adam. (2019). "How the Internet Travels Across Oceans". *New York Times*. https://www.nytimes.com/interactive/2019/03/10/technology/internet-cables-oceans.html Accessed on 4 Mar 2022.

Seabra, Pedro. (2019). "Desafios e Oportunidades do Multilateralismo no Atlântico Sul". *Nação e Defesa*, 154, 37–53.

Seabra, Pedro. (2021). "Report WS1". In "Atlantic Centre—Second Seminar". Cadernos IDN, nr. 40, National Defence Institute. https://www.defesa.gov.pt/pt/pdefesa/ac/pub/acpubs/Documents/IDN-Cadernos_40.pdf Accessed on 4 March 2022.

Seabra, Pedro, and Costa, Rita. (2021). *Mapping EU Maritime Capacity Building in the Atlantic*. The Atlantic Centre Report, nr. 1.

Silva, Alexandre Pereira da. (2013). "O novo pleito brasileiro no mar: a plataforma continental estendida e o Projeto Amazônia Azul", *Revista Brasileira de Política Internacional*, 56(1), 104–121.

Silva, Antonio Ruy De Almeida. (2020). *The Enabling Power of the Oceans and the Atlantic Center for Defence Capacity Building*. Atlantic Centre Policy Brief, (02).

Silva, Antonio Ruy de Almeida Silva. (2017). "The Enabling Power of the Oceans". *Contexto Internacional*, 39(2), 237–243.

Silva, Jorge Tavares da and Pereira, Rui. (2020). 2China and the Portuguese Atlantic: The BRI'S Last Puzzle Piece. In Francisco Leandro and Paulo Duarte (Eds.), *The Belt and Road Initiative: An Old Archetype of a New Development Model*, 389–410. Palgrave Macmillan.

Simões, José Manuel Neto. (2013)."O Mar como vector estratégico para o desenvolvimento sustentado de Portugal". *Diário de Notícias*. https://www.dn.pt/opiniao/opiniao-%20dn/convidados/o-mar-como-vector-estrategico-para-o-desenvolvimento-sustentado-de-%20portugal--3021054.html. Accessed on 4 Mar 2022.

Siying, Zhang. (2018). "Investimento direto chinês em Portugal : estratégias, desafios e oportunidades", Dissertação de Mestrado, Universidade de Lisboa. Instituto Superior de Economia e Gestão.

Songa, Annie Young, and Fabinyia, Michael. (2022). "China's 21st Century Maritime Silk Road: Challenges and Opportunities to Coastal Livelihoods in Asean Countries". *Marine Policy,* 136.

The White House. (2022). *Indo-Pacific Strategy of the United States.* Washington.

United Nations. (2018). "2018 World Oceans Day Theme: Clean our Ocean!". *UN*. https://www.un.org/depts/los/wod/. Accessed on 4 Mar 2022.

Valença Pinto, Luís. (2015). "Portugal no contexto europeu e Atlântico: Caminhos para o futuro?" Communication in the Conference "Por Portugal". https://repositorio.ual.pt/handle/11144/4431. Accessed on 4 Mar 2022.

Zhang, Gongcheng Qu, Hongjun Chen, Guojun Zhao, Chong Zhang, Fenglian Haizhang, Yang Zhao Zhao, and Ma, Ming. (2019). "Giant Discoveries of Oil and Gas Fields in Global Deepwaters in the Past 40 Years and the Prospect of Exploration". *Journal of Natural Gas Geoscience*, 4(1), 1–28.

Lusophone Cooperation Frameworks and the Expansion of the Atlantic Maritime Security

Sabrina Evangelista Medeiros
and Daniele Jacon Ayres Pinto

Introduction

In the twenty-first century, cooperation is In the twenty-first century trust in the international system, strengthening relations, and diminishing vulnerabilities and the risk of war (Lipson 1984). The relationship among actors, built both by the will and necessity, puts them in conditions where it is more harmful to act alone than together, sharing risks and amplifying interdependencies (Barbieri and Schneider 1999).

Cooperation at sea can be understood as the regulation of the waters regarding maritime commerce, shipbuilding, marine resources, environmental policies, planning, and monitoring, among others. The maritime

S. E. Medeiros (✉)
Lusófona University, Lisbon, Portugal
e-mail: sabrina.medeiros@ulusofona.pt

D. J. Ayres Pinto
Department of Economics and International Relations,
Federal University of Santa Catarina, Florianópolis, Brazil
e-mail: danielle.ayres@ufsc.br

P. A. B. Duarte et al. (eds.), *Portugal and the Lusophone World*,
https://doi.org/10.1007/978-981-99-0455-6_12

domain collective security is a top priority on the international agenda since it is an environment of intensified exploration. Additionally, the development of coastal states is closely linked to their ability to control and manage their resources in the territorial waters and the Exclusive Economic Zones (EEZ).

Maritime diplomacy brings together elements commonly dissociated from traditional literature on war, especially in the idea of sea cooperation through defence capabilities and other contributing actor schemes (Medeiros and Moreira 2017). In a broader sense, Gregory Winger (2014) states that the concept of defence diplomacy is aimed at the nonviolent use of defence for the benefit of peace through amplifying trust and collaboration to the defence and security schemes in place in the West and spreading good practices and norms of a civilian-military collaborative approach to the area. As so, maritime diplomacy may include more than military and defence capabilities, such as negotiations on biodiversity, scientific cooperation, and multistakeholder initiatives to boost international relations (Cottey and Forster 2004; Winger 2014; de Almeida Silva 2015).

If defence diplomacy was an option of states with undisputed deterring power, it seems to be the predominant choice within states of small or medium-sized military power, such as Portugal, Brazil, and African Portuguese-Speaking countries, despite being dependent on suppliers from robust military powers (de Almeida Silva 2015). This approximation strategy of medium and small military powers often brings together factors as substantive as those related to geopolitical or regional proximity, economic complementarity, the extension of consumer markets, and cultural and linguistic proximity.

Behind the marine and commercial-related cooperation is the defence cooperation, which surpasses regular trade agreements by the strategic-military content of partnerships involving joint production, purchase and sale, training and, in a greater dimension, knowledge transfer. In this regard, Kinne (2018) observes that "bilateral defence cooperation agreements, or DCAs, are now the most common form of institutionalised defence cooperation". Cottey and Foster (2004) have pointed out that the efforts around defence bilateral relations and multilateral agreements are focused on training officers and foreign civilians in visiting and establishing official ties, promoting interchange, supplying military equipment, performing training missions collaboratively, and planning multilateral simulations exercises.

Based on the concepts and definitions mentioned above, it is worth characterising the link between defence cooperation and maritime security as part of the defence diplomacy agreements that touch the maritime environments in their capabilities, regimes, and knowledge (or information) transfer.

As such, maritime security cooperation is made by efforts regarding the regulation of maritime traffic and the exploration on the seas, the cooperation frameworks in place, and the defence mechanisms at its disposal. At the same time, the growth of maritime crime networks and routes, extremism, piracy, illicit trafficking, and energy (in)security come at the same pace as development reaches state and non-state actors' interests (Bueger et al. 2020). Accordingly, the conception of maritime security can have an approach focused on the good order of the sea and an environment without threats (Bueger 2015).

It is common sense to connect maritime cooperation and maritime security to international transits (Feldt et al. 2013). Though, it's critical to recognise that the core maritime agendas include the cyber dimension. Two pieces of evidence turn the seas part of the disruptive technologies' scene affected by cyber conditioners. The first is the submarine cables infrastructures responsible for communications within continents in the revealing dimension of about 98% of the total communications. The second is the governance or the supply chains, which are decisively based on cyber means (Vichi et al. 2020; Medeiros and Ayres Pinto, 2022).

Maritime cooperation frameworks can work as a combination of material resources and immaterial capacities to strengthen cooperation between States, creating a more secure environment of resource exchanges. Yuan and Chang (2021), reporting the results of the Inaugural Symposium on Maritime Cooperation and Ocean Governance in Haikou, China, observe a trend after the COVID-19 outbreak for states to pose national policies despite international multilateral cooperative schemes based on unilateral policies towards oceans governance.

Thus, this chapter tries to observe what sources of triangulation are underway that cross Portugal, Brazil, and the Africa Portuguese-Speaking countries and their potential outcomes on Portugal's relevance in its Atlantic and European positioning. The Portuguese-speaking governments compound links that mark relations not always visible and that manifest axes of trust on which the European Atlantic relations can benefit.

Crossing Atlantic Cooperation Schemes

The Atlantic Ocean is a geopolitical interface of distinctly characterised regions. It has varied political contributions between colonial and post-colonial processes to contemporary transatlantic relations considered communally by its North axis. Cyclical periods between tensions and rapprochements have characterised the comings and goings of Atlantic relations between the United States and Europe, especially under the NATO Alliance (Anderson 2018). The political dimension has not always been a constant of stability, which can be seen in the UK's exit from the European Union (BREXIT) by creating scars in trust among allies in the North Atlantic (Ferreira-Pereira 2020 2021).

The initiatives in evidence characterise the presence of growing interest in states to empower subregions with conditions of sheltering the growing standardisation of international trade in a security, sustainable development, and the attraction of investments. Nevertheless, the initiatives that mark intercontinental relations are endorsed with old principles, qualified by twentieth-century demands. Institutional development had not come up at the same pace, and common frameworks of cooperation do not express the needs or the interests in place.

Bueger et al. (2020) point out that the set of innovations at sea in capacity-building has been related to experimentation and exploration of solutions to emerging problems. If these programmes that act in regional solutions have been developed, their interfaces with more robust frameworks occur intermittently, with advances and rapid indentations of processes that develop incrementally and horizontally.

The concept launched by NATO in 2010 of the Atlantic Basin broke, to some extent, with the imaginary line between North and South (NATO 2010). Nevertheless, it was not received as an attempt at regional conceptual unification but rather as a strategy of domination from the North guidelines. In 2019, in an opinion article published by Ambassador Rubens Barbosa of Brazil, the Brazilian mistrust regarding the concept of the "Atlantic Basin" led to resistance to the creation of the Centre for the Defence of the Atlantic (later named Atlantic Centre), which aims at rapprochement between Atlantic countries and has the official participation of Brazil, Morocco, Spain, Germany, United States, Senegal, or Uruguay, among others.

In parallel to the Lisbon Treaty (EU 2008), the NATO 2010 Strategic Concept interpretations of Atlantic security have provoked official statements such as by the Brazilian Defence Minister Nelson Jobin (2010). It is worth noting that the conception of a "wider Mediterranean region" came to represent an expansionist view of the North over the South, which led to more identity reinforcements from the Global South. Instead, the NATO strategic concept revision of 2022 (NATO 2022) calls for the "wider transatlantic community", which encompasses a more balanced view on the theme, and does not include the "Atlantic Basin" as it is in the previous edition.

Cooperative efforts between the North Atlantic and the South Atlantic countries were also part of the *European Union External Action Service* (EEAS). Latin America and the Caribbean countries (LAC) gained a bilateral summit with the European Union in 1999. Still, only twenty years after that, the relationship was formalised under a Joint Communication (Joint Communication to the European Parliament and the Council). In this regard, the initiative addressed issues that formalised shared values such as transparency, gender equality, democracy, and the fight against corruption, but also a common proposition agenda on sustainable resource governance and maritime transportation. It is worth noting that Brazil is cited as one of the contributing countries to the European Union Common Security and Defence Policy (CSDP).

The initiative between the European Union and the LAC region also highlights the focus on expanding space and earth observation cooperation, manifested by the orientation for the benefit of regional visibility through technological and satellite cooperation, which includes maritime surveillance. Cooperation in space and communications points to an increased interest in ensuring environments of economic projection with the contribution of technologies, which provoked competition with the United States during attempts to make the European market more autonomous.

The Atlantic cooperation faces, in its various dimensions, the Chinese competition, which involves the European Union, the African countries, and Latin America. Paulo Duarte states that tensions within the West regimes and their cooperation networks in the Atlantic have marked key opportunities for the Chinese economic expansion (Duarte 2019). Regarding the New Silk Road (the Belt and Road Initiative, BRI), the progressive Chinese influence in South Atlantic is strategically addressed by the BRI Maritime Program (Silva and Pereira 2020; Dos Santos and

Lobo 2021; Oliveira and Myers 2021). Some important efforts that involve Portugal towards the Atlantic can be mentioned.

The North Atlantic Coast Guard Forum (NACGF), formed in 2007 with representatives from 20 North Atlantic countries involving safety and security issues, focuses on meeting between coastal guard leaders or equivalents and a second annual meeting between Subject Matter Experts (SMEs), which qualifies a multistakeholder approach. From the EU and at the operations level, the EUROMARFOR—established in 1992 by the Petersberg Declaration, formed by the French, Spanish, Italian, and Portuguese navies—has its purpose dedicated to humanitarian missions, peacekeeping operations, crisis response operations, and peace enforcement, and can be triggered by NATO, the European Union, or the UN.

Within the South Atlantic, projects such as COAMAS (CAMAS—*Coordenador da Área Marítima do Atlântico Sul—AMAS*), created under the auspices of the "Inter- American Defense Board", and ZOPACAS (South Atlantic Peace and Cooperation Zone, 1986), with the region's maintenance as denuclearised, have become regimes of continuing and stable technical contribution, (Medeiros and Moreira 2017; Paiva et al. 2019). While ZOPACAS is a zone without a secretary office to guarantee institutional collaboration, it came to be a way to surpass regional barriers to cooperation when it comes to bilateral or trilateral partnership, and especially as an instrument of the Brazilian foreign policy in the region (Rizzi and Bueno 2021).

In addition to international regimes in the Atlantic, some are established between coastal states, which may be considered maritime-driven. This is the case of the Caribbean Community or the subregional actions in Africa, such as CRESMAC and CRESMAO, part of the Interregional Coordination Centre (ICC), a joint initiative proposed by ECCAS, ECOWAS, and the GGC. It is no wonder that maritime security-driven cooperation in the South Atlantic between Brazil, Angola, Namibia, Guinea, Guinea- Bissau, Cameroon, and South Africa is marked by regional and extra-regional relations such as the Community of Portuguese-speaking Countries (CPLP), the Friends of Gulf of Guinea (FoGG), and the IBAS framework (India-Brazil-South Africa) (Abdenur and Souza Neto 2014).

CPLP and Maritime Cooperation

The Portuguese-Speaking countries community (CPLP—*Comunidade de Países de Língua Portuguesa*) is a stable community with different areas of engagement, having as members: Angola, Brazil, Cape Verde, Guinea-Bissau, Mozambique, Portugal, São Tomé and Príncipe, Timor-Leste, and Equatorial Guinea. Timor-Leste became a member of the CPLP in 2002 after its independence process, and Equatorial Guinea was admitted as a permanent member of the community in 2014. With the possibility of having associate observers since 2010 (Ministries′ Council, Luanda), the CPLP has been opening to states such as Namibia, Georgia, Turkey, Japan, Luxemburg, Italy, India, Spain, United Kingdom, United States, and Uruguay. Currently, there are more than 250 million inhabitants among the member countries, representing 10.5 million square kilometres in territorial area, connected mainly through the southern part of the Atlantic and with the Portuguese language and cultural paradigm.

Promoting maritime security cooperation seems to boost other sources of participation to the Portuguese representations once the Portuguese-Speaking countries participate in the international agenda with some capacity to influence. Although the first meeting of Heads of States and Governments of Portuguese-Speaking countries was held in 1989, involving Angola, Brazil, Cape Verde, Mozambique, Portugal, São Tomé and Príncipe, it was just in 1996 that the Declaration of The Constitution of the Community of Portuguese-Speaking Countries was in place.

With considerable economic and political strength to interact with the international system and an agenda involving human rights to science and technology, it has been limited by its budget and national conditions to comply with and advance cooperation protocols. Despite the conditions for suspending members because of their non- compliance to budget requirements, "this mechanism has never been applied". As seen in the financial study of the CPLP by Herpolsheimer (2019), the budget had been increased in volume, representing a significant step up when it comes to the Angolan and the Brazilian contributions, with little progress in terms of the Portuguese contributions. On the other hand, those volumes represent different proportions of contribution if the Gross Domestic Product is considered, putting Portugal as the leading contributor, as it has been driving its utmost national importance (Herpolsheimer 2019).

As an initiative that congregates countries to improve their cooperation and promote countries' development, CPLP offers some challenges regarding the non-balanced importance within members to deepen commitments unless considering their common ground on maritime issues. That may explain why the naval and marine cooperation schemes had been progressing more than in other areas. South Atlantic, while representing a challenge to global maritime security, has been a conditioner of those developments (Seabra 2014).

While the CPLP secretariat progressively mobilises its autonomy as an actor, participating in works in collaboration with other organisations such as the UN and accessing exogenous funds to implement agendas that have strength in other forums, cooperative security is more limited to the actions of member states. This is one of the reasons why the extensively varied agendas end up representing two distinguishing groups: those that are included in the international agendas of other organisations, and those that are restricted to the group, such as defence cooperation (Herpolsheimer 2019).

The South Atlantic security frameworks had incrementally benefited from the CPLP partnership in the matter. The Atlantic Centre, a Portuguese-based initiative characterised as a multinational environment for defence and capacity-building in the Atlantic, has been pushing this agenda forward into an integrated Atlantic strategic incremental conception (Coker et al. 2020). Maritime and naval cooperation from then on is promoted by the CPLP, but it does not always occur within it.

The member countries' navies had been at the forefront of those cooperation ties. The improvement of Atlantic maritime awareness, which may lead to maritime security enhancement, has been a focus of the Conference of Navies among Portuguese-Speaking Countries. Although the CPLP is not organically responsible for this cooperation, like CHENS (CHiefs of European NavieS, if a member of NATO and the EU), the Portuguese-Speaking countries' navies forum addresses naval and maritime issues. However, as a regime, the CPLP has not been constituted as a defensive block or a global defence framework (Bernardino 2016). Neither the CPLP represents a security community as Adler and Barnett have set as a dependable expectation of peace (1998).

The former CPLP Marine Symposium, currently called the CPLP Navies Conference, carried the reputation of one of the most successful cooperative experiences within the CPLP. In addition, the Conference of Ministers of Fisheries and the CPLP Ports Meeting also represented initiatives that made the CPLP very focused on the seas (Bernardino 2011).

At this juncture, the Strategy of the Community of Portuguese-Speaking Countries for the Oceans was also made in 2007 and approved the following year (CPLP 2008). Among the points highlighted in the CPLP Strategy for the Oceans, the promotion of the Law of the Seas and the regulations within the scope of the UN, the improvement in the management of sea resources and the protection of the oceans, the coordinated training of human resources and a multisectoral approach, make room for the collaborative development of technologies and their protection more appropriately in national budgets and strategies.

In June of 2021, the CPLP published its Biennial Cooperation Framework 2020–2022, which includes Sectoral Strategic Cooperation Plans (PECSET). But, before the new Biennial Cooperation Framework and directed to sea cooperation, the Mindelo Declaration (CPLP 2019) was launched from the Meeting of Ministers on the Affairs of the Seas, which happened in 2019, reinforcing commitments made before and stating new ones such as the blue economy transition according to the UN Agenda 2030 and the Sustainable Development Objectives (SDO) under the Article 14. Also worthy of note is the qualification of the importance of the CPLP as a unique actor to enhance participation when it comes to ocean matters.

Strategic cooperation plan	*Validity*	*Global objectives*	*Priorities axis*
Mindelo Action Plan of the Meeting of Ministers on The Affairs of the Sea	2019–2021	• Promote the principles set out in the United Nations Convention on the Law of the Sea • Contribute to better management and sustainable development of the oceans through the implementation of the multisectoral approach (including defence, environmental, scientific, technological, social, and economic approaches) and international cooperation • Promote the establishment of marine protected areas in maritime spaces under sovereignty and jurisdiction in the CPLP member states • Promote measures to understand and adapt to climate change in coastal regions • Contribute to the strengthening of a human resources network empowered to develop an integrated ocean policy • Promote measures to make economical use of marine resources, including the encouragement of business partnerships	• Encourage scientific research • •Increased civil society's knowledge of the Oceans • Extension of the Continental Shelf and Associated Programs • •International Projection of CPLP across the Oceans • CPLP Partnership for a Waste-Free Sea • Development of Marine Clusters

Retrieved from: *Estratégia da CPLP para os Oceanos*. Translated by the authors

In addition to bilateral, multilateral cooperation, interagency relations and alliances, the Portuguese navy, the Brazilian navy, and the Portuguese-Speaking countries′ navies operate in projects that have a soft law role. As the Portuguese external policy seems to express (Palma 2013), elements of the historical path of the countries seem to be decisive to cooperation schemes and functionalities, especially due to a peace resolution condition historically oriented (Mahoney 2000).

Bilateral Contributions to the Extending Frameworks of Maritime Cooperation

Thus, it is possible to conceive that a process of cooperation built on the seas as the main scene would be divided into two fronts—the maritime and naval. In this regard, the crossing cooperation between the navies of Portugal, Brazil, and the PALOPS (Portuguese-Speaking African Countries) is decisive to the ongoing frameworks such as the CPLP, although not precisely part of it. Besides building on a dynamic of promotion of absolute gains (Grieco 1993; Snidal 1991), where the triangular relationship between these agents will strengthen a shared identity, non-equivalent repercussions may happen. For Portugal, the Lusophony has become a vital alternative for interacting in the international sphere with more strength and influence since the loss of overseas territories, reinventing the way it should be in the international system (Moreira 1984).

The Portuguese bilateral cooperation is divided into staff talks, joint staff talks, joint committees, and technical-military cooperation. Bernardino (2019) states that the Portuguese Armed Forces have been the object of foreign policy qualification through technical cooperation projects in Africa that guarantee a relevant dimension of intersection of interests through both bilateral and CPLP frameworks. The most critical bilateral initiative between Portugal and Brazil regarding defence and security is the Agreement on Cooperation in Defence of 2005 (CPLP 2000). However, it does not mention the CPLP as one of its cooperation instruments.

For the bilateral relationship between Portugal and Angola, the 1996 Defence Cooperation Agreement[1] was complemented by the Memorandum of Understanding of 2005, which expanded technical-military cooperation in scientific and medical care areas. In 2018, a Framework Programme in the Defence Domain (CDD) was implemented for the following years until 2022. In 2022, a renewed framework programme is dedicated to enhancing maritime security (as well as the Women, Peace and Security agenda), cyber- defence, and environmental projects (climate change, hydrography), launched between the countries to be under force until 2026.

Concerning bilateral defence cooperation, Guinea Bissau and Portugal have agreements dating back to 1989. Their first framework programme in 1991 was interrupted by successive domestic political crises due to the 2012 military coup and was resumed in 2015, now including a focus on the Atlantic. The Military Technical Cooperation Agreement signed in 1988 between Portugal, and Cape Verde was followed by a framework programme in 1991 and a Joint Surveillance Treaty on Maritime Spaces under Sovereignty or Jurisdiction of the Republic of Cape Verde in 2006.

The Brazilian navy's donation of military material to São Tomé and Príncipe Coast Guard in 2021 as part of the defence cooperation agreement ratified by both countries and other members of CPLP aims at improving the capacity of São Tomé and Príncipe to fight criminal groups. At the same time, a Brazil Naval Advice Mission was installed inside the São Tomé and Principe Coast Guard headquarters. That initiative intends to introduce the Brazilian military corps to the administrative routine of the Coast Guard and close the ties between both countries. At the same time, that action has a vital purpose: to reinforce the Brazilian cooperation project as a foreign policy and promote the Brazilian influence within the Portuguese-Speaking countries. Military-technical cooperation can boost synergies between CPLP countries and become the essential axis to the cooperation triangle in the Atlantic Portuguese-Speaking countries in the twenty-first century. Da Silva and De Carvalho argue:

> [...] Brazil is one of those emerging countries that seeks international insertion, where ICD (International Cooperation for Development) has become a relevant key. Therefore, Brazil tends to follow the securitisation of ICD, despite its historical discourse of non-intervention and peaceful settlement of disputes. In the Brazilian's historical approach, as elements of this securitisation of ICD, we can highlight its participation in multilateral peace operations of the UN13, including the armed forces' participation in activities of international cooperation for development by the Brazilian Agency for Cooperation of the Ministry of Foreign Affairs, the Community of Portuguese Language Speaking Countries and the Union of South American Nations. (Da Silva and De Carvalho 2019, pp. 172–173)

A relevant institutional condition in Portugal is the existence of a National Maritime Authority (AMC) supported in terms of material and human resources by the Portuguese navy and subordinated to the Ministry of National Defence. For the Brazilian case, the role of maritime authority is accumulated by the Brazilian Navy Commander, where the Maritime Authority advisor is the Armada's Command and Staff.

As part of the Maritime National Authorities' roles, maritime commerce uphold is dependent on crossing standards that are ruled by specific agreements. The Protocol amending the Agreement between the Government of the Portuguese Republic and the Government of the Federative Republic of Brazil on Transport and Navigation has been valid since 1995 and was made precisely to cover those binding considerations and requirements of the European Union that conditions the cooperation previously driven with Brazil. In other words, if the European Union policies do not dispute those of the members with third countries, they may be fulfilled by those. Thus, cooperation frameworks may create room for continuing relations that interfere with actors' choices, values, or reputations (Medeiros and Moreira 2017; Espach 2019).

In September 2015, at the facilities of the Brazilian Navy Naval War College, academics and representatives of both the navies from Portugal and Brazil met to present and discuss the convergent paths between the two strategic models and the opportunities to accentuate these points of convergence. The Seminar followed a workshop between guests of institutional representation such as the CPLP Strategic Analysis Centre and academic experts on the theme of defence cooperation that included both military and civilians, among them, Vice Admiral Antônio Manuel Silva Ribeiro and, at that time, Director-General of the National Maritime Authority.

A proposal for a Portuguese-Speaking countries Sea Forum was born in the workshop, where maritime and marine strategies could be addressed on a continuous agenda, promoted by the navies of Portugal and Brazil, but which included institutional and academic representatives from various of Portuguese-Speaking countries based on a multistakeholder approach. Although the CPLP's Centre for Strategic Analysis also had the function of dissemination and scientific production, having a Sea Forum would broaden the scope and participation in issues notified of interest for disseminating the maritime mentality among Portuguese-speaking countries. The co-adnation of these interests would simultaneously contribute to the scientific understanding of this conjuncture and its promotion. Until 2019, three editions of the Sea Forum were made, and its realisation has not only continued due to the COVID-19 outbreak.

Final Thoughts: Crossing Cooperation, Avoiding Distancing or Overlapping

As Scott Jasper (Jasper and Moreland 2012) identified, shared spaces like the oceans, cyberspace, or outer space are potentially conflictive because common interests are concentrated. The ability to focus on cooperative solutions, which is perhaps the safest way to ensure permanence in these spaces (Bernardi 2012), happens as reinforced by Keohane (1984) that conflict does not mean the absence of the chance to cooperate; contrariwise, it means an alternative scenario, where choosing to cooperate is a better decision to avoid conflict and maximise the results of the relationship.

After presenting institutional initiatives on the maritime cooperation between Portugal, Brazil, and the African Portuguese-Speaking countries, it is essential to clarify which synergies can be identified and used to improve the cooperation processes in this maritime scene and how repercussions can uphold security.

Regarding the synergies, we highlight the necessary improvement of institutional and material capacities of Atlantic countries, where Portugal, Brazil, and Angola could have a leading role in concentrating some of the tasks and obtaining transversal benefits from this triangulated cooperation. Furthermore, with the incidence of terrorist attacks, civil wars of different spectrums, attacks on merchant platforms and ships, refugee flows and maritime piracy, the combined and joint actions could be a less costly and more efficient way out for coastal states and sea security responsibility.

Because of the historical motivations which can be qualified as reasons for path dependence, spaces of power within the international system are better faced by cooperative partners (Bernardi 2012). In this case, the emergence of a renewed political will, whose alignment also permeates the leadership of the navies, can be of extreme relevance, given the historical commitments outlined over time.

Defence cooperation is still modest between Portugal, Brazil, and the Portuguese- speaking African countries at the bilateral level; however, within the CPLP, it seems to be more efficient. The initiatives that reinforce this communion of values meet the bilateral cooperation instruments to strengthen the multilateral frameworks.

Forces against the rapprochement between Portugal within the CPLP can be listed. On the one hand, the remoteness of Portugal and Brazil regarding the vision of NATO's strategic concept presented an obstacle to the cooperative effort between parties. Nevertheless, the Brazilian interest in the proposition of ZOPACAS has configured, through the UN scope, an essential vehicle of dialogue for the benefit of security towards Africa. Although not necessarily a competitive initiative, ZOPACAS brings to the South of the Atlantic the strategic design of security and defence projects, diminishing, to some degree, the cultural link dimension (Abdenur and Souza Neto 2014; Paiva et al. 2019).

Thus, a security identity project for the Atlantic that includes broad European interests may encompass the integration of those bilateral and multilateral frameworks within the European Union's external cooperation programmes. The war in Ukraine may be one of the biggest obstacles to cooperation between Portugal and other Portuguese- Speaking countries, as well as it reinforces the importance of trust building outside the European Union but among its members and as its outside assets. Within the Portuguese- Speaking countries, the difference in the understanding of war, as seen with the abstention of Angola and Mozambique in condemning the invasion by the Russians at the UN, can damage cooperation and lead it to alternative global players such as China and India, which are already traditional Russian partners.

Markedly, maritime cooperation would be vital to create within those countries a unique way to participate in and influence the international system, especially in the Atlantic scenario. Indeed, the development of coastal states, like Portugal, Brazil, and other African Portuguese-Speaking countries is intricately linked to the seas and the ability to control and manage their resources out of but also within their community of security practices.

Acknowledgements We thank Dr. Laura Ferreira-Pereira for the valuable reading, considerations and insights, and Dr. Leonardo Vichi for the final reading.

References

Abdenur, A. E., & Souza Neto, D. M. D. (2014). O Brasil e a cooperação em defesa: a construção de uma identidade regional no Atlântico Sul. *Revista Brasileira de Política Internacional*, *57*, 05–21.

Adler, Emmanuel, and Barnett, Michael. (1998). *Security Communities*. Cambridge University Press.

Anderson, J. J. (2018). Rancor and Resilience in the Atlantic Political Order: The Obama Years. *Journal of European Integration*, *40*(5), 621–636.

Barbieri, K., & Schneider, G. (1999). Globalisation and Peace: Assessing New Directions in the Study of Trade and Conflict. *Journal of Peace Research*, *36*(4), 387–404.

Bernardi, B. (2012). O Conceito de Dependência da Trajetória (Path Dependence): definições e Controvérsias teóricas. *Perspectivas*, 41(jan/jun), 137–167.

Bernardino, L. (2011). Segurança Marítima no Seio da CPLP: Contributos para uma Estratégia nos Mares da Lusofonia. *Nação e Defesa*, 5 série, n.128, 41–65.

Bernardino, L. (2016). Uma nova visão estratégica para a defesa na CPLP. *Ciclo de Conferências dedicadas à CPLP–Uma nova visão estratégica para a defesa na CPLP*. Universidade de Lisboa, Centro de Estudos Internacionais. https://repositorio.iscte-iul.pt/handle/10071/10811

Bernardino, L. (2019). As forças armadas como instrumento de política externa: contributos para a cooperação militar portuguesa em África. *Política Externa Portuguesa e África: Tendências e Temas Contemporâneos*, 101.

Bueger, C. (2015). What is maritime security? *Marine Policy*, *53*, 159–164.

Bueger, C., Edmunds, T., & McCabe, R. (2020). Into the Sea: Capacity-building Innovations and the Maritime Security Challenge. *Third World Quarterly*, *41*(2), 228–246.

Coker, C., Djinadou, M., El Houdaigui, R., Ehle, J., Moreira, J. A., Nascimento, D., and Young, R., et al. (2020). Atlantic Centre for Defence Capacity 11building. *IDN Cadernos*.

Cottey, Andrew., & Forster, Anthony. (2004). Strategic Engagement: Defence Diplomacy as a Means of Conflict Prevention. *Adelphi series* 44.365, 15–30.

CPLP. (2000). Acordo entre a República Portuguesa e a República Federativa do Brasil sobre Cooperação no Domínio da Defesa. Porto Seguro. https://app.parlamento.pt/webutils/docs/doc.pdf?path=6148523063446f764c324679626%20d56304c334e706447567a4c31684d5a5763765247396a6457316c626e527663306c7561%20574e7059585270646d45764e7a52694e44457844d5749744e6a426d4d433030597a51354%20c5745344d6d45744f47466b4d474a6d5a6a42684e4755354c6d527659773d3d&fich=74b%204111b-60f0-4c49-a82a-8ad0bff0a4e9.doc&Inline=true

CPLP. (2008). *Estratégia para os Oceanos*. VII Conferência de Chefes de Estado e de Governo da Comunidade dos Países de Língua Portuguesa. Lisboa.

CPLP. (2019). Declaração de Mindelo. São Vicente.

Da Silva, Daniele Dionisio., & De Carvalho, Carolina Ambinder. (2019). Military Technical Cooperation for Development–The Brazilian Perspective of Interaction for the 21st Century. *Revista da Escola de Guerra Naval*, *25*(1).

De Almeida Silva, A. R. (2015). A diplomacia de defesa na política internacional. *Revista da Escola de Guerra Naval*, *21*(2), 179.

Dos Santos, P. P., & Lobo, A. (2021). Geopolitical Relations Between China and the South Atlantic Portuguese-Speaking Countries: A blue evolving partnership. In *China and Portuguese-Speaking—Small Island States*, 266.

Duarte, P. (2019). China's momentum: The "One Belt One Road" Triple's Securitisation. In *Mapping China's 'One Belt One Road' Initiative* (pp. 143–165). Palgrave Macmillan.

Espach, R. (2019). Reflections on the Ends, Ways, and Means of Maritime Security Cooperation in the South Atlantic. In É. Duarte, M. Correia de Barros (Eds.), *Maritime Security Challenges in the South Atlantic*. Palgrave Macmillan.

European Commission, Treaty of Lisbon (2008). Consolidated Version of the Treaty on European Union OJ C115/13.

Feldt, L., Roell, P., & Thiele, R. D. (2013). Maritime Security–Perspectives for a Comprehensive Approach. *ISPSW Strategy Series: Focus on Defense and International Security*, *2*.

Ferreira-Pereira, L. C. (2020). The Mainstreaming of Security and Defense in the European Union Post-2016: Building Resilience in Challenging Times. In *Regionalism Under Stress* (pp. 98–115). Routledge.

Ferreira-Pereira, L. C. (2021). European Union-Brazil Relations: A Strategic Partnership in Suspended Animation. In *The European Union's Strategic Partnerships* (pp. 151–175). Palgrave Macmillan.

Grieco, J. M. (1993). Anarchy and the Limits of Cooperation: a Realist Critique of the Newest Liberal Institutionalism. In: Baldwin, D.A. (ed.). *Neorealism and Neoliberalism: The Contemporary Debate*. New York, Columbia University Press, pp. 116–142.

Herpolsheimer, J. (2019). The Finances of the Community of Portuguese-Speaking Countries (CPLP). In *The Finances of Regional Organisations in the Global South* (pp. 35–50). Routledge.

Jasper, Scott, & Moreland, Scott. (2012). Introduction: A Comprehensive Approach. *Conflict and Cooperation in the Global Commons: A Comprehensive Approach for International Security*, pp. 1–19.

Jobim, Nelson. (2010). *Lecture by the Minister of Defence of Brazil at the Closing of the International Conference: The Future of the Transatlantic*

Community. http://www.defesanet.com.br/defesa/noticia/3381/JOBIM---O-Futuro-da-Comunidade-%20Transatlantica/

Keohane, Robert O. *After Hegemony*. Princeton: Princeton University Press, 1984.

Kinne, B. J. (2018). Defense cooperation agreements and the emergence of a global security network. *International Organization*, *72*(4), 799–837.

Lipson, C. (1984). International Cooperation in Economic and Security Affairs. *World Politics*, *37*(1), 1–23.

Mahoney, J. (2000). Path dependence in historical sociology. *Theory and Society*, 29, pp. 507–48.

Medeiros, S. E., & Moreira, W. D. S. (2017). Maritime Cooperation among South Atlantic Countries and Repercussions for the Regional Community of Security Practice. *Contexto Internacional*, *39*, 281–304.

Medeiros, S. E., & Ayres Pinto, D. J. (2022). Cabos. submarinos e segurança cibernética no Atlântico. *Policy Briefs*, *11*, 1–15. Atlantic Centre.

Moreira, Adriano. (1984). Portugal e as Relações Internacionais. *Revista Nação e Defesa*, n.032, Outubro a Dezembro. pp. 23–38.

NATO. (2010). *Strategic Concept for the Defence and Security of the Members of the North Atlantic Treaty Organization*. Lisbon. https://www.nato.int/nato_static_fl2014/assets/pdf/pdf_publications/20120214_strategic-concept-2010-eng.pdf

NATO. (2022). *NATO 2022 Strategic Concept*. Madrid. https://www.nato.int/nato_static_fl2014/assets/pdf/2022/6/pdf/290622-strategic-%20concept.pdf

Oliveira, G. D. L., & Myers, M. (2021). The Tenuous Co-production of China's Belt and Road Initiative in Brazil and Latin America. *Journal of Contemporary China*, *30*(129), 481–499.

Paiva, A. L. B. E., Mendes, C. S. M., & Medeiros, S. E. A. (2019). Guinada para o Atlântico Sul: a influência do Brasil nas relações ao leste e a diversificação de parcerias com a África Ocidental. *Revista Hemisfério*, Inter-American Defense College.

Palma, F. M. V. G. D. (2013). *O quinto elemento da política externa portuguesa e o conceito de soft power* (Doctoral dissertation, Faculdade de Ciências Sociais e Humanas, Universidade Nova de Lisboa).

Portugal, Angola. (1979). Acordo Geral de Cooperação entre a República Portuguesa e a República Popular de Angola. https://gddc.ministeriopublico.pt/sites/default/files/documentos/instrumentos/lei6-%201979.pdf

Rizzi, K. R., & Bueno, P. (2021). O papel da ZOPACAS nas políticas externa e de defesa do Brasil no século XXI (2005-hoje). *Coleção Meira Mattos: revista das ciências militares*, *15*(54), 309–332.

Seabra, Pedro (2014), "A case of unmet expectations? Portugal and the South Atlantic". *Portuguese Journal of Social Sciences*, v. 13, n. 3, 331–346.

Silva, J. T. D., & Pereira, R. (2020). China and the Portuguese Atlantic: The BRI'S Last Puzzle Piece. In *The Belt and Road Initiative* (pp. 389–409). Palgrave Macmillan, Singapore.

Snidal, D. (1991). International Cooperation Among Relative Gains Maximisers. *International Studies Quarterly*, *35*(4), 387–402.

Vichi, L. P., Ayres Pinto, D. J., & De Sá, A. L. N. (2020). A Defesa da Infraestrutura de Cabos Submarinos: por uma interface entre a Defesa Cibernética e a Segurança Marítima no Brasil. *Naval War College Journal*, *26*(2).

Winger, G. (2014). The Velvet Gauntlet: A Theory of Defense Diplomacy. *What do ideas do*, 6.

Yuan, W.; Chang, Y. C. (2021). Maritime cooperation and ocean governance: Conference report. *Marine Policy*, *125*, 104388.

The Spatial Development Initiatives: The Case of African Portuguese Speaking Countries

Francisco José B. S. Leandro and Yichao Li

Introduction

Short (2022, p. 21) calls geopolitics a form of spatial imagination. Geopolitics certainly accesses both space and power, i.e., how geo-economics promote inducements and/or penalties to leverage third-party policy options, in the context of international cooperation or competition. It is in such context that *spatial development initiatives* (SDIs) become relevant. The term SDI was coined by the South African National Departments of Transport and Trade and Industry (Rogerson 2001, p. 326). SDIs were first implemented in South Africa in 1995[1] with a view to

[1] As of 1998, there were 11 SDIs throughout South Africa: The Maputo Development Corridor, the Phalaborwa SDI, the Platinum SDI, the West Coast Investment Initiative, the Fish River SDI, the Wild Coast SDI, the Richards Bay SDI, the Durban and Pietermaritzburg nodes, the Lubombo SDI, and the Gauteng Special Economic Zones (Jourdan 1998, p. 717).

F. J. B. S. Leandro (✉)
University of Macao, Macao SAR, Macao

Y. Li
ISCTE—IUL, Lisbon, Portugal

P. A. B. Duarte et al. (eds.), *Portugal and the Lusophone World*,
https://doi.org/10.1007/978-981-99-0455-6_13

serving the wider reconstruction and development of South Africa, particularly areas identified as having the greatest potential for growth (Jourdan 1998, p. 717; Rogerson 2001, pp. 324–325). After the successful implementation of the Maputo Development Corridor in 1996, southern Africa followed suit to adopt a regional SDI approach (Crush & Rogerson 2001, p. 85; Mitchell et al. 2008, p. 120). While concepts of geopolitics and geo-economics strengthened, geography itself made it possible to bring a wider understanding and utilization of SDIs to Africa. The SDI concept comprises several elements purposefully designed and co-located to advance geo-economic objectives. The commonality between these elements is that they can magnify and maximize the locational advantages of economic agglomeration. Meanwhile, where and when geopolitics and geo-economics meet, political means are employed to attain economic goals, and economic means are utilized to facilitate political goals (Mair, n.d.).

There is no single perspective on how history, geography, and security combine to shape power perceptions and expectations in Lusophony geopolitics. Lusophony shares two important geo-economic elements: relation to the sea, and language-culture. Lusophony is also a space of multiple perspectives, multiple actors, and is likely dominated by immaterial concepts (such as identity, collective memory, and shared linguistics) but with some common material elements (such as economic and trade cooperation, infrastructure, and security arrangements). This echoes Léonard's suggestion (1999, p. 483) that Lusophony is far more than just a language dimension; it also encompasses these following interconnected spaces: (1) collective memory stemming from commonalities between members' respective origins and histories, in turn inducing a sort of centric notion (Reis 1997, p. 23) (space of memory and identity); (2) a shared language-culture, despite regional splintering in identification, recognition, and adaptation (geo-linguistic space); (3) a maritime sovereign dimension despite being spread over four continents (geo-maritime space); (4) existence of some form of politically, legally, economically, and culturally structured cooperation (space of cooperation). Sousa (2005) thus argues that "utopic unity can only make sense if grounded in the recognition of difference and in the understanding of the fragmentation of [such a] cultural space."

China's Belt and Road Initiative (B&RI) is a joint vision that represents a tremendous opportunity for political concertation and cooperation through offering strategic economic options. As such, the B&RI has potentially immense impact on African Portuguese Speaking Countries (APSCs) by bringing their national visions into more prominence on the world stage. Though the notion of a unified Lusophone community faces intrinsic implementational challenges (as all agglomerations do), we rationalize the Lusophone notion from a regional geo-economic and geopolitical perspective, especially in the context of the various initiatives to integrate the APSCs' economies. The B&RI thus offers the Lusophone community a renewed sense of purpose, by establishing and developing a geo-economic space that revolves around a shared language-culture, as well as access and usage of the sea. This is indeed a crucial building block of a space of cooperation that has not only a political, economic, but also a social dimension. This chapter, therefore, endeavours to answer, in terms of national and regional development plans, this following question: To what extent does the Belt and Road Initiative contribute to designing the development of the APSCs regional economic space? In particular, we wish to identify lessons from the geo-maritime space as reference for this Lusophone space of cooperation.

An important limitation of this chapter is that it does not address how new geopolitics initiatives—such as the 2019 Blue Dot Network[2]; the 2021 Build Back Better World (B3W)[3]; the 2021 EU Global Gateway[4]; the 2016 Asia-Africa Growth Corridor (AAGC),[5] as well as other indirectly related ones such as the Master Plan on ASEAN Connectivity 2025

[2] The Blue Dot Network (BDN) is a mechanism to certify infrastructure projects that meet robust international quality standards. The United States, Japan, and Australia launched the Blue Dot Network as a multilateral effort to promote principles of sustainable infrastructure development around the world. Retrieved in December 2021, from https://www.state.gov/blue-dot-network/.

[3] Build Back Better World (B3W) is an international economic initiative undertaken by the Group of Seven (G7). This initiative is designed to provide an alternative to China's Belt and Road Initiative (B&RI) for infrastructural developments in low- and middle-income countries. Retrieved in December 2021, from https://www.reuters.com/world/g7-counter-chinas-belt-road-with-infrastructure-project-senior-us-official-2021-06-12/.

[4] The European Commission and the High Representative for Foreign Affairs and Security Policy launched the Global Gateway, the new European Strategy to boost smart, clean, and secure links in digital, energy, and transport, and to strengthen health, education, and research systems across the world. Retrieved in December 2021, from https://ec.europa.eu/commission/presscorner/detail/en/ip_21_6433.

[5] The Asia-Africa Growth Corridor (AAGC) will envisage people-centric sustainable growth strategy, details of which would evolve through a process of rigorous consultations across Asia and Africa, engaging various stakeholders. The AAGC will be raised on

(ASEAN Secretariat 2017)—have impacted Spatial Development Initiatives.[6] What is certain, however, is that the world will witness a sort of competition between these new initiatives, the B&RI, and African regional and national development plans.

Geopolitical Perspective

The B&RI is the latest impetus for regional spaces comprising Lusophone states to develop. In fact, the B&RI brings to the Lusophone community a fresh material perspective (particularly in terms of infrastructure connectivity and unimpeded trade)—calling for it to come together to form a strategic economic network—which will in more ways than one redefine world geopolitics. This perspective stems from recognizing that a common, unifying element of the Lusophone space—its maritime relations—coincides with a main component of the B&RI; herein lies the rationale for the notion of a Lusophone maritime leg of the B&RI. Complementing this maritime component with land and coast- to-coast (C2C) SDIs will give Lusophony especially the APSCs much to consider: how to re-envisage their space of cooperation, incorporating into it dimensions of political concertation, economic cooperation, and social exchanges. This idea of Lusophony not (just) as a community bound together by a common language but as a forum for concertation and cooperation in economic and trade matters is particularly compelling, as the notion will benefit from more research, discussion, and debate to gain traction within the Community of Portuguese Language Countries (Comunidade dos Países de Língua Portuguesa, CPLP). Despite not having built enough momentum, however, the notion itself does not in any way deviate from CPLP's initial purpose; rather it reinforces what its fundamental charter has always set out to achieve the following goals[7]:

four pillars = Development and Cooperation Projects, Quality Infrastructure and Institutional Connectivity, Enhancing Capacities and Skills, and People-to-People Partnerships. Retrieved in December 2021, from https://www.eria.org/Asia-Africa-Growth-Corridor-Document.pdf.

[6] Retrieved in December 2021, from https://asean.org/wp-content/uploads/2018/01/47.-December-2017-MPAC2025-2nd-Reprint-.pdf.

[7] According to Article 3—Statutes of the Community of Portuguese Language Countries (CPLP)—with amendments as of São Tomé/2001, Brasília/2002, Luanda/2005, Bissau/2006, and Lisbon/2007.

(a) Political-diplomatic consultation between its members in matters of international relations, namely to strengthen its presence in international fora; (b) Cooperation in all fields, including education, health, science and technology, defence, agriculture, public administration, communication, justice, public security, culture, sports and media (...)

The CPLP's Constitutive Declaration (1996) calls cooperation in the economic and business sphere fundamental for affirming the progressive international group of Portuguese-speaking countries. It is in this context that these following objectives are identified for the CPLP: (1) to develop economic and business cooperation among themselves and enhance existing potential through defining and implementing projects of common interests as well as exploring cooperations in various forms—bilateral, trilateral, and multilateral; (2) to promote and coordinate activities of various public and private institutions, economic associations, and non-governmental organizations engaged in the development of cooperation between countries. In accordance with these objectives, in 2005, the CPLP Council of Ministers meeting in Luanda (Angola) approved the creation of an "associate observer" status—a third state of participation—upon agreement of all full-membership states.

A growing number of sovereign states and international organizations (listed in Table 1), whose geo-economic interests can be associated with the Lusophone space, have acquired such observer status at the CPLP. Currently, the CPLP is spread across four continents, representing 5.48% of the maritime world and 7.2% of the global land dimension, with access to an estimated 2.9 billion consumers[8] and an official language that is the most spoken in the southern hemisphere. These numbers, coupled with CPLP's objectives, show that the organization will achieve full potential when its nine member states can combine their national interests into collective regional perspectives in order to explore the set of shared geo-economic advantages, based on the development of their intertwined language-cultures as well as economies driven by their sea-land locations. As of 2021, the CPLP has approved the Agreement on Mobility between its member states (Luanda, Angola, on July 17, 2021), which holds the potential to facilitate the movement of people across CPLP borders. This will prove to be an important step towards creating a new CPLP perspective in the area of development, trade, infrastructure

[8] This is an estimate based on Table 3, which shows Portuguese-speaking countries' memberships of regional economic integration areas.

Table 1 Attribution of the associate observer status

Total	*Local and date*	*New members*
2	Bissau (Guinea-Bissau) July 2006	Republic of Equatorial Guinea (since 2014 is a full member state); Republic of Mauritius
3	Lisbon (Portugal) July 2008	Republic of Senegal
6	Dili (Timor-Leste) July 2014	Republic of Namibia; Republic of Turkey; Democratic Republic of Georgia; Japan
10	Brasilia (Brazil) October 2016	Hungary, the Czech Republic, the Slovak Republic and the Oriental Republic of Uruguay
18 + 1	Sal (Cabo Verde), July 2018	Grand Duchy of Luxembourg; Principality of Andorra; United Kingdom of Great Britain and Northern Ireland; Republic of Argentina; Republic of Chile; French Republic; Italian Republic; Republic of Serbia; and the Organization of Ibero-American States for Education, Science and Culture (OEI)
27 + 4	Luanda (Angola) July 2021	Canada; State of Qatar; United States of America; Republic of Ireland; Kingdom of Spain; Republic of India; the Republic of Côte d'Ivoire; Republic of Peru; Hellenic Republic; Romania; Ibero-American Conference; the g7+; European Organization of Public Law (OEDP/EPLO)

Source Retrieved in November 2021, from https://www.cplp.org/

connectivity, and unimpeded trade. On the other hand, the B&RI can be instrumental in driving forward the infrastructural development and transformation necessary for realizing this immense Lusophone potential. Such development and transformation must be rooted in SDI geo-economics.

Geo-Economic Perspective

Even back in 1998, Tuathail, Dalby, Routledge already discussed global geopolitics in the context of a world that was no longer dominated "by territorial struggles between competing blocs but by emerging transnational problems" (p. 2). Today, we continue to find what the trio described then, that a "new geopolitical order dominated by geo-economic questions and issues" and a "world where the globalization of economic activity and global flows of trade, investment, commodities and images" were "remaking states, sovereignty and the geographical structure of the planet" (Tuathail, Dalby, Routledge 1998, p. 2) to be emphatically true and relevant still. On the other hand, the concept of geo-economics, since being identified by Luttwak in 1990, has gained importance and momentum. Blackwill and Harris (2017) have associated geo-economics with the promotion and defence of national interests; Scholvin and Wigell (2018) have defined geo-economics as the exercise of economic power to achieve strategic objectives; Klement (2021, p. XIX) has called geo-economics the study of how geopolitics and economics interact in international relations.

Nevertheless, there is currently no consensus on the definition of geo-economics to provide a common academic point of reference. In the interest of this chapter, we define geo-economics as an instrument of geopolitics that helps to correlate national interest with the construction of an economic web of state and non-state actors, as a field of study capable of identifying options to generate strategic weight, and as an instrument for promoting inducements or penalties and therefore leveraging third-party policy options. Such leveraged options must contribute to state security options and geopolitical objectives. Thus, geopolitics identifies the risks associated with economic national strategic objectives, vis-à-vis economic competitors, based on the perceived impact of geopolitical flows. Geopolitical flows with economic purposes are to be designed and created by economic diplomacy, understood as "the use of [...] political influence held by states to promote [...] economic interests in international markets" (Spanish Ministry of Foreign Affairs 2011, p. 8; Klement 2021, p. 106).

Table 2 shows the vision of an integrated network of SDIs and its opportunities. The network combines the Lusophone maritime leg of the B&RI with major existing land-based SDIs. Angola and Mozambique play particularly pivotal roles in this vision, bridging their own economic regions with several landlocked states and the Sahel region, potentially creating synergy with São Tomé e Príncipe and Equatorial Guinea in the Gulf of Guinea, as well as with Cabo Verde and Guinea-Bissau in the central parts of the Atlantic Ocean.

Table 3 lists the PSCs' partnerships with China, the status of the B&RI implementation agreements, and their regional economic integration,

Table 2 Key elements of the lusophone maritime leg of the B&RI combined with major African spatial development initiatives

Trans-African Highway network comprising transcontinental road projects being developed by the African Union, the African Development Bank (AfDB), and the United Nations Economic Commission for Africa (UNECA) in conjunction with Regional Economic Communities (African Development Bank (2019, p. 54)).

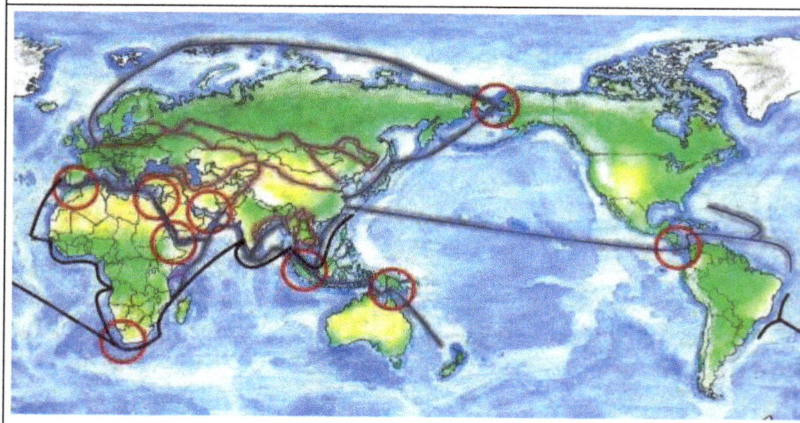

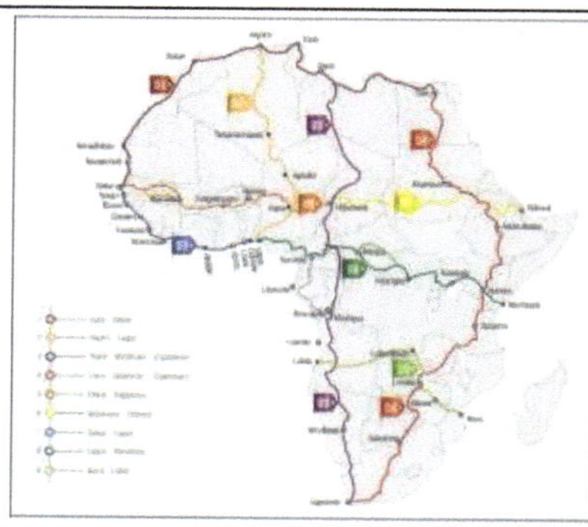

Source World Map authored by Paulo Gonçalves (2022)—Publication rights purchased by the authors. African Maps: Adapted from Laurance, Sloan, Weng, & Sayer 2015, p. 203. Retrieved in October 2021, from https://www.arcgis.com/home/item.html?id=aa6dcedfbede4b2188f90cda23ae03d0
Adapted from Kynge, Campbell, Kazmin, and Bokhari. (2017). Retrieved in July 2021, from https://ig.ft.com/sites/china-ports/
Retrieved in July 2021 from https://www.researchgate.net/figure/The-Belt-and-Road-Initiative-Metrics-Adapted-by-Ana-Thudichum-Vasconcelos_fig2_338066100 and https://www.clbrief.com/the-portuguese-speaking-countries-well-positioned-for-belt-and-road-initiative/
African Development Bank (2019, p. 54)

Table 3 PSCs B&RI and regional economic integration

PSC	*Partnerships with China*		*B&RI Agreement (Signed)*	*AfCFTA*[a]	*Regional Economic Integration*
	Date	*Types*			
Portugal	2005	Comprehensive strategic partnership	2018	Not applicable	European Union (EU)
	2017	Blue partnership			
	2018	Further strengthened			
Brazil	1993	Strategic Partnership	Not yet	Not applicable	Southern Common Market (Mercosur)
	2009	Further strengthened			
	2012	Comprehensive strategic partnership			
	2014	Further strengthened			
	2019	Further strengthened			
Timor-Leste	2014	Comprehensive cooperative partnership	2017	Not applicable	Candidate to Association of Southeast Asian Nations (ASEAN)
Angola	2010	Strategic partnership	2018	Ratified 4/11/2020	South African Development Community (SADC) Angola is also a member of ECCAS
Mozambique	2016	Comprehensive strategic cooperative partnership	2018	Signed	

(continued)

Table 3 (continued)

PSC	*Partnerships with China*		*B&RI Agreement (Signed)*	*AfCFTA*[a]	*Regional Economic Integration*
	Date	*Types*			
Cabo Verde	Not yet		2018	Signed	Economic Community of West African States (ECOWAS)
Guinea-Bissau	Not yet		2021	Signed	Guinea-Bissau is also a member of the Community of Sahel–Saharan States (CEN-SAD)
Equatorial Guinea	2015	Comprehensive cooperative partnership	2019	Ratified 2/07/2019	Economic Community Central African States (ECCAS)
São Tomé e Príncipe	2017	Comprehensive cooperative partnership	2021	Ratified 27/06/2019	

Source Authors

[a]Retrieved in November 2021, from https://www.tralac.org/documents/resources/infographics/2605-status-of-afcfta-ratification/file.html

including the latest initiative of establishing an African Continental Free Trade Area (AfCFTA). According to the B&RI's official website,[9] as of 29 November 2021, 51 out of 54 African states have at one point or another, signed B&RI-related Memoranda of Understanding (MoUs) (the only three states that have not signed are Eswatini (Swaziland), Malawi and Mauritius (Western Sahara is not considered)). In fact, despite not being legally binding, the African Union itself also signed an MoU during the 2018. Beijing Summit of the Forum on China-Africa Cooperation (FOCAC), agreeing to cooperate with China under the B&RI.[10]

Lusophony geo-economics, as shown in Table 7, can be organized through three regional geo-economic spaces: (A) the Western Europe–American space; (B) the Sahel and Sub Saharan African-American belt; and (C) the Australasia maritime space. As illustrated in the same table, and based on these spaces, we use the concept of spatial development initiatives (SDIs) to identify and categorize the roles of the APSCs, in the context of regional integration and development, into the different perspectives of the Sahel and Sub Saharan regions. The rationale for using SDIs is associated with the fact that they are substantial national-level guiding instruments for planning, investing, and supporting decision-making associated with development and economic prosperity. In the same vein, Brand (2018, p. 109) argues that "spatial planning encompasses common principles to be applied to different planning systems to provide guidance for decision-making proposals to achieve social and economic prosperity. Planning systems, in this instance, refer to policies and legislation." SDIs are particularly important not only for designing national development strategies but also for advancing those strategies to a transnational context, bearing in mind world-wide connectivity and the web of economic flows at national, regional, and inter-regional scales.

This research focuses on the two interconnected geo-economic Lusophone spaces in the Sahel and Sub Saharan African-American regions: (B1) Central and South Atlantic Ocean, Macaronesia and the Gulf of Guinea, and (B2) Indian Ocean and the African Great Lakes area, having the following national plans as main reference (Table 7). SDIs are important geo-economic instruments and their implementation is

[9] Retrieved in November 2021, from https://www.yidaiyilu.gov.cn/xwzx/roll/77298.htm (in Chinese).

[10] Retrieved in November 2021, from http://www.xinhuanet.com/english/2018-09/07/c_137452482.htm.

strongly influenced by national plans, regional development and integration plans, partnerships, locations of Special Economic Zones, and spatial arrangements of economic corridors.

(a) A spatial development initiative brings together spatial planning and development projects to include areas of unrealized economic potential (Hope & Cox 2015, p. 11). It is a large investment strategy based on main integrated policies to develop key infrastructures, involving the private and public sectors, with the objective of generating economic growth in under-developed areas or designed with the purpose of connecting production centres and markets, including mechanisms to facilitate border crossings (reducing both time and costs [Workshop Report 2015, p. 3]). SDIs are the ultimate expression of a centralized state vision of spatial planning.

Several types of SDI have proliferated: economic corridors, clusters, industrial parks, special economic zones (SEZs), and technopoles (Nogales 2014, p. 1). SDIs are spatially organized economic development schemes with the aim to develop business and investment environments in specific areas (Reeg 2017). SDIs can be further driven by economic corridors, built to connect rich hinterlands to poor ports, or vice versa.

Typical SDIs have the following characteristics and components (Hope & Cox 2015, pp. XI–XII):

(1) multiple public and private stakeholders; (2) core transport infrastructure and freight logistics; (3) institutional frameworks and procedures; (4) anchor projects and cluster projects, as well as conglomerates of local communities and small businesses; (5) are designed and implemented based on specific geographic linkages; (6) constitute a cluster of mutually reinforcing development projects (as opposed to standalone initiatives) established to help a particular geographic area thrive; (7) are embedded in an institutional framework to facilitate design, implementation, and monitoring; and (8) linking infrastructure and large-scale economic sectoral investments in defined geographic areas. As suggested before, the SDI concept encompasses such elements as economic corridors, clusters, industrial parks, SEZs, technopoles, and represents a purposeful

agglomeration of economic activities positioned to facilitate and promote interactions within a selected area where businesses and economic activities can benefit from the co-location (adapted from Nogales 2014, p. 6).

(b) National Plans—A close analysis of sample passages from the APSCs' national development plans, contained in Table 4, reveals that they all share similar concerns in relation to regional connectivity and economic integration, sea, blue economy, and exclusive economic zones (EEZs), language, and the CPLP.
(c) Regional development and integration plans—Table 5 contains sample passages from regional development plans. A close analysis reveals that they all share similar concerns in relation to regional integration, strengthening the institutional capacity, sea access, and connectivity of infrastructure.
(d) Partnerships—Per the definitions given by Li (2021, p. 42) and Tyushka and Czechowska (2019, pp. 20–24), partnerships can be conceptualized as generic bilateral agreements between two sovereign states, designed to be ad hoc, dynamic, consensual, and non-legally binding. Partnerships are political-diplomatic cooperation frameworks capable of advancing stable sovereign interests and generating mutual benefits to promote peaceful, secure, and sustainable economic development. Partnerships build synergy between national development plans, as they establish formal institutional links at various governmental and non-governmental levels, producing multiple official and unofficial interactive channels. Partnerships also facilitate more frequent summits between top-level leaders where policies can be fine-tuned according to preceding outcomes and results, as well as meetings at the subministerial and bureaucratic levels where officials can explore and discuss common interests and/or concerns, often in the form of joint task forces targeting specific issues. Whether or not they eventually lead to legally binding agreements, partnerships involving different actors in complementary scopes can promote and facilitate state- to-state, state-to-investor, and investor-to-investor relations within its cooperative framework, which brings together national development plans.
(e) Special Economic Zones (SEZs)—Located within a specific geographic area, SEZs are administered more efficiently so that

they can drive and enhance local and regional economic development more effectively. Altbeker, Visser, and Bulterman (2021, p. 3) believe that the most successful SEZs in the world are those "that have been instruments for supporting industrialisation and integration into global trade flows." This further implies that SEZs can be seen as indispensable connectors that promote the sustainable development of SDIs, as the success of SEZs also lies within such factors as access, location, infrastructure, ability to attract investments and trade, and operational effectiveness (Figueiredo, Leandro, & Li 2022, p. 276). While China's successful experience of developing SEZs may not be a one-size-fits-all solution for other sovereign states, such experience offers a wealth of lessons for others to refer to and emulate, as well as platforms for various parties to come together and discuss building and developing SEZs cooperatively, particularly under the flexible framework of Chinese partnerships.

(f) Economic Corridors—Reviewing the relevant literature—Pottier (1963), Friedmann (1972), Tuppen (1977), Geyer (1988), Andersen and Burnett (1998), Brunner (2013), Rodrigue (2020)—shows that any definition of the term "economic corridors" will inevitably encapsulate four essential ideas: (1) They comprise spatial loci of flows, various infrastructural modes, conglomeration of economic actors, and interlinked economic, infrastructural, and technological processes. When these processes involve urban development, corridors become a system of cities oriented along an axis, commonly fluvial or coastal, which gives the cities additional commercial relations (Rodrigue 2020, Chapter 2); (2) They provide rationale to link nodes, where economic opportunities of different levels, scales, and intensities can be accessed; (3) They comprise different arrangements and are represented by different types and/or modalities; (4) They can and need to be streamlined through integrating and coordinating state policies between/across nations.

Economic corridors can be thought of as programmatic models for building, developing, and structuring, physically and socio-economically, an area where there is an agglomeration of economic activities and people upon a backbone of transport infrastructure (Healey 2004). Table 6 shows a five-stage development process of an economic corridor, with

Table 4 APSCs—sample of national development plans

1	**Mozambique** National Development Strategy (2015–2035) Country Strategy Paper (2018–2022)	Opportunities—Geographical positioning—the **unique regional position as a hinterland gateway** (SP, p. 8) … Deeper integration between regions and the removal of barriers to trade and improve access to local and regional markets would further foster the environment for industrialization (SP, p. 9) … The main objective of this pillar (1) is to create an enabling business environment that is more competitive in order to incentivize and dynamize the private sector through investments in the country's energy and transport infrastructure, **which connect rural areas to development corridors** and thus **improve access to local and regional markets** (SP, p. 16) … 50… The completion of **major regional road corridor** backbones is essential to leverage the economic activity of the country and interlink rural areas with local markets and the region, in particular the trans-border regional growth poles of Niassa and Cabo Delgado, which are provinces with a high poverty incidence. (SP, p. 17) …

(continued)

Table 4 (continued)

2	**Angola** National Development Plan (2018–2022)	The country has a high agricultural potential; natural resources; **strategic geographical location that facilitates regional integration and intra-regional trade** (NDP, point 5, p. V) … The other area vital to growth is **regional integration in order to unlock the potential of local manufacturing and boost trade**. (NDP, point 6, p. V) … 2.2.9 **Regional Integration: Angola's geographical location offers a potential to provide road and railway transportation and logistical platform services for the landlocked countries.** The Lobito Corridor is central to Angola's transportation infrastructure as it crosses 4 provinces and concerns 40% of the Angolan population; provides the shortest route to the seas for Zambia's North Western Province, the Copper belt, and the Democratic Republic of Congo (DRC)'s Katanga province with a population of 16 million working for a vibrant mining activity… Potential for intra-trade is huge and Angola is already investing in a special economic zone at Lobito and an oil refinery… (NDP, p. 5) … 3.1.1 **National Priorities**: The Angola Long Term Plan, dubbed "Vision 2025" … It is based on five main dimensions: (i) … (ii) … (iv) … (v) infrastructure development and regional integration. (NDP, p. 7) … **Transport.** Angola has a road network of about 76,000 km of which only 18,000 km are paved. The government is committed to rehabilitate and expand trunk roads including **regional corridors connecting to DRC, Zambia, and Namibia**, so far about 13,000 km of roads were rehabilitated and upgraded. The country has a railway network of 2950 km out of which 2725 km were rehabilitated with the investment of more than USD 3 billion and made operational from 2012 to 2014, but the country's railway network lacks interconnection. Angola has four important ports of trade, namely: Luanda, Cabinda, Lobito, and Namibe making the country a regional transport hub for neighbouring landlocked countries. The government has plans to build a new commercial port north of Luanda at Barra do Dande to reduce traffic at the port of Luanda and the capacity of the port of Lobito has been expanded. Plans are underway to **build 44 logistical platforms to connect to railway line and trunk roads**. Total investment is estimated at USD 3.9 billion. Five platforms have already registered some progress in the civil works, namely: Lombe, Luau, Menongue, Soyo and Caala. (NDP, p. 10) … **Regional integration**: Angola can take advantage of its ports as well as the untapped regional market to boost intra-regional trade, in particular along the Lobito Corridor (NDP, p. 11)

	Country Strategy Paper (2017–2021) Long Term Plan—Vision (2025)	
3	**São Tomé e Príncipe**	Definition of a new trade policy aimed at progressive integration into the regional and world economy; Deepen relations with Economic Community of Central African States (ECCAS) and Communauté Economique et Monetaire de l'Afrique Centrale (CEMAC), in order to benefit from the provisions for the extension of a Free Trade Area (FTA); Deepen and perfect negotiations for the Economic Partnership Agreement with the European Union (EPAEU) in the regional framework (NSP, Point 2.6)
	National Sustainable Development Plan (2020–2024) Country Strategic Plan (2019–2024) Combined Country Strategy Paper (2018–2022) National Development Plan (2017–2021)	Strategic objective 1: Economic domain—Improve the exploitation of the country's development potential, accelerate economic growth, and strengthen integration into the regional and global economy (NDP, p. 23) ... 5.4.1.2 Construction, under private financing, of a port capacity transshipment in deep waters that will make the country a centre for the provision of maritime services for the sub-region of the Gulf of Guinea... 5.4.1.3. The modernization and extension of São Tomé International Airport, in order to progressively turn it into a regional centre for air transport; (NDP, p. 52) the country will continue to actively participate in the projects and programmes of the Interregional Coordination Center for Combating Maritime Piracy in the Gulf of Guinea, which contributes to the preservation of sovereignty and national security at sea (NDP, p. 51)

(continued)

Table 4 (continued)

4	**Cabo Verde**	Lack of adequate inter-island **transport connectivity constrains integration in the regional and global markets** (SP, point 5, p. 2) … Regional integration and trade: Despite the country's remoteness and insularity which constrains physical **connectivity and integration in the regional and global economy, the government has made regional integration a key priority**. The country applies the Economic Community of West African States (ECOWAS) protocol on the free movement of goods which is in line with the Bank's Regional Integration Strategic Framework 2018–2025. Cabo Verde is also finalizing an assessment for participation in the ECOWAS Common External Tariff, but is fully compliant with ECOWAS's zero non-tariff barriers such as quotas and prohibitions on intra-regional trade. Cabo Verde signed the agreement establishing the Africa's Continental Free Trade Area (AfCFTA) in March 2018 and established a diplomatic representation in Abuja to deepen dialogue with regional organizations including the ECOWAS and benefit more from intra-regional trade and transit trade (SP, point 5, p. 9) … Strategic geographic location could position Cabo Verde as a regional hub (SP, point 5, p. 12)… Outcome 2: Enhanced infrastructure **supporting value chains and regional integration** … using its comparative advantage and play a leading role in supporting efficient transport systems to foster regional integration by co-financing the feasibility studies and implementation of the **multimodal regional corridor Praia-Dakar-Abidjan**. This will provide alternative transportation services that will open up the country, reduce the transportation costs, facilitate movement of goods and people, and promote regional integration. (SP, point 5, p. 18) …

	Country Strategy Paper (2019–2024) National Sustainable Development Plan (2018–2022) Cabo Verde Programme Strategy (2015–2018)	
5	**Equatorial Guinea** Country Strategy Paper (2018–2022)	**2.2.17 REG is a member of CEMAC and ECCAS**. Its central geographical position and economic power since the beginning of the oil era make it a potentially important partner in these economic spaces. Regional integration is essential for this country, given the small size of its domestic market... The decision taken in October 2017 to abolish visas for CEMAC citizens is expected to further promote regional trade, thus stimulating the country's economic growth. **2.2.18. REG seeks to assert itself as a regional transport and trade hub in Central Africa**. To that end, it has significantly upgraded its port and airport facilities to meet the requirements of a regional goods and passenger transportation hub. As a CEMAC member country, it has embarked on the reform of its tax and customs system. Specifically, it has introduced the common external tariff (CET) comprising four rates and categories of goods. The authorities are also seeking to accelerate and modernize customs clearance procedures, but these efforts are hampered by difficulties in enforcing the law and tax evasion... Lastly, the authorities guardedly evoke plans to conclude an economic partnership agreement (EPA) with the European Union (EU) which is thought to have a negative impact on employment in the country, technology transfer and diversification (SP, p. 6)
6	**Guinea-Bissau** Country Strategic Plan (2019–2024) Country Strategy (2021–2025) Terra Ranka (2025)	Guinea-Bissau 2025 strategy will favour the emergence of a new economic map, with 9 hubs spread across the entire country, which will be dynamic reservoirs of economic activity, jobs, and urban life. The 9 hubs identified are: Bissau, the Bolama-Bijagós islands, Biombo, Cacheu, Farim, Bafatá, Gabú, Catio, and Buba (TR, p. 13) ... Guinea-Bissau's strategy: it shows the six axes (foundations and pillars) that will be necessary to the building of the house of Guinea-Bissau 2025 and which converge towards sustainable and solidarity-based development (TR, p. 14) ... Rehabilitation and construction of national and regional roads... Restructuring of Port Bissau... Construction of a deep-water port at Buba... Deep-water port at Pikil... Rehabilitation of Osvqldo Vieira airport (TR, p. 25) ...

Table 5 APSCs—sample of regional development plans

1	**Southern African Development Community** Angola Mozambique	**SADC—SADC Industrialization Strategy and Roadmap 2015–2063**—The Strategy is anchored on three pillars namely: industrialization as champion of economic and technological transformation; competitiveness as an active process to move from comparative advantage to competitive advantage; and regional integration and geography as the context for industrial development and economic prosperity (p. 5). **Southern African Development Community (SADC) Vision 2050**—SADC Vision 2050 is expressed in three pillars: I. Industrial Development and Market Integration, **II. Infrastructure Development in Support of Regional Integration**, and III. Social and Human Capital Development; and built on a firm foundation of Peace, Security, and Good Governance (p. 3). Pillar II: By 2050, SADC is to have efficient and effective, **technologically driven cross-border infrastructure services and networks** to support and facilitate deeper regional integration. **SADC Regional Indicative Strategic Development Plan (RISDP) 2020–2030**—Strategic Objectives for Pillar II: (1) Quality, interconnected, integrated, and seamless infrastructure and networks; (2) Improved capacity for conceptualization, design, construction, maintenance, and operation of regional infrastructure and services; (3) Increased access to affordable infrastructure and services (p. 52)

2	**Economic Community of West African States** Cabo Verde Guinea-Bissau	**ECOWAS**—2015 Strengthening the Institutional Capacity of the Economic Community of West African States (ECOWAS). ECOWAS Master Plan for the Development of Regional Power Generation and Transmission Infrastructure 2019–2033. **West Africa Regional Integration Strategy Paper (WA-RISP) 2020–2025**—Geographically, the ECOWAS region is characterized by an assortment of: (1) Countries with access to the sea (Benin, Côte d'Ivoire, Ghana, Guinea, **Guinea-Bissau**, Gambia, Liberia, Nigeria, Senegal, Sierra Leone, and Togo); (20 Island country (**Cabo Verde**); and (3) Landlocked countries (Burkina Faso, Mali, and Niger) (p. 6). The Priority Areas of the new WA-RISP 2020–2025 have been narrowed to: (1) Enhancing resilient cross-border infrastructure, and (2) supporting regional enterprise development (p. 2)

(continued)

Table 5 (continued)

3	**Economic Community of Central African States** Angola Equatorial Guinea São Tomé e Príncipe	ECCAS—2015 Strengthening the Institutional Capacity of the Economic Community of Central African States (ECCAS). Central Africa Regional Integration Strategy Paper 2019–2025 (CA-RISP) (included Equatorial Guinea)—However, the region has immense sources of resilience given its great agro-ecological diversity and abundant natural resources, its advantageous geostrategic location in the centre of the continent and its mining natural resources, to name but a few, which could offer reassuring opportunities. Indeed, the region is a distinct area with the co-existence of the Saharan ecological zones, located on the northern borders of the Republic of Chad, the Sahel zones of the Far North of Cameroon and part of Chadian territory, the forest areas that cover more than 50% of the surface area of the sub-region, as well as mountainous areas and a large coastal area, which extends from the Cameroonian coast to the Angolan coast. In addition, the sub-region has 346.2 million hectares of forest, 135.5 million hectares of pasture, and 26.9 million hectares of arable land. Similarly, the region has the world's greatest untapped hydropower potential, which is a major strategic asset for the sub-region to develop a competitive, low-cost, and sustainable energy supply. (p. 57). Southern Africa Regional Integration Strategy Paper 2020–2026 (SA-RISP) (included Angola and São Tomé e Príncipe)—Countries in the region can be categorized into six landlocked countries (Botswana, Eswatini, Lesotho, Malawi, Zambia, and Zimbabwe), four coastal countries (Angola, Mozambique, Namibia, and South Africa), and three island countries (Madagascar, Mauritius, and Sao Tome and Principe). (p. 2). The main objective of the new RISP is to foster an integrated and diversified Southern African region promoting structural transformation and inclusive and green growth. Reflecting this objective, the new RISP has two mutually reinforcing Priority Areas of Bank support: (i) Infrastructure Connectivity; and (ii) Market Integration and Industrialization. (p. v)
4	**The Community of Sahel–Saharan States** Guinea-Bissau	CEN-SAD—2015 Strengthening the Institutional Capacity of the Communauté Des Sahélo-Sahariens (CEN-SAD)

some possible overlap between stages, and therefore should be considered holistically rather than as individual stages (Nogales 2014, pp. 8–9). This echoes Srivastava's idea that a corridor "from 'nowhere to nowhere through nowhere' would not be very meaningful" (2011, p. 3). The same applies to SEZs. The fundamental elements of an economic corridor include access, location, infrastructure (stage 1), and the ability to attract investments and trade flows (stages 2 + 3). Corridors usually form on the basis of such existing infrastructure—it is this association with infrastructure that makes them priorities of developing countries looking to connect and develop their rural areas (Workshop Report 2015, pp. 1–3). Subsequently, an economic corridor "channels, focuses, and amplifies the potential for economic growth" (stage 4) through connecting effective economic nodes such as SEZs (Srivastava 2011, p. 3), while cross-border corridors have the ability to also accelerate regional integration. Stage 5 of the development concerns the sustainability and longevity of the economic network, and it is in this stage that the human factor becomes extremely important.

As the economic corridor model fits within the SDI concept, developing economic corridors also encounters what Mitchell et al. (2008,

Table 6 Modalities of "Economic" Corrid

Stage 1 Transport Corridor	Only Domestic	Adequate and reliable transport infrastructure; Integrated and well-maintained infrastructure, with sustainable operating costs; Transport services available, operated in line with the market demands; Security of the infrastructures and the surroundings, in a manner consistent with the market freedom. They can be land (incorporating pipelines, highways, airports, other infrastructure) or sea-based (seaports and SLOC).
Stage 2 Logistics Corridor		**Stage 1** + Logistics services with sustainability and in line with the market demands; Management and coordination, including the existence of skills and adequate technology.
Stage 3 Trade Corridor	Domestic + Domestic and International	**Stage 1 + Stage 2** + Trade facilitation mechanisms put forward by adequate legislation; Trans-border trade facilitation put forward by adequate legislation and international cooperation; Establishment of networks of cross-border agents[12].
Stage 4 Economic Corridor	Mostly International	**Stage 1 + Stage 2 + Stage 3** + Existence of multi-sectorial trade flows and multi services; Facilitation of flows of people, capital, and services, put forward by adequate legislation; Existence of a SEZ or trade connectivity between production centres and consumers; Significant local impact and engagement. They are connected with a network of other corridors.
Stage 5 Growth Corridor		**Stage 1 + Stage 2 + Stage 3 + Stage 4** + Overall investment in human social capital and a consistent state attitude to fight against corruption; Domestic integration of the trade and service flows. They are connected with a network of other corridors.

p. 121) refer to as common problems encountered during the development of SDIs: lack of communication with the public, particularly at the local level [which in fact is closest to human social capital], capacity deficiencies at various levels of government, unresolved land claims and other local sources of tension, and poor understanding on local practices. On a related note, according to Ernst and Young (2011), combining corridors with regional trading blocs can help deepen conventional country-based macro-analysis, in ways that enrich strategic thinking regarding how to spur inclusive and sustainable growth in the developing world.

According to Nogales (2014, p. 10), economic corridors have an analytical and a policy dimension. The analytical dimension defines a corridor's spatial-functional form and patterns, reinforcing the idea that corridors are linear, interconnected, and interacting clusters of land, where the whole should be greater than the sum of its parts (Albrechts & Tasan-Kok 2009). The policy dimension defines the corridor's policy and spatial planning instruments (ibid.). A definitive key feature of economic corridors is their ability to attract investment and induce economic activities with its confines. To achieve this, physical connectivity and logistics facilitation must be in place (Banomyong 2008). Economic corridors can also be "gateways" (e.g., airports and ports) linking economic nodes to a hinterland and/or to global trade routes (IDB 2011). Transport corridors may be long or short: short corridors connect local and/or regional urban and industrial centres/zones; long corridors may include roads, railway, inland waterways, and regional shipping lanes (Nogales 2014, p. 9). Corridors are most effectively developed when there are comprehensive plans. In other words, an understanding of how physical infrastructure, policy arrangements, and specific circumstances work together within a purposeful, interactive network is imperative (Nogales 2014, p. 89).

Geopolitical and Geo-Economic Associations of the Lusophone Space

The B&RI is an initiative that provides geo-economic access with consent, via the construction of key infrastructure, offering a platform to improve regional integration, taking into consideration access to the sea, which is something that all APSCs have. For the Lusophone community, the fact that there it shares a common language and culture facilitates the high-level political arrangements at the geopolitical level that is necessary to advance regional articulation. In addition, a geo-economically coherent Lusophone space has two functions: (1) It presents opportunities to generate regional economies to be integrated into larger economic corridors; (2) it acts as "access facilitators" for neighbouring landlocked states to access the sea. This latter fact is particularly important in the African and APSCs context, as 16 out of 32 landlocked developing countries (LLDCs) are in Africa[11] (Botswana, Burundi, Central Africa, Chad, Lesotho, Malawi, Mali, Niger, Zimbabwe, Rwanda, Swaziland, Uganda, Burkina Faso, Zambia, Ethiopia, and South Sudan), and 13 of these LLDCs are classified as poor and highly indebted, while 10 are in or at a high risk of being in debt distress.[12] In fact, the UN's "Landlocked Developing Countries Fact Sheet 2020,"[13] very decisively associate LLDCs with "countries that lack territorial access to the sea," implying that remoteness and isolation from markets abroad, additional border crossings, cumbersome transit procedures, inefficient logistics systems, weak institutions, and poor infrastructure all contribute to incurring substantially higher transport and other trade costs for LLDCs than coastal countries. These high costs cause tremendous reduction in trade, inducing direct negative impact on economic growth, putting the countries themselves at a disadvantage to fully realize their potential in sustainable development. According to estimates by the United Nations Conference on Trade and Development (UNCTAD), landlocked countries on average spend almost twice more on their export earnings on transportation and insurance than developing countries, and three times more than economies belonging to the Organization for Economic Cooperation and Development (OECD). According to the Vienna Programme of Action (2021)[14] "Thirty-two of the world's landlocked developing countries face an array of challenges mainly associated with lack of direct territorial access to the sea and remoteness from world markets. Their dependence on other countries for international trade and transit compounds other challenges that landlocked developing countries (LLDCs) face." The Vienna

[11] There are 32 landlocked developing countries (LLDCs) in the world, of which, 17 are landlocked least developed countries. Retrieved in December 2021, from https://unctad.org/topic/landlocked-developing-countries/list-of-LLDCs.

[12] Retrieved in December 2021, from https://www.un.org/ohrlls/sites/www.un.org.ohrlls/files/landlocked_developing_countries_factsheet.pdf.

[13] Ibid.

[14] Retrieved in December 2021, from https://www.un.org/ohrlls/content/vienna-programme-action.

Programme of Action also defines the following as key priorities: (1) Fundamental transit policy issues; (2) Infrastructure development and maintenance; (3) International trade and trade facilitation; (4) Regional integration and cooperation; (5) Structural economic transformation; and (6) Means of implementation. These are particularly relevant to the current discussion, as all continental APSCs (with the exception of Equatorial Guinea) are surrounded by at least one landlocked state (Fig. 1).

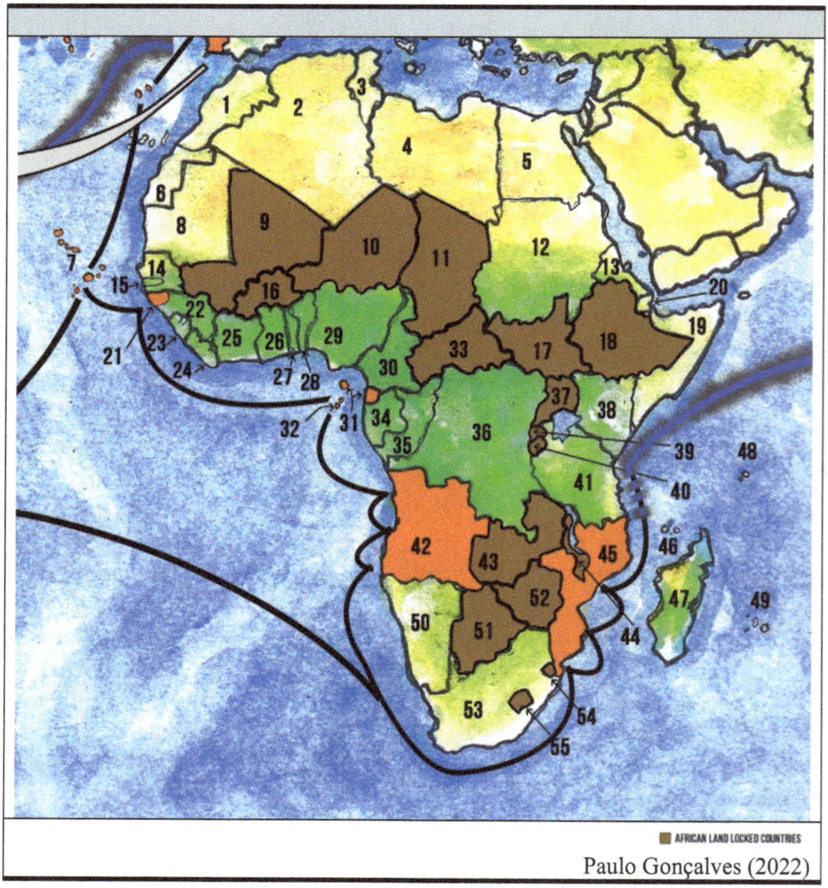

Fig. 1 African landlocked states (*Source* Badi and Pamucar [2019])

Table 7 The geopolitical and geo-economic associations of lusophone space

The regional perspective—the geo-economic axis			
A	B		C
Western Europe-Central and South American Region	Sahel and Sub Saharan African (Western and Central)—Central and South American Region		Australasia Maritime Region
North Atlantic Ocean, Mediterranean Sea and Western Africa	B1 Centre and South Atlantic Ocean, Macaronesia and Gulf of Guinea	B2 Indian Ocean and African Great lakes area	Indian-Pacific Ocean ASEAN-Australia maritime roads
Cabo Verde; Brazil; Portugal	Angola; Cabo Verde; Brazil; Portugal (insular); Guinea-Bissau; Equatorial- Guinea; São Tomé e Príncipe	Mozambique	Timor-Leste
Coast 2 Coast (C2C) and other key spatial development initiatives			
(BR) Road corridor Brazil, Paraguay, Argentina and Chile[a] (BR) Central Bi-Oceanic Railway[b] (BR) MERCOSUR-Chile Axis (BR)Paraná-Paraguay Waterways Axis[c] (BR) Guyanese Shield Axis (BR) Amazon Axis (BR) Peru-Brazil-Bolivia axis[e] (BR) South Axis (BR) Capricornean Axis (EU) The Atlantic Corridor[f] (EU) The Trás-os-Montes Railways Corridor[g] (EU) Mediterranean Corridor[h]	(1) Praia (CV)—Bissau (GB)—Madeira/Azores (POR) (2A) (GB) Dakar-Abidjan-Lagos Corridor–Gulf of Guinea (2B) Praia (CV)—Dakar (SEN)—Bamako (MAL)–Port Harcourt (NIG) (3) (GB) Trans-Sahelian[i] and Cairo–Dakar Highways (TAH 1) (4A) (STP) Duala (CAM)—N'djamena (CHD)—Khartoum (SUD)—Port Sudan (SUD) (Central Africa-Red Sea) (4B) Fernão Dias (STP) Duala (CAM)—Yaounde (CAM)—Bangui (CAR)—Bambali (CAR)—Juba (SSD)—Addis Ababa (ETH)—Djibouti or Nairobi-Lamu-Mombasa (KEN) (5A) (ANG) Lobito-Lusaka-East African Coast (Beira, Quelimane, Nacala (MOZ); Mtwara, Dar es salaam (TAZ)) (5B) (ANG) Namibe-Lubango—Ondangwa (NAB)—(SA) Johannesburg—(MOZ) Maputo (6) (NAB) Walvis Bay—(BTW) Gaborone—(SA) Johannesburg—(MOZ) Maputo		ASEAN Connectivity Master Plan 2025

(continued)

Table 7 (continued)

Major regional economic integration spaces		
Economic Community of West African States (ECOWAS) Community of Latin American and Caribbean States (CELAC) Mercado Comum do Sul (MERCOSUR) European Union (EU)	Africa Continental Free Trade Agreement (AfCFTA) Economic Community of West African States (ECOWAS) The Community of Sahel–Saharan States (CEN-SAD) Southern African Development Community (SADC) Arab Maghreb Union (AMU) East African Community (EAC) Economic Community of Central African States (ECCAS) European Union (EU)	Candidate to Association of Southeast Asian Nations (ASEAN) ASEAN Plus

[a]Retrieved in July 2021, from https://conexionintal.iadb.org/2017/07/11/corredor-vial-entre-el-atlantico-y-el-pacifico/?lang=en

[b]Retrieved in July 2021, from https://www.railway-technology.com/features/the-bi-oceanic-corridor-a-new-railroad-to-rival-maritime-freight/

[c]Pedone and Ronconi, 2017, p. 677

[d]Retrieved in July 2021, from https://repositorio.cepal.org/bitstream/handle/11362/6343/1/S0900132_en.pdf

[e]The Atlantic corridor links the western part of the Iberian Peninsula and the ports of Le Havre and Rouen to Paris and further to Mannheim—Strasbourg, with high-speed rail lines and parallel conventional ones, including the Seine as inland waterway. Retrieved in July 2021, from https://ec.europa.eu/transport/themes/infrastructure/atlantic_en and https://ec.europa.eu/transport/infrastructure/tentec/tentec-portal/map/maps.html?corridor=7&layer=8,9

[f]Lisbon—Porto (Portugal)—Madrid (Spain)—Paris (France) Retrieved in July 2021, from https://economiafinancas.com/2021/plano-ferroviario-nacional/

[h] The Mediterranean corridor links the Iberian Peninsula with the Hungarian-Ukrainian border. It follows the Mediterranean coastlines of Spain and France, crosses the Alps towards the east through Northern Italy, leaving the Adriatic coast in Slovenia and Croatia towards Hungary. Apart from the Po River and some other canals in Northern Italy, it consists of road and rail. Retrieved in July 2021, from https://orientalreview.org/wp-content/uploads/2016/07/map-eu-ten-t-corridors-railwaygazette_01.jpg

[i]Or TAH 5 or Dakar-Ndjamena Highway

Table 7 puts forward the key geo-economic associations of the Lusophone space: (1) the membership of regional economic spaces; (2) the ability to access the Sahel region, the African Great Lakes, the Gulf of Guinea, and to facilitate cost-to-cost solutions. The value of geo-economic planning in the context of all components of the SDI and the regional economic communities' rests with the fact that all APSCs are located in areas with easy access to the sea, in the vicinity of a large domestic market, all belonging to the same international organization (CPLP) where they can look for consensual- coordinated solutions, and all share the same cultural-language. "[G]eo-economics and geopolitics are sometimes interrelated strategies that complement each other" (Scholvin 2019, p. 213). All these features can be combined and potentiated by the opportunities offered in the context of the Lusophone maritime leg of the B&RI. The two geo-economic APSCs axes, identified as (B1) Central and South Atlantic Ocean, Macaronesia, and Gulf of Guinea, and (B2) the Indian Ocean and African Great Lakes area, mark an area of immense potential which should be explored further, and integrated and evaluated at national, regional, and international levels.

Conclusion

"[I]deas don't work in isolation but in amalgamation," and "have become more interconnected and interdependent" (Shahzad 2021)—these in fact are the essence of developing Spatial Development Initiatives (SDIs). SDIs link together factors related to spatial development, and comprehensively consider different combinations of national plans, regional development and integration plans, partnerships, SEZs, MoUs, gateways, hubs, economic corridors, and ad hoc national policies via perspectives of geopolitics and geo-economics. Essentially, SDIs are geo-economy's operational instruments which are available to states and other economic agents to coordinate, synergize, and transform their shared geopolitical visions into economic spaces. Seeking to examine and understand SDI development specifically in the APSCs context, this chapter has revolved around the question: To what extent does the Belt and Road Initiative contribute to designing the development of the APSCs regional economic space?

The B&RI's contributions to the design of the APSCs regional economic space lie within these ideas:

(1) Reflecting the potential of the two APSCs geo-economic axes—(B1) central and south Atlantic Ocean, Macaronesia, and Gulf of Guinea, and (B2) Indian Ocean and the African Great Lakes area—in terms of access to regional economic communities and to landlocked states; (2) laying out how an integrated vision of the space and coherent development of SDIs can unleash the potential of these axes, allowing the different components to work together to create synergy; (3) For PSCs (or at least the APSCs), the institution which can unify various existing SDI visions and offer a platform for political and economic cooperation is the CPLP—its significant potential seems to have drawn growing international interest; (4) In the same token, the CPLP can be a platform for full-membership regional economic entities to reconcile any differences in national interest and work towards geo- economic concertation; and (5) It is through SDIs that the B&RI's vision can be coherently aligned with the APSCs' national and regional development plans.

Through an integrated and cooperative SDI, the new African Continental Free Trade Area (AfCFTA) project will bring together six APSCs to create the largest free-trade area in the world by number of participant countries. Implementing the AfCFTA will help usher in the kinds of deep reforms necessary to enhance long-term growth and therefore a strong commitment to responsible multilateralism among African countries. As Perez suggests, "strategic cooperation and responsible statecraft must be part of geo-economics" (2021, p. 175), so, to some extent, multilateralism offers more possibility for participant states to maintain long-term sustainable cooperation, especially after negotiations and reiterating shared values.

Current partnerships (Table 3) between China and the APSCs will be more effective if they can have the reference of previous success stories of cooperation involving PSCs as well as their national plans and regional economic initiatives. Partnerships can be powerful bilateral political-diplomatic agreements that incorporate regional and national SDIs, but they need to be transformed into legally binding commitments, or risk becoming ad hoc solutions serving only short-term, circumstantial developmental visions.

We stated at the beginning that there is no singular perspective on how history, geography, and security combine to generate power perceptions and expectations in Lusophone geopolitics, but we have also mentioned that Lusophony shares two important geo-economic elements: access to the sea, and culture-language. Since 2021, CPLP has added a new element: the internal mobility of people. Bearing in mind that Lusophony is a space of multiple perspectives and actors, and is bound to be dominated by immaterial concepts with some common material elements, the geopolitics associated with the geo- economics of spatial development initiatives in the case of APSCs may represent a game changer in their relationships with the Chinese B&RI especially within the African continent. Indeed, recent news reports on the establishment of a new Chinese military installation in Equatorial Guinea,[15] combined with an existing one in Djibouti, may be a sign of a long Chinese presence on the African Continent. The macro African vision on SDIs, based on national and regional interests as well as the B&RI (possibly with other initiatives as well), all combine to offer the Lusophone community a new sense of purpose, commonness, and contribution, by creating and developing a shared geo-economic notion of their maritime and language-cultural spaces. The African Spatial Development initiatives represent decisive opportunities for all APSC, as they call for a comprehensive geo-economic approach, in the context of the CPLP as a platform for geopolitical concertation. These opportunities, side-by-side with policies such as B&RI (and others), are there to transform the potential of language-culture space into a geo-economic shared asset.

[15] Retrieved in December 2021, from https://ecfr.eu/article/chinas-new-military-base-in-africa-what-it-means-for-europe-and-america/. It total, there are 44 landlocked countries in the world. Retrieved in December 2021, from https://thefactfile.org/landlocked-countries-list/.

Bibliography

African Development Bank (2019). *Cross-Border Road Corridors—The Quest to Integrate Africa.*

Albrechts, L. & Tasan-Kok, T. (2009). Corridor and Axis Development. *International Encyclopedia of Human Geography*, MS no. 833. Studies, Vol. 4, pp. 43–58.

Altbeker, A., Visser, R., & Bulterman, L. (2021). *What if South Africa had a Special Economic Zone that was Actually Special?* Centre for Develoment and Enterprise (CDE). Retrieved in December 2021, from https://media.africaportal.org/documents/What-if-South-Africa-had-a-special-economic-zone-that-was-actually-special-1.pdf

Andersen, S. J., & Burnett, S. L. (1998). *Activity Corridors, Spines, Streets and Nodes and Access Management.* Johannesburg.

ASEAN Secretariat (2017). Master Plan on ASEAN Connectivity 2025. Jakarta. Retrieved in March 2023, from https://asean.org/wpcontent/uploads/2018/01/47.-December-2017-MPAC2025-2nd-Reprint-.pdf

Badi, I., & Pamucar, D. (2019). Determination of Key Factors Affecting Transient Seaport Selection for Landlocked Countries in African Continent. Retrieved in December 2021, from https://www.researchgate.net/publication/338023924_Determination_of_Key_Factors_Affecting_Transient_Seaport_Selection_for_Landlocked_Countries_in_African_Continent

Banomyong, R. (2008). Logistics development in the Greater Mekong Subregion. A study of the North-South Economic Corridor. J. Greater Mekong Subregion Development.

Blackwill, R., & Harris, J. (2017). *War by Other Means: Geo-economics and Statecraft.* Harvard University Press.

Brand, A. (2018). *The Use of Corridor Development as a Strategic and Supporting Instrument Towards the Development of National Space Economies.* Thesis submitted in fulfilment of the requirements for the degree Doctor of Philosophy in Urban and Regional Planning at the North- West University.

Brunner, H. P. (2013). *What is Economic Corridor Development and What Can it Achieve in Asia's Subregions?* Asian Development Bank (ADB) Working Paper on Regional Economic Integration, 117.

CPLP (1996). *Declaração Constitutiva da Comunidade dos Países de Língua Portuguesa—CPLP [Constitutive Declaration].* Retrieved in March 2023, from https://www.cplp.org/id-3869.aspx

Crush, J. & Rogerson, C. M. (2001). New Industrial Spaces: Evaluating South Africa's Spatial Development Initiatives (SDI) Programme. *South African Geographical Journal*, Vol. 83, No. 2, pp. 85–92.

Ernst & Young. (2011). *Eye on Africa: How to Write Yourself into the African Growth Story.* Special Issue, December/January 2011. Retrieved in

October 2021, from: http://www.ey.com/Publication/vwLUAssets/Eye_special_ed_Africanm_Growth_Story/$FILE/rican_Growth_Story.pdfEye_special_ed_Af

Figueiredo, P. G., Leandro, F. J., & Li, Y. (eds.). (2022). *Handbook of Research on Special Economic Zones as Regional Development Enablers*. IGI Global. https://doi.org/10.4018/978-1-7998-7619-9

Friedmann, J. (1972). *A General Theory of Polarized Development*. London: Collier-McMillan. Geyer, H. S. (1988). *The Terminology, Definition and Classification of Development Axes*. Potchefstroom: NWU.

Healey, P. (2004). The Treatment of Space and Place in the New Strategic Spatial Planning in Europe.

International J. *Urban and Regional Research*, Vol. 28, No. 1, pp. 45–67.

Hope, A., & Cox, J. (2015). *Development Corridors*. Coffey International Development. Retrieved in October 2021, from https://assets.publishing.service.gov.uk/media/57a08995e5274a31e000016a/Topic_Guide_Development_Corridors.pdf

IDB (2011). A study of international transport corridors in OIC member countries. Jeddah, Saudi Arabia, Islamic Development Bank.

Jourdan, P. (1998). Spatial Development Initiatives (SDIs): the Official View. *Development Southern Africa*, Vol. 15, No. 5, pp. 717-725.

Klement, J. (2021). *Geo-economics: The Interplay Between Geopolitics, Economics, and Investments*. CFA Institute Research Foundation.

Kynge, J., Campbell, C., Kazmin, A., & Bokhari, F. (2017). How China Rules the Waves—FT investigation: Beijing has spent billions expanding its ports network to secure sea lanes and establish itself as a maritime power. Financial times. Retrieved in July 2021, from https://ig.ft.com/sites/china-ports/

Laurance, W. F., Sloan, S., Weng, L., & Sayer, J. A. (2015). Estimating the Environmental Costs of Africa's Massive "Development Corridors". *Current Biology*, Vol. 25, No. 24, pp. 3202–3208. https://doi.org/https://doi.org/10.1016/j.cub.2015.10.046

Léonard, Y. (1999). As Ligações a África e ao Brasil. In Bethencourt, F., & Kirty, C. *História da Expansão Portuguesa*, Vol. 5, Navarra, Círculo de Leitores.

Li, Y. (2021). *Threefold Contributions Delivered by the Belt and Road Initiative: The Case of Portuguese-Speaking Countries*. Thesis submitted in fulfilment of the requirements for the degree Doctor of Philosophy in Research on Portuguese-speaking Countries, City University of Macau, China.

Luttwak, E. (1990). *From Geopolitics to Geo-Economics: Logic of Conflict, Grammar of Commerce*. National Interest 20 (Summer), pp. 17–23.

Mair, S. (n.d.). From Geopolitics to Geoeconomics. Retrieved in December 2021, from https://deutschland-und-die-welt-2030.de/en/article/from-geopolitics-to-geoeconomics/

Mitchell, S., Andersson, N., Ngxowa, N., & Merhi, S. (2008). A Community-based Impact Assessment of the Wild Coast Spatial Development Initiative, 1997–2004. *Development Southern Africa*, Vol. 25, No. 1, pp. 119–132.

Nogales, E. G. (2014). *Making Economic Corridors Work for the Agricultural Sector*. Food and Agriculture Organization of the United Nations.

Pedone, L., & Ronconi, G. (2017). Evolution of Brazilian Geopolitical Thought: Elements for a Contemporary Analysis in South America. *Journal of the Naval War College*, Vol. 23, No. 3. https://doi.org/10.22491/1809-3191

Perez, R. V. (2021). The Development of Geo-Economics: A Path Towards an Institutional Liberalism Approach. Austral: Brazilian Journal of Strategy & International Relations, Vol. 10, No. 19, pp. 154–180.

Pottier, P. (1963). Axes de Communication et Développement Économique. *Revue économique*, 14.

Reeg, C. (2017). Spatial Development Initiatives—Potentials, Challenges and Policy Lessons: with a Specific Outlook for Inclusive Agrocorridors in Sub-Sahara Africa Studies. German Development Institute / Deutsches Institut für Entwicklungspolitik (DIE), Vol. 97, No. 97.

Reis, C. (1997). A Questão da Lusofonia. *Jornal de Letras*, 30 de Julho.

Rodrigue, J. (2020). *The Geography of Transport Systems*: Chapter 2—Transport and Spatial Organization. New York: Routledge. Retrieved in November 2021, from https://transportgeography.org/contents/chapter2/transport-and-spatial-organization/

Rogerson, C. M. (2001). Spatial Development Initiatives in Southern Africa: the Maputo Development Corridor. *Journal of Economic and Human Geography*, Vol. 92, No. 3, pp. 324–346.

Scholvin, S. (2019). Geo-economics and Geopolitics in Sub-Saharan African Power Politics. In Wigell, M., Scholvin, S., & Aaltola, M. (eds.). Geo-Economics and Power Politics in the 21st Century: The Revival of Economic Statecraft. Routledge.

Scholvin, S., & Wigell, M. (2018). Power Politics by Economic Means: Geo-economics as an Analytical Approach and Foreign Policy Practice. Comparative Strategy, Vol. 37, No. 1, pp. 73–84.

Shahzad, A. (2021). *Geo-economics is the New Geopolitics*. Retrieved in December 2021, from https://tribune.com.pk/story/2325778/geo-economics-is-the-new-geopolitics

Short, J. (2022). *Geopolitics: Making Sense of a Changing World*. London, Powman & Littlefield.

Sousa, H. (2005). *The Mobilization of the 'Lusophony' Concept: The Case of RTP International Channels*. Communication presented at International Association for Media and Communication Research (IAMCR), Taipé, Taiwan, 26–28 July 2005.

Spanish Ministry of Foreign Affairs. (2011). Economic Diplomacy as a Strategy in International Relations. Miradas Al Exterior No. 17 (January–March). Retrieved in December 2021, from https://issuu.com/miradasalexterior/docs/miradas-17-en

Srivastava, P. (2011). Regional Corridors Development in Regional Cooperation. *ADB Economics Working Paper Series* No. 258. Asian Development Bank.

Tuathail, Ó. G., Dalby, S., & Routledge, P. (1998). *The Geopolitics Reader*. Routledge: London and New York.

Tuppen, J. N. (1977). *Axial Regions: An Appraisal of Their Formation, Evolution and Definition*. Discussion paper in geography, No. 4. Salford: University of Salford.

Tyushka, A., & Czechowska, L. (2019). Strategic Partnerships, International Politics and IR Theory. In Czechowska, L., Tyushka, A., Domachowska, A., Gawron-Tabor, K., & Lamparska, J. P. (eds.), *States, International Organizations and Strategic Partnerships*. Edward Elgar Publishing.

Workshop Report (2015). Corridors, Clusters, and Spatial Development Initiatives in African Agriculture. Durban. Retrieved in October 2021, from https://ecdpm.org/wp-content/uploads/Corridors-Clusters-Spatial-Development-Initiatives-Engel-Bizzotto-November-2015–1.pdf\

Brazil's Reach Out to Africa

Giorgio Romano Schutte, Flávio Thales Ribeiro Francisco, and Mojana Vargas Correia Silva

Introduction

Historical and cultural ties have always been "practically mandatory references in all diplomatic discourses on Brazil-Africa relations" (Gala 2019, p. 21) but gained a deeper meaning during the Lula administration. While during the military dictatorship (1964–1985), the ideology of "racial democracy" was consecrated, the Lula government presented Brazil as a country of affirmative action, determined to recognize and overcome the deep heritage of slavery.

G. R. Schutte (✉) · F. T. R. Francisco
Universidade
Federal do ABC (UFABC), Santo André, Brazil
e-mail: giorgio.romano@ufabc.edu.br

F. T. R. Francisco
e-mail: flavio.thales@ufabc.edu.br

M. V. C. Silva
Universidade Federal de Paraíba (UFPB),
Joao Pessoa, Brazil
e-mail: mvargas@ccsa.ufpb.br

P. A. B. Duarte et al. (eds.), *Portugal and the Lusophone World*,
https://doi.org/10.1007/978-981-99-0455-6_14

In both cases, Africa is given priority as part of a bold foreign policy designed to project Brazil into the world as an independent power and as part of a solidarity agenda with developing countries. In both cases, Africa represented a "new frontier" for Brazil's international insertion (Kowalski 2018, p. 8). To sustain the policy of a stand-alone player on the international stage, the shift toward Africa is strategic because it is there that the country manages to show itself as *primus inter pares* and increase its bargaining power in the political and economic sphere with the northern powers. Azeredo da Silveira, minister of foreign affairs of the Geisel government, emphasized in retrospect that "the major decision centers would never hear us if our position did not also have something African..." (Silveira 2010, l. 1641). In the words of Ambassador José Vicente de Sá Pimentel (2000, p. 5), former director-general of the Department of Africa and the Near East, he called relations between Brazil and Africa "a strategic point of support for Brazil's international insertion." Saraiva (2002, p. 9) stated, in the same vein, that Africa "(gives an) identity to the insertion of Brazil in the world" and helped it to build its vision of the world. This meant that Africa would play a role far beyond material factors.

A first attempt to implement this policy was observed in the years leading up to the 1964 military coup with the so-called Independent Foreign Policy (PEI) formulated by San Tiago Dantas (1961–1962). However, as Santos (2003) has stated, at that time there was no translation into concrete actions of significance, particularly concerning trade and investment. Nevertheless, the basic idea of the PEI was present in the justification in both periods studied: the diversification of economic and political relations in favor of national economic development and international political projection.

This paper uses a comparative methodology that helps to understand the specificity of each period analyzing it from three perspectives: geopolitical motivations, geo-economic interests, and cultural/racial identity considerations. This analysis dialogues with the structural factors identified by Fonseca (1996, p. 308) for an understanding of the foreign policies of Brazilian governments: domestic considerations (the political coalitions for support of governments, the influence of organized groups and movements), the State as a formulator of foreign policy and the international environment. Our approach also dialogues with the theoretical framework used by Halliday (1994), which understands the national State as a space of dispute between different interest groups and that this should be analyzed in its specific historical context.

The chapter consists of five sections, including this introduction. In the second section, the historical connections between Brazil and Africa are presented. In the third section, we examine the first "back to Africa movement" of the 1970s. The fourth section focuses on the experience of the Lula government in the 2000s. In the fifth section, we conclude with the final considerations.

The Trajectory of Connections Between Brazil and Africa

Brazil's relationship with the African peoples, and later with the continent's nations, was initially structured by the slave trade, which supported the fundamental economic cycles of the colonial period and later the constitution of the empire. The country endured the most significant impact with the trade of enslaved peoples, receiving about 44% of the 12.5 million Africans subjected to slavery in the Americas (Alencastro 2000; Florentino 2015). The territorial space that would become Brazil was constituted as part of the formation of a global economy that connected the Americas and the African continent.

The slave trade networks formed groups in different parts of the African coast that established trade and cultural relations (Costa and Silva, 2003). Between the eighteenth and nineteenth centuries, flows of the slave trade reached their peak, but after the process of political independence in Brazil (1822) the British started to press for the end of slavery. One of the main challenges for Brazil in the first half of the nineteenth century was to combine the supply of work by Africans, especially with the boom in coffee exports and the onslaught of British diplomacy. The end of this trade would be enacted in 1850, not only by external pressure but also due to pressure from the enslaved themselves.

In 1885, when the Berlin Congress defined the artificial borders of colonial territories, connections between Brazilians and Africans declined sharply. After the suppression of trafficking, the city of Salvador, unlike Recife and Rio de Janeiro, still maintained relationships in West Africa. Tobacco and cachaça, for example, continued to be marketed to Africans, placing the country among the main partners in Lagos. In addition, there were elite members of the returnee communities, mainly in Dahomey (present-day Benin), who circulated between the two continents, creating transatlantic family ties. Anthropologist J. Lorand Matory (1998) highlights priests' journey of Afro-Brazilian religions to Africa, seeking artifacts and improvement in rituals. These relations explain the recognition of Brazil's independence by Africans and even a project designed to incorporate Angola into the Brazilian empire (Mourão, 1999).

However, these cultural practices were not enough to maintain close relations between Brazilians and Africans. As a result, Brazil has distanced commercial and cultural relations, developing its identity as a nation that emerged from a European civilizing matrix. In addition, after the black "Malês" Revolt in 1835 in Bahia, the Brazilian authorities developed different strategies to control the enslaved (Cunha 2012) and, after the abolition of slavery in 1888, repressed sociocultural manifestations associated with African descendants (Albuquerque 2011).

In the first decades of the twentieth century, Brazil promoted whitening policies in some cities, distancing itself from Africans. In the 1930s, the country began to constitute a national identity based on narratives of racial democracy. While the country forged its image as a racial paradise for non-European populations, the only relationship on the African continent was with South Africa (Saraiva 1996).

In 1953, Getúlio Vargas signed the Brazil-Portugal Friendship Treaty, establishing a Portuguese-Brazilian Community. As Visentini (2010) points out, it was a time when the intellectual Gilberto Freyre stood out as a defender of *Luso-Tropicalism*, an idea that emphasized the Portuguese role in the formation of the first modern civilization of the tropics. The Brazilian theory legitimized the Portuguese colonial empire and, consequently, the fascist regime of Antônio de Oliveira Salazar (1932–1968). Brazil's support to the Community yielded the Coffee Agreement, which guaranteed increased coffee sales to Portugal.

During the government of Juscelino Kubitschek (1956–1961), the idea prevailed that engagement with Africa should be mediated by European metropolises (Penha 2011). Brazil did not yet have a strategic view of the continent. On the contrary, Brazil aligned with the colonial powers, which was also reflected in support of their positions in the United Nations (Saraiva, 1996).

The government of Jânio Quadros (1961) begins to form a different foreign policy for the continent, combining the theory of Brazilian racial democracy with an anticolonial approach. Although his presidency was brief, the architects of Brazilian foreign policy reoriented the country's relations with African and European countries and stressed the need for independence and autonomy of the country in order to increase exports and modernize the Brazilian economy. Brazil flirted with the third world but did not become a member of the non-aligned bloc.

Africa as a Priority

Although there was a strong movement toward Africa at the end of the previous government, there is consensus in the literature that the structuring and consolidation of this policy first occurred during the government of Ernesto Geisel (1974–1979) under a foreign policy known as "Responsible and Ecumenical Pragmatism." In his first ministerial meeting in March 1974, the President announced as part of the geopolitical realignments his intention to "give special emphasis to our relationship with the sister nations of the surrounding area below [Latin America, authors] and overseas [Africa, authors]" (Geisel 1974).

It should be remembered that Brazilian policy, in alignment with the USA, Portugal, and South Africa, discussed in the previous section, was linked to the paradigm of the Cold War. The Geisel government broke with that logic. Gonçalves and Miyamoto (1993) place this option in the context of the spirit of the time, marked by questions about the international order. Thus the new policy for Africa was part of a general movement to seek multiple partnerships. Chancellor Silveira understood that the relationship with the US had not generated the expected results (Gonçalves and Miyamoto, 1993, p. 15) and limited the options for Brazil's development. He also understood that Brazil could be a viable alternative for African countries to seek autonomy over the former colonizing countries (Kowalski 2018, p. 47).[1]

[1] As an example, in 1974, the US Congress passed the Trade Act, a protectionist act that hampered Brazil's exports, further aggravating the trade deficit. Two years later, the US foreign aid law was amended, and the State Department began preparing annual human rights reports. Added to this was the American opposition to the Brazilian desire to acquire nuclear technology. In protest in 1977, the Geisel government denounced the 1952 Brazil-U.S. military agreement.

Diplomacy and Trade Policy

The active policy toward Africa had to overcome several obstacles. First, ignorance of the terrain. A milestone in this effort was the mission of Foreign Minister Mário Gibson Barboza, who, in late 1972, for almost a month, visited nine African countries. Second, there was a need to overcome an African mistrust caused by traditional support for Portugal in its colonial policy and the friendly relations that Brazil had long maintained with South Africa. The third problem was the strong presence of European companies and brands. This privileged position of European capital was strengthened in 1975 by the Lomé Convention, which favored trade relations between Africa and Europe. Additional to diplomatic missions, there was an investment to have a Brazilian presence on the ground that could cover the whole of Africa. For this, there was a significant expansion of Embassies.[2]

The options in foreign policy were directly linked to the developmental policy that characterized the Geisel government. The years of the so-called "economic miracle" (1969–1973) had increased the need to import oil and generated an industrial capacity capable of conquering foreign markets. During this period, Geisel was President of Petrobras and, in this role, established contacts with Libya and Algeria through the subsidiary Braspetro, independently of the Ministry of Foreign Affairs itself (Jorge 2007, p. 73).

The breakdown of Breton Woods agreements on the dollar's exchange rate parity increased international competition, and on top of this in there was the first oil shock in 1973. Until then, Brazil had a trade equilibrium but depended on imports for 80% of its oil consumption. Imports in dollars doubled and, in the face of the sharp trade deficit, the government had a strong incentive to increase exports.

The great concern about oil supply led the Geisel government to strengthen relations with producing countries in the Middle East and North Africa and with Nigeria and Angola. It was not by chance that Nigeria became the leading trading partner.

Faced with the impasse generated by the new international economic environment, the government opted for a bold heterodox policy, taking advantage of the availability of international liquidity, it launched the II

[2] The exact numbers differ slightly between the authors. Rosi (2011, p. 37) stated that between 1974 and 1984, the number of Embassies in Africa increased from 12 to 21.

National Development Plan (II PND). It was an interventionist program that expanded the participation of state enterprises in the economy (Castro 2004). It contains a specific chapter dedicated to the search for integration in the world economy compatible with the plan's objectives. There is specific mention of opportunities in Africa and priority for oil-producing countries. However, there were several difficulties for Brazilian businesses: First mutual ignorance. Second, European companies, and products already mentioned as trade preferences, which had strong support from their home countries, for example, through favorable financing from development banks. Third the lack of direct transportation lines. Fourth, the precarious credit and insurance mechanisms for exports (Pimentel 2000).

The government argued in favor of doing business with the cultural affinities and a certain similarity with land and climate conditions. In addition, the technological level of Brazilian companies competed in medium complexity sectors (Pimentel 2000, p. 12). These advantages were even more present in Portuguese-speaking African Countries (Palops), particularly Angola.

It was up to the State, seen as a promotor of development, to provide financing and guarantee favorable conditions (credit, tax incentives, logistical support) to boost exports (including subsidiaries for multinationals installed in Brazil) and encourage the presence of Brazilian companies in African countries. Santana (2003) emphasized these generous government incentives as being a fundamental element for advancing economic relations.

Another factor was the performance of the Afro-Brazilian Chamber of Commerce (CCAB), created and led by Adalberto Camargo, a black businessman from the interior of São Paulo and a federal deputy. The Chamber had as one of its main objectives to organize and assist Brazilian trade missions in Africa and vice versa. It has reached its peak with about 300 medium and large companies affiliated. Although the initiative arose from the private sector, the entity had strong political and organizational support from the government (Santana 2003, pp. 545–546). In the second half of 1973, it carried out the first Brazilian trade mission to Africa through nine countries. Camargo's political influence with the government and the business was fundamental to the success of this unprecedented undertaking. Brazilian entrepreneurs knew little or nothing of the African reality. According to the reports, the delegation was received with great sympathy by African partners (Santana 2003,

p. 531). The effort resulted in a significant increase in the trade chain that jumped from US$ 259 million in 1973 to US$ 1.1 billion in 1974, according to data from Banco do Brasil, Cacex[3] (Santana 2003, p. 532). The Ministry of Development, Industry and Foreign Trade series shows an equally significant increase in Africa's share of total Brazilian exports, which jumped from 4.5% in 1979 to 8.4% in 1981, which should be interpreted as a result of the efforts made in previous years. Subsequently, exports to Africa have taken advantage more than proportionally from the positive impact of the 1980 maxi-devaluation.

It can be concluded that the government's policy of stimulating exports to Africa has found an echo among several companies and African demand. With this, he managed to overcome the various obstacles mentioned.

The Anti-Colonial Struggle and the Racial Issue

Under the management of Azeredo da Silveira as the head of the Ministry of Foreign Affairs (1974–1979), Brazil developed a new policy for Africa designed to support the new priority. Central elements were the condemnation of apartheid, support for decolonization, and the defense of the principle of non-interference. The untying of identification with Portuguese colonial policy was symbolized by the prompt recognition of the independence of Guinea-Bissau (1974), even before Portugal. Brazil also quickly recognized the government of the Popular Movement for the Liberation of Angola (MPLA) in 1975, in apparent dissonance with American policies. Saraiva (2002, p. 9) classified this as "a rebellious recognition of newborn states from the emancipationist struggle of communist bias, against the interests of the hegemonic power." Azeredo da Silveira himself commented in retrospect:

> ...if we had not had a clear position on Angola and Mozambique, we would not have any trade with Nigeria. It is important to clarify that Nigeria has only approached us by our understanding of African problems and by our anti-colonialist position. [...] We, as a traveling salesman in hand, would never have conquered the African markets. (Silveira 2010, l. 1874)

[3] Adjusted for dollar inflation, the figures in 2020 would be $1.5 billion and $5.5 billion respectively.

The joint declarations of the various missions, since the early 1970s, emphasized the recognition of the African ethnic and cultural contribution to Brazil and the repudiation of all forms of racism. For example, Corrêa (2012, p. 397) cites speeches by the 1974 Chancellor strongly repudiating any form of apartheid and "any claim of the international community to want to colonize the nations of Africa culturally."

Nevertheless, these statements did not reflect an effort in the same spirit in Brazil itself. Silveira (2010, l. 1764–1776) reported a curious episode during the II World Festival of Afro-Black Arts and Culture (Festac) in Lagos, Nigeria, in 1977. According to the chancellor at the time, Brazil was allegedly attacked by the US delegation for denying the existence of racial discrimination in the country itself but would have counted on the defense of African delegations. Abdias do Nascimento (2018, pp. 27–46) brought a completely different account of the discussion about racism in Brazil during Festac. One of the activities of the Festival was the academic Colloquium to which Nascimento was invited. However, subsequently, the Afro- Brazilian writer had his contribution to the Colloquium *("Racial Democracy" in Brazil: Myth or Reality)* denied without justification. This led to a debate at the event itself, and the Nigerian and Portuguese press gave favorable coverage. Journalist Portuguese Figueiredo (1977, apud Nascimento 2018, p. 33) dedicated a report to the incident: "Brasil Festac 77." He pointed to the root of the problem and the insistence of the Brazilian authorities to maintain the myth of racial democracy: "... the long tradition of censorship on racial issues has contributed to keeping Brazil out of the attention of the main currents of pan-Africanism and blackness." The Zambian delegation advocated the inclusion of Nascimento's contributions in the Colloquium's recommendations under protest from the official delegation of Brazil. Piaia (2012), when reporting the episode, stated: "by prohibiting the exposure of Abdias, Brazil confirmed the thesis itself combated." The author himself came to question whether gestures of friendship and political solidarity with Africa should not be understood as "mere attempt to replace the influence of colonialist Portugal... Brazilian neocolonialism" (Nascimento 2018, p. 109).

In justifying the new policy for Africa, Geisel avoided talking about African culture in Brazil, the slavery past, and the existence of racial discrimination in the country itself (Kowalski 2018). Instead, the narrative used in the President's official speeches was marked by references to the geopolitics of neighborhood, such as "they are countries bordering ours, separated only by the Atlantic, which does not separate. I think it unites us" (Geisel 1979, p. 59). With this, Africa was seen as an integral part of the strategic environment, a language that explained the new policy for Africa in terms understandable to the political-military establishment of the time. Another reference widely used in the discourses by Geisel was the common heritage of the language, although this was limited to the Palops (Kowalski 2018, p. 72).

At some unexpected moments, the racial issue appeared as an internal problem in a somewhat curious way: Adalberto Camargo recalled in an interview an impasse to be resolved in the organization of the first Brazilian trade mission to Africa mentioned above.

> I was worried about bringing a trade mission to Africa with no black businessman... I had to do certain gymnastics because I was thinking: well, I'm going to do a commercial mission from Brazil to Africa, taking forty-five Brazilian entrepreneurs, and I am going to take forty-five whites? It would be seen as a captain of the bush mission in Africa. So do you know what I did? I got eleven businessmen to allow me to pick eleven black people to go there to represent their companies and play the game. (Santana 2003, p. 529)

Crisis and Removal

Since 1979, both continents, Latin America and Africa, faced the consequences of the debt crisis from the new US monetary policy. The highly indebted countries suffered severely from this new reality. This was the case in Brazil. The last military government of João Figueiredo (1979–1985) managed to take advantage of Geisel's pro-Africa policy. Particular attention was paid to Angola for the importance of oil and the opportunity to export goods and services. Figueiredo was the first South American head of State to make an "official" visit Africa in 1983.[4]

From the mid-1985s, Africa lost its central position in foreign policy in the face of economic reality and new political priorities. Santana (2003) and Pimentel (2000) emphasized that many companies failed with the end of incentive and privilege policies, and exports fell sharply. That is, much of the more than proportional fall in exports to Africa is due to

[4] The mission included Algeria, Cape Verde, Guinea Bissau, Nigeria and Senegal (Rosei, 2011, p. 27).

the fact that the government has dismantled the set of incentives. Several direct flights were extinguished (Lagos, Abidjan, Luanda, Maputo).

As a reflection, Africa's share of total exports fell from 8.4% in 1981 to 2.9% in 1989 (Secex). However, it can be observed that large companies in infrastructure and energy maintained their position, especially Odebrecht and Petrobras. About Odebrecht, Santana notes that despite the progressive reduction in state support, it continued to expand its activities on the African continent in the 1990s (Santana 2003, p. 548). The same goes for the mining company Vale, which entered the continent in the 1980s. A characteristic of the operation of these two companies, and in a way also of Petrobras, was the direct articulation with local governments, independent of the Brazilian State (Alencastro 2020).

With the arrival of liberal-oriented governments in the 1990s, there was a readjustment to prioritize relations with Europe, the USA, and the Southern Cone (Saraiva 2002) that generated a "frustration of expectations" (Cervo 2002). Regarding the supposedly realistic arguments to justify this downsizing of relations with Africa (the insignificance to Brazilian economic and commercial interests), Pimentel (2000, p. 6) identified "... undisguised gradations of racism in its so-called realism."

The Lula Government and the Rediscovery of Africa

This section will discuss the relations between Brazil and the African continent during Lula da Silva's (2003–2010) terms. Initially, we highlight the great novelty: the construction of the racial agenda in the Workers' Party (PT) and the successive dialogues established with different organizations of the black movement. This process reflected internal pressure for public policies to combat racial inequality and anti-racist articulations internationally. We argue that the Lula administration's agenda for Africa was constructed by incorporating elements of the agenda of black movements into the party program. While bringing this element of novelty, Brazilian foreign policy of the period also recovered visions of previous periods and ran into known problems and contradictions.

The PT, Race Relations, and Brazilian Foreign Policy

As Brazil is the nation with the largest black population outside Africa, it is also one of the most unequal and with the most extended history of racial discrimination. For the black population, being a majority has never been reflected in Brazilian international relations, given its systematic exclusion from the diplomatic corps and, consequently, the international representation of the country (Dzidzienyo 2001). In the early 1960s, for example, the attempts at Brazilian rapprochement to African countries were based on the idea of historical-cultural heritage and a supposed identification between Brazil and Africa, headed by an exclusively white diplomatic corps, was seen as strange among African diplomats and leaders (Dávila 2010).

The late recognition of racism in Brazilian society has kept the country and its foreign policy operators linked to the discourse of racial democracy and averse to any reflection that associated Brazilian international relations with Africa and race relations in the domestic environment (Dzidzienyo 2001, p. 44). The Brazilian military regime continued to minimize the issue internally, as shown in the previous section. This, notwithstanding having supported and adhered to several international commitments against racism in the 1960s and 1970s, already indicated the adoption of measures to reduce racial inequality (Godinho, 2009).

With the re-democratization, black organizations could reinforce their claim against the State and promote a dialogue with the new political parties that were formed (Gala, 2019). However, during the 1980s and 1990s, these claims continued to be treated as issues of racial minority and occupy secondary spaces in party programs, including the Workers' Party (Santos 2018).

It was in 1996, with the creation of the National Secretariat for Combating Racism, that the PT made room for the debate on combating racism to be seen as an issue that should be addressed in all areas of the party's activities (Oliveira Alcione, 2014).[5]

[5] We mentioned the action of black militancy directly associated with the PT to highlight its role in the construction of what became the government agenda during the party's mandates. However, the action of other entities such as Unified Black Movement (MNU), Union of Blacks for Equality (UNEGRO), among others, went beyond the party sphere, as well as many other organizations acted politically in the anti-racist fight without maintaining direct links to the PT.

The participation of several organizations of the black movement in the "III International Conference against Racism, Racial Discrimination, Xenophobia, and Related Intolerance," held in 2001, in the city of Durban, was a pivotal moment for black militancy to consolidate a broad program of public policies to combat racism (Carneiro 2002). This led to the formulation of the program "*Brazil without Racism*," whose objective was to "harness and systematize the contributions of black militancy in the formulation and execution of policies that could denounce, bare and combat the myth of racial democracy in our country". (Partido dos Trabalhadores 2002a, p. 4)

The document, organized around eleven topics, systematized a set of propositions for promoting racial equality in the country, aiming to repair the historical debt that Brazil has accumulated to the black population at the social and racial levels. "Brazil without Racism" was not restricted to discussing domestic issues but presented racial inequality as a phenomenon that affects all peoples of the African diaspora. In line with the Durban Declaration, topic 5.9 of the document was dedicated to international relations and stipulated that "Brazil, the second country with the largest black population in the world, should turn to Africa. In addition to exploring the ethnic and cultural ties it maintains with that continent, *especially with Portuguese-speaking countries, it must seek the construction of new economic* and commercial relations (emphasis by the authors), in particular with South Africa" (Partido dos Trabalhadores 2002a, p. 16).

In other words, the development of what would become the foreign policy of the Lula government for the African continent began with the activism of the black movement close to the party. These groups disputed positions to insert the anti-racist fight as a priority agenda in both domestic and international politics. Thus, the formulation of the African policy of the Lula government is also the result of new partisan convictions about the importance of agendas of the black movement. This would also be reflected in what would become the Brazilian foreign policy.

The insertion of the black movement in the debate imprinted certain originality to the foreign policy of the Lula government when compared to other periods in the history of Brazil- Africa relations. The Brazilian State began to act concretely in deconstructing the myth of racial democracy and confronting racism while still valuing its African heritage at the rhetorical level.

The integration of domestic and international, of the national interest and the country's place in the world, became constitutive elements of Brazilian foreign policy, conceived to contribute to a multipolar world (Garcia 2010, p. 60). Thus, addressing racial and social inequalities become inseparable parts of the "new look to the south" defined in the foreign policy strategy.

Affirmative Action and the New African Agenda

The confrontation with racial inequalities was initiated with the adoption of affirmative policies specifically aimed at the black population and the creation of the Special Secretariat for the Promotion of Racial Equality (Seppir) with ministerial status. As a result, between 2003 and 2004, Brazil had, for the first time, a policy, an executive body, and a high-level collegiate dedicated exclusively to racial issues in the country.

Among Seppir's achievements, we should mention the Statute of Racial Equality (Law No. 12.288/2010), legislation that gives formal recognition to the condition of the greater vulnerability of the black population and establishing specific rights that help in promoting the improvement of their socio-economic conditions. Above all, the Statute is an essential instrument for establishing the fight against racism not only as a problem of the black population but as a human rights issue (Silva 2012b).

In the early days of the new government, Law 10.639, promulgated on January 9, 2003, established the mandatory teaching of Afro-Brazilian and African History and Culture at all levels of Brazil's educational system. It was the starting point for the adoption of different redistributive initiatives in the educational field, providing the insertion and permanence of black and brown students, especially by including racial criteria in the funding programs existing until then (Feres Jr et al., 2012).

This policy enabled the recovery of the historical contribution of the black population to the construction of Brazil and the African people, including the diaspora, to the development of human knowledge. Furthermore, it made room for expanding educational cooperation actions with the African continent (Cicalo 2014).

In his inauguration speech, in 2003, Lula presented the content of his foreign policy, based on the country's sovereign insertion in the international scenario and its link with the promotion of national development (Brasil 2003a, pp. 8–9). The African continent was among the priorities of Brazilian international action with a well-defined guideline: to expand cooperation with South Africa and the Portuguese-speaking African Countries (PALOP). Furthermore, the inaugural speech of Chancellor Celso Amorim—who remained at the head of the Ministry of Foreign Affairs throughout Lula's term—reinforced this decision by pointing to the African continent as one of the priority regions for Brazilian action (Brasil 2003b).

There was a growing recognition of the economic and political importance of the African continent for the development of this new profile of Brazilian foreign policy (Oliveira and Mallmann 2020). In this way, the strategic place that the African continent had experienced in the 1970s was recovered.

The increase in relations with the African continent also expressed a recognition of its importance in international politics. For example, African countries members of the World Trade Organization accounted for 26.8% of the votes (WTO 2022) and contributed to the election of Roberto Azevedo as the head of the organization in 2013. Similarly, the support of African countries was indispensable for the election of Brazilian José Graziano as Director-General of the United Nations Food and Agriculture Organization (FAO) in 2011.

At the opening of the 59th session of the United Nations General Assembly in 2004, the Brazilian government called for an autonomous political articulation of the peripheral countries, aiming at the effective consolidation of the independence of the formerly colonized territories, which evidenced the basis for Brazilian action in the region (Burges 2013). In this respect, the President reverberated the autonomist projects nurtured by different generations of political leaders and intellectuals critical of colonialism—such as Frantz Fanon, quoted in the speech—and the postcolonial dependence, such as José Vasconcelos, Federico Carvajal, and Celso Furtado (Valdés 2000).

At this point, the link between social policies to combat poverty and racial inequality and the development cooperation with African countries implemented by the Lula government became evident. Projects such as "Fome Zero" (Zero Hunger) and "Luz para Todos" (Light for Everyone), which were directed to the vulnerable populations in Brazil, became flagships of Brazil's international cooperation, as well as the projects developed by the Brazilian Agricultural Research Corporation (Embrapa), whose expertise in the agricultural production was attractive to several African countries.

Business Relationship

Throughout the 1990s, there was a reduction in commercial activities between Brazil and Africa. The governments led by Fernando Henrique Cardoso (1995–2002) gave priority to economic relations with developed countries and, during this period, practically ignored the growth of African economies (Ribeiro 2017, p. 10). However, after 2003, trade relations were expanded at the bilateral and multilateral levels. Contributing factors were: support for Brazilian private investors through diplomatic action in several countries, particularly in Southern Africa; the rapprochement between Mercosur and the Southern African Customs Union (SACU); the Southern African Development Community (SADC) and the financing of operations granted by the National Bank for Economic and Social Development (BNDES). This activism promoted trade growth with the continent over the years, as can be seen in the chart below (Graph 1).

Africa's relative share in Brazilian international trade grew considerably from 4% of total exports in 2003 to 6% in 2009. After a slight downturn related to the 2008 international financial crisis, exports remained stable at around 4% until 2015. Imports started at around 6% in 2003 and, after reaching a peak of 10%, stabilized at around 7% until 2015, after which

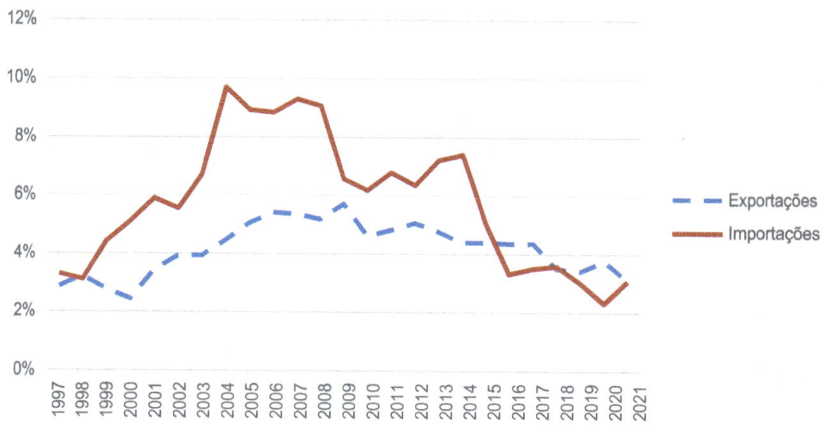

Graph 1 Trade with Africa as % of total trade between 1997 and 2021 (*Source* Prepared by the authors. *Data* COMEX STAT [2022])

they went into a downward trend due to the economic crisis. A characteristic of Brazilian exports to Africa is the predominance of manufactured products, corresponding to 66.3% of the total, unlike the strong presence of commodities in exports to developed countries and China.

The Look to the South and Cooperation

The cooperation developed by the Brazilian government on the African continent covered different areas. For its operationalization, the government opened new Brazilian diplomatic missions in all regions of the continent and promoted an internal organization to be the responsible agency (Ribeiro 2017). In the first two years of his term, Lula visited seven African countries—mostly from southern Africa—using presidential diplomacy to promote cooperation agreements in the technology area, defense and security, and commercial area. In the eight years of the Lula government, 238 documents were signed in 21 different areas, emphasizing health (Silva and Andriotti 2012).

In evaluating these numbers, Mendonça and Faria (2015, pp. 17–18) pointed out that in addition to increasing Brazilian cooperation in virtually all areas already established by its predecessors, there was an expansion of its scope, prioritizing the "sharing of Brazilian indigenous technologies, which would be specific, for example, to tropical countries." The volume of investments in technical cooperation offered by Brazil to African countries was also high, going from US$ 11.4 million in 2005 to US$ 57.8 million in 2010 (IPEA 2013, p. 15). The main recipients were the Portuguese-speaking countries, with 76.5% of Brazilian cooperation for the continent. (Milani et al. 2016; Captain, 2010).

Education was a prominent focus of cooperation, especially through the Student Agreement Program (PEC), which provides comprehensive training to undergraduate and graduate students from developing countries. Although the program existed since 1965, African countries were only integrated into the PEC in 1975, signing a technical-scientific cooperation agreement between Brazil and Angola. Until 2003, 18 countries were part of the program, which was raised to 28 during the Lula administration (Silva 2017).

A major event was the creation of the University of International Integration of Afro- Brazilian Lusophony (Unilab), headquartered in the city of Redenção, in Ceará, the first Brazilian municipality to abolish black slavery in 1883. Created in July 2010, this University is part of the cooperation agreement with PALOP. It foresees the incorporation of African academics into the faculty and the opening of courses in areas of mutual interest and strategic importance to combat inequality and eliminate poverty in Brazil and African countries, teacher training, rural development, and public health.

The evaluation of this cooperation provoked a critical debate in the literature. Several authors emphasize the strong influence of mercantilist interests (Barriviera 2016; Stolte 2015; Taylor 2014; Miyamoto 2011). Thus, despite rhetorical elements of valuing historical ties with the region (Faria and Silva 2017), the option for Africa is seen as an effort to attend to economic and political ambitions without differing qualitatively from the cooperation maintained by the central countries. (Taylor 2014; White 2013).

Others emphasized deficiencies in the implementation, despite the advances made. One of the problems was the large number of public agencies involved in the programs, generating coordination difficulties on several occasions, and even a reduction in the participation of civil society in the receiving countries, but also of Brazilian NGOs and social movements (Waisbich, 2019; Kamwengo 2017). A second issue is the lack of mechanisms for monitoring and evaluating the results. Since the technical cooperation offered by Brazil to African countries involves mostly the transfer of intangible items, such as knowledge, technology, and skills, it is more difficult to access the impact of these activities empirically (Nganje, 2016, p. 664). Kamwengo (2017) concluded that the promise of horizontal cooperation remained more rhetorical than a practice. Amaral (2013) pointed out a lack of a joint definition of priorities in educational cooperation. Silva (2017) concluded in the same way that Brazilian educational cooperation was implemented as a one-way street: there is only one initiative to seek African cooperation, in 2013, through an internship project for Brazilian teachers of primary education in African institutions. Presented through the CPLP, the project aimed to qualify Brazilian teachers to implement Law 10.639 and to reinforce the Brazilian openness to reciprocity in cooperation (Milani et al. 2016).

On the whole, we conclude that the Brazilian technical cooperation with the African continent was relatively successful. However, the institutional capacity of the Brazilian Agency for Cooperation (ABC), responsible for the elaboration and monitoring of the projects, was not strong enough to play this role, leading to problems such as lack of coordination and discontinuity. In addition, there was limited social participation in the formulation of the agenda in foreign policy—in contradiction to the proposition of Minister Celso Amorim in his inauguration speech. Moreover, in this way, the definition of the national interest that should orient the cooperation effort, was being restricted to groups with greater capacity to influence the government and, consequently, reduced the character of public and democratic policy that was intended initially by the government and the black movement that participated in the construction of the PT's government plan.

The Decline in Relations with the African Continent

President Dilma Rousseff's administration (2011–2016) of the Workers' Party did not present the same assertiveness as the previous government concerning the African continent. Her administration was responsible for downsizing representations in some countries and did not use presidential diplomacy with the same vigor as in previous years. In addition, Rousseff faced the consequences of the 2008 crisis, which contributed to the slowdown in economic activity.

Mainly beginning with Dilma Rousseff's second term, when the economic and political crisis deepened, groups interested in the agenda for the African continent lost ground. As reported, the Lula administration articulated its policy with the Brazilian black movement and business segments around a diversity of educational and commercial initiatives that were dismantled or reorganized to respond to budget constraints amid the crisis. Nevertheless, Rousseff's foreign policy did not distance itself from the agenda guidelines built throughout the 2000s, continuing to treat African countries as strategic partners for Brazilian integration into the international system.

With the government of Michel Temer (2016–2018), Brazil began, in fact, a process of distancing itself from the African continent, driven by the neoliberal agenda. The argument of the new Foreign Minister, José Serra, was that South-South relations should be directed in a "correct" manner, focusing mainly on the commercial area. Brazil's political engagement with African countries in the governments of previous Workers' Party presidents was considered ineffective and ideological (Brasil 2016). Under the new administration, Brazil deepened its ties with the United States and distanced itself from initiatives in the Global South.

This trend was accentuated under the government of Jair Bolsonaro, elected in 2018. The President did not disguise his deep sympathy for the figure of Donald Trump and tended to align himself with the United States. However, the current scenario does not necessarily indicate a lack of interest from the side of Brazilian society. Africa studies, for example have expanded significantly. And in the business community, despite the setback to foreign policy for Africa, some consider the African Continental Free Trade Zone as an arrangement capable of boosting the continent's economy. And the Brazilian agribusiness identified business opportunities disrespecting Africa's potential as a food producer, projecting Brazilian insertion through expertise in the field.

Final Considerations

In Brazil's recent history of international relations, two governments that prioritized relations with the African continent stood out: the Ernesto Geisel administration in the 1970s and Luiz Inácio Lula da Silva in the 2000s. The determinants of these policy experiences should be analyzed in their historical context considering international and national factors.

This article made a comprehensive review of the existing literature, focusing on geopolitical considerations, economic-commercial interests, and racial considerations.

We observed a remarkable similarity between the two periods. First in the domain of geopolitical motivations, both governments tried to gain greater independence from Western powers. Second, the economic motivation, aims to expand trade and identify investment opportunities. Third, in both cases, Portuguese-speaking African countries, especially Angelo and Mozambique were seen as a key priority.

Looking at the international situation, opposite situations have led to the same set of priorities. In the case of the first period, the realignment of priorities was part of a comprehensive response to the challenges caused by the oil shock, the consequent significant deficit in the trading account, and the intensification of international competition. The reach to Africa was part of the effort to face the constraints generated for national development. In the second period studied, the government wanted to take advantage of a window of opportunity based on the new dynamism in the Brazilian economy, which in its turn was provoked by a sharp increase in commodity prices and public investments. The government understood that it was an opportunity to qualify for Brazil's international insertion.

What appears to be completely different is the relationship with the racial issue in Brazil itself, which became an important component in policy formulation for Africa only in the 2000s.

In the 1930s there began a move to constitute a national identity based on narratives of racial democracy. In the 2000s, the government tried to overcome this vision and project Brazil as a country of anti-racist policies and social inclusion that mainly affected the black population. These transformations were mobilized to improve Brazil's discourse for African peoples, although not without ambiguities.

Thus, in the first period, the racial issue was part of the state narrative to reinforce diplomatic efforts toward African states. While in the second period, it became a mobilizing factor of foreign policy for Africa building upon the domestic dimension. This dimension, however, is not alone in sustaining the priority of the projection for Africa. At the same time, everything indicates that the myth of racial democracy has structurally lost its strength.

References

Albuquerque, Wlamyra R. (2011), *O jogo da dissimulação: abolição e cidadania negra no Brasil*, São Paulo: Companhia das Letras.

Alencastro, Luiz Felipe. (2000), *O trato dos viventes: formação do Brasil no Atlântico Sul*, São Paulo: Companhia das Letras.

Alencastro, Mathias (2020), A Odebrecht e a formação do Estado angolano (1984–2015), *Novos Estudos*. CEBRAP, v. 39, pp. 125–141.

Amaral, Joana B. (2013), Atravessando o Atlântico: o programa estudante convênio de graduação e a cooperação educacional brasileira, 132 f. Dissertação, Universidade de Brasília, Brasília.

Barriviera, G. de N. (2016), O Lugar da África na Política Externa Brasileira após 2003, *Conjuntura Austral*, v. 7, n. 36, pp. 57–72.

Brasil (2003a), Pronunciamento do Presidente da República, Luiz Inácio Lula da Silva, na sessão solene de posse no Congresso Nacional Brasília – DF, 01 de janeiro de 2003a, Biblioteca da Presidência da República, Available at http://www.biblioteca.presidencia.gov.br/presidencia/ex-presidentes/luiz-inacio-lula-da-silva/discursos/discursos-de-posse/discurso-de-posse-1o-mandato

Brasil (2003b), Celso Amorim – Discurso de Posse Ministro das Relações Exteriores, 02 de janeiro de 2003b, Available at https://www.gov.br/funag/pt-br/chdd/historia-diplomatica/ministros-de-estado-das-relacoes-exteriores/celso-luiz-nunes-amorim-discurso-de-posse

Brasil (2016), Discurso do ministro José Serra por ocasião da cerimônia de transmissão do cargo de ministro de estado das Relações Exteriores, Ministério de Relações Exteriores, Brasília. Available at: http://www.itamaraty.gov.br/ptBR/discursosartigos-e-entrevistas-categoria/ministro-das-relacoes-exteriore sdiscursos/14038-discurso-do-ministro-jose-serra-por-ocasiao-da-cerimonia-detransmissao-do-cargode-ministro-de-estado-das-relacoes-exteriores-brasilia-18-demaio-de-2016, Acesso em: 04 de junho de 2019.

Burges, S. W. (2013), Brazil as a bridge between old and new powers? *International Affairs*, v. 89, n. 3, pp. 577–594.

Captain, Y. (2010), Brazil's Africa Policy under Lula, *The Global South*, vol. 4, n.1, pp. 183–198.

Carneiro, S. (2002), *A Batalha de Durban, Estudos Feministas*, v. 10, n. 1, pp. 209–214.

Castro, Antônio Barros (2004), *A Economia Brasileira em Marcha Forçada,* São Paulo: Paz e Terra.

Cicalo, A. (2014), From Racial Mixture to Black Nation: Racializing Discourses in Brazil's African Affairs, Bulletin of Latin American Research, v. 33, n. 1, pp. 16–30.

Corrêa, Luiz Felipe de Seixas (2012), *O Brasil nas Nações Unidas: 1946–2011,* Brasília, DF: Fundação Alexandre de Gusmão.

Costa e Silva, Alberto (2003), *Um Rio chamado Atlântico: A África no Brasil e o Brasil na África.* Rio de Janeiro: Nova Fronteira.

Cunha, Manuela Carneiro (2012), *Negros, estrangeiros: os escravos libertos e sua volta à África,* São Paulo: Companhia das Letras.

Dávila, J. (2010), *Hotel Trópico: Brazil and the Challenge of African Decolonization, 1950– 1980,* Duke University Press: Durham.

Dzidzienyo, A. (2001), Race and international relations: Brazil and South Africa, South African *.Journal of International Affairs,* v. 8, n.1, pp. 41–52.

Feres Júnior, João.; Daflon, V. T.; Campos, L. A. (2012), Ação Afirmativa, Raça e Racismo: uma análise das ações de inclusão racial nos mandatos de Lula e Dilma, *Revista de Ciências Humanas*, v. 12, n. 2, pp. 399–414.

Florentino, Manolo (2015), *Em costas negras: uma história do tráfico negreiro de escravos entre a África e o Rio de Janeiro (Séculos XVIII e XIX),* São Paulo: Fundação Editora UNESP.

Fonseca Jr, Gelson (1996), Notas sobre aspectos doutrinários da política externa independente e do pragmatismo responsável, In: Albuquerque J. A., *Sessenta Anos de Política Externa brasileira. Crescimento, Modernização e Política Externa.* São Paulo: Cultura Editores Associados.

Gala, Irene Vida (2019), *Política Externa como Ação Afirmativa, Projeto e Ação do Governo Lula na África 2003–2006,* Santo André: Editora UFABC.

Garcia, Marco Aurélio (2010), O lugar do Brasil no Mundo, A política externa em um momento de transição, In: SADER, Emir; GÁRCIA, M. A. *Brasil entre o Passado e o Futuro*, São Paulo: Editora Fundação Perseu Abramo/ Boitempo.

Geisel, Ernesto (1974), Pronunciamento feito na primeira reunião ministerial em 19 de março de 1974, Biblioteca da Presidência da República. Brasília.

Geisel, Ernesto (1979), *Discursos:* Volume V -1978. Brasília, DF: Assessoria de Imprensa da Presidência da República.

Geisel, Ernesto (1997), *Ernesto Geisel: depoimento*, Entrevistadores: Maria Celina D'Araújo e Celso Castro, Rio de Janeiro: Editora Getúlio Vargas.

Godinho, R. de O (2009), Normas e redistribuição: um estudo sobre condicionantes internacionais das políticas de combate ao racismo no Brasil. *Revista Brasileira De Política Internacional*, v. 52, pp. 71–88.

Gonçalves, Williams da S.; Miyamoto, Shiguenol (1993), Os Militares na Política Externa Brasileira, Estudos Históricos, Rio de Janeiro, v. 6, n. 12, pp. 211–246.

Halliday, Fred (1994), *Rethinking International Relations*, Macmillan.

IPEA (2013), *Cooperação Brasileira para o Desenvolvimento Internacional 2005–2009*, Brasília.

Jorge, Fernando (2007), *Geisel: o presidente da abertura,* São Paulo: Companhia Editora Nacional; Lazuli.

Kamwengo, C. (2017), China and Brazil as Southern Africa's Non Interfering Development Partners: Rhetoric or Reality?, *Journal of Southern African Studies,* v. 43, p. 5.

Kowalski a, Camila C. (2018), *África na política externa brasileira: uma análise dos discursos de Ernesto Geisel (1974–1979) e Luiz Inácio Lula da Silva (2003–2010),* Dissertação apresentada ao Programa de Pós- Graduação em Estudos Estratégicos Internacionais da Faculdade de Ciências Econômicas da UFRGS, Porto Alegre.

Matory, J. Lorand (1998), Yorubá: as rotas e as raízes da nação transatlântica, 1830-1950, *Horizontes Antropológicos*. Porto Alegre, v. 4, n. 9, pp. 263–292.

Mendonça, Wilson Jr; Faria, Carlos. A. P. (2015), A cooperação técnica do Brasil com a África: comparando os governos Fernando Henrique Cardoso (1995-2002) e Lula da Silva (2003–2010), *Revista Brasileira de Política Internacional,* v. 58, n. 1, pp. 5–22.

Milani, Carlos. R. S.; Conceição, Franciso, C., e Saba M'Bunde, Timóteao (2016), Cooperação Sul-Sul em Educação e Relações Brasil-PALOP, *Caderno CRH*, v. 29, n. 76, pp. 13–32.

Miyamoto, S. (2011), As Grandes Linhas da Política Externa Brasileira, *Textos para Discussão CEPAL-IPEA*, nº 45, Brasília: CEPAL Escritório no Brasil/IPEA.

Mourão, Fernando Augusto A. (1999), A evolução de Luanda: aspectos sociodemográficos em relação à independência do Brasil e o fim do tráfico, In

Pantoja, Selma; Saraiva, José Flávio Sombra (org.), *Angola e Brasil nas rotas do Atlântico Sul*. Rio de Janeiro: Bertrand Brasil.

Nascimento, Abdias (2018), *O Genocídio do Negro Brasileiro: processo de um racismo mascarado*, 4ª edição, São Paulo: Perspectivas.

Nganje, Fritz (2016), Brazilian Cities in Mozambique: South–South Development Co-operation or the Projection of Soft Power? *Journal of Southern African Studies*, v. 42 n. 4, pp. 659–674.

Oliveira, Alicianne G. de; Barbalho, Alexandre A. (2014), O Movimento Negro no Poder? O PT, o Governo Lula e a SEPPIR, *O público e o privado*, v. 12 n. 23, pp. 151–172.

Oliveira, Guilherme Z.; Mallmann, Vinícius H. (2020) *Revista Carta Internacional*, v. 15, n. 3, pp. 129–150.

Partido dos Trabalhadores (2002a), *Compromisso com a Soberania o Emprego e a Seg. do Povo Brasileiro*. São Paulo: Fundação Perseu Abramo, Available at https://fpabramo.org.br/csbh/programas-de-governo/.

Penha, Eli A. (2011), *Relações Brasil-África e geopolítica do Atlântico Sul*, Salvador: EDUFBA.

Partido dos Trabalhadores (2002b), Programa Brasil sem Racismo, Available at: https://fpabramo.org.br/csbh/wp-content/uploads/sites/3/2017/04/02-brasilsemracismo.pdf.

Piaia, Victor (2012), Trabalho sobre o Festival Negro e Africano das Artes e da Cultura, Festac, *África em questão*, julho.

Pimentel, José Vicente de Sá (2000), Relações entre o Brasil e a África subsaárica, *Rev. Bras. Polít. Int.*, v. 43, n. 1, pp. 5–23.

Ribeiro, C. O. (2017), Brazilian African policy and the experience of the first Lula government (2003 to 2006), *African Journal of Political Science and International Relations*, 11(5), 92-102.

Rosi, Bruno Gonçalves (2011), As relações Brasil-África no regime militar e na atualidade, *Revista Conjuntura Austral*, vol. 2, n. 3–4.

Penha, Eli A. (2018), Imagem e Representação Social da África no Brasil: A Geopolítica Africana do Governo Lula, *Geo UERJ*, v. 33. pp. 1–17.

Santana, Ivo (2003), Relações Econômicas Brasil-África: A Câmara de Comércio Afro- Brasileira e a Intermediação de Negócios no Mercado Africano, *Estudos Afro-Asiáticos*, v. 25, n. 3, pp. 517–555.

Santos, F. B. dos (2018), Estado e movimentos sociais negros (1980–2010), *Tempo e Argumento*. Florianópolis, v. 10, n. 25, pp. 144–182.

Santos, Luiz Cláudio Machado (2003), A política externa brasileira para a África negra: Da "interdependência" ao "pragmatismo responsável" (1964–1979), *Universitas: História* (Uniceub), v. 1, pp. 71–87.

Saraiva, José Flávio S. (2002), Política exterior do Governo Lula: o desafio africano. Brasília, *Rev. Bras. Polít. Int.*, v. 45, n. 2, pp. 5–25.

Saraiva, José Flávio Sombra (1996), O lugar da África: a dimensão atlântica da política externa brasileira (de 1946 a nossos dias), Brasília: Editora UnB.

Silva, M. V. C. Da (2017), A Cooperação Brasileira para o Desenvolvimento no Âmbito do Ensino Superior: o Programa de Estudantes-Convênio e a Política Externa Brasileira para os PALOP, In: Freire, J. C. da S.; Varela, B. L.; Pacheco, J. A.; Baptista, M. G. (orgs), *Educação Superior, Desenvolvimento e Cooperação Sul-Sul,* Belém: UFPA, 2017 Praia: Edições Uni- CV, 2017, pp. 227–248.

Silva, André L. R. D (2010), As Transformações Matriciais da Política Externa Brasileira Recente (2000–2010), *Meridiano 47*, v. 11, n. 120, pp. 18–24.

Silva, André L. R. D.; Andriotti, Luiza S. (2012), A cooperação sul-sul na política externa do governo Lula (2003–2010), *Conjuntura Austral*,, v. 3, n. 14, pp. 69–93.

Silva, T. D. (2012b), O Estatuto da Igualdade Racial. Texto para Discussão n°1712, Instituto de Pesquisa Econômica Aplicada (IPEA), Brasília. Available at: http://hdl.handle.net/10419/90923.

Silveira, Azeredo (2010), *Azeredo da Silveira: um depoimento,* Entrevistadoras: Maria Regina Soares de Lima e Monica Hirst, Rio de Janeiro: FGV. E-book.

Stolte, C. (2015), *Brazil's Africa Strategy,* Londres: Palgrave Macmillan.

Taylor, Ian (2014), *Africa Rising? BRICS–Diversifying Dependency,* Melton: James Currey.

Valdés, E. D. (2000) *El pensamiento latinoamericano em el siglo XX, Entre la modernización y la identidade, tomo I, Del Ariel de Rodó a la CEPAL (1900–1950),* Buenos Aires: Editorial Biblos.

Visentini, Paulo Fagundes (2010), A África na política internacional: o sistema interafricano e sua inserção mundial, Curitiba: Juruá Editora.

Waisbich, Laura T. (2019), Participation, Critical Support and Disagreement: Brazil-Africa Relations from the Prism of Civil Society, In: Alencastro, Mathias; Seabra, Pedro (2019), *Brazil-Africa Relations in the 21st Century*, pp. 113–132. Springer.

White, Lyal (2013), Emerging Powers in Africa: Is Brazil any different? *South African Journal of International Affairs,* v. 20, n. 1, 117–136.

World Trade Organization (WTO), About WTO-Members and Observers, Consulted January, 15, 2022. https://www.wto.org/english/thewto_e/whatis_e/tif_e/org6_e.htm.

The Nativist Movement in Angola: A Proposal for a Modern State and Society in the Lusophone Context

Cátia Miriam Costa

Introduction

Nativist movements characterized the African political environment of the early twentieth century (in the 1910' and 1920' decades). Angola was no exception, with ongoing debates between different actors: creole elite, sons of the soil (mestizos and African elite educated in the Portuguese culture but identifying themselves as Angolans). and the colonial regime within which they were brought up and educated. Before we expand on the importance of the nativist movements in the early twentieth century, it is important to offer the historical context in which the movement emerges.

In 1845, the introduction of official typography and newspapers in Angola profoundly contributed to the increase of debates until censorship and persecution of Angolan intellectuals' curtailed the discussions. The first periodical publication in Angola was the *Boletim do Governo-Geral da Província de Angola* (Bulletin of the General Government of the

C. M. Costa (✉)
ISCTE-Instituto Universitário de Lisboa, Lisbon, Portugal
e-mail: Catia.Miriam.Costa@iscte-iul.pt

P. A. B. Duarte et al. (eds.), *Portugal and the Lusophone World*,
https://doi.org/10.1007/978-981-99-0455-6_15

Province of Angola, first edition 13 September 1845). The Bulletin was central in disseminating and standardizing colonial processes and administration. It also provided local printing houses with the necessary resources to produce newspapers, magazines, books, and leaflets. It was this access to local production of reading materials that informed Angolan intellectual elites' ambitions because it provided a way to print locally produced texts. Instead of merely receiving others' intellectual production, local elites could print their discourses and distribute or sell locally produced and printed documents. Therefore, since the official typography services in Luanda started operating, they were allowed to print materials deemed harmless by the colonial administration. Until the arrival of the independent periodical press in 1866, the local elites depended on the official printers to produce and distribute their addresses, which were mostly literary texts. The first poetry book published in the Portuguese African colonies was printed in Angola in Portuguese. The author was José da Silva Maia Ferreira. The book reflects the style and kind of literature tolerated by the colonial regime as inoffensive. It was an example of shared aesthetic tastes that brought together local elites and the colonizer.

Only some years later, the introduction of the independent periodical press with their typographies ushered in another type of published content. There was a direct connection between the independent printed press and local creole elites' discourse autonomy. This was particularly useful when addressing political issues. The construction of a proto-nationalist political and spatial union, during the wars for colonial occupation of the territory, was one of their contributions to the conception of the modern state in Angola. The spatial and political union of Angola was part of the imagination of local elites who saw themselves as mediators between the colonial administration and local populations with no contact with the colonizer. Through literature and journalism, creole elites publicly debated issues like identity, culture, and the need for cooperation between the colonizer and the colonized to improve the colony's political, economic, and social development. The case of Angola takes specific contours which are significant in the contestation of the colonial system implemented. We should look at the African context of the time to better make sense of the lines of connection between intellectual elites and the emergence of a more sophisticated colonial administration. Similarly, the connection between local elites and the growing numbers of European settlers who worked within the colonial administration deserves specific investigation.

Nativist Movements in Africa

Most individuals involved in the so-called nativist movements were born while the colonial map of Africa was being designed by European powers in the late nineteenth century, and was brought up and educated during the consolidation of colonial regimes. The First World War offered additional opportunities for the solidification of colonial regimes, and these young adults attempted to participate in a fast-changing world which was leaving behind creole elites' ambitions. African intellectuals moved and acted under the restrictions of the colonial regime, which would directly affect how they drove their Africanist affirmation through proto-nationalist movements or pan-African movements. The colonial system imposed an external power above all local authorities, compelling them to conform to the social and political norms to participate in the colonial society they were part of. The abundant critical literature related to colonial law or suggesting new solutions and alternative political paths such as autonomy and, afterwards, nationalism suggests that every colonial regime imposed similar restrictions on local intellectuals, namely creoles or, under their particular characteristics, sons of the soil. However, even with restrictions over intellectual production, the desire for nationalism evolved from a surreptitious expression to an explicit claim (Oloruntimehon 2010).

In general, African intellectuals demanded the education of African populations, even when this reinforced colonial institutions. Nevertheless, education could also raise political awareness and, simultaneously, provide the tools for Africans to participate in the colony's public sphere, and demand more equality and opportunities to take part in the development plans of the colony. The creole elite regarded education as the only means of becoming a citizen with full rights. Despite colonial narratives that emphasized civilizing and development efforts, education was far from a priority. Colonial authorities introduced basic education, schools, and technical skilling needed to develop the local economic activities, and bring understanding and acceptance of colonial dominance to a small proportion of the local population. Therefore, colonial administrations did not proceed to the universalization of education, maintaining most of the population away from the knowledge required for more skilled participation in the colonial economy or society.

For the sons of the soil the education opportunities led to a paradox: placing them between two worlds, as sons of mixed relations and/or as individuals brought up between two cultures. Part of the dissatisfaction of the sons of the soil came from being brought up as mixed individuals, educated as white, but despite being active actors in the colonizer culture and society, denied full citizenship. Settlers coming from the metropolis surpassed them in public or private contracts even when less skilled. The ability to write and the level of education attained, gave them the opportunity to lead social movements and local civil society institutions, to write and publish leaflets, petitions, and articles, which contributed to local awareness about the colonial regime. These abilities were determinant in disseminating ideas that contested the colonial regime. Therefore, education and science became paradoxical. On one hand, justifying the civilizing arguments, on the other hand, giving the tools for colonized individuals to express and demand transformation in their societies (Betts 2010). Consequently, this situation resulted in a competition between metropolitan and local creole elites for the public sphere and discourse. However, colonial regimes always considered educated colonized individuals as similar but never equal (Caldwell 2010). When colonized elites became fully aware of this, they started to use the colonizer's discourse to introduce their own words and dissatisfaction expression (Soyinka 2010).

Internationally, the nativist movements presented similar arguments and organization. They problematized diverse colonial issues such as racial barriers, access to resources, education, and civic participation. These questions were further presented and problematized at the Pan-African Congresses that took place in European capitals between 1919 and 1923. Held in 1919, in Paris; in 1921, in London, Brussels, and Paris; and in 1923, in London and Lisbon, the congress questioned the arbitrary division of Africa. These congresses brought together the African diaspora of the New World, as well as European and African intellectuals. The American sociologist W. E. B. Du Bois (American sociologist and historian, organizer of the Pan-African Congress) had an important role in emphasizing a common heritage and a shared African past (Ralston and Mourão 2010). Nevertheless, these congresses still had higher participation of Europeans and Africans coming from the New World than African intellectuals, revealing how difficult it was for African intellectuals to take the lead in an international setting (Alfieri, 2021).

The development of nativist movements shed light on local issues, concerning colonial administration and the rights of the colonized peoples. These questions endured through the twentieth century, with some changes after the First World War. It is during and after the Great

War that the massive and generalized persecution of nativist movements takes place. The modern colonial regime was fully established in Africa, after the late nineteenth-century scramble for Africa. It is important to take into consideration that the period between 1880 and 1935 shaped colonial regimes and relationships in the colonies. The definition of frontiers (even without real territorial occupation) contributed to the process of occupation and the creation of a locally imposed administration, based on the principles of modern European states. The interest in Africa grew gradually, and the diversification of knowledge and discourses (political, scientific, cultural) developed alongside it. However, while there is a diversification of topics and contribution of Africans to the construction of European knowledge about Africa, colonial historiography often only considers European narratives (Boahen 2010). For some years, African inputs to knowledge and discourses about Africa were ignored and erased.

This Eurocentric perspective did not consider that African elites tried to contribute to shaping local administration and deepening the development of the territories. Although local elites received the modernization of the colonies with enthusiasm: the installation of infrastructures such as ports, railways, and the telegraph, and saw this process as a way to really develop local societies and establish a partnership, becoming mediators of this modernization process, they were considered a threat by colonial authorities on their claims and action. The recognized deletion of African intellectuals from colonial history (Boahen 2010). departs from the fact that local elites when having access to public discourse, used cultural texts to express their political concerns. The influence and the impact these intellectuals had on civil society institutions and generally in the population, directly produced repercussions in the way they were seen by the colonial authorities. The success of the reception of their public discourse was the determinant argument for their persecution. The cases of Madagascar (Crowder 2010). Senegal, Equatorial Guinea, and Ghana are evidence of the trend in the African Continent. These cases have some resemblance with the anti-nativist processes in Angola and Mozambique. In these cases, there was the persecution and imprisonment of individuals accused of nativism and anti-white movements, during and immediately after the First World War.

The aftermath of the period that saw the persecution of the sons of the soil led to the complete subordination of local elites to the colonial power, while raising the spectre of resistance (Issacman and Vansina, 2010). Instead of looking for cooperation with colonial authorities, local elites looked for other ways of resistance that preceded a most frontal opposition. The valorization of African values and cultures, and the teaching of African history and culture through orality are part of the initial resistance of the 1930s. While resisting, local elites also created an imagined political space, which accepted the frontiers that were designed by colonial powers but introduced an ideal of harmony between all the ethnic groups. These elites were mainly urban and still marked by a creole culture. Afterwards, there was a shift in this paradigm when the opposition to colonial powers became stronger and called for the participation of the rural populations.

Where the Portuguese colonies are concerned, researchers compare the formation of local elites in Angola and Mozambique. Generally, scientific works evidenced some specificities of the Portuguese empire: the lack of own capital, a large temporal difference in the occupation of the coastal and inland areas of the colonies, and the fact the Portuguese colonial regime became progressively more authoritarian. Some authors even refer to the role of journalism in the colonies and the metropolis in denouncing the abuses that became increasingly more frequent (Davidson et al. 2010). The same authors also refer that the sons of the soil conquered a place in the public sphere through literature. Therefore, in the Portuguese colonies, the nativist movements had similar characteristics and followed similar paths as movements in other African colonies, dealt with the same kind of challenges, although we can also identify some specific characteristics.

Angolan Nativist Movement: The Progressive Autonomy Under a Modern State Model

In Angola, the nativist movements became relevant during the First World War and in its immediate aftermath. The persecution of nativists has several episodes (1913, 1914, 1915, and 1917). It is notable that during the Republican period, with the contribution of the Free Masons, the printed press boosted the appearance of new projects, often connecting the colonies with the metropolis. Therefore, the persecutions start precisely local elites become excited about the new regime and new projects for the public sphere, which seemingly confirmed their expectations (Lopo 1962, 1964). However, the First World War and the competition to keep the territorial domains agreed in the Berlin Conference untouched, the European Empires centralized their power and persecuted those who posed a threat to their hegemonic power. The ambitions of the creole elites were dashed.

Nevertheless, out of all the persecutions, the one taking place in 1917 was the most significant, because it involved individuals from the local elite from every area of colonial society, including lawyers, journalists, civil servants, merchants, etc., for a considerable time, and reached every municipality in the colony. Most of the detainees were taken by surprise and were unaware of the reason for detention. Another element that contributed to the relevance this episode gained, was the publication of the testimony of one of the detainees in a newspaper and in two books, printed in the newspaper's typography. The newspaper, titled *O Angolense*, already called attention because it connected directly with the local political identity of the colony and the sons of the soil. The author of the report was António Assis Júnior, a very well-known intellectual, who regularly wrote for the public sphere. António Assis Júnior was also recognized for defending the interests of local property owners at a time when colonial authorities tried to commercialize land and transfer properties to settlers from the metropolis or metropolitan companies.

António Assis Júnior describes the impact of this event and the political reasons for it in his *Relato dos Acontecimentos de Dala Tando e Lucala, I and II* (Report of the events of Dala Tando and Lucala). published in 1917 and 1918 respectively, reflecting the significance the event had in the Angolan society. It is important to remember that since 1913/1914, all the European colonies were going through a process of centralization of power and authority in white hands. Local intellectuals were seen as a threat, and there was a need to control them. The involvement of colonies in the First World War partially explains this tendency, the other part is explained by the need for effective occupation by European powers and the fear of manipulation of local populations.

António Assis wrote in his book:

> For us, the revolt of the natives in Angola is an old and worn-out thing, with no shape or form of any kind – it's a bogeyman that no longer frightens children. For others, it is still a powerful lever for achieving their ends – good or bad, we don't know. (…) An indigenous revolution was invented, guided by the most civilized: and the occasion is fortunate to coincide with the events of Amboim and Seles, making their immediate arrest necessary, all difficulties disappeared and we served not only private interests but also collective: we want to see the back of a man they, or most, are afraid to keep. (Assis Júnior 1917 translation mine)

If, on the one hand, Assis Júnior speaks of ancient persecution, on the other hand, he refers to the Seles and Amboim revolts (1916/1917) directly linked to the coffee fields, property rights, and to the commercialization of products, with an emphasis on this area, which was an export product. This Angolan region was under the close attention of the colonial authorities. António Assis Júnior defended that native owners of Amboim and Seles lands had the right to maintain their properties and be included in the new capitalist way of exploring products such as coffee.

For intellectuals such as António Assis Júnior the development of the colony was possible under an alliance or partnership between settler and colonized, with the creole elite as middlemen that could introduce African natives into the projects of colonial administration. The concept of political territory and administration was clear for the Angolan creole elite: they asked for the introduction of the modern state in the colony but without the alienation of African natives. They saw themselves as individuals that could cooperate with the colonizer in the transition to a more "civilised" territory and ensure a soft transition to autonomy, and, possibly, independence if the territory developed. Therefore, addressing these movements as nativists was a way to highlight their demands for African participation in the colony's present and future. However, the colonial authorities easily began a process to misrepresent the concept, identifying nativism with anti-white movements, while knowing these movements recognized the colonial frontiers and political territory, and that they defended the implementation of a modern administration in the territories. It was never the aim of these African intellectuals to return to the traditional African governments.

Nevertheless, the situation of being in between two worlds brought suffering to the creole elite. Their aspirations of modernization of the colonies and, simultaneously, the respect and involvement of local populations, were compromised by the persecution of the colonial administration, and by local communities' misunderstanding of their position. Assis Júnior explains how mestizos or creoles integrated colonial society by using the image of what we can call "the burden of the mestizo". Assis writes in his book:

> Some, attending the same schools in the metropolis, are here condemned to the most flagrant contempt; the most unfortunate is the one who appears to have civilized habits and enjoy rights that only education confers, because, as that other black Mozambican mentioned by Freire

Andrade said, "before (he said) they always let me stay with those of my race, living like them than to educate me and throw me into the current situation, repelled by the whites who see me black, and I repel those of my colour with whom I cannot get used to living because I have contracted, by education, the habits of whites. (Assis Júnior 1918 translation mine)

Belonging to two worlds was, in fact, one of the difficulties faced by these intellectuals, not only during their lives but in the way their intellectual work was received, seeming to occupy an inhospitable middle ground (Memmi, 1973). Their work was frequently ignored, not only due to the conditions of production, but also of reception, and the cultural and conceptual of an era, strongly dominated by rationalism and positivism that saw indigenous cultures as only a starting point for the civilization that would be brought by scientific methods of colonization (Victor, 1975).

When handling European knowledge, the educated African occupied a pivotal position, between sameness and otherness, rejected by some, and pushing away others who did not accompany him. A common feature of these authors and intellectuals is, undoubtedly, their care for their lands and people, which they recognize as differentiated and with their own identity and projects designed according to the principles, learned in those societies where they are educated. It is in alterity that they find the answers to sameness, which makes them not far from so many others who trace national destinies, who, assuming positions of foreignness, propose solutions tried in different situations (Soares 2001). Their identification with the "civilizational" principles of the colonial administration made them believe they could fully integrate into colonial society, without being identified as "others". However, the persecution of the so-called nativist movements proved to them they were identified as other, much like the rural populations with no access to colonial institutions. Assis Junior quotes in his report the official document that justified his and other African intellectual's detention:

And, more than the constant words of the initial auto, revealing the intentions of the natives against the Europeans, they are only the complement of what they agreed in secret conversations. And so much so, that on August 15th of that year, at a banquet I presided over (!) and attended by Xavier de Lemos [who also collaborated with the press], recipient, at Guilherme Silva's house (!). there In toasts and speeches by António Galiano (...) and other natives, exchanged, the desire to carry out the revolt was affirmed,

> with the massacre already established, at least, of the Europeans residing in Dala-Tando. (...) These men were very seers: On that date I arrived, with Augusto Bastos, in Loanda, coming from Bié. By the same process, Jorge Gurjel (...) and others were also seen, at Maritz's house, at a large conference!... Holy people are here!.(Assis Júnior b). 1918 translation mine)

The involvement of these sons of the soil appears here as having been invented and the result of their professional, social, and political activity, but which was carried out within the normal framework of action. This means that there was a concerted initiative against the sons of the soil, whether these small autochthonous landowners or those who could stand the most in front of the colonial power, through the sharing of knowledge and semiosphere (meaning African and colonial elites shared the same processes of signification and conceptualization). having acquired all the necessary tools to decode, interpret and react within what is acceptable by that society. In fact, the imminent danger for colonialism was this group that should have been controlled and only as an intermediary of colonial power, never as its executor. Assis Júnior publishes this report because he has access to colonial institutions and to the means to enter the public sphere. The report echoed beyond the Angolan public sphere, and other newspapers than *O Angolense* also published texts about the events and this particular publication, inclusively in the metropole.

Thus, there is a certain complementarity between metropolitan and colonial journalistic writing (the term is used herein in the sense of produced in colonized soil). which allowed us to understand colonial reality, but which, in fact, also reminds us that the circulation was more in the metropolis/colony direction than in the opposite direction. Although periodical publication in colonial cities means access to publication by local elites, from there its dissemination in metropolitan cities goes some distance and it is verified that authors from colonial cities acquire greater recognition from readers when they publish in the metropolis. However, in circles of friendship, the fact that the African theme jumped to the front pages of newspapers throughout Europe led Portuguese intellectuals to develop an interest in the production of intellectuals from the colonies and scrutinize further the colonial context. This complementarity was determinant for the generation of nativists who were persecuted. Their connections in the metropole assured that many of them still had the freedom to exercise their professions and to, somehow, participate in colonial society.

The circulation of newspapers and other printed materials was only possible because part of the colonial society population shared the same language and semiosphere as the metropolitan society. This shows that there was a readership, formed, of course, by education of Portuguese roots, therefore with deep contact with the culture of the colonizer, but already drawing on local needs, and leading to articles, sometimes harsh, but received with avidity and satisfaction. If this was the situation with the autochthonous Creole elite, it was not always the case with the settler elite, who often had divergent interests from those of the natives. However, there was no perfect dichotomy, and it can be said that, in a way, these two worlds interpenetrated.

What made these sons of the soil a threat to colonialism? Were they really challenging colonial authorities or trying to participate in the modernization processes and development of the colony? In general, they were literate, part of a petty bourgeoisie, and very close to the colonizer, through education and participation in administrative services or economic activities that serve the colonial regime, and through personal, professional, and social relationships. However, despite this proximity, they were aware of their difference and yearnings for the colony. They even propose, even if implicitly, to continue a colonial process that would lead to greater autonomy. It is interesting to see how the term "Angolense" takes shape, knowing its genesis in colonial urban centres in Angola, especially Luanda, Benguela, Moçâmedes, and small points dotted on the map of the colony, such as Catumbela or Dondo, among others. The building of an Angolan identity precedes the territorial occupation of the borders of the province, drawn in Berlin and in the subsequent crisis of the Mapa Cor-de-Rosa (1891). based on an idea of territory and belonging to a certain space, but whose borders are still volatile (Henriques, 2004).

In fact, the effective occupation of territory offered the possibility of tracing unity between urban centres and guided the expansion of concepts created in the cities to the population within the borders. The autochthonous elite bore their own culture, made from the interpenetration of diverse influences in which the Bantu and Portuguese stand out, and firmly rooted in that space. It considered that all those who were outside the orbit of this concept of Angolan culture (which was nothing more than this Creole culture) should be brought to this Angolan culture, that is, somehow civilized (Soares 2001). However, it is undoubted that Angolans were much more committed than Portuguese settlers to the local territory and communities. Nevertheless, they managed to intertwine both heritages and, if formally Portuguese culture could dominate, in content the Bantu presence gave rise to something singular. The sons of the soil, created their own culture, a mestizo culture, intrinsically linked to the cities of these lands ancestrally touched by the Portuguese and with permanent cultural exchanges. Although more urban than *sertanejos*, and more coastal than the territory's interior, the solidarities and correspondences between both universes were maintained, making them even more different from the traditional settlers. The notion of difference combined with an ability to project this characteristic fed the beginnings of Angolanness, that is, the then evoked character of being Angolan. This ability to interconnect the diverse communities and semiospheres (from each ethnic group) frightened the Portuguese colonial authorities because they knew this Angolan elite contributed to the construction of this political space and defended the modernization of the colony through the installation of infrastructures but also by spreading education and integrating local population into the development projects.

The Angolan creole elite aimed to transform the cultural project of mixed influence to be applied to the political solution of the colonies. Their main objective was to blend the best of the modern colonial state (education, infrastructures, administrative organization, etc.) with the traditional cultures and societies. They saw themselves as mediators and individuals with adequate skill to lead or help to lead the process of modernization of the colonies. Therefore, they dreamed of autonomy that assured them to maintain the connection with the metropolis for a comfortable period without being occupied by other European imperial powers (Costa, 2015). Simultaneously, they foresaw autonomy as a first step to achieving the path to independence. Using colonizer techniques in the public sphere, they could spread their message through newspapers, books and leaflets (Costa, 2010). At the same time, they endorsed the modernization of the territory; they also transmitted their identity, somehow different from the colonizer one. The aesthetic look beyond the ethnographic research, fostering the taste and curiosity for local cultures and bringing them to modernity was also a mission taken by these intellectuals, who saw the dominance of the artistic and scientific discourses to call attention to their political demands. The printed press represented an excellent tool for their aspirations and was frequently used in the colonies and the metropolis.

The First Portuguese Republic which represented a moment of hope for local aspirations, ended a disappointment. The beginning of the control of the sons of the soil discourse happens during the Republican regime. The aftermath of these persecutions is not immediate. The repercussions were slowly implemented and some of the persecuted in these events, mostly in the one of 1917, were able to develop their careers and go on publishing until the Military dictatorship and the subsequent Estado Novo Regime. Nevertheless, the seed of a differentiated identity was rooted as well as the notion of the colonial territory not as an extension of the metropolis, but as a specific political space. The nativist movements, based on proto-nationalist ideas, were determinant for the ascension of the independent movements, led by the next generation. Simultaneously, the triangle between the colony of Angola and the metropolis involving the diverse colonies assured connections within the Lusophone political and cultural space, which were determinants for the solidarity between the creole elites and then between the liberation movements.

Conclusion

The nativist movements appeared in an urban colonial context and generally gathered African intellectuals or skilled Africans who experimented with the colonial institutions and integrated the colonial society. They represented the local elites and accepted the modernization of the colony but claimed participation in the process. The Angolan case is no exception to this international trend, reflecting the existence of European Empires that were in the process of occupation and administrative modernization of the African colonies. The Republican regime (1910–1926). which gave hope to these sons of the soil, did not assure their participation as full citizens and the situation deteriorated as time passed. The colonial administration's centralization became more evident, and in the middle of the 20' to the twentieth century, the creole elite was utterly removed from the higher positions of public colonial administration.

The generation of nativists that claimed autonomy in a proto-nationalist stage inspired the future movements that struggled for independence. Their ability to enter the public sphere in the colony and, sometimes, in the metropolis allowed them to create networks within the Lusophone world. These connections were also determinant for the support these political movements gathered, somehow protecting the first generation of nativists from being completely erased from Angola's history. Despite this native elite disappointment, they always embraced the principles of the modernization of the colony, including the new administrative rules. Their most relevant legacy was the reception and acceptance of the modernization of the territory and the creation of an identity corresponding to the colonial political space they appropriated as their reference.

References

Alfieri, Noémia (2021). Noémia de Sousa, or being an "African from head to toe" in times of colonization, In: Journal of Lusophone Studies. Jan 2020, 4, 2, pp. 219–233.

Allen Isaacman e Jan Vansina (2010). "Iniciativas e resistência africanas na áfrica Central 1880–1914",in Albert Adu Boahen [Editor], História Geral da África, VII: África sob dominação colonial, 1880–1935, Brasília: UNESCO, 2.ª Edição revista.

Betts, Raymond F (2010). "A dominação europeia: métodos e instituições", in Albert Adu Boahen [Editor], História Geral da África, VII: África sob dominação colonial, 1880–1935, Brasília: UNESCO2.ª Edição Revista.

Boahen, Albert Adu (2010). "A África diante do desafio colonial", BOAHEN, in Albert Adu [Editor], História Geral da África, VII: África sob dominação colonial, 1880–1935, Brasília: UNESCO, 2.ª Edição Revista, pp. 1–20.

Caldwell, John Charle (2010). "As repercussões sociais da doutrinação colonial: aspetos demográficos", Albert Adu Boahen [Editor], História Geral da África, VII: África sob dominação colonial, 1880–1935, Brasília: UNESCO, 2010, 2.ª Edição Revista.

Corrado, Jacopo (2010). "The Fall of a Creole Elite? Angola at the Turn of the 20th Century: the decline of the Euro-African Urban community", Luso-Brazilian Review.

Costa, C. M (2015). Continuidades e descontinuidades da colonização portuguesa: literatura e jornalismo entre a utopia e a realidade. Tese de doutoramento em Literatura, na Universidade de Évora.

Costa, Cátia Miriam (2010). "Pensamento republicano e africanismo: o caso de José de Macedo". In Viagens e missões científicas nos trópicos: 1883–2010. Lisboa: Instituto de Investigação Científica Tropical, pp. 34–38.

Crowder, Michael (2010). "A Primeira Guerra Mundial e suas consequências", Albert Adu Boahen, História Geral da África, VII: África sob dominação colonial, 1880–1935, Brasília: UNESCO, 2010, 2.ª Edição Revista pp. 333–353.

Davidson A. Basil, Isaacman, Allen Pélissier, F., René (2010). "Política e Nacionalismos nas Áfricas Central e Meridional", in Albert Adu Boahen [Editor], História Geral da África, VII: África sob dominação colonial, 1880–1935, Brasília: UNESCO 2.ª Edição Revista.

Dodney, Walter (2010). "A economia colonial", in Albert Adu Boahen [Editor], História Geral da África, VII: África sob dominação colonial, 1880–1935, Brasília: UNESCO, 2.ª Edição revista.

Henriques, Isabel Castro, Território e Identidade (2004). A construção da Angola colonial (c.1872–c.1926). Lisboa: Centro de História da Universidade de Lisboa.

Júnior, António Assis Junior a) (1917). Relato dos acontecimentos de Dala Tando e Lucala, Parte I, Loanda: Tipografia Mamã Tita.

Júnior, António Assis b) (1918). Relato dos acontecimentos de Dala Tando e Lucala, Parte II, Loanda: Tipografia Mamã Tita.

Lopo, Júlio de Castro (1962). Para a história da imprensa de Angola, Luanda: Edição do Museu de Angola.

Lopo, Júlio de Castro (1964). Jornalismo de Angola: subsídios para a sua história, Luanda: Centro de Informação e Turismo de Angola.

Memmi, Albert (1973). Portrait du Colonisé, Paris: Petite Bibliothèque Payot Mortimer, Henry (1899). L'Utopie Coloniale, s/local, Bureau du Voltaire.

Oloruntimehon, B. Olantuji (2010). "A política e o nacionalismo africano 1919–1935", Albert Adu Boahen [Editor], História Geral da África, VII: África sob dominação colonial, 1880–1935, Brasília: UNESCO, 2.ª Edição Revista, pp. 657–659.

Ralston, Richard David, Mourão, Fernando Augusto de Albuquerque (2010). "A África e o Novo Mundo", Albert Adu Boahen [Editor], História Geral da África, VII: África sob dominação colonial, 1880–1935, Brasília: UNESCO, 2.ª Edição Revista.

Soares, Francisco (2001). Notícia da Literatura Angolana, Lisboa: Imprensa Nacional—Casa da Moeda.

Soyinka, Wole (2010). "As artes na África durante a dominação colonial", Albert Adu Boahen [Editor], História Geral da África, VII: África sob dominação colonial, 1880–1935, Brasília: UNESCO, 2.ª Edição Revista, pp. 648–656.

Victor, Geraldo Bessa (1975). Intelectuais angolenses dos séculos XIX e XX: Augusto Bastos, I, Lisboa: Edição do Autor.

Cabo Verde's Geopolitical Relevance in the Mid-Atlantic

João Paulo Madeira

Introduction

In January 2011, Cabo Verde approved the Strategic Concept of Defense and National Security, which highlighted the areas considered by the country of strategic interest. Such areas include countries where there are large Cabo Verdean communities; the West African region, where the country is located; and the African continent as a whole. The archipelago's location in the Atlantic space, between the parallels 17°12′ and 14°48′ North and the meridians 22°44′ and 25°22′ West, is of particular interest to other countries, institutions, and international organizations, due to the relevance of such space for the current critical geopolitical challenges. The country's relations with Portugal, Spain, and France, in Europe, and with the United States in the northern hemisphere are particularly noteworthy. Countries like Brazil, Angola, and South Africa are in focus on the southern hemisphere. Considering the European space, Cabo Verde deepens its foreign relations with the European Union, developing a Special Partnership since 2007. There is also an incentive to strengthen

J. P. Madeira (✉)
Universidade de Cabo Verde (Uni-CV), Paria, Cape Verde
e-mail: joao.madeira@docente.unicv.edu.cv

P. A. B. Duarte et al. (eds.), *Portugal and the Lusophone World*,
https://doi.org/10.1007/978-981-99-0455-6_16

the ties with the Macaronesia Islands, made up of the Azores and Madeira archipelagos (Portugal) and the Canary Islands (Spain), where links of historical, cultural, linguistic, and complementary nature have always been woven.

The Community of Portuguese-Speaking Countries (CPLP), with which Cabo Verde shares the language and culture, is also indisputably an element that raises feelings of belonging. At its core is a multilateral forum that materializes the idea of partnership, promoting cooperation between its members, political-diplomatic consultation, and the deepening of friendly relations based on its main foundation: the Portuguese language (Marchueta 2003). The CPLP is, after all, an Intergovernmental Organization based on the historical, cultural, and linguistic bond that unites its nine member-states (Angola, Brazil, Cabo Verde, Guinea-Bissau, Equatorial Guinea, Mozambique, Portugal, São Tomé and Príncipe and Timor-Leste). Its mission is to develop and promote cooperation in various fields and contribute to the sustainable development of its members. It also aims to consolidate its projection as an International Organization to face the challenges of globalization with greater determination. Without losing sight of its focus, Cabo Verde has recently been witnessing a growing emphasis on the axis made up of China and, to a lesser extent, Japan and other areas of the globe where national interests are at stake. Ultimately, these new partners could provide new opportunities in the scope of police and judicial cooperation and security, as well as in the areas of finance, education, culture, science and technology, and the environment.

Indeed, the archipelago is located in a complex chess game of geopolitical dispute. Firstly, due to the growing interest of China, which has been financing several infrastructures in Cabo Verde, among which the National Assembly, the Government Palace, the National Auditorium, the National Library, the Jorge Barbosa Auditorium, the Amílcar Cabral Memorial, the Poilão Dam, the National Stadium, the neonatal services of the Agostinho Neto Hospital and other emblematic constructions located in the country's capital (Ferreira and Madeira 2020). In addition, other initiatives that have fostered rapprochement and exchange between the archipelago and the People's Republic of China are worth noting. For instance, the Cabo Verde-China Friendship Association (AMICACHI), created in 2011, contributes to the operationalization of this relationship. It is a Cabo Verdean non-governmental organization with financial autonomy and a support structure that aims to strengthen ties of friendship and cultural exchange between both countries (Madeira 2017). Moreover, it constitutes a reference, as in the case of the civil society platform for China-Cabo Verde-Africa intercultural dialogue.

On July 23, 2021, the Chinese government handed over the New Campus of the University of Cabo Verde (Uni-CV) to the country's Government. This complex, located in Palmarejo Grande, covers almost 28,000 m2 of total area and houses eighteen buildings (Governo de Cabo Verde 2021b). On the 4th of July, the date which marks the United States Independence Day, the US Ambassador to Cabo Verde, Jeff Daigle, publicly announced the launch of the new U.S. Embassy construction on the land adjacent to the Government Palace, with an area of 4.5 hectares (U.S. Embassy in Cabo Verde 2021). The friendly relations between Cabo Verde and the US date back more than two centuries to the moment when the American government installed its first Consulate in all of Sub- Saharan Africa in the city of Praia in December 1818. Samuel Hodges, a Massachusettsan Merchant, presented himself before Governor António Pusich as the first American Consul in Cabo Verde. The installation of this Consulate is the result of an essential element from a historical and diplomatic perspective (Tolentino 2019). Regarding this, the US highlights Cabo Verde as an important partner that, since its independence in July 1975, has been committed to building the rule of law that promotes democracy, transparency, and accountability of public institutions (Madeira 2021).

The Biden administration has made it clear that it will favor the countries which speak up for such values. In this sense, the US Secretary of State, Anthony Blinken, has described Cabo Verde as "a model of democratic governance and human rights in Africa" (U.S. Department of State 2021). It is no coincidence that Cabo Verde obtained, as in 2020, 92 points out of a possible 100 in the freedom ranking of the Freedom House. According to this ranking, this score places Cabo Verde as the freest country in Africa. The island state, placed in the group of "free" countries, scored 38 (out of 40) in terms of "Political Rights" and 54 (out of 60) considering Civil Liberties (Freedom House 2021).

The archipelago is located 455 km from the northwest African coast at the crossroads of some of the main international air and sea routes. To the south is Santiago Island, the. the largest island with its capital, Praia, and to the North is São Vicente Island, which is smaller but has better ports, bays, and coves. In the port city of Mindelo, China uses the repair station for merchant ships, cabotage vessels, and maritime support vessels (Hill 2021).

However, it is worth mentioning that since July 2020, Cabo Verde has been benefiting from the Special Economic Zone of Maritime Economy in São Vicente (ZEEEM-SV), which provides for an Integrated Free Zone, as well as for land-use policies and concessions of exploration of the seafront. It also prescribes special conditions for procedures of registration, granting, and revocation of special benefits and certification of entities or companies in the ZEEEM-SV, and incentives for contracting services from companies or entities with Cabo Verdean capital (National Assembly 2020).

This positioning places Cabo Verde not only at the nodal point of the most important trade routes but also of Transnational Organized Crime such as drug trafficking, money laundering, arms trafficking, and related crimes. The location of the island nation, far beyond the territorial waters of its closest neighbors such as Senegal, could represent, in these same countries, the development of surveillance and covert operations against terrorist groups such as Boko Haram, Al-Qaeda in the Islamic Maghreb (AQIM), the Islamic State in the Greater Sahara (ISGS); Ansarul Islam or the (MUJAO)/Al- Mourabitoun (OBE and Wallace 2021), which is currently deepening new alliances with radical Islamist organizations in Somalia, Nigeria, and Mali (Matos 2014). Local and international actors try to prevent and combat terrorist activities, but their actions usually fall far short of expectations.

Therefore, it is necessary to answer clearly the following research problem: what is the role of Cabo Verde in the fighting against phenomena such as transnational crime, drug trafficking, terrorism, and maritime piracy that threaten the safety of States bordering the Atlantic? Answering this question requires adopting a qualitative study with an interdisciplinary basis and a hypothetical-deductive approach. In general terms, the starting point is geographic and historical analysis, proceeding with the collection, analysis, and processing of information concerning the archipelago's placement in the region, considering that it influences national strategic options directly or indirectly. Adopting this approach is useful as it makes it possible to interpret and relate the interdependence of political events in relation to the geographical environment.

Cabo Verde in the Mid-Atlantic: Privileged Geographical Positioning

Cabo Verde comprises ten islands and thirteen islets, covering a total land area of 4033 km^2, spread over an ocean area of approximately 87 miles. The country also has 1000 km of coastline and a maritime area of 734,265 km^2, including the archipelagic waters, the territorial sea, the contiguous zone, and the Exclusive Economic Zone (EEZ). Furthermore, the maritime vocation of the archipelago and the associated responsibilities concerning security in the Mid-Atlantic must be under the country's ambition and possibilities, as expressed in the Cabinet of Ministers Resolution No. 5/2011 of January 17, 2011. This document approves the CEDSN, considering the challenges of developing the capacity of monitoring and controlling the jurisdictional space, which can only be achieved through cooperation agreements with partner countries that have expertise in ocean intervention. To this end, the country is strengthening partnerships in defense and security policy to protect the immense sea under its jurisdiction. In this regard, it is worth remembering that Cabo Verde is a country whose total area is 99% composed of the ocean, in a dynamic region in terms of activities related to this sector (Fortes 2014).

The Mid-Atlantic, an expression used here, represents an attempt at geographical delimitation of a maritime space whose configuration is limited by the Tropic of Cancer to the North, the African coast to the East, the meridian that passes close to Barbados to the West, and Strategic Geographic Ecuador to the south. Such space reaches 5,000 km at its greatest length and 3241 km at its greatest width. This attempt to delimitate this region is justified for reasons related to the geographical location of Barbados, which is the easternmost island in the Caribbean. Due to the fact that this island belongs to the American Mediterranean, the limitation to the West of the Mid-Atlantic meridian was reconsidered. Such a limitation is accepted in the vicinity of Port of Spain, the capital of Trinidad and Tobago (Amante da Rosa 2007). This "new" meridian constitutes a vital maritime and air space in the traffic and distribution of ships, aircraft, and submarine cables.

Cabo Verde's success comes from the consolidation of its strategic position between Europe, the African continent, and the Americas, in a geographical situation that integrates it in a vast and special space and makes its experience interesting and worthy of study. It is also noteworthy that Cabo Verde is part of the bio-geographic region of Macaronesia, which includes the volcanic archipelagos of the Azores, Madeira, Savage, and the Canary Islands. In addition to sharing identical elements of its fauna and its volcanic origin, this island space shares a set of historical and cultural ties. This is a relevant repository of information and one of the primary sources for studying fauna, flora, uses and customs, genealogy, toponymy, and settlement (Chaves 2020).

If we look at the last forty-seven years since national independence, it is possible to highlight the country's extraordinary progress. In addition to Amante da Rosa (2007), several other researchers have paid particular attention to the geopolitics and foreign policy in Cabo Verde, such as Varela (2007), Pinto (2008, 2009), Costa and Pinto (2014), Graça (2014), Tolentino (2016) and e Madeira (2016b, 2019a, 2019b). According to these authors, since the country's independence, some elements of foreign policy have accompanied successive governments, namely: [1] the privileged geostrategic position in the Mid-Atlantic Ocean; [2] political stability and good governance; [3] the perspective of territorial security and the non-alignment in ideological blocks, however, maintaining political-diplomatic relations with several States such as Brazil, Russia, India, China, and South Africa (BRICS), Commonwealth of Independent States, Gulf Cooperation Council, and high net worth individuals (Lilyblad 2020); [4] the culture of social peace reflected in domestic and foreign policy; [5] the commitment to diplomacy characterized by modesty and proximity and based on the principles of peace aimed at resolving or circumventing socioeconomic constraints.

Cabo Verde, a territory of reduced dimensions and a resident population of 491,233 inhabitants (INE 2021), assumes an integrating role in the Mid-Atlantic that must be preserved. Its geographic location gives rise to different feelings of belonging. Cabo Verde has also been a member of the Economic Community of West African States (ECOWAS) since 1977 and has, since 2007, under the Portuguese presidency, a Special Partnership Agreement with the European Union based on six pillars: good governance; security/stability; regional integration; technical and normative convergence; knowledge society; fight against poverty and development (EU 2007). An important point refers to the fact that this approach goes beyond the mere "donor-beneficiary relationship" and does not constitute an alternative to the Cotonou Agreement (2000–2020). In this sense, besides considering regional integration in its plan of action, it allows the archipelago to establish a bridge between two continents (Madeira 2015). On the one hand, it enhances the approximation to the Outermost Regions and the rest of the Union and, on the other, allows to intensify relations within the scope of ECOWAS (EU 2007). In July 2008, Cabo Verde became the 153rd Member States in the World Trade Organization (WTO). It was the first African country and the third, still as a Least Developed Country (LDC), to join the WTO through direct negotiation, constituting an essential element of the strategy for its insertion in the global market (Governo de Cabo Verde 2009). The remaining countries that are part of the WTO signed the Marrakech Agreement (1994) that created the organization. The Cabo Verde archipelago was the second in the world, following Tonga, to do so as a Least Developed Country (LDC).

Cabo Verde develops close relations with Portugal, Brazil, and other CPLP countries. In July 1996, these countries formed an organization for political-diplomatic consultation between its Member States to strengthen the Community's presence and promote cooperation in defense and security, science and technology, education and health, culture, and promotion, and dissemination of the Portuguese language. Cabo Verde joined the Francophonie in 1997 and, in 2003, the Parliamentary Assembly of La Francophonie, becoming part of the International Organization of La Francophonie (OIF), which houses countries from all continents, having reinforced the status of the French language in the country.

In addition, an analysis of the CPLP Strategic Document of Cooperation 2020–2026 should also be carried out, making it possible to state, directly or indirectly, that cooperation in the CPLP could be more expressive. Several reasons lead to this conclusion: the Community is not a contiguous space, as the African Union, ECOWAS, ECCAS, SADC, ASEAN, and Mercosur, for instance. The States are geographically distant from each other, which makes cooperation difficult—especially with regard to the mobility and circulation of people, goods, capital, and services—hindering the development of projects of common interest. A typical example concerns the fact that most cooperation projects require the involvement of at least three Member States. However, when it comes to practice, the project often does not have the same interest and level of impact in each Member States. Each State is different and uses different approaches to implement these projects in practice since they have different levels of development and distinct priorities, which may result in a lack of interest in at least one of the States. The CPLP does not have reliable and effective mechanisms to finance cooperation projects, and Member States' contribution to funding cooperation is voluntary, creating a lack of financial availability.

Another issue that must be addressed within the scope of subsidiarity is related to the financial difficulties experienced by most CPLP Member States. The difficult conditions in which each country lives—not only due to the territorial smallness, resulting from the geographical situation, but also due to political and social instability, lack of transparency, and governments' leadership—make cooperation immensely difficult. Without hurting susceptibilities and without excluding anyone, only Portugal and, sometimes, Brazil and Cabo Verde comply with the payment of annual fees for CPLP cooperation (Inforpress 2020; Deutsche Welle 2019). Noteworthy is the fact that CPLP Member States are geographically distant and dispersed. They assume commitments with the Organizations of their respective regions: Portugal with the EU, Angola and Mozambique with SADC, Cabo Verde and Guinea-Bissau with ECOWAS, São Tomé and Principe and Equatorial Guinea with ECCAS, and Timor-Leste with the possibility of becoming a member of ASEAN. We believe that the best solution is to define the priority areas on which cooperation will focus in the coming years. Financing in all domains requires regular meetings of the cooperation focal points in order to establish partnerships between the various sectors and thus obtain funding for their implementation. In practice, this model translates into the proliferation of small projects and, therefore, reduces its impact. In fact, the pillars of diplomatic and political consultation and the promotion and dissemination of the Portuguese language work best within a Community of cultural values, traditions, and cultural specificities.

Another significant point refers to the fact that Cabo Verde hosted the first exercise of the NATO Response Force (NRF) outside the traditional space of the organization. Held between 15 and 28 June 2006, the exercise called Steadfast Jaguar aimed to test its capacity for projection and interoperability (Reis 2014). These exercises follow on from the November 2002 Prague Summit, which discussed the enlargement and capacity building of the North Atlantic Treaty Organization (NATO). In addition, it debated the creation of the multinational rapid reaction force, which would act at any level of conflict and wherever the North Atlantic Treaty Council deems necessary. Approximately one year before the exercises, the then Minister of Foreign Affairs of Bulgaria, Solomon Passy, formally proposed the inclusion of Cabo Verde in the Atlantic Alliance.

In 2009, Passy was a candidate for the Secretary-General of NATO position, having lost to the Danish Anders Fogh Rasmussen, who held this post between 2009 and 2014. Although Cabo Verde was not accepted by member states such as Greece, among others, some advances have certainly been made. Portugal and Spain joined together in a semi-formal way with the 2009 "Lanzarote Declaration" aimed at designing a soft security architecture (oriented toward the fight against organized crime, health, and the environment) for the southern Atlantic space that extends to the south of the allied jurisdictional space (Guedes 2012).

In July 2019, the Prime Minister of Cabo Verde, Ulisses Correia e Silva, admitted the possibility of asking for the integration of the archipelago into NATO, considering the country's need for partnerships to reduce vulnerabilities. Such a need was particularly significant given the archipelago's geostrategic location (Expresso das Ilhas/LUSA 2019). Following that decision, some progress has been made. In November 2021, the Prime Minister of Cabo Verde—celebrating the National Defense Day at Amílcar Cabral Avenue, Plateau, and after receiving a courtesy visit of the Portuguese Minister of National Defense, João Gomes Cravinho, in his office at the Government Palace—considered that the archipelago plays an important role in the relations with the European Union and the triangulation with the United States of America. Cabo Verde's current intention is to get closer to NATO, as security issues are important, not only because "we have a vast maritime area, we are 99% sea, but because we need to have surveillance and monitoring of our seas" (Inforpress 2021).

However, this is a complex and delicate issue, and the arguments presented on the subject sometimes have unfavorable repercussions in the press. In July 2019, when the Prime Minister of Cabo Verde announced the possibility of the country asking for integrating NATO, reactions soon arose. The African Party for the Independence of Cabo Verde (PAICV), the main opposition party, recalled that a possible accession to NATO would require greater internal concertation. However, the party's general secretary, Julião Correia Varela, recognizes that Cabo Verde must strengthen partnerships with international organizations and foreign countries in terms of defense and security. According to the law professor and security specialist João Santos, in order to take this step, it is necessary to promote the revision of the Constitution first, since the current Magna Carta does not allow the installation of any foreign military base in the country. An eventual entry of Cabo Verde into NATO would be established with the aim of having structures to guarantee security and prevent enemy actions and their entry into the territories of Member States (VOA 2019).

Cabo Verde is also part of the South Atlantic Peace and Cooperation Zone (ZOPACAS), an international organization created in 1986 at the initiative of Brazil during the United Nations General Assembly and which currently comprises twenty-four countries. In practical terms, this organization constitutes another Forum to protect the South Atlantic region from tensions or conflicts in developing countries. Significant is the fact that the ZOPACAS went through a stagnation period during the 1990s, resuming its work in the late 2000s, when its spheres of cooperation were renewed (Carvalho and Nunes 2014). On January 15, 2013, the organization was revitalized on the occasion of the VII Ministerial Meeting of the Zone—held in Montevideo, Uruguay's capital. In that context, Brazil had already discovered its oil deposits in the pre-salt layer of the coast of São Paulo. Besides, the United States had reactivated the Fourth Fleet, nearly 60 years after its dissolution in 1950; and China was increasing its presence in South America and on the African Atlantic coast (Garcia 2017).

Following that, Cabo Verde hosted between the 20th and 21st of May 2015 in the city of Mindelo, São Vicente Island, the VIII Ministerial Meeting of the ZOPACAS with the participation of all twenty-four member countries with the aim of promoting regional cooperation and the maintenance of peace and security in African and South American countries, whose coast is bordered by the Atlantic Ocean. This meeting focused on cooperation in maritime safety, oceanographic research, maritime transport, university cooperation, and information and communication technologies (Portugal Digital 2015).

Several attempts to create a security architecture were made. However, they faced internal and regional difficulties and the fragmentation of regional cooperation, low institutionalization, and a high degree of overlapping. Such elements prevented a greater institutionalization of the ZOPACAS project, for instance, threats to security, environmental protection, peaceful conflict resolution, and respect for the rule of law principles, despite a greater geostrategic interest in the South Atlantic, notably for coastal countries. The definition of security governance is suitable for characterizing this region. This concept expresses a configuration of regional security that contributes to intensifying South Atlantic relations (Pimentel 2016).

Cabo Verde's position arouses particular geopolitical interest in other countries, international organizations, and institutions. Its region is composed of fifteen member countries that share historical and cultural ties, in addition to common interests and values. Among these states, eight are francophones (Benin, Burkina Faso, Côte d'Ivoire, Guinea-Conakry, Mali, Niger, Senegal, and Togo), five anglophones (Gambia, Ghana, Liberia, Nigeria, and Sierra Leone), and two lusophones (Cabo Verde and Guinea-Bissau).

Regarding Cabo Verde's position in ECOWAS, although the Constitution of the Republic of Cabo Verde (CRCV, 1992, article 11, no. 7) establishes that the country should be committed to African unity and integration, what is seen in political-diplomatic practice is that this expectation has not been met. The candidacy in early 2015 by Cristina Duarte, at the time Minister of Finance and Planning, for the presidency of the African Development Bank (AfDB) deepened the certainty that, in recent years, there has been a loosening of relations between Cabo Verde and Africa. The campaign director, Jorge Brito, argued that Cabo Verdean political leaders lack the political will to get to know the African continent and, for this reason, they should adopt an adequate policy of sub-regional integration, as these factors somehow affect the performance in elections (Monteiro 2016). This issue raised a wave of criticism in Cabo Verde regarding the integration of the archipelago into Africa, stating that the country has not been able to take advantage of its relations with the continent and that it is necessary to adopt a geopolitical view that values regional integration (Madeira 2015).

The problem of regional integration is transversal to Cabo Verde. The country seeks to include its economy in a safe and stable global space, essentially through multilateralism, seeking to mobilize political-institutional solutions capable of circumventing the vulnerabilities of an island State (Monteiro 2016). Whatever the actors, visions, and projects, regional integration will always be a complex and slow process, encompassing internal factors that interact with geopolitical, economic, cultural, and religious factors (Tolentino 2013). This reality has directly contributed to a less successful relationship between Cabo Verde and ECOWAS.

To circumvent this situation, the Ministry of Foreign Affairs, Cooperation and Regional Integration (MNEIR) of Cabo Verde has sought, together with its strategic partners, to boost political-diplomatic activity concerning the African continent. Cabo Verde has few diplomatic representations/embassies in Africa, but even so, it considers them as strategic for its development. We refer here, more specifically, to the Embassies in Bissau (Guinea- Bissau); Dakar (Senegal); Luanda (Angola); São Tomé (São Tomé and Principe); Abuja (Nigeria)—which simultaneously represents the country in ECOWAS—and Addis Ababa (Ethiopia), although in the latter one, there is only one permanent mission to the African Union. Indeed, this interest has been highlighted by José Maria Neves, President of the Republic elected in October 2021, who considers that Cabo Verde is only of strategic importance if properly anchored in Africa. In this sense, strategic cooperation should be strengthened with the Government for a competitive insertion of Cabo Verde in the African continent, starting with ECOWAS (VOA 2021).

In this study, we start with the analysis of the geographical situation of Cabo Verde, considering that it is an essential factor in foreign policy and the most permanent (Gray 1999). We understand that it is clear that the geographic factor is directly related to several others, including the position of the State. Geopolitics, on the other hand, is characterized as a method of analyzing the intersection of two diluted dimensions: the spatial location of the various powers (namely the conflicting phenomena, the offensive or defensive strategies), and physical and human geography and the arguments, political motivations, and trends and continuities of history (Encel 2011). There is usually a tendency to relate geopolitics to geostrategy since both are closely related, despite being different sciences. Thus, they form a homogeneous relationship that offers, both the political and the military, the same method of approaching the necessarily interconnected problems of the world today (Célèrier 1969). Geostrategy emerges as an element or part of geopolitics. It is fundamentally distinguished by its focus on studying problems related to the links between geography and the use of coercion in conflict situations and by its method. Considering the premise that geostrategy deals with the study of the constants and variables of space and that it aims at the construction of models of evaluation and employment (or threat of employment) of forms of coercion, it ends up projecting geographic knowledge in the strategic activity (IAEM 2000).

This study is based on geographic knowledge and involves the interaction between not only internal and external factors but also physical (territory) and human (population) elements, natural resources, circulation, technology, and structures (Dias 2005, p. 223). Because it is an insular and peripheral region in relation to the continental area, we believe it is necessary to draw attention to other approaches concerning Cabo Verde's geopolitics since it involves a multiplicity of highly complex issues beyond those usually discussed regarding security and possible threats to the country. We refer, for example, to territorial smallness and insularity; dispersion between islands; and low agricultural productivity due to the hot and dry winds that blow from the Sahara Desert toward the archipelago. Natural watercourses are scarce due, on the one hand, to cyclical droughts and seasonal rains and, on the other, to water scarcity and desertification risks. When precipitation occurs between August and October, it takes the form of sometimes torrential rains that cause significant damage and water erosion (Neves 2017). However, whenever possible, responses and solutions suited to the characteristics of this insular region are sought, not only because it is peripheral but because it has its own geographical characteristics and specificities based on the territorial constraints to which it is attached and which require joint responses. These responses may be carried out between countries, partners, and institutions involved.

Supposing the adoption of an approach based on strengthening the means available to combat crime—taking into account the seriousness of a certain type of transgression, highlighting, for example, money laundering and drug trafficking, which require institutional articulation and exchange of experiences—the solution must go through a cooperative effort of several international partners in order to guarantee safe, effective and cost-efficient operations and the optimal use of available resources. An illustrative example is that the Cabo Verde Judiciary Police (PJ) seized on January 31, 2019, in the Praia Harbour 9570 kg of cocaine on the Panama-flagged cargo ship ESER. Following the operation, the PJ detained eleven citizens of Russian nationality. The freighter from South America was bound for the port of Tangier in Morocco The PJ confirmed that the.

ship stopped at Praia Harbour to comply with legal procedures related to the death, onboard, of one of the crew members. In this mega operation of search, unloading, packaging, transport, and storage of the seized product, the PJ had the cooperation and technical support of the Portuguese Judicial Police and the French National Police. It also involved the collaboration of the national security forces, namely, the Armed Forces (FA), the Maritime Police, the National Company for Port

Management S.A. (ENAPOR), and the Administration of the Port of Praia.

The operation was developed following an instruction process resulting from the exchange of operational information with the Maritime Analysis and Operation Centre—Narcotics (MAOC (N), based in Lisbon (UNODC 2019). UNODC has warned that the country is becoming an important pivot in transatlantic drug trafficking due to a set of factors that cross the unitary, regional, and systemic levels, making this situation extremely difficult to manage. In fact, the status quo greatly mitigates the chances of success. Added to the lack of necessary financial, material, and human resources are the handicaps resulting from the country's geographical location and configuration and the security dynamics of the international system, factors that the country can do little or nothing about (Évora 2014). There is no doubt that Cabo Verde's participation in multilateral mechanisms is fundamental in the framework of mutual assistance, cooperation, and respect for sovereignty. Territorial integrity must be preserved to maintain stability in the region (Madeira 2019b). We refer here to the need for internationally coordinated control, for cooperation programs to reduce threats, for political and economic instruments, for the prohibition of illegal activities, and, ultimately, the use of coercive measures in accordance with the UN Charter.

However, it is also widely accepted that geostrategy and geopolitics use the same data or a working basis. However, while the former uses them to support policy, geopolitics uses them to support strategy. On the other hand, geopolitics is part of geostrategy mainly in the design of scenarios that may involve potential conflicts of interest that may come up (Dias 2005).

Cabo Verde, but also the Canary Islands, Azores, and Madeira are far from the coast and, for this reason, are less exposed to border problems, including epidemics, territorial disputes, and religious issues (Madeira 2019a). For instance, in just eighteen months, in the ECOWAS Region, of which Cabo Verde is a part, three coups d'état took place—on May 24, 2021, in Mali, on September 5 of the same year in Guinea-Conakry, and on January 24, 2022 in Burkina Faso. A week later, on February 1, 2022, an attempted coup d'état took place in Guinea-Bissau (Dabo 2022). The consolidation of democracy depends on several factors, especially the attitude, behavior, and trust that civil society places in a given political regime. Given the insularity and climatic conditions, the Cabo Verdean population sought to survive and one of the key behaviors contributing to this survival was the hospitality and good coexistence of its inhabitants, which has also contributed to political stability (Madeira and Reis 2018).

The way Cabo Verdeans internalize democratic rules allowed democratic consolidation to effectively constitute a reality, especially in the post-conflict phase, in which the behavior of its inhabitants constituted a reference in the African region (Madeira 2016a). If we analyze the historical and social foundations of Cabo Verde, it can be deduced that it is different in relation to all other Member States. The archipelago had no inhabitants when it was discovered, and the settlement resulted in a process that created both homogeneity and heterogeneity between the islands with the Euro-African heritage. There, the nation emerged, and the national identity, appreciated by the cultural elite, created a State that currently has peaceful relations with Portugal and, in particular, with the EU (Madeira 2018).

Being an open country, Cabo Verde attracts many tourists. For this reason, this sector corresponds to one of the country's main economic activities. However, there are several important constraints to the security of the Cabo Verde archipelago, with particular emphasis on organized crime of economic and financial nature, drug and arms trafficking, and money laundering. A growing need for cooperation in disaster prevention also represents a significant limitation. Besides, it is essential to establish an information mechanism that guides the performance of professionals from the National Police (PN), the Judiciary Police (PJ), the Armed Forces (FA), and the National Civil Protection Service (SNPC), in any eventuality, in a given territory. These proposals seem indispensable, but for them to function fully, they must be accompanied by training programs and reforms in the judicial system and other bodies responsible for security and defense. Perhaps in this context, the Information Services of the Republic (SIR) and the National Security System (SSN) were created. The latter was established to reinforce national security and generate a system of support, articulation, and coordination of the different forces responsible for security in the national territory. According to Article 2 of Decree-Law no. 51/2013, of December 20, the SSN involves the coordinated and integrated use of forces and services aimed at the prevention and protection of risks and threats against the population and patrimony, the repression of hostile and illegal actions, and the assistance, rescue, and aid to populations affected by attacks or other catastrophes.

This system encompasses all state institutions that are engaged in security matters, depending on the Prime Minister and having the following composition: the PN, the PJ, the SIR, the FA, the Maritime Authority bodies, the Aeronautical Authority bodies, the bodies responsible for the radio spectrum control and the protection of the information and communication systems, and also other bodies with security functions. Cabo Verde's security and defense policy will only have results if it implies interoperability between the Armed Forces and the Police and other services related to security, articulating such bodies whenever necessary.

The security activity started even before independence in July 1975. In 1962, for example, a new organization of the Cabo Verdean police took place, with its transformation into the Public Security Police (PSP), a civilian organization modeled on the structure and functioning of the Portuguese Public Security Police. Following Cabo Verde's independence, the PSP was transformed into the Public Order Police (POP) (Rodrigues, 2016). Due to historical ties and the fact that several of its officers were trained in Portugal, POP maintained a close connection with the Portuguese PSP, keeping, for example, uniforms, structure, organization, operating model, and common rules and procedures. However, the lines of continuity embodied in the State security and public order services were guaranteed. The Cabo Verdean legal framework is very positive in preventing and repressing the crime of laundering, money, assets, rights, and values (Law no. 120/VIII/2016, of March 24) and in combating the financing of terrorism (Law no. 119/VIII/2016, of March 24) (UIF 2017). The latter establishes measures of a preventive and repressive nature against terrorism, its functioning and organization establish a penal framework that goes up to 20 years in prison and the sentencing of anyone who participates in or supports terrorism.

Conclusion

Cabo Verde presents vulnerabilities arising from its dispersion in islands, surrounded by an extensive ocean surface, the extension of the coast, and the size of the jurisdictional waters, which facilitates the practice of transnational and related crimes, namely drug trafficking and the trafficking of arms and people. In defense planning, this vulnerability is taken into account, as well as the sustainability of resources, the preservation of marine biodiversity, and the prevention of pollution. Cabo Verde's maritime vocation generates responsibilities for the country in the security of the Mid-Atlantic that has been politically defined and that are assumed in accordance with the country's ambition and possibilities. The situation of drug trafficking in West Africa and the flow of irregular immigration across the sea demand the full attention of the security and defense sector with the aim of creating national capacities to oppose them and develop effective cooperation with other affected states and organizations dedicated to combating such issues.

Transnational terrorism in the Sahel region, close to Cabo Verde, is viewed with particular attention and should be the subject of the necessary defense planning measures. For these identified situations, efforts have been made to obtain a proper capacity for surveillance and control of the jurisdictional space, which is complemented by agreements with friendly and cooperating countries endowed with the capacity for ocean intervention. For example, the CPLP is an instrument that, in the context of defense and national security, develops actions to strengthen its defense and security dimension through Technical-Military Cooperation, Technical-Police Cooperation, and support to Justice, particularly with Portugal. For example, on November 6, 2021, a framework program for Cooperation in Defense was signed between Cabo Verde and Portugal for the period 2021–2026 aimed at training and building capacity in the Armed Forces of Cabo Verde, particularly the Coast Guard. It also states the possibility of exploring, namely the execution of the Treaty concluded in terms of joint supervision, the continuity of the Open Sea Program and the Integrated Program for Reinforcement and Maritime Security (SWAIMS) (Governo de Cabo Verde, November 6, 2021a).

Political-diplomatic consultation, the promotion and dissemination of the Portuguese language, and cooperation in all domains constitute fundamental pillars of the CPLP. Cabo Verde has the privilege of having in Praia, Santiago Island, the headquarters of the International Institute of the Portuguese Language (IILP), which, despite the need to be more dynamic, has as its objectives the planning and execution of promotion, defense, enrichment, and dissemination of the Portuguese language as a vehicle for culture, education, information and access to scientific and technological knowledge and to be used in international forums. A critical point should be highlighted here: the problem of the historical consensus of the Portuguese-speaking area and the possible dysfunctional elements, and the respective destructuring effects they can generate. Details on this are explored in Pedro Borges Graça (2008, p. 137) who draws attention to the lesson of history, including the Present, in a combination of the various factors that substantiate the real difficulties of institutionalizing the CPLP. In summary, the author points to the need to build consensus since we are faced with a common heritage undervalued or devalued most of the time. Moreover, reciprocal images are divergent; public opinion is disconnected; there is an excessive politicization and personalization of the process; and there is a tendentially more expressive Luso-Brazilian dynamics and passivity of Lusophone African Countries. These factors combine and translate into the difficulties of institutionalizing the CPLP, along with those exclusively related to the financial and material feasibility of the project, considering the number and nature of the institutions simultaneously envisaged: Parliament of the Portuguese Speaking Peoples, International Institute of the Portuguese Language, and Arbitration Court.

However, concerning technical-military cooperation projects with Portuguese-speaking Countries, as well as cooperation in the area of defense within the framework of the CPLP, Cabo Verde participates in military exercises carried out on an annual basis, alternating the version of Exercises on the Chart (EC) with that of Forces on the Ground (FT). An example is the 2017 FELINO Exercises, which had their seventeenth edition held in the Military Academy of the Black Needles (AMAN), in Resende, Rio de Janeiro, between the 18th and 29th of September. Military personnel from the nine CPLP member states were present. The Joint and Combined Task Force (FTCC) was composed of representatives of the Brazilian Armed Forces (Navy, Army, and Air Force), in addition to military personnel from Angola, Cabo Verde, Guinea-Bissau, Equatorial Guinea, Mozambique, Portugal, São Tomé and Principe and Timor-Leste (Rizzi and Cruzich 2018).

These exercises represent a multi-dimensional and comprehensive vision of national defense established by the Constitutions of the Member States. In the Cabo Verdean case, the CEDSN also complements the Grand Options of the Plan approved in April 2005 in relation to those contained in the Government's strategic agenda. This contributes to building a "shared vision" of the future, in which the Cabo Verdean Nation successfully overcomes the challenges for its affirmation as a middle-income country, capable of responding to the risks, namely in terms of inspection, informing the population, protecting civilians, and developing defense capabilities.

Regarding Cabo Verde's accession to NATO, a point needs to be clarified. In addition to the USA and Canada, NATO has European countries as members and is essentially intended to improve the coordination between security and defense activities. As an open organization, other European States may join the organization, provided that they fulfill a set of requirements and are in a position to defend the principles contained in the Treaty. They are also required to participate in the debate on NATO's budget and contribute to peace and security in Europe. Also, the countries must not be seen as threatening to their neighbors, and the membership application should be approved unanimously. Outside this scope, NATO has established dialogue and cooperation with other countries. Cabo Verde is not part of NATO, but it could eventually be considered a preferential non-NATO ally. This designation means that the archipelago is close to the countries that make up NATO in political and military terms, which could benefit Cabo Verde in commercial terms through exchanges of services and technologies between the organization's member countries and Cabo Verdean companies. In October 2021, the President of Cabo Verde, José Maria Neves, advocates closer relations with NATO toward a pragmatic, realistic and also intelligent and wider vision of the country's position in the world (VOA, 2021).

Furthermore, Cabo Verde's maritime space could also constitute an important platform for the region where it is located, transforming the Atlantic into a corridor of peace and stability (Madeira and Monteiro 2017), and recognizing that, in addition to the mobility of people and goods, the country's social and economic needs should be addressed. Besides, the region is not limited to the North or the South so that the Geographic West can cover both shores of the entire Atlantic Ocean. In this way, it is possible to figure out why Cabo Verde can serve as a mediator in the tensest situations through strategic support. Due to its insular and archipelagic position and for being a democratic state that respects the rule of law and fundamental rights, the country can contribute and benefit from its contribution in support of defense and security throughout the Atlantic area. However, we consider that it is not plausible that this possibility excludes neighboring countries such as Senegal. Additionally, there is no possibility that it does not involve the installation of a military base of some kind. If so, it presupposes a prior amendment of the CRCV.

Finally, the archipelago should continue highlighting the prestige capital it enjoys, which constitutes one of its most relevant assets (Tolentino 2016). Here, when we refer to being different, we refer to preserving the image that generally stands out of stable political, economic, and social institutions. Also noteworthy is that the country values good governance, democracy, respect for human rights, socioeconomic development, and regional integration, meeting the population's needs without exclusions. We believe that this is the most effective way of taking advantage of the geographic location, dealing with its vulnerabilities, and being a useful country (Tolentino 2016). Building partnerships with States, international organizations, and agencies that contribute to implementing policies and respecting principles and values is essential to ensure that citizens can live with the security and dignity to which they are entitled.

References

Amante da Rosa, Manuel. (2007). Geoestratégia de Cabo Verde no Atlântico Médio. *Revista Direito e Cidadania* 25/26, pp. 163–187.

Carvalho, Josiane Rocha; Nunes, Raul Cavedon. (2014). A ZOPACAS no contexto da geopolítica do Atlântico Sul: história e desafios atuais. *Revista Perspetiva* 7, 13, 83–102.

CEDSN. (2011). Council of Ministers. Resolution nº 5/2011. January 17. Approves the Strategic Concept of National Defense and Security. I Series, no 3: 129–140. https://kiosk.incv.cv/V/2011/1/17/1.1.3.37/p129.

Célèrier, Pierre. (1969). *Géopolitique et Géostratégie*. Paris: Presses Universitaires de France.

Chaves, Duarte Nuno. (2020). *Questões de Identidade Insular na Macaronésia*. Ponta Delgada: Santa Casa da Misericórdia das Velas & CHAM – Centro de Humanidades.

Costa, Suzano, and Pinto, Jorge Nobre. (2014). A Política Externa Cabo-verdiana num Mundo Multipolar: entre a Ambivalência Prática e a Retórica Discursiva? In: Delgado, J. P., Varela, O. B., and Costa, S. (orgs.). *As Relações Externas de Cabo Verde: (Re)leituras Contemporâneas*, pp. 163–228. Praia: ISCJS.

CPLP. (2019). Documento Estratégico de Cooperação da CPLP 2020–2026. Retrieved on 1 March 2022, from https://www.cplp.org/id-4176.aspx.

Dabo, Alberto. (2022). Guinea-Bissau president: Failed coup may have been linked to drug trade. *Reuters*, 2 February.

Deutsche Welle. (2019). CPLP: Maioria dos países com quotas em atraso, 14 novembro. Retrieved on 1 March 2022, from https://www.dw.com/pt-002/cplp-maioria-dos-pa%C3%ADses-com-quotas-em-atraso/a-51246146.

Dias, Carlos Manuel Mendes. (2005). *Geopolítica: Teorização Clássica e Ensinamentos*. Lisboa: Prefácio.

Encel, Frédéric. (2011). *Comprendre la géopolitique*. Paris: Éditions du Seuil.
EU. (2007). Communication from the Commission to the Council and the European Parliament on the future of relations between the European Union and the Republic of Cape Verde. Brussels, 24.10.2007 COM (2007) 641 final. Retrieved on 1 March 2022, from https://eur-lex.europa.eu/legal-content/EN/TXT/?uri=CELEX:52007DC0641.
Évora, Maurino. (2014). A Evolução do Processo de Securitização do Narcotráfico em Cabo Verde: Das Limitações do Estado à Displicência da Sociedade Civil. In: Delgado,
J. P., Varela, O. B., and Costa, S. (orgs.). *As Relações Externas de Cabo Verde: (Re)leituras Contemporâneas*, pp. 451–473. Praia: ISCJS.
Expresso das Ilhas/LUSA. (2019). Primeiro-ministro admite adesão de Cabo Verde à NATO, 30 july. Retrieved on 1 March 2022, from https://expressodasilhas.cv/politica/2019/07/30/primeiro-ministro-admite-adesao-de-cabo-verde-a-nato/64977.
Ferreira Ivete Silves, and Madeira, João Paulo. (2020). China and the Great Urban Projects in Cabo Verde. In: Leandro F., Duarte, P. (eds). The Belt and Road Initiative. An Old Archetype of a New Development Model, pp. 343–362. Singapore: Palgrave Macmillan.
Fortes, Gracinda Marísia da Cruz. (2014). A dimensão marítima da segurança nacional : os desafios do Arquipélago de Cabo Verde. Dissertação de Mestrado em Ciência Política e Relações Internacionais. Lisboa: Universidade Nova de Lisboa.
Freedom House. (2021). Freedom in the World. Retrieved on 1 March 2022, from https://freedomhouse.org/country/cabo-verde/freedom-world/2021.
Garcia, Francisco Proença. (2017). Cabo Verde e o Espaço do Atlântico. *Austral: Revista Brasileira de Estratégia e Relações Internacionais* 6, 11, pp. 99–117.
Governo de Cabo Verde. (2009). Cabo Verde comemora um ano de adesão à OMC. 20 July. Retrieved on 1 March 2022, from https://www.governo.cv/cabo-verde-comemora-um-ano-de-adesao-a-omc/.
Governo de Cabo Verde. (2021a). Cabo Verde e Portugal assinam programa-quadro de Cooperação no domínio da Defesa para período de 2021–2026. 06 November. Retrieved on 1 March 2022, from https://www.governo.cv/cabo-verde-e-portugal-assinam-programa-quadro-de-cooperacao-no-dominio-da-defesa-para-periodo-de-2021-2026/.
Governo de Cabo Verde. (2021b). Governo recebe novo Campus Universitário da UNI- CV. 23 July. Retrieved on 1 March 2022, from https://www.governo.cv/governo-recebe-novo-campus-universitario-da-uni-cv/.
Graça, Camilo Leitão da. (2014). A Noção de "Pragmatismo" na Política Externa de Cabo Verde: Interesse Nacional e Opções Identitárias. In: Delgado, J. P., Varela, O. B., and Costa, S. (orgs.). *As Relações Externas de Cabo Verde: (Re)leituras Contemporâneas*, pp. 267–283. Praia: ISCJS.

Graça, Pedro Borges. (2008). O Problema do Consenso Histórico na Área Lusófona. *Revista de Ciências Sociais e Políticas* 2, pp. 123–139.

Gray, Colin S. (1999). *Modern Strategy*. Oxford: Oxford University Press.

Guedes, Armando Marques. (2012). Da desregulação ao recentramento no Atlãntico Sul, e a construção da "Lusofonia". *Janus.net, e-journal of International Relations* 3, 1, pp. 1–37.

Hill, Geoff. (2021). United States and China chess up in Africa's smallest country: Cape Verde. Modern Diplomacy. 11 August. Retrieved on 1 March 2022, from https://moderndiplomacy.eu/2021/08/11/united-states-and-china-chess-up-in-africas-smallest-country-cape-verde/.

IAEM. (2000). Geografia, Geopolítica e Geoestragégia: Realidade Geopolítica. NC 71–00–15. Lisboa: IAEM.

INE. (2021). V Recenseamento Geral da População e Habitação (RGPH—2021). Resultados Definitivos. Praia: INE.

Inforpress. (2021). Cabo Verde quer aproximar-se da NATO para melhorar a segurança—Primeiro-Ministro. 06 November. Retrieved on 1 March 2022, from https://inforpress.cv/cabo-verde-quer-aproximar-se-da-nato-para-melhorar-a-seguranca-primeiro-ministro/.

Inforpress. (2020). Estados-membros devem à CPLP 3,8 ME em quotas, com Brasil a liderar. 15 March. Retrieved on 1 March 2022, from https://inforpress.cv/estados-membros-devem-a-cplp-38-me-em-quotas-com-brasil-a-liderar/.

Lilyblad, Christopher Marc. (2020). Cape Verde Is Emerging as a Global Pivot Point. Foreign Policy. 20 October. Retrieved on 1 March 2022, from https://foreignpolicy.com/2020/10/20/cape-verde-is-emerging-as-a-global-pivot-point/.

Madeira, João Paulo. (2015). Cape Verde: Geopolitics and Projection of a Small Island State in West Africa. *Austral: Brazilian Journal of Strategy & International Relations* 4, 8, pp. 58–77.

Madeira, João Paulo. (2016a). A morabeza cabo-verdiana: contributos para a sua análise. *Revista de Estudos Cabo-verdianos*, Atas IV EIRI, Número Especial, pp. 51–56.

Madeira, João Paulo. (2016b). Cabo Verde: De um "Estado inviável" ao Pragmatismo na Política Externa. *Revista de Relaciones Internacionales, Estrategia y Seguridad* 11, 1, pp. 85–101.

Madeira, João Paulo. (2017). The Dragon Embraces Africa: Cape Verde-China Relations. *Austral: Brazilian Journal of Strategy & International Relations* 6, 12, pp. 127–141.

Madeira, João Paulo. (2018). *Nação e Identidade - A singularidade de Cabo Verde*. Praia: Pedro Cardoso Livraria.

Madeira, João Paulo. (2019a). Política Externa Cabo-verdiana: evolução, perspetivas e linhas de força. *Revista de Relações Internacionais da PUC Minas* 7, 1, pp. 87–109.

Madeira, João Paulo. (2019b). Security Challenges for Small Island Developing States: The Case of Cape Verde. *Revista de Relaciones Internacionales, Estrategia y Seguridad* 14, 2, pp. 155–177.

Madeira, João Paulo. (2021). Cabo Verde e Estados Unidos da América: uma ligação bicentenária. *Janus.net, e-journal of International Relations* 12, 2, pp. 94–113.

Madeira, João Paulo, and Monteiro, Nataniel. (2017). Cabo Verde na segurança e defesa do Atlântico: Dimensões da parceria Norte-Sul e Sul-Sul. *Revista Geográfica Venezolana* 58, 1, pp. 102–117.

Madeira, João Paulo e Reis, and Bruno Carriço. (2018). A construção da democracia em Cabo Verde: do condicionalismo colonial português ao reconhecimento internacional. Notas. *Janus.net, e-journal of International Relations* 9, 1, pp. 183–198.

Marchueta, Maria Regina. (2003). *A CPLP e o seu enquadramento.* Lisboa: Ministério dos Negócios Estrangeiros.

Matos, Antero. (2014). A Visão Integrada da Segurança no Conceito Estratégico de Defesa e Segurança Nacional. In: Delgado, J. P., Varela, O. B., and Costa, S. (orgs.). *As Relações Externas de Cabo Verde: (Re)leituras Contemporâneas*, pp. 425–449. Praia: ISCJS.

Monteiro, Nataniel Andrade. (2016). África, a nova fronteira estratégica no desenvolvimento global: A geo-política de Cabo Verde no contexto da CEDEAO. *Revista de Relaciones Internacionales, Estrategia y Seguridad* 11, 2: 93–109.

National Assembly. (2016). Law nº 120/VIII/2016, March 24. Establishes measures to prevent and repress the crime of laundering money, assets, rights and values. I Series, nº 3: 749–792. https://kiosk.incv.cv/V/2016/3/24/1.1.21.2165/p729.

National Assembly. (2016). Law n.º 119/VIII/2016, March 24. Establishes preventive and repressive measures against terrorism, its functioning and organization. I Series, nº 21: 729–749. https://kiosk.incv.cv/V/2016/3/24/1.1.21.2165/p729.

National Assembly. (2020). Law nº 94/IX/2020, June 13. Establishes the Special Maritime Economic Zone in São Vicente, abbreviated ZEEMSV or Special Economic Zone in São Vicente and establishes the special legal regime for its organization, development and functioning. I Series, nº 82: 1644–1653. https://kiosk.incv.cv/V/2020/7/13/1.1.82.3314/p1644.

Neves, Danielson Jorge Delgado et al. (2017). Aspectos gerais do clima do arquipélago de Cabo Verde. *Ambiência - Revista do Setor de Ciências Agrárias e Ambientais* 13, 1, pp. 59–73.

OBE, Alex Vines, and Wallace, Jon. (2021). Terrorism in Africa. 15 September. Chatham House. Retrieved on 1 March 2022, from https://www.chathamhouse.org/2021/09/terrorism-africa.

Pimentel, Cauê Rodrigues. (2016). O ressurgimento da ZOPACAS e a agenda de segurança no Atlântico Sul. *Tensões Mundiais* 12, 22, pp. 113–143.

Pinto, José Filipe. (2008). Adimplendum est hodie. *Africanologia: Revista Lusófona de Estudos Africanos* 1, pp. 1–14.

Pinto, José Filipe. (2009). *Estratégias da ou para a Lusofonia? O Futuro da Língua Portuguesa.* Lisboa: Prefácio.

Portugal Digital. (2015), Cabo Verde acolhe Encontro da Zona de Paz do Atlântico Sul. 16 May. Retrieved on 1 March 2022, from https://portugaldigital.com.br/cabo-verde-acolhe-encontro-da-zona-de-paz-do-atlantico-sul/.

Reis, Carlos. (2014). Cabo Verde/NATO: Que Relações. In: Delgado, J. P., Varela, O. B., and Costa, S. (orgs.). *As Relações Externas de Cabo Verde: (Re)leituras Contemporâneas*, pp. 553–564. Praia: ISCJS.

Rizzi, Kamilla Raquel e Cruzichi, Isabella. (2018). Os Exercícios Felino 2017 e a cooperação em defesa e segurança na CPLP. *Boletim de Conjuntura - NERINT* 3, 8, pp. 7–15.

Rodrigues, Nilton Delgado. (2016). Polícia Nacional de Cabo Verde: análise histórica e de competências. Integrated Master's Thesis in Police Sciences. XXVIII Training Course for Police Officers . Lisboa: ISCPSI.

Sistema de Segurança Nacional. (2013). Conselho de Ministros. Decreto-Lei nº. 51/2013, de 20 de dezembro. Diploma que estabelece o Sistema de Segurança Nacional. 2277- 2281. Retrieved on 1 March 2022, from https://kiosk.incv.cv/V/2013/12/20/1.1.69.1778/p2277.

Tolentino, André Corsino. (2013). A Difícil Integração Africana. In: Sarmento, C. M., and Costa, S. (orgs.). *Entre a África e a Europa: Nação, Estado e Democracia em Cabo Verde*, pp. 609–622. Coimbra: Almedina.

Tolentino, Jorge. (2016). Tempos de InCertezas. Praia: Spleen Edições.

Tolentino, Jorge. (2019). *Estados Unidos da América e Cabo Verde: Uma Parceria Histórica e Estratégica.* Praia: Arnaldo França Livraria.

U.S. Department of State. (2021). Secretary Blinken's Call with Cabo Verdean Minister of Foreign Affairs and Defense Figueiredo. 23 February. Retrieved on 1 March 2022, from https://www.state.gov/secretary-blinkens-call-with-cabo-verdean-minister-of-foreign-affairs-and-defense-figueiredo/.

U.S. Embassy in Cabo Verde. (2021). Article by U.S. Ambassador to Cabo Verde, Jeff Daigle – Land Dedication. 30 June. Retrieved on 1 March 2022, from https://cv.usembassy.gov/article-by-u-s-ambassador-to-cabo-verde-jeff-daigle-land-dedication/.

UIF - Unidade de Informação Financeira. (2017). Cabo Verde é um país de "elevado risco" em matéria de lavagem de capitais e financiamento do terrorismo. 25 November. Retrieved on 1 March 2022, from http://www.uif.gov.cv/index.php?option=com_content&view=article&id=14:onad-cv-participa-no-2-congresso-mundial-de-nutricao-e-prevencao-da-obesidade-em-londres&catid=14&Itemid=108.

UNODC. (2019). Grande operação de drogas pelas autoridades cabo-verdianas apreende com sucesso 9,5 toneladas de cocaína na Praia. 5 July. Retrieved on 1 March 2022, from https://www.unodc.org/westandcentralafrica/pt/2019-02-05-massive-cocaine-seizure-in-cabo-verde.html.

Varela, Odair Bartolomeu Barros Lopes. (2007). A Encruzilhada da Defesa e Segurança no Atlântico Médio: Cabo Verde entre a "Espada" da NATO e a "Parede" Africana? *Revista Direito e Cidadania* VII, 25/26, pp. 219–248.

VOA Português—Voz da America. (2021). José Maria Neves: "Cabo Verde só tem importância estratégica se estiver ancorado em África". 26 October. Retrieved on 1 March 2022, from https://www.voaportugues.com/a/presidente-eleito-cabo-verde-s%C3%B3-tem-import%C3%A2ncia-estrat%C3%A9gica-se-estiver-devidamente-ancorado-em-%C3%A1frica/6285562.html.

VOA Português—Voz da America. (2019). Cabo Verde e a adesão à NATO: Constituição tem de mudar. 31 July. Retrieved on 1 March 2022, from https://www.voaportugues.com/a/cabo-verde-e-a-adesao-%C3%A0-nato-constitui%C3%A7%C3%A3o-tem-de-mudar/5023663.html.

Mozambique Geopolitics in the Lusophone World: Challenges and Perspectives

Emilio J. Zeca

Introduction

Mozambique is a State that emerged in the International System in 1975, after proclaiming its National Independence from the Portuguese Colonial System. In the Postcolonial Period which held the process of its State Building, Mozambique had several national and international experiences influenced by its geopolitical factors, therefore, this chapter discusses about the challenges and perspectives of Mozambique's geopolitics in the Lusophone world. It analyzes the contours of challenges and perspectives of Mozambique geopolitics in the Lusophone World, focusing on the period between 1992 and 2020. It also analyzes the Mozambican geopolitical factors with emphasis on human, economic, circulation and military factor, as elements of attainment, maintenance and projection of Mozambican national power in the contemporary international system.

In 1992, after the signing of the General Peace Agreement—AGP, which ended one of the most destructive wars in Africa, Mozambique

E. J. Zeca (✉)
Center for Strategic and International Studies – CEEI/UJC, University Joaquim Chissano, Maputo, Mozambique
e-mail: emilio.zeca@ujc.ac.mz

P. A. B. Duarte et al. (eds.), *Portugal and the Lusophone World*,
https://doi.org/10.1007/978-981-99-0455-6_17

began a process of international strategic insertion. In this process, the Lusophone World had a privileged place and the Mozambique's Foreign Policy proposed to maintain special ties of friendship and cooperation with countries whose official language is Portuguese and with countries that host Mozambican emigrants. In this context, the Lusophone World became a space of national strategic interest and an opportunity to operationalize the national strategic and geopolitical potential. Thus, this study is guided by the following research question: what are the challenges and perspectives of Mozambique geopolitics in the Lusophone world?

The question above is answered with a study based on a qualitative methodology research, supported by the historical method, the document research, the systematic desktop review and the content analysis. The theoretical framework uses the Geopolitical Analysis Model that match human, economic, circulation and military factor, as elements of attainment, maintenance and State projection in international system (Leal 2007, pp. 233–285; Martín 2016, pp. 21–26; Wache 2019, pp. 155–172). This text has a structure divided in four blocks, namely, brief historical of Mozambique; geopolitics, defence and security in Mozambique; international strategic insertion of Mozambique in the Lusophone World; opportunities and challenges for Mozambique in the Lusophone World.

Brief History of Mozambique

Mozambique is a State located in Southern Africa and was a Portuguese colony until 1975. The contemporary history of Mozambique is marked by three historical periods: the first historical period covers the National Liberation Struggle, led by FRELIMO—Liberation Front of Mozambique against the Portuguese Colonial Regime. The second historical period covers the post-Independence moment, marked by the existence of one-party system, Socialism and Marxist-Leninist orientation. The third historical period covers the Post-General Peace Agreement, marked by the implementation of a guided liberal and democratic system. These three periods must be analyzed as sequential and not isolated analytical blocks.

In Mozambique, the National Liberation Struggle took place between 1964 and 1974. In 1962, in Dar Es-Salaam, Tanzania, FRELIMO emerged as a result of merger from three nationalist movements, namely, National Democratic Union of Mozambique—UDENAMO, Mozambique African National Union—MANU and African National Union of

Independent Mozambique—UNAMI. The National Liberation Struggle ended, in 1974, with the signing of *Acordos de Lusaka* (an agreement), signed in Zambia, between the Portuguese State and FRELIMO, as the legitimate representative of the Mozambican People. The colonial power was transferred to FRELIMO through a Transitional Government, that ruled until the proclamation of National Independence on June 25, 1975.

After the proclamation of National Independence, Mozambique was marked by national euphoria, resulting from the collapse of the Portuguese Colonial Regime and the powers transfer to FRELIMO. In this euphoria, in 1976, has been registered the first armed attacks by RENAMO supported by Rhodesian Forces of the Government of Ian Smith against the Mozambique. The Ian Smith's Rhodesian Intelligence Services formed, armed and guided strategically and militarily RENAMO (Antunes 1996) until 1980. The independence of Zimbabwe in 1980, changed the situation and RENAMO gained support from the Apartheid Regime established in South Africa. The Apartheid regime welcomed RENAMO, because FRELIMO supported the African National Congress (ANC) struggle against the racist and segregationist regime in South Africa. To solve this problem, Mozambique and South Africa signed the Nkomati Agreement, in 1984. It was a peace, security and good neighbourliness agreement, where Apartheid pledged to stop supporting RENAMO and the Government of Mozambique would do the same to the ANC, but both parties did not comply with the agreement and the war continued until the beginning of the 1990s.

In 1977, FRELIMO held its 3rd Congress where the socialist and Marxist-Leninist model was adopted as a form of organizing the State, Society and FRELIMO Party. The transformation of FRELIMO into a Marxist-Leninist Party was a strategy for the Government of Mozambique to have access to COMECON—Council for Mutual Economic Assistance. However, the request to join these mechanisms of socialist cooperation was refused, because Mozambique was considered a State with a socialist orientation and not a Socialist State. To deal with this situation, Mozambican decided to realign its economic, ideological policy and Foreign Policy. Thus, the Mozambican Government allied to the West countries and joined the Bretton Woods Institutions—World Bank and International Monetary Fund. So, the Mozambique's decision to join the World Bank and IMF brought with it Structural Adjustment Programs and social, economic and political changes.

The civil/destabilization war reached its escalation stage in the mid-1980s. Worn out by the effects of the war, the Mozambican Government, led by FRELIMO, and RENAMO concluded that the armed way would not be the best way to solve their problem and it was a time to start a political negotiation. The negotiation process started at the end of 1980s and extended until the 1990s, ending with the General Peace Agreement—AGP, in Rome, on October 4, 1992. Before the signing of the AGP, the Government of Mozambique initiated a process of political, economic and social reforms, influenced by the Structural Adjustment Programs. Thus, in 1990, Mozambique adopted a new Constitution that introduced multiparty political system, free elections and universal suffrage, liberal economy, respect and promotion of civil, economic and political rights. The AGP came to embody these rights creating non-partisan Armed Forces, Police and Intelligence Services.

The Post-General Peace Agreement period was marked by national reconstruction efforts, creation of stable and durable peace and international insertion of Mozambique in the concert of nations, within the logic of the Post-Cold War. With support of United Nations—ONUMOZ—the first general and multiparty elections took place in 1994. Subsequently, Mozambique organized general elections in 2009, 2014 and 2019, won by FRELIMO and its presidential candidates, namely, Joaquim Alberto Chissano, Armando Guebuza and Filipe Jacinto Nyusi. Between two decades, Mozambique experienced a situation of stable peace and was considered an example of war to peace transition, resorting to the implementation of the democratic model and multiparty elections. Unfortunately, in 2012, the political violence returned through the Military Political Tension, with a small interregnum, where were signed two peace agreement: Agreement for the Cessation of Military Hostilities (2014) and National Peace and Reconciliation Agreement (2019).

In October 2017, an irregular insurgency began in Cabo Delgado Province (Northern Mozambique), where high quantities of natural gas were discovered putting Mozambique in the global geopolitics of natural gas. Nevertheless, the few studies on this issue, the insurgency is carried out by a group called *Ansar al-Sunna wa al-jama'ah*. The group is guided by the principles of Sunism (Morier-Genoud 2021, p. 11), with Salafist and Wahhabite roots. The actions of this insurgent group combine guerrilla, terrorism, political mobilization, religious instrumentalization, propaganda, recruitment, clandestine actions and transnational jihadism.

These acts seek to weaken the state's capacity for controlling this region and increase the legitimacy of the insurgents. Since 2019, this terrorist group has had direct support from the Islamic State (ISIS), through the Central Africa Province (IS-CAP). Since this time, the Islamic State propaganda bodies have indicated that the Cabo Delgado insurgents have been accepted into the Islamic State's Central African Province and claim the attacks taking place in this region.

Geopolitics, Defence and Security in Mozambique

The contemporary history of Mozambique is marked by attacks against the physical base of the State and national efforts to guarantee its existence and survival. In this context, Mozambican geopolitics has been oriented towards dealing with disputes for power resulting from the meanings that are given to the different spaces that need to be preserved, taking into account situations of internal and external aggression (remnants of PIDE/DGS, Southern Rhodesia aggressions, RENAMO and Apartheid), which Mozambique experienced in the process of State building and consolidation. This effort can fit into the geopolitical vision of famous Brazilian General Carlos de Meira Mattos (1913–2007), who mentioned that "geopolitics is the policy applied to geographic spaces under the inspiration of historical experience". In other words, we can refer geopolitics as "the study of the relationship between politics and space" (Dias 2010, p. 19). In the relationship between politics and its geographical spaces, Mozambique has a complex geopolitical factor. In geopolitical analysis models, scholars favoured the physical, human, economic, circulation and military factor, as determining elements that "positive or negatively influence the state power attainment, maintenance and projection" (Wache 2019, p. 155).

In terms of physical geopolitical factors, Mozambique has a territory of 801.590 km^2. The Mozambican state is located in South-eastern Africa bordered by the Indian Ocean to the east, Tanzania to the north, Malawi and Zambia to the northwest, Zimbabwe to the west, and Swaziland and South Africa to the southwest. Its hydrographic network is mostly made up of international rivers flowing towards the Indian Ocean. In terms of inland waters, Mozambique has four notable lakes, namely, Niassa Lake, shared with Tanzania and Malawi, Chiuta Lake, Amaramba Lake and Chirua Lake, all in the north. The Indian Ocean bathes the Mozambican coast in an extension of 2.470 km, being a source of marine resources and several maritime threats, such as unreported and unregulated illegal fishing, maritime border disputes, drug trafficking and illegal immigration by sea, trafficking in resources and seabed's; maritime terrorism and other military, non-military and hybrid threats. In Mozambique, the humid and tropical climate predominates, influenced by monsoons and warm currents of the Mozambique Channel. The relief is formed by plateaus and mountains, in the interior, and plains, towards the sea (Chichango 2009, pp. 13–16).

In terms of human geopolitical factor, Mozambique has a population around 30 million habitants and population density of 34.8 inhabitants/km^2. There are several ethnic, linguistic, cultural and religious groups in Mozambique, where predominates the Bantu peoples (97.80%). The remaining part of population is composed by white African people of Portuguese origin, Euro-Africans and Indians (Singhvi 2000, p. 94). In terms of religious practices, 56.10% are Christians; 18.70% don't practice any religion; 17.90% are Muslims; and 1.20% practice African Traditional Religions. Portuguese is the official language of the State, but there are others native languages, namely, Macua, in the North region; Sena, in the Centre region; and Tsonga, in the southern region.

In terms of geopolitical resources factor, Mozambique has several mineral and energy resources: coal; precious, ornamental and semi-precious stones; gold; graphite; mineral water; gabbro; agates; tourmaline, rose quartz; uranium; iron; copper; black granite; limestone; vanadium; fluorite and others resources. The Cahora-Bassa Hydroelectric Power Plant is located in Tete Province and is one of the largest dams in Africa and eighteenth in the world, with a maximum annual production of 18.000 GWh of energy. In 2012, natural gas was discovered, in large quantities, approximately, 4.200 billion cubic metres (150 trillion cubic feet), in the offshore area of the Rovuma Basin, in Cabo Delgado. This discovery could make Mozambique one of the largest producers of liquefied natural gas in the world. The natural gas is already explored by SASOL, in the Districts of Pande and Temane, in Inhambane Province.

In terms of economic geopolitical factor, in the Republic of Mozambique, agriculture shall be the basis for national development. The State shall guarantee and promote rural development in order to meet the growing and diverse needs of the people, and for the economic and social progress of the country (Article 103, Mozambique's Constitution of 2018). Regarding the circulation geopolitical factor, Mozambique has a National Road (N1) that connects the national territory from Rovuma to Maputo. The Mozambique Channel is the principal maritime communication route. The Mozambican railway system is a colonial heritage and links the national ports (Maputo, Beira and Nacala) with the hinterland Commonwealth neighbours (Zimbabwe, Zambia and Malawi). The Mozambican ports and railways system are parts of SADC development corridors. Between Mozambique and Zimbabwe, there is an oil pipeline for the transport of refined petroleum products, from Port of Beira to Zimbabwe, managed by the Mozambique-Zimbabwe Pipeline Company.

In terms of Defence and Security Sector and military geopolitical factor, the National Security architecture is oriented by the Mozambique's Constitution and Defence and Security Policy, approved by Act 17/97, October 1 and revised by Act 12/2019, September 24. This security architecture is composed by Armed Forces, in Portuguese, *Forças Armadas de Defesa de Moçambique* (FADM), Police of the Republic of Mozambique—PRM and the State Information and Security Service, in Portuguese, *Serviço de Informações e Segurança do Estado* (SISE). These legal instruments establish that "Mozambique does not have a paramilitary force" (Macuácua 2006, p. 149) and the Mozambique's Defence and Security Sector consists of these three forces.

According to de Articles 145 and 264 of Mozambique's Constitution (2018), the President of the Republic is the Commander-in-Chief of the Defence and Security Forces and is advised by the National Council for Defence and Security, a consultation and advisory body to the President of the Republic, in matters related to Defence and National Security.

> The National Defence and Security Council shall be the State consultative body for matters pertaining to national sovereignty, territorial integrity, the defence of democratically established authority, and security. The National Defence and Security Council shall be Chaired by the President of the Republic and the law shall determine its composition, which shall include two members appointed by the President of the Republic and five members appointed by the Assembly of the Republic. The National Defence and Security shall have the following powers, in particular: to pronounce upon a state of war before such is declared; to pronounce upon the suspension of constitutional guarantees and the declaration of a state of siege or of a state of emergency; to issue an opinion on the criteria and conditions governing the use of total or partial protection zones for the purposes of defence and security of the national territory; to analyse and monitor the initiatives of other State offices aimed at guaranteeing the consolidation of national independence, the strengthening of democratic political power,

> and the maintaining of law and order; and to pronounce upon overseas peace missions. (Articles 264 and 265 Articles, Mozambique's Constitution 2018)

The Mozambican Armed Forces—FADM were created by the Protocol IV—"*On Military Issues*"—of the General Peace Agreement of 1992. According to Adriano Malache, Paulino Macaringue and Paulo Borges Coelho (2005) refer, in your text "*Profound Transformations and Regional Conflagrations: The History of Mozambique's Armed Forces from 1975/2005*", published in the book "*Evolutions and Revolutions: A Contemporary History of Militaries in Southern Africa*", edited by Martin Rupiya, that "The origin of the Mozambican armed forces can be found in the liberation struggle against Portuguese colonial occupation" (Malache et al. 2005, p. 155). In the same text, these authors add that:

> The creation of the Mozambican Armed Forces was the leitmotif of post-colonial nation building; and the force that exists today – the Armed Forces for the Defence of Mozambique (FADM) – is a product of the 1992 political settlement and its provisions. Mozambique's recent history has created formidable challenges when it comes to attempts to professionalise its armed forces. As a result, the FADM is torn between the 'push' of its socio-political guerrilla heritage (the party) and the 'pull' of the need for a new and preferred apolitical, professional ethos. (Malache et al. 2005, p. 155)

The General Peace Agreement of 1992 refers that FADM was constituted to ensure the National Defence, safeguarding of Sovereignty, Independence and Territorial Integrity. In this context, the FADM were created on non-partisan with 30.000 soldiers: 24,000 from Army; 4.000 from the Air Force; and 2000 from Navy. The soldiers would come from FAM/FPLM (Governmental Forces) and RENAMO Forces, in the proportion of 50% for each side. The definition, responsibility and mission of FADM were further defined by Act 17/97, October 1, which approves the Defence and Security Policy Act, revised by Act 12/2019, September 23 and Act 18/97, October 1, which approves the Law on National Defence and Armed Forces for the Defence of Mozambique, revised by Act 18/2019, September 24.

According to the Defence and Security Policy Act approved by Act 17/97, October 1, the National Defence is the activity carried out by the

State and the citizens, which aims to ensure independence and national unity, preserve sovereignty; the integrity and inviolability of the country and guarantee the normal functioning of institutions and the security of citizens against any threat or armed aggression. The military component of National Defence is ensured by the Armed Forces for the Defence of Mozambique (FADM) and the non-military component through the other State organs. The President of the Republic is responsible for the superior direction of the war, in his capacity as Commander-in-Chief. In a State of Siege or State of War, the Defence and Security Forces are placed, for operational purposes, under the command of the Chief of the General Staff of the Armed Forces, who is responsible for the military conduct of the war. Thus, the Armed Forces have fundamentally the following missions:

> [...] to defend the vital interests of the country against all forms of threat or aggression; guarantee the integrity of the national territory, the sovereignty, the freedom of the citizens and the security of the Nation means of development; ensure the normal functioning of the institutions in all circumstances and in the face of any direct or indirect threats; participate in the protection of bodies, installations or civilian means that are decisive for the maintenance of the populations lives, as well as take preventive and relief measures that are required in certain circumstances by decision of the competent authority; participate in actions aimed at maintaining peace and respect for international law; contribute to the defence and security of the region and the continent by supporting actions to prevent and solve conflicts; and ensure the defence of the national territory against all types of threats, including terrorism. (Article 10, Act 12/2019, September 23)

The Mozambican Police Forces were created during the Transitional Government, as a Police Corps. Later, they became Popular Police of Mozambique—PPM, during the one-party and socialism system. The Protocol IV of General Peace Agreement created the Police of the Republic of Mozambique—PRM, as a non-partisan and paramilitary police force, with the mission of guaranteeing public security, order and public tranquillity. By the Act 19/92, December 31, the PRM replaced the Popular Police of Mozambique—PPM. Thus, the function of the Mozambican Police in collaboration with other State institutions

> [...] shall be to guarantee law and order, to safeguard persons and property security, to keep public peace and to ensure respect for the democratic rule of law and the strict observance of the fundamental rights and freedoms of citizens. The Police shall not adhere to any particular party. In the exercise of its functions, the Police shall owe obedience to the law and shall serve citizens and public and private institutions with impartiality and independence. The Police of the Republic of Mozambique shall be headed by a General Commander. The law shall establish the general organization of the Police and shall determine its branches, functions, structure and the rules regarding admission into the Police". (Articles 253 and 254, Mozambique's Constitution 2018)

According to the Defence and Security Policy Act, approved by Act 17/97, October 1, revised by Act 12/2019, September 23, the Internal Security is the activity carried out by the State to guarantee public order, security and tranquillity, protect people and property, prevent crime, contribute ensuring the normal functioning of institutions, the exercise of citizens' fundamental rights, freedoms and respect for the Constitution and legality. The Public order, security and tranquillity are ensured by the Police of the Republic of Mozambique and other institutions created by law, to support the society in general. Thus, the missions in the field of public order, security and tranquillity are:

> [...] to ensure respect for legality, taking appropriate measures to prevent and combat crime and other acts contrary to the law; guarantee the necessary measures for the borders surveillance, as well as the control of people and goods movement across them; guarantee public order, the citizens security, as well as the protection of their property and promote police measures; guarantee the personal protection and safety of high national and foreign entities, as well as other persons, when subject to situations of relevant threat; and ensure the necessary information to the public about crime and the actions carried out in the context of public order and security, and carry out educational programs that contribute to increasing the participation of citizens in preventing and combating crime. (Article 13, Act 12/2019, September 23)

In Mozambique, the intelligence service is framed in State Security Sector. According to Articles 15, 16, 17, 18 and 19 of Act 12/2019, September 1, the State Security is the activity carried out by the State aimed at ensuring, in compliance with the Constitution and the law, the production of information necessary to safeguard national independence, to guarantee national security, the functioning of sovereign bodies and other institutions within the framework of constitutional normality and the protection of the vital interests of society. The State Information and Security Service—SISE is the body responsible for collecting, researching, producing, analyzing and evaluating information useful to the State security, preventing acts that violate the Constitution, against the functioning of the State power organs, State fight against espionage, sabotage and terrorism. Therefore, research activities, processing and dissemination of information comply with the provisions of the Constitution and the law, namely with regard to guarantees of the rights and of citizen's freedom. In Mozambique, it is forbidden for other services to pursue the objectives and activities reserved for SISE, but this orientation does not affect the activities carried out by the services responsible for the research, production and processing of strategic information of a military or police nature from operational nature, necessary for the mission's performance assigned to them.

Finally, in terms of international relations and diplomacy principles, Articles 17 and 22 of Mozambique's Constitution (2018) establish that:

> The Republic of Mozambique shall establish relations of friendship and cooperation with other States on the basis of mutual respect for sovereignty and territorial integrity, equality, non-interference in internal affairs and reciprocity of benefits. The Republic of Mozambique shall accept, observe and apply the principles of the Charter from the United Nations and from the Organization of African Unity. Validly approved and ratified, international treaties and agreements shall enter into force in the Mozambican legal order once they have been officially published and while they are internationally binding on the Mozambican State. Norms of international law shall have the same force in the Mozambican legal order as have infra-constitutional legislative acts from the Assembly of the Republic and the Government, according to the respective manner in which they are received. The Republic of Mozambique shall be in solidarity with the struggle of the peoples and States of Africa, for unity, freedom, dignity and the right to economic and social progress. The Republic of Mozambique shall seek to strengthen relations with countries engaged in the consolidation of their national independence, democracy and the recovery of their natural wealth use and control for their respective peoples. The Republic of Mozambique shall join with all States struggling for the establishment of a just and equitable economic order in international relations. The Republic of Mozambique shall support and be in solidarity with

> the people struggles for their national liberation and for democracy. The Republic of Mozambique shall grant asylum to foreigners persecuted on the grounds of their struggle for national liberation, for democracy, for peace and for the protection of human rights. The law shall define political refugee status. The Republic of Mozambique shall maintain special ties of friendship and cooperation with the countries of the region, with countries whose official language is Portuguese and with countries that host Mozambican emigrants. The Republic of Mozambique shall pursue a policy of peace and shall only resort to the use of force in the case of legitimate self-defence. The Republic of Mozambique shall support the primacy of negotiated solutions to conflicts. The Republic of Mozambique shall uphold the principle of general and universal disarmament of all States. The Republic of Mozambique shall advocate the transformation of the Indian Ocean into a nuclear free zone of peace.

The Resolution 32/2010, of August 30, approves the "White Paper" of Mozambique's Foreign Policy, which is based on the principle of "making more friends, avoiding enemies and diversifying partnerships". Mozambique's Foreign Policy includes bilateral, regional, multilateral cooperation and assistance to Mozambican communities abroad. Mozambique privilege great importance to the UN System, as a privileged forum for multilateralism. This privilege is given also to other multinational forums, such as SADC, African Union, Commonwealth, Community of Portuguese Language Countries (CPLP), Organization of Islamic Cooperation, International Organization of Francophonie and other international organizations. In the UN and others international forums, Mozambique defends the reform of the Security Council and engages in issues related to human rights, disarmament, terrorism, transnational organized crime, food security, combating HIV/AIDS and other pandemics, gender issues, migration, environment, climate change, international trade, international financial system and sustainable development.

International Strategic Insertion of Mozambique in the Lusophone World

The Mozambique's international insertion strategy is guided by the Resolution 32/2010, August 30, and the Resolution 34/2010, August 30, according to its strategic environment. The Mozambique's strategic environment includes Southern Africa, Africa, Middle East, Europe, America,

Asia, Oceania and International Organizations. These spaces have a direct relationship with the geopolitics of Mozambique and in all of them we have Lusophone States: Portugal, in Europe; Brazil, in America; East Timor, in Oceania; and Angola, Cape Verde, Guinea-Bissau, Equatorial Guinea and São Tomé and Príncipe, in Africa. The Article 21 of Mozambique's Constitution (2018) refers that the Mozambican State agrees on "special bonds of friendship and cooperation with [...] Portuguese-speaking countries".

In the Lusophone World, the Mozambican interactions are oriented towards the PALOPs and the CPLP. This relationship started ate the National Liberation Struggle and the Post-Independence context. With the collapse of the Portuguese Colonial System, in 1975, the historical ties united the peoples of Angola, Cape Verde, Guinea-Bissau, Mozambique and São Tomé and Príncipe. The "Five States" began to coordinate their actions and constituted the Forum of Portuguese-speaking African Countries, whose main objective was the search for "solve common problems; strengthening of unity and solidarity among its members and promotion of development" (Guebuza 2010, p. 449), through political-diplomatic consultations and other types of initiatives.

Since the National Independence proclamation period, Mozambique has favoured international cooperation and a growing relationship with Portuguese-speaking African States—Angola, Cape Verde, Guinea-Bissau and São Tomé and Príncipe. So, this group has been a relevant forum for objectives and interests' concertation in Africa and in others international forums. For Mozambique, the Forum of Portuguese-speaking States is a multilateral cooperation platform with the potential for conception, materialization and continuation of cooperation initiatives in the fields of culture, education, economy, defence, diplomacy and preservation of the Portuguese language in Africa. However, it is imperative that a set of efforts be carried out that should focus on improving and strengthening the instruments and mechanisms for consultation, to improve the "monitoring and materialization of programs and action plans resulting from the decisions of the States" (Guebuza 2010, p. 450).

Regarding multilateral cooperation within the CPLP framework, this has a great importance for Mozambique, as a forum where there are possibilities to carry out joint efforts to solve problems and materialize common objectives in various areas. In this context, CPLP has been a forum for multilateral cooperation in the areas of health, food and nutrition security, energy, defence, economic and business sphere and a platform for materialization of Lusophone States. The Lusophone World is a field to operationalize a cooperation agenda in areas such as higher education, science and technology, culture, education, administrative modernization, social protection, social inclusion, employment and education for citizenship, which should continue in the future.

In addition to the areas mentioned above, in the Lusophone World, we can highlight sectors and priority of community agenda that are not yet well materialized and need more attention such us: "youth and sports, seas, civil society and social participation, environment, tourism, industrial development, agriculture and forests" (CPLP 2015, p.10). For Mozambique, these areas of cooperation have functioned as fundamental elements for the progressive international affirmation of the group of Portuguese-speaking States in the Portuguese-speaking world and contemporary, since the Lusophone World has a geographically discontinuous in terms of international organization.

Opportunities and Challenges for Mozambique in the Lusophone World

Recently, in the past 1990s decade, Mozambique began a process of international and strategic insertion, using resources from its geopolitical factors, where the Lusophone countries were always considered vital and strategic spaces, nevertheless the geographic discontinuity, for materialization of permanent national's goals and interests. So, Mozambique has explored the Lusophone World as a geopolitical and geostrategic space that primarily contributes "to maintenance peace and security, strengthening of democracy and collective search for mechanisms that promote and increase cooperation for development, in favour of progress and the well-being of its people" (Resolution 32/2010, August 30).

For Mozambique, the Lusophone World represents a great opportunity for its strategic international insertion, through multilateral cooperation operated by CPLP and PALOPs. In relation to CPLP, "cooperation has a great importance not only for development, but also for consolidating the solidarity that guide the relations between the states member". The multilateral cooperation at Lusophone World focus on "developing economic and business cooperation among themselves and enhancing existing potential, through the projects of common interest definition and implementation, exploring the various forms of bilateral, trilateral and multilateral cooperation; promoting the coordination of various public institutions and private entities activities, economic associations and non-governmental organizations engaged in the development of cooperation between their States; and encourage bilateral and multilateral cooperation for the protection and preservation of environment in States members and promoting sustainable development".

The Lusophone World constitutes a strategic space for multilateral and bilateral cooperation for Mozambican State. In this strategic space, Mozambique has cooperative relations in many different areas, such as macroeconomics governance, economic development, poverty, human capital development, security and defence and transversal issues, including education, health, food and nutrition security, energy, economic and business, culture and sport. So, it is a space that Mozambique has as forum for cooperation in areas of and for materialization of the Lusophone agenda. Thus, the Lusophone world become a privileged space for the operationalization of Mozambican geopolitical factors, where we can highlight the human, economic, resources and factors as well as the defence sector.

Mozambique has taken advantage of the Lusophone World to promote the technical, scientific and higher education training for students, with emphasis on higher education institutions in Portugal and Brazil. In Mozambique, there are robust investments from Portugal and Brazil in the health sector (construction of antiretroviral factory), civil construction and mining, as the case of coal mines in Tete Province. The discovery and exploration of energy resources in Mozambique (natural gas and mineral coal) creates several business and investment opportunities, as happens with the Brazilian company VALE and the Portuguese company GALP, which have been operating in the energy mining sector. It is important to note the experiences of Angola and Brazil, in the energy sector. These experiences can contribute to the international insertion of Mozambique in this sector. In the Defence and Security Sector, the military technical cooperation agreements with Portugal, Brazil, Angola and within the scope of the CPLP are relevant instruments to guarantee the national security of Mozambique.

It is also important to mention that in the field of bilateral and multilateral cooperation with Portuguese-speaking countries, Mozambique has registered relevant advances when we look at areas related to youth and sports, seas, civil society and social participation, environment, tourism, industrial development, agriculture and forests (CPLP 2015, p. 10). These areas have functioned as strategic tools for the progressive international affirmation and insertion of Mozambique in the contemporary

International System. However, there are still great challenges that involve mechanisms of cooperation instruments operationalization in the CPLP and in the Portuguese-speaking African Countries (PALOPs); creation of platforms for coordination, monitoring and evaluation of the cooperation process; consolidation of instruments for assessing the degree of agreements implementation signed in the bilateral and multilateral domain; performance evaluation in terms of plan executions, programs and development projects that benefit the multilateral and bilateral cooperation in the Lusophone World.

Conclusion

The analysis and discussion of Mozambique geopolitics aspects and factors in the Lusophone World shows that this is a Portuguese-speaking State that is in the process of consolidation of a democratic system, implemented since the 1990s, as a result of General Peace Agreement and political, social and economic transformations imposed by the Bretton Woods Institutions. So, in the last decade, several potentialities have emerged in Mozambique. The discovery of natural resources such as natural gas, coal and heavy mineral sands, economic growth and political stability are aspects that facilitate the international insertion of Mozambique on the international agenda. These are positive aspects, nevertheless the emergence of terrorist attacks, in Cabo Delgado, since October 2017, and military-political tension, in the central region of the country. All these potentialities of Mozambique create positive externalities for the countries of Lusophone World. The countries of Lusophone World should seize and capitalize all these opportunities, otherwise, other States and hegemonic Powers will gain qualitative and quantitative advantages in their relationship with Mozambique. The common history and linguistic approach is a strategic aspect to capitalize on the relationship between of Lusophone World and Mozambique.

The Lusophone World is a special and privilege geopolitical area in the process of international and strategic insertion of Mozambique. Thus, the Mozambique's Foreign Policy maintains special ties of friendship and cooperation with countries whose official language is Portuguese. The Lusophone World is a space of national strategic interest and an opportunity to operationalize the Mozambican national strategic and geopolitical potential. Among the different Mozambican geopolitical factors, the Lusophone World is a special space that can contribute for promote and operationalization of human, economic, resources and military factors, as elements that can attainment, maintenance and projection the influence and nation power of Mozambique in the contemporary international system.

The international and strategic insertion process, using the Lusophone World is vital for Mozambique, nevertheless the geographic discontinuity of the Portuguese-speaking countries. The CPLP and PALOP are two important platforms for materialization the Mozambican bilateral and multilateral cooperation at Lusophone World. This cooperation should focus on political and diplomatic cooperation, education, health, science and technology, defence, agriculture, public administration, communications, justice, culture, sports, media and civil society. So, it is necessary to create the mechanisms, platforms and initiatives for operationalization, coordination, monitoring and evaluation of Mozambican bilateral and multilateral cooperation in the Lusophone World.

References

Act 12/2019, September 24th – Revised Act 17/97, October 1st. Maputo: Imprensa Nacional.

Act 17/97, October 1st – Approves the Defence and Security Policy Act. Maputo: Imprensa Nacional.

Act 18 /97, October 1st – Approves the Law on National Defence and Armed Forces for the Defence of Mozambique. Maputo: Imprensa Nacional.

Act 18/2019, September 24th – Revised Act 18 /97, October 1st. Maputo: Imprensa Nacional.

Antunes, J. F. (1996). *Jorge Jardim: Agente Secreto*. Lisboa: Bertrand Editora.

Chichango, I. P. (2009). *A Geopolítica de Moçambique*. Lisboa: IESM.

CPLP (2015). *Cooperação na CPLP – Uma Visão Estratégica no Pós 2015: Contribuição dos Pontos Focais de Cooperação da CPLP*. Bissau: CPLP.

Dias, C. M. (2010). *Geopolítica: Teorização Clássica e Ensinamentos*. Editora Prefácio, Lisboa.

Guebuza, A. E. (2010). *PALOP: Passado Comum – Uma Alavanca Para o Desenvolvimento*. Coletânea de Discursos Volume VI. Maputo: CEDIMO.

Leal, J. L. R. (2007). Análise Geopolítica e Geoestratégica de Portugal: Factores Físico, Humano e Circulação. *Revista Militar*, 2463, 825–875.

Macuácua, L. (2006). 'Mozambique', in Omitoogun, W. and Hutchful, E. (Ed.) *Budgeting for the Military Sector in Africa: The Processes and Mechanisms of Control*, New York: SIPRI and Oxford University Press, pp. 138–153.

Malache, A.; Macaringue, P.; and Coelho, P. B. (2005) 'Profound Transformations and Regional Conflagrations: The History of Mozambique's Armed

Forces from 1975/2005', in RUPIYA, M. (Ed.) *Evolutions and Revolutions: A Contemporary History of Militaries in Southern Africa*, Pretoria: ISS Africa, pp. 155–197.

Martín, M.l Á. B. (2016). Method for the Analysis of Geopolitical Regions. *Journal of the Spanish Institute for Strategic Studies*, 6, 1–43.

Morier-Genoud, E. (2021). *A Insurgência Jihadi em Moçambique: Origens, Natureza e Início*. Cadernos IESE nº 21/2021. Maputo: IESE.

Mozambique's Constitution (2018). Maputo: Imprensa Nacional.

Resolution 32/2010, of August 30th – Approves the Mozambique's Foreign Policy. Maputo: Imprensa Nacional.

Resolution 34/2010, August 30s – Approves the Strategy of Implementation of Mozambique's Foreign Policy. Maputo: Imprensa Nacional.

Singhvi, L. M. (2000). *Other Countries of Africa*. Report of the High Level Committee on the Indian Diaspora. New Delhi: Ministry of External Affairs.

Wache, P. (2019). *Geopolítica: Teorias, Doutrinas e Factores*. Maputo: ISRI.

Luso-Mozambican Diplomatic Cooperation in the Case of the Terrorist Conflict in Cabo Delgado

Célia Taborda Silva

Introduction

Throughout 2021, the province of Cabo Delgado in Mozambique has had the attention of political circles and the media due to attacks on the population by radical groups that profess Islam. Although the conflict in the region has been dragging on for some years, it has only now achieved great media visibility due to the violence of the latest attacks.Please check and confirm if the author, mail ID and their respective affiliation have been correctly identified. Amend if necessary.Is amended

Cabo Delgado is a province located in the northern part of Mozambique and occupies a territorial area of 82,625 km^2, bordering the United Republic of Tanzania to the north. It is a territory with natural wealth, agriculture, forestry, fishing, mineral resources, and natural gas, although the gas has only recently begun to be economically exploited by several multinational companies. This wealth, however, does not benefit a population that is still dependent on family agriculture, poor, with a low level of

C. Taborda Silva (✉)
CICANT/Universidade Lusófona, Porto, Portugal
e-mail: celia.taborda@ulusofona.pt

P. A. B. Duarte et al. (eds.), *Portugal and the Lusophone World*,
https://doi.org/10.1007/978-981-99-0455-6_18

education among young people and who, historically, feel exploited by the Makondes or Christians, a large part of the population being Mwanis or Islamists. The Mwanis consider the ancestral Makondes enemies because they have exploited them over time through mining companies, and at present they feel marginalized and excluded from the economic and social benefits of natural gas exploitation. The 2014 victory of Filipe Nyusa, who is of Makonde origin, and the generalization of ethnic Makonde elements within Frelimo and the government have sharpened ethnic rivalries. As João Feijó[1] states, in Cabo Delgado, a constellation of factors has come together to potentiate social conflicts: "unemployed youth, fragility of public institutions, corruption, and a feeling of injustice" (Rodrigues, 2021). This exclusion to which the youth felt themselves condemned made them vulnerable to alternative Islamic proselytism that appeared with new approaches and ideas, having created a network of Muslim cults parallel to the one existing in the region, from which Mozambican religious leaders demarcated themselves. Here, international terrorism saw a population that was permeable to radicalization processes, in which propagandistic discourses of justice, equality, and prosperity were included. According to Fernando Cardoso, what is at the core of this conflict is the fact that the population is against the state and against the way of life of the overwhelming majority of the population, particularly the Muslim population, an ideological and civilizational conflict motivated by sectarian religious convictions (rejected by local Muslim leaders) and using terrorist methods (Cardoso 2021).

Nevertheless, in recent years, the province has been the target of several terrorist attacks, and the violence of the 2020 terrorist attacks on local populations has made it jump into the diplomatic and journalistic spotlight.

Thus, based on a news *corpus* and on the available bibliography, we intend to verify whether there was effective diplomatic cooperation in the case of Cabo Delgado between Portugal and Mozambique, given that both share the same Lusophone space and that many Portuguese live and work in Cabo Delgado.

[1] João Feijó is a researcher at the Observatório do Meio Rural, a Mozambican NGO dedicated to rural development, and is author of several studies on the conflict in Cabo Delgado.

The Expansion of Terrorism to the Lusophone Space

Terrorism is a concept of little consensual definition and historically in evolution, but it was defined by the League of Nations as "criminal acts directed against a state and with the calculated intention of creating a state of terror in the minds of specific persons or groups of persons or the public at large" (1937, art. 1). Aron (2002, 242) defines it as "violent action whose psychological effects are disproportionate to the purely physical results". In this conception, psychological terror is highlighted as the main characteristic of terrorism, which is highly potentiated in fundamentalist terrorism since the pattern seems to change from attack to attack, intensifying insecurity. Therefore, as Pereira (2016, 13) argues, some characteristics persist: Terrorists are willing to kill and die; terrorists are waging a "holy war"; terrorists are tolerated by some states, which allows them to move around; and terrorists do not have massive weapons but imaginative actions. Regardless of the type of strategy used by terrorist groups, the ultimate goal of terrorism is to influence through fear. When we talk about the concept of terrorism today, the reference point is the attack on the World Trade Center in the United States on 11 September 2001, although "no definition of terrorism can possibly cover all varieties of terrorism throughout history" (Laqueur 2001, 7). However, terrorism, from the mid-1980s, of the twentieth century, was a latent concern, mainly because of the emergence of terrorist groups, such as Al-Qaeda, founded by soldiers from the Afghanistan War, which boosted international terrorism from the 1990s onwards. The attacks on the Twin Towers in 2001 gave terrorism a new significance, ushering in a new era of transnational terrorism in which "one of the unfortunate signs of barbarism is that terrorists have discovered that as long as it is within reach of the world's screens, the mass murder of insignificant men and women has greater news value than the most celebrated or symbolic targets for their bombs (Hobsbawm 2008, 119).

The transnational dimension of Islamic terrorism is characteristically driven by religious fanaticism. It is "based on religious ideals to justify terrorist activities" (Adkins 2013, 2) and by extreme violence, without targeting specific victims: "indiscriminate attacks against 'soft' targets" (Martin 2006, 212) and the way terrorists use technology and the media as a way to disseminate their activity. Apart from Al-Qaeda, Daesh is another important movement. This terrorist group gained prominence on the international scene in the early twenty-first century, at the time of the reconstruction of jihadism, and was then affiliated with Al-Qaeda. In 2014, Daesh proclaimed itself a caliphate, expanded beyond Syria and Iraq, and proceeded to vie with Al-Qaeda for the leadership of global jihadism (Tomé 2015, 144). Daesh bases its ideology on Islamic fundamentalism, that is, an adaptation of Islam as a religion (because it does not follow the Koranic precepts) to obtain certain political and economic goals, namely the formation of an Islamic state that expands Islam worldwide.

Globalization turned the world into a global village and the Lusophone space was not left out of it and, as such, has also become subject to the threats of transnational terrorism and subject to its maximum expression, which is violence on a large scale, without space or time barriers (Viana 2011). Terrorism entered Mozambique through the Al-Shabaab group, better known throughout Mozambique as mashababos (free translation for the plural of Al-Shabaab, youth in Arabic) with affiliation to the African branch of Daesh. Founded in 2004, the Al-Shabaab militia controlled much of Somalia's capital, Mogadishu, and large areas in central and southern Somalia for several years. In 2011, the Somali government, with the support of Ethiopian and Kenyan troops, succeeded in driving the group out of the capital and most other cities. However, the Al- Shabaab militia continued to carry out various attacks, both in Somalia and neighbouring Kenya. From Kenya, they expanded to Tanzania and from here to Mozambique. Initially, they did not have the recognition of the Islamic State, which did not happen until late 2019. From then on, experienced fighters joined the Mozambican group from the northeast of the Democratic Republic of Congo, from where they left for southern Tanzania due to a military offensive by the Congolese army against the base of the recently decreed Islamic State Province for Central Africa. As of 2020, there is a reference that the jihadist groups act under the direction of Abu Yasir Hassan, of Tanzanian origin and according to the US, the designated leader of the jihadist movement in Cabo Delgado (Avó, 2021) . However, this has not been confirmed. As of March 2021, the US State Department considers the Islamic State of Iraq and Syria-Mozambique (ISIS-Mozambique) as foreign terrorist organizations and the alleged leaders as global terrorists.

Most of the jihadists are Mozambican, both in terms of leadership and fighters, young (under 40), and many of them were probably radicalized in madrassas in Tanzania. According to Feijó, among the leadership of the jihadists are Bonomado Omar, born in the village of Ncumbi, in Palma; the chief executive Mustafá "Shinpwateka", from Mocímboa da Praia; Maulana Ali Cassimo, born in Lichinga, capital of Niassa province, one of the most respected commanders; and Rosa Cassama, of whom is only known that she was born in Cabo Delgado, the "queen of black magic", whom the jihadists call their mother, responsible for recruiting many women to the cause (Rodrigues, 2021).

The terrorist contingent has between 1000 and 2000 men, a number that has varied over time, comprising mainly Mozambicans. Only in large-scale attacks, such as in Mocímboa in 2020 and Palma in March 2021, "the group used foreign mercenaries, most of them from Tanzania, and there are references to 'white' individuals among the machababos", says the study by Feijó (Rodrigues, 2021). However, Mourier has no doubt that the presence of Daesh in Mozambique is real. There was shouting and swearing in the name of Al Shabaab, and there are several other signs of the presence of this organization in Cabo Delgado (Rodrigues 2020a, 2021).

The jihadist group's attacks in Cabo Delgado have already caused more than 3,100 deaths, half of them civilians, and resulted in almost 817,000 displaced persons (Lusa 2021a, b, c, d, e), triggering a humanitarian crisis similar to that caused during the civil war in Mozambique (1977–1992). Al-Shabaab's violent tactics, burning villages and beheading local inhabitants, ignited panic among the population who fled and sought protection (DN/AFP 2021).

The media coverage of the conflict in Cabo Delgado has led ISIS to claim responsibility for many attacks, although with frequent errors about the locations and names of the attacks.

Methodology

The theme chosen for this research is related to a current and still developing theme, and for this reason it is not a subject about which there is a large body of literature. Our objective was to verify what was being written about the subject, and we had to use Portuguese national newspapers as a primary source, which have provided good coverage of the conflict in Cabo Delgado. Our intention is to verify if there was effective diplomatic cooperation between Portugal and Mozambique in the case of terrorism in Cabo Delgado, since Portugal and Mozambique are part of the Lusophone area, have a historical relationship and many Portuguese live in the region. On the other hand, if this cooperation is verified, we wished to establish whether it was effective and fast, and if it speeded up the collaboration between the two countries. To do this, we use a qualitative methodology. Qualitative research is concerned with a level of reality that cannot be quantified and seeks to understand and interpret as reliably as possible the subject under study, revealing its "truth" (Minayo 2012). Of course, the subjectivity that is implicit in this methodology can raise criticism regarding the study, but the studies are not exhaustive by themselves; they are inputs for new investigations. The qualitative method allows for the use of various sources of information, such as empirical materials, case studies, personal experiences, life stories, interviews, observations and historical, journalistic, interactive, and visual texts. Thus, our information gathering focused on the journalistic news in the Portuguese reference newspapers of the years 2019–2021. We established a corpus by researching and collecting the news that was coming out in the various newspapers referring to Cabo Delgado. According to Cunha and Peixinho, the corpus can be delimited, taking into account a theme, or themes, questions of periodicity and volume, but above all the representativeness of the selected material (2020). In this context, this survey was conducted from the collection of news from the national press by theme, removing the content related to the subject under research. After this heuristic phase, we moved on to hermeneutics, content analysis of our documentary sources and confrontation of the various news sources with other sources of official information or theoretical studies.

Terrorism in Cabo Delgado

Terrorism in Cabo Delgado, related to religious extremism, dates back to at least 2015. However, the first armed attack in northern Mozambique occurred on 5 October 2017 when insurgents occupied the town of Mocímboa da Praia for 48 h and stole armament, only fleeing to the bush when police reinforcements arrived (Morier-Genoud 2020). In November of that year, local Muslim religious leaders were banning the sale and consumption of alcohol, arguing that it would be against the principles of the Muslim religion and that they would be the main cause of behavioural deviance among young people in the region (Chichava 2020). This prohibition on the sale of alcoholic beverages led to clashes and, consequently, police intervention. Following the clashes that took place, one police officer died and two civilians were seriously injured. These were the first victims of a religious conflict that was beginning to gain momentum in the region. In 2016, the authorities of the administrative post of Quiterajo were reporting that the number of students dropping out of the Pequeué Complete Primary School was increasing at an alarming rate. According to the same authorities, these school dropouts were attributed to "certain Islamic religious influences from a local sect" (Chichava 2020, 1). While the province's public schools were losing students, the madrasahs were attracting these young people and spreading their radical ideals among them. This accentuation of the youth's entry into Quranic schools manifested itself in the way the youth interpreted and expressed Islam, more radicalized and sectarian than the majority of the region's inhabitants who were of the same creed. At the end of 2016, these different religious views led to the people of the village of Cogolo destroying a mosque belonging to Al Shabaab because they considered the members of the mosque as "young people who do not follow roots of the ancient Islamic religion" (Chichava 2020, 1). This divergence between various groups belonging to the same religion is not something new in the province, as clashes of this kind had been occurring since the late 1980s (Morier-Genoud 2020, 6).

In 2016, the religious disturbances in the province gained even greater momentum when the religious leader Saíde Bacar, belonging to CISLAMO (Islamic Council of Mozambique), was forced to issue a statement referring to the emerging Islamic groups for being "anti-Islamic, having their origin in Somalia and their aim being to destroy the Islam practiced in Mozambique" (Chichava 2020, 1). Among the principles espoused by Al Shabaab that contradicted Mozambican Islam were: Praying shoes; rejection of secular education in favour of Islamic religious education; mandatory wearing of Islamic veil covering the face, leaving only the eyes open; restricting women's work to house care; prohibition of the use and carrying of civil identification documents; not greeting state leaders; not participating in national events; rejecting the national flag; amputating adulterers and thieves; not collaborating with or being part of the government and (of) state institutions; and the rejection of state courts in favour of Islamic courts (Chichava 2020, 2).

Both Chichava and Morier-Genoud report that the new Islamic groups were infiltrating mosques belonging to CISLAMO and were preaching Islam in a way that opposed what was practised in Mozambique (Chichava 2020; Morier-Genoud 2020). On 5 October 2017, armed attacks began by these Islamic religious groups that opposed CISLAMO. The attack on the city of Mocímboa da Praia lasted for two days (Morier-Genoud 2020). From this moment, the conflict in the region took on an increasing scale, with aspects of a "guerrilla war", in Morier-Genoud's opinion (2020, 1). Since 2017, the attackers were gaining confidence, and in 2018, daylight attacks began. In the following year, the targets of the attackers shifted to include small towns, military warehouses, and road transport. That same year, the attackers swore allegiance to ISIL (Islamic State of Iraq and the Levant), also known as ISIS (Morier-Genoud 2020). As early as 2020, attacks could be seen on district capitals and videos were circulating showing fighters waving black flags and swearing allegiance to ISIS (DN/AFP 2021), with clear calls for a Holy War. They advocated the implementation of Koranic law and the creation of a zone liberated from Frelimo under the black banner of jihad. District capitals were attacked and, within them, the police commands, showing off their evil deeds and claiming the attacks for Daesh through its official news agency, Amaq. In one of the videos circulating, they even advocated the implementation of "Koran law" and the removal of the Frelimo flag (Rodrigues 2020a b). The chiefs of the attacked villages were considered collaborators of Frelimo, and this party is identified with the state, so the motive behind the violent actions is, among other causes, a reaction to the state.

In March 2021, they attacked the town of Palma, killing and wounding several residents and also workers from gas projects in the region, leading the French multinational energy company Total to suspend work there (DN/AFP 2021). On the afternoon of 24 March, residents and about 200 workers of the gas exploration plant were forced to flee and seek refuge in the Amarula Hotel, from where they tried to leave to the gas exploration project facilities. At least seven of them were killed in an ambush, in which a Portuguese man was also wounded (DN/AFP 2021).

As of July, the situation was more under control, with the recovery of Mocímboa da Praia, located 70 km from the natural gas exploration project, which had been occupied since August 2020. An offensive of the government troops with the support of Rwanda allowed for an increase in security, recovering several areas where rebels were present, including the aforementioned village. According to the president of Mozambique, Filipe Nyusa, the military advances in Cabo Delgado "open good prospects for the restoration of the environment of stability" (Lusa 2021a, b, c, d, e).

Portuguese-Mozambican Diplomatic Cooperation on Terrorism in Cabo Delgado

The Lusophone space is a traditional vector for Portuguese foreign policy because of the Atlantic vocation that has marked Portugal's history. Decolonization weakened the African dimension of Portuguese foreign policy due to the Euro-Atlantic positioning assumed by the country (Teixeira 2005), which had become a democracy and needed to be consolidated as it lacked development and modernization.

However, the "African vocation" has always been present, and Portugal has always maintained bilateral relations with its former colonies. This Portuguese will to strengthen ties with its former colonies materialized with the creation of the Community of Portuguese Language Countries (CPLP) in 1996 (Pinto, 2005). Cooperation with the Portuguese-speaking African Countries (PALOP) is built on a "common legal-legal matrix" and has practical consequences in a wide range of areas, which are very relevant in terms of security, such as reducing crime and trafficking networks, and is also extremely important to facilitate the lives of Portuguese living or working in Portuguese-speaking countries (Ferreira et al. 2015, 60).

Relations between Portugal and Mozambique started as early as 1975, after the recognition of Mozambique's independence and the signing of a cooperation agreement between the two states. To strengthen the ties of friendship and cooperation, the heads of state of each country visited each other. First, Ramalho Eanes went to Mozambique (1981), and then President Samora Machel visited Portugal (1983). The current president of the republic, Marcelo Rebelo de Sousa, also made a point of going to Mozambique at the re-election of President Filipe Nyusi in 2019 to reaffirm the good relations between the two countries. The president of Portugal highlighted the "bonds of brotherhood with Mozambique, which are unique", to emphasize that "the presence of Portugal and the fact that the Portuguese president is the only head of state of the member countries of the European Union" to attend the inauguration of Nyusi, shows the significance of this connection (Lusa 2020). In 1983, 1985, and 1995, several cooperation agreements were signed in various areas, ranging from the economy to education, culture, science, and internal security. The 1995 agreement, signed in Maputo, was about cooperation in internal security. The last foreign policy document signed by the two states was in 2017, the "Strategic Programme of Cooperation between

Portugal and Mozambique", for the period from 2017 to 2021 (Diplomatic Portal, Portuguese Government, 2021 Governo Português, Portal Diplomático, 2021).

Terrorism in Cabo Delgado has increased the need for bilateral cooperation between Portugal and Mozambique, and what is certain is that bilateralism has not disappeared, although Teixeira maintains that: "Portuguese diplomacy notes the progressive decline of bilateral diplomacy in favour of multilateral diplomacy that leads Portugal to a presence in multilateral organizations in its areas of strategic interest: the EU in Europe, NATO in the Atlantic and the CPLP for post-colonial relations" (Teixeira 2005, 116).

Portugal is seen as "a solid, constant and permanent partner, which is present in the long term and to whom the authorities and organizations of partner countries can turn whenever there is an urgent situation, or a need not met by other donors" (Ferreira et al. 2015, 60). Portugal and Mozambique reinforced bilateral cooperation on 10 May 2021. The new cooperation agreement was signed in the Portuguese city of Oeiras between the defence ministers of the two countries and includes an increase in the presence of Portuguese military personnel in Mozambique, as well as a substantial increase in investment. This new cooperation foresees a fourfold increase in the number of military personnel and a tripling of investment in Mozambique over the next five years (Ribeiro 2021a, b).

Terrorism in Cabo Delgado has made international aid urgent. With the successive increase in violence, instability, and uncertainty in the province of Cabo Delgado, the Portuguese government made itself available to help (Carlos, 2021). However, as the prime minister of Portugal said, this aid would only be effective if requested by the Mozambican president Filipe Nyusi. The Portuguese defence minister, João Gomes Cravinho, reiterated Lisbon's willingness to support the Mozambican authorities in whatever they deemed useful. It was now up to the Mozambican authorities to define the needs considered useful for fighting terrorism in northern Mozambique.

In addition to bilateral cooperation, the Portuguese defence minister pointed out that: "there is also a dialogue with the European Union, and if there were a mission from the European Union (EU), naturally Portugal would participate, but we have our bilateral cooperation that will continue and will certainly be strengthened in this area" (DW, 2020). Thus, the Portuguese intervention could be done individually, within the EU or the CPLP; in the end, the cooperation within the EU stood out.

In a letter sent to the EU High Representative for Foreign Affairs and Security Policy, Joseph Borrell, the Mozambican foreign affairs and cooperation minister, Veronica Macamo, formally asked the Europeans for specialized support to combat terrorism, given the jihadist insurgency in Cabo Delgado.

Specifically, the military support requested by Mozambique included "training, logistics for counter-terrorism forces, medical assistance equipment in combat zones and technical training of personnel", said the letter sent by minister Macamo to the EU High Representative for Foreign Affairs and Security Policy, Joseph Borrell. The Portuguese government had shown itself available to be an active part of the European response (Geada 2021).

The EU's reply would involve Portugal, not only because of the shared language, but also because of the historical connection. The aid presupposed sending troops to train Mozambican soldiers. In fact, this cooperation in the training of, for example policemen, is nothing new between the two countries (Geada 2021).

The EU's inaction after having committed itself to helping Mozambique led several deputies in Brussels to demand a more active and urgent role by the EU in the face of the humanitarian crisis in Mozambique (Lusa 2020). In response to these appeals made within the EU itself, Joseph Borrell appointed the future president of the EU Council, Augusto Santos Silva, as his representative (Lusa 2020) on an official visit to the country. In addition to the prominent role that Foreign Minister Augusto Santos Silva is playing in European diplomacy related to the Mozambican conflict, the presence of Portuguese diplomats working for the EU present in the resolution of the conflict does not stop there. Rita Laranjinha, who took on the portfolio of European foreign policy in Africa, is also working to resolve the conflict. Speaking to the European Parliament, she revealed that she is "shocked and horrified by the reported atrocities, which require all of Mozambique's partners, including the EU and its member states, to provide the necessary support" (Lusa 2020).

Already in March 2021, the two Portuguese diplomats working for the EU refuted the criticism of "paralysis" regarding the resolution of the situation in northern Mozambique. Laranjinha explained to the Parliament that the diplomatic process takes time because of the need to take consolidated and coherent steps that do not jeopardize the European position. The MEP said that "I anticipate that some members of this

Parliament may consider that we are not moving fast enough, but I want to assure you that we are moving in a consolidated and coherent way" (Lusa 2021a, b, c, d, e). Augusto Santos Silva's position is to demonstrate the concrete advances that have already been made in the region and where the EU has actively participated. The minister stated that: "we have already started to deal with armed violence in Cabo Delgado with concrete projects, namely in preventing and fighting radicalization and launching actions for dialogue and policies for the communities and support for the populations. We are already very active in terms of humanitarian assistance" (Lusa 2021a, b, c, d, e).

In military terms, the Portuguese would not fight side by side with Mozambican troops, but would allow the "strengthening of the capacity to combat terrorism in Cabo Delgado" (Rodrigues, 2021). Although this military support was approved at the beginning of the year, by March 2021, the Portuguese troops had not yet departed. These delays were due to the Mozambican government's unwillingness to receive multinational military contingents (Rodrigues, 2021).

Only in June 2021 did the EU approve a military training mission in Mozambique to train the Mozambican Armed Forces to restore security in Cabo Delgado. This mission would be led by Portuguese Brigadier General Nuno Lemos Pires. The SADC (Southern African Development Community) also approved sending troops to northern Mozambique. To speed up the process, Minister Gomes Cravinho said that Portugal had decided to move forward bilaterally, without waiting for multilateral cooperation. Therefore, there are 45 Portuguese troops on the ground training 100 Mozambican troops, and as the minister stressed: "We do not have and will not have combat troops for the exercise of sovereign functions".

Brigadier General Lemos Pires emphasize that "as a European", he was "very proud of the European solidarity" in helping Mozambique, "both in terms of security and development. The brigadier stressed that it was "very important this help that the EU is giving", which is part of the "values that it defends—helping peace and development" (Lusa 2021a, b, c, d, e).

The request for aid made by the Mozambican authorities directly to Portugal does not appear in the news, only the request to the EU. On 6 April 2021, Rádio Renascença asked the secretary of state of the province, Armindo Ngunga, how Portugal could help and the answer focused on humanitarian aid (Costa 2021). During this interview, Ngunga gave two examples of aid that Portugal could provide Mozambique at this time of need. One was in the creation and transport of shelter kits "that provide help to those who do not have a roof to sleep under, giving conditions for accommodation" (Costa 2021). The secretary of state also mentioned that with the existing wave of violence, many children in the region had been left without a classroom and that this was another type of assistance that "Portuguese friends" could provide (Costa 2021).

Given the emergency experienced in Cabo Delgado, the Portuguese government activated the Rapid Response Instrument for Emergency Actions (IRR), providing 250 thousand Euros for various non-governmental development organizations (NGDOs) operating in the province of Cabo Delgado (Lusa 2021a, b, c, d, e). In this context, two NGDO projects were approved: HELPO and OIKOS. The main objective of the HELPO project is to increase food security for displaced families with pregnant women and dependent children in the city of Pemba through the distribution of more than 2,000 survival kits and nutritional screening for pregnant and lactating women, children, and youth.

The OIKOS project aims to ensure that people displaced by the conflict in Palma have access to basic essentials to resume hygiene and food preparation routines in the host families and temporary shelter centres set up in the district of Montepuez, statement from the secretary of state for foreign affairs and cooperation (Soares 2021).

The Portuguese government mobilized its embassy in Mozambique to the region affected by the conflict. At the end of March 2021, the consul general in Maputo went to Pemba to meet the Portuguese community living in the area, to verify the needs of Portuguese citizens and companies based in this conflict zone and to be able to intervene from the capital Maputo (Ribeiro 2021a, b). In April, the diplomat António Costa Moura met with the Portuguese community, who worried about security issues and their economic survival. The Portuguese residents in Mozambique are very apprehensive about their future in the region, given the impact the paralysis of Total's work has had on other activities. The Portuguese ambassador has touched on the possibility of national companies operating in the area in the construction projects of reception villages or in the EU's More Employment project, worth 4.2 million euros, aimed at training Mozambicans and which Portugal is coordinating in the country.

Ambassador Costa Moura is confident that this training will lead to Portuguese companies being able to create more jobs in Mozambique, as well as visiting the region with the aim of monitoring the projects supported in the context of emergency humanitarian support to Cabo Delgado and development cooperation (Lusa 2021a, b, c, d, e).

Conclusion

Cooperation between Portugal and Mozambique has existed since the independence of the former colony in 1974. There is a historic relationship between the two countries that share the same language and cultural habits. However, it is this same history that unites them that also brings distrust, due to the many years of colonialism. As we have seen, there is a bilateral cooperation between the two countries, but in the case of Cabo Delgado, since there was a need for military intervention, the Mozambican government asked for formal and institutional help from the EU. It is true that Portugal is part of the EU, but it could have first appealed for bilateral cooperation instead of multilateral cooperation. It is also a reality that the Mozambican state's position was that the Cabo Delgado question was an internal question, one of national sovereignty, and therefore they refused help from various states, namely Algeria and Morocco, countries that offered support because they had experience in terrorism.

Portugal was always willing to help. However, the resistance of Mozambique to accept international support extended to Portugal. The Mozambican government's main concern was to avoid the appearance of not being in control to investors and international states. With regards to Portuguese cooperation, it can be said that the members of the government most directly involved in resolving the conflict in Cabo Delgado, such as the ministers of foreign affairs and of defence, committed themselves through diplomacy, military and humanitarian aid to be helpful to the Mozambican government and help to defuse the crisis in the region. Bilateral cooperation in the area of defence has manifested itself essentially in the area of training that military personnel from the special forces of the Portuguese Army, Navy, and Air Force gave to the Mozambican forces. In multilateral terms, the role that Portugal assumed of leading the EU Training Mission to train Mozambique's defence and security forces for two years stands out. The CPLP has not intervened in resolving this conflict because it was not asked to cooperate and because it does not have the structures to be able to help.

The Portuguese consul general in Maputo and the Portuguese ambassador in Mozambique have been attentive to the needs of the Portuguese community and have travelled to the conflict region to meet with the Portuguese community and help find solutions to minimize the damage of the conflict for these nationals.

We conclude that the Portugal-Mozambique cooperation agreements worked when they were most needed, in times of conflict or crisis, and that Portugal also played a very important role as a member of the EU in speeding up its response to the conflict in Cabo Delgado in diplomatic, military and humanitarian terms. The support was not greater or faster because of the position of the Mozambican regime.

What media reports have highlighted, but which needs to be studied in greater depth, is a certain resistance on the part of the Mozambican government to ask Portugal for military aid, with the stigma of colonialism still seeming to taint relations between these two states.

References

Adkins, Gary (2013), "Red teaming the red team: Utilizing cyber espionage to combat terrorism". *Journal of Strategic Security* 6, nº 5: 1–9

Aron, Raymond (2002), *Paz e Guerra entre as Nações*. São Paulo: Editora Universidade de Brasília.

Avó, César (2021), "Missão militar tem como inimigo número 1 Ibn Omar, o "rei da floresta"". *Diário de Notícias*, 10 de setembro de 2021. https://www.dn.pt/internacional/missao-militar-tem-como-inimigo-numero-1-ibn-omar-o-rei-da-floresta-14020097.html

Cardoso, Fernando (2021), "Cabo Delgado: insurgentes, jihadistas ou terroristas?". *Observador*, 5 de maio de 2021. https://observador.pt/especiais/cabo-delgado-insurgentes-jihadistas-ou-terroristas/

Carlos, João (2021), "Apoio a Cabo Delgado: Portugal em contacto com Moçambique". *DW*, 5 de setembro de 2021. https://www.dw.com/pt-002/apoio-a-cabo-delgado-portugal-em-contacto-com-mo%C3%A7ambique/a-57440536

Chichava, Sérgio (2020), "Os primeiros sinais do 'Al Shabaab' em Cabo Delgado: algumas histórias de Macomia e Ancuabe." IDeIAS, no. 129: 2 pp.

Costa, Maria João (2021), "Em Cabo Delgado, "há necessidades específicas em que os amigos portugueses podiam ajudar". Rádio Renascença. https://rr.sapo.pt/noticia/mundo/2021/04/06/em-cabo-delgado-ha-necessidades-especificas-em-que-os-amigos-portugueses-podiam-ajudar/233357/

Cunha, Isabel Ferin e Ana Teresa Peixinho (2020), *Análise dos Média*. Coimbra: University Press.

DN/AFP (2021), "Quem são os jihadistas que aterrorizam Moçambique?". *Diário de Notícias*, 29 de março de 2021. https://www.dn.pt/internacional/quem-sao-os-jihadistas-que-aterrorizam-mocambique-13510634.html

DW, 15 de dezembro de (2020), "Cabo Delgado: Chefe da diplomacia da UE escolhe um enviado para Moçambique". https://www.dw.com/pt-002/cabo-delgado-chefe-da-diplomacia-da-ue-escolhe-um-enviado-para-mo%C3%A7ambique/a-55951046

Ferreira, Patrícia Magalhães, Fernanda Faria e Fernando Jorge Cardoso (2015), *O papel de Portugal na arquitetura global do desenvolvimento. Opções para o futuro da cooperação* portuguesa. Lisboa: IMVF & ecdpm.

Geada, Hugo (2021), "Moçambique. O apoio de Portugal". Sol, 27 de setembro de 2021. https://sol.sapo.pt/artigo/709989/mocambique-o-apoio-de-portugal

Governo Português (2021), Portal Diplomático. https://www.portaldiplomatico.mne.gov.pt/relacoesbilaterais/paises-geral/mocambique

Hobsbawm, Eric (2008), *Globalização, Democracia e Terrorismo.* Lisboa: Editorial Presença.

Laqueur, Walter (2001), *A History of Terrorism.* Nova Jersey. Transaction Publisher.

Lusa (2020), "Cabo Delgado: Chefe da diplomacia da UE escolhe um enviado para Moçambique". *DW*, 15 de dezembro de 2020. https://www.dw.com/pt-002/cabo-delgado-chefe-da-diplomacia-da-ue-escolhe-um-enviado-para-mo%C3%A7ambique/a-55951046

Lusa (2021a), "Chefe da diplomacia europeia diz que a missão da UE em Moçambique pode arrancar na terça-feira". *Público*, 17 de janeiro de 2021. https://www.publico.pt/2021/01/17/mundo/noticia/chefe-diplomacia-europeia-missao-ue-mocambique-arrancar-tercafeira-1946671

Lusa (2021b), "Avanços militares em Cabo Delgado estão a abrir "boas perspetivas" para a estabilização da região norte de Moçambique". *Observador*, 30 de agosto de 2021. https://observador.pt/2021/08/30/avancos-militares-em-cabo-delgado-estao-a-abrir-boas-perspetivas-para-a-estabilizacao-da-regiao-norte-de-mocambique/

Lusa (2021c), "Embaixador português confrontado com receios de segurança em Cabo Delgado". *Observador*, 27 de abril de 2021. https://observador.pt/2021/04/27/embaixador-portugues-confrontado-com-receios-de-seguranca-em-cabo-delgado/

Lusa (2021d), "Portugal defende reforço da cooperação da UE e da comunidade internacional em Moçambique". *Observador*, 13 de fevereiro de 2021. https://observador.pt/2021/02/13/portugal-defende-reforco-da-cooperacao-da-ue-e-da-comunidade-internacional-em-mocambique/

Lusa (2021e), "Primeiro avião de ajuda humanitária já chegou a Cabo Delgado. Lisboa quer envolvimento de outros membros da EU". *Público*, 3 de julho de

2021. https://www.publico.pt/2021/07/03/mundo/noticia/aviao-ajuda-humanitaria-ja-chegou-cabo-delgado-lisboa-quer-envolvimento-membros-ue-1969030

Martin, Gus (2006), *Understanding Terrorism: Challenges, Perspectives, and Issues*. Nova Iorque. Sage Publications.

Minayo, Maria Cecília (2012), "Análise qualitativa: teoria, passos e fidedignidade". *Ciênc. saúde coletiva* 17, nº 3: 621–626

Morier-Genoud, Eric (2020), "The jihadi insurgency in Mozambique: origins, nature and beginning". *Journal of Eastern African Studies* 14 (129):1–17

Pereira, Rui (2016), "O Daesh enquanto ameaça ao sistema político internacional vigente". In Adalberto Centenico e Teresa Rodrigues (Coord.). O *DAESH. Dimensão, Globalização, Diplomacia e Segurança*, 11–21. Lisboa: Cadernos do IUM.

Pinto, José Filipe (2005), *Do Império Colonial à Comunidade dos Países de Língua Portuguesa: Continuidades e Descontinuidades*. Lisboa: Ministério dos Negócios Estrangeiros.

Ribeiro, Nuno (2021a), "Consulado de Maputo faz trabalho de campo em Pemba". 30 de março de 2021. https://www.publico.pt/2021/03/30/politica/noticia/consulado-maputo-faz-trabalho-campo-pemba-1956525

Ribeiro, Nuno (2021b), "Novo acordo com Moçambique quadruplica presença de militares portugueses".*Público*,10demaiode2021. https://www.publico.pt/2021/05/10/politica/noticia/novo-acordo-mocambique-quadruplica-presenca-militares-portugueses-1961893

Rodrigues, António (2020a), "Eric Morier-Genoud: "A presença do Daesh em Moçambique é real". 18 de novembro de 2020. https://www.publico.pt/2020/11/18/mundo/entrevista/eric-moriergenoud-presenca-daesh-mocambique-real-1939741

Rodrigues, António (2021), "Cabo Delgado: jihadistas defendem implantação da lei corânica e criação de zona libertada da Frelimo". *Público*, 26 de março de 2021. https://www.publico.pt/2020/03/26/mundo/noticia/mocambique-pemba-mantemse-calma-presos-transferidos-dentro-cidade-1909699

Soares, Miguel (2021), "Portugal reforça ajuda a Cabo Delgado". Notícias RTP, 27 de abril de 2021. https://www.rtp.pt/noticias/mundo/portugal-reforca-ajuda-a-cabo-delgado_a1315470

Teixeira, Nuno Severiano (2005), "Entre a África e a Europa: A Política Externa Portuguesa 1890–2000". In *Portugal Contemporâneo*, 87–116. Lisboa: Dom Quixote.

Tomé, Luís (2015), "Estado Islâmico" percurso e alcance um ano depois da auto- proclamação do "Califado"". *JANUS.NET e-journal of International Relations* 6, nº 1, (maio-outubro): 125–149

Viana, Vítor (2011), "Consequências Estratégicas do 11 de Setembro de 2001", *Relações Internacionais 3*1, (setembro): 25–31

Lusophone Geopolitics: Blue Economy and Maritime Security in Contemporary Mozambique's Geopolitics

Francisco Proença Garcia and *Sónia Ribeiro*

List of abbreviations

EEZ	Economic Exclusive Zone
GVA	Gross Value Added
MSP	Maritime Spatial Planning
SADC	South Africa Development Community
SWIO	Southwestern Indian Ocean
SIDS	Small Island Developing States
WB	World Bank

Introduction

The global economic relationship with the ocean is developing and expanding rapidly, influenced not only by our growing familiarity with its environment but also by the advent of new technologies that make

F. P. Garcia (✉) · S. Ribeiro
Institute of Political Studies – Portuguese Catholic University, Lisbon, Portugal
e-mail: fmgppg@hotmail.com

P. A. B. Duarte et al. (eds.), *Portugal and the Lusophone World*,
https://doi.org/10.1007/978-981-99-0455-6_19

it possible and economically viable to exploit ocean resources. Long-term growth and demographic trends also add pressure on food security and alternative sources of minerals and energy. In this context, while established ocean industries should maintain their relevance (in a framework of transformation for greater environmental sustainability), the so-called emerging activities—*offshore renewable* energy, aquaculture, deep-sea mining, and marine biotechnology—will bring new opportunities, growth, and greater diversity to the ocean economy, affirming the ocean as a "new" source of economic growth, employment, innovation, and competitive advantage.

Data from the World Bank (WB) (Bosquet 2019) suggests that the world's ocean economy is worth more than USD 1.5 trillion (approximately 2.5% of the world GVA), with 1/3 of the GVA of the ocean industries being generated by the offshore oil and gas sector (OECD 2016), followed by maritime and coastal tourism, maritime equipment, and ports. The largest employing sectors are industrial catch fishing (with more than a third of the total), and maritime and coastal tourism, with almost a quarter (out of a total of about 31 million jobs in 2010).

An important restriction on the development of the ocean economy is the current deterioration of its environmental sustainability conditions because of the increasing acidification of the ocean and increase in seawater temperatures and levels, in addition to the loss of biodiversity and habitat due to changes in ocean currents, with implications in the fish source and migration patterns and higher frequency of the ocean's adverse climatic events.

In this context, governments have underlined their intention to promote a more sustainable balance between economic growth and ocean preservation/conservation. The idea of a "blue economy" or "blue growth" has become a synonym of a more sustainable ocean economy, where there is a better alignment between economic growth and ocean health, within a framework of limited availability of ocean resources (UNDP 2018), thus creating the potential for increased conflicts.

On the other hand, the volatility of the international system is also a source of insecurity and potential conflict, when the previously established order is challenged by new actors of different natures and with different capacities and dimensions, creating new—or reinforcing old—geopolitical tensions that now become global very rapidly.

In the last two decades, the Indian Ocean has become an area of tension and projection of conflicting powers, extending from east Asia to the African coast and beyond, exerting extraordinary external pressure on African countries through economic cooperation and direct financing to economies, but also in terms of the presence on African territory of external military or militarized forces.

Relevant already during the Cold War period, the security dynamics in the Indian Ocean at the beginning of the twenty-first century are more complex and dangerous than in any previous period (Kaplan 2011), opposing India (US ally) against its traditional opponent Pakistan, now supported by a rising RP China seeking international affirmation. China's main Maritime Lines of Communication cross the entire length of the Indian Ocean, from East Africa and the Middle East to the Strait of Malacca.

Due to the dispute with India for political influence in Asia, there is a mutual distrust of their respective maritime intentions. In this context it should also be noted that France and England maintain archipelagos there and a direct military presence, and that together, the French archipelagos form a considerable Exclusive Economic Zone. The geopolitical framework of the Indian Ocean is thus not only complex but unstable in the current context, and the Mozambique channel assumes a great strategic relevance on the eastern African coast.

The African continent has a clear blue economy potential (UNECE 2016), with a special focus on fishing, aquaculture, tourism, transport/shipping, ports, coastal mining, and energy, but it also faces major structural weaknesses that need to be addressed. The blue economy is especially important for SIDS, particularly dependent on their ocean economies.

The African Union has also recognized the relevance of the Blue Economy as part of Africa's "first aspiration" for 2063 (UA 2015): "A prosperous Africa based on inclusive growth and sustainable development". The blue economy is noted as "the biggest contributor to the transformation and growth of the continent", encouraging advances in the areas of marine biotechnology, the exploration of mineral resources and the shipbuilding, transport, and fishing industries.

At a subregional level, SADC is a relevant regional interlocutor with four island states (Comoros, Madagascar, Mauritius, and Seychelles) and six coastal states (Angola, Democratic Republic of Congo, Mozambique, Namibia, South Africa, and Tanzania). The regional block covers a territory that is bathed by two oceans (Atlantic and Indian Ocean)—and contiguous to the Antarctic. On the other hand, it serves as a hub for cooperation and articulation between three of the five countries with the largest coasts on the African continent: Madagascar, South Africa, and Mozambique (the other two being Egypt and Somalia); four of the five countries with the continent's largest EEC—South Africa, Seychelles, Mauritius, and Madagascar (the other one being Somalia) and four of the five countries with the continent's largest continental platforms—South Africa, Madagascar, Mozambique and Namibia (the other one being Morocco), as well as being a relevant player in the development of strategies for the region.

When acknowledging the main Blue Economy centers and activities in Africa the WB points out Mozambique for Ocean tourism and oil & gas (Bosquet 2019). But, as noted by Gove (2019) the relevance of the ocean to the SADC region—and particularly to Mozambique—also encompasses other realities that should be considered, namely activities that are labor-intensive and thus highly relevant for employment, such as fishing and seafood.

In fact, the relevance of coastal communities must be acknowledged in SADC's SIDS (Comoros, Mauritius, and Seychelles) and coastal states, such as Mozambique, where about 70% of the population lives up to 100 km from the coast. In fact, the SADC's region most important cities (in Tanzania—Dar es Salaam; in Mozambique—Maputo, Matola, and Beira: in Madagascar—Toamasina and Mahajanga; in South Africa—Durban and Cape Town; in Namibia—Walvis Bay and Swakopmund; and in Angola—Luanda and Lobito) are coastal, making fishing and aquaculture/mariculture relevant. Coastal tourism is also a relevant reality in several SADC states and regions (e.g., Maputo, Zanzibar, Dar es Salaam, Seychelles, Mauritius, Durban, Cape Town, Swakopmund, Luanda), representing about 70% of the total "ocean asset base" of the Western Indian Ocean region, estimated at least US$ 333.8 billion (Gove 2019).

The SADC region also includes some of the main African ports (namely fishing ones), including those facing the Indian Ocean—Dar es Salaam, Port Victoria, Port Louis, Moroni, Toamasina (Tamatave), Maputo, Beira, Nacala, and Durban.

Regional blue economy is thus an opportunity for the countries in the region, namely Mozambique, with high potential for development, but also faces some threats that must be taken into account, relating to: climate change, the degradation of critical coastal habitats, and negative impacts on the ecosystem due to poor fishing practices and overfishing; natural and anthropogenic erosion and pollution; and to security issues, namely relating to maritime piracy and armed robbery (in 2018, the International Maritime Bureau recorded 201 incidents) and illegal and undocumented fishing.

Mozambique's Contemporary Blue Geopolitics

There is no consensus on what the expression "blue geopolitics" stands for—as well as for the term "geopolitics" itself. In fact, the expression expression does not appear to be commonly used by academics or politicians in the integrated sense we typically find useful, to shed a light on the understanding of tensions and cooperation relations that are developing around the world.

Developing from the broader discussion on the term "geopolitics", the expression "blue geopolitics" may be of use when the discussion is focused on maritime spaces and resources, leaving aside other factors which, although relevant for the country's "global" geopolitics, are of limited or no relevance when focusing one's attention on maritime-related issues, strategies, and capabilities.

"Blue geopolitics" can then be understood as those geographic, economic, political, and social ocean-related factors influencing the ability of defending a country's own interests and affirming them within the regional and global international context, based on its maritime geography and resources.

Though a thorough geopolitical analysis of Mozambique's contemporary blue geopolitics should imply a deeper analysis of each geopolitical factor, we shall focus our discussion on three major factors: geography, economy, and security, which we consider to be the baseline for the discussion, given—and considering—the purpose and limits of the present text.

Geopolitical Challenges and Opportunities

Mozambique is located along the southeastern coast of the African continent and occupies an estimated total area of about 1,371,380 km^2, of which 786,380 km^2 are of dry land and about 572,000 km^2 are of maritime area (República de Moçambique 2020a). It is divided into 10 provinces, of which seven are coastal facing the Indian Ocean: from North to South, Cabo Delgado, Nampula, Zambezia, Sofala, Inhambane, Gaza, and Maputo.

To the West, the country extends into the region of Southern Africa, bordering landlocked countries such as Malawi, Zimbabwe, and Zambia, who depend, for access to the coast, on Mozambique's road and railway corridors of Nacala (Malawi), Beira (Zimbabwe) and Zambezia (Zambia). The country is also crossed by the Maputo corridor to South Africa and Swaziland.

To the East, Mozambique's maritime space borders the Republic of Tanzania to the north, South Africa to the south, the Indian Ocean to the east and—north to south—the Comoros Islands, Madagascar, and France (the overseas regions of Bassas of India and the islands Juan de Nova, Europa, Glorioso and Mayotte). It has around 2700 km of coastline, and a continental shelf of around 104,300 km^2 (República de Moçambique 2020a).

Decree No. 55/2020 of July, 13th established the baseline, making it possible to define the inland waters, the territorial sea, and the EEZ, where the EEZ line does not coincide with the EEZ lines of other countries. In fact, there only exists an official delimitation of the borders with Tanzania and Comoros, since negotiations are still pending with Madagascar, France, and South Africa. The area of approximately 572,000 km^2 considered for the EEZ by Mozambique's Maritime Spatial Planning Plan is thus an estimate (República de Moçambique 2020a).

The Mozambican coastal and maritime area has a high socio-economic value. The "Mozambique channel" is an important transport route, due to its strategic location. Along this area Mozambique has three of the main ports in Southern Africa: those of Maputo, Beira and Nacala, which are not only important for Mozambique, but also for hinterland landlocked countries such as Zimbabwe, Zambia, and Malawi which integrate the SADC prioritized regional development corridors.

In addition to being a vital transport route, the Mozambique channel is also important since it is rich in a variety of resources. Activities such as, among others, fishing, tourism, and exploration of energy resources (oil and natural gas) are carried out in this area.

The discovery, in 2010, of the largest natural gas reservoirs in the Rovuma Basin in Cabo Delgado—with an estimated 180 trillion feet (Monjane Junior 2019)—which placed the country on the list of the 20 largest reservoirs of natural gas in the world and 3rd in Africa (Selemane 2013, p. 2), as well as of oil in sufficient quantities for commercial exploitation (POLMAR, p. 21), and the high potential of the offshore area of Zambezia—with the possibility of the existence of oil and natural gas (Simango 2013)—brought new attention to the region which had been a focus for large multinational companies' investment in the past two decades, namely: Anadarko in the Rovuma Basin, Petronas, and Terraliance in the Zambezi Delta and the DNO in the Inhaminga Block (Selemane 2013, p. 3).

Most of these resources are in offshore areas where there is still no official delimitation of the borders, raising a high potential for conflicts, namely in the Mozambique Basin, Angoche, and Rovuma. With this in mind, Mozambique's government has adopted what Monjane Junior has described as a "first delimit and then explore strategy", hence so far, only areas near its coast or areas with already officially delimited borders, without the great potential for dispute with other countries, have been subject to prospect and exploitation authorizations (Monjane Junior 2019, p. 91).

A Critical Point: Maritime Borders Definition

The definition and delimitation of Mozambique's maritime borders in relation to its neighbouring countries is a critical point for the development of the blue economy in the country, but also for the prevention of potential political and territorial conflicts, an ongoing process that has had many advances and setbacks.

The agreement on the delimitation of the northern border with the Republic of Tanzania was reached in December 1988, with the limits on inland waters, territorial sea, and Exclusive Economic Zone being fixed. It was only in 2011 however that an agreement was concluded, following the trilateral pact on the common tripoint of Mozambique, Comoros Islands, and Tanzania which established the intersection of borders, and defined the territorial limit that would be under the jurisdiction of each state.

With the Republic of South Africa, with which Mozambique shares both land and sea borders, the situation regarding the delimitation of maritime borders is more complex. The first attempt for an agreement occurred in 1993 and consensus was reached on the methods and points to be used for the fixing of borders, the great obstacle however continues to lie in the definition of the point of intersection between land and sea borders at the confluence of the Pongolo and Maputo Rivers with the Indian Ocean.

The most complex cases in the process of delimiting the maritime borders of Mozambique are nonetheless those with Madagascar and with the French Possessions in the Indian Ocean, with which Mozambique borders to the west, and which are disputed between Madagascar and France.

The dispute with Madagascar is due to the existence of a convergence zone between both countries' Exclusive Economic Zones, but the onset of negotiations on the issue depends on the solution of the dispute between Madagascar and France for sovereignty over the Islands along the Indian Ocean, namely: European Island, Isle of India, and Juan da Nova (Jamine 2007; Monjane Junior 2019). Such territorial disputes also exist between France and the Comoros Islands over the island of Mayote. Overall, France claims about 123,700 km^2 of EEZ for the Bassa da Indica island; 127,300 km^2 of the Europa Island's; 61,050 km^2 of Juan Nova Island; and 43,614 km^2 of Ilha Glorioso, totalling more than half of the Mozambique Channel (Monjane Junior 2019).

In addition to these cases of the definition of borders, a decision by the UN on the intention of extending the Continental Shelf of Mozambique to around 321 miles is still pending. On July 7, 2010, Mozambique deposited at the UN General Secretariat the definitive proposal to extend the Continental Shelf beyond 200 miles. This is also expected to become a subject of dispute given that in the Indian Ocean, to the South and Southwest of Madagascar, there are four States with potential demands for the expansion of the platforms: Mozambique, Madagascar, South Africa, and France. If this is indeed the case, the process will be suspended until the dispute is resolved between the States involved, thus postponing the delimitation.

This process has a special relevance for Mozambique at a stage in which the discovery of relevant mineral and energy resources has been added to the recognition of high-value living resources that the country needs to exploit for its development. In fact, as argued by Jamine, "the lack of maritime boundary delimitation and a comprehensive integrated ocean management limits the sovereignty of the State and renders the exclusive economic rights imaginary" (Jamine, E.B. 2006/7: 32).

Blue Economy in Mozambique: Developmental Potential and Challenges

Until the hidden debt scandal burst in 2016 with heavy consequences for the country's development and poverty recovery, Mozambique had recorded sustained economic growth, with an average of 7.5% per year between 2000 and 2015, making the country one of the highest performing non-oil growths for that period, having continuously outperformed global and sub-Saharan Africa's growth. The country's medium and long-term projections were those of positive change, relying on the foreseen production and exportation of liquefied natural gas (LNG); growth rates were expected to begin recovering, increasing to around 6.8% in 2021, according to IMF forecasts. The launching of gas projects, which are due to start only after 2023 (previously 2021) due to delays in final investment decisions (FID), once achieved should contribute to double-digit growth.

Though fragilized by the hidden debt scandal consequences, the government's comprehensive policy objective has been that of the stimulation of inclusive economic growth, underpinned by the exploitation of natural resources, particularly coal and gas. Increased activity in various other sectors such as agriculture, fisheries, aquaculture, tourism, and services, have also been set as a priority, with the intention of increasing added value and employment.

In this context, Mozambique has begun to recognise the potential of the blue economy and the impact it can have on the country's economic and social development. President Nyusi's inauguration speech focused on this potential, revealing a strong political interest in developing a sustainable Blue Economy by preserving and ensuring the "safe, integrated and responsible use of the Indian Ocean, lakes, lagoons and rivers, to benefit Mozambicans" (República de Moçambique 2020b).

The Blue Economy in Mozambique is still at an early stage. Although it currently contributes with a very low percentage to the economy considering the large maritime territory and its geostrategic location, blue economy activities can come to play a key role in the future of the Mozambican economy, especially regarding added value, inclusion, and employment.

Mozambique's fisheries sector plays an important role, both for the economy and as an inclusion agent. The fisheries sector plan for 2019 pointed to a growth of 6.0% with generally positive indicators for fishing production. Fishing is still mostly rudimentary in nature, with low inputs from industrial fishing and even smaller ones from aquaculture. Though the domestic market for marine products is minor with the consumption of such products being mainly restricted to coastal areas, about half a million people depend on the sector for their livelihood, so much so that the sector's relevance to the population food and nutritional security was recognized by the 2019 Social and Economic Plan (República de Moçambique 2018).

Aquaculture has been a major addressee of international assistance. The Nordic Development Fund (NDF), a joint developmental financial institution comprising of five Nordic countries, approved at the end of 2014 a $6.2 million donation for the sustainable growth of the sector. The donation is being used to link small-scale producers with large private operators through a community-based promotional scheme. Aquaculture is therefore expected to remain at a low developmental level in the medium term but has the potential to serve as a key source of international trade exchanges for the country in the long term.

Tourism, especially coastal tourism, together with nautical and sporting activities, can also come to play a decisive role in the economy in the coming decades. The latest available data from the World Travel & Tourism Council (WTTC) revealed that in 2019 Mozambique's tourism industry directly employed about 270,000 people and contributed about USD 488 million (3.2% of GDP) to the economy. The tourism industry is a key component of the economy, but incomes have recently been declining due to a slow performance from South Africa—the main gateway to Mozambique's tourism market—and to perceptions of some growing political and security instability and risk in the country.

In addition to fisheries and tourism and to being an important crossing point for cargo ships (30% of global tanker traffic), the Mozambique Channel holds within itself a treasure trove of natural wealth as the second richest coral bank in the world in terms of biodiversity (coral reef biodiversity) (Nunes and Ghermandi 2015). Moreover, according to the US Energy Information Administration, the Rovuma Basin in Mozambique "holds 100 trillion cubic feet (Tcf) of proven natural gas reserves and is the third largest holder of proven natural gas reserves in Africa" (EIA 2020).

This makes the Mozambique Channel an important economic asset to explore and defend. Maintaining security at sea and the resolution of border conflicts/indefiniteness is thus indispensable for economic development. However, it should not be forgotten that fulfilling this sovereignty function of the State also contributes directly to the economic development of the country as a value-generating function in industries and services, and a staff trainer and partner in projects with a strong economic impact. Promoting security at sea is thus also a potential contributor to the economy, since the Mozambican Navy with the necessary human resources may play a significant role in the economic promotion of industries and services directly linked to its logistical support, namely regarding monitoring and safety, and in nautical equipment life cycle maintenance, thus adding significant business opportunities and jobs to the economy.

Maritime Security in Mozambique: Threats and Opportunities

Threats to Maritime Security in the Mozambique Channel

Having such relevance as a transit route and natural resources *reservoir* for fisheries, minerals, and natural gas, the Mozambique Channel faces several threats to security in the region. Today the most significant of these threats is the Islamic insurgency in the Cabo Delgado district in Mozambique, which presents a real danger of causing a spill-over effect to other regions and countries. The insurgents occupied Mocímboa da Praia village in August 2020, and in March 2021 through a disembarkation, occupied Palma village, an important support harbor for the region's oil&gas mega-projects. They have also occupied several islands in the Quirimbas archipelago. This situation "has reinforced a number of concerns about maritime security in the Mozambique Channel" (Decis 2021).

There are also other phenomena that affect security in the region and that may be related to the financing of the insurgency, such as drug trafficking which through the "so-called "Smack Track" has long brought heroin grown in Afghanistan down the East African coast where a substantial portion has now landed in northern Mozambique before being transported to Europe and elsewhere" (Brewster 2021a, b, c).

Piracy and sea robbery are also a clear example of a threat to security, as those criminal activities prevent the free movement of goods, including hydrocarbons (Garcia 2019). The examples of maritime piracy cases that occurred in 2010 in the Mozambique Channel, namely the Vega 5 case (Eunavfor 2011), caused a great impact and serious damage to the country—both economically and in terms of image. Following these attacks, the discursive rhetoric in relation to maritime security began to focus on piracy (MIMAIP 2021).

Alongside these threats, there are also risks of an environmental nature with a direct impact on the security of maritime spaces in Mozambique, and on national security, such as: the unsustainable and unauthorized exploitation of natural and marine resources, illegal, unreported, and unregulated fishing, environmental degradation by illegal or accidental discharge and the potential impact of natural disasters, extreme phenomena, and climate change (Lampreia 2019).

Mozambique and the Affirmation of Sovereignty, Defense, and Security at Sea

The sea constitutes an important strategic asset, although, as we have seen, there are those who use it for illegal or risky purposes. Its defense and security is one of the fundamental duties of States with maritime spaces, and is essential to any activity that takes place in that space, given that without development and prosperity there will be no conditions for the maintenance of lasting peace. In this context, the approach to the security and safety dimensions should not be seen as a goal *de* per se, but as a fundamental concern, namely for preemptive or preventive action targeting the causes of fragility and instability (Garcia 2019).

It is through the Defense and Security Policy (PDS 1997) that Mozambique defined a coherent set of principles, objectives, and guidelines, with the purpose of preserving the sovereignty and integrity of the country as well as guaranteeing the normal functioning of institutions, and the security of citizens against any armed aggression. Mozambique's Sea Policy and Strategy (POLMAR 2017), defined a vision for the Sea aiming at sustainable development, stating that it desired it to be secure, and managed in an integrated and responsible manner, and to bring socio-economic benefits to Mozambique. Among the objectives mentioned in the Law, we highlight the following for this analysis:

1. Strengthening the exercise of State sovereignty over maritime jurisdictional waters;
2. Developing a blue, profitable, and sustainable economy at sea.

To fulfill objective 1, POLMAR (2017) defines as a political line: to ensure the existence of a defense, control, and security capacity of maritime and coastal spaces and to repress the real and potential threats that prove to be against Independence, Sovereignty and Territorial Integrity, as well as repression, in compliance with national laws and in conjunction with international instruments ratified by Mozambique.

According to Lampreia (2019) we can consider, among others, three types of effects that contribute to the affirmation of Sovereignty, Defense, and Security at Sea, namely:

- Defense, which aims to permanently guarantee the protection of maritime spaces under national and citizens' sovereignty and jurisdiction;
- Authority of the State at sea, which aims to ensure that illicit activities are eradicated or deterred from maritime spaces under national sovereignty and jurisdiction;
- Safeguarding human life at sea, which aims to permanently guarantee navigation assistances and the safeguarding of human life in maritime spaces under national sovereignty and jurisdiction.

The Mozambican Navy (MGM) and the Air Force (FA) are identified within the scope of Defense, for fulfilling their missions under the Law (LDNFA 2019) and the Constitution (2011). MGM is seen as the guarantor of sovereignty, the protector of the State's interests, and the executor of State authority in and by the Sea (Madeira 2010).

Within the regional framework, the SADC's Organ on Politics, Defense and Security Cooperation is responsible for creating and strengthening mechanisms of cooperation, coordination and "exchange intelligence on potential threats undermining the stability of member states (...), on the prevention and combating of terrorism" and on maritime piracy (SADC 2010). Mozambique has also established a Tripartite Memorandum of Understanding on maritime security cooperation with South Africa and Tanzania for the joint conduct of combined maritime operations in the territorial waters of each of the three countries, thus seeking to ensure greater regional maritime security (MdE, 2011).

At the level of the Authority of the State at sea, 14 entities are identified as guaranteeing compliance with the law in maritime spaces under national jurisdiction, and, therefore, exercise the power of maritime authority and constitute the Maritime Authority System (SAM). They are:

- Mozambican Armed and Defense Forces (FADM), namely through its branches of the MGM and the FA;
- Police of the Republic of Mozambique (PRM), through its branches (Coastal, Lake and River Police [PCLF], Public Order and Security Police [POSP], and Border Police [PF]);
- National Fisheries Administration;
- National Directorate of Operations;
- National Directorate of Maritime and Fisheries Policies;
- National Directorate of Fisheries Inspection, Ministry of Culture and Tourism;
- National Directorate for the Environment;
- National Migration Services;
- Tax Authority;
- General Directorate of Customs;
- Institute of the Sea and Borders;
- National Institute of the Navy;
- National Institute of Hydrography and Navigation;
- National Directorate of Medical Assistance.

This architecture, with a vast set of entities and their respective roles which often overlap and sometimes also act in the true competition, requires a very close relationship between the structures of Defense and Security and civil society in its multiple strands of economic, academic, cultural, and recreational activities.

The 2019 Sea Law (LM 2019) made an important contribution to the Authority of the State at sea, by defining the inspection in the Mozambican maritime space, its objective, scope, and how the coordination of maritime inspection should be carried out. With this Law, the Center for Coordination of Maritime Inspection Operations (CEFMAR) was created, integrating all entities with inspection functions in the maritime domain.

MGM is responsible for ensuring the safeguarding of human lives at sea and maritime rescue; maritime beacons, aids, and warnings to navigation; civil protection with implications for the sea and the coastal strip and the protection of public health (Madeira 2010).

Mozambique has limited capacities to fulfill all the sovereignty responsibilities over the sea it has been assigned, of these we highlight: a single Conejera class patrol boat donated by Spain, two Namacurra class patrol boats donated by South Africa, about ten small patrol boats offered by Portugal and two fast interceptor patrol vessels offered by India. Portugal also offered two Cessna FTB 337 aircrafts with maritime surveillance capability (MIMAIP 2021).

To these capacities we can add those of the acquisitions from the French shipyard *Constructions Mécaniques de Normandie*, of three trimarans Ocean Eagle 43s and three HSI32 interceptors (Gallois, S. 2021). These acquisitions also provided for the supply of a multipurpose vessel—the Africa Storm—which offers mobile maintenance and logistics capacity.

Based on this data we can verify a deficit of surface oceanic capacity to ensure a permanent oceanic structure, so, we believe that the three types of effects mentioned above which contribute to the affirmation of Sovereignty, Defense and Security at Sea, will hardly be carried out effectively. Consequently, the local, regional, and international maritime community will lose confidence in Mozambique ability to ensure a maritime secure environment, leading to a negative impact on maritime activities and in the economy of the sea (MIMAIP 2021).

Considerations on a Maritime Security Strategy for Sustainable Development

Despite still being at an early developmental phase, the available data on the Blue Economy's potential in Mozambique makes it possible to affirm that it holds a key to the country's sustainable development in the short and medium term, and most likely also in the long term. In fact, as stated, despite contributing to a very low percentage to the economy today and considering the large maritime territory and its geostrategic location, blue economy activities can play a key role in the future of the Mozambican economy, especially regarding added value, inclusion, and employment.

The fisheries sector will most likely keep its relevance because of its contribution to food and nutritional security, but, due to both economical, technological, and environmental constraints, one shouldn't expect it to grow into an industry. Aquaculture is an emerging sector, with high development potential and can be a key source of international trade exchanges for the country in the long term. A third sector is also key at this phase—coastal tourism, which can also play a decisive role in the economy in the coming decades, taking advantage of the transition to a new developmental model deriving from the value generated by the exploitation of gas and other mineral resources.

There are many challenges to achieving a sustained and sustainable economic development in Mozambique, namely governance ones. It is nonetheless clear that the Mozambique Channel is an important economic asset to explore, given: its abundance in living and non-living resources, its relevance to international trade and its enhanced geopolitical importance, where maritime security plays a decisive role as a basic condition for socioeconomic development and environmental preservation and sustainability.

It is the responsibility of the coastal State to create conditions that guarantee a maritime security environment. For this to be accomplished, at first, it is necessary to have a maritime security strategy and public policies for the development of capabilities so that the Armed and Police Forces can face the various threats and risks at sea.

Mozambique has promoted several initiatives amongst the various actors with responsibilities at sea, however, despite all this effort and good intentions the results are insignificant, as the country continues to have weak capacities and autonomy to ensure maritime security in its exclusive economic zone (EEZ) and remains lacking a maritime security strategy guiding the effort (Chingotuane and Freixo 2016).

Mozambique must therefore define a Maritime Security Strategy that considers, among others, the following objectives (Chingotuane and Freixo 2016; POLMAR 2017; Roughead 2019; Decis 2021):

- Enforcing the sovereign rights of Mozambique;
- Improving maritime domain awareness;
- Bolstering maritime capacity-building efforts;
- Ensuring the free movement of goods and people at sea while preserving its Lines of Communication;
- Respecting treaties, international obligations, and national laws;
- Enhancing cooperative arrangements with nations of adjacent EEZs;
- Making the use of the Automatic Vessel Monitoring System (VMS) mandatory for all economic activities that use vessels and/or platforms.

To operationalize these objectives and given the myriad of stakeholders in SAM, we believe that it is necessary to create a department at the highest level of the government where a secure and sustainable exploitation of the sea is planned, organized, and coordinated in an integrated manner, i.e., the creation of a true National Maritime Authority (AMN), already conceived in 2012 (Francisco 2018). This should be a superior structure of administration and coordination of all national departments and agencies that have competencies or carry out actions within the scope of the SAM. The Authority will allow the conjugation of synergies with those various departments and agencies that deal with maritime security issues, clarifying the degree of authority and competencies that each one enjoys, eliminating overlaps and duplication of means in the marine space such as those that already occur. It is also important to maintain the principle of coordination at all levels of the current related structures, namely with regards to the continuity of action from the high seas and to the limits of the public maritime domain.

To face the different types and degrees of security threats in the maritime area, an Operational Concept must be studied and implemented that allows for the identified objectives to be achieved.

AMN's organic structure must be established in a way such as to make it effective and quantified, and as to guarantee the necessary means to carry out its authority, regardless of the ministry that oversees it. Thus, it is necessary to identify the relevant resources, plan their use and train the various stakeholders involved, as to create optimal conditions for the facing of, in a logical and organized way, serious incidents requiring resources from different departments, (MIMAIP 2021).

The Maritime Security Strategy to be defined by Mozambique must consider both the SADC Regional Integrated Response and the MoU with South Africa and Tanzania.

Mozambique must also optimize international cooperation policies within the scope of Defense and Security, bilaterally and multilaterally, in areas such as: training, information sharing, joint operations, support for capacity building, and the development of regional regulation.

As part of the Maritime Security Strategy, there must be a continuous and uninterrupted investment in the acquisition and maintenance of capabilities, including the construction and modernization of infrastructure. To achieve this, it is necessary to approve and publish Procurement Laws for equipment and armaments both for the Defense (LPM) and Security (LPS) sectors that ensure the regularity of budget allocations for Strategic

Defense and Security projects, complying with article 3 of the CEDN (2006), and thus complying to national and international commitments. This thus would signalize the abandoning of the current dominant, short-term, ad-hoc paradigm initially targeted towards the search for military donations that results in accepting vessels that donor countries offer (Chingotuane and Freixo 2016).

Regardless of the organizational structure, the capabilities acquired from French shipyards are a "suitable foundation to provide maritime security for a country with an underdeveloped maritime infrastructure" (Roughead 2019) and a weak capacity of qualified and experienced human resources. We recall that those acquisitions were also intended to create a tuna fishing fleet (21 tuna vessels), which would integrate the MDA system. Basically, what was looked for was an integrated solution that would include locations for the deployment of maritime domain reconnaissance radars, operation centers, patrol vessels, aircraft, a maintenance vessel, and a fishing fleet (Roughead 2019).

After the situation known as "hidden debt" the project resulting from the acquisitions made in France stopped. It is thus necessary to reanimate this project or its respective capabilities, so that, at least, the patrol vessels then acquired can once again play their role of surveillance of the EEZ. This would contribute to maritime security production while at the same time serve as a suitable foundation for the growth of that same maritime capability (Roughead 2019), thus mitigating the country's situation of external dependence in this area.

Mozambique needs to know how to manage perceptions, accordingly, the State must develop a narrative to enlighten the Mozambican people for the imperative of a need to invest in Maritime Security and the important return this would have for the well-being of society. At the same time it should seek to raise awareness and sensibility to issues related to the Sea and its Defense and Security, though, for example, the dissemination of awareness programs for the population that uses maritime and coastal spaces. Without a true culture of national defense, it is not possible in a broad sense to create a moral environment or ensure the availability of indispensable resources for the development of an adequate security system.

References

Bosquet, B. (2019) The Blue Economy. An integrated and sustainable approach, Conf.ª Crescendo Azul, Maputo, 2019

Brewster, D. (2021) The Mozambique Channel is the next security hotspot. Lowy Institute, Sidney. Available in https://www.lowyinstitute.org/the-interpreter/mozambique-channel-next-security-hotspot

Chingotuane, É.; Freixo, A. (2016) Segurança Marítima e a Necessidade do Fortalecimento da Marinha de Guerra de Moçambique: Estratégias, Políticas e a Parceria com Brasil. Centro de Estudos Estratégicos e Internacionais – CEEI/ISRI. Ano III, Nº 09 – Fevereiro

Decis, H. (2021) The Mozambique Channel – troubled waters? In: Military Balance Blog. International Institute for Strategic Studies, London. Available at The Mozambique Channel – troubled waters? (www.iiss.org)

EIA. (2020). International. U.S. Energy Information Administration (EIA). Country analysis Moozambique. Available at https://www.eia.gov/international/analysis/country/MOZ, accessed on Oct 6, 2021

EUNAVFOR. (2011). Mozambican fishing vessel pirated, EUNAVFOR. Available at https://eunavfor.eu/mozambican-fishing-vessel-pirated/, accessed on Oct 6, 2021

Francisco, F. (2018) Estudo dos Sistemas de Segurança das Fronteiras Estatais em Moçambique face às Novas Ameaças à Segurança Interna. Dissertação com vista a obtenção do grau de Doutor em Direito e Segurança. Universidade Nova de Lisboa, Lisboa

Gallois. S. (2021) Lourdement endetté, le Mozambique accuse le groupe naval Privinvest de corruption. In: ouest-france. Available in Lourdement endetté, le Mozambique accuse le groupe naval Privinvest de corruption (www.ouest-france.fr)

Garcia, F. (2019) Africa and the Threats to its Security. Austral: Brazilian Journal of Strategy & International Relations v.8, n.16, Jul./Dec

Gove, D. (2019). Prospects for the Development of the Blue Economy and Governance of Oceans in the SADC (Southern Africa Development Community), Conf.ª Crescendo Azul, Maputo, 2019

Jamine, E. B. (2006/7). Delimitation of the Mozambique delimitation of the Mozambique maritime boundaries with neighbouring maritime boundaries with neighbouring states (including the extended states (including the extended continental shelf) and management of continental shelf) and management of ocean issues ocean issue, United Nations – The Nippon Fellowship Programme 2006/7. Available at https://www.un.org/depts/los/nippon/unnff_programme_home/fellows_pages/fellows_papers/jamine_0607_mozambique_PPT.pdf, accessed on Sept 29, 2021

Kaplan, R. D. (2011). Monsoon: The Indian Ocean and the Future of American Power. New York: Random House.

Lampreia, R. (2019). Uma análise prospetiva sobre a segurança marítima nacional, no horizonte 2030. Dissertação com vista a obtenção do grau de Doutor em Relações Internacionais. Universidade Nova de Lisboa, Lisboa

Madeira, A. (2010). Missão da Marinha de Guerra de Moçambique em tempo de paz e prespectiva de desenvolvimento. Breve estudo. Instituto de Estudos Superiores Militares. Lisboa.

Ministério do Mar, Águas Interiores e Pescas (MIMAIP). (2021) Plano de Ordenamento do Espaço Marítimo.

Monjane Junior, Z. (2019). A importância da delimitação das fronteiras marítimas de Moçambique no contexto das descobertas de gás natural offshore. In Revista Moçambicana de Estudos Internacionais. Vol 1, n.°1, pp. 71–95. Available at https://www.academia.edu/39042252/A_Importância_da_Delimitação_das_Fronteiras_Mar%C3%ADtimas_de_Moçambique_no_Contexto_das_Descobertas_do_Gás_Natural_Offshore, accessed on Sept 24th, 2021

Nunes, P.A.L.D., Ghermandi, A. (2015). Understanding and Valuing the Marine Ecosystem Services of the Northern Mozambique Channel, UNEP (2015). Available at https://cordioea.net/nmc/key-publications/ andat https://www.unep.org/resources/report/understanding-and-valuing-marine-ecosystem-services-northern-mozambique-channel, accessed on Oct 10, 2021

OECD. (2016). The Ocean Economy in 2030, OECD Publishing, Paris

República de Moçambique. (2018). Plano Económico e Social para 2019, Maputo, Dezembro de 2018

República de Moçambique. (2020a). *Marítime Spatial Planning Plan. Inventory and Environmental Characterization*, version for public consultation. TPF Consultores & Biodesign for Ministério do Mar, Águas Interiores e Pescas (MIMAIP). Available at https://poem.gov.mz/relatorios/, accessed on Sept 24, 2021

República de Moçambique. (2020b). Presidência da República, A Nossa Agenda é Desenvolver Moçambique. Discurso de Sua Excelência Filipe Jacinto Nyusi, Por Ocasião da Cerimónia de Investidura como o Presidente da República de Moçambique. Maputo, 15 de Janeiro de 2020

Roughead, G. (2019). An analysis of Mozambique's maritime security. In Africa Briefing. Available at https://africabriefing.org/2019/08/an-analysis-of-mozambiques-maritime-security/

SADC Water Fund Project Selection. (s.d.). https://www.sadc.int/opportunities/sadc-water-fund/eligibility/project-selection/, accessed on Sept 27, 2021

SADC. (2010). Strategic Indicative Plan for the Organ on Politics, Defence and Security Cooperation. Maputo.

Selemane, T. (2013). *Moçambique tenta entrar na lista dos maiores produtores de carvão e gás*. Boletim sobre o processo político em Moçambique. N° 53 de 15 de Fevereiro. Maputo: CIP e AWEPA. Available at https://www.open.ac.uk/technology/mozambique/sites/www.open.ac.uk.technology.mozambique/files/files/Mo%C3%A7ambique_Boletim_53_carv%C3%A3o-gas.pdf, accessed on Sept 24, 2021

Simango, S. (2013). O exercício do poder público em Espaço de Soberania e Jurisdição Marítima: Um Potencial Estratégico para o Desenvolvimento Económico de Moçambique. Dissertação de Mestrado. Universidade Católica Portuguesa. Available at https://repositorio.ucp.pt/handle/10400.14/13829, accessed on Sept 2, 2021

UNECE – UN Economic Commission for Africa. (2016). Africa's Blue Economy: A policy handbook, Addis Ababa, Ethiopia, available at https://www.afdb.org/, accessed on Mar 4, 2020

UNDP. (2018). Blue Economy for Inclusive and Sustainable Growth, UNDP Policy Brief n°6/2018, April 2018

União Africana (UA). (2015). Agenda 2063 "A África que queremos", April 2015

Legislation

Conceito Estratégico da Defesa Nacional (CEDN). (2006). Resolução n.° 42/2006, do Conselho de Ministros.

Constituição da República de Moçambique. (2011). Maputo, Imprensa Nacional de Moçambique, E. P.

Lei da Defesa Nacional e Forças Armadas (LDNFA). (2019). Lei n.° 18/2019, de 24 de Setembro.

Lei da Polícia da República de Moçambique. (2013). Lei n.° 16/2013, de 12 de Agosto. Memorando de Entendimento entre o Governo da República de Moçambique, República da África do Sul e República Unida da Tanzânia sobre Cooperação em Segurança Marítima (MdE, 2011).

Lei da Política de Defesa e Segurança (PDS). (1997). Lei n.° 18/97, de 1 de Outubro

Lei do Mar (LM). (2019). Lei n.° 20/2019, de 8 de Novembro.

Lista de coordenadas geográficas dos pontos que definem a Linha de Base da República de Moçambique, que resulta da combinação de segmentos de Linhas de Base Rectas (adiante designadas "LBR") e da Linha de Base Normal (adiante designada "LBN") (2020). Decreto n° 55/2020 de 13 Julho, do Conselho de Ministros

Política e Estratégia do Mar (POLMAR). (2017). Resolução n.º 39/2017 de 14 de Setembro que aprova a *Política e Estratégia do Mar (POLMAR)*, BR - I SÉRIE — Número 144, pps 1035–1085

Resolução do Conselho de Ministros nº 12/2015, de 1 de Julho, aprova o Estatuto Orgânico do Ministério do Mar, Águas Interiores e Pesca.

Influence and Institutional Cooperation in the Lusophone World

The Geopolitics of the Portuguese Language: Knowledge and Influence

José Paulo Esperança

Introduction

The community of Portuguese-speaking countries represents 3.7% of the world's population and about 3.5% of the world's gross domestic product (GDP). In some dimensions, such as natural resources, namely renewable energy, fresh water, and maritime economic exclusive zones, the relative size of the Portuguese-speaking nations is even larger. This community is also integrated into many international organizations and many of its citizens have occupied relevant positions in different types of international organizations. However, the role of the Portuguese language in international organizations is still underrated and the number of students interested in learning Portuguese is limited by comparison with many other languages with a much smaller number of speakers as a mother tongue. As a language of culture and science, the Portuguese language faces several challenges although it has enjoyed robust consolidation on the internet. The soft power associated to the sharing of a common language with a global dimension is under exploited and it is important

J. P. Esperança (✉)
ISCTE-Instituto Universitário de Lisboa, Lisbon, Portugal
e-mail: josepaulo.esperanca@fct.pt

P. A. B. Duarte et al. (eds.), *Portugal and the Lusophone World*,
https://doi.org/10.1007/978-981-99-0455-6_20

to discuss the main challenges and opportunities to consolidate the presence of the Portuguese language as a language of communication, culture, science, and values, to the benefit of both native speakers and users as a second language.

Despite some recent studies on the rising presence of the Portuguese language in scientific communication (Gradim and Piñero-Naval 2019), this dimension has been scarcely present in the academic literature, as well as its overall impact in key areas of economic and social relevance, leading to its impact in a geopolitical dimension.

This chapter provides an overview of the major trends in the development and expansion of the Portuguese language before analyzing its cultural, scientific, and economic dimensions, illustrating the double impact of language commonality—among Portuguese-speaking countries—and language proximity—with Spanish speaking countries. Finally, several recommendations for its future support and development are provided.

Language as an Element of Geopolitical Influence

Language has become a key element of geopolitics. Indeed, international relations are affected both by physical geography as well as cultural and economic factors. As Muller (2008, p. 323) states:

> Adopting a constructivist perspective, critical geopolitics examines the very construction and social effects of geopolitical imaginations and geopolitical identities of the imaginary spatial positioning of people, regions, states and the shifting boundaries that accompany this positioning.

Languages have sparked a concern similar to the worry with biodiversity loss in the natural world. The most threatened languages are spoken by small communities, most of which live in developing countries. Lack of support in education and literature renders these languages more fragile, with significant loss of cultural identities. Watson (1999) draws attention to the need that donors and aid agencies such as IMF and the World Bank to developing nations support the consolidation of local languages instead of carrying all communication in English. A recent study by Paz (2021) on social crowdfunding, based on the crowdlending campaigns mediated by the KIVA platform, found an overwhelming predominance of campaigns expressed in the English language which involuntarily discriminates potential beneficiaries unfamiliar with the English language.

The role of language has become ever more important as the world has never seen the dominance of a specific language as strongly as today. Swales (1997) definition of English as the language tyrannosaura has been echoed by many students of geopolitics as the overall influence on both popular culture and scientific communication has become ever more pervasive. Mendieta et al. (2006) focus on the Scandinavian countries to illustrate the challenges posed to local scientists as they struggle with the need to internalize "subtle forms of self-censorship and self-colonization". Although the economic and cultural clout of these countries is large, the overall knowledge of their languages is relatively small, compelling local researchers and scientists to choose English rather than their mother tongues.

The Unexpected Emergence of the Portuguese Language

This chapter focuses on the specific case of the Portuguese language and the contrast between its robust growth potential and the barriers to its consolidation as a language of culture and scientific communication.

The emergence and diffusion of the Portuguese language is due to a set of factors with a very low probability. Originated in a small country with a very small population, it succeeded in expanding to at least four different continents. The Maddison database estimates that in the year 1500 the Portuguese population was just 1 million, less than 1% of the Chinese population at that time. Indeed, as shown in the "Novo Atlas da Língua Portuguesa" Portuguese enjoyed that fastest expansion of a set of languages spoken in different parts of the World and is now the mother tongue of about 3.7% of the current world population, enjoying high growth prospects, especially in Portuguese-speaking African countries. This expansion stems from the innovations in sailing techniques that allowed the navigation throughout the Atlantic and, soon after, the Indian Ocean. However, the consolidation of the Portuguese language owes as much to two key factors, beyond navigation and trade. The first is the definition of a set of common rules that unify the characteristics of the language. Spanish enjoyed an early attempt with the first grammar being published by Antonio de Nebrija in 1492. About half a century later, two grammars of the Portuguese language were published—by Fernão de Oliveira in 1536 and by João de Barros, whose influence remains, in 1540. Still, this is much earlier than the famous "Pamphlet for Grammar" by William Bullokar, showing that English was a rule-based language, such as Latin, published only in 1586.

The second is the set-up of a regulatory framework that standardizes the language as a tool of communication. This means that public authorities played an important role in fostering the use of a shared language which, simultaneously, facilitated the emergence of a more centralized type of government. One interesting document was the 1656 royal decree (16 years after the end of the 60-year rule under the Spanish monarchs) requiring that doctors and surgeons write all prescriptions, addressed to pharmacies, in plain Portuguese language while defining heavy fines for those who failed to do so (Reto et al. 2020, pp. 24 and 25). This rule shows that several alternatives, including Spanish and Arabic, were still used by many Portuguese. A similar situation existed in Brazil. For centuries, after the Portuguese first arrival in 1500, the main language was based on indigenous language (tupinambá) absorbed by European migrants as well, called "general language". It is only in 1758 that Portuguese becomes compulsory and widely spoken in Brazil, although with native, African, and other influences that have also had some impact in Portugal and later in African-speaking countries. However, the expansion of the Portuguese language is very much a phenomenon of the twentieth century due to sheer population growth and more widespread education. Data from the United Nations shows that the population of the current Portuguese-speaking countries went up from 85 million in 1955 to about 284 million in 2017.

Although the Portuguese language is far more consolidated than in the past and has expanded faster than most other global languages, its relative weight is lower than three or four centuries ago. The geopolitical clout of a language can be measured by the number of non-native speakers interested in its learning. In this regard, English, beats all other languages, having become the undisputed lingua franca. However, as Casteleiro (2016) observes, between early in the sixteenth century and the middle of the eighteenth century the Portuguese language was the lingua franca of that long period, often used by two parties with different mother tongues. He adds that French took over until the second world war when English became the predominant second language. Despite rising interest in Portuguese as a second language, from most Spanish-speaking countries to China, the relative position is still lower than the number of native speakers would predict. In the US, Portuguese was number 12 among the most spoken languages (Reto et al. 2018, p. 86).

In the last centuries, the comparative advantage of the Portuguese-speaking countries declined as England and the Netherlands could compete in maritime access to valuable spices and other raw materials and were later much more advanced in the industrialization process. Therefore, the populational rise was not followed by a similar economic progress. Moreover, the Portuguese speaking countries are geographically dispersed, without sharing a single land border, which made political and diplomatic coordination more difficult.

Boundaries are a key element in the study of geopolitics, as they shape the peoples' identities (Paasi 1998). However, as transportation and communication costs decline sharply due to the technologies at hand, physical distance tends to become less relevant. For this reason, the lack of land borders, unique among global languages, renders Portuguese an interesting case for the study of language influence on geopolitical identity and the relation with other cultures. Rajagopalan (2008) explores the importance of the Portuguese language in shaping the cultural identity of Brazil and the capability of building a unified country sharing a border with 10 countries. Paasi (1999) discusses the case of Finland to illustrate the geopolitical implications of borders in an evolving context. Although it became a full member of the European Union on 1 January 1995, it is committed to pursue a sustained cooperation with Russia, with stronger social and economic implications on border towns. However, Paasi highlights the possible differences between official discourse and local practices regarding trade and freedom of movement. In a different context, the Itaipu dam, on the border between Paraguay and Brazil, the largest hydropower plant until the construction of the Three Gorges Dam in China, is an example of complex border relations. Although it has reached the production of 100 GWh of clean energy in a single year, it had a huge environmental impact and led to the displacement of over 40,000 people. It required a long negotiation engaging Brazil, Paraguay, and Argentina and a broad set of compensations, namely to the Guaíra municipality in Paraguay, the most affected by the construction of the dam. However, despite enduring complaints, especially from Paraguay, regarding the terms of the deal, it was possible to reach an agreement that led to the construction of one of the world's largest international infrastructures. This is particularly significant because it engaged three parties with occasionally strong rivalries. Rajagopalan (2008) refers that

Argentina and Brazil have occasionally regarded each other as the most significant rival. One may conclude that geopolitical interests can be best supported by active diplomacy that underlines the common interests.

The Emergence as a Language of Culture and Science: Economic and Social Implications

From the geopolitical perspective, the Portuguese language is relatively strong in two dimensions:

i. natural resources and sustainability as countries such as Brazil, Angola, and Mozambique enjoy large access to fresh water, mineral resources, arable land and, together with Portugal, vast economic exclusive zones in their maritime platforms; and
ii. the growth potential as the population of African Portuguese-speaking countries is expected to experience a significant growth in the next decades. Population estimates by the UN predict that by 2050 the population of Portuguese-speaking countries will be close to 400 million, with most speakers as a mother tongue located in Africa. Reto et al. (2020, ch. IV) provide a synthesis of an extensive comparison of the 94 languages with over 10 million native speakers. The resulting ranking places the Portuguese language in the third position, immediately after English and Spanish, by natural resources and sustainability and in the sixth position on economic and demographic predictions. By contrast, the Portuguese language is only ninth on the dimensions of communication and education, culture, and science.

Translations are a useful proxy for the cultural influence of a language and can provide a measure of its "trade" balance as well as the level of consumption of cultural goods. Portuguese-speaking countries are strong net importers of cultural goods. In Reto and Gutierrez-Rivilla (2020, pp. 246 and 247) we find that Portuguese is the 8th destination country for translations from works originally written in other languages while it is only 18th as a source of translations, from Portuguese into any other language. Using data from Unesco's Index Translationum, for 2020, they registered a total of 78,904 translations into Portuguese against only

11,853 translations from Portuguese into other languages. By comparison, German, the largest importer of translations from other languages, with a total of 301,935, is also a heavy exporter and the third most important language in this parameter, after English and French, with 208,240 works originally written in German and translated into other languages.

The strong asymmetry between cultural imports and exports shows that Portuguese is a net recipient of cultural influences from other languages although recent evolutions, such as José Saramago's literature Nobel Prize (1998) have sparked a rising interest in the literature produced by Portuguese-speaking authors, both contemporary and past such as Fernando Pessoa, Luís de Camões, Machado de Assis or Jorge Amado. It is also worth noting that although most authors with a global reach were born in Brazil and Portugal, a cohort of authors from African-speaking countries enjoy a rising global influence such as Pepetela and Luandino Vieira (Angola), Mia Couto and Paulina Chiziane (Mozambique) or Manuel Lopes (Cabo Verde). In Reto et al. (2018, p. 213) we observe that the 5 most translated authors are Paulo Coelho, José Saramago, Jorge Amado, Fernando Pessoa, and Leonardo Boff. Interestingly, for all these authors, Spanish is the first destination language. This is clear evidence of the cultural proximity because, as the two languages are significantly close, many Spanish-speaking readers can also understand and use the original texts. German is the second most important destination language, for José Saramago, Jorge Amado, and Leonardo Boff, versus Hungarian for Paulo Coelho and French for Fernando Pessoa. The geopolitical dimension of a language is strongly influenced by its position as a language of science. This is perhaps the dimension in which the English language is most pervasive, having replaced Latin as the lingua franca of choice for many scholars until late in the nineteenth century. As Mendieta et al. (2006) observed, in the context of Scandinavian countries, with relatively small populations speaking their native languages and a strong understanding of English as a second language, there is a trend to replace the mother tongues with English in most scientific communications. A similar situation can be observed In the case of the Portuguese language. Although it is shared by a large community of about 260 million people, the emergence of different variants, namely between Brazil and Portugal has led the two scientific communities to often interact in English rather than their mother tongue. This is particularly significant in relatively recent fields such as computer sciences or more technical domains such as medicine or chemistry in which many technical expressions have diverged. Moreover, the attempt to reach a broader number of researchers, specialized in the same academic domain, has led many technical papers to choose English instead.

Is Portuguese (and Spanish, which shares several common characteristics, namely the significant expansion in the last decades) facing a persistent decline as a language of science? Apparently, there are some indicators that challenge the more pessimistic view. Gradim and Piñero-Naval (2019) compare the Science Citation Index (SCI) and the Social Sciences Citation Index (SCI) in two periods—1960 and 2015 and they observe that Portuguese, out of the 10 first positions in 1960 progressed to number 6 in 2015 (SCI) and number 5 in SSCI. Spanish went up from number 6 to number 3 in both rankings (see Table 1).

These figures, based on a database of 51 million documents show that Portuguese was the fastest-growing language climbing to sixth and fifth position in SCI and SSCI, respectively. This result is the outcome of a steady policy of investment in science and higher education in the two countries, Brazil and Portugal, with larger economies and more established universities. However, the largest growth potential, in the next decades, is expected to come from African countries, namely Angola and Mozambique whose nascent higher education and research institutions have been experiencing significant upgrades.

Table 1 Sample of languages considered

SCI—Science Citation Index		*SSCI—Social Science Citation Index*	
1960	*2015*	*1960*	*2015*
1. English	1. English	1. English	1. English
2. Russian	2. German	2. French	2. German
3. German	3. Spanish	3. German	3. Spanish
4. French	4. Chinese	4. Russian	4. French
5. Dutch	5. French	5. Dutch	5. Portuguese
6. Spanish	6. Portuguese	6. Spanish	6. Russian
7. Japanese	7. Polish	7. Italian	8. Czech
8. Italian	8. Japanese	8. Afrikaans	8. Italian
100% coverage in the years considered	98.8% coverage in the years considered	100% coverage in the years considered	98.7% coverage in the years considered

Source Gradim and Piñero-Naval (2019, p. 149)

Data collected by OEI (2021) shows that in 2019 Portuguese R&D investment as a percentage of GDP, at 1.4%, was the highest of Iberian and Latin American countries. Next came Spain (1.25%) and Brazil (1.16%). However, this weight still pales in comparison with countries such as Israel (4.95%), Sweden (3.34%), Germany (3.09%), the US (2.83%), China (2.19%), or Canada (1.59%). In an ever more global world, the Portuguese language has much to catch up so that the science and technology produced in the Portuguese-speaking countries can match the high investment produced in other parts of the world including Asia, Northern Europe, and the English- speaking countries, namely.

The economic dimension is another important metric for analyzing the geopolitical clout of a language. Esperança (2016) carried out a comparative analysis of 8 global languages considering their relative weight in wealth and trade as well as their commercial interactions, as presented in Table 2.

Table 2 summarizes the relative weight of the countries whose predominant languages are included in this summary. These 61 countries,

Table 2 GDP and Trade of global languages

	German	Arabic	Chinese	Spanish	English	Other	Portuguese	Total
Number of countries	4	17	4	16	8	170	8	231
% GDP	6.39%	3.13%	14.14%	6.36%	30.87%	35.60%	3.50%	100%
Natural Share - % of World trade	10.29%	4.94%	16.31%	6.31%	19.38%	40.85%	1.93%	100%
German	31.6%							
Arabic	-51.2%	98.6%						
Chinese	-55.0%	3.6%	74.3%					
Spanish	-38.0%	-43.5%	-43.1%	44.4%				
English	-25.0%	-33.6%	-9.7%	115.2%	52.7%			
Other	39.7%	23.1%	-5.8%	-37.7%	-27.9%	9.4%		
Portuguese	-35.2%	-13.4%	15.9%	172.3%	-15.7%	-18.6%	74.6%	

Source Esperança (2016), 2014 data

associated to 6 languages spoken in at least 3 countries, accounted for 64% of the global wealth of 58.7 trillion (1012) euros in 2014, and 59% of the 36.2 trillion (1012) euros of world trade. In rows 2 and 3 we can observe that English is a language of wealth, as in 2014 the 8 English-speaking nations produced 31% of the World's wealth.

However, they are relatively closed economies as they generated less than 20% of the World trade. The main reason is that the largest English-speaking economy, the US, is relatively closed as imports and exports account for a relatively small share of its GDP. Large nations tend to be more self-sufficient as internal trade covers many of the consumption needs of the country. By contrast, German is the language of trade as the 4 German-speaking countries, although relatively rich at 6.4% of the World's wealth, control an even larger share of trade—10.3%. In the trade versus wealth relation, the Portuguese language is similar to the English language, as the share of wealth, at 3.5% is much larger than the share of trade—than 2%. There are two common characteristics that explain this similarity. The first is that English and Portuguese-speaking countries are spread in several distant regions—more so the Portuguese-speaking countries which do not share any land border. There is an exception for the English-speaking countries as the US and Canada share the largest land border on Earth. The second similarity, even more extreme in the case of the Portuguese-speaking countries is the overwhelming weight of one country—Brazil—with a very diversified economy, explained its relative closeness. Again, the emerging African economies are likely to be more integrated in the World economy and make a larger contribution to the international trade flows as they become richer.

The "natural share" in the third row represents the relative weight in global trade. The links between each language with itself and all the others measure the deviation from the natural share. All deviations within each linguistic community are positive, confirming that language proximity has a positive impact on trade, as observed by many researchers of the determinants of trade (Ghemawat 2001 and Melitz 2008). Trade flows are strongly explained by the gravitational model (Ghemawat 2001): closer and larger economies attract a larger volume of trade. However, language and other cultural factors also have a strong impact on trade and other dimensions of economic relations such as foreign direct investment. As the gravitational model would predict, the deviation from the natural share is larger within language communities who are regionally clustered as is the case with Arabic and Chinese.

Perhaps equally significant is the analysis of the links among language communities. Here we can observe the geographic and cultural factors present. We see that trade between Chinese and German-speaking countries is lower that their relative trade weight. This illustrates the impact of geographic distance as well as cultural linguistic barriers. Of course, other factors such as similar specialization in certain industrial products may also be at play, but the two factors illustrated in Table 2 are certainly significant. The highest positive deviation is observed for the relation between Portuguese-speaking countries showing that geographic as well as cultural and linguistic factors are responsible for a very high level of economic integration with very intense levels trade made stronger by the joining of trade associations such as the European Union for Portugal and Spain and the Mercosul for Brazil, Argentina, Uruguay, and Paraguay.

These data confirm an analysis frequently exploited by students of the economics of language—that language commonality and proximity curb transaction costs, therefore facilitating trade, especially of goods and services of a high cultural content. Advertising and communication spill overs are much stronger among countries who share a common or easily understandable languages. Moreover, this impact is equally relevant in other fields such as foreign direct investment (FDI), migration, tourism, or student mobility. Multinational firms face significant organizational and communication costs caused by language differences (Ly et al. 2018), especially when they need to create a homogeneous corporate culture. There is strong evidence that emerging multinationals from Latin American countries chose other countries of similar language in their first ventures abroad. Similarly, in the case of Brazil and Portugal FDI relations, in both directions, are far more intense than in trade. This particularly significant at the early stage of internationalization as many firms from Brazil and Portugal chose the other country as the first location abroad. African the same language Portuguese-speaking countries have also attracted multinationals from these countries, while hosting a few emerging multinationals who also venture abroad first in countries from community. Secondly, geographic and language proximity, render Spanish-speaking countries significant hosts and home countries for FDI flowing in both directions as was observed with trade.

We find a similar pattern in migration flows. A strong preference for countries and communities sharing a common language shows that the communication costs and other cultural barriers are a significant deterrent when moving to countries with significant language differences. Several studies on the integration of migrants show that a lack of comprehension of the host country's predominant language cause a significant loss of income by comparison with those who acquire that capacity (Lazear 1999).

The international movement of students is also strongly affected by language and cultural factors. UIS (Unesco) data on international students enrolled in tertiary education programs show that Angola provides the largest cohort of foreign students in Brazil, with 1785 out of 21,803 foreign students hosted. In the opposite direction, 15,373 Brazilian students enrolled in Portuguese higher education, lower only than Argentina as the host country as it took 18,663 Brazilian students. Next, Cabo Verde with 3338 and Angola with 3246 were significant sources of foreign students. Closer French (1510) and Spanish (1002) students were in fourth and sixth position, out of a total of 35,755 higher education students hosted in Portugal. By comparison with trade, FDI and migration there is strong evidence that language commonality can strongly supersede the pure gravitational impact that pulls higher education students to universities from nearby countries.

Conclusions and Recommendations

The study of geopolitics has been focused mainly on the role played by geographic boundaries on international relations. The impact of technology namely means of transport—navigation, railways, aviation—has not been ignored as hypotheses of world predomination were raised based on the emergence of each disruptive technology. Alfred Mahan (1890) published an influential book—"The influence of sea power upon history, 1660–1783" crediting the emergence of the British empire with the contribution of the industrial revolution to its global trade and military influence. Railways were later associated with the emergence of vast land nations such as Russia and the US. Throughout these technological advancements, declining transport costs led to increasing specialization and rising world trade. Communication costs have fallen even more sharply, compounded by the emergence of the internet.

As physical borders become less relevant, the focus of geopolitical studies is moving to "intangible borders", in which culture and language play a key role. English has reached a leading status as a lingua franca and the most valuable second language as part of the human capital of non-native speakers. Mandarin Chinese has enjoyed a significant growth anchored by the rising economic clout of the Chinese Economy and is now searched by many, beyond the direct support of the Confucius institutes. Portuguese and Spanish also enjoy a relatively strong position due to favorable history and demographics. Their study can shed light on the rising impact of new determinants of geopolitical influence as, among global languages, they are on opposite poles of geographic location—Spanish is highly clustered in Latin America while Portuguese is unique by its absence of land borders between any two countries. While the vast majority of Portuguese speakers now reside in the Southern Hemisphere, they are present mostly in South America (Brazil), Africa (Angola and Mozambique), with a smaller presence in Timor and Macau.

This study should both enhance the knowledge of the impact of language commonality on the international influence of a given language community and provide insights for policymakers and the business community about the most efficient modes of supporting a language and extracting societal and economic benefits.

Portuguese shows four significant patterns: (i) Sharing a common language is a powerful influencer of trade for the community of Portuguese-speaking countries. As seen in Table 2, the internal deviation from the natural share (74.6%) is second only to Arabic. This is remarkable as all other global languages enjoy stronger geographic proximity. The positive impact on trade can be observed on other dimensions such as foreign direct investment, tourism, migrations, and student mobility. (ii) The stronger deviation, however, is found on trade between Spanish and Portuguese-speaking countries. This can be explained by two factors—geographic proximity, in the Iberian Peninsula and Latin America—and the language proximity that makes both languages much more accessible to inter understanding than most other pairs of languages. This suggests that studies on the impact of languages should analyze the role of proximity instead of commonality alone. (iii) Portuguese is weaker as a language of culture and science than its relative size by the number of speakers and the natural resources of the community would justify. It is a net importer of cultural goods and the scientific production is significantly challenged by the attraction for publishing in English. However, the recent expansion of the number of publications, both in scientific journals and the internet shows a positive trend. (iv) Finally, the cultural proximity with Spanish-speaking countries is as remarkable as the one found for trade. Most leading authors are translated primarily into Spanish, adding to the pool of readers who can access the original works.

These patterns show that the Portuguese language lags in international influence, despite the opportunities stemming from demographic, economic, and geographic advantages. To extract the potential benefits for the community and enhancing the cultural and scientific a number of policies engaging different language stakeholders, it is required: (i) Language promotion, building upon the current efforts carried out by Camões Institute and IILP (International Portuguese Language Institute). This is also an opportunity for private business in both education and translation. (ii) Strengthening international cooperation and coordination in international fora. CPLP, the association of Portuguese-speaking countries is a key tool to promote broader usage of the Portuguese language in international organizations. (iii) Creating incentives for scientific publication in Portuguese. Publishing in English tends to obtain a higher valuation than in the mother tongue. This will require the commitment of governments, universities and research units. (iv) Forging an alliance with the Spanish speaking community. The level of integration already existent in trade, FDI and culture paves the way for a strong level of inter comprehension and the creation of a critical mass that can support the emergence of a larger number of highly ranked journals that will publish in Portuguese and Spanish. This is not entirely new as a rising number of journals insert texts in both languages, often accepting also original publications in English.

The consolidation of Portuguese as a language of culture and science is fundamental to enhance the geopolitical influence of the Portuguese-speaking countries and to consolidate their values and contribution to global understanding. Enjoying a critical mass is not sufficient as public policies in international fora as well as in the design of appropriate incentives for academics and scientists to publish in their mother tongue, play a key role in fostering the use of Portuguese as a language of science.

References

Casteleiro, J. (2016). "A importância crescente da língua portuguesa no contexto mundial", em *A Língua Portuguesa no Mundo: Passado, Presente e Futuro*. Lisboa: Edições Colibri.

Esperança, J. (2016). "Efeito da proximidade linguística no comércio internacional: o português no conjunto das línguas globais" em *O português como língua num mundo global: problemas e potencialidades*. Ed. Humus, coordination by José Teixeira.

Ghemawat, P. (2001). "Distance still matters". *Harvard Business Review*, 79(8): 137–147.

Gradim, A. and V. Piñero-Naval (2019). "Políticas para português e Espanhol: a segunda língua de publicação do mundo em teia de ciência", *Informação e sociedade: Estudos*, 29(2): 146–160.

Lazear, E. (1999) "Culture and Language", *Journal of political Economy*, 107(6): 95–126.

Ly, A.; J. Esperança and N. Davcik (2018). "What drives foreign direct investment: The role of language, geographical distance, information flows and technological similarity", *Journal of Business Research*, 88: 111–122.

Melitz, J. (2008). "Language and foreign trade". *European Economic Review*, 52(4): 667–699.

Mendieta, E., R. Phillipson and T. Skutnabb-Kangas (2006). "English in the geopolitics of knowledge". *Revista Canaria de Estudios Ingleses,* 53: 15–26.

Muller, M. (2008). "Reconsidering the concept of discourse for the field of critical geopolitics: Towards discourse as language and practice". *Political Geography*, 27: 322–338.

OEI. (2021). El estado de la ciência: Principales indicadores de ciencia y tecnología ibero-americanos/interamericanos. Buenos Aires.

Paasi, A. (1998). "Boundaries as social processes: Territoriality in the world of flows". *Geopolitics*, 3: 69–88.

Paasi, A. (1999). "Boundaries as social practice and discourse: The Finnish-Russian border". *Regional Studies*, 33: 669–680.

Paz, F. (2021). "Acabar com a Pobreza é Urgente: Determinação dos Fatores que Afetam o Sucesso do Crowdfunding Social". Master Dissertation, Lisbon: ISCTE-IUL.

Rajagopalan, K. (2008). "The role of geopolitics in language planning and language politics in Brazil". *Current Issues in Language Planning*, 9(2): 179–192.

Reto, L., F. Machado and J. Esperança. (2018). "Novo Atlas da Língua Portuguesa". Lisboa: INCM.

Reto, L., N. Crespo, R. Espanha, J. Esperança and F. Valentim. (2020). *A Língua Portuguesa como Ativo Global*, Lisboa: Imprensa Nacional da Casa da Moeda.

Reto, L. and R. Gutierrez-Rivilla. (2020). "A projeção internacional do espanhol e do português: o potencial da proximidade linguística". Lisboa: Imprensa Nacional da Casa da Moeda.

Swales, J. (1997). "English as "Tyrannosaurus Rex"". *World Englishes*, 16/3: 373–382.

Watson, K. (1999). "Language, power, development and geopolitical changes: Conflicting pressures facing plurilingual societies". *Compare: A Journal of Comparative and International Education*, 29(1): 5–22.

The Portuguese Science Diplomacy and EU's External Activities with Lusophone Africa: Looking at the Co-building Approach

João Mourato Pinto and *Laura C. Ferreira-Pereira*

Introduction

Science diplomacy is an emerging field which has been gaining traction in the achievement of the goals and priorities enshrined in the EU Global Strategy of 2016 and, ultimately, in the ambition of the organisation to assert itself as a "model power" in the world (Ferreira-Pereira 2012; Duarte and Ferreira-Pereira 2021; Ferreira-Pereira and Mourato Pinto 2021). Against this background, the present chapter will look at Portuguese science diplomacy to explore its contributions to the EU's

J. Mourato Pinto (✉)
Research Centre in Political Science (CICP-UMinho), University of Minho, Braga, Portugal
e-mail: jmouratopinto@eeg.uminho.pt

L. C. Ferreira-Pereira
Department of Political Science and Research Centre in Political Science (CICP-UMinho), University of Minho, Braga, Portugal
e-mail: lpereira@eeg.uminho.pt

P. A. B. Duarte et al. (eds.), *Portugal and the Lusophone World*,
https://doi.org/10.1007/978-981-99-0455-6_21

external science activities with the Portuguese-speaking countries, also known as Lusophone countries, in Africa.[1] Portugal constitutes an interesting case to understand the limitations of EU's science diplomacy and how its reach is extended through the science diplomacy of member states. The country has been an active part in the construction of the European Research Area (ERA), giving particular attention to its creation during its 2000 Presidency of the Council and to its reform during its 2021 Presidency.[2] Being a small peripheral country, Portugal has dedicated significant investment to the improvement of its research profile, launching a legal framework for its science diplomacy in November 2016, shortly after the publication of the EU Global Strategy and just as science diplomacy was gaining momentum in the Juncker Commission. Since then the country became a liquid beneficiary of Horizon Europe (MCTES 2022: 10), the EU research and innovation programme, and continues to expand its research goals through a dedicated strategy launched in 2019.

Furthermore, due to its historical ties to the Lusophone countries, Portugal has traditionally acted as a bridge-builder between them and the EU. This is related to the relevance of the Lusophone world as a critical axis of the Portuguese foreign policy, alongside the European axis structured around the EU and the Atlantic one founded on NATO membership. Therefore, the Portuguese authorities have been exploring opportunities to embed relations with the Portuguese-speaking countries in the EU's external agenda, namely in the realm of the Common Foreign and Security Policy (CFSP). This has been made mainly through uploading national foreign policy priorities into the EU's agenda (Ferreira-Pereira 2008). Emphasis placed upon Africa is part of the DNA of Portuguese foreign policy. Hence the country's interest in the continent, particularly the African Lusophone countries. In the context of its EU membership, this was particularly noticeable during the 2000 and 2007 Portuguese presidencies of the Council, when Portugal organised the first and second EU-Africa Summits, respectively. African issues received further attention during the Portuguese Presidency of 2021, despite the disruptive pandemic context in which it took place. The

[1] The Lusophone countries in Africa are Angola, Cabo Verde, Guinea-Bissau, Equatorial Guinea, Mozambique, and São Tomé and Príncipe.

[2] Interview with an official of the Portuguese Permanent Representation to the EU, online, 29/03/2022.

approval of the Amendment to the Visa Facilitation Agreement, reducing the cost and simplifying the requirements for short-term Schengen visas for Cabo Verdean citizens, the launching of the negotiations of the first-ever bilateral agreement on investment facilitation with Angola stood out alongside the launching of a military training mission in Mozambique (EUTM).

Incidentally, Africa has grown as a priority for the EU's science diplomacy and external action in general. The EU Global Strategy of 2016 mentions science diplomacy as a relevant tool to find better solutions for conflict settlement, energy transition and in the case of Africa, "support peace and security efforts in Africa, and assist African organisations' work on conflict prevention, counterterrorism and organised crime, migration and border management, but also to increase collaboration with Africa" (EEAS 2016: 36). The Council has its own monitory body, assuring that the member states are involved in a policy where the Commission has limited room. Portugal is also involved in this monitoring, particularly given its interest both in Africa and in higher education and research cooperation with Lusophone countries, a field that has been crucial in shaping post-colonial relations (Carvalho 2019: 147). EU higher education and research programmes, such as Erasmus+ and Horizon Europe, respectively, have been fundamental to structure relations between Portugal's science diplomacy towards and the Lusophone states in Africa. In turn, these programmes have developed themselves as EU soft power tools, conveying the values the Union aspires to project across the world by means of science diplomacy, among other domains.

This chapter aims at examining Portugal's science diplomacy vis-à-vis the Lusophone Africa against the backdrop of the growing relevance of EU's external science activities and science diplomacy, in particular. In so doing, it highlights how the EU higher education, research, and innovation programmes, particularly, Horizon Europe—the Union's main science diplomacy tool—have become instrumental for providing financial support to the Portuguese science diplomacy in Lusophone countries. As this study demonstrates, such diplomatic endeavours rely largely on a co-building approach engaging the country's representatives and the EU institutions and have become a centrepiece of a developing relationship between the EU and Lusophone Africa. While having direct access to the EU funding, Portugal has showed the capacity to mould the content of normative conditionalities underlying European science activities implemented in Portuguese-speaking African countries. The chapter argues that a symbiotic relation has been fostered as a result of the co-building approach in the management of EU's external science activities. The Union has been able to expand the reach of the normative agenda embedded in its education and science programmes through Portugal's science diplomatic activities in Lusophone Africa. At the same time, given access to the much-needed EU funding and other tools, the Portuguese authorities have succeeded in deepening the country's relations with the former colonies in Africa, which are part of the broader Community of Portuguese-Speaking Countries (CPLP). Furthermore, they are ultimately contributing to improve the EU's standing as a 'model power' in the Lusophone world.

As far as timeframe is concerned, the analysis ranges from 2016 to 2021, a period during which both the EU and Portuguese science diplomacy gained momentum, moving from a conceptualisation stage to an implementation phase. The year of 2016 is a landmark for two major reasons. It was the year of the launching of both the EU Global Strategy and of the "Open Innovation, Open Science and Open to the World" strategy, one of the first comprehensive EU strategies operationalising science diplomacy. This was also the year of the publication of the Portuguese Council of Ministers Resolution 78/2016, which is the main science diplomacy legal framework in the country. The year of 2021 corresponds to the first year of a new cycle of EU programmes (i.e. Horizon Europe, Erasmus+ and the Neighbourhood, Development and International Cooperation Instrument—Global Europe—NDICI), which ascribed a more prominent role to science diplomacy. Moreover, this year saw the release of the "Global Approach to Research and Innovation", which inaugurates a new phase of the EU's science diplomacy; and it is the first year of the implementation of "Portugal in Science and Research Network" (PERIN), that is the Portuguese strategy for the field.

Given the scarcity of scholarly studies focused on such issues, this chapter relies on the analysis of legal documents originated from the main EU institutions, such as the Commission's "Towards a comprehensive Strategy with Africa" or "Global Approach to Research and Innovation", as well as different regulations adopted by the Parliament and reports by the Council. The chapter also analyses documents from the Portuguese government, including its PERIN strategy or the Council of Ministers Resolution 78/2016. To fill in the gaps of information, an interview was conducted with a member of the Portuguese Permanent Representation to the European Union in March 2022. Additional first-hand information was obtained upon authors' request from the Portuguese National Agency Erasmus+ for Education and Training, the Portuguese Ministry of Science, Technology and Higher Education, the Portuguese Foundation for Science and Technology and the Directorate-General for Education, Culture, Youth and Sport of the European Commission. Such data generated added-value to the present work.

This chapter begins by mapping the structure of the EU's science diplomacy and the power dynamics underlying its external science activities. Then, it outlines the legal and political framework of the Portuguese science diplomacy framework, while paying particular attention to how the EU programmes and initiatives have been used by Portuguese authorities to back up the country's science diplomacy outreach in Lusophone Africa. Finally, this study focuses on the relationship between the Portuguese and EU science diplomacy, exploring their symbiotic relation resulting from the co-building approach in the management of EU's external science activities. Overall, this chapter aims to shed further light to the relevance of the articulation between the latter and science diplomacy of member states through co-building approaches (Mourato Pinto 2022); and be an addition to the debate on the EU's public diplomacy and soft power (Duarte and Ferreira-Pereira 2021; Ferreira-Pereira and Mourato Pinto 2021; Dominguez et al. 2022).

Science Diplomacy and the Powerness of the European Union's External Science Activities

Generally, science diplomacy results from the continued interaction between the foreign affairs of a state, conducted by the Ministry of Foreign Affairs, and its technological and scientific policy, which is coordinated by the Ministry of Science. While a "fluid concept" (Royal Society 2010: v), in essence it is "a series of structured practices at the intersection of science, technology and foreign policy" (Melchor et al. 2021: 4), originating a rather broad field encompassing different approaches with no single definition or a single implementation model (Flink and Schreiterer 2010: 667). In its joint publication "New Frontiers in Science Diplomacy" (2010), The Royal Society and the American Association for the Advancement of Science broke the concept down to three components: *science in diplomacy*, referring to the need to formulate science-informed foreign policy; *diplomacy for science*, involving diplomatic initiatives that support the creation of scientific collaboration; and *science for diplomacy* pointing to conditions in which the science and technology community supports the development of diplomatic relations. In any case, these components are not the only definitions of science diplomacy and others have been published in the past years (Aranda 2019). In that regard, while the terms "external science activities" and "science diplomacy" are often used interchangeably (San Román and Schunz 2018: 250–251), the latter places a stronger emphasis on the involvement of diplomatic agents.

Science diplomacy is implemented through several strategic tools such as joint declarations between states and institutions. At a more operational level, science diplomacy translates into, for example, international cooperation agreements, such as the European Organisation for Nuclear Research (CERN), the creation of university branches abroad (as done by the United Kingdom), centres of language, science, and culture (as the German Houses of Research and Innovation), and the articulation between embassies and the national scientific diaspora. In the case of the latter, Portugal can be presented as an illustrative case (Mourato Pinto 2022).

In this context, science diplomacy is composed of comprises two apparently opposite principles: on the one hand it is about promoting diplomatic and scientific cooperation; on the other, it is also about increasing the competitive advantages of a group of countries or regions towards another. Implementing science diplomacy "can thus be grounded in an interest-driven motivation" where science is a tool "to compete on the global market for knowledge and talents or on the wish to exploit the potential of science by integrating it into foreign policy to enhance co-operation with third parties" (San Román and Schunz 2018: 248).

The potential of science diplomacy has been increasingly explored by the European External Action Service (EEAS). The EU Global Strategy (EEAS 2016), which outlines the priorities of EU external action, states the importance of "creative approaches to diplomacy" which, among others, include "having more systematic recourse to cultural, inter-faith, scientific and economic diplomacy in conflict settings" (EEAS 2016: 31). From the perspective of the Council, science diplomacy "has the potential to benefit both diplomatic and international relations and the scientific endeavour and its impact" (SFIC Secretariat 2020: 6). Science diplomacy is therefore understood as an integral part of the Union's soft power dynamic within the realm of the CFSP, which became manifested in such relevant elements as engagement with civil society and people-to-people contacts through education research and science (Duarte and Ferreira-Pereira 2021: 4). Hence, following the definition first presented by Joseph Nye (2004), science diplomacy supports the EU's ability to influence another state's actions and ultimately persuade it, without using coercion, to embrace EU values.

The EU's interest in science diplomacy grew particularly during the Juncker Commission (2014–2019). In June 2015, Carlos Moedas, European Commissioner for Research, Science, and Innovation (2014–2020), while outlining the condition of the EU as a latecomer to the field, observed that "science diplomacy presents a matchless opportunity, to address the political, demographic and environmental challenges of the age through the universal language and expression of scientific endeavour" (Moedas 2015). In the following year, Moedas put forward the somewhat utopian idea of a global research area much in line with the core values of EU as a "normative" and "model" power like democracy, academic freedom, and responsible and sustainable innovation (Ferreira-Pereira 2012: 293; San Román and Schunz 2018: 249). To be sure, the understanding is that, in an increasingly competitive world, science diplomacy has a role to play in the promotion of EU values and in deepening relations with countries and regions of strategic interest to the EU. As a tool bridging science and external action, the values underlying EU science diplomacy are defined in Title 5, Article 21 of the Treaty of the EU: "The Union's action in the international scene should be guided by principles which have inspired its own creation, development and enlargement, and which it seeks to advance in the wider world: democracy, the rule of law, the universality and indivisibility of human rights and fundamental freedoms" (OJEU 2007). That being said, as stated by Article 2C.3 of the same treaty, in the areas of research and technological development the competence of the Union to carry out activities "shall not result in member states being prevented from exercising theirs" (ibid.). Thus, in practice, the EU, and particularly the European Commission, has limited legal space and, consequently, limited resources to implement a science diplomacy strategy, largely depending on the consent and performance of the member states.

Despite the more recent developments, the EU's engagement in international science and technology cooperation can be traced back to the first framework programme, in 1983, and perhaps more importantly, to the addition of a limited science competence through the Single European Act in 1987. In 2008, the Commission launched a "Strategic European Framework for International S&T Cooperation" which was complemented by a 2012 "Strategic Approach" to international cooperation in research and innovation (San Román and Schunz 2018: 247). Commissioner Moedas' (2015) speech builds on these earlier efforts and was translated into a strategy his team launched in 2016. The three main goals for the EU's research and innovation policy were set in the title of the document: "Open Innovation, Open Science and Open to the World". Science diplomacy is identified as key to make the latter a reality. The evolution of the designations and ambition of these documents illustrate that "the primary rationale of the framework programmes and the Commission's research policy in general was – and arguably still is – to strengthen Europe's competitiveness against other states and world regions, particularly the US, Japan and, more recently, the BRICS" (Rüffin 2020: 3).

These strategies have been operationalised through the progressive inclusion of science diplomacy in the goals of the external science activities of different generations of EU research and innovation framework programmes, such as Horizon 2020 (2014–2020) and Horizon Europe, its 2021–2027 successor. Other programmes relevant for the EU's science diplomacy include, for example, the Marie Sklodowska-Curie Actions and Erasmus+. Since 2014, the latter has received budget contributions from the European External Action Service (EEAS), particularly through the Partnership Instrument, as an acknowledgement to its role in the EU's external action (Ferreira-Pereira and Mourato Pinto 2021: 78). These programmes are managed by a combination of different EU agencies coordinated by the Directorates-General for Education, Culture, Youth and Sport and for Research and Innovation. There is a degree of coordination undertaken by the EEAS, but most of the work on the ground is left to administrative bodies dedicated to higher education and science.

Horizon Europe, with a budget of 95.5 billion euros, is the latest evidence of the EU's global science diplomacy ambitions since according to its regulation, one of its goals is to "promote and integrate cooperation with third countries and international organisations and initiatives based on the Union's interests, mutual benefits, international commitments, science diplomacy and, as far as possible, reciprocity" (OJEU 2021a: point 50). In this regard, the programme includes a "Global Challenges and European Industrial Competitiveness" pillar which, among other goals, points to Horizon Europe's contribution to the achievement of the SDGs through science diplomacy (point 24). To achieve this goal, the programme has a built-in associate membership status that grants third countries an access to its opportunities similar to that of the EU member states. Associate membership schemes can be used to reinforce the EU's attraction "because of their perceived inherent reward value to the recipient countries" (Ferreira-Pereira 2012: 299). In this case, the scheme is "an expression of the EU's commitment to international openness", particularly to countries "which share European values and with a strong science, technology and innovation profile" (European Commission 2021a: 3).

It must be noticed that this "international openness" is conditioned by the "science technology and innovation profile" of associated countries and by the principle of "reciprocity", which was one of the hardest to be negotiated—as evidenced by the nuanced "as far as possible"—because it entails the notion that other states' programmes must be equally open to EU participation.[3] These criteria for cooperation create a hierarchy regarding who is allowed to be associated to Horizon Europe and highlight that science diplomacy is as much about cooperation with those who share the EU's values—condensed in the word "profile"—, as it is about competition, particularly with other major powers that do not share said profile.

Horizon Europe's regulation puts in evidence that ultimately science diplomacy is framed by political decisions. This aspect is further detailed in the EU's "Global Approach to Research and Innovation: Europe's strategy for international cooperation in a changing world" (hereinafter 'Global Approach'). The communication with the same name was adopted by the Commission in May 2021 and is meant as "a guide in implementing the international dimension of the new EU programme for civil research and innovation, Horizon Europe, and its synergies with other EU programmes" (European Commission 2021a: 1). The document departs from two main ideas: "the EU is a major catalyst for internationalisation in research and innovation", which puts the tone on cooperation, and "other major science powers are now spending more on science than the EU as a percentage of gross domestic product" (ibid.), thereby fostering a competition dynamic. In this regard, the strategy

[3] Interview with an official of the Portuguese Permanent Representation to the EU, online, 29/03/2022.

acknowledges that putting "a stronger focus on science and technology in the EU's foreign and security policies in terms of "Science Diplomacy" would help the EU to project soft power and pursue our economic interests and values more effectively, meeting demand and interest from partner countries and playing to the EU's strengths as a research and innovation powerhouse" (ibid.: 4).

The Global Approach also identifies the NDICI as the key synergetic programme for Horizon Europe. This is the successor of the Partnership Instrument, European Neighbourhood Instrument, and several other EU external action instruments dedicated to different agendas and regions of the world. The regulation of the NDICI, which runs from 2021 to 2027, also mentions the importance of "promoting cooperation in the areas of science, technology and research, digitalisation, open data, big data and artificial intelligence and innovation, including the development of science diplomacy" (OJEU 2021b: ANNEX II, point 5r). The synergetic approach embedded in both regulations and the Global Approach can be seen, for example, in the work of a network of science and technology councillors that the EU allocates to third countries of strategic interest. They work at EU delegations, which are coordinated by the EEAS, and are employees paid by the Commission's Directorate-General for Research and Innovation. They promote the EU's research and innovation programmes to increase their profile and stimulate the collaboration between the member states' own science attachés or councillors through periodical meetings (Rüffin 2020: 6).

Besides underlining the relevance of the EU's external science activities in EU external action, the Global Approach also puts a strong tone on the need to adopt a "Team Europe" approach. This is a term used by the Von der Leyen Commission to describe the potential of the joint work by the European Union, financial institutions, and member states in third countries. In essence, this means that the besides mobilising its own budget, the Commission is pushing the member states to act more together and increase impact.[4] In this regard, the Global Approach is a guideline to member states regarding how to coordinate their science diplomacy strategies with the EU's "to maximise the effectiveness and impact of the actions" (European Commission 2021a: 2).

[4] Interview with an official of the Portuguese Permanent Representation to the EU, online, 29/03/2022.

Member states have their own science diplomacy initiatives, but they also contribute directly to the formulation of the EU's science diplomacy through a co-building approach. Much of that engagement takes place in the Council, particularly through the Strategic Forum for International Scientific and Technological Cooperation (SFIC). The latter is one of the sub-groups of the ERA and Innovation Committee which is the body of the Council responsible for monitoring the field. More concretely, SFIC is responsible for "the further development, implementation and monitoring of the international dimension of ERA, with focus on the external dimension of the European Union and member states' research and innovation activities, by the sharing of information and consultation between its members (member states and the Commission) with a view to identifying common priorities which could lead to coordinated or joint initiatives, and coordinating activities and positions vis-à-vis third countries and within international fora" (Council of the EU 2016: 2). It is composed by representatives of the Commission and delegates of the member states and countries associated to the Horizon Europe programme. In 2020, SFIC launched the Working Paper "Anchoring Science Diplomacy In Horizon Europe—Developing Specific Subjects And Activities" which recognises that "Horizon Europe itself is a Science Diplomacy tool", whose "benefits go beyond the EU" (SFIC Secretariat 2020: 1), allowing for "a much more informed and inclusive debate around the use and role of «knowledge» for Europe's internal and external relations" (ibid.: 6). As in the Horizon Europe and NDICI regulations, this document places a strong tone on how "science diplomacy can contribute to the strengthening of the European identity and values" (ibid.: 3).

However, the matter of values is not consensual, leading the European Commission to recommend, in its "Proposal for a Council Recommendation on a Pact for Research and Innovation in Europe", that member states "agree on a common set of values and principles for research and innovation in the Union" and promote them "in their interactions with third countries in order to achieve a level playing field and common framework conditions" (European Commission 2021b). The Commission's external action is bound to the guiding principles of article 21 of the Treaty of the EU, but this is not necessarily the case for the member states' initiatives. As a result, the EU's and member states' narratives on values are not fully aligned on the ground. This disagreement can emerge from the fact that while the agenda is set as a result of the institutional trilogue (involving the Commission, the Council and Parliament), when it comes to programme implementation "the Commission is not a simple agent of member states' interests but possesses some degrees of freedom to engage in science diplomacy" (Rüffin 2020: 5). This is particularly visible through the work of the EU delegations that, despite limited financial and human resources, engage in a coordination effort to maximise the impact of European science and technology in third countries. Eventually, this often comes down to the promotion of the education and research programmes (ibid.: 7), which means that much of the heavyweight is lifted by member states.

All in all, the relationship between the science diplomacy of individual member states and EU external science activities, which is another tangible expression of the Union's hybrid dynamics (i.e. intergovernmental and supranational), reflects the co-building approach underlying EU science diplomacy. Given that research and innovation is not an EU competence, member states have kept the authority over the field, while allowing for an appropriate degree of coordination by the European institutions provided there is added-value involved, as foreseen by the Lisbon Treaty. On the other hand, the EU has been circumventing its limitations by providing funding opportunities for member states through programmes such as Horizon Europe, whose legal and political framework is ultimately the reflection of member states' own priorities. Thus, science diplomacy, undertaken under the aegis of the Commission, have been complementing national endeavours, including in negotiations with third countries; and concrete actions are expected to originate from the member states rather than the Commission (ibid.: 6).

The Portuguese case is an illustrative example of the co-building approach underlying the EU's science diplomacy, and of how each member state's science diplomacy can extend the Union's science diplomacy outreach, by means of access to European funds for cooperation with third countries in research and innovation.

The Portuguese Science Diplomacy: Political and Legal Frameworks

In November 2016, just a few months after the release of the EU Global Strategy and the launching of the Moedas-led "Open Innovation, Open Science and Open to the World" strategy, the Portuguese government published the legal framework upon which the Portuguese science diplomacy approach has been built to date. This is the Council of Ministers Resolution 78/2016, which defines science diplomacy in the following terms: "the coherent and systematic use of resources and initiatives belonging to the field of science and technology, in the framework of the Portugal's European and foreign policy, in order to pursue the aims of this policy and, namely, the promotion of the national image and interests, of knowledge opportunities, reciprocal communication and collaboration between Portugal and other states, people-to-people contacts and public diplomacy" (Presidência do Conselho de Ministros 2016: 4253).[5]

The actions laid out in the resolution are especially concerned with the internationalisation of Portuguese science through a greater engagement with the country's foreign policy. In order to create a "policy of internationalisation in higher education and in science and technology", the resolution outlines the contribution of the Ministry of Foreign Affairs to increase cooperation with third countries and in giving "support to consortia and strategic partnerships that assert Portugal and the Portuguese in Europe and in the world". The resolution sets five key goals for Portuguese science and technology, among which is the role of science and higher education in the cooperation with third countries and the promotion of science diplomacy. The multidisciplinary dimension of the field requires shared responsibilities between the Ministry of Foreign Affairs and its embassies and the Ministry of Science and its agencies (Presidência do Conselho de Ministros 2016).

Moreover, the resolution points to different instruments in fields, such as information (e.g. Study and Research in Portugal initiatives), promotion (e.g. promotion of exchange programmes), cooperation (e.g. CERN), and stronger links between the scientific and diplomatic communities (e.g. through the establishment of science councillors). The priorities of Portuguese science diplomacy include the Atlantic Ocean and Portuguese language and culture, with target countries including the Portuguese-speaking countries in Africa and East Timor. Emphasis is placed upon multilateralism, which is sought through the Portuguese participation at the UN, OECD, and the CPLP, all of this with the aim of supporting the Portuguese ability to influence research-related priorities at the international level. Finally, the resolution highlights how the relations between scientists might spill over to the broader society, thereby

[5] All quotations in this chapter originating from Portuguese sources are the author's own translation.

promoting the Portuguese external image abroad and contributing to the country's soft power (Flink and Schreiterer 2010; Aranda 2019).

The section "Portugal's European and foreign policy" in the Council of Ministers resolution 78/2016 conveys two important ideas. First, there is an official recognition that science can contribute to Portuguese diplomacy. Secondly, there is a clear acknowledgement of the close connection between Portuguese science diplomacy and EU science diplomacy to the extent that the former is also framed within Portugal's European strategy (Presidência do Conselho de Ministros 2016: 4253). This unveils national policy-makers' understanding that Portuguese science diplomacy relies on EU external science activities in order to be effective. To some extent, this is the result of decades of integration in higher education through the European Higher Education Area and Erasmus+; and in the domain of research, through ERA and the science and innovation framework programmes. Furthermore, it has also stemmed from the fact that such agencies and programmes are the result of the co-building approach, while engaging the Commission and member states. In essence, this means that Portuguese diplomats have worked towards uploading the national priorities into the political and legal framework and priorities of the European programmes, in order to secure that European activities are in line with the national goals and priorities. These are either technical, such as "brain circulation" and the rights of young researchers; or historical and geographical like the promotion of Portuguese language, relations with its former colonies (via CPLP) and the Atlantic-related issues.[6] Hence, the Portuguese representatives have been endeavouring to shape the agenda-setting to ensure that national preferences are reflected both in the official regulations and programme guides.

The strategy for the field is supported by PERIN, which was officially created in 2019 and brings together different Portuguese governmental agencies and institutions dedicated to research and innovation, higher education, and related fields. The network has presented its completed strategy in March 2021 (updated in February 2022), setting as major goals: "to duplicate, in 2021–2027, the Portuguese presence in European programmes as compared in relation to 2014–2020, attracting about two billion euros in European Union financing in the fields of research and innovation during that period, and triplicate the number

[6] Interview with an official of the Portuguese Permanent Representation to the EU, online, 29/03/2022.

of mobility students in higher education". These goals are linked to the network's general purpose, which is to "mobilise and more effectively articulate public and private resources, particularly through European Union funding programmes in the fields of research and innovation, Erasmus+, Space and Digital (...)" (MCTES 2022: 2). Hence, it is clear from both the legal framework and the respective implementation strategy that EU funding is key to achieve the Portuguese science diplomacy goals; and, therefore, Portugal must actively strive to increase its capacity to secure and execute EU funding.

Under the aegis of this strategy, national authorities have been underlining the value of higher education and research in the training of future leaderships of strategically relevant states, allowing the former to disseminate the country's views of the world (Carvalho 2019: 144). This is particularly the case of Portuguese-speaking African countries. Given that Africa ranks high on the EU's priorities, the close relationship that Portugal has created with its former colonies through higher education and research is very interesting and useful for Brussels.

European Union's External Science Activities and Portuguese Science Diplomacy Towards the Lusophone Africa

The EU does not have a single policy targeting just the African Portuguese-speaking countries. Instead, the latter are included in EU-Africa relations, which comprise a long-lasting scientific cooperation. The importance of science and technology to strengthen bilateral relations was already highlighted in the 2007 Joint Africa-EU Strategy. Later, in 2010, at the 3rd AU-EU Summit in Tripoli, an EU-Africa High-Level Policy Dialogue (HLPD) on science, technology and innovation was launched. The collaboration gained momentum with the adoption of the document "Towards a Comprehensive Strategy with Africa" by the Commission and the High Representative for Foreign Affairs and Security Policy. Starting with the sentence "Africa is Europe's closest neighbour" (European Commission and High Representative of the Union for Foreign Affairs and Security Policy 2020: 1), the strategy recognises that "the African Union and the EU are committed to the international rules-based order and the multilateral system, with the United Nations at its core" (ibid.: 15). Against this background, the document proposes five partnerships, broken down into ten actions, upon which the new EU-Africa strategy could be built, including the scale up of EU-Africa academic and scientific cooperation (ibid.: 10).

The Global Approach provides a direction on how to enhance this collaboration, particularly under an "Africa Initiative" proposed by the EU and African Union (AU) Commissions. Under this initiative, which is the technical result of a political agreement reached at the July 2020 Ministerial meeting of the EU-AU HLPD on Science, Technology, and Innovation, a new "EU-AU Innovation Agenda" is being created (European Commission 2021a: 17). This Agenda is to be financed "by the biennial work programmes of Horizon Europe, the regional and national multi-annual indicative programmes of the Neighbourhood, Development and International Cooperation Instrument—Global Europe, (…), and other relevant AU-EU programmes. Furthermore, several EU member states have shown an interest to increase their support to AU-EU STI cooperation in African countries and contribute to the implementation of this AU-EU Innovation Agenda" (European Commission 2022: 2–3). Therefore, this Agenda will be implemented through both the synergies created by science diplomacy and the concept of Team Europe, generating a background which can enhance science diplomacy between the EU and AU, namely through strengthening cooperation within higher education institutions and research centres/organisations (ibid.: 5).

It is against this background that Portugal engages in its own science diplomacy efforts towards African Portuguese-speaking countries. At this point, it must be highlighted that, since its accession to the European project, Portugal has looked for a differentiated voice and profile which could distinguish it from other southern European countries, especially Spain (Ferreira-Pereira 2022: 652). Drawing on a comparative advantage derived from its longstanding historic and cultural ties with Africa, as well as close relations with the Lusophone states, Portuguese political and diplomatic authorities endeavoured to cultivate the role of constructive bridge-builder between the two continents (Ferreira-Pereira 2008: 65). Consequently, the first EU-Africa summit was organised in 2000 during the Portuguese Presidency of the Council. The second bilateral summit, resulting in the formal endorsement of the Africa-EU Strategic Partnership, which included a Joint Africa-EU Strategy and an Action Plan, took place in Lisbon on 8–9 December 2007 in the context of the Portuguese

Presidency of the Council. Thus Portuguese policy-makers proud themselves in being initiators of Euro-African dialogue, something that has been seen as an added-value by the EU itself since the country's accession to the European Economic Community in 1985. The same argument as a bridge-builder and as a representative of all Lusophone countries was presented by the Portuguese candidacy to the UN Security Council 2011–2012, which the country eventually won in 2010. It was later speculated that "Portugal's allies in the CPLP worked to, in turn, gather *their* allies in support of Portugal's bid, thus fanning support across the globe in a show of Lusophone solidarity" (Ashby 2017: 47). A similar type of support was relevant to elect António Guterres as UN Secretary General (Carvalho 2019: 163). Hence, Portugal's self-perception as bridge-builder is rooted in concrete and successful examples and CPLP serves as an instrument that has progressively increased Portuguese leverage in the EU, allowing the country to punch above its weight.

Much of this effort has been taking place in two distinct yet intertwined dimensions. On the one hand, there is the multilateral dimension *strictu sensu* in the framework of which Portuguese authorities rely on the EU education and research programmes to increase the country's collaboration with and weight in the African Lusophone countries. In this case, relations with each country are managed within the realm of EU-Africa relations.[7] On the other hand, there is the bi-multilateral dimension as Portugal maintains, at the same time, bilateral relations with each African Lusophone country and multilateral through international organisations, particularly CPLP. Looking at the multilateral dimension, it must be highlighted that using the EU framework to foster relations with countries of strategic interest to member states is a somewhat common practice. This is shown in the report on "European Countries" Innovation Collaboration with Africa', launched in April 2021 by the SFIC "Working Group for Africa", which is composed of nine member states, including Portugal, and the European Commission (SFIC Secretariat 2021a: 4). The report, whose conclusions are based on the results of an "Innovation Survey" answered by 15 countries, including Portugal, lists several initiatives towards Africa that member states have implemented through the funding of EU research and innovation programmes. Such initiatives range from development cooperation to the support of think tanks on

[7] Interview with an official of the Portuguese Permanent Representation to the EU, online, 29/03/2022.

strategic knowledge with Africa, showcasing a "widespread cooperation between European and African stakeholders when projects were funded by the EU or other international schemes" (SFIC Secretariat 2021b: 4). With regard to Portugal, this report emphasised, for example, the creation in 2020 of the Atlantic International Research Centre, which brings together American, European and African countries to address common challenges in the Atlantic; the "Ciência LP – International Centre for Advanced Training of Scientists from Portuguese-Speaking Countries in Basic Sciences", created in 2011, in Lisbon, under the auspices of UNESCO; and the initiative "Science 4 COVID-19" (SFIC Secretariat 2021a: 11), a framework through which Portugal provided African Portuguese-speaking countries with medical equipment.

According to Carvalho, collaboration through education and research has been the subject of investment of successive Portuguese governments because it contributes to overcoming the colonial past with the African Portuguese-speaking countries. This strategy relies on "the attractiveness of the Portuguese university system to students from African Portuguese-speaking countries" which is "one of the main vectors of Portuguese foreign policy towards these countries" (Carvalho 2019: 147). As anticipated in the previous lines, it underlines the overall value of higher education and research in the training of future leaders of states with strategic interest in the eyes of national authorities, allowing them to disseminate Portugal's worldview (ibid.: 144). The EU funding has been essential to achieve this goal. Through the framework of Erasmus+, Portuguese universities have signed bilateral agreements with most Portuguese-speaking countries. For example, looking at the Erasmus Mundus Joint Master Degrees, a study programme jointly delivered by a consortium of higher education institutions, including in non-EU countries, between 2014 and 2020, out of 369 institutions which participated in the programme, 17 were Portuguese, making the country the 6th with most institutions involved (European Commission 2021c: 5). Portugal hosted 859 out of 13,248 hosted mobility flows, making it the 7th highest placed country (ibid.: 9). These numbers have provided a basis for the conception of the PERIN strategy for Erasmus+, which states clearly that it aims to "strengthen the national participation in the external dimension of the programme, including in the cooperation with Africa" (MCTES 2022: 25). Besides Erasmus+ and Horizon Europe, other EU programmes identified by the PERIN strategy as relevant to foster cooperation with Portuguese-speaking countries in Africa, include the "Connecting Europe Facility 2021–2027", promoting Portugal as the centre of high-speed submarine cables connecting America and Africa to Europe (MCTES 2022: 28) and several initiatives of the EU Space Programme.

As for the bi-multilateral dimension of Portugal's science diplomacy efforts towards African Portuguese-speaking countries, much of the work takes place within CPLP, particularly through the meetings of Ministers of Science, Technology, and Innovation, which have taken place regularly since 1999. One of the most relevant achievements of these meetings was the creation of the "Strategic Plan for Multilateral Cooperation in the Domains of Science, Technology and Higher Education 2014–2020", approved at the VI Meeting of Ministers of Science, Technology and Higher Education of CPLP held in 2014, in Maputo. The document identifies six strategic axes to enhance cooperation, including the creation of a CPLP higher education area and of a CPLP science and technology space (CPLP 2014: 9–12). The strategic plan takes stock of different initiatives and programmes, including Erasmus+, to which CPLP countries have access, something that is identified as an opportunity to increase multilateral cooperation "having in mind the optimisation of resources" (CPLP 2014: 4). In other words, the document suggests using an EU funding scheme to increase collaboration among CPLP member states (CPLP 2014: 29). As mentioned earlier, this document, which was published around the time Erasmus+ gained a much stronger international dimension and relationship with the EEAS (Ferreira-Pereira and Mourato Pinto 2021: 78), looks at EU funding as an opportunity, providing an insight into how the "other side" perceives the relationship with the EU.

Hence, there is a perceived mutually beneficial relationship between EU and CPLP informed by a co-building approach. On the one hand, the EU invests in programmes whose conditionalities imply the acceptance and incorporation of EU values and principles in joint projects. On the other hand, the CPLP accepts those principled or normative conditions to fund its own internal cooperation goals. Equally important, Portugal is the centrepiece of this relationship since it is the only country with direct access to EU funding and, more importantly, with the capacity to mould and sometimes steer the content of those conditionalities. Consequently, although it is clear that CPLP increases the Portuguese weight within the EU, Portugal anchors the CPLP to the EU, thereby providing access to EU funds, markets, programmes, promotional platforms, among other assets (Ashby 2017: 52).

As a result of Portuguese endeavours as regards both the multilateral and bi-multilateral spheres already refereed, in the academic year 2020–2021, out of 58,960 foreign students fully enrolled in Portugal, nearly 30% were from the Portuguese-speaking countries in Africa, particularly from Angola and Cabo Verde, and about 33% were Brazilian (DGEEC 2021a). Looking at the 6056 foreign students completing their Ph.D. in Portugal, in 2020, about 18% were Angolan, 14% were Brazilian and 13% were Mozambican. Additionally, these are the top three countries of provenience of foreign Ph.D. students in Portugal (DGEEC 2021b). This means that nearly two thirds of the foreign students and almost half of foreign successful Ph.D. students in Portugal come from Portuguese-speaking countries. This can be explained by two major factors. On the one hand, the existence of a common language, which is undoubtedly a key and independent factor. On the other hand, the scientific cooperation agreements signed not only between Portuguese authorities and the governments of these countries, but also between Portuguese universities and Brazilian and Lusophone African universities, often under the aegis of Erasmus+ or Horizon Europe funding.

Overall, the two above-mentioned dimensions of Portugal's science diplomacy towards African Portuguese-speaking countries are quite aligned with that of the EU's. They reflect a symbiotic relationship in which the EU extends the reach of its external science activities, including the EU values embedded in them, to regions where Portugal has far more influence and knowledge, Portugal gets funding to deepen its relationship with the region, and the region gets funding to train its future professionals and deepen its internal collaboration. This relationship is a result of the co-building approach of EU science diplomacy, through which Portuguese authorities have been able to upload a selection of priority regions and themes to programmes such as Horizon Europe, particularly during Portugal's presidencies of the Council. Thus, even though the Commission's actions in this field are limited by the treaties, the co-building approach allows for its direct actions to be complemented by the member states' through the funding provided by its programmes. Ultimately, this is an expression of a Team Europe approach, as envisioned by both the Global Strategy (2016) and the Global Approach (2021) in a joined-up implementation effort to raise both the EU's and individual member states' soft power in Africa, a priority region at the centre of the global battle for values, showcasing the essential competitive nature of modern science diplomacy.

Conclusion

This chapter has examined the legal and political frameworks of both the Portuguese science diplomacy and EU external science activities, highlighting how their intertwined and symbiotic character, which is a result of a co-building approach, has reinforced EU science diplomacy. After introducing science diplomacy as a concept, it has showed that this field can further contribute to the EU position as a global role model and leader at the multilateral level (Melchor et al. 2021: 4), a premise which has become embedded in the political and legal framework of the main EU programmes and strategies like Horizon Europe, Erasmus+, and NDICI. Nevertheless, as this chapter has outlined, even though the Treaty of the European Union has opened some space for the Commission to act externally on the basis of the so-called "EU values", because neither research nor innovation are part of its exclusive competences, the EU faces important limitations on the ground. For this reason, Horizon Europe or Erasmus+, for example, were designed to stimulate member states' initiatives mirroring EU core values in third countries. This has resulted in the construction of a rather unique science diplomacy model, in which national and European strategies complement each other on the basis of a co-building dynamics. Indeed, the Global Approach was created to foster the alignment of the Commission's and member states' science diplomacy initiatives, in an attempt further circumvents this institution's limitations and promote the spirit of a Team Europe.

This chapter has analysed how Portuguese science diplomacy makes full use of the European framework to deepen its relations with the African Lusophone countries. The Portuguese Council of Ministers Resolution 78/2016 foresees that national science diplomacy is both part of Portugal's relations with third countries and part of its national policy or strategy towards the EU. Therefore, the PERIN strategy strives to maximise Portugal's access to EU funding in higher education and in research and innovation, not only to increase Portugal's weight in the African Portuguese-speaking countries, but also to enhance its position within the EU. By acting as a bridge-builder between Lusophone Africa, either bilaterally or multilaterally via the CPLP, Portugal has attempted to raise its status among its European peers. By acting as the sole EU member state in CPLP with direct access to EU funding, which is considered by the Portuguese-speaking Community as being relevant for the economic and social development of its member states, Portugal adds a different constructive layer to its post-colonial relations in Africa.

Such strategically good use of the EU external science activities made by the Portuguese authorities display the symbiotic relationship Lisbon has established with Brussels, in which access to and implementation of the European funds needed to achieve national goals increases the reach of EU values, thus overcoming the Commission's practical limitations. Yet, as this study has demonstrated, it cannot be said that Portuguese authorities—or any other member states' authorities for that matter—have been simply implementing the initiatives and programmes created by Brussels. This is so because the major priorities of such programmes are the result of a trilogue negotiation process between the Commission, the Council and the Parliament. Like in most European policies, EU science diplomacy stems from a co-building approach developed with the member states. In that regard, Portuguese authorities have been able to upload the country's own national priorities into the EU agenda in this domain, thereby shaping the design of the implementation-related programmes. In other words, the values, norms, and target countries of the EU science diplomacy have been reflecting Portugal's own preferences and target states, besides the values and norms enshrined in the European treaties and strategic documents like the Global Strategy. Along these lines, by means of the co-building approach, Portuguese science diplomacy has been contributing to improve the EU's standing as a "model power" (Ferreira-Pereira 2012) in the Lusophone world.

Acknowledgement The authors would like to thank the Portuguese National Agency Erasmus+ for Education and Training, the Portuguese Ministry of Science, Technology and Higher Education, the Portuguese Foundation for Science and Technology and the Directorate-General for Education, Culture, Youth and Sport of the European Commission for their collaboration in the information provided for this chapter.

References

Aranda, J. (2019) *Diplomacia Científica: Saber é Poder*. Lisbon: Edições Colibri.

Ashby, Sarah (2017) *The Lusophone World: The Evolution of Portuguese National Narratives*. Chicago: Sussex Academic Press.

Carvalho, C. (2019) "A cooperação Portugal-PALOP no domínio da educação: um instrumento de *soft power* para a política externa portuguesa?" *in* Raimundo, António, *Política Externa Portuguesa e África: Tendências e Temas Contemporâneos*. Lisbon: Centro de Estudos Internacionais do Instituto Universitário de Lisboa, pp. 141–165.

Comunidade dos Países de Língua Portuguesa (2014) *Plano Estratégico de Cooperação Multilateral no Domínio da Ciência, Tecnologia e Ensino Superior da CPLP (2014–2020).*

Council of the European Union (2016) *Revised mandate for SFIC.*

Direção-Geral de Estatísticas da Educação e Ciência (2021a) *Inscritos no ano letivo 2020/2021.* Lisbon: DGEEC.

Direção-Geral de Estatísticas da Educação e Ciência (2021b) *Inquérito aos Doutorados 2020.* Lisbon: DGEEC.

Dominguez, R., Hoffmann, A. R., Sandrin, P., Quiroga, A. (2022) "EUPD Performance in Latin America: Assessing the Cases of Brazil, Mexico and Colombia", *Journal of Contemporary European Studies.*

Duarte, P. A. B., Ferreira-Pereira, L. C. (2021) "The Soft Power of China and the European Union in the Context of the Belt and Road Initiative and Global Strategy", *Journal of Contemporary European Studies.*

European External Action Service (2016) *Shared Vision, Common Action: A Stronger Europe. A Global Strategy for the European Union's Foreign and Security Policy.*

European Commission and High Representative of the Union for Foreign Affairs and Security Policy (2020) *Joint Communication to the European Parliament and the Council Towards a comprehensive Strategy with Africa.*

European Commission (2021a) *Communication from the Commission to the European Parliament, the Council, the European Economic and Social Committee and the Committee of the Regions on the Global Approach to Research and Innovation.* Brussels: European Commission. 18 of May.

European Commission (2021b) *Proposal for a Council Recommendation on a Pact for Research and Innovation in Europe.* Brussels: European Commission. 16 of May.

European Commission (2021c) Erasmus+ Programme, Statistical Factsheets on the Achievements of the Erasmus Mundus Joint Master Degrees (2014–2020). Brussels: European Commission.

European Commission (2022) *The AU-EU Innovation Agenda—Working Document.* Brussels: European Commission. 14 of February.

Ferreira-Pereira, L. C. (2008) "Portugal and the 2007 EU Presidency: A Case of Constructive Bridge-Building", *Journal of Common Market Studies*, 46(1), 61–70.

Ferreira-Pereira, L. C. (2012) "The European Union as a 'Model Power': Spreading Peace, Democracy and Human Rights in the Wider World", *in*

Federica Bindi (ed.), *The European Union Foreign Policy: Assessing Europe's Role in the World*. Washington, D.C.: Brookings, pp. 293–305.

Ferreira-Pereira, L. C. (2022) "Portugal in the European Union: Chronicling a Transformative Journey", *in* Jorge Fernandes, Pedro Magalhães and António Costa Pinto (eds.), *Oxford Handbook of Portuguese Politics*. Oxford: Oxford University Press, 2022, pp. 648–665.

Ferreira-Pereira, L. C., Mourato Pinto, J. (2021) "Soft Power in the EU's Strategic Partnership Diplomacy: The Erasmus Plus Programme", *in* Laura C. Ferreira-Pereira and Michael Smith (eds.), *The European Union's Strategic Partnerships: Global Diplomacy in a Contested World*. London: Palgrave MacMillan.

Flink, T., Schreiterer, U. (2010) "Science Diplomacy at the Intersection of S&T Policies and Foreign Affairs: Toward a Typology of National Approaches", *Science and Public Policy*, 37(9), 665–677.

Melchor, L., Elorza, A., Lacunza, I. (2021) *Calling for a Systemic Change: Towards a European Union Science Diplomacy for Addressing Global Challenges*. S4D4C Policy Report, February.

Ministério da Ciência, Tecnologia e Ensino Superior (2022) *PERIN – Portugal in Europe Research and Innovation Network. Estratégia de promoção da participação nacional nos programas de financiamento da União Europeia 2021–2027 Investigação & Inovação, Erasmus+, Espaço e Digital*.

Moedas, C. (2015) *The EU Approach to Science Diplomacy*. Speech at the European Institute, Washington DC, United States. 1st of June.

Mourato Pinto, J. (2022) "Portuguese Science Diplomacy and the Networks of Portuguese Professionals, Researchers and Graduate Students Abroad: From the Escape to the Circulation of Brains", *Janus.net, E-journal of International Relations*, 13(1), May–October.

Nye, J. (2004) "Soft Power and Higher Education", *Forum for the Future of Higher Education*.

Official Journal of the European Union (2007) *Treaty of Lisbon Amending the Treaty on European Union and the Treaty Establishing the European Community, Signed at Lisbon*, 13 December 2007.

Official Journal of the European Union (2021a) *Regulation (EU) 2021/695 of the European Parliament and of the Council of 28 April 2021 establishing Horizon Europe—The Framework Programme for Research and Innovation*.

Official Journal of the European Union (2021b) *Regulation (EU) 2021/947 of the European Parliament and of the Council of 9 June 2021 Establishing the Neighbourhood, Development and International Cooperation Instrument—Global Europe*.

Presidência do Conselho de Ministros (2016) *Resolução do Conselho de Ministros n.º 78/2016*. Diário da República, 1.ª série – N. 230. 30 November, Lisbon, 4250–4253.

Royal Society and American Association for the Advancement of Science (2010) *New Frontiers in Science Diplomacy: Navigating the Changing Balance of Power*. London: Royal Society.

Rüffin, N. (2020) "EU Science Diplomacy in a Contested Space of Multi-level Governance: Ambitions, Constraints and Options for Action", *Research Policy*, 49(1).

San Román, A. L., Schunz, S. (2018) "Understanding European Union Science Diplomacy", *Journal of Common Market Studies*, 56(2), 247–266.

SFIC Secretariat (2020) *SFIC Task Force on Science Diplomacy Working Paper "Anchoring Science Diplomacy in Horizon Europe Developing Specific Subjects and Activities"*. 21 September, Brussels.

SFIC Secretariat (2021a) *European Countries' Innovation Collaboration with Africa—SFIC Africa Working Group—Innovation Survey Results*. 14 April, Brussels.

SFIC Secretariat (2021b) *Summary Conclusions of the 44th Meeting of the Informal Videoconference of the Members of the ERAC-SFIC on 10-03-2021*. 10 March, Brussels.

The Nets That Empires Weave: The Commonwealth of Nations and the Community of Portuguese-Speaking Countries

Fernanda Ilhéu

Introduction

Both the Commonwealth of Nations and the CPLP—Community of Portuguese-Speaking Countries are free associations of sovereign states that chose to maintain ties of friendship and cooperation among themselves. These countries have in common the existence of diasporas which share the same language and culture as a result of their colonial past in the British and Portuguese Empires. It is perhaps difficult to understand the cohesive factor that has united them for many generations as their colonial pasts cannot be forgotten, especially bearing in mind the bloody wars that they had to fight to gain independence. As Rostow (1971, p. 111) affirmed "the exit from imperial status, with a few exceptions, took the form of a bitter, bloody war, or it was accompanied by a major

F. Ilhéu (✉)
CEsA-ISEG—Lisbon School of Economics and Management, Lisbon University, Lisbon, Portugal
e-mail: fernandailheu@iseg.ulisboa.pt

P. A. B. Duarte et al. (eds.), *Portugal and the Lusophone World*,
https://doi.org/10.1007/978-981-99-0455-6_22

political and diplomatic crisis at home". In fact, the majority of decolonialization processes were disruptive processes, resulting in dramatic social and economic consequences for colonies and metropoles, as well as for colonists and the indigenous populations. In certain colonies this process provoked the discontinuity on the countries' development and long-term local wars in some cases. Several European countries were obliged to receive thousands of refugees as a result of these independence conflicts. For instance, almost 600,000 Portuguese returned from the Portuguese colonies in Africa in 1975. Critics of these communities tend to analyze them through the lens of the past, whereby these relations only subsist within officialdom and governments structures and consider that without these they are irrelevant institutions that have been affected by "*imperialist amnesia*", as Professor Murphy (2021) considers the British Commonwealth to be. However none of these critics analyze them through the lens of the present and future, an example being Lord Howard, who in a debate in the House of Lords of the British Parliament on the *The Commonwealth meets tomorrow* on the 5th of May 2021 affirmed that in "the age of networking and digital connectivity the linkages in a voluntary, non-treaty organization like the Commonwealth are joined as much by enterprise and trade, by civil society concerns and by common everyday life and work interest as through governments – or even more so".

In the twenty-first century, economic leadership, rather than military strength can be considered to be the index of a country's national power. A critical factor for the economic superiority of a nation is the trade leadership of their companies in the global market. The Network Theory stresses the importance of the relationship between independent companies to achieve the development of trade and investment in international market, creating long-term relationships, where mutual trust and knowledge implies a high degree of connectedness and commitment by different types of bonds (Johanson and Mattsson 1988; Madsen and Servais 1997). The diaspora networks of kinship and language, based in the Network Theory, are considered to be, a potent economic force, which easier the business networks across the borders by fostering trust based on the mutual cultural understanding of the diaspora's bonds.

Till the present we didn't find any academic research work comparing Commonwealth of Nations and the CPLP—Community of Portuguese-Speaking Countries similarities and differences, the explanations for them, as well as, their future prospects.

We analysed trade and power models from the classic Comparative Advantage theory and its developments till trade and power in the age of Network theory and, for framing our empirical case, we had also to perform an historic documents analysis of trade and power relations, between Britain and Portugal and their colonies, as well as, the outcome of the British and Portuguese decolonization processes and relate them with the Commonwealth of Nations and CPLP origins. Summarising, we concluded that there is indeed a future for both these international voluntary communities, as long as they become less government-based and more people-based.

Trade and Power During the Colonial Period

From the sixteenth to the eighteenth centuries, economic theorists defended a mercantile system based on the idea that the material wealth of nations is achieved by increasing exports and restricting imports through tariffs and achieving a favourable trade balance that creates wealth which is manifested by large stocks of gold and silver, which is used for payments. In this context the ascendance of a state is achieved at the expenses of others and in competition with others, as global wealth is limited and has attained a mature stage in Europe, where an increase in a state's wealth was only possible by expansion in the New World. Accordingly, the European nations competed in various overseas regions and colonialism emerged together with conflicts to dominate colonies in order to control raw materials and many other commodities, such as tropical products, wood, spices, sugar, fish, tea, cocoa, coffee, silk, furs, porcelain, gold and silver, and precious stones, as well as labour in the form of slaves. In turn, the European nations sold goods produced in Europe in their colonies. This trade was carried out within the context of protective national policies in the form of tariffs and the monopoly of concessions by conglomerates. Trade and military conquest advanced hand on hand and progressed from trade to governance and the extension of kingdoms and prestige (Andrews 1915; Wilson 1959; Rostow 1971; Pinto 2021).

From the end of the fifteenth century onwards, European countries begun to compete in various overseas locations for trade domination. The Iberian countries initiated this movement when the Ottoman Empire obstructed the land trade routes with Asia and the Portuguese merchants initiated the maritime trade routes to East, along the Atlantic coast to the Indic, Pacific, and China seas. Portuguese ships regularly sailed from Lisbon to Africa, India, the Far East, establishing trading stations in locations such as Goa, Oman, Colombo, Malacca, Macau, Canton, Fukien, and Nagasaki, where they collected pepper, cinnamon, cloves, and nutmeg, among other products. On their return journey they stopped off at the African coast for food and slaves. In the beginning, in this route to East the Portuguese expeditions were limited to the occupation of trade ports.

This movement was followed by ships from Spain, who instead sailed to the Americas, to be followed by the Portuguese, who settled in Brazil. New World influence and trade was divided among the two powers in the Treaty of Tordesillas, which was signed by the two Iberian countries on the 7th of June, 1494. The enormous wealth and prestige of Spain and Portugal earned from this trade aroused the attention of the other European countries which begun to follow and pressurize them that on the beginning of the seventeenth century. First it was Holland that attacked the Spanish and Portuguese ships and colonies, followed by France and Britain (Short 1982). Military action and strategic alliances with native populations where the only way to keep or gain trade overseas. The European colonial powers established a system of organization based on a political framework similar to that of the mother country. This was a condition for the expansion of this trade and was designed to keep its benefits in the hands of the European colonial elites which were transferred and shared within their nations, enriching themselves while conferring national power and prestige. Colonies were established by merchants, the military, and religious orders (whose mission was to convert the local populations to Christianity), and the local populations were educated and organized to perform their social and economic role. The overseas trade and power of certain European countries influenced their balance of power in Europe and in the whole world. The alliances and wars between these countries were driven by the ultimate strategy to maintain the governance of their resources-rich overseas colonies under their sovereignty and by doing so, guarantee their dominance of overseas trade.

Trade and Power in the Age of Networking

In the twenty-first century, economic leadership, rather than military strength can be considered to be the index of a country's national power. A critical factor for the economic superiority of a nation is the trade leadership of their companies in the global market. This competition is not achieved anymore just by the Ricardo's (1817) Comparative Advantage theory, which was based on differences in labour productivity. Nor is it even explained by the more comprehensive two-factor model of comparative advantage trade theory presented by Heckscher (1919) and Ohlin (1933), which included not only labour as a factor of production, but also capital. This latter theory defends that the countries that are rich in capital export capital-intensive products, and that those countries that are rich in labour, exports labour-intensive products, and that the two resources can in many cases be obtained either through a labour-intensive process or a capital-intensive process. An example is textile production, which can be carried out in labour-intensive countries, such as Pakistan, Vietnam, or Bangladesh, or in capital-intensive ones, such as the USA, England, or Germany.

Both processes can be internationally competitive, although their companies' competitive advantages can be different, as one group competes on cost, while the other competes on differentiation, which includes innovation, technology, design, and marketing. Companies can also choose a strategy that focusses on both cost and differentiation (Porter 1990). For to be competitive in today's international market, companies have to be truly international, where they can benefit from the advantages of different countries' competitive resources endowments, whether they be labour- or capital-intensive. Porter (1980, 1985, 1990, 1992) introduced and developed the concept of value chain, staring in 1980 with the conceptualization of a company as a floating organization, made up of interdependent and interchangeable modules. Porter defended the idea that these modules can either belong to the company or can be outsourced, also can be located in the domestic market or in different parts of the word, this benefitting from capabilities and other advantages abroad, while enabling the company to have access to new customers and to enter new markets. These capabilities can take the form of being less labour-expensive or more effective processes, either by mastering intangible assets such as technology, or by achieving superior management. By internalizing the advantages of their presence abroad, companies can become competitive in many markets, including their domestic market.

To be internationally competitive, a company must know how to spread its activities in the value chain among countries, seeking locations where strategic factors have competitive advantages (Porter 1985). Porter went on to introduce the idea of regional or global value chains, where multinational companies invest worldwide and manage trading inputs and outputs in cross-border value chains which are often highly complex, whereby such value chains can either be intra-company or inter-company, or regional or global.

In the regional or global value chains model, two dimensions have to be considered:

> 1) the international dimension of a company's activities, "where in the world each activity in the value chain is performed including in how many places"; 2) and the coordination dimension, or "how like activities performed in different countries are coordinated with each other". (Porter 1992, p. 67)

Downstream activities in the chain create competitive advantages that are largely country-specific, whereas upstream activities and support activities are obtained in the entire network system of activities spread around the world.

As a consequence, many companies outsource and coordinate all their manufacturing activities, either by investing in subsidiaries or by integrating networks around the world in order to minimize costs. The tendency is to concentrate the core critical competitive factors in the head office of the company, such as research, innovation, and marketing as a means to increase added value of the brand. Downstream activities are usually performed by subsidiaries, whereas the upstream activities are carried out by the head office (Porter 1992).

To enhance "innovation and flexibility, companies are focusing their resources on core competences and outsourcing all other activities" (Achrol and Kotler 1999, p. 147). Nike, for example, does not manufacture its own shoes, as certain Asian producers are more competitive in this task. For Nike's core competences are shoe design and shoe merchandising, which is what the company concentrates on, as it knows well that today's competition is "between networks not companies. The winner is the company with better network" (Kolter 2003, p. 72). According to Ilhéu (2020, p. 146), "Global investment and trade are thoroughly entwined in international production networks", where communication technology integrates producers into networks of suppliers' processes and customers' lifestyles and consumer habits. These networks are business networks that can be defined as being sets of connected companies or alternatively sets of connected relationships between companies (Anderson et al. 1994). These authors used the Social Exchange Theory of Kelley and Thibaut (1978) to define business networks as being sets of two or more business relationship or sets of interlinked relationship connections, where each commercial exchange is carried out by enterprises that are collective voluntary actors, be they suppliers, clients, distributors, or even competitors or governments.

Achrol and Kotler (1999, p. 148) define the network organization as "an independent coalition of task-or-skill-specialized entities (independent companies or autonomous organizational units) that operates without hierarchical control but is embedded, by dense lateral connections, mutuality, and reciprocity, in a shared value system that defines «membership» roles and responsibilities". Häkansson and Snehota (1995) refer to the essence of the network as being a business relationship, saying that from the beginning, networks include a structure of actor bonds, activity links, and resource ties. The organizational members of the networks, the actors, are bound together by bonds, which can be simply an interest in a specific topic. There are many types of bonds, namely: technical bonds, which are related with technologies employed by the companies; knowledge bonds, which are related to parties' knowledge about their business; social bonds, in the form of personal confidence; or administrative bonds, which are related to companies' administrative routines and procedures (Häkansson and Johanson 1988).

The Network Theory stresses the relationship between independent companies, where such a kind of relationships often take time to be established and developed, especially in the case of long-term relationships, where mutual trust and knowledge implies a high degree of connectedness and commitment by different types of bonds (Johanson and Mattsson 1988; Madsen and Servais 1997).

Sharing one's expertise with other network members requires trust that the shared knowledge will not be used against one-self. Newly-created organizations make less use of capital to guarantee control over system activities, but rather rely on the commitment of their members to behavioural norms, based on trust. Rodríguez and Wilson (2002, p. 55) suggest that "trust is dependent on goal congruence and cultural similarity between partner's values and methods". Another key dimension in the network model is cooperation, which can be defined as "similar or complimentary coordinated activities performed by companies in a business relationship to produce superior mutual outcomes or singular outcomes with expected reciprocity over time" (Anderson et al. 1994, p. 10). A basic assumption of cooperation in business relationship is called the "relationship understanding", which in contrast to trust that calls upon affective, moral, ethic, behaviours in business relations between partners, instead places attention on a more cognitive aspect of cooperation, investing in a greater commitment by the partners, which is known as "relationship commitment".

Commitment is a central construct of the model of relationship development and contributes. An example is commitment to the understanding of international joint-ventures, where the partners are mutually committed to understanding regarding how to coordinate their activities in a foreign market where they are prepared to invest in their relationship (Holm et al. 1996).

Iborra et al. (1998) consider that there are three types of networks: interchange, communication, and social. The interchange and communication networks are formalized between different partners and participants, however, social networks are informal, where the different members make up a close socio-economic environment, with common objectives, trust, and moral commitment, with no need for written contracts.

Social networks are much more flexible than the formalized ones, which makes them more efficient in terms of adjustments to environmental changes. An example of this kind of network is expressed by Yeung (1997, p. 41), as "Chinese business in Asia is largely embedded in business networks which rely substantially on pre-existing social relations in terms of family businesses, ethnic ties, trust mechanism, and institutional bondage". Networks usually have a social dimension characteristic, but they can also have a cultural one, in the sense that they can be based on beliefs about the basis of social activity and behavioural rules within the network (Easton 1992). Broadly speaking, they are embedded in the cultural characteristics of their members. Ranging from restaurants to real estate, through to plastic-sandal makers to semiconductor manufacturing, the "Chinese Commonwealth" consists of "many individual enterprises that nonetheless share a common culture" (Kao 1993, p. 24).

In fact, the diaspora networks of kinship and language as the Economist (2011, p. 68) pointed out, are a potent economic force which makes it easier to carry out business across borders, because "they have three lucrative virtues": "they speed the flow of information across borders, they foster trust, and they "create connections that help people with good ideas collaborate with each other within and across ethnicities". The Economist provides examples of these diasporas, including the Chinese, Indiana, or Jews, among others. These diaspora networks of kinship and language are based on societies that have collective cognitive styles that affect perception, behaviour, thinking patterns, and business practices which characterize their national cultures. Social scientists define national culture as being "patterns of thinking, feeling and acting rooted in common values and conventions of society" (Nakata and Sivakumar 2001, p. 257). Lord Howell considers that it is impossible to understand the Commonwealth today or in the future without the worldwide communications of today and its impact on global networks, of which Commonwealth happens to be the largest, he goes on, to add that the cultural similarity of the societies of the diaspora networks of kinship and language also facilitates trust through the basic assumption of cooperation, as well as the relationship understanding and commitment of its members.

British Decolonization and the Origins of the (British) Commonwealth of Nations Origins

The British Commonwealth of Nations, which is now just called the Commonwealth of Nations (after the conditions imposed by India on joining as a member state), might as well have been an inspiration for the creation of the CPLP—Community of Portuguese-Speaking Countries, although its origin, motives, and reasons for existence are very different. The Commonwealth of Nations is the oldest world organization of nations, and is rooted in the decolonization process of the British colonies. It is a long-term consequence of the American Revolution and the following independence from the British of the 13 colonies on the 4th July, 1776. The drive for independence conquest came from the British colonists' elite, rather than being an initiative of the native populations and it can be explained by ideological reasons, but mostly by settlers' dissatisfaction. The ideological illuminist ideals were taken to America by Freemasons, such as George Washington and Benjamin Franklin, among others. The first Masonic lodge in North America, the St. John's Lodge, was created in 1733 in Boston, by the Grand Lodge of England, which served as the catalyst for the distrust of British settlers in the American colonies. In fact, this colonial dissatisfaction was mostly due to the high tax burden imposed by England on its British colonies in America during the eighteenth century, resulting from the emptying of its public coffers after the wars in Europe, including the Spanish War of Succession (1701–1714), the War of Jenkins' Ear (1739–1748), and the Seven Years War (1756–1763).

The Seven Years War, which is also known in America as the French and Indian War, was the first global war, it was mainly fought in Europe, but was also rooted in colonial geopolitics and geo-economics competition, and thus extended to India and America. This war was driven by commercial and imperial rivalry between Great Britain and France and by the antagonism between Prussia (allied with Great Britain) and Austria (allied with France). Imperialism here is used it in the Leninist sense, where the overseas powers had the objective to economically exploit the dominions, as well as Montesquieu's Spirit of Laws, which affirmed that the purpose of colonies is to permit commerce with better conditions than with neighbouring peoples with whom all the advantages were reciprocal, whereby in the case of colonies, only the mother country trades with the colony and benefits from the advantages.

The fight was for trade and power in this war. Pinto (2021, p. 121) refers to a letter by Governor Shirley of Massachusetts to London, where he writes "that if Great Britain expels France from America, the profits from all the trade in these colonies will gradually develop her navigation, and the balance of trade with North America will forever be in Great Britain's favour". Indeed, this is in part what happened, as the outcome of the Seven Years War was that France was defeated and had to sign the Peace Treaty of Paris with Great Britain, Spain (allied with France), and Portugal (allied with Great Britain) in 1763. In the ensuing process of reconfiguration of overseas possessions, France had to formally cede to Great Britain territories in different parts of the world, namely in North America, including Nova Scotia in Canada, six West Indies Islands, and the land east of the Mississippi River. However. if the results were good for Great Britain, the British colonists in America were disappointed, as in a move to pacify the local populations, the British Crown did not allow them to occupy these territories in North America, but instated insisted that the colonists pay the expenses of British army military protection for the American colony.

The British Parliament passed several Acts to raise money in the colonies, such as:

a. The Sugar Act (1764), which levied taxes on different types of sugar imported from British territories (it was a common practice to smuggle molasses and sugar from French and Dutch Indies at more competitive prices), as well as Madeira wine, silk, coffee, indigo, and textiles;
b. The Currency Act and the Hostage Act (both in 1764). The former forbade the issue of paper money in the New England colonies, (Connecticut, Rhode Island, Providence, Massachusetts Bay, Plymouth and New Hampshire) and stipulating that payments should be made in gold or silver; while the latter obliged the colonists to feed the British soldiers;
c. The Stamp Act (1765), which directly taxed all the colonial commercial and legal journals, newspapers, pamphlets, almanacs, and obliged the emission of all official documents to be subject to the payment of an official British stamp;
d. The Townshend Acts (1767), whereby these four acts reasserted the British government's authority over the colonies and taxed goods imported to the American colonies;
e. The Tea Act (1773) was passed in the British Parliament to give the British East India Company the exclusive rights to sell tea in America and to award monopolies to certain colonial tea merchants, with the objective to save the Company from insolvency and to promote the selling of taxed British tea in America, rather than non-British tea.

These Acts were all passed by the British Parliament where the colonists had no representation and consequently considered these Acts to be an abuse of power and an attempt against the interests of the colonies.

The colonial resistance to these new laws was high and several incidents took place, the most famous one being the "Boston Tea Party", which took place on the 16 December, 1773 in Boston, when thousands of citizens protested against the taxes and a group known as the "Sons of Liberty", a clandestine political organization against British rule, organized opposition to the Stamps Act and boarded three ships in the

Boston harbour and threw the cargoes of tea weighing approximately 46 tonnes into the sea (Carp 2011). This attitude divided the American citizens between those who favoured resistance but without the destruction of property, and the others, who in turn were divided between those who wanted to resolve the problems in dialogue with Great Britain and those who wanted independence. As Carp (2011, p. 218) affirmed "the unknown planners of The Boston Tea Party probably did not intend that the consequence of their action would be a break from Great Britain and the formation of a new nation". The Boston Tea Party was very controversial, for was it a cynical act of group of discontent colonial merchants, or was it a collective anticolonial action driven by ideological principles? Although the idea of the Sons of Liberty was a message to the British Parliament to limited the above-mentioned Acts in the colony, over time this dangerous action of destruction became seen to be a signal of the principle of self-determination, as independence was evermore defended as the solution. Massachusetts was declared to be in a state of rebellion in February 1775 and the military action of the American Revolution War begun that year when the colonists opposed the British Army. Indeed, this War is classified by historians as an ideological and political revolution. The Declaration of Independence was signed by the Continental Congress on the 4th July, 1776, which declared the American colonies to be free and independent states, however, the War only terminate in 1783 with the creation of a modern, constitutional, liberal, and democratic country. It should be recalled that the Patriots professed the political philosophies of liberalism and republicanism, and rejected the idea of a monarchy (Middlekauff 2005).

The majority of other British colonies in other continents were decolonized after the Second World War. In 1947 the Jewel of the Crown, India, gained its independence, and when British forces were expelled from the Suez Canal in 1955, Britain lost its influence in the Middle East and during the government of Harold MacMillan (1957–1963) other colonies in Africa, Asia, and Middle East were decolonized.

Nevertheless, the creation of the British Commonwealth did not wait for this decolonization process to begin. According to Hall (1953, pp. 997–998), "The evolution of the Commonwealth was one of the long-range consequences of the American Revolution". For this author, the Commonwealth is the lesson learned by the British from the American Revolution, as what happened there could happen in any of the other colonies, and it was the "*inevitability of change*". He goes on to add that the British learned in America "That there could be no continuity of relations with the colonies unless there was freedom, consultation, and association, and elasticity in any institutional arrangements". The question was how to maintain historical continuity and avoid catastrophic change or revolution? The answer began to be put into practice in the mid-to-late nineteenth century, with the implementation of responsible governments in the British colonies, following the publication of the Durham Report (1839), where appointed governors could act in domestic matters only upon the advice of ministers who enjoyed the confidence of the elected chamber, such as in Canada, Australia, New Zealand, South Africa, and Ireland.

Dependent self-governing states attained growing but limited measures of independence and in 1926 the Imperial Conference considered that these states were autonomous communities within the British Empire, equal in status, but in no way subordinated to others in both domestic and external affairs, yet united by its common alliance with the British Crown, as stipulated in the Balfour Declaration of 1926, which later became law in Section 4 of the Statute of Westminster in 1931. This law stated that "No Act in the Parliament of the United Kingdom passed after the commencement of this Act shall extend, or deemed to extend, to a Dominion as part of the law of that Dominion, unless it is expressed declared in that Act that the Dominion has requested, and consented to, the enactment therefore".

In Section 1 of this law the Dominions (semi-independent countries that gradually all become completed independent states) were named as Canada, Australia, New Zealand, the Union of South Africa, and the Irish Free State. Although India was mentioned in the Balfour Declaration, it was not considered in the Statute of Westminster, due to the worsening British-Indian relations during the period of 1926–1931. Nevertheless India, as well as Pakistan and Ceylon signed the London Declaration in 1949, accommodating the new statute of India, which had become independent in 1947 (bringing with it the creation of Pakistan) and Ceylon, which became independent in 1948. These nations all declared that they remain united as free and equal members of the Commonwealth of Nations, cooperating with free will in the pursuit of peace, liberty, and progress.

The Empire Parliaments Association was founded in 1911, which included the Dominions mentioned above in 1948, the name of this organization being changed to the Commonwealth Parliament Association, which currently incorporates all the Commonwealth member parliaments. It meets once a year to support good governance, democracy, and human rights and issues a quarterly Journal of Commonwealth Parliaments.

From the above-mentioned first group of countries that joined the British Commonwealth only Ireland definitely withdrew from the organization as a member, but since then many other countries joined the organization, which presently consists of 54 member countries, all of which are ex-British colonies, with the exception of Mozambique and Rwanda.

The Commonwealth represents 2.5 billion people, of which 60% are aged 29 years old or less, and the members states are spread over Europe, Africa, Asia and the Caribbean, and the Americas. Economically, some are among the more advanced countries in the world, while others are developing ones, and as a whole they generate approximately 14% of the world's GDP. Reaffirming their commitment to the core principles, the member states signed the Commonwealth Charter in 2012. These principles contemplate: democracy, human rights, freedom of expression, sustainable development, access to health, food and education, gender equality, international peace and security, tolerance, respect and understanding, separation of powers, the rule of law, good governance, the importance of young people in Commonwealth, protecting the environment, recognition of the needs of small states, recognition of the needs of vulnerable states, and the role of civil society.

Queen Elizabeth II serves as the Head of Commonwealth, which is a symbolic position that is now beginning to be contested by the populations of some countries, as was witnessed during the recent visit of Prince William to the Caribbean in 2022 (Barry 2022). The Commonwealth's organic bodies include the Commonwealth Secretariat, which comprises a Secretary-General, a Board of Governors, and a Chair-in-office. To supports the members to achieve their common goals, the Commonwealth has created two communities, namely the Commonwealth Foundation, which supports members to achieve democracy and development, and Commonwealth Learning, which promotes open learning and distance education.

To increase trade and investment between its members, Commonwealth Learning organizes several programmes, including: a Commonwealth competitiveness agenda, which is a platform for member countries to share best solutions and experiences in trade and investment; and a trade opportunities agenda, where Commonwealth experts help member countries to improve global trade competitiveness by developing their export capacities. The Commonwealth Secretariat runs a Debt Management Unit, which organizes a public debt programme to support the efforts of member countries to manage their debt portfolios. Another important finance programme is the Commonwealth Fintech Toolkit, which is designed to strengthen the capabilities of senior leaders and teams to understand and work with fintech blocks. The Commonwealth Secretariat also supports the members' implement sustainable development goals, especially by providing technical assistance for members to manage their natural resources, one of them being the ocean, including the blue economies or land-based ones. The Commonwealth Secretariat also identifies and proposes responses to challenges faced by small or vulnerable states, namely through the utilization of innovative financial instruments to create finance resilience to economic or financial shocks. In addition, global funds are being established to help countries deal with climate change. As Lord Howard stated in its article of the 5 May, 2021, "Networks never sleep. The future pattern of international relations is going to be (is already) far more through interest groups, all the professions, twinning and dialogue between cities, business conferences and initiatives, universities, research and discovery, projects both social and physical, shared technology and innovation, and a thousand other connections, than through any formal or official channels and agreements". He placed a strong emphasis on bodies such as the Commonwealth Learning community.

Portuguese Decolonization and the Origins of the CPLP

The colonization process of Portuguese colonies, began centuries earlier than the British one and the decolonization process ended, two years later, if we consider the handover of Hong Kong and Macau in China, which occurred respectively in 1997 and 1999. These two territories although they had governments nominated by England and Portugal, were both territories managed with an almost-full degree of autonomy, in that they had their own parliaments and judiciary systems, however, these territories did not have diplomatic autonomy. Indeed, in the case of Hong Kong, the military forces garrisoned there were British and in Macau no military forces had been stationed there since 1975, when a special statute for Macau was approved by the Portuguese Parliament, which considered it to be Chinese territory, but with Portuguese administration. Either way, the handover process of these two ex-colonies of England and Portugal were both negotiated on good terms with the Chinese government.

The two decolonization processes were similar in their final stage, and there is also a similitude in the timing and causes of their beginning, although in between they were very different.

Brazil was a Portuguese colony since 1500 and declared its independence in 1822, being the first colony to leave the Portuguese Empire. It can be said that both the independence of American colonies and the illuminist ideals contributed to the movements that opened the way for this independence, however, in reality, a series of events locally and in Portugal can explain it. The first notable independence movement in Brazil occurred in Minas Gerais in 1770, as in this region a progressive social and economic decline resulting from the collapse in gold production had made it very difficult to pay the fixed annual Crown tax, in gold. Of note is the fact that the discovery of gold in Minas Gerais had attracted a lot of prospectors, even from Portugal, because contrary to the exploitation of sugar, which required huge plantations and much capital and slave labour, gold exploitation could be carried out by small enterprises that did not required technical skills or the ownership of land and could be family-managed with just two or three slaves. This latter kind of colonization enabled the development of a white middle class, which spread the Portuguese language and culture into the interior of Brazil. However, this kind of mono-product rapidly led to extensive exploitation, which had two negative effects. The first was hunger, as agriculture production was insufficient to feed the increasing population of Minas Gerais, and the second was that the gold mines entered in a situation of diminishing levels of production.

According to Thomaz (2021), the total production of gold in 1752 was 8.878 tonnes per year. However, ten years later it was only 5.840 tonnes. Since the Crown received a mine tax of 20% of annual production, to avoid the decrease of this revenue which supported a great deal of the financing of Portugal's public budget, especially for the reconstruction of Lisbon after the devastating earthquake of 1755, the Viscount of Barbacena, the Governor of Minas Gerais, imposed a fix tax for exploitation of gold. Furthermore, coincidently the Portuguese Crown authorized the implementation of the so called *derrama*, which was a type of personal tax, which obliged the miners to pay with their own funds to cover any shortfall in the fixed tax for gold production. In Portugal, the Marquis of

Pombal, the Prime Minister of King D. José I, defended the doctrine that the colonies should only serve the metropole of the mother company and thus they should specialise in the production of raw materials, and they were forbidden to directly trade with other countries or even develop local industries in the colonies. Pombal also created the General Trade Companies of Grão-Pará, Maranhão, Pernanbuco, and Paraiba in Brazil.

These events provoked the *Inconfidentes* rebellion in 1788, which was led by Lieutenant Joaquim José da Silva Xavier, whose pseudonym was Tiradentes. The mostly European local elite, who were mainly members of the army, the church, lawyers, judges, miners, and poets among others, developed a project to turn the Captaincy of Minas Gerais into an independent country from Portugal.

In 1789, Governor Barbacena suspended the leverage of taxes on the population and all the rebels were jailed, and Tiradentes was judged in 1792 and executed after he assumed the full responsibility for the revolt. This rebellion was aborted, however, Tirandentes is still considered a hero in Brazil as an icon of liberty and the precursor of the independence of the country, a patron of the Brazilian Nation.

Even though the *Inconfidentes* rebellion provoked many reforms and policies from the metropole government in Portugal to attempt to lessen discontent (Disney 2020), the catalyst of the independence movement in Brazil occurred a few years later in 1798, in the form of the Bahian Conspiracy rebellion, better known as the Revolt of the Tailors, as many of its leaders and members were tailors working in the Captaincy of Bahia. This was a popular rebellion, which had the support of many *baianos*, including poor whites, freed blacks, black slaves, artisans, tailors, shoemakers, *mulatto* half-breeds, and radicals from the upper echelons of society—all of whom were in some way or another oppressed or discontented classes which were very much influenced by the French Revolution and freemasonry ideals. Indeed, the first Masonic lodge to be founded in Bahia, the Cavaleiros da Luz, counted with the participation of intellectuals who supported this movement. The objectives of the rebellion were "full independence, the creation of a republic, racial equality, and the complete abolition of slavery". The background of this rebellion was ideological, albeit also economic, resulting from the transfer of the capital of the colony of Brazil from Salvador de Bahia to Rio de Janeiro in 1763, which led to a period of economic decline. This rebellion was put down by the Governor of Bahia, Fernando de Portugal e Castro, and those rebels who were caught were jailed and the leaders were condemned to death.

However, unbeknown, Brazil's independence was fast approaching, albeit in an unexpected way. For in 1807, the Portuguese Regent, D. Joao VI, and all his Court were forced to relocate to Brazil when Napoleon's troops invaded Portugal, resulting in the metropole of Portugal then being located in Brazil, leading to the subsequent proclamation of the United Kingdom of Portugal, Brazil, and the Algarves in 1815. This led to a period of great development for Brazil in economic and social terms. The embassies of numerous European countries moved from Lisbon to Rio de Janeiro and Brazilian ports were open to international trade. However, the hostility between the local colonial Portuguese and the newly-arrived Portuguese increased, as the local taxes on sugar and cotton were increased significantly to pay for the expenses of maintaining the Court (Koster 1978). This hostility was especially strong in Pernambuco, whose Captaincy was the richest of the colony of Brazil and which had developed a strong identity since its inhabitants had repelled an attempted Dutch invasion in 1654 unaided. This discontent increased in 1817 with the crash of the sugar price worldwide, the increase in taxes, and the delay in paying soldiers their salaries. The local producers of sugar and cotton also complained that the Portuguese merchants dominated the trade of sugar and prevented them from trading directly with the buyers, who were mainly from Britain.

Furthermore, the Brazilian Portuguese were banned from occupying important posts in the public administration and in the army. This climate of discontent led to the spread of the illuminist and liberal ideas which were to drive the independence movements of the American colonies and the French Revolution. These ideas were promoted by Academies, the Masonic Lodges, and also the Catholic Seminar of Olinda, and were progressively accepted by local elites. The Masonic Lodges of Rio de Janeiro, which were linked to the Portuguese Masonic Lodges, wanted to implement a Constitutional Monarchy and the Lodges of Pernambuco, which were exclusively loyal to Brazil, favoured the Republic. In 1817, a group of Patriots therefore stormed the Pernambuco government, declared a Republic, and formed a new government which lasted 75 days and was then suppressed by D. João VI's troops. The similarity with the independence of the American colonies is very great and even extends to the use of the word "Patriots" both during the Boston Tea Party and in the Pernambuco rebellion. In effect, Brazil's independence came about as an indirect outcome of the defeat of Napoleonic troops in Portugal. For as a result of the sending of British armed forces to Portugal in compliance with the centuries-old alliance between the two countries, a Regency government was implemented in Portugal which was subject to the leadership of the British military, and it soon turned to be unpopular and intolerable to the Portuguese people who raised the cry "Portugal for the Portuguese". The King, D. João VI, was thus obliged to return to Lisbon, leaving his son D. Pedro to govern Brazil. D. Pedro was an ardent admirer of the parliamentary system and also the Grand-Master of the Brazilian Masonic Lodge which strongly advocated a liberal constitution and the complete independence of Brazil, and it was he who proclaimed Brazil's independence in 1822 (Stephens 2017).

There are many similarities between the independence of the American colonies and that of Brazil, in both timing and form, including the British and Portuguese strategies and policies, but after that those occurrences, the decolonization processes of the two Empires were very different. In fact, the Portuguese "*Estado Novo*" government headed by Salazar refused to decolonize after the II World War as the British government had, as for him the possessions in Africa and Asia were overseas provinces which were inalienable parts of the country and the progressive process of self-determination of those colonies was not to be even discussed, as Pinto (2017, pp. 320–321) affirmed "In Africa we defended above all the borders of the Nation".

Correia (2017) concluded that after World War II the colonial powers of Great Britain and Portugal followed different politic-administrative models, with the former following a policy of autonomy and progressive emancipation of its colonies, while the latter adopted to integrate its colonies in the whole national territorial system as overseas provinces centred on the metropole in Portugal, pursuing an homogeneous unity, although foreseeing regional differentiations to adjust to the cultural identities, religious creeds, and uses and customs of local populations.

This model proved to be unsuitable for the economic and social development of the Portuguese colonies, both in Africa and in Asia. The white Portuguese elites in the colonies had their expectations of progress frustrated by the lack of vision of the metropole, its slow autocratic and bureaucratic processes and ignorance of the local cultures and business environments. In addition, the indigenous populations complained as in general they were poor, illiterate, low-cost labour working in big plantations and factories, and those who had managed to achieve a better education felt excluded from the leading professional positions and from political decision making, as in reality the differences in the centres of power and the standard of living between the leading white elites and the indigenous population were enormous. Furthermore, the policy adopted by Portugal during this period of history was also in complete opposition to the mainstream international idea of indigenous populations gaining self-determination and the granting of independence to colonies which was defended by international organizations such as the United Nations. The end of the World War I had created a sense of unfairness among the colonized populations that had fought shoulder to shoulder during the war with the colonial powers and who had expected that after their contribution during the War that they would have a more equalitarian social position, however, this was not to pass. According to Correia (2017), the first claim of a colonized society is peace and justice in general, the second is equality among individuals, and the third its autonomy.

After the independence of India negotiated with the British in 1947, Portugal refused a similar negotiation and this decision was condemned by the UN Assembly and the International Court, with the latter to a degree legitimizing the military invasion by India in 1961 of the Portuguese State of India, which included the territories of Goa, Damão, and Diu. In 36 hours, Portugal was defeated and was obliged to leave India after 451 years. This acted as a touch light for the independence movements of the other Portuguese colonies, mostly in Africa, where these movements were anchored in different African ethnicities, but all had external support from either the USA and South Africa, or the USSR. A bipolar international system was installed at the end of the World War II which was dominated by the two superpowers of the USA and the USSR, and with the emergence of non-aligned countries, the geopolitics theory's concept of "spheres of influence" was developed.

The tug-of-war by the two superpowers to include the Portuguese colonies in their "spheres of influence" was largely justified by the wealth of the resources of these colonies. Both supported different independence movements by sending military equipment and training and also finance. As a consequence, starting in 1961, a guerrilla war was waged against the Portuguese colonialists in the majority of Portugal's colonies by different movements. In defence, Portugal sent professional soldiers to the colonies and formed militias. Simultaneously, a development plan for these colonies was launched by the Portuguese government. However, the cost of supporting all this during almost 13 years profoundly weaken

Portugal's economy and society and the country became exhausted, with the majority of the population viewing negatively the conscription of its young male population to fight in these wars. The military leaders were divided regarding the continuity of this war as a solution for the future of the colonies, as well as the justification for the non-democratic Portuguese political regime. Then the whole world was struck by the oil crisis of 1973, which in turn created the conditions for a military putsch in Portugal on the 25 April, 1974.

This completely changed the direction of domestic Portuguese politics and consequently the destiny of the Portuguese colonies in Africa and Asia. From the 25th April onwards, the Portuguese initiated a process of democratization, which at the beginning was led by the Portuguese Communist Party, which was aligned with the USSR, which resulted in the nationalization of all the most important means of production and created the conditions for placing Portugal within the "sphere of influence" of the USSR. This revolutionary process lasted for 19 months and was only stopped by another military putsch on the 25 November, 1975, which re-established a full representative democracy in Portugal that realigned Portugal with the "sphere of influence" of the USA. Nevertheless, during those 19 months the decolonization process was carried out and independence was negotiated and the Portuguese colonies were delivered into the hands of their freedom movements, which were all aligned with the USSR.

This rapid process of decolonization was not accepted pacifically in all the ex-Portuguese colonies. In the case of Timor, for instance, the neighbouring country, Indonesia, took exception to having a communist regime in its backyard and invaded Timor in 1976. China refused to negotiate the handover of Macau, as the historical lease was not yet due. In Angola and Mozambique, deadly fratricidal civil wars began respectively in 1975 and 1976. In Angola UNITA fought the MPLA during 27 years, giving rise to 500,000 military and civilian casualties, and in Mozambique RENAMO fought the FRELIMO in a civil war which lasted 16 years and provoked 1 million deaths and 3 million refugees. In the middle of the Cold War, both the MPLA and FRELIMO movements to whom Portugal had handed over government in Angola and Mozambique were backed by the USSR and these respectively fought against the USA-backed UNITA and RENANO movements. After the 25th of November, 1975 the diplomatic relations between Portugal and their colonies become quite complicated, as they were situated in different "spheres of influence", each with opposing political and economic models and philosophies. This dire situation was compounded by the fact that dialogue became even more difficult as both Angola and Mozambique were embroiled in civil war (Pinto 2008; Correia 2017).

The situation at the time of the Portuguese colonies was difficult for although they had great proximity as a family, they were like a separated family. The historical heritage, common language, and cultural affinities were responsible for a big weight of the shared ambition to create a Community of Portuguese-Speaking Countries. The idea was expressed and launched in 1983 during the official visit to Cape Verde by the then Minister of Foreign Affairs of Portugal, Jaime Gama, who suggested the organization of both biennial rotating meetings of Heads of State and Government and annual meetings of Ministers of Foreign Affairs. The objective was to hold frequent political consultations between political leaders and regular meetings of representatives in the form of international organizations and forums, such as the UN, and it was even proposed to proceed with the constitution of a Portuguese-speaking group at the Inter-parliamentary Union (CPLP 2022).

However, only six years after holding the first meeting of Heads of State and Government which took place in Brazil, was decided to create the IILP—International Institute of Portuguese Language on the suggestion of the Brazilian President José Sarney. During a meeting which also took place in Brazil, in 1994, the Foreign Affairs Ministers of the seven Portuguese-Speaking Countries (Angola, Brazil, Cape Verde, Guinea-Bissau, Mozambique, and São Tomé and Principe) came to the decision to recommend a Summit of Heads of State and Government to adopt a constitutive act for a Community of Portuguese-Speaking Countries and a Permanent Concertation Group based in Lisbon to prepare the Summit and a Constitutive Declaration. This Summit took place in Lisbon on the 17th of July, 1996, and the Constitutive Declaration of the Community of Portuguese-Speaking Countries (the CPLP) was signed with the objective of strengthening the bonds of solidarity and cooperation that unite the ex-colonies, the dissemination of the Portuguese language, and the promotion of joint initiatives to develop the economic and social development of their peoples. East Timor joined the Community six years later after its independence from Indonesia in 2002. The fall of Berlin Wall in 1989 and the end of Cold War facilitated the diplomatic dialogue that finally brought to an end the civil wars in Mozambique (1992) and Angola (2002) and the creation of the CPLP. On the 2 November,

2007, the Statutes of the CPLP as a multilateral forum were signed, thus consecrating Article 9 of the IILP—International Institute of Portuguese Language as a CPLP institution that has as its objective, the planning and execution of programmes to promote and perpetuate the Portuguese language. The same Statutes foresees that beyond its founding members, the organization can integrate other states members, provided that they have Portuguese as an official language. Accordingly, after a controversial process, Equatorial Guinea was accepted as a full member in 2014.

The organizational bodies are: the Heads of State Conference that meets every two years, which defines the general policies and the strategies and elects the President and the Executive Secretariat, both of which have a two years mandate; the Ministers Council (Foreign Affairs Ministers), which coordinate the activities of the CPLP, supervises its management and development, and approves the budget; and a Permanent Consultation Committee, which consists of a representative from each member State and is led by the representatives of the country that holds the Presidency and is responsible for monitoring the IILP as well as for coordinating the activities of the CPLP, supervising its management, policies, and programmes and approving its budget.

During the 26 years of its existence, the CPLP has carried out the role of the diplomatic and political coordination of its member states, namely reinforcing their presence in international forums, cooperating in domains such as education, wealth, defence, science and technology, agriculture, justice, public administration, culture, sports, media, and implementing projects for the promotion of the Portuguese language. Economic and business cooperation was not a priority for the CPLP, as the organization has been much bore an official entity, which is more concentrated on inter-governmental diplomatic relations, and public administrations, military, and legal cooperation programmes.

According to Ambassador Ribeiro Telles, who was the Executive Secretary from 2020 to 2022 as Portugal's representative, the CPLP has three main pillars, namely: (1) the promotion and diffusion of the Portuguese language; (2) political concertation and cooperation; and (3) diplomatic concertation and cooperation. He also lobbied during his mandate for the creation of a fourth pillar—an economic one, with the development of a Business Confederation, whose role would be to organize a kind of Davos Forum every two years preceding the Summit of Heads of State (Ribeiro Telles 2020). This came about with the holding of the

1st Business Confederation Summit which was organized in Malabo in May, 2021.

There is a possibility that a fifth pillar will be launched, that of civil society, which is very important as it has the potential to further the development of a Portuguese diaspora network, for some 291.4 million people that constitute the CPLP countries, of which 73% are from Brazil. When analyzing the demographic age groups, it can be concluded that the youngest population is from Angola, where 46% of the population is less than 14 years old, and the oldest is Portugal, where 22% is aged 65 or older (UN 2019). The wealth of the CPLP accounts for approximately 2.1% of the total world gross domestic product, and if it were an integrated economy, then it would be the tenth largest economy in the world, after Canada and before South Korea (IMF 2021).

Conclusions

Both Great Britain and Portugal had trading and political colonial empires which explains the current day existence of vast networks of diaspora with a common kinship and language. The cultural similarity of the societies of these ex-colonies foments understanding and trust, which are two basic conditionals for cooperation which enhance their relationship between members of understanding and commitment to the communities of peoples of the Commonwealth of Nations and the CPLP.

Even though much similarity exists concerning the geographic spaces of the ex-colonies of Great Britain and Portugal and their processes of trade colonization, and also the coincidence regarding how and when the de-colonization of their colonies began and finished, both communities are very different. The first British colony to become independent was in North America, in 1776, while the first Portuguese one was Brazil in South America, in 1822. However, both Empires terminated their presence in Asia at virtually the same time—the British in 1997 in Hong Kong, and the Portuguese two years later in Macau. However, the decolonization processes of the two former Empires and the outcome of both of them are far from being similar.

The origins of the British Commonwealth date back to 1926 with the Balfour Declaration, which paved the way for the founding of an institution designed to welcome the independent member countries that were former colonies and which were connected through their common use of the English language and historical ties. These countries share common values of democracy, human rights, and the rule of law, as enshrined in the Commonwealth Charter. In the case of the Portuguese colonies, it was only a good few years after their independence that it became possible to constitute the CPLP, principally because some important former colonies, namely the African ones, had fallen under the "sphere of influence" of the USSR, and communist ideology, whereas Portugal and Brazil remained within the sphere of influence of the USA, with a capitalism ideology. Accordingly, it was only possible to carry out dialogue between these opposite countries on the basis of the emotional links which remained very strong, albeit the political context made this convergence very complicated. It was only after the fall of the Berlin Wall in 1989 and the end of the Cold War that diplomatic dialogue became possible, leading to the creation of the CPLP.

Apart from the difference in size of these two communities, both have a high potential as networks of diasporas which contribute to the construction of multinational business communities, although the CPLP has yet a long way to go to emulate the importance and efficiency of the Commonwealth of Nations. Networking and digital connectivity based on voluntarily-linked business and civil society models will be very important for the future of both Commonwealths. In conclusion, we surmise that there is indeed a future for both these international voluntary communities, as long as they become less government-based and more people-based. In addition, the British Commonwealth has to resolve the problem of the British Monarch being the Head of the Commonwealth in a democratic way where the position could be held on a rotating basis. In the case of the Portuguese Commonwealth, the CPLP, apart from enhancing the three pillars that have already been developed in the community, there is a need to develop other pillars, all of which encourages inter-community activities, namely: (1) a business community, which organizes business conferences, product and services exhibitions, provides investment funds, and promotes value-added chains with intertwined projects; (2) a knowledge community, created through the association of universities and cooperation in scientific research projects and funding; (3) a professions community, centred on meetings and conferences between professional associations; (4) an inter-cities community; (5) a cultural community, devoted to cultural initiatives, such as biannual events and shows, etc.; and, (6) a sports community, which organizes championships in different sports.

References

Achrol, R. S. and Kotler, P. (1999) "Marketing in the Network Economy", *Journal of Marketing*, 63 (Special Issue): 146–163.

Anderson, J. C., Häkansson, H. and Johanson J. (1994) "Dyadic Business Relationships within a Business Network Context", *Journal of Marketing*, 58: 1–15.

Andrews, C. M. (1915) "Anglo-French Commercial Rivalry, 1700–1750: The Western Phase", *The American Historical Review*, 20 (3): 539–556.

Balfour Declaration (1926) https://www.foundingdocs.gov.au/item-sdid-95.html (Accessed: 16 February 2022).

Barry, E. (2022, 24 March) https://time.com/6160376/prince-william-kate-royal-tour-controversy-caribbean/ (Accessed: 28 March 2022).

Carp, B. L (2011) *Defiance of the Patriots, The Boston Tea Party & The Making of America*, New Haven and London: Yale University Press.

Commonwealth Parliament Association https://www.cpahq.org/ (Accessed: 18 February 2022).

Correia, P. P (2017) da Descolonização. Do protonacionalismo ao pós-colonialismo. Book Cover Editora.

CPLP (2022) https://www.cplp.org/ (Accessed: 22 February 2022).

Disney, A. R. (2020) *A História de Portugal e do Império Português*, Vol. II, University of Oxford, Clube do Autor.

Durham Report (1839) https://www.cpsa-acsp.ca/papers-2007/Ajzenstat.pdf (Accessed: 16 February 2022).

Easton G. (1992) "Industrial Networks: A Review", in B. Axelsson and G. Easton (eds.), *Industrial Networks: A New View of Reality*, London: Routledge: 3–27.

Häkansson, H. and Johanson, J. (1988) "Formal and Informal Cooperation Strategies", in F. J. Contractor and P. Lorange (eds.), *Cooperative Strategies in International Business*, Lexington, MA: Lexington Books: 369–379.

Häkansson, H. and Snehota I. (1995) *Developing Relationships in Business Networks*, London: Routledge.

Hall, D. H. (1953) "The British Commonwealth a Symposium. The British Commonwealth of Nations", *American Political Science Review*, 47 (4): 997–1015.

Heckscher, E. (1919) *The Effect of Foreign Trade on the Distribution of Income*, Ekonomisk Tidskriff: 497–512. Translated as chapter 13 in American Economic Association, Readings in the theory of international trade. Philadelphia: Blakiston, 1949, and a new translation is provided in Flam and Flanders (1991).

Holm, D. Blankenburg, Eriksson K. and Johanson J. (1996), "Business Networks and Cooperation in International Business Relationships", *Journal of International Business Studies* (Special Issue): 1033–1053.

Howard, D. (British Parliament, May 5, 2021). https://www.cweic.org/the-commonwealth-meets-tomorrow-article-by-lord-howell/ (Accessed: 12 February 2022).

Iborra, M., Menguzzato M. and Ripollés M. (1998), "Creation de Empresas Internacionales: Redes Informales y Obtención de Recursos", *Revista Europea de Dirección y Economía de la Empresa*, 7 (3): 147–160.

Ilhéu, F. (2020) "The Global Value Chains and the Evolution of Chinese Economic Model", *International Relations and Diplomacy*, 8 (4). ISSN 2328-2134.

IMF (2021) https://www.imf.org/external/datamapper/NGDPD@WEO/OEMDC/ADVEC/WEOWORLD (Accessed: 25 March 2022).

Johanson, J. and Mattsson L. G. (1988) "Internationalization in Industrial Systems: A Network Approach", in N. Hood and J. E. Vahlne (eds.), *Strategies in Global Competition*, New York: Croom Helm: 287–314.

Kao, J. (1993) "The Worldwide Web of Chinese Business", *Harvard Business Review*, March–April: 24–36.

Kelley, H. H. and Thibaut, J. W. (1978) *Interpersonal Relations: A Theory of Interdependence*. New York: Wiley-Interscience.

Kolter, P. (2003) *Marketing Management*, 11th Edition, Prentice-Hall International Inc.

Koster, H. (1978) *Viagens ao Nordeste do Brasil*. Recife: Secretaria de Educação e Cultura, Brasil.

Madsen, T. K. and Servais, P. (1997), "The Internationalization of Born Globals: An Evolutionary Process?" *International Business Review*, 6 (6): 561–583.

Middlekauff, R. (2005) *The Glorious Cause, The American Revolution, 1763–1789*, Oxford University Press.

Montesquieu, in the in 'The Spirit of the Laws' (1989). Translated by Anne M. Cohler, Basia Carolyn Miller, and Harold Samuel Stone. Cambridge, UK: Cambridge University Press.

Murphy, P. (2021) *The Empire's New Clothes; The Myth of Commonwealth*, C. Hurst (Publishers) Limited.

Nakata, C. and Sivakumar, K. (2001) "Instituting the Marketing Concept in a Multinational Setting: The Role of National Culture", *Journal of the Academy of Marketing Science*, 29 (3): 255–275.

Ohlin, B. (1933) *Interregional and International Trade*, Cambridge, MA: Harvard University Press.

Pinto, J. N. (2008) *Jogos Africanos*, 1st Ed. Esfera dos Livros.

Pinto, J. N. (2017) *Portugal Anos do Fim—A Revolução que Veio de Dentro*, 2nd Ed. Dom Quixote.

Pinto, J. N. (2021) *Hegemonia 7 Duelos pelo Poder Global*, Critica.

Porter, M. E. (1980) *Competitive Strategy: Techniques for Analyzing Industries and Competitors*, New York: Free Press.

Porter, M. E. (1985) *Competitive Advantage, Creating and Sustaining Superior Performance*, New York: Free Press.

Porter, M. E. (1990) *The Competitive Advantage of Nations*, Macmillan, London.

Porter, M. E. (1992) "Changing Patterns of International Competition", in F. R. Root and K. Visudtibhan (eds.), *International Strategic Management, Challenges and Opportunities*, Taylor & Francis, Inc.: 61–85.

Ribeiro Telles, F. (2020) https://estrategizando.pt/2020/01/01/um-quarto-pilar-para-a-cplp/ (Accessed: 25 March 2022).

Ricardo, D. (1817) *Principles of Political Economy and Taxation*, Cosimo Classics, NY.

Rodríguez, C. M. and Wilson, D. T. (2002) "Relationship Bonding and Trust as a Foundation for Commitment in U.S.-Mexican Strategic Alliances: A Structural Equation Modeling Approach", *Journal of International Marketing*, 10 (4): 53–76.

Rostow, W. W. (1971) *The Stages of Economic Growth a Non-Communist Manifesto*, Cambridge University Press.

Short, J. R. (1982) *An Introduction to Political Geography*, London: Routledge & Paul Ltd.

Stephens, H. M. (2017) "*Portugal a História de uma Nação*" Alma dos Livros.

The Economist (Nov. 19, 2011) "Weaving the World Together": 68.

Thomaz, L. F. F. R. (2021) *A Expansão Portuguesa Um prisma de muitas faces*, Gradiva.

UN (2019) https://news.un.org/pt/story/2019/04/1667931 (Accessed: 24 March 2022).

Wilson, C. (1959) "The Other Face of Mercantilism", *Transactions of the Royal Historic Society*, 9: 81–101.

Yeung, H. W. (1997), "Transnational Corporations from Asian Developing Countries: Their Characteristics and Competitive Edge", in H. V. Wortzel and L. H. Wortzel (eds.), *Strategic Management, in a Global Economy*, Wiley: 22–45.

The Soft Power of the Community of Portuguese-Speaking Countries

José Palmeira

Introduction

When it was thought that the so-called classical geopolitics of the first half of the twentieth century was outdated, due to the emergence of a networked, globalized and interdependent society, based on multilateralism, Europe is once again witnessing a war in its midst, in 2022, with Ukraine as its epicentre and ideological (alleged denazification) and imperialist (defence of Russian-speaking space) factors as motivation. This time, the main European troublemaker is the Russian Federation, led by Vladimir Putin, whose offensive generating widespread condemnation of the West and the collaborative neutrality of some of its allies at the moment, particularly the People's Republic of China, with which the Kremlin had conceived a "strategic partnership".

The argument for the defence of the Russian-speaking space takes us back to the era of empires that devastated a significant part of Eurasia

J. Palmeira (✉)
Research Centre in Political Science (CICP), University of Minho, Braga, Portugal
e-mail: palmeira@eeg.uminho.pt

P. A. B. Duarte et al. (eds.), *Portugal and the Lusophone World*,
https://doi.org/10.1007/978-981-99-0455-6_23

and whose construction and deconstruction shaped successive international orders, until it culminated in the post-World War II era, in the mid-twentieth century, with the Cold War and the bipolar world that would collapse in 1991, with the implosion of the Soviet Union and the end of the Warsaw Pact.

What was described as the "End of History" (Fukuyama 1989) opened the door to what others described as the "Clash of Civilizations" (Huntington 1993), allegedly proven by the terrorist attacks of September 11, 2001, in the United States of America (USA). Meanwhile, economic and financial globalization is gaining ground and is being ridden, with particular success, by the People's Republic of China, the new emerging power with global skills that rivals the USA, in the face of the Russian Federation's secondary status, which, however, with Putin, regains military capacity and becomes the largest power in terms of number of nuclear warheads.

In this complex context, one would think that Soft Power, using the expression coined by Joseph Nye (1990)—the ability of a country to persuade others to do what it wants without force or coercion—(e.g. China's Belt and Road Initiative), would be more relevant than Hard Power (e.g. Russian invasion of Ukraine). However, international actors, namely the states and the intergovernmental organizations, move based on multiple geometries, all with a view to maximizing their power in the international system.

Among the empires that were forged over the centuries, the most recent are the colonial ones, with European powers as protagonists, such as the United Kingdom, France, Spain, the Netherlands and Portugal. After the 2nd World War and the creation of the United Nations (UN), the decolonization process was accentuated, putting an end to the colonial empires. One of the last to resist was Portugal, which only after the democratization of its political regime, in 1974, concluded what its European counterparts had done decades before. As remnants of these empires we have today international organizations such as the Commonwealth, the Organization Internationale de la Francophonie (OIF) and the Community of Portuguese-Speaking Countries (CPLP).

Founded in 1996, the CPLP has completed a quarter of a century as an intergovernmental organization that strives for political and diplomatic consultation (Moreira 2001) among its nine members states (Angola, Brazil, Cape Verde, Guinea-Bissau, Equatorial Guinea, Mozambique, Portugal, Sao Tome and Principe and East Timor). Established in the wake of the epilogue of the Portuguese colonial empire and the collapse of the Cold War, the CPLP made its way in parallel with the increasing globalization of world economic and financial markets, a process that cooled down with the military conflict in Ukraine.

The armed forces of the Russian Federation invaded Ukrainian territory on February 24, 2022. Most countries condemned the attitude of the Kremlin, which already, in 2014 had annexed Crimea and supported the separatist movements in Lugansk and Donetsk, in eastern Ukraine. Only with the support of four more States in the United Nations General Assembly, the Russian military intervention deserved the abstention of the majority of the BRICS (China, India and South Africa) and the opposition of Brazil that, however, did not align with the economic sanctions imposed on Moscow. Among the abstentionist countries were Angola, Mozambique and Guinea-Bissau, three Portuguese-speaking countries (Lusophone) that have economic and military cooperation ties with Russia (Hugon 2015; Palmeira 2021). Among the Portuguese-speaking countries, Portugal, Cape Verde, Sao Tome and Principe and East Timor expressed their condemnation of President Putin's decision.

The harbinger of a new international order, with a realignment of global and regional powers, represents a challenge for the CPLP, whose members are divided into different spheres of geopolitical influence. It is interesting, for now, to analyse what has been the path of the CPLP as an actor in the contemporary international system and to discern some of its most striking features. The observation lens is based on the instruments of geopolitics and geostrategy, having as main methodological tool the qualitative analysis, based on primary and secondary sources. The analysis focuses on the organization's history in terms of areas of cooperation, its geopolitics and member states at the regional level, as well as its ability to influence the international system. It was found that the power of the CPLP is based mainly on the intercontinental Portugal-Brazil-Angola "strategic triangle" and that there is added value in specific sectors such as maritime security and energy. This provides the CPLP with Soft Power characteristics that are embodied in the positions held by Portuguese-speaking citizens in international organizations and in the interest of third states in joining the CPLP, albeit with the status of Observers.

Portuguese-Speaking Countries Geopolitics

The Community of Portuguese-Speaking Countries was created following the end of the cold war, in 1996, as a corollary of Portuguese decolonization, promoted in 1975, following the democratization of the Portuguese political regime, which took place a year earlier. Angola's independence was marked by a civil war between 1975 and 2002, involving the government of the Popular Movement for the Liberation of Angola (MPLA), supported by Moscow, and the National Union for the Total Independence of Angola (UNITA), supported by South Africa, then under apartheid, and Western countries, in what was considered one of the last conflicts of the cold war (Almeida 2011; Pavia 2011; Ramos 2018). The conjuncture of blocs was also decisive in the occupation of East Timor by Indonesia, in 1975, undertaken by that country, a member of the Non-Aligned Movement, following the unilateral proclamation of the independence of that territory by the Revolutionary Front of Independent East Timor (Fretilin), considered pro-communist.

Most Portuguese-speaking African countries that gained independence remained in the orbit of the Soviet Union, which had previously supported the liberation movements that, in the meantime, had come to power. This fact, as well as the traditional post-colonial acrimony, between the colonized and the colonizer, justifies the birth of the CPLP five years after the end of the cold war.

The initial unifying element, common to the seven founding states, was the defence and promotion of the Portuguese language, adopted as official in the countries that emerged from colonization. Having as precedent models the British Commonwealth, more pragmatic and focused on economic cooperation, and the Organization Internationale de la Francophonie, more intergovernmental and committed to cultural dissemination, the CPLP ended up emphasizing more the intergovernmental aspect and cooperation in public sectors, such as the Defence policy (Bernardino and Azevedo 2015).

The seven founding states were joined in 2002 by East Timor, concluding that it was a troubled process of independence after the Indonesian occupation, managed by the United Nations, and later, in 2014, Equatorial Guinea, a country led by one of the oldest African dictators (Teodoro Obiang, since 1979) who went so far as to introduce the Portuguese language (not spoken in that country) as an official language (along with Spanish and French) to comply with the organization's statutes and break the international isolation of its regime. If in the case of Timor, the historical connection to Portugal prevailed, in the case of the accession of Equatorial Guinea its energy power spoke louder (Santos 2014), which strengthened the range of Lusophone producing countries, joining Angola as member of Organization of Petroleum Exporting Countries (OPEC), Brazil and Timor, in addition to neighbouring Sao Tome and Principe, in the Gulf of Guinea, and Mozambique, with significant hydrocarbon reserves (Eiras 2012).

The CPLP evolved, in 2014, from the organization of Lusophony to the organization of "Petrophony", at a time when access to fossil energy still represented a significant geopolitical power factor, an aspect, however, lessened, due to its impact on climate change and investment in renewable energies, alternatives to hydrocarbons. Since that date, Energy has been one of the areas of cooperation within the CPLP, with the first meeting of ministers in the sector taking place in 2015, while Lisbon hosted a conference of the organization on energy for development.

The establishment of this community coincided, temporarily, with the entry into force of the United Nations Convention on the Law of the Sea (1994) and the entry into operation of the World Trade Organization (1995), responsible for the increasing liberalization of world trade, facts that, together, they dynamized international maritime flows, given that the largest tonnage of freight transport takes place across seas and oceans (Dias 2014). Portugal, as a former maritime power of the fifteenth and sixteenth centuries, created an overseas colonial empire, with anchors in three oceans (Atlantic, Indian and Pacific), dominating key strategic points, such as the Straits of Hormuz and Malacca, and the Gulf of Guinea, the Mozambique Channel and the Timor Sea, in addition to its proximity to the Strait of Gibraltar (Palmeira 2016; Alves 2017). Five hundred years later, these chokepoints maintain geostrategic relevance, not only due to the increasing flow of their maritime routes but also to the emergence of the phenomenon of piracy in points such as the Gulf of Guinea and the Gulf of Aden at the access to the Suez Canal (Guedes 2012). The nine CPLP member states have in common the fact that they are coastal, some are archipelagic (Cape Verde and Sao Tome and Principe), spanning four continents (Europe, Africa, America and Asia) and three oceans (Atlantic, Indian and Pacific) vast maritime areas under its sovereignty and jurisdiction. Hence, cooperation in the field of the Oceans has developed, not only from the perspective of its environmental component, but also in the field of security, regarding its location in the route of flows of world transport of goods. An example of this cooperation is established within the scope of the Macaronesia Commission, a geopolitical space created in 2010, involving the archipelagos of three States—Cape Verde, Portugal (Azores and Madeira) and Spain (Canary Islands).

Each of the nine CPLP member states has its own regional geopolitical insertion. Portugal is a member of the European Union, the North Atlantic Treaty Organization (NATO) and the Union for the Mediterranean, while Brazil is a member of the Organization of American States (OAS), Southern Common Market (Mercosur), the Union of South American Nations (Unasur), the Latin American Integration Association (ALADI), the Community of Latin American and Caribbean States and the BRICS (Brazil, Russia, India, China and South Africa), among other organizations. Angola and Mozambique are part of the Southern African Development Community (SADC), and Angola is also a member of the Community of Central African States (alongside Sao Tome and Principe and Equatorial Guinea), of the Gulf of Guinea Commission and of the International Conference of the Great Lakes Region, in addition to being a member of the OPEC. Guinea-Bissau and Sao Tome and Principe are members of the Community of Sahel-Saharan States and Guinea-Bissau and Cape Verde are members of the Economic Community of West African States (ECOWAS), an organization that has played a mediating role in resolving several internal conflicts that have affected the Bissau regime. On the contrary, the Cape Verdean islands are an example of good governance, a fact that led the European Union to celebrate a special partnership with that archipelago in 2007. A year earlier, NATO carried out its first military exercise outside its area of jurisdiction in that African territory (Palmeira 2014, 2015). East Timor, in turn, awaits its integration into the Association of Southeast Asian Countries (ASEAN), where it has observer status, as is the case with the Pacific Islands Forum, where Australia pontificates (Durand 2010). Of all the Portuguese-speaking countries, East Timor is, perhaps, the one where membership in the CPLP has the most geostrategic significance (Palmeira 2010a, 2010b), since its small territory is situated between two geopolitical giants (Indonesia and Australia) has been political cooperation and technique of countries such as Portugal and Brazil fundamental for the pursuit of objectives such as the delimitation of their maritime borders.

In turn, Brazil is the member state for which the CPLP will have less geopolitical relevance, given its autonomous potential (Rouquié 2009), as evidenced by its soft participation in the organization.

Elements of Soft Power

The greatest interest sometimes seems to come from outside. Among the third countries that have expressed interest in cooperation with the CPLP, the People's Republic of China (PRC) (Dan 2009) and India stand out. These two partners of Brazil in the scope of the BRICS have historical links with Portugal, which until 1999 was the administrative power of Macau, since then the Special Administrative Region of the PRC, and Goa, a federal state of India that until 1961 was under Portuguese administration, along with Daman and Diu. It was Macau and Goa that in 2006 and 2014 respectively hosted the Lusophone Games, a sporting event that involves athletes from member states.

The Nine have diplomatic cooperation as one of their pillars, supporting each other when it comes to applying for governing bodies of international organizations. Thanks also to its ability to mobilize support at the regional level where they are inserted, Portuguese-speaking countries have been able to see their citizens elected to relevant bodies, such as the UN Secretary General António Guterres (since 2017)—previously United Nations High Commissioner for Refugees (2005–2015)—the Director General of the International Organization for Migration (IOM), António Vitorino (since 2018), and the President of the Global Alliance for Vaccines, José Manuel Barroso (President of the Commission European Union between 2004 and 2014). Prior to that, Brazilian Roberto Azevêdo was Director General of the World Trade Organization (WTO) (2013–2020) and former Portuguese Head of State Jorge Sampaio was appointed High Representative of the United Nations Secretary General for the Alliance of Civilizations (2007–2013). The presence of Portuguese-speaking politicians in prominent positions in global and regional international organizations has contributed to the transfer of some of the national's values to these international organizations. The multilateralist and globalist vision of Portuguese foreign policy (Silva 2018) is present in the conduct of António Guterres as Secretary-General of the UN, as well as the openness to refugees and cooperation in the field of migration guides António Vitorino's mandate at the head of the IOM (Palmeira 2019a). Furthermore, the traditional Euro-Atlanticism that marks Portuguese foreign policy as a historical constant (Lima 2016) may have influenced the choice of Barroso as President of the European Commission, in 2004, in the aftermath of the military intervention of the USA and its allies in Iraq, in 2003, following the terrorist attacks of September 11, 2001. The division of Europeans between supporters of US intervention (as in the United Kingdom, Spain, Italy and Portugal) and opponents (as in the Franco-German axis) opened up fissures in the euro-Atlantic relationship that later there was interest in overcoming. Barroso's choice benefited from the victory of the European People's Party in the elections to the European Parliament and the support of British Labour Tony Blair, who with President Bush attended the summit in the Azores (Portugal) that preceded the aforementioned military operation.

Once president, Barroso took to Brussels his vision of an integrated maritime policy for the EU, which he ended up promoting and encouraging, culminating in its approval at the Lisbon European Council in 2007. The Portuguese presidencies of the European Union were also marked by the opening of the continent to other markets (Ferreira-Pereira 2008), through the holding of summits European Union-Africa (2000 and 2007), European Union-Brazil and Europe-India (2007), regions of the world where there are historical marks of Portuguese culture (Palmeira 2019b).

When analyzing the CPLP from a geopolitical perspective, some peculiar characteristics emerge. Like its counterparts Commonwealth and OIF, it has a multi-continental dimension, as its members are spread over four continents (Europe, America, Africa and Asia). All the States are coastal (Atlantic, Indian and Pacific) and most of them are concentrated in the South Atlantic (Palmeira 2012). They integrate regional geo-economic spaces (or aspire to do so, in the case of Timor-Leste in relation to ASEAN), with different idiosyncrasies. Another characteristic is the territorial disproportionality of the member states, including the fifth largest country in the world (Brazil, 8,515,770 square kilometres) and one of the smallest countries in Africa (Sao Tome and Principe, 974 square kilometres) (CIA 2022c).

The economies of the nine members states represent, as a whole, the tenth largest economy in the world (1.8 billion dollars), situated between Canada and South Korea, in a list led by the United States, prepared with data from the International Monetary Fund (Lusa 2021). The main contribution is made by Brazil (US$1.4 billion), followed by Portugal (US$257 billion) and Angola (US$66.4 billion), with Sao Tome and Principe being at the tail of the Portuguese country's speakers (485 million dollars). Brazil is the seventh most populous country in the world, with 217 million inhabitants (CIA 2022a), and an average age of 32.3 years (2015), much lower than the Portuguese (44.6 years), but well above the Angolan (15.9 years) which is one of the lowest in Africa and the world (CIA 2022b). Brazil is also characterized by having the largest tropical forest in the world (Amazon)—considered a lung of humanity—and one of the largest reserves of fresh water (15.44% of the world total) (Reto et al. 2016).

The Portuguese language is considered the ninth most spoken language in the world, with an estimated number of 257.7 million speakers (Ethnologue 2022). Portuguese is the official language of the nine states that make up the CPLP and the working language of the international organizations that they are part of, such as the European Union, African Union and Organization of American States (Reto 2012; Teixeira 2016). The CPLP limits the possibility of being effective members of the organization to Portuguese-speaking States. Its statutes (CPLP 2007) are, in this regard (Article 6), more restrictive than those of the Commonwealth or the OIF, the Anglophone comprising a Portuguese-speaking state (Mozambique) and the Francophone two (Cape Verde and Guinea-Bissau). For this reason, the number of effective member states of the CPLP (9) is significantly lower than that of the Commonwealth (54) and the OIF (54), although the Portuguese-speaking community, like the French-speaking one, has a significant number of States with the status of Observer, which allows them to participate in the Conferences of Heads of State and Government of the CPLP, although without the right to vote (Article 7, nr. 3).

Among the Observer states of the CPLP there are three permanent members of the United Nations Security Council (France, United Kingdom and USA), six members States of the G7 representing the largest economies in the world (USA, Canada, France, Italy, Japan and the United Kingdom) and several of the G20 member states (Argentina, Canada, France, India, Italy, Japan, Turkey and the United Kingdom) such as Brazil. The other Observers are members of the European Union (Czech Republic, Greece, Hungary, Ireland, Italy, Luxembourg, Romania, Slovakia and Spain) or the European continent (Andorra, Georgia and Serbia). There are also African countries (Ivory Coast, Mauritius, Namibia and Senegal) and South America (Argentina, Chile,

Peru and Uruguay) and the Asian country Qatar. International organizations such as the Conference of Iberian-American States, the Organization of Iberian-American States for Education, Science and Culture and the G7+ have the same statute (CPLP 2022).

Portugal-Brazil-Angola "Strategic Triangle"

When analyzing the CPLP member states based on the quantity and quality of their natural and human resources, their political stability and their ability to influence regionally and globally, there are three that stand out from the rest: Brazil, Angola and Portugal.

Brazil is the CPLP member state with the greatest influence in the international system, presenting itself as one of the candidates for permanent member of the United Nations Security Council, in a scenario of reformulation of this body. This country, together with Germany, India and Japan, is part of a group (G4) that at the diplomatic level support each other with a view to that objective. The largest South American country is part of other economic and political forums such as the BRICS, with Russia, India, China and South Africa, as well as the G20, which brings together the world's largest economies, and the Group of 77, created in 1964, within the scope of the United Nations, to support development and which includes a more restricted group of countries (G24), of which Brazil is a part and Angola is an observer, to promote their insertion in the Bretton Woods institutions (International Monetary Fund and World Bank). The Portuguese-speaking African countries and Timor-Leste are also part of the G77+ China, a country that became associated with the group in terms of development aid.

Portugal and Brazil are among the twenty-two States that make up the Iberian-American Conference which, since 1991, has periodically brought together the heads of State and Government of the Iberian countries (including Andorra) and Latin American countries. The same geopolitical area energizes the Iberian-American Organization for Education, Science and Culture.

In addition to developed countries such as Brazil and Portugal, which is a member of the European Union and the Organization for Economic Cooperation and Development (OECD), the CPLP is mostly made up of developing countries, some of which are affected by chronic internal conflicts, such as this is the case of Guinea-Bissau (Nóbrega 2003), harming its governability and good governance. This country integrates with East Timor, Sao Tome and Principe and more seventeen States the G7+, a forum established in 2010, in the Timorese capital, Dili, to support vulnerable or conflict-affected States.

Portuguese-speaking-African countries are among the 79 members of the Organization of African, Caribbean and Pacific States, established in 2020 as a corollary of the Georgetown Agreement (1975), which created the ACP group, the oldest partnership between the European Union and developing countries, responsible for the Lomé (1975) and Cotonou (2000) conventions (Palmeira 2017).

The CPLP was created with the aim of promoting diplomatic consultation among its members in matters of international policy, namely to strengthen its presence in international forums. Furthermore, it cooperates in the most diverse areas, namely in the field of Defence (CPLP 2015), with a Permanent Secretariat for Defence Affairs, established in Lisbon in 1999, a Strategic Analysis Centre, created in Maputo (Mozambique) and the periodic joint and combined military exercises (Felino), started in Portugal at the beginning of the century (CPLP 2016). The technical-military cooperation between member states makes it possible to articulate a military doctrine within the CPLP (2018) and allow the availability of personnel to operate in peacekeeping forces with the coverage of the United Nations (EMGFA 2022).

At the military level, Brazil was the seventeenth country with the highest expenditure in the world, in 2021, with 19.2 billion dollars, in a ranking led by the United States of America (SIPRI 2022). According to the Stockholm International Peace Research Institute, Brazil is a regional leader (Latin America) in military spending and despite the 4.3% cut in spending, in 2021, the country "was still able to make the planned payments for its strategic armament programmes, which include the acquisition of 36 Gripen combat aircraft from Sweden" (SIPRI 2022).

An African Lusophone country, Angola, was in 2021 the fifth largest military spenders in sub-Saharan Africa (SIPRI 2022). Between 2012 and 2021 military spending by Angola fell by 66% due to "the worsening economic conditions in Angola from around 2015 — largely caused by low oil prices and slumps in its oil production — and the slow pace of economic recovery in more recent years were central to the sharp drop in Angolan military spending over the decade" (SIPRI 2022).

Portugal, for is part, is the seventeenth member state of NATO in terms of military expenditure as a percentage of Gross Domestic Product

(1.55%), falling short of the 2% that is the organization's guideline (NATO 2022).

Due to their manifest or latent power, relative to their intrinsic potential and their regional and global influence, it can be said that Portugal, Brazil and Angola constitute a "strategic triangle" within the CPLP with a view to maximizing the organization's power in the international system (Palmeira 2006).

The South Atlantic as "Lusophone Sea"

Considering the size of the maritime areas under its jurisdiction, it can be said that the South Atlantic is largely a "Lusophone sea" in terms of the rescue area. It turns out that only Brazil, on the Portuguese-speaking side, has the naval capacity for this purpose, a fact that justifies the investment that the CPLP has made through instruments such as a Strategy for the Oceans (2009) and an Identity in the Domain of Defence (2015).

At the proposal of Brazil, ratified by the United Nations, a South Atlantic Peace and Cooperation Zone was established in 1986, bringing together South American and African coastal countries (UN 1986). South-south cooperation is a feature of Brazilian geostrategy (Patriota 2013), which has been engaged in projects such as relations with South America-Africa (ASA) and with India and South Africa (IBAS), not neglecting the regional scope (Common Market of South, since 1991) and cooperation with the European Union (Ferreira-Pereira 2015), while an agreement between the two blocs (Mercosur and EU), signed in 2019, is being ratified by member states.

In the Portuguese-speaking bilateral sphere, the Brazil-Angola relationship stands out, with the South American country being the first to recognize the independence of the African country, in 1975. The Angolan civil war (1975–2002) affected their cooperation, which would be resumed in 2010, through the celebration of a strategic partnership, promoted by the respective Presidents, complemented in 2015 with the signing of a technical memorandum in the field of Defence (Stuenkel 2012; Sousa 2014).

Angola is one of the African Union countries with the greatest regional interconnections, given its status as a member of the Economic Community of Central African States (since 1991), Southern African Development Community (since 1992), Gulf of Guinea Commission (since 2001), International Conference of the Great Lakes Region (since 2008) and Forum of Portuguese-Speaking African Countries (since 2014). The Great Lakes region, in terrestrial terms, and the Gulf of Guinea, in the maritime space, are two particularly unsafe areas, with the involvement of African and extracontinental military forces (IMO 2014). Luanda has hosted, since 2007, the headquarters of the Gulf of Guinea Commission, which is made up of two other Portuguese-speaking countries, Sao Tome and Principe and Equatorial Guinea, and in whose fight against maritime piracy third countries, such as Portugal, participate in the European Union's mission (Bernardino 2013; Barros 2014; Cunha 2014).

West Africa is another problematic area in terms of maritime security, in this case due to its insertion in the narcotics trafficking route that develops between Latin America and Europe (Almeida and Bernardino 2013). Cape Verde, due to its archipelagic condition, and Guinea-Bissau, as a coastal State, are two Portuguese-speaking countries that are part of the ECOWAS which, in addition to economic cooperation, promotes regional security. In this transition zone between the European, African and South American continents (Middle Atlantic), is located the geopolitical block of Macaronesia, consisting of 28 islands, inhabited by three million people, under the sovereignty of three States: Cape Verde, Portugal (Azores and Madeira) and Spain (Canary Islands).

Cape Verde has a Special Partnership with the European Union, concluded in 2007, having among other objectives the "security and stability, through actions implemented on a cross-border and regional basis in particular, in the areas of the fight against transnational organized crime, efficient management of migration flows and maritime security" (EU 2008). Located on the Euro-African and Euro-Latin American axes, on the routes of the Strait of Gibraltar and the Panama Canal, Macaronesia saw its geostrategic potential recognized by NATO, which in 2006 carried out the Steadfast Jaguar operation of the NATO Response Force in Cape Verde, in what was the first military exercise outside its natural area of action, which is north of the Tropic of Cancer. In the geopolitical space of Macaronesia, which is a transition area between the North Atlantic and the South Atlantic, several regional geostrategies converge: CPLP Strategy for the Oceans (2009), European Maritime Security Strategy (2014), Integrated Maritime Strategy for Africa 2050 (2014) and ECOWAS Integrated Maritime Strategy (2014). Maritime security is a common concern in several areas of the African continent, both on the Atlantic coast and in the Indian Ocean, in this case in the

Gulf of Aden, between Somalia and Yemen and in the access to the Suez Canal, where cases of piracy led to the intervention of NATO naval assets.

The Portuguese-speaking country most recently affected by security issues was Mozambique, whose region of Cabo Delgado, rich in natural gas, has since 2017 been the object of terrorist actions unleashed by Islamic fundamentalist groups. The conflict, which led several multinationals in the energy sector to suspend their economic activity there, led to the intervention of Rwandan and SADC forces in 2021, with the aim of helping the Mozambican military forces restore peace in the region (ICG 2022).

The seas under the jurisdiction of the CPLP member states represent 2.5% of the globe's maritime surface and are crossed by busy routes of world trade in goods (Bernardino 2011). This fact, combined with the lack of naval resources capable of inspecting such extensive areas by Portuguese-speaking African countries, has led the CPLP to invest in maritime cooperation, promoting initiatives such as the congress "The Seas of Lusophony", the symposium of the Navies of the CPLP and an Association of Portuguese-Speaking Ports.

Conclusion

A quarter of a century after its creation, the CPLP is an intergovernmental organization that pursues two objectives: to consolidate its internal cohesion and to integrate itself into the international system. In the first case, cooperation in various political, economic and social sectors has allowed its members to find added value, one of the most recent being the institution of a Portuguese-speaking citizenship that promotes mobility within the community. From a practical point of view, cooperation in the military domain has created synergies and developed capabilities in sectors such as maritime security, which is a critical point for several member states, especially African ones.

Given the potential and vulnerabilities of the CPLP, one can conclude that the organization's capacity is underdeveloped due to internal conflicts that in the past affected some states (Angola, Guinea-Bissau, Mozambique) or due to the lower political commitment of its main asset (Brazil), but remains active and is waiting for better days thanks to the resilience of members such as Portugal, Cape Verde and East Timor.

Due to their potential, whether manifest or latent, Brazil, Portugal and Angola prove to be the member states most capable of projecting the

CPLP to a global level, not only because of their intrinsic potential (such as natural resources, in the case of the two countries in the South) but also to the regional blocs they are part of (maximum EU and NATO, in the Portuguese case).

Objectives such as Brazil's ascension to permanent member of the United Nations Security Council remain to be materialized, a status only possible to achieve within the scope of a reformulation of the body. Also, to be concluded is the ratification of the European Union-Mercosur agreement, which has deserved the commitment of Portugal and Brazil.

Established ten years after Portuguese decolonization in Africa, which resulted in the independence of five new Portuguese-speaking countries, and five years after the end of the cold war (implosion of the Soviet Union and the Warsaw Pact), the CPLP is confronted, in 2022, with the war in Ukraine and the division of its members between Kremlin critics and neutrals in the face of the conflict.

The organization fulfils the objectives of the United Nations by promoting cooperation among its members and regional and global multilateralism, towards economic and social development and peace.

The CPLP member states are part of influential international organizations on a regional scale, with particular relevance to Portugal, Brazil and Angola, members, respectively, of the European Union, Mercosur and SADC.

On the economic front, Brazil is one of the BRICS and is part of the G20, while Portugal is a member of the OECD and Angola is part of OPEC. Other Portuguese-speaking countries have significant hydrocarbon reserves—notably Brazil, Equatorial Guinea (also a member of OPEC), Mozambique and East Timor—and Energy was introduced as a new area of ministerial cooperation within the CPLP in 2014.

In the political-military context, Portugal is a founding member of NATO and the cooperation in the field of Defence is developed within the CPLP, through a permanent secretariat, a strategic analysis centre and joint and combined exercises that form an Identity in the Domain Defence (2015).

The sea is a common concern for Portuguese-speaking states, endowed with extensive exclusive economic zones, both in terms of the environment and maritime safety, which is why an Ocean Strategy was established in 2009. Brazil is also distinguished by the size of its forestry and freshwater reserves that are of universal interest.

For reasons of a geopolitical nature that show the power of States at the regional and global level, it is considered that Portugal, Brazil and Angola found a "strategic triangle" with the potential to project a Lusophone "brand" in international relations.

On a global scale, and depending on the current international context, marked by conflicts, migrations and a pandemic crisis, influential entities such as the United Nations, the International Organization for Migration and the Global Alliance for Vaccines are led by Portuguese-speakers (António Guterres, António Vitorino and Jose Manuel Barroso). Previously, a Portuguese-speaker had headed the WTO (Roberto Azevêdo, 2013–2020), responsible for the liberalization of world trade, and another the European Commission (Barroso, 2004–2014), coinciding with the enlargement of the EU from 15 to 28 members and the approval of his reform treaty (Lisbon, 2007).

The organization is attractive to third countries (the most recent is Australia) that cannot be effective members due to the fact that they have not an official Portuguese language so they adhere with the status of Observers. The quantity (three tens) and quality (permanent members of the UN Security Council, the G7, the G20, the European Union, the African Union and the OAS) of the Observer States highlight the centripetal character of the CPLP.

The placement of Portuguese-speaking politicians in high international positions and the quantity and quality of states that want to join the CPLP are elements that show the Soft Power of the organization.

References

Almeida, Eugénio (2011), *Angola: Potência Regional em Emergência*. Lisboa: Colibri.

Almeida, Eugénio; Bernardino, Luís (2013), "A Comissão do Golfo da Guiné e a Zona de Paz e Cooperação do Atlântico Sul. Organizações interzonais para a persecução da segurança marítima na Bacia Meridional Atlântica", *Revista Militar* (2532), 43–61.

Alves, Duarte Bué (2017), *Diplomacia Azul: O mar na política externa de Portugal*. Sintra: Caleidoscópio.

AU (2014), "Integrated Maritime Strategy for Africa 2050", https://wedocs.unep.org/bitstream/handle/20.500.11822/11151/2050_aims_srategy.pdf [accessed on 5 April 2022].

Barros, Manuel (2014), "A Segurança no Golfo da Guiné: Uma Visão Marítima Angolana", *Revista Militar* (2553), https://www.revistamilitar.pt/artigo/964 [accessed on 11 April 2022].

Bernardino, Luís (2011), "A Segurança Marítima no seio da CPLP: Contributos para uma Estratégia nos Mares da Lusofonia", *Nação e Defesa* (128), 41–65.

Bernardino, Luís (2013), *A Posição de Angola na Arquitetura de Paz e Segurança Africana: Análise da Função Estratégica das Forças Armadas Angolanas*. Coimbra: Almedina.

Bernardino, Luís; Azevedo, Francisco (2015), "A nova identidade da CPLP no domínio da Defesa. Impactos para a centralidade geoestratégica de Portugal", *Lusíada - Política Internacional e Segurança* (12), 105–129.

CIA (2022a), "The World Factbook: Population", https://www.cia.gov/the-worldfactbook/field/population/country-comparison/ [accessed on 22 April 2022].

CIA (2022b), "The World Factbook: Median age", https://www.cia.gov/the-world-factbook/countries/#people-and-society [accessed on 22 April 2022].

CIA (2022c), "The World Factbook: Area Country Comparisons", https://www.cia.gov/the-world-factbook/field/area/country-comparison/ [accessed on 22 April 2022].

CPLP (2007), "Estatutos da Comunidade dos Países de Língua Portuguesa", https://www.cplp.org/Files/Filer/Documentos%20Essenciais/Estatutos_CPLP_REVLIS07.pdf [accessed on 11 April 2022].

CPLP (2009), "Estratégia da CPLP para os Oceanos", https://cplp.defesa.pt/Normativos/20090720_CPLP_Estratégia_Oceanos.pdf [accessed on 14 April 2022].

CPLP (2015), "Identidade da CPLP no Domínio da Defesa", https://cplp.defesa.pt/Normativos/20150526_IDENTIDADE%20DA%20CPLP%20NO%20DOMINIO%20DA%20DEFESA.pdf [accessed on 13 April 2022].

CPLP (2016), "Protocolo de Cooperação da CPLP no Domínio da Defesa", https://cplp.defesa.pt/Normativos/20060915_Protocolo%20Cooperacao%20CPLP%20Dominio%20Defesa.pdf [accessed on 13 April 202].

CPLP (2018), "Componente da CPLP em Defesa", https://cplp.defesa.pt/Pages/home.aspx [accessed on 13 April 2022].

CPLP (2022), "Observadores Associados", https://www.cplp.org/id-2765.aspx [accessed on 23 April 2022].

Cunha, Augusto (2014), "Angola compra navios patrulha no Brasi", http://www.angonoticias.com/Artigos/item/44026/ [acessed on 13 April 2022].

Dan, Wei (2009), *Os Países de Língua Portuguesa e a China num Mundo Globalizado*. Coimbra: Almedina.

Dias, Carlos Manuel Mendes (coord.) (2014), *Geopolítica e o Mar*. Lisboa: MGI.

Durand, Fréderic (2010), *Timor-Leste: País no Cruzamento da Ásia e do Pacífico – Um atlas histórico-geográfico*. Lisboa: Lidel.

ECOWAS (2014), "Integrated Maritime Strategy", https://www.ecowas.int/wp-content/uploads/2019/05/EIMS-English-final.pdf [accessed on 4 April 2022].

Eiras, Ruben (2012), "A era do petróleo em português", *Expresso* (22 November, 2012).

EMGFA (2022), "Missões militares portuguesas no estrangeiro", https://www.emgfa.pt/miss%C3%B5es/miss%C3%B5es-no-estrangeiro [accessed on 22 April 2022].

Ethnologue (2022), "What Are the top 200 Most Spoken Languages"', https://www.ethnologue.com/guides/ethnologue200 [accessed on 27 April 2022].

EU (2008), "Special Partnership with Cape Verde', https://eur-lex.europa.eu/legalcontent/EN/TXT/HTML/?uri=LEGISSUM:r13018&from=MT [accessed on 12 April 2022].

EU (2014), "European Maritime Security Strategy", https://data.consilium.europa.eu/doc/document/ST%2011205%202014%20INIT/EN/pdf [accessed on 5 April 2022].

Ferreira-Pereira, Laura C. (2008), "Portugal and the 2007 EU Presidency: A Case of Constructive Bridge-Building", *JCMS Annual Review* (46), 61–70.

Ferreira-Pereira, Laura C. (2015), "The European Union's Partnership Policy Towards Brazil: More Than Meets the Eye", https://doi.org/10.1080/09557571.2015.1103973 [accessed on 22 April 2022].

Fukuyama, Francis (1989), "The End of History?", https://www.jstor.org/stable/24027184 [accessed on 4 April 2022].

Guedes, Henrique Portela (2012), "Pirataria Marítima", in Cajarabille, V. et al. (coord.), A Segurança no Mar – Uma Visão Holística. Aveiro: Mare Liberum, pp. 69–77. Hugon, Philippe (2015), Geopolítica de África. 3rd. Ed., Lisboa: Escolar Editora.

Hugon, Philippe (2015), *Geopolítica de África.* Lisboa: Escolar Editora.

Huntington, Samuel (1993), "The Clash of Civilizations?", https://www.foreignaffairs.com/articles/united-states/1993-06-01/clash-civilizations [acceded on 4 April 2022].

ICG (2022), "Winning Peace in Mozambique's Embattled North", *Crisis Group Africa Briefing* (178).

IMO (2014), "Fortalecimento de la Protección Marítima en Africa Occidental y Central", https://www.imo.org/es/OurWork/Security/Paginas/Strengthening-Maritime-in-West-and-Central-Africa.aspx [accessed on 15 April 2022].

Lima, Bernardo Pires de (2016), *Portugal e o Atlântico.* Lisboa: FFMS.

Lusa (2021), "CPLP: Países lusófonos juntos seriam a 10ª maior economia mundial", https://observalinguaportuguesa.org/cplp-paises-lusofonos-juntos-seriam-a-10-a-maior-economia-mundial [accessed on 22 April 2022].

Moreira, Adriano (coord.) (2001), *Comunidade dos Países de Língua Portuguesa – Cooperação*. Coimbra: Almedina.

NATO (2022), "Defence Expenditure of NATO Countries (2014–2021)", *NATO E- Library*, 31 March 2022, https://www.nato.int/nato_static_fl2014/assets/pdf/2022/3/pdf/220331-def-exp-2021-en.PDF [accessed on 19 April 2022].

Nóbrega, Álvaro (2003), *A Luta pelo Poder na Guiné-Bissau*. Lisboa: ISCSP.

Nye, Joseph (1990), "Soft Power", https://www.jstor.org/stable/1148580 [accessed on 4 April 2022].

Palmeira, José (2006), *O Poder de Portugal nas Relações Internacionais*. Lisboa: Prefácio.

Palmeira, José (2010a), "O potencial estratégico de Timor-Leste na geopolítica da CPLP", in Leach, M. et al. (eds), *Understanding Timor Leste: Proceedings of the Timor- Leste Studies Association Conference*. Hawthorn: Swinburne Press, 41–45.

Palmeira, José (2010b), "O aprofundamento das relações UE-NATO: Oportunidades, Desafios e Opções para Portugal", *Sínteses EuroDefense* (17), 26–33.

Palmeira, José (2012), "Cooperação entre Estados Lusófonos: A Segurança no Atlântico", *Eixo Atlântico* (19), 39–50.

Palmeira, José (2014), "Potencial geopolítico da CPLP na segurança internacional", in Martins, M.; Cabecinhas, R.; Macedo, L.; Macedo, I. (eds), *Interfaces da Lusofonia*. Braga: CECS, 191–198.

Palmeira, José (2015), "Potential Lusophone Role in Atlantic Security", *Portuguese Studies Review*, 23 (1), 97–115.

Palmeira, José (2016), "O Mar na Geopolítica de Portugal", *Biblos* (2), 117–125.

Palmeira, José (2017), "Relações Externas – ACP", in Brandão, A. et al. (coord.), *Enciclopédia da União* Europeia. Lisboa: Petrony, 379–381.

Palmeira, José (2019a), "Estratégia multilateral portuguesa na ordem global", in Fernandes, S.; Simão, L. (coord.), *O Multilateralismo: Conceitos e Práticas no Século XXI*. Coimbra: Imprensa da Universidade de Coimbra, 213–237.

Palmeira, José (2019b), "Desafios Geopolíticos à Estratégia Global da UE: Abalo no Pilar Euro-atlântico", in Camisão, I.; Brandão A. (coord.), *O Estado da União Europeia: Da(s) crise(s) à mudança?* Lisboa: Petrony, 125–143.

Palmeira, José (2021), "Geopolítica de África: A influência das grandes potências", in Sarmento, J. (ed.), *Áfricas: mobilidade, violência, memória e criatividade*. Braga: Humus, 37–41.

Patriota, António de Aguiar (2013), "VII Reunião Ministerial da Zona de Paz e Cooperação do Atlântico Sul" (Basic text of the speech by the Minister of Foreign Affairs António de Aguiar Patriota, Montevideo, January 15, 2013), https://www.gov.br/mre/pt-br/centrais-deconteudo/publicacoes/discursos-artigos-e-entrevistas/ministro-das-relacoesexteriores/discursos-mre/vii-reuniao-ministerial-da-zona-de-paz-e-cooperacao-do-atlantico-sul-zopacas-texto-base-do-discurso-do-ministro-antonio-de-aguiar-patriota-montevideu-15-de-janeiro-de-2013 [accessed on 8 April 2022].

Pavia, José (coord.) (2011), *A Política Externa de Angola no Novo Contexto Internacional*. Lisboa: Quid Juris.

Ramos, Justino da Glória (2018), *Angola pelos Caminhos da Paz – Guerra e Diplomacia (1975–2002)*. Luanda: Mayamba.

Reto, Luís (coord.) (2012) *Potencial Económico da Língua Portuguesa* (Lisboa: Texto Editores)

Reto, Luís Antero; Machado, Fernando Luís; Esperança, José Paulo (2016), *New Atlas of the Portuguese Language*. Lisboa: INCM.

Rouquié, Alain (2009), *O Brasil do Século XXI*. Lisboa: Piaget.

Santos, Carlos Pinto (2014), "Cimeira de Díli e Guiné Equatorial", *África 21* (88), 5.

Silva, Augusto Santos (2018), *Argumento Necessários – Contributos para a Política Europeia e Externa de Portugal*. Lisboa: Tinta da China.

SIPRI (2022), "Trends in World Military Expenditure 2021", *SIPRI Fact Sheet* (April 2022), https://www.sipri.org/sites/default/files/2022-04/fs_2204_milex_2021_0.pdf [accessed on 19 April 2022].

Sousa, Carlos (2014), "Brasil, possibilidades de cooperação para a segurança da África", https://idi.mne.gov.pt/images/docs/conferencias/guine/017.pdf [accessed on 14 April 2022].

Stuenkel, Olivier (2012), "O Brasil na África: uma ponte sobre o Atlântico?", http://www.postwesternworld.com/2012/04/02/ [accessed on 8 April 2022].

Teixeira, José (org.) (2016), *O Português como Língua num Mundo Global*. Braga: CELUM.

UN (1986), "Declaration of a Zone of Peace and Co-operation in the South Atlantic", https://digitallibrary.un.org/record/123188 [accessed on 12 April 2022].

United Nations Convention on the Law of the Sea (1994). https://www.un.org/depts/los/convention_agreements/texts/unclos/unclos_e.pdf [accessed on 22 April 2022].

World Trade Organization (1995), https://www.wto.org/english/thewto_e/whatis_e/wto_dg_stat_e.htm [accessed on 22 April 2022].

Wavering or Privileged Cooperation? Portugal and Lusophone Africa at the UN General Assembly

Pedro Seabra and Rafael Mesquita

Introduction

The legacy of colonialism in the reformulation of new bilateral relations remains a key topic in contemporary history. The lasting memory of independence wars enmeshed with a shared historical-cultural background has come to supply a set of intersected relations that remains as central as unpredictable in equal measure. The creation of post-colonial intergovernmental organizations (IGOs) as instruments to ensure structured ties between former metropoles and former colonies further ensures the issue continues routinely open for debate. The creation of the Commonwealth, with the UK at its core, or the French-led *Organisation Internationale of la Francophonie* (OIF) stand out as the two most well-known examples of such lingering collective dynamics (Glasze 2007; Shaw 2010).

P. Seabra (✉)
ISCTE-University Institute of Lisbon, Lisbon, Portugal
e-mail: pedro.seabra@iscte.iul.pt

R. Mesquita
Federal University of Pernambuco (UFPE), Recife, Brazil
e-mail: rafael.mslima@ufpe.br

P. A. B. Duarte et al. (eds.), *Portugal and the Lusophone World*,
https://doi.org/10.1007/978-981-99-0455-6_24

However, analyses are often hamstrung by a recurring lack of empirical data and quantitative studies attesting to the intensity and variation in this kind of relationship. This omission is particularly striking when turning to the Lusophone case. Formed in 1996, the Community of Portuguese Speaking Countries (CPLP) is often relegated to a secondary role in the broader canvas of IGOs. Yet, its institutional longevity on par with its centrality amidst the foreign policy agendas of countries like Portugal makes the CPLP an intriguing case study to explore linkages between envisioned designs at the time of creation and its perceived utility in the current world order.

This chapter directly targets the expectation of privileged contacts in such kind of formal contexts and its translation into possible mutual alignment in other international fora. We aim to deconstruct how former colonial powers cooperate or interact with their former colonies at the international level by testing these propositions within the framework of the United Nations General Assembly (UNGA). This common multilateral platform stands out as particularly useful by allowing to measure high-level consultations from a longitudinal perspective. Given its expressed purpose to be used for high-level political consultations and concertation worldwide, our main query thus resides on answering to what extent the CPLP has succeeded or not in promoting greater joint projection between Portugal and African Lusophone countries, namely with Angola, Cape Verde, Guinea-Bissau, Mozambique and São Tomé and Príncipe.

Two methodological notes are first warranted. On one hand, even though our original point resides in Portuguese relations with its former African colonies, as a more direct testament of contemporary intricacies associated with post-colonial relations, our analysis invariably takes stock of what has also been achieved within the overall CPLP scope, thus including Brazil and Timor-Leste in the mix. On the other hand, we choose to centre our efforts on the 2000–2020 timeframe for the quantitative analysis of work carried out at the UNGA. This decision is grounded on both issues of data availability as well as on matching a period of increased international visibility for the CPLP.

The chapter is organized as follows. It begins by providing an overall snapshot of post-colonial relations between Portugal and African Lusophone countries in order to showcase the level of priority that is often attributed to regular high-level political cooperation. We then examine the potential of the CPLP as a multilateral propeller for joint endeavours in the world stage. The third section focuses on specific efforts made within the UN institutional framework, followed by the actual unpacking of expectations surrounding higher concertation at the UNGA. We conclude by summarizing our results and indicating additional areas worthy of further research in this context.

Portugal and Lusophone Africa

Any attempt to holistically address the political-diplomatic relations between Portugal and Africa inevitably faces a considerable pre-existent historical weight. The challenge of exploring these ties proves particularly sizeable when dealing with a relationship as complex as prolific in official announcements, high-level visits, and political-media rhetoric (Seabra 2019; Carvalho 2018). Indeed, running counter to some prevailing notions, the "dissolution of Portugal's African empire was every bit as brutal and nasty as many other imperial endgames, and the managing of the postcolonial relationships was also fraught with incidents and misunderstandings" (Oliveira 2017, p. 13).

For all intents and purposes, the post-April 25th period represented a perfect storm in terms of obstacles to the planning and execution of a new relationship agenda with the African continent. On the one hand, short-lived governments and serious domestic economic difficulties, together with around 600,000–800,000 Portuguese citizens who left the former colonies, led to a recurrent degree of paralysis in political terms, as well as hesitation about external options. On the other hand, the East–West geopolitical divisions and the option of many newly independent countries to follow the communist bloc also implied management of expectations and interests susceptible to cyclical crises (Figueiredo 1986; Gaspar 1988). Assessments have therefore hardly differed about the structural problems underlying the planning and execution of Portuguese foreign policy towards Africa since then. Franco (2006), for one, mentions how, in "the name of a 'perfect' bilateral relationship, affections or political friendships are confused with the formality that guarantees relations between States" (p. 29). For his part, MacQueen (2003) characterizes the national efforts carried out in this area as equivalent to a set of "relations, variable objectives and uncertain rapprochements with the former territories, both psychological and political" (p. 182).

The inexistence of binding bilateral legal instruments in the immediate period following decolonization that allowed for consultations on issues in the international order did not help move the needle along either. In fact, the preference was initially placed on agreements of a more diffuse and ambiguous scope, which did not elaborate on how a post-colonial relationship could translate itself into a different international context. On that note, Portugal signed a General Cooperation and Friendship Agreement with Guinea-Bissau and São Tomé and Principe, and Mozambique in 1975, followed by Cape Verde in 1977. Angola was next in 1979 with a General Cooperation Agreement. None of these instruments, however, managed to incite substantial political discussions.

This did not mean that issues of common interest did not occasionally surface. For example, during the 1980s and 1990s, the main topic of interest to both parties resided in how Portugal presented itself as an informal representative of the interests of African Lusophone countries within the European Communities, especially when considering the negotiations then underway with African, Caribbean and Pacific (ACP) countries, under the Lomé and Cotonou frameworks (Raimundo 2014). But following several false starts in the late 1980s and early 1990s (Monteiro 1996), enough political consensus was found in 1996 to then create a new multilateral organization, with an international legal stand that could bring Angola, Brazil, Cape Verde, Guinea-Bissau, Mozambique, Portugal, and São Tomé and Príncipe—and after 2002, East Timor—to the same table (Seabra 2019).

However, from the start, the CPLP also had to face a considerable number of challenges. On the one hand, it exhibited a lingering centrality by Portugal, which, in turn, came to incite at times a sensitive cohabitation with the remaining members (Seabra 2021). Indeed, the "fact that the organization is sometimes referred to as 'lusophone' hints at the existence of an invisible centre/periphery construct, which can seldom be either flattering or beneficial to members other than Portugal" (Santos 2003, p. 75; Reis and Oliveira 2018). The very aggregating concept of "Lusophony" led to consensus and unity only to a certain point given how its limits were also stretched in the name of new geopolitical considerations. The adhesion of Equatorial Guinea in 2014 (Seabra 2021), in particular, exposed the internal divergences regarding the course intended for the CPLP. On the other hand, a shifting focus from a cultural-based project, to a business-friendly facilitator, to a resource-driven accelerator, and back to more shared-cultural/educational leitmotivs, also fuelled a generalized perception of a structural ambivalence over what its role and purpose ought to be (Hewitt et al. 2017).

The CPLP and Political Cooperation Between Member States

Mandate-wise, the focus of the CPLP has been unequivocally set on inwards cooperation since the organization's early inception. The thematic list stands as wide as ambitious, but also on par with other similar multilateral arrangements of the sort: economic and social development, easier transit of citizens, diffusion of the Portuguese language, cultural exchanges, interparliamentary cooperation, business cooperation, scientific and technological cooperation, shared support in humanitarian and emergency crises, civil society exchanges, cooperation in immigration policies, protection and preservation of the environment and sustainable development, eradication of racism, racial discrimination and xenophobia, improvement of children's living conditions, promotion of corporate social responsibility, and youth exchanges.[1]

However, external efforts concerning political coordination also figure prominently amidst this sprawling mandate. In fact, the CPLP's stated purpose consists of enhancing the "international affirmation of all Portuguese-speaking countries that constitute a geographically discontinuous space but identified by the common language". Two sub-domains stand out in this regard, namely, (1) promoting "coordination at the multilateral level to ensure the respect for human rights in the respective countries and around the world"; and (2) extending cooperation in "the area of political and diplomatic consultations, particularly within international organizations, in order to give increasing expression to the common interests and needs within the international community".[2] Moreover, the ensuing statutes consecrated "Political and diplomatic consultation between its members in matters of international relation, namely to reinforce its presence in international fora" as one of the organization's

[1] Although not included in the original purview, intra-defence cooperation was subsequently added in 2002.

[2] CPLP Constitutive Declaration, 17 July 1996.

main goals.[3] Among its constituent bodies, the Permanent Concertation Committee, made up of one representative from each of the CPLP member states, is in charge of providing more direct monitoring of all activities carried out within the organization. But the role of the so-called CPLP Groups, made up of a minimum of three Representatives of member states to other foreign Governments or international organizations, is also relevant in this regard as they coordinate positions on common interests, ensure CPLP representation at conferences, seminars, and international meetings, carry out joint efforts, exchange information on the political and governmental reality of the country where they are located, support the holding of events organized within the scope of the CPLP and publicize the activities and achievements of the organization itself.

Overall, their activities have been diversified, ranging from accompanying UNESCO programs for the protection of the cultural heritage of Portuguese-speaking countries to sensitizing FAO agencies in relation to food programs, supporting the implementation of development aid to African member countries and Timor-Leste, or promoting the use of Portuguese in the world and as a working language in international organizations. General evaluations continue to posit that "(…) while often not spectacular in nature, the CPLP does offer meaningful returns for its members. The organisation provides a platform that can be leveraged by members to advance specific agendas if they are willing to devote the necessary resources to coordinating their counterparts and driving their programme forward" (Hewitt et al. 2017, p. 307; Sanches 2014). However, more nuanced assessments of sectorial progress remain amiss.

The CPLP and the UN

Part of the CPLP's original mandate consisted in trying to translate prior cultural affinities among its members into political dividends in other multilateral settings, while at the same time aiming to stand on an equal playing field with other intergovernmental organizations (IGOs) in world stages. The most immediate route to both ends inevitably went through the UN. Two reasons underlined such an option: on the one hand, it

[3] CPLP Statutes, consolidated 2007 version, n. 3, a.

granted a measure of international legitimacy unlike any other international organization; on the other hand, it comprised the sole other venue where all Lusophone member states stood equally invested in its success, utility, and longevity.

In that sense, in 1999, just three years after its creation, the CPLP applied for and obtained permanent observer status at the UN General Assembly.[4] The reasoning provided at the time was straightforward: given how the coincidence of purposes with the UN and how "mutually advantageous" it would be to establish working cooperation channels, the CPLP would be officially allowed to participate in the sessions and ensure work of the General Assembly, on par with 76 other IGOs.[5] Soon afterwards, relations between the CPLP and the UN also began to be framed under Chapter VIII of the UN Charter as well as under successive UN Security Council resolutions call for cooperation between the UN and regional/sub-regional organizations on maintaining international peace and security. The latter dispositions would become increasingly paramount in light of the CPLP's increasing involvement with successive political-military crises in Guinea-Bissau and ensuring mediation efforts.

The exact same mould of the first resolution would then be reissued, almost to the letter, in 2004, 2006, 2008, 2010, 2013, 2015, 2017, and 2019.[6] Two explicit requests were also routinely made through such procedures. The first consisted of having the UN Secretary-General regularly submit a report on the implementation of the desired state of relations between the two organizations, which has been carried out

[4] The UN Charter and the General Assembly Rules of Procedure have no provisions related to granting permanent observer status to third parties. However, it has been agreed the UNGA would restrict observer status to States and intergovernmental organizations whose activities cover matters of interest to the Assembly. Under A/RES/54/195, the UNGA Sixth Committee is bound to consider all applications for observer status before they are considered in the plenary session. Permanent Observers may participate in the sessions and workings of the General Assembly and maintain missions at UN Headquarters.

[5] See A/RES/54/10, 18 November 1999.

[6] See A/RES/59/21, 8 November 2004; A/RES/61/223, 20 December 2006; A/RES/63/143, 11 December 2008; A/RES/65/139, 16 December 2010; A/RES/67/252, 26 March 2013; A/RES/69/311, 6 July 2015; A/RES/71/324, 8 September 2017; A/RES/73/339, 12 September 2019.

with increasing regularity in recent years.[7] The second request entailed initiating further consultations towards the establishment of a formal cooperation agreement between the UNSG and the CPLP, to no avail.

In parallel, the most visible result of this concertation resided in the endorsement of national or individual candidacies for institutions and positions within the UN system. This process began in full in 2002, during the III Summit of Heads of State and Government in Brasília, where 3 candidacies to a non-permanent seat at the UN Security Council—from Angola (2002–2003), Brazil (2003–2004) and Portugal (2010–2011)—were collectively endorsed. In the following years, as seen in Fig. 1, other additional 58 candidacies were also endorsed.[8] On all these occasions, member states pledged to reinforce such a practice as well as the concertation in world forums on matters of common interest on the international agenda.

When taken together, these cumulative inroads amount to tokens of political cooperation within CPLP as manifested through the UN. However, if these countries managed to reach such a consensus with regard to candidacies for international positions, it is worth questioning if such dynamics also translated themselves into the long-standing forum for more recurrent interactions between countries worldwide, namely the UNGA.

Lusophone Cooperation at the UNGA

UNGA votes provide a first cut into the collective behaviour of CPLP countries in multilateral arenas. Figure 2 is derived from the Bailey et al. (2017) data and shows the ideal point scores calculated for all 9 members, based on their voting position from 2000 to 2020. The authors recommend interpreting these scores as measures of satisfaction with the US-led international order. As such, there seems to be early evidence of a split

[7] For UNSG reports on relations with the CPLP see: A/61/256, 16 August 2006; A/63/228–S/2008/531, 8 August 2008; A/65/382–S/2010/490, 20 September 2010; A/67/280–S/2012/614, 9 August 2012; A/69/228–S/2014/560, 4 August 2014; A/71/160–S/2016/621, 15 July 2016; A/73/328–S/2018/592, 17 August 2018; A/75/345–S/2020/898, 11 September 2020.

[8] 2018 proved the only exception, when the Heads of State and Government of the CPLP gathered at Praia opted to not make any explicit commitment in this regard, choosing instead to reaffirm previous commitments to a permanent UNSC seat for Brazil and Africa.

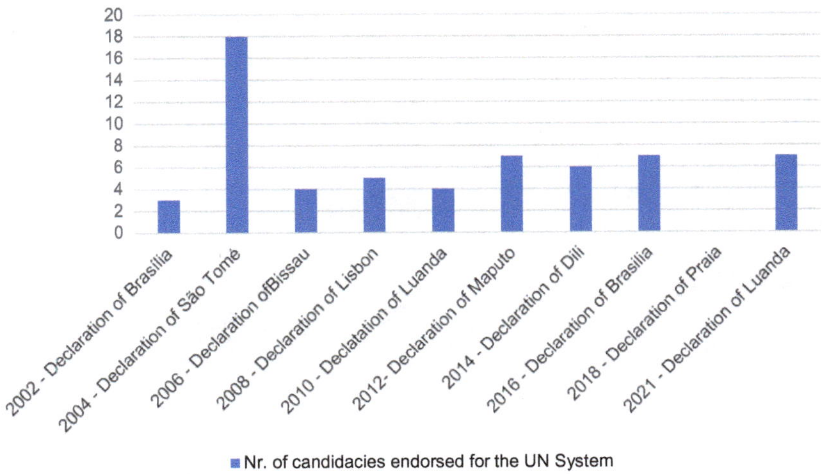

Fig. 1 Number of individual and national candidacies endorsed by CPLP member states to the UN system (*Source* Elaborated by the authors based on the final declarations of Heads of State and Government Summits)

between Portugal, tied to the rest of its European partners, and the rest of CPLP.

Knowing, however, that voted resolutions are only a fraction of the total UNGA output, these results fail to depict the complete story. As highlighted in additional research on this topic (Seabra and Mesquita 2022), given that only contentious themes are settled through the ballot box, cooperation between countries can be underestimated by such indices if their partnership is strong on topics that are less controversial. As a remedy, we turn to the sponsorship of draft resolutions as a more encompassing metric.

Institutional rites of the UNGA in that regard remain fairly stable and predictable. Every session, an item is put on the agenda, as previously discussed by the General Committee of the UNGA. Most draft resolutions are then initiated and drafted by a member state (the "main sponsor") and usually subscribed by other supporters ("co-sponsors"). Every draft then turns into a so-called L-document and is normally tabled in one of six different committees, each referring to a different policy area (Mesquita and Seabra 2020). Once a draft is tabled, its trajectory can vary considerably. In an ideal-type scenario, a draft will cruise unmodified

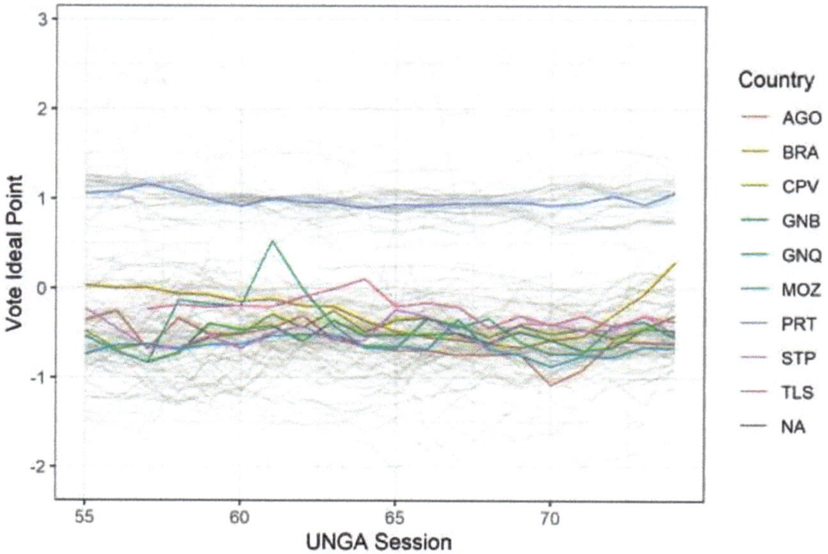

Fig. 2 Roll-call votes ideal point scores (*Source* Elaborated by the authors, based on data from Bailey et al. 2017)

through the original committee, before being adopted as a full resolution by the plenary, either through a vote, by consensus, by acclamation, without objection, or without any vote (Peterson 2006, p. 54). However, L-documents frequently receive additional contributions along the way. These can alter either their original sponsors (via Addenda), their content (via Corrigenda and Revisions), or even both (via Revisions). The range of opportunities for member states to engage with the process by sponsoring a draft remains therefore very wide, without any major caveats or preconditions (Mesquita and Seabra 2020).

To map the sponsorship behaviour of the CPLP countries, we rely on sponsorship information drawn from the UN General Assembly Sponsorship Dataset.[9] Following two previously proposed indices, priority and ownership (Seabra and Mesquita 2022), we seek to better ascertain draft relevance for member states. Priority indicates how early (or late) a country adhered to a draft resolution. Ownership, in turn, is

[9] Available at https://doi.org/10.7910/DVN/MPQUE2.

a count of total sponsors, aimed at discriminating between resolutions that embody widespread interests (many sponsors, low ownership) and those conveying peculiar preferences (few sponsors, high ownership). In essence, the indices attempt to separate "the wheat from the tares" (p. 3), i.e. differentiate initiatives near to core interests of member states from those that were ritualistic and unimportant, based on their urgency and exclusivity. We use these indices as a complement to raw sponsorship information, so as to obtain a finer assessment of peculiar initiatives arising from the CPLP.

Between 2000 and 2020 (sessions 55 to 74), there were 5,010 draft resolutions tabled at the UNGA.[10] From this total, at least 3,709 counted with the sponsorship of one or more CPLP members. On 101 occasions—on average 5 times per session—we observed all 9 CPLP participants sponsoring a proposition together. If we consider that group size changed over the years, with the entrances of East Timor and Equatorial Guinea as of UNGA sessions 57 and 69, respectively, then the total number of occasions when all CPLP members endorsed a draft reaches 120. From these 120 drafts, 15 were initiatives from the African Group, 75 from the G77, 2 from the Non-Aligned Movement, and 20 were not attributed to formal groups. Figure 3 shows these totals over time.

This reveals that joint sponsorship by all CPLP members, more often than not, is a side effect of the activity of larger and more traditional UNGA groupings. This is not to say the group is lost amid these bigger factions. Though less frequent if compared to this type of output driven by large groups, the CPLP has nonetheless a distinctive and intentional production of its own. Its signature product resides in the recurring draft resolution "Cooperation between the United Nations and the Community of Portuguese-speaking Countries", previously mentioned. This proposal is tabled every two years at the UNGA plenary. It is not placed under the responsibility of any formal political or geographical group, and different members of CPLP have taken turns in introducing the draft to the Plenary. Similar to other proposals concerning the cooperation between the UN and external organizations, the content of this draft acknowledges summits held by the group, joint statements, and

[10] We call "draft" the collection of sequenced L-Documents, starting from an original root proposition until its revisions and addenda.

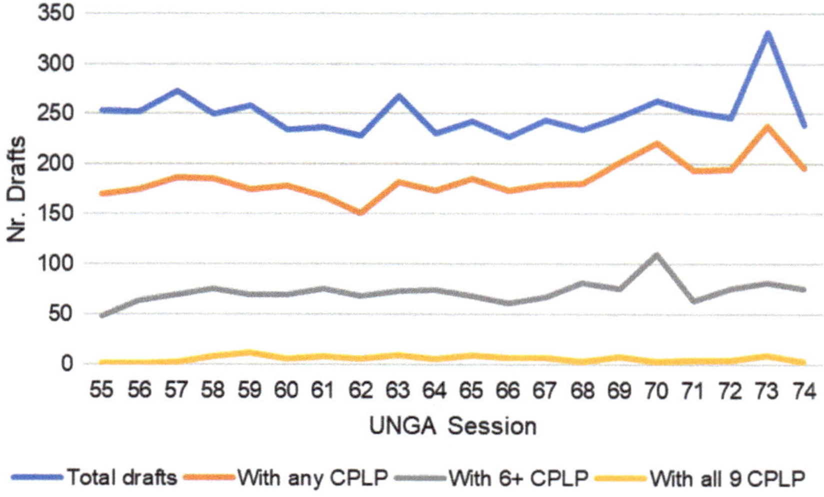

Fig. 3 Sponsorship of UNGA drafts by CPLP members (*Source* Elaborated by the authors, based on Seabra and Mesquita 2022)

laudatory developments in its countries. Approximately 20 other organizations tabled similar drafts, for instance, the African Union, the OIF, and the Organization of Islamic Cooperation.

Interestingly, CPLP-UN cooperation drafts stand out as the ones with the most co-sponsors in this sort of initiative. Though in 2004 the proposal only garnered 8 backers, by 2010 this number reached 49, and in 2017 a total of 118, averaging 61 sponsors across the whole period. This performance can be considered surprising if we consider how small the CPLP is with just 9 members. Figure 4 puts this into perspective by comparing several regional organizations that tabled such UN cooperation drafts. The horizontal axis refers to the number of members each entity had and the vertical axis compares how many supporters it garnered on average on its recurring drafts under this topic. Each organization was observed twice: with average values for 2000–2009 and then 2010–2020. Results show that, though very small, CPLP resolutions had more endorsers than large groups like the African Union or the OIC, and, most impressively, had the highest surge in a mean number of co-sponsors from one decade to the next.

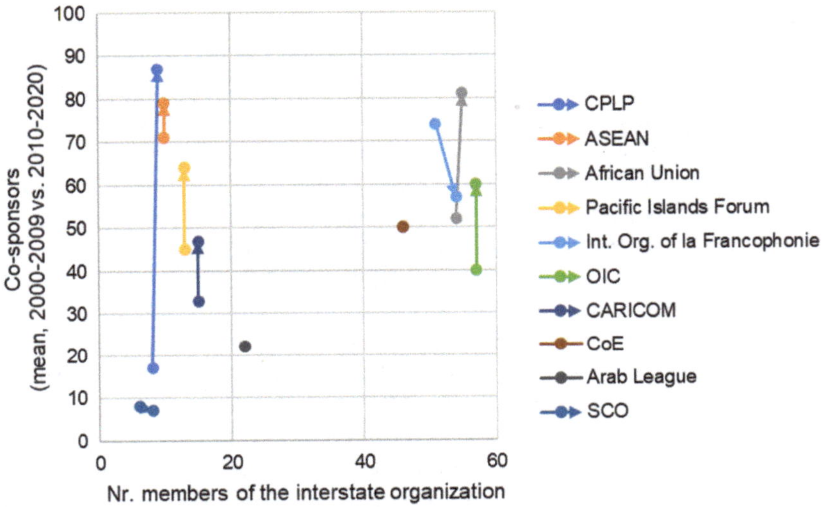

Fig. 4 Comparison of the mean number of final co-sponsors for drafts on cooperation between the UN and regional groups (2000–2009 and 2010–2020) (*Source* Elaborated by the authors, based on data from Seabra and Mesquita [2022]. Data on number of members in each organization are from Wikipedia)

If we monitor the dimensions of priority and ownership, that is, focusing on drafts sponsored early by CPLP countries and not too diluted among the UNGA crowd, we find next in order of importance drafts attached to the African continent and its different social-political predicaments. CPLP members have essentially supported drafts on health programs,[11] refugees and displaced persons,[12] economic development

[11] Recurring drafts "Intensification of efforts to end obstetric fistula" (A/C.3/69/L.20/Rev.1, A/C.3/71/L.16/Rev.1, A/C.3/73/L.20/Rev.1), "Prevention and control of non-communicable diseases" (A/64/L.52), "Consolidating gains and accelerating efforts to control and eliminate malaria in developing countries, particularly in Africa, by 2030" (A/70/L.62, A/71/L.89, A/72/L.68, A/73/L.109, A/74/L.91).

[12] See, for example, "Assistance to refugees, returnees and displaced persons in Africa" (A/C.3/65/L.56).

programs,[13] and memorials about the transatlantic slave trade,[14] all focused on Africa.

This thematic pull is not surprising if we consider that CPLP countries bring forward relatively little as original produce of the 9 members and share instead a more loaded agenda with larger political and regional groups. All members tend to nurture denser workloads with neighbouring partners. Just as Angola co-sponsored most of its drafts with Nigeria in these 10 years (1799), Brazil did it with Chile (1804), and Portugal with Italy (1677) (see also Mesquita and Seabra 2020). This trend corroborates the accumulated findings from past UNGA scholarship. Studies using roll-call voting ideal points customarily identify a North vs. South cleavage at the Assembly and consistently place Portugal on the Northern faction pitted against Brazil and PALOP countries (Bailey et al. 2017). Novel research using sponsorship, in turn, joins Portugal and Brazil in the Western bloc while remaining CPLP members are placed in a broader African, Caribbean, and Pacific cluster (Seabra and Mesquita 2022), confirming a split nonetheless between Lusophone countries.

Conclusion

The New Strategic Vision of the CPLP for 2016 to 2026, adopted by the XI Heads of State and Government Summit in Brasília, in November 2016, aimed to revamp the organization's activities and stake out new a working agenda. In this context, two axes of action, in particular, were brought up: (1) "Broadening the participation of actors, calling for the cooperation of other relevant partners to achieve the programmatic objectives"; and (2) "Diversification of Partnerships and identification of additional sources of financing, promoting joint work with other actors and seeking to increase the resources available for CPLP cooperation".[15]

[13] See, for example, drafts on the "New Partnership for Africa's Development" (A/58/L.17/Rev.1, A/59/L.33/Rev.1, A/60/L.16/Rev.1, A/62/L.10/Rev.1, A/63/L.60/Rev.1, A/64/L.38/Rev.1, A/65/L.69/Rev.1, A/66/L.40/Rev.1, A/67/L.57/Rev.1, A/68/L.41/Rev.1, A/69/L.64/Rev.1, A/70/L.48/Rev.1, A/71/L.70/Rev.1, A/72/L.57/Rev.1, A/72/L.71, A/73/L.96/Rev.1, A/73/L.112).

[14] See, for example, "Permanent memorial to and remembrance of the victims of slavery and the transatlantic slave trade" (A/62/L.32, A/63/L.5, A/64/L.10, A/65/L.36, A/66/L.25, A/67/L.41, A/68/L.7, A/69/L.19, A/70/L.5, A/73/L.119).

[15] CPLP Strategic Cooperation Document 2020–2026, 16 July 2019, available at: https://www.cplp.org/id-4176.aspx.

The organization's global aspirations for the coming years would therefore appear to remain contingent on a set of practical requirements, indicating where the main priority will likely continue to fall.

This chapter focused on exploring the evolution of this type of relationship as well as the practical result through which they translate themselves, in multilateral terms. As expected, the manifestation of a Lusophone front in UNGA inner dynamics has proven difficult to emerge over the years. On one hand, Portugal stands out as more closely aligned with its European partners than with the rest of CPLP. On the other hand, whenever joint sponsorship is recorded by all CPLP members, more often than not, it represents a side effect of what was agreed upon within other larger UNGA groupings, where each country is more involved or has a more direct stake. However, the unexpected popularity of drafts on cooperation between the UN and the CPLP also merits further analysis as it indicates that political-diplomatic cooperation in the Lusophone space might actually entice considerable interest across the board of the remaining international community. But for the time being, UNGA inner dynamics demonstrate that the CPLP has not necessarily succeeded in promoting greater joint projection between Portugal and African Lusophone countries, therefore leaving ample room to improve the translating of political consultations in the context of the CPLP into the world at large.

References

Bailey, Michael, Anton Strezhnev and Eric Voeten (2017), "Estimating Dynamic State Preferences from United Nations Voting Data", *Journal of Conflict Resolution* 61(2): 430–456.

Carvalho, Clara (2018), "Africa and Portugal", in D. Nagar & C. Mutasa (eds.), *Africa and the World: Bilateral and Multilateral International Diplomacy*. Cham: Palgrave Macmillan, 143–165.

Figueiredo, António (1986), "Portugal and Africa", in Kenneth Maxwell (ed.), *Portugal in the 1980s: Dilemmas of Democratic Consolidation*. Westport: Greenwood Press, 89–108.

Franco, Manuela (2006), "Petróleo em Português? Em Prol de uma Política Africana", *Nação e Defesa* 114: 15–34.

Gaspar, Carlos (1988), "Portugal's Policies toward Angola and Mozambique since Independence", in R. J. Bloomfield (ed.), *Regional Conflict and U.S. Policy: Angola and Mozambique*. Algonac: Reference Publications, 40–74.

Glasze, Georg (2007), "The Discursive Constitution of a World-Spanning Region and the Role of Empty Signifiers: The Case of Francophonia", *Geopolitics* 12(4): 656–679.

Herpolsheimer, Jens (2020), "The Finances of the Community of Portuguese-Speaking Countries (CPLP)", in Ulf Engel and Frank Mattheis (eds.), *The Finances of Regional Organisations in the Global South: Follow the Money*. Abingdon: Routledge, 35–50.

Hewitt, W. E., Sean Burges and Inês Gomes (2017), "The Comunidade dos Países de Língua Portuguesa at 20 Years: An Impact Assessment", *South African Journal of International Affairs* 24(3): 291–309.

MacQueen, Norrie (2003), "Re-defining the 'African vocation': Portugal's post-colonial identity crisis", *Journal of Contemporary European Studies* 11(2): 181–199.

Mesquita, Rafael and Pedro Seabra (2020), "Go Global or Go Home: Comparing the Regional vs. Global Engagement of Brazil and South Africa at the UN General Assembly", *Politikon* 47(3): 361–384.

Monteiro, António (1996), "A Comunidade dos Países de Língua Portuguesa", *Nação e Defesa* 77: 49–62.

Oliveira, Pedro Aires (2017), "Decolonization in Portuguese Africa", in *Oxford Research Encyclopedia of African History*. https://doi.org/10.1093/acrefore/9780190277734.013.41.

Peterson, M. J. (2006). *The UN General Assembly*. London: Routledge.

Raimundo, António (2014), "Mapping the Agency of a Small, Former Colonial Power: Portugal and EU Political Conditionality in Sub-Saharan Africa", *Perspectives on European Politics and Society* 15(4): 589–605.

Reis, Bruno Cardoso and Pedro Aires Oliveira (2018), "The Power and Limits of Cultural Myths in Portugal's Search for a Post-Imperial Role", *The International History Review* 40(3): 631–653.

Sanches, Edalina Rodrigues (2014), "The Community of Portuguese Language Speaking Countries: The Role of Language in a Globalizing World", *Atlantic Future Scientific Papers* 14.

Santos, Luís António (2003), "Portugal and the CPLP: Heightened Expectations, Unfounded Disillusions", in Stewart Lloyd-Jones and António Costa Pinto (eds.), *The Last Empire Thirty Years of Portuguese Decolonization*. Bristol: Intellect, 67–81.

Seabra, Pedro (2019), "Um produto de tempos passados? Portugal e África no domínio político-diplomático", in António Raimundo (ed.), *Política Externa Portuguesa e África: Tendências e Temas Contemporâneos*. Lisboa: Centro de Estudos Internacionais, Iscte – Instituto Universitário de Lisboa (CEI-Iscte), 73–99.

Seabra, Pedro (2021), "From Opportunity Seeking to Gap Filling: Reframing Brazil in Lusophone Africa", in Mathias Alencastro and Pedro Seabra (eds.), *Brazil-Africa Relations in the 21st Century: From Surge to Downturn and Beyond*. Cham: Springer, 25–41.

Seabra, Pedro and Rafael Mesquita (2022), "Beyond Roll-Call Voting: Sponsorship Dynamics at the UN General Assembly", *International Studies Quarterly* 66(2): sqac008.

Shaw, Timothy M. (2010), "Comparative Commonwealths: An Overlooked Feature of Global Governance?", *Third World Quarterly* 31(2): 333–346.

Transition to a New Geopolitics of Energy: The Lusophone World

Carla Fernandes and António Paulo Duarte

Introduction

Geopolitics is the instrument that questions the relationship between space and politics. Defarges (1994) defines it as "the study of the relations between a power policy raised to the international stage and the geographic framework in which it is inserted". Energy and geopolitics are inextricably linked in "both old and new formulations" of power as countries have always made and continue to make strategies to meet their "energy needs, reach markets and secure national positions and interests" (Austvik 2018, p. 25).

This chapter obtained the FCT funding from the IPRI-UN Multiannual project, under Reference UIDB/04627/2020.

C. Fernandes (✉)
Instituto Português de Relações Internacionais (IPRI-NOVA), Lisbon, Portugal
e-mail: carlafer@fcsh.unl.pt

A. P. Duarte
Portuguese Military Academy, Lisbon, Portugal

P. A. B. Duarte et al. (eds.), *Portugal and the Lusophone World*,
https://doi.org/10.1007/978-981-99-0455-6_25

Energy geopolitics analyses, among others factors, the relations between the geography of energy resources and the effects that they can have on the balance of the power of the states in their relations with other actors, as framed by the dynamics of energy and energy security. In accordance with Mel Conant (1993 cit. by Skeet 1996, p. 265), it studies "the effects that the location of energy resources has on countries policies, namely in decision-making". From this concept, two dimensions are inferred, the first is the "location of resources" and the second is the "decision-making of the states".

Although location is an important factor, all internal and external characteristics must be considered, such as the type of resource, whether it is abundant or scarce in the territory, its market importance, the methods and techniques of extraction and transportation used within the global supply chain, and the location of the resources in the international market.

According to Yu and Dai (2012, pp. 94–95) the influence of resources is not static, changing over the years with the "advances in technology, the shifting demand for raw materials, the changes in domestic and international political goals, as well as the changing in the judging standards of the legality of the means to the pursuit of political goals". As a result, these changes have an impact on the actors and the energy market.

With regard to the second dimension, all actors in the energy sector who can be identified by their location and the resource characteristics in their territory, as producing, transit and consuming countries, should be included (Conant 1993 cit. by Skeet 1996, p. 266). If the supply-demand relationship is balanced, none of the parties will feel threatened or endangered. However, if there is no balance, one of them may be vulnerable, with the potential to have a "significant loss of production or well-being" (Fernandes 2019). In order to decrease this vulnerability, governments devise strategies, which for Lucas Kerr de Oliveira (2015, p. 1) refers to "the ability to plan, operate, modify and implement a strategy for the complete and integrated development of different sectors of the economy and society that depend on or are directly related to the generation, distribution and consumption of Energy". Among the various strategies, diversification is one of the main priorities. Reflecting for consumer countries, in the development of endogenous energy resources in order to reduce external dependence, and, for producers, in the diversification of energy buyers, in order to ensure the security of demand and to have the ability to return on investment in their energy resources (Fernandes 2019, p. 81).

Although conventional fossil fuels continue to be the primary global source of energy, they are also the least desirable sources, either due to the high level of dependence that they represent for most consuming countries, or to their negative effects on human, environmental, and climate security. With this in mind, switching from non-renewable energy resources, such as oil, natural gas, and coal to renewable energy is the main goal of every government. This transition will redraw the geopolitical map in the twenty-first century and will reconfigure "many elements of international politics that have shaped the global system since at least World War II, significantly affecting the sources of national power, the process of globalization, relations among the great powers" (Bordoff and O'Sullivan 2022). It will also rearrange trade alliances and flows, and forge new interdependencies around new commodities (IRENA 2019). This new energy order will restructure the traditional geopolitical dimensions of energy supply and demand (Yang and He 2021), and lead to the same or to new types of conflicts, or, on the contrary, to the reduction of energy-related conflicts (Bordoff 2020; IRENA 2019; Bordoff and O'Sullivan 2022).

A new energy geopolitics is emerging, which is, for many authors (Roman et al. 2020) the geopolitics of renewable energy, translated into structural changes in the organization of the energy system and in the social and power relationships established through it and driven by the need to reduce the carbon intensity of the energy system (Blondee et al. 2021).

Within this framework, we integrate the relationship between the energy dimension of the Portuguese-speaking countries and the process of the energy transition. In some of these countries, particularly in Angola, Brazil, Mozambique, and East Timor, fossil energies have dominated consumption, development, and exploitation. While, others, such as Portugal and Brazil, are already leaders in the generation of renewable energy, for instance, in solar photovoltaic and wind power, and currently are investing in green hydrogen as well. In this chapter, we propose to assess the potential of the Portuguese-speaking space for the current energy paradigm shift and for the energy transition. Through a mixed analysis and based on the multiple case study method, we will first analyze and frame the energy cooperation strategies of Portuguese-speaking countries for the energy transition. Addressing our objective, in a second section, we will analyze the potential of these countries using the

World Economic Forum's Energy Transition Index (WEF),[1] regarding the "energy access and security" indicator. This indicator integrates the performance of the energy system and incorporates six sub-items: electrification, quality of electricity supply, access to clean cooking fuels, net energy imports, fuel mix diversification, and import diversification (WEF 2021)

For a greater uniformity of the data under analysis, we will essentially use statistics from the International Renewable Energy Agency (IRENA), complementing with information from the energy agencies of the Portuguese-speaking countries, the International Energy Agency (EIA), and the World Economic Forum.

Theoretical Framework of the Energy Transition

The energy transition is not a uniform process, being important to understand what this process entails and to explain major currents of research. As with energy security (Fernandes 2019, pp. 78–82), there are numerous concepts of energy transition. IRENA (2021i) defines it as "pathway toward transformation of the global energy sector from fossil-based to zero-carbon by the second half of this century". In turn, Smil (2016, p. IX) denotes that it is "the change in the composition (structure) of primary energy supply, the gradual shift from a specific pattern of energy provision to a new state of an energy system". The Dictionary of Energy (Clevaland and Morris 2017, p. 201) defines it as a "change in the primary form of energy consumption of a given society"; e.g., the historic transition from wood to coal and then to oil and gas in industrial Europe; the current shift from biomass fuels to commercial energy in some areas of the developing world. It can also be understood as "a timely transition towards a more inclusive, sustainable, affordable and secure energy system that provides solutions to global energy-related challenges, while creating value for business and society" (WEF 2020, p. 12).

[1] This Index is divided into two parts: the performance of the power system and the enabling environment for transition. The first is, in turn, divided into three analysis factors that allow to evaluate the energy system in relation to three priorities: (*i*) the capacity to support economic development and growth, (*ii*) security, reliability and universal accessibility of energy, and (*iii*) environmental sustainability throughout the energy value chain. The objective of a country's energy transition must be to simultaneously fulfill these three priorities, thus maintaining a balanced "energy triangle" (WEF 2021).

The plurality of concepts exposes what many authors (Guimarães 2020; Valkenburg and Gracceva 2016) refer to as the "complexity and irreducibility" of the energy transition process. This complexity increases with the variety of perspectives regarding the speed at which a transition can take place and its nature. There are two main dominant currents in terms of temporal dynamics. The first integrates the authors (Fouquet 2016; Grubler et al. 2016; Smil 2016; Myhrvold and Caldeira 2012) who advocate that the transition is a long and protracted process, often taking decades or centuries to occur. The other current includes authors (Sovacool 2017) who defend that rapid transitions can occur within a decade or a few years, with the change in the end of energy usage at a smaller geographic scale, mainly at a national level.[2]

The nature of transitions fluctuates with the endogenous and exogenous factors that can influence them. Endogenous factors include the national energy policy decision-making and strategic planning, the countries' resources characteristics and innovation, and technological development. Exogenously, other factors can act as catalysts and accelerate the transition process, such as global energy crises (e.g. 1973 crisis); military conflicts (e.g. War in Libya, Iraq and Afghanistan), or even the COVID-19 pandemic and the "green recovery" plans (Kuzemko et al. 2020).

There are few academic studies that include Portuguese-speaking countries and the energy transition process (Eiras 2013; Losekann and Tavares 2019), and most of the analysis is fragmented rather than comprehensive. Or resorting to an individual analysis of each of the Portuguese-speaking countries, e.g., Portugal (Prados et al. 2022; Henriques 2011; Domingues 2021) and Brazil (Lazaro et al. 2022), separately or alternatively, by integrating each of the countries in the geographical spaces that they belong to, for instance, Portugal in the Iberian Peninsula (Pérez-Franco et al. 2020). Therefore, this chapter intends to contribute to the study of the energy transition in the Portuguese-speaking space understood by the group of countries that share the Portuguese language. This process is linked to the increased importance of energy in Portuguese-

[2] For a more in-depth analysis of the temporal dynamics of energy transitions, see the study of Benjamin K. Sovacool "How long will it take? Conceptualizing the temporal dynamics of energy transitions" (2016).

speaking countries since 2000 and also with their potential to become key players on the global energy map and being able to support the United Nations Sustainable Development goal 7 "Ensure Access to Affordable, Reliable, Sustainable and Modern Energy for all" by 2030 (SDG 7).

Energy Cooperation in the Lusophone World and the Energy Transition

The "Lusophone world" did not originate due to energy interests. The basis for uniting the eight countries that make up the Portuguese-speaking space—Cape Verde, Mozambique, São Tomé and Príncipe, Guinea-Bissau, Brazil, East Timor, Portugal, and Angola, is cultural, linguistic, and historical. It is no coincidence that the foundation of an organization that brings these countries together is based on their common language—Community of Portuguese Language Countries (CPLP).

When the CPLP was formed in 1996, the energy dimension was not relevant, nor could it be assessed how it could come to be. At that moment, only Angola was important in the global energy market as an oil producer. It was only since the beginning of the twenty-first century that this relevance has gradually spread to other CPLP countries, such as Brazil and Mozambique. Thus, this transformation was mainly due to the application of new technologies for the extraction of unconventional energy resources as the Brazilian pre-salt and the deepwater and ultra-deepwater oil and gas exploration in Angola. As a result, the energy dimension of CPLP has expanded and, currently as a group, CPLP can be considered the world's fourth largest oil producer (Lima 2016).[3]

In this context, at the CPLP's 10th Summit of Heads of State and Government in 2014, held in Dili, the Member States attached importance to the establishment of joint actions in the energy field, with the coordination of political-diplomatic cooperation initiatives in the energy sector, namely within the framework of the "CPLP Energy" project (CPLP 2014). As a result, the "Technical Study Group for the Joint

[3] Within the CPLP framework, there is a fifth hydrocarbon producer, Equatorial Guinea, which is also a member of OPEC. However, Equatorial Guinea does not have Portuguese speakers, and so it is not part of the Portuguese-speaking space. Its entry into the CPLP was, in fact, due to its relevance as a producer of hydrocarbons, in a space similar to that of São Tomé and Príncipe, and Angola.

Exploration and Production of Hydrocarbons in the CPLP Space" was created. This group would propose to extend the energy cooperation through the creation of Focal points of the Member States in the Energy area, working as an organization that coordinates energy cooperation within the scope of the CPLP.

At the First Meeting of Energy Ministers of CPLP held in Cascais, Portugal, on 23rd of June 2015, the energy institutional cooperation was reinforced with the set-up an "Energy Network" responsible for designing and implementing policies, programs, and measures in the sectors of energy efficiency, renewable energy, and environment. In addition to hydrocarbons, this meeting included, for the first time, the discussion of renewable energies, electricity, energy efficiency, and bio energy (CPLP 2015b).

The relevance of CPLP as a global player in the world energy system was also discussed, particularly for the sustainable development of energy resources and energy efficiency (CPLP 2015). These objectives were enshrined in the Strategic Plan for Energy Cooperation for the Development of CPLP, launched one year after the I Technical Meeting of Energy in CPLP, under the motto "The Economic Potential of Energy in CPLP", in Malabo, Equatorial Guinea, on October 2016. Taking into account the United Nations Sustainable Development energy goals, this plan established the CPLP global vision for the energy, with the identification of global and specific objectives. Of the global goals stands out the promotion of cooperation in the energy field, to combat energy poverty, promote a sustainable development, and the transition to low-carbon resilient and sustainable economies. Among the specific objectives, it was agreed the exchange of experiences by facilitating the transfer, access, and development of technologies, knowledge, legislation, and standards in the areas of energy and the environment, as well the promotion of information sharing on business opportunities, taking into account view possible partnerships and investments in the energy field (CPLP 2017b).

However, an examination of the priority areas of cooperation identified in this plan reveals that, while energy security is one of the CPLP's cornerstones, and the CPLP aspires to be a global energy player, there are internal challenges that must be overcome. Specifically, on universal access to energy, improving access to rural electrification coverage, and modernization of supply technologies; increasing the contribution of renewable energies in the energy mix through greater complementarity of renewable energies and biofuels; and strengthening energy training, capacity building, and development of human resources (CPLP 2017a).

This strengthening of institutional initiatives among CPLP members reflects the importance that energy has taken within the CPLP framework, which initially focused on fossil energies, but has since 2015 shifted also to renewable energies. It also demonstrates how cooperation in the energy sector can be a valuable economic asset within the context of the CPLP, enhancing the development of each of its members both individually and collectively. In terms of the energy transition, the CPLP member states' renewed political commitment and cooperation demonstrate the benefits of working together to create a favorable and equitable energy environment in the Portuguese-speaking space. Together with the willingness to continue to promote policies that support the energy transition, particularly the promotion of access to clean energy for all (SDG 7), as well as the goals of the United Nations Framework Convention on Climate Change and the Paris Agreement (CPLP 2021).

Energy in the Portuguese-Speaking World and the Energy Transition

The countries that are part of the Portuguese-speaking space are geographically present in four continents—Africa, Europe, America, and Asia—occupying about 7.2% of the planet's area (CPLP 2010), with very different economic and social realities, which places them at very unequal levels of development in the energy field (CPLP 2015d). Whereas, its position and influence in the energy market differs with the endowment of their resources, only three countries have global relevance in terms of oil and gas reserves and production: Angola, Brazil, and Mozambique. In turn these can be separated by the nature of resource explored, being the first two oil and gas and the third mainly gas and coal.[4]

Concerning the proven oil reserves, Brazil has the largest in the Portuguese-speaking space and the second largest in South America, after

[4] Although East Timor is also an oil and gas producer, it is nearing the end of its export era as its oil and gas reserves are practically depleted or nearly depleted (Scheiner 2021), therefore it will not be included in this analysis.

Venezuela (12.7 billion barrels in January 2021) (EIA 2021a). In second place is Angola with 8.2 billion barrels at the beginning of 2020 (EIA 2021b). In terms of oil production, Brazil is the largest in the Portuguese-speaking countries and the seventh largest in the world, representing 4% of total global production (EIA 2021b). Angola is the second largest in the Portuguese-speaking group and in the Sub-Saharan Africa and the sixteenth in the world (Worldometers 2021; EIA 2021b).

The energy transition implies, as noted, a drastic reduction of energy based on fossil resources. However, even in this situation, some resources are better suited to decarbonization than others, such as natural gas, a fuel with a much lower carbon footprint than oil or coal. It is therefore worth noting that, either Brazil, Angola, or Mozambique has, in terms of natural gas, a potential that can offset a reduction in global oil production. In terms of proved gas reserves, Mozambique stands out with around 100 trillion cubic feet (Tcf), the third largest reserves in Africa, after Algeria and Nigeria, and the largest of the Portuguese-speaking countries (EIA 2020). In second place is Angola with 13.5 Tcf, followed by Brazil with 12 Tcf in early 2020. Although they have the capacity to increase production due to vast offshore reserves, both Brazil and Angola prioritize crude oil production over natural gas production, reinjecting the majority of natural gas to recover oil fields. Consequently, only Mozambique stands out for the production of natural gas, and for its substantial deposits of natural gas discovered in Area 1 and Area 4 in the deep waters of the Rovuma Basin, as well for the possibility of becoming an exporter of liquefied natural gas (LNG) (EIA 2020). Nevertheless, this potential is, for the time being, conditioned by the insecurity situation in the Cabo Delgado region, with constant attacks by militants in that area since 2017 (Seabra 2021). These attacks, in addition to leading to serious human rights violations, exacerbate the country's precarious situation resulting from several challenges that have occurred since the discovery of the large natural gas reserves in 2010. Firstly, after the debt cover-up scandal, in 2013 and 2014, several bilateral donors withdrew their support from development programs, exacerbating the country's weaknesses. This weakness was further aggravated by the devastating effects of the cyclone IDAI in 2019, and by the pandemic that since 2020, as in other Portuguese-speaking developing countries, has caused a reduction in economic activity, triggering extreme poverty levels (Silva 2021).

There is a big difference between renewable and fossil energy in the geography of energy resources. The former is available in one form or another in most countries and on four continents, while the latter, as we have seen, has very specific locations. This difference is also reflected in the importance of Portuguese-speaking countries, with Brazil and Portugal having a greater diversified economy and scientific-technological complexity, especially, but not only, in the area of renewable energies. While Angola, Brazil, East Timor, and Mozambique are more related to the trade raw materials, mainly fossil energies. Considering that their economies are highly dependent on hydrocarbon revenues, particularly Angola and East Timor, they are also the most vulnerable countries to economic decarbonization of the energy transition process in the Portuguese-speaking space.[5]

Based on the differences presented, we evaluated the energy systems of Portuguese-speaking countries for the energy transition process, based on the indicator "energy access and security" from the WEF Energy Transition Index. Despite the fact that one of the primary goals of the energy transition is to "ensure access to affordable, reliable, sustainable and modern energy for all", there are still significant inequalities between regions and countries. Inequalities that also prevail in the Lusophone world with only two countries, Portugal and Brazil, achieving 100% of the population's access to electricity. Very close are Cape Verde (93%), East Timor (89%) and São Tomé Príncipe (71%). At a lower level, with almost or more than half of the population without access to energy are Mozambique, Guinea-Bissau, and Angola (IRENA 2021a, b, c, d, e, f, g, h) (see Table 1).

It should be noted that access to electricity is not uniform across the Portuguese-speaking countries, with greater access in urban areas at the expense of rural or interior areas. This challenge also stands out in the energy poverty characterized by the population's insufficient access to other basic needs such as food preparation, lighting, refrigeration, and the thermal comfort of housing. As can be seen from Table 2, the percentage of the population with access to cooking methods considered non-polluting, efficient, convenient, and safe (SDG 7) is significantly low in Guinea-Bissau, Mozambique, São Tomé and Príncipe (<5%) and in East Timor (11%). On the opposite side, with a better access by the population to so-called clean kitchen technologies, such as electric stoves

[5] "The study Beyond Petrostates" of Carbon Tracker Initiative predicts that East Timor will hit the potential oil and gas revenue shortfalls of 93% and Angola 76% (Coffin et al. 2021).

Table 1 Sustainable Development Goal 7: Energy Indicators (2018)

Country	*Access to electricity (% of population)*	*Access to clean cooking (% of population)*
Angola	45	49
Brazil	100	>95
Cabo Verde	93	77
Guinea-Bissau	29	<5
Mozambique	31	<5
Portugal	100	>95
São Tomé and Príncipe	71	<5
East Timor	89	11

Source IRENA (2021a, b, c, d, e, f, g, h)

are Portugal and Brazil with more than 95%, followed by Cape Verde with 77% (IRENA (2021a, b, c, d, e, f, g, h). Angola is at an intermediate level, with 49% of the population with access to clean cooking technologies, although in terms of sub-Saharan Africa, it has one of the highest proportions due to government policies to support natural gas (EIA 2021c).

These data also reflect the negative impact that the use of traditional fuels in food production has on the health and well-being of the Lusophone population. In Guinea- Bissau, Mozambique, São Tomé and Príncipe, and East Timor the use of firewood, harvest residues, and coal in closed environments causes indeed an increase in health problems, such asthma or bronchitis, and increases the risk of lung cancer. Furthermore, these problems are more exacerbated in the poorest rural areas of the countries, with the greatest impact on women and children (The World Bank 2021).

The differences that Portuguese-speaking countries have between themselves in access to energy also reflects the disparities not only "in terms of economy and wealth, but also in health systems, service structure, coverage of health professionals, basic sanitation, schooling in the population" (Malta et al. 2019). They also express the countries' potential and differential for the energy transition process in terms of research and development (R&D) and investment capacity. In fact, the energy transition is rich in new knowledge and requires a large amount of human capital to disseminate and produce it (WEF 2021).

Table 2 Human Development Index (HDI) Ranking

Rank	*Country*	*HDI value (2019)*	*Life expectancy at birth (years) SDG3*[a]	*Expected years of schooling (years) SDG 4.3*[b]	*Mean years of schooling (years) SDG 4.6*[c]	*Gross national income (GNI) per capita (PPP $) SDG 8.5*[d]
38	Portugal	0.864	82.1	16.5	9.3	33,967
84	Brazil	0.765	75.9	15.4	8.0	14,26
126	Cabo Verde	0.665	73.0	12.7	6.3	7,01
135	Sao Tome and Principe	0.625	70.4	12.7	6.4	3,95
141	East Timor	0.606	69.5	12.6	4.8	4,44
148	Angola	0.581	61.2	11.8	5.2	6,104
175	Guinea-Bissau	0.480	58.3	10.6	3.6	1,996
181	Mozambique	0.456	60.9	10.0	3.5	1,25

Source UNDP (2020)
SGD 3—to ensure health and well-being for all, including a bold commitment to end the epidemics of AIDS, tuberculosis, malaria and other communicable diseases by 2030
SGD 4.3—to ensure equal access for all women and men to affordable quality technical, vocational and tertiary education, including university by 2030
SGD 4.6—to ensure that all youth and a substantial proportion of adults, both men and women, achieve literacy and numeracy by 2030
SGD 8.5—to achieve full and productive employment and decent work for all women and men, including for young people and persons with disabilities, and equal pay for work of equal value by 2030

Nonetheless, with the exception of Portugal and Brazil, which have a socio- political framework that drives R&D in renewable energies and a reasonable scientific- technological capacity within this industry, almost all other countries have significant weaknesses in the educational dimension of their populations, particularly low levels of literacy. According to the United Nations Development Program (UNDP 2020), Portugal and Brazil are the only countries in the Lusophone group with very high and high human development (HDI). Meanwhile, Guinea-Bissau and Mozambique have low HDI levels. In the education dimension, both Portugal and Brazil have the highest averages of years of schooling and expected higher education, while Mozambique, Guinea-Bissau, and East Timor have the lowest averages of years of schooling (see Table 2).

Advances in technological research in Portugal and Brazil are also visible in the evolution of the number of patents in renewable energies, particularly in the period between 2009 and 2012, in wind, thermal and photovoltaic solar power and biofuels (see Fig. 1).

In terms of total primary energy supply, Portuguese-speaking countries can be divided into two groups: the first, in which supply is dominated by renewable energies and which includes Angola, Mozambique, and Guinea-Bissau; and the second, in which fossil energies are dominant, contains Portugal, Cape Verde, São Tomé and Príncipe and East Timor. Only two countries—Brazil and Portugal—have a more diversified energy mix, with Portugal being the only country in the Lusophone world with nuclear energy production (see Fig. 2).

Regarding the renewable energy supply, biofuels are the primary source in all the countries, accounting for an average of 85% of the total Portuguese-speaking space in 2018 (see Fig. 3). Following biofuels,

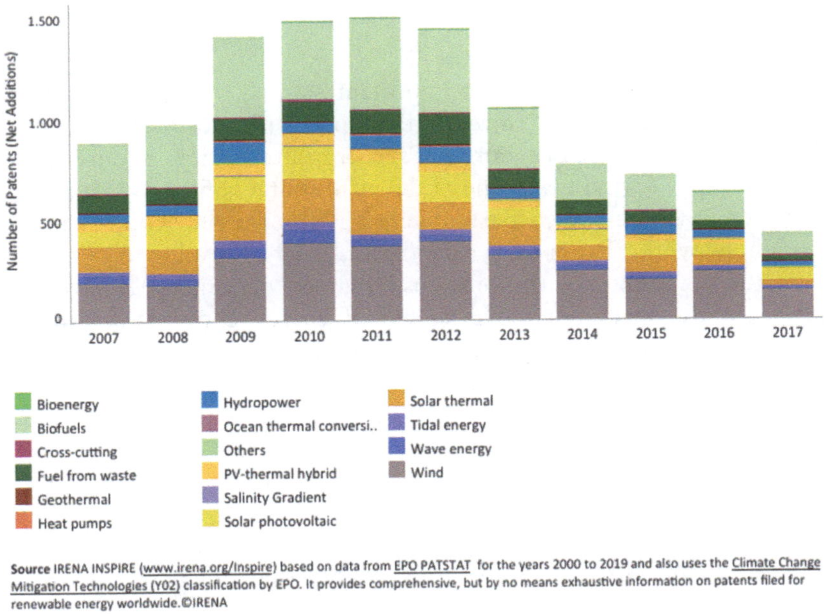

Fig. 1 Portugal and Brazil renewable energy Patents Evolution (*Source* IRENA (2021a, b, c, d, e, f, g, h))

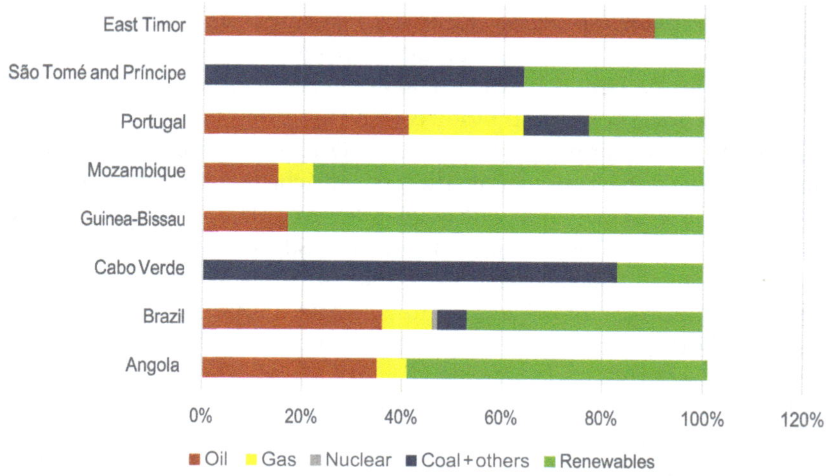

Fig. 2 Total primary energy supply in 2018 (*Source* IRENA (2021a, b, c, d, e, f, g, h))

hydropower is the second most important source, with particular relevance for Brazil, which is currently the world's second-largest producer after China (EIA 2021a). Portugal's energy production is once again diverse, with the wind being one of the main sources of renewable energy produced in the country, after biofuels. It is also the only country in the Lusophony world that produces geothermal energy (see Fig. 3).

In the continuity of the previous observed data, in 2018, biofuels were also the main renewable source of energy consumption in the Portuguese countries, with the exception of Portugal, Brazil, and Mozambique, which also consumed electricity (see Fig. 4). This disparity in the Portuguese-speaking world reflects the difficulties that some of these countries face in gaining access to electricity. Guinea-Bissau, São Tomé and Principe, and East Timor, in particular, have electricity grids that are limited in terms of extension and connectivity. This, along with insufficient investment capacity and a lack of human resources, explains the poorest and inland regions' poor access to the electricity grid and reliance on biomass.

To increase the security of supply, the Lusophone countries are implementing a variety of strategies, including the diversification of the energy mix and the endogenous energy development. The analysis in Table 3

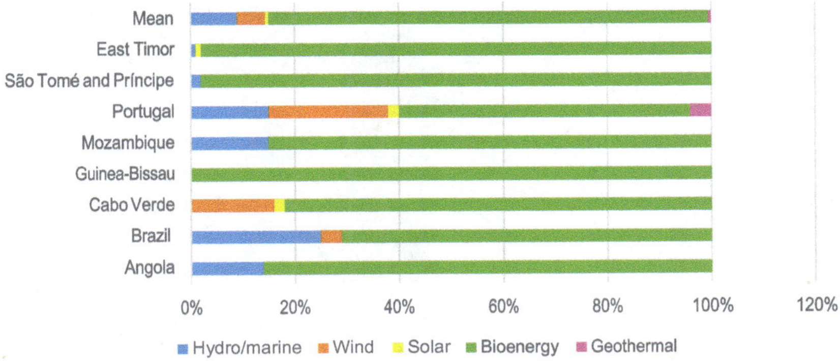

Fig. 3 Renewable energy supply in 2018 (*Source* IRENA (2021a, b, c, d, e, f, g, h))

shows that, while all of these countries are still energy importers, there was an increase in energy self-sufficiency in some of them between 2013 and 2018, particularly in Angola, Brazil, Mozambique, and East Timor. This increase occurred in countries with very favorable geo-energetic conditions, namely those with fossil energy reserves and endogenous production capacity, and was associated with the increased demand for fossil resources in the energy market, especially by developing countries like China.

Between 2015 and 2020, the capacity and generation of electricity from renewable energy increased in some Portuguese-speaking countries, particularly in Angola and Guinea-Bissau. Mozambique was the only country unable to keep up with the others, which could be explained by the same difficulties mentioned above in developing the country's gas potential.

With the regard to the sources used, solar and hydro power were the main sources of electricity capacity grown during this period. Apart from Angola, which boosted its electricity capacity from hydropower, the remaining countries invested in the development of solar energy. Highlighting Brazil, which managed to increase its production capacity by 170 times, as well as Portugal for being the only country to obtain an increase, albeit residual in some sources, in all renewable energy (see Table 4).

The shift to more renewable energy production and consumption will enable countries to increase their energy self-sufficiency, create better

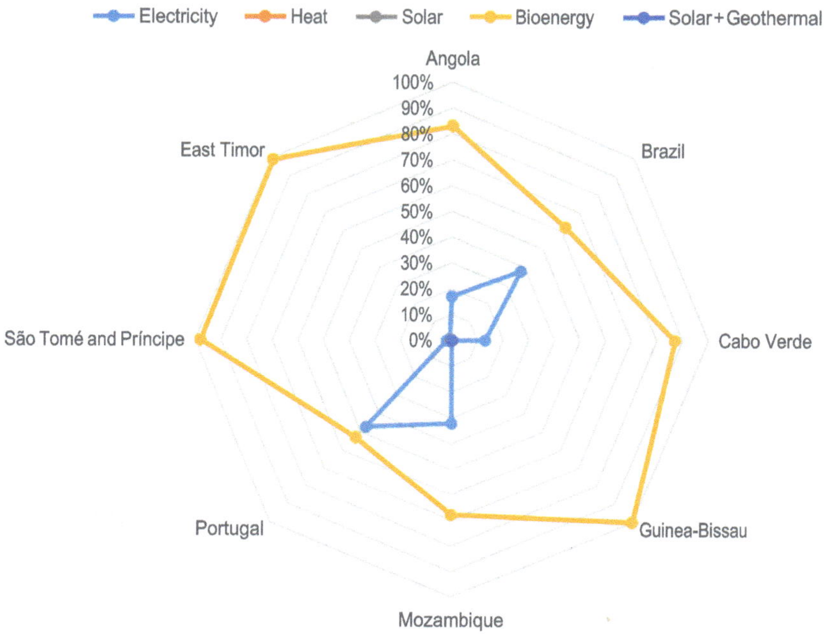

Fig. 4 Renewable energy consumption in 2018 (*Source* IRENA (2021a, b, c, d, e, f, g, h))

living conditions for people and rebalance their trade balances. According to IRENA data (2021), in broad terms, the Portuguese-speaking countries have a diversified spectrum of energy potential for this transition. With Cape Verde, Guinea-Bissau, and East Timor with less potential, both in terms of resources they use today to guarantee their energy supply, and in terms of potential that they can presumably develop for the energy transition. The first country bases its energy supply essentially on biomass and oil, and has great potential in regards to wind and solar energy (IRENA (2021a, b, c, d, e, f, g, h). The second uses biomass as the main source of energy consumption and will have the potential for energy transition in terms of solar energy (IRENA (2021a, b, c, d, e, f, g, h). São Tomé and Príncipe and East Timor appear to have their energy potential for the transition in hydro and solar power (IRENA (2021a, b, c, d, e, f, g, h).

Angola already has a significant hydro potential, with hydroelectric power, in combination with oil as the basis of its energy supply (IRENA

Table 3 Primary energy trade

		Primary energy trade							
		Imports (TJ)	*Exports (TJ)*	*Net trade (TJ)*	*Imports (% of supply)*	*Exports (% of production)*	*Energy self-sufficiency (%)*	*Net trade (USD million)*	*Net trade (% of GDP)*
Angola	2013	203,007	3,603,118	3,400,111	33	89	656	64,445	47.1
	2018	147,859	3,439,869	3,292,010	28	90	721	36,489	36.0
Brazil	2013	3,199,737	1,198,607	−2,001,130	26	12	85	−31,370	−1.3
	2018	2,649,406	2,716,067	66,661	22	22	103	477	0.0
Cabo Verde	2013	11,234	0	−11,234	128	0	21	−155	−8.4
	2018	14,087	0	−14,087	129	0	17	0.98	−5.0
Guinea-Bissau	2013	4924	5	−4919	17	0	85	n.a.	n.a
	2018	5888	3	−5885	19	0	83	n.a.	n.a.
Mozambique	2013	88,012	277,445	189,433	18	37	154	−1623	−9.6
	2018	103,065	539,709	436,644	23	63	192	967	6.5
Portugal	2013	967,904	270,257	−697,647	109	110	27	−8273	−3.7
	2018	1,057,647	271,402	−786,245	117	116	26	−6503	−2.7
São Tomé and Príncipe	2013	2012	0	−2012	79	0	38	−40	−13.4
	2018	2390	0	−2390	81	0	36	−33	−7.9
East Timor	2013	6406	167,419	161,013	88	99	2326	145	−10.4
	2018	7285	264,316	257,031	92	100	3342	n.a.	n.a.

Source IRENA (2021a, b, c, d, e, f, g, h)

Table 4 Electricity capacity and generation

	Angola		*Brazil*		*Cabo Verde*		*Guinea-Bissau*	
Capacity change (%)	*2015–2020*	*2019–2020*	*2015–2020*	*2019–2020*	*2015–2020*	*2019–2020*	*2015–2020*	*2019–2020*
Non-renewable	55	0	10	6.3	−3	0	0	0
Renewable	267	9.7	33	3.8	6	0	275	0
Hydro/marine	285	9.8	19	0.2	0	0	0	0
Solar	4		17,191	70.8	24	0	275	0
Wind	0	0	125	11.4	2	0	0	0
Bioenergy	0	0	18	1.9	0	0	0	0
Geothermal	0	0	0	0	0	0	0	0
Total	146	6	28	4.2	−1	0	3	0

	Mozambique		*Portugal*		*São Tomé and Príncipe*		*East Timor*	
Capacity change (%)	*2015–2020*	*2019–2020*	*2015–2020*	*2019–2020*	*2015–2020*	*2019–2020*	*2015–2020*	*2019–2020*
Non-renewable	147	0	0	0	25	0	1	0
Renewable	5	0	17	1.1	9	0	4	0
Hydro/marine	1	0	18	0	0	0	0	0
Solar	850	0	129	13.8	181	0	6	0
Wind	0	0	6	0.3	0	0	0	0
Bioenergy	0	0	25	2.3	0	0	0	0
Geothermal	0	0	16	0	0	0	0	0
Total	19	0	11	0.7	24	0	1	0

Source IRENA (2021a, b, c, d, e, f, g, h)

(2021a, b, c, d, e, f, g, h)). Its potential lies in hydropower, which can be combined with wind and photovoltaic (solar) power and biomass. Finally, Mozambique's potential today is essentially based on biomass, hydroelectric power (Cahora Bassa) (IRENA (2021a, b, c, d, e, f, g, h), and on the opportunities created by the vast gas reserves of the Rovuma Basin.

Portugal has integrated renewable energy into its energy mix and is progressively reducing its dependence, which went from 81.2% in 2009 to 74.2% in 2019 (Observatório da Energia 2021). It has a high mix of renewable energy, from biomass, wind, solar, hydro (which already provides much of part of the country's electricity), and geothermal (IRENA (2021a, b, c, d, e, f, g, h) and it plans to begin using green hydrogen by 2025 (Mendes 2021).

Conclusion

Energy has been a fundamental component of power for more than 100 years, and it has been transitioning from fossil to clean energies since the mid-2000s. This transition is not a uniform and one-of-a-kind process. It reflects different priorities, particularly overcoming environmental and climate challenges, as well as countries' energy vulnerability, and entails a combination of resources, policies, strategies, technologies and investments. Countries approach the energy transition in different ways, prioritizing goals based on their unique circumstances. Transforming the global energy system in accordance with the 1.5 °C climate target has the potential to be an excellent equalizer, making the world more resilient, fairer, and more inclusive.

This chapter examined the Portuguese-speaking countries in terms of "energy access and security" using the WEF Energy Transition Index. This indicator combines the performance of the energy system through the analysis of six sub-items: electrification, quality of electricity supply, access to clean energy and food security, energy dependence, diversification of the energy mix, and imports diversification.

The Portuguese energy countries differ in their trajectories for the energy transition. With different geographies and energy potential, all of them are developing the production of renewable energies and gradually incorporating them into energy consumption. However, some Portuguese-speaking countries continue to have significant internal constraints in making this potential into an effective reality. Especially the Portuguese-speaking African and Asia-Pacific countries, which, unlike

Portugal and Brazil, have a reduced human capital and a limited economic and scientific-technological complexity, which mutually combines and weakens their development prospects, in general, and in terms of the energy transition, in particular. Currently, biofuels are the dominant source in all countries, despite the fact that all of them have the potential to increase production and consumption of other sources, such as hydropower and solar power. These constraints are also reflected in their countries' high rates of energy poverty and internal imbalances in access to clean energy, as well as the negative effects on their people's living conditions, health, and well-being.

On the one hand, Portugal and Brazil dominate technologies for renewable energy sources, which are critical for decarbonizing the electricity sector; on the other hand, the other countries in the Portuguese-speaking world continue to face challenges in implementing them. Moreover, despite the CPCLP's intention to adhere to the United Nations' sustainable development agendas, the energy transition in the Portuguese-speaking world as a whole is moving slowly.

Given the multiplicity of dimensions associated with it and the density of interactions that it consequently streamlines, the energy transition is a complex process. The potential for energy transition is an advantageous condition, but it is only meaningful if it is virtualized.

In this sense, the potential obviously has to be linked to another indicator of the WEF's energy transition Index: the development and economic growth. Energy transition processes rely on being integrated into more complex economies, which means they must emerge from advanced economic structures, in order to be successful. This is one of the first challenges in the Portuguese-speaking space's energy transition, because, with the exception of Portugal, almost all other countries—Brazil, Angola, Mozambique, and East Timor—essentially extractive economies, heavily reliant on the extraction and export of fossil resources. As a result, because their economies rely heavily on this, they are the countries in the Portuguese-speaking world that are most resistant to the necessary transitional changes. Future challenges may be greater for these countries with the need for a post-Covid-19 green recovery and the greater need for funding to recover their economies.

International cooperation is a way of overcoming national weaknesses in almost all areas of human activities. Since 2015, the CPLP has been interested in developing mechanisms for cooperation in the energy sector, as well as the relationship between energy and the energy transition. The main goal is to increase the energy potential of this space while also contributing to the promotion of the diversification of the energy mix, to the development of renewable sources and to greater access to clean energy for all. In this regard, the greater potential of Portugal and Brazil, with greater economic complexity and greater scientific-technological capacity, particularly in the areas of energy, should be highlighted as a factor that can facilitate and promote a greater energy capacity of Lusophone world and for strengthening the mechanisms that facilitate the energy transition. However, we can question how and with what resources this area can be virtualized as a synergistic instrument for the dissemination of the energy transition process, given the constraints of each of the Portuguese-speaking space's economies and their integration into different regional spaces (European Union, Mercosur, Community for the Development of Southern Africa), to which are added the economic weaknesses that each country's economic matrix possesses and which limits its possibilities for foreign investment and international cooperation.

References

Austvik, O. G., 2018. *Concepts of Geopolitics and Energy Security*, Cleveland: International Association for Energy Economics.

Blondee, M., Bradshaw, M. J., Gavin, B. & Kuzemko, C., 2021. The Geopolitics of Energy System Transformation: A Review. *Geography Compass*, Volume 15, no. 7, pp. 1–22.

Bordoff, J., 2020. Everything You Think About the Geopolitics of Climate Change Is Wrong. *Foreign Policy*, 5 October.

Bordoff, J. & O'Sullivan, M. L., 2022. Green Upheaval. The New Geopolitics of Energy. *Foreign Affairs*, January–February.

Clevaland, C. & Morris, C., 2017. *Dictionary of Energy*, Amsterdam: Elsevier.

Coffin, M., Dalman, A. & Grant, A., 2021. *Beyond Petrostates*, London: Carbon Tracker Initiative.

CPLP, 2010. *Estados Membros.* [Online] Available at: http://www.cplp.org/id-22.aspx [Accessed 14 March 2011].

CPLP, 2014. *Declaração de Díli, X Confêrencia de Chefes de Estado e de Governo da Comunidade de Países de Língua Oficial Portuguesa.* Dili, CPLP.

CPLP, 2015. *Plano Estratégico de Cooperação em Energia Para o Desenvolvimento na CPLP*, s.l.: CPLP.

CPLP, 2017a. *Plano Estratégico de Cooperação em Energia para 2018-2023*, s.l.: CPLP.

CPLP, 2017b. *O Plano de Ação da Energia para 2018-2019*, s.l.: CPLP.

CPLP, 2021. *Resolução sobre a Emergência Climática na CPLP. XXVI Reunião Ordinária do Conselho da CPLP*, Luanda: CPLP.

Defarges, P. M., 1994. *Introduction à la Géopolitique*. 1ª edição ed, s.l.: Éditions du Seuil.

Domingues, N., 2021. The Contribution of Natural Gas to the Paradigm of Energy Transition in Portugal: Economy, Continuity of Supply and Welfare. *Journal of Business Strategy, Finance and Management*, pp. 56–67.

EIA, 2020. *Mozambique*. [Online] Available at: https://www.eia.gov/international/analysis/country/MOZ [Accessed 13 December 2021].

EIA, 2021a. *Brazil*. [Online] Available at: https://www.eia.gov/international/content/analysis/countries_long/Brazil/brazil_background.pdf [Accessed 11 December 2021].

EIA, 2021b. *Angola Energy Analysis*. [Online] Available at: https://www.eia.gov/international/analysis/country/AGO [Accessed 13 December 2021].

EIA, 2021c. *What Countries Are the Top Producers and Consumers of Oil?* [Online] Available at: https://www.eia.gov/tools/faqs/faq.php?id=709&t=6 [Accessed 26 November 2021].

Eiras, R., 2013. Segurança Energética na CPLP: um Imperativo Estratégico. *Nação e Defesa*, Volume 136, 5.ª Série, pp. 234–252.

Fernandes, C., 2019. Segurança Energética: Para Quem, Por Quem e De Que Ameaças? *Nação e Defesa*, Volume 153, pp. 73–100.

Fouquet, R., 2016. Historical Energy Transitions: Speed, Prices and System Transformation. *Energy Research & Social Science*, Volume 22, pp. 7–12.

Grubler, A., Wilson, C. & Nemet, G., 2016. Apples, Oranges and Consistent Comparisons of the Temporal Dynamics of Energy Transitions. *Energy Research & Social Science*, Volume 22, pp. 18–25.

Guimarães, L. M., 2020. *The Regulation and Policy of Latin American Energy Transitions*, Amsterdam: Elsevier.

Henriques, S., 2011.*Energy Transitions, Economic Growth and Structural Change: Portugal in a Long-Run Comparative Perspective*. Lund Studies in Economic History 54 ed. Lund: Lund University.

IRENA, 2019. *A New World: The Geopolitics of Energy Transformation*, Abu Dhabi: IRENA.

IRENA, 2021a. *Angole Energy Profile*, Abu Dhabi: IRENA.

IRENA, 2021b. *Brazil Energy Profile*, Abu Dhabi: IRENA.

IRENA, 2021c. *Portugal Energy Profile*, Abu Dhabi: IRENA.

IRENA, 2021d. *East Timor*, Abu Dhabi: IRENA.

IRENA, 2121e. *Cabo Verde Energy Profile,* Abu Dhabi: IRENA.

IRENA, 2021f. *Guinea-Bissau Energy Profile*, Abu Dhabi: IRENA.

IRENA, 2021g. *Mozambique Energy Profile*, Abu Dhabi: IRENA.

IRENA, 2021h. *Sao Tome and Principe Energy Profile*, Abu Dhabi: IRENA.

IRENA, 2021i. *Energy Transition.* [Online] Available at: https://www.irena.org/energytransition [Accessed 4 October 2021].

Kuzemko, C., et al., 2020. Covid-19 and the Politics of Sustainable Energy Transitions. *Energy Research & Social Science,* Volume 68, p. 101685.

Lazaro, L. et al., 2022. Energy Transition in Brazil: Is There a Role for Multi-level Governance in a Centralized Energy Regime? *Energy Research & Social Science*, Volume 85, p. 102404.

Lima, B. P. d., 2016. *Portugal e o Atlântico.* Lisbon: Fundação Francisco Manuel dos Santos.

Losekann, L. & Tavares F. B., 2019. *Política Energética dos BRICS. Desafios da Transição Energética*, Rio de Janeiro: Instituto de Pesquisa Económica Aplicada (IPEA).

Malta, D. C., et al., 2019. *Avaliação das metas dos Objetivos de Desenvolvimento Sustentável relacionadas à saúde nos países de língua portuguesa.* Lisbon, s.n.

Mendes, A. C., 2021. Projeto de hidrogénio verde de Sines arranca com investimento de 76 milhões. *Jornal Económico*, 9 November.

Myhrvold, N. & Caldeira, K., 2012. Greenhouse Gases, Climate Change and the Transition from Coal to Low Carbon Electricity. *Environmental Research Letters*, Volume 7, p. 014019.

Observatório da Energia, 2021. *A Energia em Números, Edição de 2021.* Lisbon: ADENE.

Oliveira, L. K. D., 2015. *Geopolítica Energética dos Países Emergentes.* [Online] Available at: https://www.ufrgs.br/sicp/wp-content/uploads/2015/09/OLIVEIRA-2015-Geopol%C3%ADtica-Energ%C3%A9tica-dos-Pa%C3%ADses-Emergentes.pdf [Accessed 12 December 2021].

Pérez-Franco, I., García-García, A. & Maldonado-Briegas, J., 2020. Energy Transition Towards a Greener and More Competitive Economy: The Iberian Case. *Sustainability,* Volume 12, no. 8, p. 3343.

Prados, M.-J., Iglesias-Pascual, R. & Barral, Á., 2022. Energy Transition and Community Participation in Portugal, Greece and Israel: Regional Differences from a Multi-Level Perspective. *Energy Research & Social Science*, Volume 87, pp. 10246.

Roman, R., Overland, I. & Scholten, D., 2020. Renewable energy and geopolitics: A review. *Renewable and Sustainable Energy Reviews*, Volume 122, p. 109547.

Scheiner, C., 2021. Timor-Leste Economic Survey: The End of Petroleum Income. *Asia Pac Policy Studies*, Volume 2, pp. 253–279.

Seabra, P., 2021. O Conflito de Cabo Delgado em Perspetiva. *IDN Brief*, fevereiro, pp. 2–4.

Skeet, I., 1996. Geopolitics of Energy. *Energy Exploration & Exploitation.* Volume 14, nos. 3–4, pp. 265–272.

Silva, J. M. d., 2021. Uma tempestade perfeita em Moçambique. *Diário de Notícias*, 1 April.

Smil, V., 2016.*Energy Transitions: Global and National Perspectives.* 2nd revised ed. Westport: ABC-CLIO.

Sovacool, B. K., 2016. How Long Will It Take? Conceptualizing the Temporal Dynamics of Energy Transitions.*Energy Research & Social Science*, March, Volume 13, pp. 202–215.

Sovacool, B. K., 2017. The History and Politics of Energy Transitions. In: *The Political Economy of Clean Energy Transitions.* s.l.: Oxford Scholarship Online, pp. 1–22.

The World Bank, 2021. *Tracking SDG7. The Energy Progress Report 2021*, Washington: International Bank for Reconstruction and Development.

UNDP, 2020. *Human Development Report 2020. The Next Frontier Human Development and the Anthropocene*, New York: United Nations Development Programme.

Valkenburg, G. & Gracceva, F., 2016. Towards Governance of Energy Security. In: P. Lombard & M. Gruenig, eds. *Low-Carbon Energy Security from a European Perspective.* Amsterdam: Academic Press, pp. 207–229.

Vasconcelos, J., 2019. *A Energia em Portugal.* 1ª Edition ed. Lisbon: FFMS.

WEF, 2020. *Fostering Effective Energy Transition 2020 edition*, Geneva: World Economic Forum.

WEF, 2021. *Fostering Effective Energy Transition 2021 edition*, Geneva: World Economic Forum.

Worldometers, 2021. *Oil Production by Country.* [Online] Available at: https://www.trade.gov/country-commercial-guides/angola-oil-and-gas [Accessed 25 November 2021].

Yang Yu & He Ze, 2021. Energy Geopolitics and Power. *Progress in Geography*, Volume 40, pp. 524–540.

Yu, Jianhua & Dai, Yichen 2012. Energy Politics and Security Concepts from. *Journal of Middle Eastern and Islamic Studies (in Asia)*, Volume 6, no. 4, pp. 91–120

The Role of Forum Macao in the People's Republic of China Foreign Policy

Pedro Paulo dos Santos

Introduction

The People's Republic of China (PRC)'s stance on international collaboration has been shifting ever since Deng Xiaoping's economic and structural reforms were first introduced in the 1980s: To attain a new role in global affairs, China first had to restructure how it set out to engage with its foreign counterparts. Then, after decades of rather a stagnant diplomacy, it was time for China to assert itself in the international arena, so in the early 2000s, there was a new development in the PRC's foreign policy—the establishment of "Chinese" forums. These frameworks, sharing structural elements of international organizations and institutions, have come to define China's approach to contemporary geopolitics. Such forums have been established through the PRC's initiative and placed under the Ministry of Commerce (MOFCOM)'s tutelage. Nevertheless, they would not have existed without other nations agreeing to participate. These initiatives, mainly aimed at developing nations in the southern hemisphere, would present an alternative to the "Washington

P. P. dos Santos (✉)
City University of Macau, Macao, China
e-mail: pedro@cityu.mo

P. A. B. Duarte et al. (eds.), *Portugal and the Lusophone World*,
https://doi.org/10.1007/978-981-99-0455-6_26

consensus" and the current order of main international organizations. The forums' principal calling card would be to act as multilateral platforms where dialogue would abound and equality would be prevalent among all member nations. To achieve this purpose, China insisted on a set of norms that set the path for the future success of these mechanisms: non-conditionality, equality, mutual benefits, and non-interference in internal affairs (Alden and Alves 2016).

Zhang (2010) conducted research to track Chinese diplomatic activities over the years. The study demonstrates that new trends in China's foreign policy have been instrumental for the rapid rise of China as a global superpower. According to the research, China's foreign policy in the mid-1990s revolved around challenging the United States regarding global, regional, and bilateral issues. Zhang (2010) also demonstrates that China has forged strategic alliances with other nations in an effort to enhance its position as a global superpower, and that China's diplomatic policy has been centered on reshaping its position concerning regional affairs. This new behavior is exemplified by China adopting measures to reshape events in various regions including Southeast Asia and Central Asia. For instance, China entered into a free-trade agreement with the Association of Southeast Asian Nations (ASEAN) in 2004.

Boon et al. (2017) conducted a study to evaluate new developments in Chinese foreign policy. According to this research, new foreign developments have occurred after China hosted the 18th Party Congress in 2012. The study demonstrates that China has adopted various strategies to enhance its foreign policy, including changing Beijing's strategic thinking, rebalancing its views on Western countries, and creating a flexible brand. The country has also adopted a new strategy of handling maritime disputes and has adopted new policies to enhance global governance. In addition, the study demonstrates that China is dedicated to creating a more enabling environment for its economic development. The study moreover shows that China seeks to enhance its international diplomacy through various diplomatic initiatives.

In another research, Zhang (2017) studies the diplomatic policies adopted by China toward different regions, particularly toward Pacific Island Countries (PICs). China strives to establish diplomacy with the PICs based on economic development and cooperation. Xi Jinping's 2014 visit to Fiji was the first by a Chinese president. There, Xi launched the China-Pacific Economic Development and Cooperation Forum, which would evaluate areas of strategic cooperation between China and the

PICs. Additionally, research has shown how China's aid to the PIC region has increased over the years, totalling USD 1.45 billion by the year 2013. China's aid to the region contributed significantly to persuading the eight-country PIC region to support the One-China Policy. The collaboration between China and the PICs has also ensured that the region supports China's international policies.

Vangeli (2018) conducted a research to evaluate China's diplomatic policy based on the Bourdieusian concept which focuses on symbolic power. In particular, the study evaluated the diplomatic relationship between China and the 16 countries that form Central, Eastern, and Southern Europe. According to the Bourdieusian concept, power has three dimensions. First, power focuses on winning conflicts and influencing decision-making. Second, power aims at limiting alternatives and setting agendas. The third aim of power is to shape normality. Vangeli's study demonstrates that China's diplomatic policy is based on the third dimension of power. China's foreign diplomacy can be viewed as being based on sharp power as the country focuses on creating a strong relationship with other countries in Africa and Asia. The study also demonstrates that China's new diplomatic policy focuses on establishing China-centric international institutions and initiatives.

Alden and Alves (2016) state that China started creating multilateral mechanisms, mostly formed with developing nations from the southern hemisphere, to strengthen ties, open stronger dialogue channels, and promote cooperation on several levels. These mechanisms are aptly called "forums." These include the Forum on China-Africa Cooperation (FOCAC) founded in 2000, Forum Macao in 2003, the Forum of China, and Community of Latin American and Caribbean States (China—CELAC) in 2014, among others. The multilateral approach to these platforms also aims to address concerns about China's growing economic power and expanding interests.

The Forum Macao was created to strengthen economic and trade ties with the PSCs, while promoting Chinese businesses and culture to the lusophone world. This particular forum presents unique characteristics in its structure that makes it stand out from other similar initiatives. The success of this organization in achieving its original goals has not been entirely disclosed. This study will attempt to clarify what level of achievement has the Forum Macao had in promoting and improving relations between China and the nations that are part of the lusophone world.

This study aims to divulge Forum Macao's role in China's international approach, by investigating the purpose of the forum, applying as a theoretical framework the Theory of Chinese Leadership, and analyzing the relationships and importance of PSCs to China. Thus, this research is driven by a qualitative approach where an extensive study of existing literature, analysis of documentation and reports, and careful examination of the existing discourse of the main topics are applied. A main and a secondary research question are proposed: (main) What is the role of Forum Macao in China's foreign policy? (secondary) How important are Portuguese-speaking countries to the People's Republic of China?

The rest of the chapter will present an overall picture of Forum Macao, followed by a section on Chinese Leadership Theory, explaining its concept and structure, and a section that shows how Chinese forums—specifically, Forum Macao—fit into the framework of the Chinese Leadership Theory. Two subsequent sections will present an overview of the relations between Portuguese—speaking countries and the PRC, and the importance that these countries have in China's foreign policy. The final chapter contains findings and discussions which focus on the role that Forum Macao plays in China's vision and the important link that it provides between China and the Portuguese-speaking countries.

The Forum for Economic and Trade Cooperation Between China and Portuguese-Speaking Countries (Macao)

Forum Macao was created in 2003 upon its first ministerial conference in Macao. There were seven PSCs that joined the initiative: Angola, Brazil, Cabo Verde, Guinea-Bissau, Mozambique, Portugal, and Timor-Leste. São Tomé and Príncipe became a full-fledged member in 2017, after cutting diplomatic ties with the Republic of China, commonly known as Taiwan, and becoming a supporter of the One-China Policy. Forum Macao's name stems from the fact that its Permanent Secretariat is based in the city of Macao, a location that serves as a platform that enhances the relationships between PSCs and China. This particular forum presents some elements that make it stand out from other forums. It is the only forum where there is a membership criterion on having Portuguese as a sovereign official language. It is also the only forum that has a permanent secretariat, in this case, based in the gambling hub of Macao. Forum

Macao, together with the Belt and Road Forum for International Cooperation (BRF), is the only forum whose member nations cover more than two continents, having a global reach, and therefore, unlike most Chinese forums who have regional focuses.

Organisationally, Forum Macao comprises representatives from the PSCs, coordinators of different offices, deputy secretary-generals appointed by the PRC, the PSCs, and the MSAR, and a secretary general selected by China. In this arrangement, we not only observe a leading role of the PRC but also proactive and important roles for the PSCs. Macao, serving as a platform between China and the PSCs, is also strongly engaged in the forum, as most of the forum's administrative processes are managed by Macao officials. The MSAR government is responsible for financially supporting the forum, including all expenses and remunerations of its members.

Macao has retained Lusophone characteristics, and therefore Forum Macao capitalizes on its association with other Portuguese ex-colonies. Mendes (2014) observes that the birth of Forum Macao in the early 2000s has allowed the special administrative region of Macao to connect Beijing with other Lusophone nations, using the Portuguese language as an element of soft power. It was in fact Forum Macao's intention to maximize Macao's Lusophone advantage. The 1st Lusophone Games, an event that aimed to bring together Portuguese speakers, was held in Macao in 2006. It was organized by the Institute for Civic and Municipal Affairs and the Tourist Office of Macao's government. This initiative would go on to be organized by other PSCs every three or four years. An example of the events organized or supported by Forum Macao is the Cultural Week of China and Portuguese-speaking Countries, a week-long cultural exchange event where the PSCs' products are showcased, Lusophone art is featured in exhibitions, and musicians from the Portuguese-speaking world participate in concerts and events such as the Lusofonia Festival.

Education and human resources constitute another element of soft power used by China (King 2020). This element involves scholarships and short-term modules of training for human resource development. For FOCAC, high in their agenda is the development of higher education in Africa. The forum has thereby facilitated the training of African healthcare professionals and the development of disease control centers as well as regional medical research institutes within Africa. Additionally, the forum offers hundreds of scholarships, and, by the fifth conference, there had already been plans to build more vocational training facilities, and training hundreds of personnel to ensure the facilities are managed effectively. Forum Macao operates a similar venture, the Cooperation on Training and Human Resources, which is a mechanism where PSC, Chinese, and Macao nationals and citizens can study and learn about such fields as governance, public administration, formulation of tax policy, use of commercial and international law, formation of community-based initiatives, quality control and product certification, use of topography, application of customs services, environmental protection, and Chinese- and Portuguese-language teaching (Platformchinaplp.mo. 2021).

Chinese Leadership Theory Framework

The Chinese model of leadership entails mutual benefits, cohesion, and humility in individuals in power. Han (2013) examines the logic behind the success of China's leadership in the modern era and discovers that the Chinese theory of leadership embodies Confucian views. The theory argues that karma is a reality, and leaders should not take advantage of other people or subjects, since, over time, the tables may turn and they may be on the receiving end. Further, the theory prioritizes religious influences on morality and conduct, thereby explaining that it is the ancient knowledge of Chinese culture and history that supports the religious, economic, and political outlooks of the nation. As a result, it commends leaders who are humble, focused, and just in their deeds. The model denounces evildoings such as corruption and bigotry as being detrimental to one's rule of power.

Ling and Fang (2013) discuss two predominant Chinese outlooks on leadership—the C-P-M outlook and the somewhat modest Chinese Leadership Theory. Considering that in C-P-M the C stands for character, P for personality, and M for maintenance, this paper argues that the Chinese expect not only high moral conduct and charisma from a leader, but also performance. Additionally, maintenance implies balance in the execution of duties, human association, and a track record of achievements. In other words, the Chinese favor a leader who performs and behaves consistently and morally.

Chinese Forums Under the Chinese Leadership Theory

Devika (2019) reviews and analyses the Chinese-powered China-CELAC Forum, through which she particularly identifies positivity in China's intentions for and in Latin America, arguing that Chinese cooperations there have entailed influential policies that help nations to achieve political and social stability. Moreover, she observes that CELAC states enjoy economic help from the Chinese government, which helps them stimulate local exchanges. China's relations with CELAC have a multilateral structure governed by principles, where exchanges are associable with post- liberal engagements, in which the rights of independent nations to exercise freedom and liberty are ensured.

Herman (2020) outlines China's unique approach toward FOCAC leadership and argues that China uses a trust-building strategy to manage businesses in Africa. In particular, Chinese officials share and learn from the African experience, enhancing social behavior via trust. Additionally, Chinese representatives engage in personal interactions with African leaders to discuss the sharing of objectives, through which they come to understand the goals and needs of individual states. Similarly, the Chinese use trust to facilitate group meetings, presenting genuine, clear ideas that are accessible to all participants of the discussions.

Mendes (2014) focuses on the Forum Macao of 2013, rationalizing how it represented a transformation of Chinese leadership toward Lusophone nations, as that particular forum, instead of being established by the Ministry of Foreign Affairs, was held under the Ministry of Commerce (MOFCOM). Mendes explains that such a move prevented the forum from becoming politicized, reducing other nations' susceptibility toward (perceived) Chinese domination. China in turn retains social and economic interests in the Lusophone nations, reinforcing its pursuit of a legacy of honesty and trustworthiness on the international front. The author ascertains that political meetings such as those held at Forum Macao seek to legitimize cooperations between companies of Lusophone nations and in the Chinese mainland, with a view to creating a political framework for human resource development in both the Lusophone states and in China. Furthermore, they aim to improve social exchanges such as the spread of Chinese language and Chinese culture in the Portuguese-speaking nations, and vice versa.

Chinese Foreign Affairs Relations with Portuguese-Speaking Countries

Da Silva Horta (2012) identifies five primary motivators for China to develop and enhance relations with Portuguese-speaking countries: (1) energy resources, particularly oil and gas; (2) Beijing's interest in Lusophone energy products and raw materials; (3) uranium reserves, large deposits of gold, bronze, nickel, iron, mercury, and manganese, as well as the Amazon, the world's largest rainforest; (4) oil and gas, diamond, marble, ruby, sapphire, and emerald specifically from Angola; and (5) rich natural resources in Guinea-Bissau, Mozambique, and Timor-Leste. Additional motivators include specific markets and purposes: Angola's energy security; Brazil's trade importance; negate Taiwan's diplomatic space; and to enhance China's prestige in world affairs.

A brief introduction to historical and contemporary relations between the PRC and each of the PSCs is presented below to help understand their statuses. Most of the economic data presented refer to pre-COVID times of 2019. This time frame can better elucidate the success levels of partnerships between these nations under normal conditions, without constraints or difficulties of transactions and transportation caused by the pandemic.

Angola is China's most essential relationship in Africa, with trade amounting to around $25 billion in 2009 and Angola being a primary source of crude oil. In 2010, China gave Angola a $1 billion loan to promote its agriculture. Chinese presence in Angola has however increase the likelihood of the country falling under Chinese control. An article written in the *Yale Global Online Magazine* indicates growing tension between the locals and the increasing number of Chinese immigrants, potentially leading to conflicts. China has also been accused of mistreating Angolan employees, and there has been concerns regarding the quality of Chinese constructions, the most infamous example occurring at Luanda General Hospital soon after its inauguration (Da Silva Horta 2012). Nevertheless, the Republic of Angola and the PRC have had strong diplomatic relations established since 1983. In 2019, China was Angola's largest trading partner, with a 62.4% share of the African nation's exports, and 21.6% of Angolan imports originating from the Asian country (OEC 2021a).

Diplomatic relations between the Federative Republic of **Brazil** and the PRC, two of the largest countries and economies in the world, commenced upon the establishment of Brazil's first embassy in Beijing and China's embassy in Brasilia in 1974. China became Brazil's most significant trading partner in April 2009, with trade reaching $36 billion. The nations have cooperated technologically and have collaborated on developing four satellites. In 2009, PRC navy pilots started training in São Paulo to prepare for the deployment of China's first aircraft carrier. Both countries have grown very close, supporting each other politically, in trade regimes, human rights, and UN reforms (Lopes 2021). After China replaced the United States as Brazil's main trading partner in 2009, the strong commercial ties between the countries have gone from strength to strength. In 2019, China accounted for 28% of Brazil's exports (the U.S. accounted for only 13%). A large portion of Brazilian imports (20.5%, largest by percentage) also originate from the PRC (OEC 2021b).

China's first relations with **Cabo Verde**, which consisted of cultural exchanges and visits, were established in April 1976. The relationship began to intensify in the mid-1990s when Chinese small-scale private investors arrived. Macao millionaire David Chaw reportedly set up a $100 million fund to construct an enormous amusement park on the island of Santa Maria to be finished in 2009, and promised $300 million for other projects. Various Chinese business tycoons such as Stanley Ho have requested to build casinos on the same island. China's influence in Cabo Verde grows despite the locals complaining about low salaries and going on strike. Cabo Verde's ambassador to Beijing has highlighted that the two countries would establish more direct cooperation in the foreseeable future (Vogt 2017). As Cabo Verde is one of the most politically stable countries in Africa, it is no surprise that China has funded large infrastructure projects in the country, the most recent being the University of Cabo Verde.

China's relations with **Guinea-Bissau** started back in the mid-1960s, which explains China's shock when Guinea-Bissau shifted diplomatic identification to Taiwan in the 1990s. Less than a year later, upon China's persuasion, Guinea-Bissau abandoned support for Taiwan and restored diplomatic ties with China. China calls this relation "friendly" with "no strings attached," which is evidenced by the Chinese funding a massive dam construction in Guinea-Bissau in 2006 (Lopes 2021). In March 2021, a Sino-Guinean agreement worth approximately US$7.5 million was signed between the two nations, focusing on economic and technological cooperations. In November of the same year, China and Guinea-Bissau signed a memorandum of understanding on the BRI, making the small West African nation one of the most recent additions to the project.

China's contemporary relationship with **Mozambique** started in the 1960s when Mozambique fought Portuguese colonizers for independence. China provided training and financial support to FRELIMO during the ensuing decade (1964–1974). Throughout the mid-1990s, Beijing continued to be a crucial participant in Mozambique, and, by the early 2000s, the growing Chinese economy generated new priorities for Beijing in the energy market. Trade between China and Mozambique reached around $208 million in 2007 and $690 million in 2010. China Development Bank funded Mozambique in $110 million to construct a cement plant. Since the early 2000s, China has been known to exploit the country's timber and fisheries, which has been somewhat controversial (Dos Santos and Lobo 2021).

China's relationship with the Portuguese Republic is more historical than with any other Western nation, dating as far back as 1513 when Jorge Alvares landed in Zhujiang (the Pearl River estuary). The first major diplomatic effort took place in 1517–1518, when Tomé Pires and Fernão Pires de Andrade led the first official visit to Guangzhou. This mission proved to be a success, leading to the first trading post being established in Zhujiang and an embassy in Beijing to follow. Later, the Portuguese settled in the peninsula of Macao, and went on to benefit immensely from exclusive trade agreements with imperial China. This mutually beneficial relationship suffered a setback when the Portuguese declared Macao a colonial territory of the Portuguese Empire during the Opium Wars. In the late 1940s, **Portugal**'s neutrality in World War II aggravated the ambivalence of its earlier existence in China. Immediately after the war, these uncertainties gave rise to numerous political and diplomatic discussions as the Chinese and Portuguese regimes attempted to work on their different sovereignty concepts in the new uncertain post-WWII scenario (Lopes 2021). The return of Macao to PRC sovereignty allowed Sino-Portuguese relations to flourish once again; Portugal went on to manifest support for the One-China Two-Systems policy, and provided for treaties and agreements to be signed thereon on a regular basis. Recently, Chinese state companies have invested in the purchase of shares of some major companies in Portugal, and, according to figures from MOFCOM, Chinese investment in Portugal reached 2.525 billion euros at the end of 2018. Energy, banking, insurance, communications, engineering design, and catering are among sectors where Chinese corporations are now investing in Portugal (Global Times 2021).

According to the Ministry of Foreign Affairs of the PRC (2014), China instituted diplomatic relationships with **São Tomé e Príncipe** (STP) in mid-1975. In 1997, the STP government, together with Taiwanese authorities, signed a joint communiqué on instituting diplomatic relations, which stated that the two parties would initiate diplomatic relations the following day. Later, the small African nation changed its allegiance to the PRC. This move allowed STP to join Forum Macao and be a future recipient of Chinese investments. In 2020, the PRC government committed to funding the redevelopment and expansion of STP's international airport.

The relationship between **Timor-Leste** and the PRC dates as far back as imperial China, when the first Chinese merchants developed an interest in sandalwood, which was prevalent on the island. The first significant number of Chinese immigrants however did not arrive until the early 1900s. Since 2002, China's presence and relations with Timor has grown significantly. In 2011, a delegate from China came to Dili to discuss the feasibility of providing a loan to Timor to develop infrastructure. The expected $3 billion worth of soft loans would make China Timor's leading economic partner and significantly change its economic status. In 2002, China approached Timor and requested for an electronic eavesdropping spot to be opened on Timor's south coast (Alves 2002). In sum, China-Timor relationship has provided infrastructure investment on the island such as in power plants, highways and roads, a container port, foreign ministry, military headquarters, and the presidential palace.

Importance of PSCs to the PRC

The value of Lusophone states goes far beyond its historical ties with Macao. With a combined population of around 290 million spread over four continents, the Lusophone world represents immense trade, financial, and commercial cooperation opportunities and benefits to China. Portugal, first of all, being situated in Western Europe and a member of the European Union (EU) is of great relevance (Alden and Alves 2016). In turn, the EU has been China's largest trading partner for the past 14 years with a total volume in 2019 reaching US$ 561 billion. For Angola, Brazil, Mozambique, and Timor-Leste, the most significant fact is that they sit on massive natural resources and mineral reserves. For China, the PSCs' support of One-China Two Systems, and the votes they hold in international organizations elevate their lure for China to maintain with them strong diplomatic ties and effective cooperation terms.

Table 1 demonstrates how the Portuguese-speaking countries are relevant to China, and in the following sections we will present its relevance level. First discussion is the trade potential of the PSCs. A comparative analysis of China's biggest trade partners is presented and is also referenced in Fig. 1. Here, countries that belong to the European Union (EU) are classified together, as are the PSCs. The figures relating to trade statistics show that total trade between the PRC and PSCs totalled US$129 billion. These numbers lagged behind the US$532 billion with the United States and US$561 billion with the EU. In fact, the EU and the U.S. are China's current biggest trading partners, and China in turn is the EU's second-biggest trading partner. Nevertheless, the PSCs as a block may present an interesting perspective: pre–COVID-19, all of these states, most of which developing countries with economies very much reliant on foreign investment, were growing. As this paper has presented, China has been investing in infrastructure in these countries, and the trade figures have been growing steadily. As a post–COVID-19 return to trade "normalcy" looms, a similar ascending trend can be expected.

The combined population of the PSCs is almost 291 million, representing only 4.85% of the world's population, but is forecasted to rise to 390 million by 2050 and 515 million by the year 2100 (United Nations, n.d.). This represents a not only growing but potentially enormous consumer market, which China's manufacturing industry, the largest in the world, can tap into to export its massive output of goods.

In terms of land area, the PSCs cover roughly 7% of global territory above sea level, which is more than China's 6.3%. In particular, Brazil has some of the most fertile terrain in the world, is home to the largest tropical rainforest, and has extensive agriculture and cattle industries. Angola and Mozambique are large countries even by African standards, though both have underdeveloped farming and food production industries. The other PSCs are considered small in size, but—along with Brazil, Angola, Mozambique—they are all coastal countries with considerable Exclusive Economic Zones (EEZs). Brazil currently has the 11th largest EEZ in the world, while Portugal, if requests to extend its current EEZ are accepted, will possess the 7th largest EEZ in the world (Migiro 2018), bringing to this PSC numerous possibilities in natural resources and marine industries.

Table 1 Data regarding Portuguese-speaking countries

Portuguese-speaking countries	Population (2022) [1]	Land area km² [2]	Gross Domestic Product (GDP) US$ (2020) [3]	GDP per capita US$ (2020) [4]	Trade exports to PRC US$ (2019) [5]	Trade imports from PRC US$ (2019) [5]	Natural resources [6]
Republic of Angola	34,438,114M	1,246,700	$62,306.91B	$6,198	$20.5B	$2.06B	petroleum, diamonds, iron ore, phosphates, copper, feldspar, gold, bauxite, uranium
Federative Republic of Brazil	214,887,107M	8,515,767	$1,444,733.26T	$14,064	$36.3B	$63.5B	alumina, bauxite, beryllium, gold, iron ore, manganese, nickel, niobium, phosphates, platinum, tantalum, tin, rare earth elements, uranium, petroleum, hydropower, timber
Republic of Cabo Verde	565,288k	4,033	$1,703.70B	$6,045	$95.8k	$59.5M	salt, basalt rock, limestone, kaolin, fish, clay, gypsum
Republic of Guinea- Bissau	2,039,562M	36,125	$1,431.76B	$1,847	$7.55M	$31.9M	fish, timber, phosphates, bauxite, clay, granite, limestone, unexploited deposits of petroleum
Republic of Mozambique	32,602,113M	801,590	$14,021.42B	$1,229	$652M	$1.96B	coal, titanium, natural gas, hydropower, tantalum, graphite
Portuguese Republic	10,150,890M	92,090	$231,226.74B	$32,181	$741M	$3.73B	fish, forests (cork), iron ore, copper, zinc, tin, tungsten, silver, gold, uranium, marble, clay, gypsum, salt, arable land, hydropower
Democratic Republic of São Tomé and Príncipe	225,423k	963	$472.91M	$4,052	$13.6k	$12.4M	fish, hydropower, unexploited oil deposits
Democratic Republic of Timor-Leste	1,357,095M	14, 874	$1,821.00B	$3,181	$22.5M	$144M	gold, petroleum, natural gas, manganese, marble
Totals	296,265,592M		$1,757,713T		$58.22B	$71.48B	

Created by the author with data from https://www.worldometers.info/, https://www.worldometers.info/geography/largest-countries-in-the-world/, https://data.worldbank.org/indicator/NY.GDP.MKTP.CD, https://ourworldindata.org/grapher/gdp-per-capita-worldbank?tab=table, https://oec.world/en, https://www.nationmaster.com/country-info/stats/Geography/Natural-resources

The overall GDP of the PSCs stood at US$1.7 trillion in 2020. When compared to China's largest trading partners, the EU's US$15 trillion, and the U.S.'s US$20 trillion, these numbers pale by comparison. Nonetheless, when taking into consideration the expectable population rise and especially the fact that most PSCs have emerging economies, potential and opportunities abound for China to gain economic footholds in these nations. The GDP per capita of the PSCs, except for Portugal (US$32,181) and Brazil (US$14,064), all lag behind the world's average of US$10,925. Such a low level of economic development pertaining to Lusophone countries in fact presents opportunities for cheap labor and infrastructure development.

In terms of natural resources, Brazil and Angola stand out. Brazil, with its massive land area (5th largest the world) and EEZ, is already one of the most resource-rich countries in the world. Angola is one of the richest nations in natural resources in Africa; it sits on massive oil deposits and China has already been the main destination for its oil crude exports (62.4% in 2019). To put it into perspective, next on the destination list for Angolan oil is India, at 10.3% (OEC 2021a). The other PSCs have more modest levels of natural resources, although Timor-Leste with its Greater Sunrise oil fields and the yet-to-be-explored oil fields off the coast of Guinea-Bissau and near the islands of Sao Tomé e Principe may be a game changer for the respective small economies. Another natural

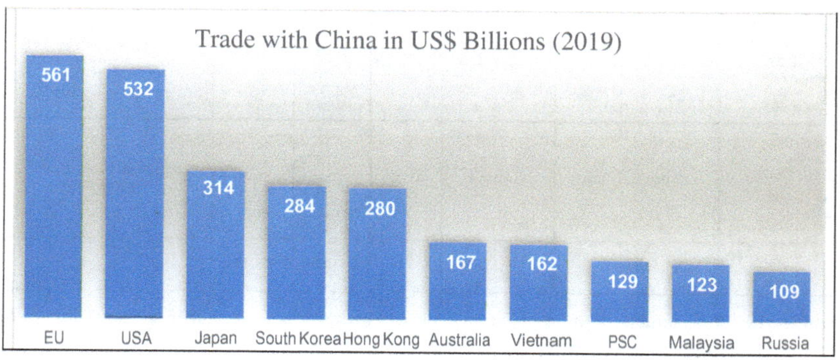

Fig. 1 Overall trade statistics between China and its biggest trade partners (Created by the author with data from https://ec.europa.eu/trade/policy/countries-and-regions/countries/china/, https://oec.world/en, https://wits.worldbank.org/Default.aspx?lang=en)

resource that the PRC has a great interest in is fisheries. China is one of the largest consumers of seafood in the world, and the fact that all PSCs have large coastal areas and EEZs presents an opportunity for China to explore a resource that the EU and Japan also seem to be vying for.

Another key area of interest for the PRC is the geographic locations of the Lusophone nations. Mozambique is located near the end of the Maritime Silk Road (MSR) in East Africa, a section of the enormous Belt and Road Initiative (BRI). If the MSR is to expand southward and go around the Cape of Good Hope, then it will necessarily need to cross into the Mozambique channel, a large maritime area between the EEZ of Mozambique and the island of Madagascar.

The port of Beira in Mozambique has been renovated by China Harbour Engineering Company Ltd. Angola's coastline would also become part of a possible extension of the MSR, as it goes up the west coast of the African continent. The PRC has invested in a deep-sea port in the enclave of Cabinda and has shown interest in getting a concession of the Port of Lobito. China has also been heavily involved in financing the restructuring and extension of the railway line linking Dar es Salaam in Tanzania to Lobito in Angola. The location of the islands of São Tomé e Príncipe in the Gulf of Guinea, a major global maritime transport highway, is also extremely relevant. Moreover, for any potential extension of the BRI through an area that suffers from piracy and instability, maintaining security in that region will be paramount for China. This would include measures to protect international trade and Chinese interests in the region. Guinea-Bissau too would be part of a continuation of the MSR up the African west coast, where Chinese companies are involved in exploring oil fields. Also, contained in Guinea-Bissau's EEZ is one of the most biodiverse marine systems in the world. Finally, Cabo Verde, sitting at a crossroads between three continents—Africa, Europe, and South America—is of great interest to China. Cabo Verde has one of the most stable political situations in Africa, which has attracted large infrastructural investment. This includes investment in Sao Vincente's Special Maritime Economic Zone.

Portugal is the westernmost country in Europe, a possible extension of the MSR through West Africa to reach Europe would most likely terminate in this European country. Portugal was the first EU country to sign memoranda relating to the BRI. In addition, Portugal has several important ports, but it is the Port of Sines, located in its southern region, that is perhaps most relevant to China—it is the closest European deep-sea port to the U.S. and the Panama Canal. China already owns a stake in one of the four terminals at Sines, and is set for more investment. The United States has also shown interest in investing in the port.

Brazil's massive coastline and potential extension of its EEZ—awaiting approval from the Commission on the Limits of the Continental Shelf (CLCS)—will also warrant interest from the PRC. In fact, most of the eastern coast of South America is under Brazilian sovereignty, so any maritime corridor linking Africa and South America would be heavily influenced by Brazil. As for Timor-Leste, China has funded several infrastructural projects (mentioned previously). The ongoing interest in oil fields off the coast of Timor, which are located in a Joint Petroleum Development Area with Australia—a potential regional rival—is of great importance to the PRC's interests in the region.

Findings and Conclusions

PSCs are greatly connected not only by a common language but also in terms of culture, traditions, business, and mentality. These countries share long-term ties and frequently engage in bilateral negotiations or dealings. Moreover, they are all part of the Comunidade dos Países de Língua Portuguesa (CPLP), an international organization made up of the PSCs. Forum Macao was not intended to replace or compete with CPLP. As stated on their website, "Forum Macao is a multilateral, intergovernmental cooperation mechanism aimed at promoting economic and trade exchanges between China and Portuguese-speaking Countries, by using Macao as a connecting platform between those places" (Forum Macao 2021). While CPLP aims to promote the Portuguese language and foster stronger ties between the PSCs, Forum Macao targets the promotion of better economic terms and further trade with Lusophone countries.

Forum Macao differs from CPLP and other similar organizations in that it provides a setting where representatives of the Portuguese-speaking countries are in direct contact with Chinese governmental authorities via appointed officials who have a direct line to Beijing. Here, it is worth noting that the African country of Equatorial Guinea has become a Portuguese-speaking country when it adopted Portuguese as a co-official language in 2011, and at the time of writing, were in the process of joining this forum. Forum Macao was established with a focus on promoting trade and economic ties between China and the PSCs, but in reality (although this is yet an under-studied subject), its impact on trade figures and on the economies of all concerning parties has been minor, and the forum has taken on a somewhat different role: it has become an instrument for the PRC to demonstrate its leadership skills, its support for open dialogue and equality, to promote its culture, and to gain support for its foreign policy.

In any event, Forum Macao stands out from other Chinese initiatives: It exhibits unique characteristics such as having a common language, and being the only forum with a permanent location as well as secretariat in the city of Macao. Moreover, it serves as a platform for the PRC to show its strong commitment toward the PSCs. For a country and economy as large and strong as China('s), its priorities must be focused on business, trade, and economic goals. Nevertheless, China sees enough value in these forums despite their limited trade and economic contribution thus far. In fact, China treats these forums as a tool to embrace member nations, as well as to cultivate and strengthen long-term relationships with them, in the process providing visibility to Chinese soft power.

China has demonstrated in the international arena that it has the capability and ingenuity to establish unique frameworks—forums—to equip itself with communication channels unlike conventional international organizations, to engage with other nations. Doing so has brought China prestige and recognition—albeit mostly from developing countries in the southern hemisphere—as the forums present a friendlier, more approachable, and accessible side to the world's second-largest economy. In the past, China has closed itself to the world for decades, therefore incurring significant misgivings, speculations, and apprehension from other nations regarding its new and rampant development. Forums, particularly Forum Macao, through culture- and education-related initiatives, have helped ease such concerns. Today, PSCs have all experienced close diplomatic and economic ties with China, and everything has pointed toward that upward trend to continue. Forum Macao's impact on these relationships is difficult to quantify, but it is undeniable that it must have contributed to the sharing of knowledge of each other's cultures, histories, business procedures, education, and communication identities. This study has shown that Forum Macao helps project Chinese ideal, appeal, and soft power to the PSCs, and therefore plays a particularly impactful role on the PRC's relations with these countries. During the COVID-19 pandemic, for example, China donated millions of masks and medical products to members of its forums. Later, the supply of Chinese vaccines (which has come to be known as "vaccine diplomacy"), even though having enjoyed only limited success, has also exemplified China's readiness and willingness to support developing nations.

In terms of leadership, China approaches Forum Macao much like it does other Chinese forums, and the approach encompasses several elements of the Chinese Leadership theory. China assumes leadership roles in these forums with clear initiative and charisma, its objectives are cohesive, and it shows versatility in adapting to diverse cultures and customs from different parts of the world. In addition, China's goals and objectives are implemented under guidelines and agreements, and even when results have not been fully delivered, China remains patient and hopeful. It is through such approach that we see elements of Confucianism on multiple levels in China's leadership and management of not only Forum Macao but also other forums as well.

Further research on the economic impact of Forum Macao and other Chinese forums on bilateral relations would be warranted. Another line of study would be to ascertain the different characteristics of Chinese forums and the role they play in China's foreign policy. Forums are still a somewhat misunderstood and under-researched Chinese phenomenon. Despite their international and multilateral aura, they seem to have limited visibility. Nevertheless, they are growing in stature, number, and members. As a case in point, Portuguese-speaking countries have already recognized and acknowledged the value of being a part of Forum Macao, as they regularly send ministers (including prime ministers) and/or high governmental representatives to the forum. Although most of the significant bilateral dealings continue to occur in Beijing at the embassy level, all parties understand that Forum Macao helps to maintain another line of communication between them, that it strengthens their common goals, enables better understanding of each other's cultures and business practices, and perhaps most importantly, it helps to build a foundation of trust that will further impact relations between the People's Republic of China and Portuguese—speaking countries.

References

Alden, C., & Alves, A. C. (2016). China's Regional Forum Diplomacy in the Developing World: Socialisation and the 'Sinosphere'. *Journal of Contemporary China, 26*(103), pp. 151–163. https://doi.org/10.1080/10670564.2016.1206276.

Alves, A. (2002). China's Lusophone Connection-Africa Portal. *China in Africa Project Reporting*. Retrieved September 13, 2021, from https://media.africaportal.org/documents/Chinas_Lusophone_connection.pdf.

Boon, H. T., Li, M., & Char, J. (2017). *New Trends in Chinese Foreign Policy*. Retrieved April 15, 2021, from https://www.tandfonline.com/doi/full/10.1080/14799855.2017.1286158.

Da Silva Horta, M. L. (2012). China's Relations with Portuguese-Speaking Countries: A Growing but Unnoticed Relation. *Naval Postgraduate School Monterey CA*. Retrieved September 4, 2021, from https://calhoun.nps.edu/handle/10945/17351.

Devika, M. (2019). The China-CELAC Forum—Missed Opportunity for India? *JSTOR*, *23*(4), pp. 58–71. Retrieved May 21, 2020, from https://doi.org/10.4103/0028-3886.96400.

Dos Santos, P. P., & Lobo, A. (2021). Geopolitical Relations Between China and the South Atlantic Portuguese-Speaking Countries: A Blue Evolving Partnership, chapter 3A, pp. 269–299, in *China and Portuguese-Speaking Small Island States: From Sporadic Bilateral Exchanges to a Comprehensive Multilateral platform*, by Leandro, F. J. B. S., dos Santos, P. P. and Li, Y. (Eds). City University of Macau.

Forum Macao. (2021, June 29). *Forum Macao* | 中葡論壇 | 中葡论坛 | *Fórum de Macau*. Forum Macao | 中 葡 論 壇 | 中 葡 论 坛 | Fórum de Macau. Retrieved September 14, 2021, from https://www.forumchinaplp.org.mo/.

Global Times. (2021). *Portugal Opens Arms to Welcome Chinese Investment: Embassy*. Global Times. Retrieved September 4, 2021, from https://www.globaltimes.cn/content/1205057.shtml.

Han, P. (2013). Confucian Leadership and the Rising Chinese Economy. *The Chinese Economy*, *46*(2), pp. 107–127. https://doi.org/10.2753/ces1097-1475460205.

Herman, F. (2020). Does Trust Facilitate Cooperation in the Forum on China–Africa Cooperation (FOCAC)? A Socio-Psychological Approach. *Africa Review, 13*(1), pp. 76–93. Retrieved May 21, 2021, from https://doi.org/10.1080/09744053.2020.1840900.

King, K. (2020). China–Africa Education Cooperation: From FOCAC to Belt and Road. *ECNU Review of Education*, *3*(2), pp. 221–234. https://doi.org/10.1177/2096531119889874.

Ling, W., & Fang, L. (2013). *The Chinese Leadership Theory | Emerald Insight*. Emerald.com. Retrieved November 17, 2021, from https://www.emerald.com/insight/content/doi/10.1016/S1535-1203(02)03010-1/full/html.

Lopes, H. F. S. (2021) Ghosts of War: China's Relations with Portugal in the Post-War Period, 1945–9. *Historical Research*. Retrieved February 21, 2021, from https://doi.org/10.1093/hisres/htab020.

Mendes, C. (2014). Macau in China's Relations with the Lusophone World. *Revista Brasileira De Política Internacional*, *57*(spe), pp. 225–242. Retrieved May 20, 2021, from https://doi.org/10.1590/00347329201400214.

Migiro, G. (2018). *Countries with the Largest Exclusive Economic Zones*. World Atlas. Retrieved November 18, 2021, from https://www.worldatlas.com/articles/countries-with-the-largest-exclusive-economic-zones.html.

Ministry of Foreign Affairs of the PRC. (2014). *São Tomé and Príncipe*. https://www.Fmprc.Gov.Cn/. Retrieved March 19, 2021, from https://www.fmprc.gov.cn/mfa_eng/wjb_663304/zzjg_663340/fzs_663828/gjlb_663832/3069_664164/.

OEC—The Observatory of Economic Complexity. (2021a). *Angola (AGO) Exports, Imports, and Trade Partners | OEC*. Retrieved May 21, 2021, from https://oec.world/en/profile/country/ago.

OEC—The Observatory of Economic Complexity. (2021b). *Brazil (BRA) Exports, Imports, and Trade Partners | OEC*. Retrieved May 21, 2021, from https://oec.world/en/profile/country/bra.

Platformchinaplp.mo. (2021). *Economic and Trade Co-operation and Human Resources Portal between China and Portuguese-Speaking Countries*. Retrieved May 2, 2021, from https://www.platformchinaplp.mo/?lang=en.

United Nations. (n.d.). *World Population Prospects—Population Division—United Nations*. https://Population.Un.Org/. Retrieved August 13, 2021, from https://population.un.org/wpp/.

Vangeli, A. (2018). Global China and Symbolic Power: The Case of 16+ 1 Cooperation. *Journal of Contemporary China, 27*(113), pp. 674–687. Retrieved June 18, 2021, from https://sci-hub.se/10.1080/10670564.2018.1458056.

Vogt, W. J. (2017). China and Lusophonia. *World Scientific Publishing*. Retrieved May 21, 2021, from https://www.worldscientific.com/doi/pdf/10.1142/S2377740017500312.

Zhang, B. (2010). Chinese Foreign Policy in Transition: Trends and Implications. *Journal of Current Chinese Affairs, 39*(2), pp. 39–68. Retrieved April 7, 2020, from https://www.researchgate.net/publication/45655571_Chinese_Foreign_Policy_in_Transition_Trends_and_Implications.

Zhang, D. (2017). China's Diplomacy in the Pacific: Interests, Means and Implications. *Security Challenges, 13*(2), pp. 32–53. Retrieved May 21, 2021, from https://www.jstor.org/stable/pdf/26457717.pdf.

The Geopolitics of Timor-Leste: Belt & Road Initiative (B&RI), ASEAN and CPLP

Francisco José B. S. Leandro, José Eduardo Garcia Leandro, and Carlos Martins Branco

Introduction

Timor-Leste has been at the center of the geopolitical and geo-economic debate in South-East Asia since its inception as a sovereign state in 2002, and a point of convergent interests of several Asian states. With the launch

---

This chapter with the original title—The Geopolitics of Timor-Leste in the Context of the Belt & Road Initiative (B&RI) vis-à-vis ASEAN and CPLP—has been initially published in lhéu, Fernanda; Leandro, Francisco; Duarte, Paulo (2019). The New Silk Road and the Portuguese-speaking Countries in the New World Context. Sumaoriental. In 2022, all chapter has been extensively revised and updated and the publisher Sumaoriental has authorized its republication in a written declaration.

F. J. B. S. Leandro (✉)
University of Macau, Macau, China
e-mail: fleandro@um.edu.mo

J. E. G. Leandro
Fundação Jorge Álvares, Lisbon, Portugal
e-mail: garleandro@sapo.pt

C. M. Branco
Portuguese Institute of International Relations (IPRI), Lisbon, Portugal
e-mail: carlos.branco@netcabo.pt

P. A. B. Duarte et al. (eds.), *Portugal and the Lusophone World*,
https://doi.org/10.1007/978-981-99-0455-6_27

of the Chinese Belt and Road Initiative (B&RI) in 2013, Timor-Leste became part of the equation of the South Asian maritime component of the B&RI, especially because of its location between Indonesia and Australia. It is in this context that Timor-Leste's request for accession to ASEAN must be evaluated, along with the implications of its affiliated groups, bearing in mind Timor-Leste's national commitment to development. Moreover, Timor-Leste is the only Asian member state of the Community of Portuguese Language Countries (CPLP), with historical and symbolic political bilateral ties to all Portuguese-speaking countries.

Timor-Leste faces a sort of 'trilemma'. On the one hand, the history of Timor-Leste compels it to carefully balance all the interests at stake, especially in relation to the possibility of deeper economic relations with China, because this may affect the perceptions of Indonesia and Australia. On the other hand, Timor-Leste perceives accession to ASEAN as the way forward in terms of regional integration, but that integration could give the small island state, with the help of China, a functional power which may not be well received by others. Finally, CPLP membership links Timor-Leste to a set of geographic, cultural, and diplomatic rationales, which are difficult to reconcile with regional economic interests. All of this exists in the context of national development and the accompanying challenges, which calls for long-term political stability within this young country.

Discussion

Geopolitics of Timor-Leste

The discussion on B&RI tends to focus on the Eurasian region and in particular takes the Sino-European perspective as these are the two leading commercial blocks. We, however, view the B&RI as an access strategy, combining the land corridors and the maritime routes to establish a network of trade and commercial flows across continents. Therefore, our discussion starts from the assumption that the geopolitical relevance of Timor-Leste should be viewed in the context of its maritime dimension. In fact, the six economic land corridors and the Maritime Silk Road were initially developed in Central and Eastern Europe, but the B&RI has turned global and now extends far beyond Eurasia. Three Chinese domestic development axes were initially extended into six economic corridors and the Maritime Silk Road. This 3 = 6 + 3 structure (3 domestic axes = 6 international land corridors + 3 maritime blue passages) (Fig. 1) is the core network of a global strategy spanning Central and Eastern Europe (the B&RI for the Western Balkans, the Arctic Silk Road and the Greenland Arctic Base[1]); Africa (the Maghreb-Sahel Silk Road, Great Lakes Silk Road, the Trans-Africa Highway, the Western Africa Railways, the Angola-Tanzania Railways, and the Great Lakes infrastructure plan); Asia (the ASEAN integrated master plan network of connectivity—The Thailand Regional Connectivity Plan,[2] the Southeast Asia Railways Plan—The Pan-Asia Railway Network,[3] the Mekong India Economic Corridor), the Pacific (Trans-Pacific Maritime Silk Road); and the Americas (the Latin America Silk Road, the Inter-Oceanic Railway, the Nicaraguan Canal, and the Cartagena-Caribbean Railway). All of these material components of the B&RI are complemented by pathways in other domains, such as the Digital Silk Road, the Green Silk Road, Cultural Silk Road, Education Silk Road for the future (EU/China), and the Space Silk Road. Timor-Leste is located on none of the land routes, but its location on a natural sailing route between the Indian Ocean and Pacific Ocean is significant and cannot be ignored, especially in the context of the maritime Silk Road. Timor-Leste seats on the natural extension of the COSPBEP (China—South Pacific—Blue Economic Passage), as it connects China and the Torres Strait, 'travelling southward from the South China Sea into the Pacific Ocean' (State Council of PRC 2010). Furthermore, Timor-Leste is indeed the only alternative sovereign state, in an immense area dominated by Indonesia and Australia.

According to State Council of PRC (2010), 'The Chinese government supports the development of mechanisms for ocean cooperation and the formulation of policies and rules under the Asia Pacific Economic Cooperation (APEC), the East Asia Leaders' Meetings, the China-Africa Cooperation Forum and the China-Pacific Island Countries Economic Development and Cooperation Forum. China will boost cooperation with multilateral cooperative organizations and support the Intergovernmental

[1] Retrieved on December 19, 2021, from https://www.bbc.com/news/world-europe-46386867.

[2] Retrieved on December 19, 2021, from https://canchamthailand.org/thailands-infrastructure-plans-and-canadian-capabilities/.

[3] Retrieved on December 19, 2021, from https://photos.nomadicnotes.com/img/s7/v163/p368258383.png.

	China Internal Development Axis	China International Economic Corridors	
Land	Axis 2 Guangdong-Harbin	China-Mongolia-Russia-Economic Corridor	CMREC
		New Economic Land Belt	NELB
	Axis 1 Urumqi-Shanghai-Kashgar	China-Central Asia and Western Asia-Economic Corridor	CCWAEC
		China-Pakistan-Economic Corridor	CPEC
	Axis 3 Kunming-Shanghai	China-Bangladesh-India-Myanmar-Economic Corridor	CBIMEC
		China-Indochina Peninsula-Economic Corridor	CICPEC
Maritime	China-Indian ocean – Africa-Mediterranean - Blue Economic Passage (Extension to Lusophone B&RI)		CIOAMBEP
	China – South Pacific - Blue Economic Passage		COSPBEP
	China – Arctic – Europe - Blue Economic Passage (Silk Polar Maritime Road)		CAEBEP

Fig. 1 B&R Physical Dimensions (partial)

Oceanographic Commission of UNESCO (IOC/UNESCO), the Partnership in Environment Management of Seas of East Asia (PEMSEA), the Indian Ocean Rim Association, and the International Ocean Institute in jointly organizing and promoting major programs and projects (…) The Chinese government has mobilized domestic resources and set up the China-ASEAN Maritime Cooperation Fund and the China-Indonesia Maritime Cooperation Fund. China have also implemented The Framework Plan for International Cooperation for the South China Sea and its Adjacent Oceans. Meanwhile, the Asian Infrastructure Investment Bank and the Silk Road Fund have provided capital support for major ocean cooperation programs'.

Chauprade (2003, pp. 130–131) asserted that island states benefit from maritime routes, particularly in the establishment of land points of support. Timor-Leste is a young island nation state, a fragile state,[4] and low-income country, exercising sovereignty over a non-continuous island territory. It lies in South-East Asia between the Timor Sea and Banda Sea, in the group of the Lesser Sunda Islands at the eastern end of the Indonesian archipelago. It comprises the eastern half of Timor Island (approximately 5400 square miles, bordering Indonesia's Nusa Tenggara province), the separate exclave of Oecusse in West Timor, and the small offshore islands of Atauro and Jaco. The Wetar Strait, in particular the passage between Atauro and Timor-Leste, which connects it to Ombai

[4] Listed by the World Bank in 2021, http://www.worldbank.org/en/topic/fragilityconflictviolence/brief/harmonized-list-of-fragile-situations.

Strait, has a depth of close to 3000 m and approximately 30% of water movement between both the Pacific and Indian oceans.[5] Timor-Leste shares land and maritime borders with Indonesia, and a maritime border with Australia. Timor-Leste and Australia are separated by the Timor Sea at a distance of approximately 300 nautical miles. Situated between the Indian Ocean and Pacific Ocean, Timor-Leste is at the center of the Coral Triangle, home to the most biodiverse marine ecosystem in the world. Its territorial waters are part of the Western Pacific Warm Pool. Positioned between Wallace's line, Weber's line, and Lydekker's line, Timor-Leste is situated in an area of abundant fauna and flora diversity.

The abundance of natural resources and Timor-Leste's position make it natural choice for other actors to consider using the island as a sea-land platform to support commercial shipping. The Timor-Leste archipelago is at approximately the same latitude as the Torres Strait, which is an important maritime passage and one of the maritime bottlenecks in commercial navigation. The distance between Díli and Port Moresby (Papua New Guinea) is approximately 2400 km and the Torres Strait is a natural maritime access point, connecting the Pacific and Indian oceans. Almost all maritime traffic from the eastern edge of the Indian Ocean to the South Pacific must pass through the Timor Sea, one of the most biodiverse regions on the planet. Timor-Leste sits on the outer Banda Arc, a west-facing horseshoe-shaped arc near eastern Indonesia, which is the locus of three converging major plates, the Indo-Australia Plate, the Pacific Plate, and the Eurasian Plate. The climate is tropical and generally very hot and humid, depending upon the altitude, which reaches 2963 m (Mount Ramelau). It is characterized by distinct rainy and dry seasons, floods, landslides, earthquakes, tsunamis, and tropical cyclones. The mountainous terrain that dominates Timor-Leste impacts human activities, especially in terms of domestic transportation. The deep valleys, semi-permanent water courses, small and isolated communities spread out around the territory and a variety of microclimates make it difficult to access populations and immensely increases the costs of road maintenance. The only way to access some communities is by small-sized horses. The different microclimates also facilitate the production of agricultural

[5] Adapted from Sebille, E., J. Sprintall, F. U. Schwarzkopf, A. S. Gupta, A. Santoso, M. H. England, A. Biastoch, and C. W. Böning (2014). Pacific-to-Indian Ocean connectivity: Tasman leakage, Indonesian Through flow, and the role of ENSO. *Journal of Geophysical Research Oceans*, 119, 1365–1382, https://doi.org/10.1002/2013JC009525, p. 1373.

goods and timber. Being part of an archipelago, Timor-Leste fisheries are abundant, especially along the southern coast. Local people refer to the Timor Sea as '*Mar Homem*' (Tasi Mane[6]) because of its violent and rough waters.

The history of Timor-Leste could be summarized as a strong native cultural history mixed with the long-standing presence of foreigners, more recently shaped by the circumstances of the Portuguese departure and the U.S. and Indonesian Cold War fears. The small size of Timor-Leste also played a role in its fortunes, alongside the watershed media coverage of the Santa Cruz graveyard massacre in 1991, which brought international attention to the suffering of the Timorese people. Timor-Leste's history has profoundly shaped its national identity, a result of a diverse native population, Portuguese colonial rule, Japanese occupation, Indonesian occupation, the proximity of Australia, and the recent significant international presence. Sahin (2014, p. 11) summarized Timor-Leste's history in the following words: 'four centuries of Portuguese colonial administration, 24 years of Indonesian occupation and two-and-half years of UN transitional rule'. The population of Timor-Leste is approximately 1.1 million according to a 2016 estimate,[7] approximately 25% of whom live in Díli, the capital city (in 2022, the population is estimated to be 1,364,035 based on Worldometer elaboration of the latest United Nations data). The country's two official languages are Portuguese and Tetum, with English and Indonesian as working languages as well as a myriad of local dialects. According to a 2005 World Bank report, 98% of the population is Catholic, 1% is Protestant, and less than 1% is Muslim. Most citizens also retain some vestiges of animistic beliefs and practices, which some regard as more cultural than religious. With all of these factors in mind, the national character of Timor-Leste is aptly described in the following statement displayed at the National Archive and Museum of Timorese History (Díli)—'To resist is to win. To resist is to know how to accommodate past divergences to address the challenges of the present and the future'.

[6] Male Sea—the Tetum name for the Timor Sea between Timor-Leste's south coast and Australia.

[7] Retrieved in November 2021, from East-Timor Strategic Development Plan 2011–2030, p. 107, and http://www.statistics.gov.tl/pt/census-2/key-census-results/, and Retrieved in April 2022, from https://www.worldometers.info/world-population/timor-leste-population/.

According to the Timor-Leste Strategic Development Plan 2011–2030, the country is pursuing a strategy of regional development corridors[8] and is making a significant investment to develop the nation's social capital. The Timor-Leste spatial development vision (Fig. 2) (p. 118) organizes the national space according to two Regional Development Corridors (North and South), divided by a protected forest, with two land connectivity hubs (Dili and Suai) and a maritime linkage to the Oe-Cusse Ambeno exclave. The framework will include two Regional Development Corridors, the northern corridor development and the southern corridor development as well as a number of special zones designed to guide development based upon the specific characteristics of certain regions... Timor-Leste National Planning Framework will guide the acceleration of sustainable economic growth and equitable development from national level to 'sucos' level, while protecting Timor-Leste's biodiversity and natural environment in conservation zones (p. 114).

According to the same document (p. 47), the traditional gender biases affect all aspects of life in Timor-Leste. Adult male illiteracy rates are lower than women's (21% compared to 32% for women; albeit some progress made by the latter), and more men are in higher education (83 women for every 100 men). Nearly 40% of women over the age of 15 in Timor-Leste have experienced physical violence. Of women who have been married, 34% have experienced physical violence from their husbands and many have not been able to obtain justice and redress for their grievances. Fertility rates are still among the highest in the world, and while health statistics are improving, too many Timorese women still die in childbirth. The Timor-Leste maternal mortality rate remains high, with 42% of all deaths of women aged 15–49 related to pregnancy. Timor-Leste ranked 132 on the human development index (HDI) (2017). For this reason, Timor-Leste's public budget allocation gives a high priority to the education and health sectors, followed by the justice sector and the public sector.[9]

Alongside investment in human social capital, the priority development areas seem to be connectivity (roads, airports, and seaports), energy production, and tourism. Timor-Leste is heavily dependent on a single national port in Díli for all of its general cargo imports and exports.

[8] Timor-Leste Strategic Development Plan 2011–2030, p. 114.

[9] Timor-Leste Strategic Development Plan 2011–2030, p. 208.

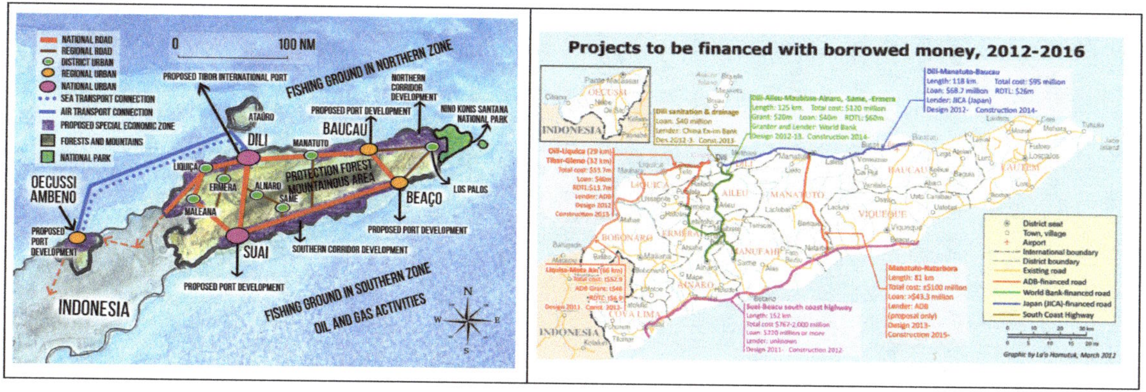

Fig. 2 Timor-Leste national planning framework and projects financed (*Sources* Timor-Leste Strategic Development Plan 2011–2030, p. 118, https://oretornodaasia.wordpress.com/2013/10/03/o-banco-asiatico-de-desenvolvimento-alarga-a-sua-presenca-em-timor-leste/)

Regular direct shipping services are currently provided to Darwin in Australia, Kota Kinabalu in Malaysia, Surabaya in Indonesia, and Singapore. Other services also operate to Indonesian ports. A ferry service runs between Díli and Oecusse Ambeno twice a week and between Dili and Atauro once a week. There is a strategy of regional development corridors which includes two regional development corridors, the northern and southern corridor developments, as well as a number of special zones designed to guide development based upon the specific characteristics of certain regions. The proposed national strategic zones are: (1) Dili—Tibar—Hera; (2) Suai—Betano—Beaço Liquiça—Ermera—Aileu; (3) Manatuto—Baucau—Lautem; (4) Bobonaro—Cova Lima; and (5) the Oe-Cusse Ambeno exclave. A logistics base for the petroleum sector will also be established in Suai (Timor-Leste Strategic Development Plan 2011–2030, p. 94). This base will provide capacity for the south coast to develop a domestic petroleum sector along with related and supporting industries and businesses. The centerpiece of this development will be the construction of a new port at Suai. This facility will open up the south coast to investment and growth and provide an international access point to Timor-Leste. The new Suai Port will provide an entry point for the materials and equipment needed to build infrastructure and plants for the petroleum industry. Suai Port will be a multi-purpose seaport and include a container park, a warehouse logistics area, and fuel storage facilities. The port may also provide shipbuilding and repair facilities. Construction of the port will require a breakwater to provide protection from the Timor Sea. The port will be part of the Suai Supply Base, which will become a national industrial base and logistics center to drive job creation and economic development on the south coast. The base will also support the establishment of petroleum centers at Betano-Manufahi and Beaço-Viqueque. The centerpiece of the Timor-Leste government's development strategy is Tasi Mane, a corridor of petroleum infrastructure along the southwest coast of the country. This ambitious project is described in the Timor-Leste Strategic Development Plan 2011–2030 (p. 138) as 'a multi-year development of three industrial clusters on the south coast which will form the backbone of the Timor-Leste petroleum industry'.

Furthermore, according to the Timor-Leste Strategic Development Plan 2011–2030 (p. 101), the country will pursue a connection to either an Indonesian cable, such as the PT Telkom fiber-optic backbone that will soon connect Kupang in West Timor, or to an Australian cable.

Such a connection would be operated either on a commercial basis by private telecommunications operators or by the government. Concerning energy production, Timor-Leste has access to vast reserves of gas in the Timor Sea. The availability of natural gas for electricity generation has the potential to provide much cheaper and cleaner fuel than liquid fuels. In environmental terms, for the same amount of electricity produced, the carbon emissions from natural gas-generated electricity are considerably lower than from diesel-generated electricity. The development of renewable energies in Timor-Leste will help drive economic growth and allow Timor-Leste to embrace new technologies that will make the country a model of sustainable development. Population growth and the needs of an expanding economy are likely to increase electricity consumption in Timor-Leste from the current level of about 160 GWh to 800 GWh by 2020. At least half of the country's future energy needs will be provided by renewable energy sources. Analysis undertaken for the Strategic Development Plan (p. 87) identified more than 450 MW of potential renewable energy projects across the following technologies: hydro (wire-to-water and regulation): 252 MW; hydro pumping: 100 MW; wind: 72 MW; solar: 22 MW; and biomass/solid waste: 6 MW.

In relation to the tourism industry, the government has pursued a policy of establishing national protected areas such as the Nino Konis Santana National Park, Timor-Leste's first national park. The park, established on August 3, 2007, covers 1236 square kilometers. Timor-Leste's Strategic Development Plan 2011–2030 (p. 128) observed that 'Timor-Leste is blessed with tropical waters rich in marine life, white sand beaches, spectacular mountain ranges, unique Timorese culture, Portuguese colonial heritage and resistance history'. The value of international tourism in Timor-Leste can be measured by the number of arrivals. In 2015 this was 62,000 and in the 9 years between 2006 and 2015 arrivals reached a maximum of 79,000 in 2013.[10] Overall, there is an increasing trend in the number of tourist arrivals. Investment in the country by international brands such as Heineken and Hilton Hotels also shows an upward trend.

Timor-Leste seems to have a clear view of its past, a strong national will, and balanced plans for the near future. Development, investment,

[10] Retrieved on December 21, 2021, from https://www.indexmundi.com/facts/timor-leste/indicator/ST.INT.ARVL.

infrastructure, and human capital are at the center of its efforts to consolidate what was previously a fragile existence into a nation with real sovereign capacities, especially in relation to its neighbors. Timor-Leste's determined commitment to development, its abundant natural resources, and its location in the context of the Indian Ocean-Pacific Ocean sea lines of communication have attracted China to include it in the Maritime Silk Road.

Timor-Leste Foreign Affairs: Australia, Indonesia, and China

'As a small nation in a highly strategic geographic location, Timor-Leste's security will depend upon forging strong relationships with our neighbors and friends, making a positive contribution to a stable and peaceful region, and participating in global peacekeeping missions and cooperative international forums and initiatives' (Timor-Leste Strategic Development Plan 2011–2030, p. 176). Despite its limited resources and a small diplomatic corps, Timor-Leste has made a tremendous effort on the diplomatic front to increase its strategic power and room for maneuver, both bilaterally and multilaterally, in its aim to be listened to and to be relevant. For that reason, Timor-Leste has established diplomatic relations with almost 100 states and international organizations, and is a founding member state of g7+, a voluntary association of countries that are or have been affected by conflict and are now in transition to the next stage of development. Timor-Leste is not a regional power and does not intend to be. However, the 'functional balancing' of this 'small' territory could make the difference, especially in the vast region dominated by Indonesia and Australia.

In case of a global or a regional crisis, the strategic importance of the sea lines between the Pacific and Indian oceans will leverage the functional power of Timor-Leste. The country's future accession to ASEAN could also play a very important regional role, especially in relation to future ASEAN-China relations. Likewise, from a regional economic standpoint, the possibility of setting up some sort of support to Chinese interests should be considered, in terms of communication, sea resources exploration, scientific research, and shipping infrastructure. From the perspective of Australia, and bearing in mind Chinese activities in the Pacific Islands (especially Vanuatu), it is crucial for Australia not to allow an antagonistic power free access to Timor-Leste.[11] If controlled or strongly influenced by a hostile power, Timor-Leste could be used as a platform to prevent Australian ships entering the northern Indian Ocean or from reaching Java and the Banda Sea. From this perspective, Timor-Leste can be considered a geopolitical pivot by Australia. Controlling Timor-Leste seems strategically more important to Australia than to China. China, as a regional power, has other options in relation to the Indian Ocean. Australia, Indonesia, and the ASEAN member states have to develop their existing relations with Timor-Leste, knowing that this small country needs them all to balance its small size and to make the most of its presence in this part of the world.

Timor-Leste's agency in the international arena has been dependent on the cooperative and constructive relations it has established with its neighbors and world powers, balancing its relationships with them, and avoiding creating enemies. Timor-Leste has pursued a hybrid strategy of neutrality, practicing 'leadership in niche diplomacy and active multilateral diplomacy'. On the one hand, it has sought to strengthen its independence vis-à-vis its neighbors, while on the other hand it has not ignored Australia's security shadow and intends to join ASEAN, a regional group dominated by Indonesia (Tomé 2016, p. 72). It is important to understand the nuances of this strategic positioning.

Nevertheless, Timor-Leste did not adopt an ad hoc neutrality to conflicts led by major powers, such as the US invasion of Afghanistan and Iraq. It did not contribute with troops but also did not refrain from supporting the former and condemning the latter. Timor-Leste has not pursued a de jure neutrality, or neutrality by international law, nor has it adopted a de facto neutrality. The young state does not host foreign military bases, although it benefits from military cooperation programs with China, the U.S., Australia, Portugal, and Indonesia and is willing to join Asian regional arrangements, such as ASEAN and the ASEAN Regional Forum (ARF). Security is not ASEAN's primary role, but it is a domain to which the organization pays particular attention.

Timor-Leste and Australia

Unlike Indonesia, Timor-Leste does not perceive Australia as a security threat. Rebecca Strating (2014, pp. 242–243) asserted that Timor-Leste

[11] 'A secure, resilient Australia extends into our northern approaches, our Exclusive Economic Zone, and our offshore territories', 2016 Defence White Papers, §3.5, p. 69.

faces low-level external security threats such as illegal movement of goods and people and illegal fishing, and that its most serious security threats to date have been internal, largely due to the weaknesses of state security institutions. Díli looks to Canberra as a security provider that will help preserve its sovereignty. Australia was there in 1999, leading the INTERFET, and again in 2006 in response to a request from the government of Timor-Leste during another difficult period. Moreover, Australia has been the primary provider of equipment and training for the Timor-Leste Defense Force. Timor-Leste is conscious of the limits to setting up a formal defense relationship with Australia due to the negative reaction this might provoke in Indonesia. For obvious reasons, Timor-Leste cannot alienate Indonesia, but at the same time it cannot do without Australian defense and security assistance. It has to find a cooperative security solution with Australia which does not involve a formal military pact or alliance.

'Australia's hardball tactics in the convoluted negotiations over oil and gas reserves in the Timor Gap' (Smith 2005, p. 26) caused rising anti-Australian sentiment in Timor-Leste. As Timor-Leste never agreed to be a province of Indonesia (Díli rejected the principle of *uti possidetis iuris*), it effectively had no maritime boundaries in place.[12] The lengthy negotiations over the resources in the Timor Gap have poisoned relations between Australia and Timor-Leste. Australia negotiated from a position of strength, acting as a primus inter pares, treating its 'partner' in an overbearing way, something that Timor-Leste considered unfair. Australia wanted access to resources to which their rights were very questionable under the United Nations Convention on the Law of the Sea (UNCLOS), but this did not prevent them maneuvering Timor-Leste into a corner. Australia withdrew early on from the legal process for resolving maritime boundaries within the International Court of Justice (ICJ) and from the dispute settlement mechanism under UNCLOS. Timor-Leste was helpless to bring them back to the negotiating table, which revealed how weak Timor-Leste's bargaining position was, and how far major powers play deviate from norms and rules when these do not serve their interests. '[Xanana] Gusmão has spoken of an 'unequal relationship' and likened the stakes surrounding the negotiations for the Timor Gap as akin to the independence struggle itself' (Smith 2005, p. 27). Maritime borders

[12] China-Lusophone Brief, 2018. Retrieved in October 2021, from https://clbrief.com/greater-sunrise-at-last.

between Timor-Leste and Australia remained unsettled until March 6, 2018, when the governments of Timor-Leste and Australia signed a boundary delimitation agreement that should open the way for the development of the Greater Sunrise oil and gas project. This agreement will first of all increase Timor-Leste's control over oil and gas deposits in the Timor Sea. Despite the apparent setback to Australia's ambitions caused by Timor-Leste initiation of compulsory nonbinding conciliation proceedings against Australia, and the finding by the Conciliation Commission that the Australian position was unfair, the 2018 boundary delimitation agreement is not the end of the story. Timor-Leste will continue to foster a relationship with Australia because it needs services, education, and basic goods, but the boundary delimitation agreement will position Australia closer to Timor-Leste, preventing excessive proximity to Indonesia. This agreement also expands the economic potential of Timor-Leste and may facilitate its accession to ASEAN. Nevertheless, Australia will continue imposing bilateral dispute management, an adverse situation for Timor-Leste, and the country might have no choice but to acquiesce. Australia has supported Timor-Leste, because it needs a strong and stable partner in the region. The latest developments in the light of the Pacific Maritime Security Project (PMSP)[13]—'Australia and Timor-Leste are collaborating as Timor-Leste prepares to receive (until 2023) two Australian-built Guardian-Class Patrol Boats for its military's naval component, along with a comprehensive package of Australian support to operate these vessels' confirm precisely that. Timor-Leste strives to continuously consolidate its relationship with Australia because there are few other alternatives for regional balance.

Timor-Leste and Indonesia

Timor-Leste's political elite have dealt very cautiously and strategically with Indonesia. They have been able to put geography (and its security implications) before history, prejudices, and hard feelings, even with many important issues unresolved. Cognizant of their constraints, they understand very well what state survival requires and what is at stake. Developing and maintaining good relations with Indonesia is a top priority for Timor-Leste's foreign policy. In this way, Timor-Leste's government hopes to create the necessary goodwill in Jakarta to facilitate

[13] Retrieved on April 11, 2021, from https://www.asiapacificsecuritymagazine.com/australia-and-timor-leste-step-up-defence-engagement/.

open sea lanes, cross-border trade (especially food, oil and gas), access to the Oecussi exclave (inside West Timor), movement of people, and general territorial security with special concern for a common border (Smith 2005, p. 20). Timor-Leste's government is well aware that the 24 traumatic years under Indonesia rule and the brutal attacks carried out by pro-Jakarta militias after the referendum had a psychological effect that is difficult to reconcile, at least in the short term. According to Rebecca Strating (2014, p. 238), 'the prioritization of good relations with Indonesia above the pursuit of senior Indonesian inductees was further highlighted in June 2014, when President Xanana Gusmão met with his "dear friend" General Wiranto less than two weeks after the former Tentara Nasional Indonesia (TNI) chief's indictment by the Serious Crimes Unit (SCU) ... Timor-Leste's leaders obstructed the achievement of retributive justice in order to advance other national interests, presenting problems for Timor-Leste in developing political order through rule of law and separation of powers' Timor-Leste has also learned how to live in disadvantageous conditions, appease aggressive behavior and promote conciliatory policies. Such is the balance between Timor-Leste and Indonesia, a relationship which depends on the ability of the weaker party to please (or at least to have good relations with) the giant, knowing that it can bite, because there is no other option but to work for mutual advantage.

Timor-Leste's decision makers have often surprised foreign observers, who expected to see Timor-Leste at the vanguard of human rights promotion. But this has not always been the case, as this topic puts Timor-Leste in a delicate relationship with its neighbors. Moderation has prevailed in Díli when it comes to human rights activism, thus avoiding misinterpretations by Jakarta, especially with regard to human rights in Indonesia and the prosecution of those involved in serious crimes during the 24 years of Indonesian occupation. Forgetting the past—or conveniently pretending to forget it—has become a fundamental principle of Timor-Leste's foreign policy. Smith (2005, p. 35) suggested that Timor-Leste leaders, who were once seen as left-wing radicals that would upset the regional order, have proved to be cautious and conservative in their foreign policy approaches'. The same author further proposed that this principle was determinant in Timor-Leste's decision to give up the trial of those implicated in the 1999 acts of violence. In line with this, Timor-Leste did its best to avoid cooperation with UN efforts to secure their trials. They understood that, at the end of the day, that no matter the outcome, these trials would not do Timor-Leste any good. Smith (2005, p. 22) suggested that, in the interests of remaining in Indonesia's good books, Timor-Leste's leadership not only opposed the UN trials but went further by maintaining 'that the two countries involved would jointly decide on what course of action would be taken', thus avoiding international embarrassment to Indonesia. Timor-Leste's government never protested the ludicrous outcome of trials held in Indonesia, which were challenged by many, including the U.S. State Department. It is easy to say that Díli engaged in realpolitik for its own benefit, especially since Díli has avoided making negative comments on any of Indonesia's domestic issues, let alone secession matters, such as Aceh or Papua. Díli's official line has been to support Indonesia's territorial integrity and distance itself from any possible perception of tacit support to secessionist movements, 'an issue that Jakarta is obsessive about' (Smith 2005, p. 23). To be quite clear, as observed by Rebecca Strating (2014, pp. 240, 242, 246, 252 and 253), Timor-Leste faces a pressing dilemma. On the one hand, the state needs to instill trust in its new judicial institutions, to curb possible domestic unrest; on the other, the country's economic and social dependence on Indonesia (particularly for foodstuff—such as rice) and its foreign affairs objectives (especially candidacy to ASEAN) makes it vital to develop harmonious relations with its nearest neighbor. Perhaps this is why Timor-Leste has made it clear that it will not offer support to any secessionist movements within Indonesia, to make sure that Indonesia does not entertain any illusion of a presence in Timor-Leste.

It was not by chance that Timor-Leste's March 2011 revised application for ASEAN membership was submitted when Indonesia was ASEAN Chair. It was also not by chance that in 2012, Prime Minister Xanana Gusmão declared 'when building a State and Nation, there is no room for nurturing past hatreds'. It was not a coincidence that in 2008, the Commission of Truth and Friendship issued a report (From Memory to Hope), which stated 'To this end, the two nations desire conducive circumstances for peace and development, including harmonious relations'. Eagerness to please Jakarta has turned Díli into an advocate of Indonesia in the international arena: supporting Indonesia's bid for a non-permanent seat on the UN Security Council; requesting 'greater western assistance to Indonesia, including debt write-offs' (Smith 2005, p. 23); and appealing to the U.S. 'to resume military-to-military ties, which were severed in the first place because of violence in Timor Leste in 1999' (Smith 2005, p. 24). Timor-Leste also joined international efforts to provide aid to Indonesia following the devastating earthquake and subsequent tsunami that ravaged Indonesia in 2005, contributing US$60,000 (Smith 2005, p. 24).[14] This act was full of symbolic meaning and entirely in line with Díli's strategic diplomatic choice to appease Jakarta. Timorese leaders also cultivated (or tried to cultivate) a relationship with Indonesian presidents and members of the elite. Díli did its best to reassure the Indonesian presidents of its willingness to develop close ties with Jakarta, not even excluding those who were politically responsible during the occupation. Despite being imprisoned in Indonesia during Suharto's presidency, Xanana Gusmão attended his funeral in January 2008 (Kingsbury and Leach 2007). At the same time, Timor-Leste avoided at all costs getting involved in territorial disputes with Indonesia over the demarcation of the border between the eastern and western parts of the island, and over misunderstandings around the exact location of Batek Island, which is part of Indonesia but is located near the Timorese exclave of Oecussi, and whose waters are used by fishermen from both countries. Progress was also made in border coordination and management, and in visa exemptions for travel between Timor-Leste and the Indonesian province of West Timor (World Politics Review 2012).

On August 21, 2011, Prime-Minister Xanana Gusmão and the Indonesian Minister of Defence, Purnomo Yusgiantoro, signed a Memorandum of Understanding on Defence Cooperation, showing a will to heal old wounds and proving that Timor-Leste does not intend to enter into a formal military alliance with Australia. 'It is vital to Timor-Leste to assure Indonesia that it will not become an offshore base for an outside power' (Smith 2005, p. 29), and that it will not pursue any formal military alliance with Australia. Díli had to balance the pressing need for assistance, notably in the military field, provided by other countries, especially Australia, while reassuring Indonesia that it will not host military bases of foreign powers, including China. In this context, we have spoken of appeasement before. We understand 'appeasement' in an international sovereign context as a diplomatic policy of making political, diplomatic, and/or material concessions to a dominant power in order to avoid conflict. This applies in this context as Timor-Leste pursues good relations

[14] Margesson, R., Coordinator (2005). CRS Report for Congress. Indian Ocean Earthquake and Tsunami: Humanitarian Assistance and Relief Operations. Updated February 10, 2005. Retrieved on October 2, 2018, from https://fas.org/sgp/crs/row/RL32715.pdf.

with Indonesia not only to avoid conflict, but also to facilitate cooperation. The location of Timor-Leste and its territorial discontinuity provides no other smart options. A dominant alliance with any of the contenders for deeper cooperation with Timor-Leste will trigger negative perceptions from others, something that Timor-Leste cannot afford.

Timor-Leste basically relies on diplomatic action for its security. However, it also created a domestic defense capability to be prepared for the worst. The FALINTIL-Timor-Leste Defense Force (F-FDTL) has made significant strides in its development as a conventional military force from its origins as a guerrilla force[15] and it has already sent members to serve in peacekeeping operations in Lebanon (integrated with the Portuguese Peacekeeping Force operating with UNIFIL) and in South Sudan. This participation requites the international community for what it has done for Timor-Leste and it is also an act of foreign policy. Timor-Leste's patient approach to foreign affairs is bearing fruit. There are some signs of change, as shown by the Indonesian support of Timor-Leste's candidacy to ASEAN and Indonesian promotion of the development and economic diversification of the nascent manufacturing industry in Timor-Leste (Hägerdal and Berlie 2018, p. 98). Timor-Leste's relationship with Indonesia remains an enormous challenge, requiring careful balancing in each and every foreign policy, particularly toward Australia and China. In the areas of security (border control and illegal fishing), trade (e.g. Timor-Leste's dependence on manufactured goods), and international support (ASEAN accession), cooperation is the only way forward.

Timor-Leste and China

When Timor-Leste unilaterally declared independence on November 28, 1975, the People's Republic of China was one of the few countries which immediately granted it official recognition, an act that would shape future friendly relations between Timor-Leste and China. The Hakka Chinese community in Díli was guaranteed full citizenship in the new country by the FRETILIN[16] government. In 2002, soon after the restoration of independence, China was the first to initiate consistent diplomatic

[15] Australian Government, Department of Defence, Supplementary Submission (76) to the Joint Standing Committee on Foreign Affairs, Defence and Trade, Australia's Relationship with Timor-Leste. On the model adopted by Timor-Leste Armed Forces, see Simões's (2012) essay on the implementation of 'Força 2020'.

[16] Revolutionary Front for an Independent East Timor (FRETILIN).

relations with Timor-Leste. Today, Timor-Leste is an active member of the Forum for Economic and Trade Cooperation between China and Portuguese-speaking Countries (Forum Macau), established by China in Macau in October 2003.

The Forum Macau is the result of an initiative by China's central government in coordination with seven Portuguese-speaking countries—Angola, Brazil, Cabo Verde, Guinea-Bissau, Mozambique, Portugal, and Timor-Leste—and with the collaboration of the Government of the Macau Special Administrative Region (Macau SAR).[17] Equatorial Guinea has joined Forum Macau formally in 2022, during an extraordinary online ministerial meeting. Forum Macau institution facilitates Chinese economic and trade policies for Portuguese-speaking countries, for which the government of Macau provides effective support and facilitates multilateral action. The bulk of the relations between Timor-Leste and China takes place at a bilateral level. Nevertheless, the Forum Macau and the funds associated with it have a complementary role, especially in terms of promotion of trade, the attraction of investment[18] and the enhancement of human resources.[19] It seems that the Forum Macau has the potential to help Timor-Leste divert its economy from excessive dependence on gas and oil, by initiating new projects and industries. Among the different projects are the establishment of the Oecussi special economic zone, and the contribution of the Greater Bay Area, composed of Macau, Guangdong, and Hong-Kong. From China's perspective, the role of the Forum Macau is supported by three very important elements: a common language (Portuguese), the China and Portuguese-speaking Countries Cooperation and Development Fund, and the practical opportunities offered by the Closer Economic Partnership Arrangement (CEPA).

Timor-Leste has no issues with China about its existence. China is neither a threat nor a security provider for Timor-Leste. However, Timor-Leste perceives China as an important diplomatic partner. It has turned to China as a counterbalance in critical moments in its troubled relationship with Australia, showing that it has other alternatives and is not entirely

[17] Retrieved in December 2021, from http://www.forumchinaplp.org.mo/about-us/mission-and-objectives/.

[18] Retrieved in January 2021, from http://www.plataformamacau.com/china/timor-leste-aposta-na-cooperacao-com-o-sul-da-china/.

[19] Retrieved in January 2021, from https://expedientesinico.com/2018/12/05/timor-leste-forum-macau-pode-ter-papel-reforcado-na-formacao-de-recursos-humanos.

at Australia's disposal. Timor-Leste has been a recipient of Chinese assistance and aid, and has also signed a number of bilateral trade and aid agreements with China, including conferring most favored nation status on one another. Chinese companies have constructed two heavy oil power plants under a US$360 million contract as part of the national power grid. Timor-Leste also paid US$25 million for two petroleum tankers from China.

The number of Chinese projects in Timor-Leste is remarkable and is likely to increase. Among the most significant are the Díli sanitation and drainage project (US$50 million),[20] the Suai-Beaco highway connecting three industrial clusters on the southern coastline (US$171 million), and the Tibar Bay Port, a public–private partnership (US$278 million). According to the *Asia Times* (2018) quoting[21] the Macau News Agency in early 2019, negotiations are underway to establish an airline connection between Timor-Leste and Guangzhou in southern China. As of February 2019, the only direct flights to Díli are from Bali and Darwin. Several Macau-based firms, including Charlestrong Engineering Technology and Consulting Ltd, are building housing and resorts in Timor-Leste's special region of Oecusse. There are also persistent rumors that Ina Chan Un Chan, a prominent Macau-based businesswoman and wife of Macau's casino tycoon Stanley Ho Hung Sun, is interested in investing in Timor-Leste's tourism sector.

Beijing also cooperates with Timor-Leste in the military field. China donated nonlethal equipment (uniforms, tents, transport vehicles, etc.) to the Timorese armed forces, built barracks and houses for their soldiers, and set up a program of practical military cooperation which included education and training courses in China. Military cooperation also involved Timor-Leste making acquisitions from China. In 2006, Díli signed a contract with a Chinese vendor to purchase eight light armed jeeps. Díli further turned down an Australian invitation to join the Australian Pacific Patrol Boat Program in favor of Poly Technologies, a Chinese company with close links to the People's Liberation Army

[20] Approved by the Council of Ministers to take place in 4 phases between 2011 and 2025. Retrieved on March 8, 2019, from http://mucp-mfit.org/wp-content/uploads/Joao.pdf.

[21] Retrieved in January 2021, from http://www.atimes.com/article/will-timor-leste-become-chinas-next-debt-trap/.

(PLA). In 2010 it signed a US$25 million contract to buy two Shanghai-class patrol boats mounted with 30-millimeter cannons, to combat illegal activities in Timor-Leste's exclusive economic zone.[22] This, Timor-Leste's largest defense acquisition to date, was seen by some observers as a slap in the face for Australian diplomacy, a sort of retaliation for Australia's disregard of Timorese demands in the negotiations over their maritime boundaries.

Some believed that Díli bought these boats to 'demonstrate to Canberra that it has other choices when it comes to defence partners' (Murdoch 2010). We see these military agreements are part of Timor-Leste's balancing strategy, extending cooperation with China into the traditional hardline sectors to send a message to Indonesia and Australia. Likewise, this purchase was evidence of Timor-Leste willingness to assume more responsibility for its territorial waters and therefore to increase its particular-intrinsic power. Such cooperation will probably continue in the near future. However, Timor-Leste's cooperation with China is unlikely to lead to a substantial Chinese military presence in the country. As Sahin (2014, p. 13) suggested, with this action Timor-Leste hopes to leverage its competitive position to reinforce Indonesia's and Australia's support for its accession to ASEAN and to avoid being heavily dependent on either of its powerful neighbors.

The importance of China in the context of Timor-Leste foreign relations has grown over the course of time. Timor-Leste has established an embassy in Beijing and China has the largest diplomatic presence in Díli. China has raised its profile in several other ways, exercising 'symbolic structural charm diplomacy'. According to Sahin (2014, p. 12), China has provided funding for the construction of a new Presidential Palace, the Ministry of Foreign Affairs, defense buildings and military residential quarters in the capital city. China has also allegedly financed the construction of Timor-Leste's embassy in Beijing. China's efforts to establish closer contact with Timor-Leste included participation in all the UN peacekeeping missions deployed in Timor-Leste, mainly contributing civilian police officers.[23] In 2017, a Chinese PLA Navy hospital ship

[22] Storey (2012, p. 299), citing *The Australian*, April 16, 2008 'Alarm Grows at China's Influence in Timor-Leste.

[23] UNTAET—UN Transitional Authority East Timor (1999–2002); UNMISET—Mission of Support in East Timor, 2002–2005; and UNMIT—UN Integrated Mission in Timor-Leste, 2006–2012.

visited Díli, the second time that a PLA Navy vessel had visited the country. In January 2016, a Chinese Navy task force arrived in Dili to pay a five-day official visit to the country. This task force comprised a destroyer, a frigate, and a supply ship (Xinhua).[24]

Timor-Leste is rich in sandalwood, coffee, minerals (copper, zinc and rare blue marble), marine resources, and hydrocarbons (oil and gas). The competition for oil and gas is high. PetroChina, one of China's largest state-owned energy companies, financed a US$1.6 million onshore seismic study for oil and gas exploration in the country's interior, and it expected to be involved in offshore oil field development (Storey 2012). However, the exploitation of offshore deposits was won by Australian and other international companies. Although advancing its interests and slowly establishing a stronger foothold in Timor-Leste would increase Beijing's political clout, we must bear in mind Timor-Leste's relative importance to China. To quote Loro Horta, 'Timor-Leste is not a priority for China, but Beijing is definitely keeping an eye on it'.[25] This statement expresses the situation well. However, geopolitical dynamics may dictate so far unforeseen developments. From being just a good friend, Beijing may become Díli's closest friend in the future.

Heine (2013, p. 58) asserted that 'One of the greatest contributions of the B&RI is its potential to push states out of an exclusive narrow domestic definition of self-interest'. The Maritime Silk Road for South Asia provides context for a dialogue between Timor-Leste and China on their interests, with two different but complementary perspectives. China needs Timor-Leste as a sea-land support platform in a region dominated by Indonesia and Australia. Timor-Leste needs China to aid the development of its functional ability as a sea-land support platform to promote stable and balanced relations with Indonesia and Australia. China sees Timor-Leste's candidacy to ASEAN as another element in favor of solving the South China Sea disputes by peaceful means. For economic, political, and historical reasons, it seems unlikely that China will displace Australia and Indonesia as the main players in Timor-Leste's foreign relations in the near future. Timor-Leste's leadership certainly appreciates.

[24] Retrieved in March, 2021, from http://en.people.cn/n3/2016/0118/c90786-9005098.html.

[25] Loro Horta interviewed by Sunanda Creagh and Tito Belo. Retrieved in January 2022, from https://www.reuters.com/article/us-timor-china-idUSTRE58D0GD20090914.

Beijing's support of its independence since 1975, but this does not mean that China will occupy a position comparable to Australia and Indonesia in Timor-Leste's foreign affairs, at least in the short and medium term. China achieved an important foreign affairs objective when it induced Timor-Leste to recognize the principle of 'one China', in which Taiwan is an inalienable part. This will be one of the core issues governing relations between the two countries.

Timor-Leste and International Organizations

International organizations are receptive to small states, since they offer good opportunities to small states to operate and to defend their interests. In contrast to the immediate post-Cold War scarcity of institutions promoting regional integration in Asia, today there is a dense and complex network of institutions all set up in less than two decades. This is a dimension of foreign policy that states must explore, especially small states. Despite its limited assets, Timor-Leste has dedicated considerable resources to participate in multilateral forums. Timor-Leste's leaders are actively engaged in an 'assertive campaign' of multilateral diplomacy with multiple alignments beyond the Lusophone world or the non-aligned movement, which according to them is sliding into irrelevancy. Timor-Leste has joined various international and regional organizations. It is a full member of the UN as well as a number of UN organs, and has ratified a wide range of international conventions. It joined the Community of Portuguese Speaking Countries in 2002, a few months after independence, which opened the way to connection with regions on five continents.

The next section specifically addresses the process of Timor-Leste's accession to ASEAN. However, it is worth noting here that Timor-Leste's membership in ASEAN[26] is probably one of the most important aspirations in its national strategy, because such membership will give Timor-Leste a functional power as a land support platform for commercial shipping and sea resource exploration in the context of ASEAN and its affiliated groups, namely the East Asian Community (10 ASEAN+

26 (ASEAN member states) Indonesia, Malaysia, the Philippines, Singapore, Thailand, Brunei, Vietnam, Laos, Myanmar, and Cambodia.

3[27]), the Regional Comprehensive Economic Partnership (10 ASEAN+ 6[28]), the Asia–Pacific Economic Cooperation (10 ASEAN+ 8[29]) and the ASEAN+ 9.[30] As Sahin (2014, p. 11) observed, by choosing ASEAN (which does not allow double membership) rather than the Pacific Islands Forum (dominated by Australia and New Zealand), Timor-Leste's leadership has indicated their interest in becoming part of a bigger, more flexible and stable regional grouping, with perhaps more to gain also in terms of security. Timor-Leste is part of a free trade zone, the Timor-Leste–Indonesia–Australia Growth Triangle (TIA-GT). On December 7, 2016, the General Council of the World Trade Organization agreed to establish a Working Party on the Accession of Timor-Leste and granted it observer status. This allows attendance at meetings of the General Council and 'as appropriate, [at] meetings of other WTO bodies as observers' during the accession process. According to official WTO information,[31] the Trade Ministers, led by Afghanistan and Liberia, officially inaugurated the g7+ WTO Accessions Group on December 10, 2017, on the margins of the 11th WTO Ministerial Conference in Buenos Aires, Argentina. Timor-Leste has also been pursuing 'leadership in niche diplomacy'.[32] In 1997, Ramos-Horta gained much attention headlining a 'People's Summit' in Vancouver which hosted the Asia–Pacific Economic Cooperation (APEC) summit. The summit offered a vision of human rights counterpoised against the economics-first philosophy of APEC leaders, including Indonesia's Suharto.

Within the g7+, Timor-Leste has made an effort to shift the language of development from state 'failure' toward hope in the face of long odds, very much echoing the themes of the earlier campaign for Timor-Leste

[27] (ASEAN member states plus 3) China, Japan and South Korea.

[28] (ASEAN member states plus 6) China, Japan, South Korea, India, Australia, and New Zealand.

[29] (ASEAN member states plus 8) China, Japan, South Korea, India, Australia, New Zealand, the United States and Russia.

[30] (ASEAN member states plus 9) China, Japan, South Korea, India, Australia, New Zealand, the United States, Russia, and Canada.

[31] Retrieved in January 2021, from https://www.wto.org/english/thewto_e/acc_e/mc11g7group_e.htm.

[32] Retrieved on November 23, 2021, from https://www.asiapacific.ca/canada-asia-agenda/15-years-after-independence-whatever-happened-east-timor.

independence. This effort is aimed at a group of states placed in a position of weakness or even helplessness in the global system, and seeks to shift their weakness into collective moral strength. Timorese diplomats do not try to intervene in every global issue, but they are far from shy in asserting leadership in targeted areas, such as the economic development of 'fragile states'. Timorese diplomats are very active, as in the example of Milena Pires, an East Timorese politician and women's rights activist who served as director of the United Nations Development Fund for Women (UNIFEM) in East Timor. Since 2016, Milena Pires has been the Permanent Representative of Timor-Leste to the United Nations. The country still has a long way to go in combatting violence against women, but it has taken on a leadership role in the region on this issue. While Timor-Leste aspires to feature more prominently at the regional level, with ASEAN membership as the primary foreign policy goal, so far it has been unable to gain more than candidate status.

Timor-Leste and ASEAN

On May 20, 2002, soon after regaining independence, Timor-Leste was granted observer status to ASEAN. Timor-Leste also joined the ASEAN Regional Forum in 2005 and signed the Treaty of Amity and Cooperation in Southeast Asia on January 13, 2007, during the ASEAN Summit in Cebu, the Philippines. The formal effort to become the 11th ASEAN member state began on March 4, 2011, when Timor-Leste officially applied for membership. So far Timor-Leste is still considered a guest, and was addressed as such at the 31st ASEAN Summit in 2017 (Zamora 2017). Timor-Leste's full membership in ASEAN has been vetoed by some member states. It has often aligned its foreign policy with Western countries on issues such as humanitarian intervention and human rights, which has not helped its cause. A number of ASEAN members do not support humanitarian intervention. Boasting of being a Western liberal democracy in a region where autocratic regimes and illiberal democracies has created a negative impression. Another argument against Timor-Leste's accession to ASEAN is its CPLP membership, which, according to a few member countries, could cause other, conflicting regional loyalties. Windraskinasih and Afriansyah (2018, p. 88) observed,

> The CLMV[33] countries ... were accorded observer status during their "candidacy-in-waiting," [while] Timor-Leste has only the status of a guest in attending open sessions of ASEAN Foreign Ministers Meetings and ASEAN Summits.

And, further (Windraskinasih and Afriansyah 2018, p. 96),

> the case of membership application by CLMV countries as well as Timor-Leste truly signifies the changes [in] the membership system of ASEAN. During the era of the ASEAN Declaration, as the constituent instrument, the membership system was informal to which the conditions of membership only [required] two factors, namely: geographical location and subscription to aims, purposes and principles. Evidently, the ASEAN Charter prescribes additional requirements, such as one's capacity in carrying out obligations of membership. Said condition becomes a huge obstacle for a Southeast Asian country to enter into ASEAN, as illustrated by the case of Timor-Leste...

Despite of the inapplicability of the Master Plan on ASEAN Connectivity (MPAC) 2025, this suggests that Timor-Leste is regionally 'relatively well integrated', and that the ASEAN decision-making process is now more demanding, especially in relation to the capacity of a country to carry out the obligations of membership. This is why the position of Singapore in relation to Timor-Leste's accession to ASEAN is unclear. Nevertheless, in March 2022,[34] Timor-Leste Ambassador Joana Veneranda Amaral, speaking in Kuala Lumpur, mentioned '... It is a national and strategic priority for Timor-Leste to become an Association of Southeast Asian Nations member (...)'. "It is the dream of our people and the political leaders. Integration into ASEAN will give a positive impact for us because the Southeast Asian region is more economically dynamic in the world". Indeed, the process did not stop as, in April 2022,[35] Timor–Leste received the delegation team from Indonesia to discuss the process of preparation in accession to ASEAN.

[33] Cambodia-Laos-Myanmar-Vietnam Membership Admission to ASEAN.

[34] Retrieved in April, 2022, https://www.nst.com.my/news/nation/2022/03/780504/becoming-asean-national-and-strategic-priority.

[35] Retrieved in April, 2022, from http://www.tatoli.tl/en/2022/04/11/timor-leste-receives-the-delegation-team-from-indonesia-to-discuss-the-process-of-preparation-in-accession-to-asean/

With the support of Indonesia and the Philippines, a steadily developing economy and a stable political system, Timor-Leste seems to meet all the requirements for a smooth accession: (1) location in Southeast Asia; (2) the political recognition of all ASEAN member states; (3) the agreement of the Timor-Leste government to be bound to and to be abide by the ASEAN Charter; and (4) the ability and willingness to carry out the obligations of membership. In relation to requirement (4), there are not reasons to doubt that Timor-Leste's accession to ASEAN would be economically beneficial to all. Its market is so far untapped by Southeast Asian trade institutions and the region similarly represents a largely unexplored market for Timorese goods. In our view, it would benefit all involved, and there are no objective reasons to deny or postpone Timor-Leste's accession to ASEAN, especially since the Economist Intelligence Unit's 2016 Democracy Index[36] ranked Timor-Leste the most democratic in Southeast Asia.

The Community of Portuguese Language Countries (CPLP)

Timor-Leste joined the United Nations and the Community of Portuguese-Speaking Countries in 2002, and since then the CPLP has made an important contribution to the country in terms of infrastructure, justice, education, and human rights. Timor-Leste shares three factors in common with the CPLP member states: culture and language, maritime domain and political values. Timor-Leste is not only the youngest CPLP member after Equatorial-Guinea, but also the only Asian CPLP member state. Timor-Leste's CPLP membership enables it to reinforce its identity vis-à-vis its dominant regional neighbors. Sahin (2014, p. 21) observed that 'although strategically positioning Timor-Leste in South east Asia, the government has also sought to distinguish the sovereign identity of the state from its two powerful neighbors, Australia and Indonesia, by referencing Portuguese heritage'. The CPLP continuously reinforces the identity of Timor-Leste, providing a non-Asian reference, which is one of the determinants of its existence as a sovereign state. The CPLP is an international forum where Timor-Leste can be more active, since its relative power is equal (at least de jure) to all other 8 member states.

[36] Retrieved in December, 2021, from www.eiu.com/topic/democracy-index.

The more Timor-Leste develops diplomatic, cultural and economic relations with the CPLP, the more its relative regional importance will be asserted, despite reservations put forward by a few ASEAN member states. A small, young state surrounded by large states such as Indonesia and Australia must strengthen its position through partnership with other states and relevant international organizations. Thus, the more the CPLP gains prestige internationally, the better Timor-Leste will be equipped to develop balanced relations with its regional neighbors. The CPLP could also see Timor-Leste as a sort of platform for developing economic relationships in South-East Asia, especially in the context of ASEAN if its political leadership takes steps in that direction. To this date, the benefits for Timor-Leste in relation to key infrastructure in the context of CPLP and the extension of the Lusophone B&RI in the context of the China-Indian Ocean-Africa-Mediterranean—Blue Economic Passage, are yet to be seen. This will only be possible if the CPLP invests seriously in developing its common economic strengths and if Timor-Leste manages to overcome its difficulties in terms of accessing markets. In both cases, infrastructure and social capital appear to be the essential factors.

The prevalence of several languages in Timor-Leste (Tetum, Portuguese, English and Bahasa Indonesia) could boost regional competitiveness in the long term, if the skills and quality of the country's labor force match those of its ASEAN counterparts. Timor-Leste's position in the maritime domain close to Australia and embedded in the Indonesia Archipelago, not far from Philippines (Banda and Celebes seas), and midway between the Pacific islands, will only be relevant to the CPLP if projects such as the Tibar Bay port (10 km West of Dili) are successfully developed. However, CPLP participation in this kind of infrastructural investment is almost nonexistent and is not expected. Another maritime factor is the opportunities provided by the Timor-Leste Economic Exclusive Zone (EEZ) and Kitan fields. 'Australia and Timor-Leste have agreed that the companies which hold the production sharing contracts [in the Bayu-Undan and Kitan fields] will be subject to the same fiscal and regulatory regimes although under Timor-Leste's jurisdiction not joint Australian and Timorese jurisdiction as is the case under existing treaty arrangements'. Bearing in mind this new agreement and the map in

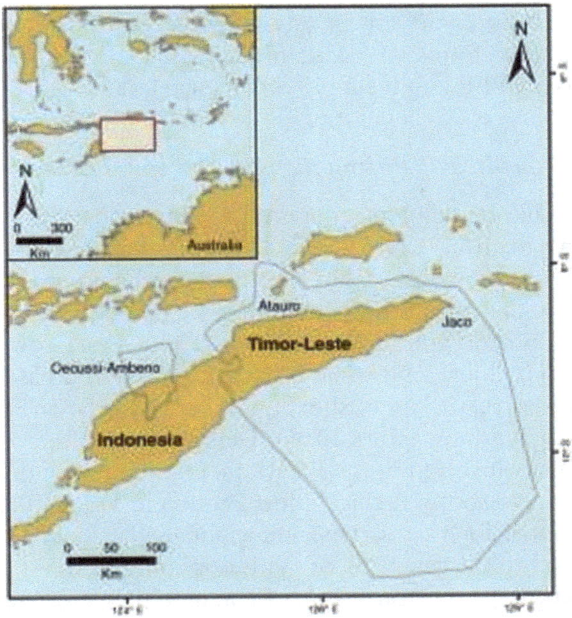

Fig. 3 Timor-Leste EEZ (*Map Source* https://www.researchgate.net/figure/Map-of-Timor-Leste-East-Timor-including-islands-of-Atauro-and-Jaco-and-exclave_fig1_311511099)

Fig. 3,[37] CPLP membership should represent an opportunity to fully explore the possibilities offered by such a large area. Unfortunately, the economic cooperation within CPLP is far from this level of ambition.

One of the main standards of CPLP membership is the unity of political values, with democracy, human rights, and respect for sovereign rights at the top of a long list. However, none of these political values appear to have spurred fellow member states to cooperate on large investment projects, capable of generating significant revenues. The CPLP seems to be happy with niche diplomacy (developed by Timor-Leste), without extending to other forms of cooperation. But for Timor-Leste,

[37] Retrieved on December 21, 2021, from https://www.researchgate.net/figure/Map-of-Timor-Leste-East-Timor-including-islands-of-Atauro-and-Jaco-and-exclave_fig1_311511099.

CPLP membership could still be advantageous if the Community were to embrace other forms of economic activism. If not, Timor-Leste's membership in CPLP might simply become irrelevant.

China and the B&RI: Filling the Gap Left by CPLP and ASEAN?

Chinese and Timorese diplomacy are marked by strong historic ties and a very clever pragmatism. China needs Timor-Leste as a regional presence and influence. Economically, China means cheaper imports and potential exports for Timor-Leste. Timor-Leste needs China for regional empowerment, development, and 'balancing'. The Timor-Leste government has been wary about China, and while it has accepted aid, it has also refused some of its advances, such as offshore oil rights and radar arrays ostensibly to counter illegal fishing (Hutt 2016). Despite the fact that Timor-Leste is not yet directly involved in the B&RI, its maritime component (particularly the China—South Pacific—Blue Economic Passage—COSPBEP) provides potential for two parties aiming for further cooperation. Likewise, in relation to the extension of the Lusophone B&RI—China-Indian Ocean—Africa-Mediterranean—Blue Economic Passage. As previously stated, Timor-Leste's accession to ASEAN is probably one of the most important of the country's national aspirations. A good part of the Chinese interest in Timor-Leste lies with its potential as a sea-land platform, a geopolitical alternative to regional dominant powers, in the context of the COSPBEP, located in the area of the Torres Strait, to support commercial shipping in the context of the ASEAN member states, once it accedes to the organization. The 2022 China—Solomon Islands security pact, which provides China a new platform for cooperation with Honiara on maintaining social order, protecting people's safety, aid, combating natural disasters, and helping safeguard national security, reinforces the argument about the importance of Timor-Leste. Nevertheless, the absence of ASEAN and CPLP support for national structural development projects in Timor-Leste will contribute to the deepening of Sino-Timorese relations, particularly in the context of the B&RI. The two main limitations to cooperation between China and Timor-Leste are Timor-Leste's aversion to excessive debt (or other forms of dependency on China), and the Indonesian and Australian authorities' perception of China. The symbolic, cultural, and language ties between Timor-Leste and the CPLP are important for the next generation, but if not properly cultivated, these ties will lose their real importance within two or three generations.

Conclusion

Timor-Leste's foreign affairs policy has been to keep the country's options open, to balance multiple relationships, and to increase its geopolitical relevance. Any foreign affairs strategies and tactics adopted by Díli have taken into account the need to preserve the special partnerships Timor-Leste has developed with its two nearest neighbors. As Ramos Horta summarized, Timor-Leste's foreign policies are based on the need 'to consolidate and maintain good relations with Indonesia and Australia'. Timorese authorities are well aware of the importance to their security of retaining Australian support, without alienating Indonesia. It has not been easy, especially in the first decade to gain the support Australia needed to underpin its security without, at the same time, alienating Indonesia. Timor-Leste's relational network also includes the United States, China, and the ASEAN member-states. Dealing with and satisfying both a rising China and the United States, with their conflicting interests, is an overwhelming task. To be everyone's friend is not without stress and tension. For Timor-Leste to be everyone's friend, it has to carefully manage its relationships with all its neighbors, with particular attention to China's place in the balance.

Timor-Leste is building its armed and police forces with the help of its partners, to increase its power and to achieve a deterrent capability against external asymmetric threats. These forces will also be an instrument of Timor-Leste's foreign policy to fight threats to regional and global stability. Aware of the limitations of its power and reflecting a careful reading of the regional structure, correlation of forces and distribution of power, Timor-Leste has avoided bandwagoning and has carried out a careful positive sum game foreign policy strategy. Its acquisition of military equipment from China showed Australia and Indonesia that Timor-Leste is not entirely at their disposal... the two Australian-built Guardian-Class Patrol Boats as part of the PMSP, which were announced in 2019 is a result of that movement. This could be interpreted as Timor-Leste leveraging its particular-intrinsic power to appease its neighbors, placing itself as a contributing partner in that region of the world. On the other hand, diversification of foreign investments and international loans for development is an assurance to all regional partners that none will gain an upperhand in relations with Timor-Leste nor gain control, directly or indirectly in Timor-Leste's economy. This is why Timor-Leste should consider all options in its association with the B&RI. The B&RI is an opportunity for Timor-Leste as well as for China, to advance further existing economic and diplomatic relations. From this perspective, the Forum Macau will complement bilateral relations between Timor-Leste and China.

It seems clear that Timor-Leste is keen to create a sort of functional power between giant actors in the region, shaping the conditions that would serve all interests, with Timor-Leste as a sea-land platform supporting shipping and international trade in that area of the world. To attain the goals, it has set and to gain a rightful place in the region, Timor-Leste is focusing its resources and efforts in the following areas:

1. National development within the perimeters of controlled debt;
2. Reform of domestic institutions to increase their credibility and curb domestic threats;
3. Balanced economic and diplomatic interests vis-à-vis Indonesia, Australia and China;
4. Full regional integration and ASEAN membership;
5. Development as Timor-Leste's national priority, developing human social capital, agriculture, oil, gas and tourism, alongside massive investments in sewage, potable water distribution, and roads; and
6. Active membership in the CPLP and a strong commitment to development and human rights in this organization.

All in all, Timor-Leste is important to Indonesia, Australia, ASEAN, China, and CPLP. All these actors have Asian interests and perspectives, except the CPLP whose center of gravity is in the South Atlantic.

Therefore, the existing CPLP symbolic capital vested in Timor-Leste must be used to promote effective large-scale cooperation and development. Otherwise any ensuing gap will be filled by others, namely China, Indonesia, Australia, and eventually ASEAN.

Bibliography

Chauprade, A. (2003). Geopolitique, Constants et Changements dans l'Histoire. Paris, Ellipses, 2nd edition.

Hägerdal, H., and J. Berlie (2018). Timor-Leste and ASEAN. In Berlie, J., ed., East Timor's Independence, Indonesia and ASEAN. The Education University of Hong Kong, Palgrave, pp. 91–112.

Heine, J. (2013). From Club to Network Diplomacy, The Oxford Handbook of Modern Diplomacy, Edited by Andrew F. Cooper, Jorge Heine, and Ramesh Thakur, Oxford University Press.

Hutt, D. (2016). Is China's Influence in Timor-Leste Rising? While There Are Indications of Beijing's Growing Reach, Its Role Needs to Be Kept in Perspective. The Diplomat. Retrieved in April 2022, from https://thediplomat.com/2016/11/is-chinas-influence-in-timor-leste-rising/.

Kingsbury, D., and M. Leach, eds. (2007). East Timor: Beyond Independence. University Press, Melbourne.

Leandro, F. (2018). Steps of Greatness: Geopolitics of OBOR, University of Macau.

Leandro, F. (2018). The OBOR Global Geopolitical Drive: The Chinese Access Security Strategy, in the Belt and Road Initiative—Law, Economics, and Politics, Brill Nijhoff, Chapter 5, pp. 89–106.

Margesson, R., and Coordinator (2005). Indian Ocean Earthquake and Tsunami: Humanitarian Assistance and Relief Operations. CRS Report for Congress. Updated February 10, 2005. Retrieved on October 12, 2018 from https://fas.org/sgp/crs/row/RL32715.pdf.

Murdoch, L. (2010). Relations Strained as East Timor Buys Chinese Navy Boats. *The Sidney Morning Herald*, June 7. Retrieved on August 19, 2018 from https://www.smh.com.au/world/relations-strained-as-east-timor-buys-chinese-navy-boats-20100606-xn5y.html.

Sahin, S. (2014). Timor-Lente's Foreign Policy: Securing State Identity in Post-Independence Period, *Journal of Current Southeast Asian Affairs*, 33, 2, pp. 3–25.

Sebille, E., J. Sprintall, F. U. Schwarzkopf, A. S. Gupta, A. Santoso, M. H. England, A. Biastoch, and C. W. Böning (2014). Pacific-to-Indian Ocean Connectivity: Tasman Leakage, Indonesian Through Flow, and the Role of ENSO, *Journal of Geophysical Research Oceans*, 119, 1365–1382, p. 1373.https://doi.org/10.1002/2013JC009525.

Simões, J. (2012). Novo Modelo das Forças Armadas de Timor-Leste (FALINTIL-FDTL). *JDRI*. Retrieved on September 11, 2018 from http://database.jornaldefesa.pt/assuntos_diversos_defesa/Novo%20modelo%20das%20For%C3%A7as%20Armadas%20de%20Timor%20Leste%20Falantil%20FDTL.pdf.

Smith, A. (2005). Constraints and Choices: East Timor as a Foreign Policy Actor, *New Zealand Journal of Asian Studies*, 7, 1 (June), pp. 15–36.

State Council of PRC (2010). Vision for Maritime Cooperation Under the Belt and Road Initiative, to Synchronize Development Plans and Promote

Joint Actions Among Countries Along the 21st Century Maritime Silk Road. Retrieved in January 2022, from https://uaf.edu/caps/resources/policy-documents/china-vision-for-maritime-cooperation-under-the-belt-and-road-initiative-2017.pdf.

Storey, I. (2012). China's Bilateral Defense Diplomacy in Southeast Asia, *Asian Security*, 8, 3, pp. 287–310.

Strating, R. (2014). The Indonesia-Timor-Leste Commission of Truth and Friendship: Enhancing Bilateral Relations at the Expense of Justice, *Contemporary Southeast Asia*, 36, 2, pp. 232–261.

Timor-Leste Government. (2010). Timor-Leste Strategic Development Plan 2011–2030.

Tomé, L. (2016). Multilateralismo e Regionalismo na Ásia-Pacífico. *Janus 2015–2016*. p. 72.

Van Sebille, E., J. Sprintall, F. U. Schwarzkopf, A. S. Gupta, A. Santoso, M. H. England, A. Biastoch, and C. W. Böning (2014). Pacific-to-Indian Ocean connectivity: Tasman leakage, Indonesian Throughflow, and the Role of ENSO, *Journal of Geophysical Research Oceans*, 119, 1365–1382. https://doi.org/10.1002/2013JC009525.

Windraskinasih, M., and A. Afriansyah (2018). The Struggle of Becoming the 11th Member State of ASEAN: Timor-Leste's Case, *Brawijara Law Journal*, 5, 1 (April 2018), pp. 74–101. https://doi.org/10.21776/ub.blj.2018.005.01.06.

World Politics Review (2012). A New Partnership Emerges for Timor-Leste and Indonesia, 2 July. Retrieved on July 3, 2018, from http://www.worldpoliticsreview.com/trend-lines/12116/global-insi-der-a-partnership-emerges-for-timor-leste-and-indonesia.

Zamora, R. (2017). Government Bares Preparations for 31st ASEAN Summit, Business World. Retrieved on November 23, 2018, from http://bworldonline.com/govt-bares-preparations-31st-asean-summit/.

Index

P. A. B. Duarte et al. (eds.), *Portugal and the Lusophone World*, https://doi.org/10.1007/978-981-99-0455-6

FSC
www.fsc.org
MIX
Papier | Fördert gute Waldnutzung
FSC® C083411

Kolibri 360 GmbH
Ferdinand-Jühlke-Straße 7
99095 Erfurt, Deutschland
produktsicherheit@kolibri360.de